THE COLLECTED PAPERS OF
FRANCO MODIGLIANI

VOLUME 1
Essays in Macroeconomics

THE COLLECTED PAPERS OF
FRANCO MODIGLIANI

Edited by Andrew Abel

The MIT Press
Cambridge, Massachusetts, and London, England

Portrait of Franco Modigliani by Bachrach Photographers of Boston, Massachusetts.

See pages 447–448 for acknowledgments to publishers.

Library of Congress Cataloging in Publication Data

Modigliani, Franco.
  The collected papers of Franco Modigliani.

  Includes bibliographical references and indexes.
  CONTENTS: v. 1. Essays in macroeconomics.—v. 2. The life cycle hypothesis of saving.—v. 3. Essays in the theory of finance. Stabilization policies. Essays in international finance. The role of expectations and plan in economic behavior. Miscellanea.
  1. Economics—Addresses, essays, lectures. I. Abel, Andy.
HB171.M557   330   78-21041
ISBN 978-0-262-13150-6 (v.1; hc.: alk. paper), 978-0-262-51932-8 (pb.)
ISBN 978-0-262-13151-3 (v.2; hc.: alk. paper)
ISBN 978-0-262-13152-0 (v.3; hc.: alk. paper)

TO SERENA

CONTENTS

Volume I   Essays in Macroeconomics

PREFACE

The essays collected in these volumes represent a selection of my scientific contribution to economics published over a span of nearly four decades. The volumes do not include more popular writings in newspapers, magazines, and the like.

This collection has been on the drawing board for a good many years. But I kept postponing it on the grounds that there were one or more nearly finished papers whose inclusion in the collection seemed to me essential to elucidate my thinking. As it turned out, those essays took much longer than expected to reach publication. By the time they were ready, there were always some new, almost completed papers to take their place. I have finally been persuaded by many friends not to tarry any longer, especially since I have at long last come to realize that there is no such thing as "the final word."

I wish to express my gratitude to Andy Abel for undertaking the task of editing these volumes. He waded patiently through most of my writings, helped me in the final selection, and also meticulously looked out for needed corrections due to misprints or more serious errors. Such corrections are reported in the errata at the end of each essay. Fortunately, and to my pleasant surprise, Andy's zealous effort has yielded a surprisingly meager crop of errors. All the essays have been reprinted in their original form, with the single exception of an unpublished paper with Richard Brumberg, which appears in volume 2.

Throughout my career I have had the good fortune to be associated with stimulating colleagues. Many of these associations have blossomed into scientific collaborations, as evidenced by the substantial number of joint papers included in this selection. I wish to express my appreciation for permission to reprint these joint papers and extend my thanks to these coauthors for their contribution to these volumes: Albert Ando, Hossein Askari, the late Richard Brumberg, Kalman J. Cohen, J. Phillip Cooper, Jacques Drèze, Emile Grunberg, the late Franz Hohn, Dwight Jaffee, Peter Kenen, Giorgio La Malfa, Merton H. Miller, Tommaso Padoa-Schioppa, Lucas Papademos, Robert Rasche, Robert Shiller, Richard Sutch, Ezio Tarantelli, Stephen J. Turnovsky, H. Martin Weingartner.

My thanks go also to my secretary, Judy Mason, who not only helped with these volumes but patiently typed countless, almost illegible, drafts of many of the essays collected here.

Finally, I want to acknowledge my gratitude to my wife Serena, knowing that words can not adequately accomplish this task. Throughout the forty years of our married life she has given me the encouragement to aim for the stars while trying her best to see that my feet remained planted on the ground.

INTRODUCTION

I have chosen to arrange the papers collected in these three volumes by topic—except when a paper covers more than one topic. Under each topic the order is generally chronological. The major exceptions are the lead papers in volumes 1 and 2. In volume 1 the first paper is one of my most recent contributions, the Presidential Address to the American Economic Association in 1976. I feel that this essay serves as an overview of my present thinking on macroeconomics, the focus of my contribution to economics and of these volumes. Its numerous references to other papers contained in the volumes make it a useful guide to the entire collection.

The topical arrangement helps to bring into relief the basic theme that has dominated my scientific concern, namely that of sorting out the lasting contribution of the Keynesian revolution by (1) integrating the main building blocks of the *General Theory* with the more traditional and established methodology of economics that rest on the basic postulate of rational maximizing behavior on the part of economic agents; (2) testing and estimating the resulting structure by means of empirical data; and (3) applying the results to policy issues, including the issue raised by the monetarist counterrevolution as to whether there is a valid case for active policies.

The first line of endeavor has been pursued from my very first significant scientific contribution in 1944, which appears as the second essay in part I of volume 1. Its main purpose was to examine to what extent the novel results of the *General Theory,* including its explanation of "equilibrium" unemployment, could be traced to the unorthodox assumption of wage rigidity. My conclusion was that the ability of the model set out in the *General Theory* to explain the persistence of unemployment could be traced primarily to the assumption of wage rigidity. The one exception was the so-called liquidity trap, or "Keynesian case." It is logically of undeniable importance, although its empirical relevance appears now very limited, especially once the message of the Keynesian revolution served to innoculate the economy against the repetition of the Great Depression.

The same basic issue, as well as the analysis of the working of monetary and fiscal policies in a system with rigid wages (at least in the short run), was picked up some twenty years later in the third essay, a more polished and rigorous presentation benefiting from later developments, including valuable criticisms of the previous essay. This paper also attacked a new issue, namely how the working of the system is affected if the standard assumption of competitive money and credit markets is replaced by that of systematic credit rationing.

The conclusion of these two essays concerning the monetary mechanism is supported and illustrated in the last two papers of part I, but this time with the benefit of specific estimates of the relevant parameters. The estimates were the result of a lifelong concern with empirically modeling and testing the main behavioral equations of the Keynesian system, a concern that is evidenced by many of the essays collected in these volumes. This endeavor found a synthesis with the construction of the so-called FMP (Federal Reserve-MIT-University of Pennsylvania) Econometric Model of the United States in the second half of the 1960s, in collaboration with Albert Ando—an invaluable lifelong associate in this as well as numerous other undertakings—Frank deLeuw, and many others.

As is well known, the Keynesian system rests on four basic blocks: the consumption function, the investment function, the demand for and supply of money and other deposits, and the mechanisms determining wages and prices. The two essays in part II of volume 1 deal with the derivation and estimation of demand and supply functions for currency and deposits, based on the assumption of (expected) profit maximization on the part of banks and deposit holders, with proper allowances for U.S. institutional features and the cost of adjustment.

The original streamlined Keynesian model assumed that one interest rate controlled both the demand and supply of money and the rate of investment in various types of physical assets. In reality what is determined in the money market is a short-term nominal rate (or a family of closely interrelated short-term rates), whereas investment in physical assets, whose very nature is durability, must respond to long-term real yields of a maturity commensurate to the life of the asset. Furthermore, the yields also must generally reflect the uncertainty of the cash flow generated by physical assets in contrast with the contractual certainty of the return from loan instruments. The three essays in part III are devoted to modeling the relationship between short- and long-term nominal yields on loans. Earlier work had provided a definitive answer to the nature of that relation in a world of certainty; to wit, that the long-term rate depends, in a well-defined fashion, on the path of short-term rates over the life of the long-term instrument. The first essay in part III, written with Richard Sutch—one of the many outstanding graduate students with whom I have been blessed—proposes and tests an extension of this earlier model to a world of uncertainty, dealing with both the formation of expectations of future rates and the effect of their uncertainty. The second essay, also written with Richard Sutch, uses the same framework to test the then-fashionable view that the term structure could be readily and significantly manipulated through changes in the maturity structure of the national debt (''operation twist''); the results were negative. The third essay, the result of collaboration with another outstanding graduate student, Robert Shiller, extends the model to a world characterized by significant and uncertain inflation—an extension inspired by the experience of recent years. It also shows that the hypothesis about the formation of expectations embedded in the model is consistent with rational expectations.

The relationship between the bond yield and the return required to justify an investment in risky physical assets is developed in three essays, the results of a long and productive cooperation with Merton H. Miller. Because the issue examined and the method of attack fall somewhat outside traditional macroeconomics and lie close to the heart of the theory of corporate finance, the essays are grouped under the heading of ''Essays in the Theory of Finance'' in volume 3. Indeed, their greatest impact has been in the field of corporate finance—at least if one is to judge from the efforts devoted to refute them. The basic message that has caused all the furor is that (1) in a world of uncertainty, the maximization of profit criterion is ill defined and must be replaced by the maximization of market value and (2) with well-functioning markets (and neutral taxes) and rational investors, who can ''undo'' the corporate financial structure by holding positive or negative amounts of debt, the market value of the firm—debt plus equity—depends *only* on the income stream generated by its assets. It follows, in particular, that the value of a firm should not be affected by the share of debt in its financial structure or by what will be done with the returns—paid out as dividends or reinvested (profitably). In essence, it will be determined by the capitalization of the expected stream of returns before interest at the rate which differs from the sure loan rate by a risk factor reflecting the risk characteristics of that stream. From the viewpoint of macroeconomics, the main implication of the analysis is that there exists one further slip between monetary policy and the investment component of aggregate demand, namely the risk premium required by the market to induce it to hold equities (or directly physical assets) instead of bonds.

Part IV of volume 1 deals with another major critical building block, investment in physical capital, which the early Keynesians (if not Keynes himself) tended to regard as largely unpredictable and capricious. The essay reproduced in this part— the result of teamwork with three coauthors, Albert Ando, Robert Rasche, and Stephen Turnowsky—endeavors to derive an aggregate investment function from the classical postulates of maximization over the relevant horizon, allowing for both technological progress and the effect of (anticipated) inflation. The function relies on the twin assumptions of a putty-clay technology—whose implications for aggregate investment were developed earlier in a path-breaking contribution by Charles Bischoff—and of oligopolistic pricing behavior as elaborated in the essay, "New Developments on the Oligopoly Front," reproduced in part V. The resulting aggregate investment function appears to account quite well for the behavior of investment in the postwar U.S. economy.

The concluding part V of volume 1 contains my main published contributions to the analysis of the mechanism determining wages and prices. I must acknowledge that the models of wage determination proposed and tested in these papers— aside from the analysis of the dynamics of the flows through the labor market inspired by the work of Charles Holt—remain, in good part, in the old Keynesian tradition of empirical generalization and are not supported by a rigorous analysis based on maximizing behavior. But then I do not believe that anyone else has yet provided a convincing analysis satisfying this requirement while accounting for the distressing slowness with which wages and prices appear to respond to unutilized labor and plant capacity. Indeed, the modeling of wage behavior remains to this day the Achilles heel of macroeconomic analysis.

The remaining basic building block of the Keynesian system, the consumption or saving function, is the one to which I have unquestionably dedicated the greatest attention, and it in turn has provided me with the greatest reward. Volume 2 is entirely devoted to twelve essays dealing with this subject.

The second contribution offers a recent overview of the life cycle hypothesis of saving (LCH), the empirical support for it that has been built over the years, and some major implications of both an analytical type and a policy type, providing appropriate references to other papers collected in volume 2. It first reviews the foundations of the model, as laid out in the early 1950s, by relying on the classical postulates of utility maximization applied to a decision horizon consisting of the household's life cycle. It then shows that this framework, once supplemented by some plausible assumptions about the nature of tastes and combined with well-established regularities about the profile of the life cycle of earnings, can provide a unified explanation for many well-known, but sometimes puzzling, empirical regularities in saving behavior. These include such disparate phenomena as the short-run cyclical variability and the long-run stability of the saving ratio; the long-run tendency for the proportion of income saved by a family at any given level of real income to decline as an economy develops; the evidence that family net worth tends to rise with age through much of life but tends to fall beyond dome point; or the finding that black families tend to save more than white families at any given level of income. At the same time, the model has yielded a number of implications, sometimes counterintuitive, that were not known at the time the model was proposed and have since been largely confirmed. Among these implications one might cite the apparent lack of significant association of the aggregate (private) saving rate with the economic well being of the country as measured by per capita real income or with the retention policies of corporate enterprises, and the very striking association of the saving rate with the rate of growth of per capita income and the age structure of the population.

Part II of volume 2 covers the basic LCH theory. The first two essays, which are the result of collaboration with a young graduate student, Richard Brumberg, lay the foundation for what has become known as the Life Cycle Hypothesis. The first contribution is well known, but the second was never published, as Richard Brumberg's untimely death sapped my will to undertake the revisions and tightening that would no doubt have been required to make the paper acceptable to one of the standard professional journals. Much of the content of the second essay has since become known through other papers and even through some limited private circulation. But some portions are still novel, notably the analysis of the implications of the LCH for the working of the so-called Pigou effect. It is shown that this effect is transient rather than permanent, as is usually supposed, and that it can maintain full employment equilibrium through time only on condition of a constant rate of deflation. As I see it now, this result has one further interesting "general equilibrium" implication that I intend to pursue at some future time. Once the nominal interest rate has been reduced to its institutional minimum, a steady (and hence fully anticipated) rate of deflation implies a real rate of interest at least as high as the rate of price decline. Accordingly, while steady deflation would reduce the rate of saving, it would (at least under neo-classical assumptions) also reduce the rate of investment. To establish that the Pigou effect can maintain full-employment equilibrium, one must, therefore, consider whether and under what conditions steady deflation can be expected to reduce saving more than investment.

The third essay of part II, the result of a collaboration initiated with Jacques Drèze when he too was a graduate student, examines the implications of uncertainty for saving within the general framework of the life cycle. Among the many results reported, one that is of particular interest for macroeconomics is the derivation of the rather restrictive sufficient conditions that allow for the saving decision to be independent of portfolio composition decisions—an independence that is usually taken for granted in macroeconomic models.

Part III focuses on the empirical verification of LCH. The first essay is the abstract of a much longer monograph, written with Albert Ando, devoted to cross-sectional verification. It also deals with clarifying the relationship between the LCH and its contemporary, the Permanent Income Hypothesis of Milton Friedman, which shares with LCH the postulate of utility maximizing over time as well as the powerful intellectual influence of Margaret Reid's work and teachings. The second and third essays, coauthored respectively with Albert Ando and Ezio Tarantelli, are devoted primarily to time series tests, one for the United States and the other for a developing country like Italy. The second essay also explores the implications of LCH with respect to the short- and long-run propensity to consume out of labor and property income, respectively. It is shown that these propensities will in general be different, a result qualitatively consistent with Kaldor's model of two castes—parsimonious capitalists and spendthrift laborers. However, according to the LCH, the long-run propensity to consume out of property income could very well exceed that out of labor income and, in fact, could exceed unity. These quantitative implications, shown to be consistent with the empirical evidence, are altogether irreconcilable with the Kaldorian paradigm and the many applications thereof.

The fourth essay examines and tests the implications of LCH with respect to the short- and long-run relationship between wealth and income, including inferences about the effect of the national debt on the stock of private wealth and private tangible wealth developed in the first essay of part 4. Finally, the last essay applies the LCH to the explanation of intercountry differences in the long-run saving rate, confirming the insignificant role of per capita income and the dominant role of the rate of growth of per capita income predicted by the model.

The two contributions in part IV apply the LCH to policy issues. In the first essay, the conceptual framework is used to throw new light on the classical issue of the burden of the national debt. It implies that the burden can be attributed to the public debt "crowding out" productive private capital with a resulting loss of income. To a first approximation, this loss is commensurate with the future flow of debt service, although it might be somewhat smaller or larger, depending on a variety of circumstances such as tax laws and the responsiveness of the demand for wealth to the rate of interest. The second essay shows that the LCH implies a novel channel by which monetary policy affects consumption, namely through the market value of wealth responding to changes in the capitalization rate of property income induced by changes in market interest rates. Furthermore, simulation experiments with empirically estimated parameters suggest that this mechanism could play a major role in the working of monetary policy, since the response to consumption is not only appreciable but also fast relative to other channels. However, these results must be regarded as tentative until a number of remaining conceptual issues have been clarified.

Volume 3 includes the balance of my selected works in macroeconomics and closely related areas, as well as a selection of papers in other areas. The first three essays in part I—"The Theory of Finance"—were discussed earlier in the introduction. The remaining two contributions examine the impact of inflation on financial markets and investment decisions, with special reference to the disruptive effects of inflation on the mortgage and housing markets. They also explore the role and consequences of the introduction of indexed loan contracts and summarize some results of a larger monograph on "Mortgage Designs for an Inflationary Environment," written by a research team at the Massachusetts Institute of Technology.

Part II brings together a number of contributions in which the view of the macroeconomic system set forth in all the preceding essays is brought to bear on various issues of policy. The lead essay, coauthored with Giorgio LaMalfa, analyzes the first Italian endeavor at dealing with a nominal wage explosion in 1963–64 still in a world of fixed parities. The second essay criticizes the U.S. economic policy in 1973 and warns that the Federal Reserve's announced policy of adhering strictly to a no-more-than 6 percent growth rate of the money supply would lead to a serious contraction—as it did. The main relevance of the third contribution, coauthored with Lucas Papademos, is found not in the policy recommendations as such but in its analysis of the reasons for the sharp differences in policies prescribed by different schools for dealing with the great stagflation beginning in 1974–75. It attempts to sort out the role of different views of the monetary mechanism, different estimates of the relevant parameters in contrast with different valuations of the cost of tolerating inflation and unemployment, and different assessments of the risks of entrusting government with discretionary powers. It concludes that analytical differences play a minor role compared to value judgments and even political philosophy. In other words, contrary to the popular stereotype, economists do not really disagree on policy as economists—they disagree as men.

The last essay in part II, coauthored with an Italian colleague, Tommaso Padoa-Schioppa, was again inspired by the recent Italian experience. It examines the nearly hopeless task confronting stabilization authorities in an economy in which, with the help of 100 percent indexation, powerful unions are able to fix the real wage rate arbitrarily. In a closed, and even more clearly in an open, economy the authorities are confronted with a Phillips-curve type trade-off between permanent inflation and unemployment that is worse the higher the real wage, and which cannot be improved by conventional demand policies. It is shown, in particular, that the inflation does not significantly depend on the size of the government deficit (within limits) and that, in fact, an endeavor to reduce the deficit by measures such as raising indirect taxes or reducing government employment is likely to increase rather than decrease inflation. Other means of improving the trade-off are explored, with disappointingly meager results.

Part III of volume 3 brings together a number of essays in international economics. This is an area to which I first devoted major attention in the second half of the 1940s while working on the book *National Income and International Trade* in collaboration with Hans Neisser. This collaboration proved to be of great educational value to me.

The first of the essays in part III marks my return to international economics fifteen years later. This contribution, as well as the second essay, represents an endeavor—not very successful—to improve the tottering Bretton Woods system by attacking some of the major shortcomings of the day. The first paper, coauthored with Peter Kenen, was written at a time when the U.S. balance of payment deficit was the main source of international liquidity, and yet the rest of the world was deeply troubled by the size and persistence of that deficit. We proposed as a solution the creation of a new international fiat money—the Medium for International Transactions, or MIT. Its quantity was to be regulated by the agreed upon reserve targets of the participating countries, thus solving the troublesome problem of the potential instability in the demand for reserves. At the same time, the adjustment mechanism was to be improved by symmetrical penalties on the deviations of reserves from the target in either direction, and through more flexibility in changing parities. A mechanism was even suggested for stabilizing the purchasing power of the new money. An international money was later created—though with the much less colorful name of Special Drawing Rights (SDR)—but the other more novel suggestions had no visible impact.

The second essay, written with Hossein Askari, came five years later, by which time an even larger U.S. balance of payment deficit, compounded by a deteriorating current account balance, had brought the Bretton Woods System to the verge of collapse. Now the major difficulty was arising from the inability of the United States to devalue its currency relative to other currencies and from the threat of mass demands for conversion of foreign official dollar claims into gold or an equivalent. The two demands made on the United States—that it should make the dollar freely convertible while forsaking the right of changing parity unilaterally— were clearly inconsistent. The inconsistency would be resolved by the United States giving up control over its exchange rate, which would be entrusted to the other countries, but at the same time making the dollar inconvertible de jure. In addition, holders of dollar reserves would be given an option of exchange rate guarantees in terms of the SDR, which was to be turned into a stable purchasing power money by letting the rate of exchange between the dollar and the SDR vary inversely with an index of the purchasing power of the dollar. As it turned out, by the time the proposal came out in print, the Bretton Woods system had already received its death blow through the unilateral suspension of convertibility of the dollar.

The third essay takes issue with the then-popular view that fixed parities could be made consistent with full employment and freedom of capital movements even in the presence of price rigidities, provided fiscal policy was used to offset the gap between full-employment saving and the sum of investment at the world interest rates and whatever current account balance might result from the given exchange rate and domestic price level. The essay shows that, in fact, this approach is highly wasteful because it is inconsistent with capital flowing from countries with a potential surplus of saving to those with a potential deficit. In the absence of price flexibility, the flow can be achieved only via adjustment in exchange rates. The purported solution, instead of preserving freedom of capital movement so that capital would move, relied, in effect, on fiscal policy to control the movement of capital for the sake of preserving freedom of capital movement.

The next essay in part III, written in cooperation with Hossein Askari, endeavors to analyze the effectiveness of alternative exchange regimes, ranging from fixed parities through crawling pegs to free floating rates, in terms of the twin criteria of allowing long-term capital movements and minimizing the international transmission of internal disturbances. The analysis points to the crawling peg as the most promising solution, with floating rates as a second best.

The last essay is one sample of my many testimonies offered over the years to congressional committees. It was given in the spring of 1974, but is based on two articles written in January 1974 for the Italian newspaper, "Il Corriere della Sera," at the height of the oil crisis. It provides an analysis of the problems created for the world economy by the rise in the price of oil and how they should have been handled to minimize the negative consequences, which, I feel, still makes good reading.

From 1949 to 1952, I was in charge of a research project on "Expectations and Business Fluctuations" financed on a generous scale (for the time) by the Merrill Foundation for the Advancement of Financial Knowledge. Part IV of volume 3 contains two contributions that have come out of the project. Both deal with the role of expectations and plans in economic behavior and with the nature of the relevant expectation and planning horizon. Although limitations of space have made it possible to include only a token representation of the outcome of the project, I want to stress that the impact of that research on my professional development goes well beyond what one might infer from the relative allotment of space. For instance, as is pointed out in the first note of each of the joint papers with Richard Brumberg, the Life Cycle Model was partly inspired by the analysis, undertaken in the course of that project, of the role of inventories in permitting smoothing of the production schedule, with attendant cost advantages, in the face of variability—predictable and unpredictable—of sales. Another fallout from that project is reflected in my contribution to the book *Planning Production, Inventories, and Work Force,* coauthored with C. C. Holt, H. Simon and J. Muth.

The single essay in the concluding part V was written with Emil Grunberg while we were colleagues at the then-Carnegie Institute of Technology. It was originally conceived as a clever essay in methodology but has since acquired a new interest. The problem posed in the essay, whether it is possible to make correct public forecasts given that those whose behavior is forecasted respond to the forecast was answered by means of Brower's fixed point theorem. But that problem is formally the same as the one posed by the analysis of the working of an economic system in which agents form rational expectations in the Muthian sense. These expectations must be correct on the average after allowing for the fact that the future realization depends on these expectations.

PART I
The Monetary Mechanism

The Monetarist Controversy or, Should We Forsake Stabilization Policies?

By FRANCO MODIGLIANI*

In recent years and especially since the onset of the current depression, the economics profession and the lay public have heard a great deal about the sharp conflict between "monetarists and Keynesians" or between "monetarists and fiscalists." The difference between the two "schools" is generally held to center on whether the money supply or fiscal variables are the major determinants of aggregate economic activity, and hence the most appropriate tool of stabilization policies.

My central theme is that this view is quite far from the truth, and that the issues involved are of far greater practical import. There are in reality no serious analytical disagreements between leading monetarists and leading nonmonetarists. Milton Friedman was once quoted as saying, "We are all Keynesians, now," and I am quite prepared to reciprocate that "we are all monetarists"—if by monetarism is meant assigning to the stock of money a major role in determining output and prices. Indeed, the list of those who have long been monetarists in this sense is quite extensive, including among other John Maynard Keynes as well as myself, as is attested by my 1944 and 1963 articles.

In reality the distinguishing feature of the monetarist school and the real issues of disagreement with nonmonetarists is not monetarism, but rather the role that should probably be assigned

to stabilization policies. Nonmonetarists accept what I regard to be the fundamental practical message of *The General Theory*: that a private enterprise economy using an intangible money *needs* to be stabilized, *can* be stabilized, and therefore *should* be stabilized by appropriate monetary and fiscal policies. Monetarists by contrast take the view that there is no serious need to stabilize the economy; that even if there were a need, it could not be done, for stabilization policies would be more likely to increase than to decrease instability; and, at least some monetarists would, I believe, go so far as to hold that, even in the unlikely event that stabilization policies could on balance prove beneficial, the government should not be trusted with the necessary power.

What has led me to address this controversy is the recent spread of monetarism, both in a simplistic, superficial form and in the form of growing influence on the practical conduct of economic policy, which influence, I shall argue presently, has played at least some role in the economic upheavals of the last three years.

In what follows then, I propose first to review the main arguments bearing on the *need* for stabilization policies, that is, on the likely extent of instability in the absence of such policies, and then to examine the issue of the supposed destabilizing effect of pursuing stabilization policies. My main concern will be with instability generated by the traditional type of disturbances—demand shocks. But before I am through, I will give some consideration to the difficult problems raised by the newer type of disturbance—supply shocks.

I. The Keynesian Case for Stabilization Policies

A. *The General Theory*

Keynes' novel conclusion about the need for

*Presidential address delivered at the eighty-ninth meeting of the American Economic Association, Atlantic City, New Jersey, September 17, 1976. The list of those to whom I am indebted for contributing to shape the ideas expressed above is much too large to be included in this footnote. I do wish, however, to single out two lifetime collaborators to whom my debt is especially large, Albert Ando and Charles Holt. I also wish to express my thanks to Richard Cohn, Rudiger Dornbusch, and Benjamin Friedman for their valuable criticism of earlier drafts, and to David Modest for carrying out the simulations and other computations mentioned in the text.

stabilization policies, as was brought out by the early interpreters of *The General Theory* (for example, John Hicks, the author, 1944), resulted from the interaction of a basic contribution to traditional monetary theory—liquidity preference—and an unorthodox hypothesis about the working of the labor market—complete downward rigidity of wages.

Because of liquidity preference, a change in aggregate demand, which may be broadly defined as any event that results in a change in the market clearing or equilibrium rate of interest, will produce a corresponding change in the real demand for money or velocity of circulation, and hence in the real stock of money needed at full employment. As long as wages are perfectly flexible, even with a constant nominal supply, full employment could and would be maintained by a change of wages and prices as needed to produce the required change in the real money supply—though even in this case, stability of the price level would require a countercyclical monetary policy. But, under the Keynesian wage assumption the classical adjustment through prices can occur only in the case of an increased demand. In the case of a decline, instead, wage rigidity prevents the necessary increase in the real money supply and the concomitant required fall in interest rates. Hence, if the nominal money supply is constant, the initial equilibrium must give way to a new stable one, characterized by lower output and by an involuntary reduction in employment, so labeled because it does not result from a shift in notional demand and supply schedules in terms of real wages, but only from an insufficient real money supply. The nature of this equilibrium is elegantly captured by the Hicksian *IS-LM* paradigm, which to our generation of economists has become almost as familiar as the demand-supply paradigm was to earlier ones.

This analysis implied that a fixed money supply far from insuring approximate stability of prices and output, as held by the traditional view, would result in a rather unstable economy, alternating between periods of protracted unemployment and stagnation, and bursts of inflation.

The extent of downward instability would depend in part on the size of the exogenous shocks to demand and in part on the strength of what may be called the Hicksian mechanism. By this I mean the extent to which a shift in *IS*, through its interaction with *LM*, results in some decline in interest rates and thus in a change in income which is smaller than the original shift. The stabilizing power of this mechanism is controlled by various parameters of the system. In particular, the economy will be more unstable the greater the interest elasticity of demand for money, and the smaller the interest responsiveness of aggregate demand. Finally, a large multiplier is also destabilizing in that it implies a larger shift in *IS* for a given shock.

However, the instability could be readily counteracted by appropriate stabilization policies. Monetary policy could change the nominal supply of money so as to *accommodate* the change in real demand resulting from shocks in aggregate demand. Fiscal policy, through expenditure and taxes, could *offset* these shocks, making full employment consistent with the initial nominal money stock. In general, both monetary and fiscal policies could be used in combination. But because of a perceived uncertainty in the response of demand to changes in interest rates, and because changes in interest rates through monetary policy could meet difficulties and substantial delays related to expectations (so-called liquidity traps), fiscal policy was regarded as having some advantages.

B. *The Early Keynesians*

The early disciples of the new Keynesian gospel, still haunted by memories of the Great Depression, frequently tended to outdo Keynes' pessimism about potential instability. Concern with liquidity traps fostered the view that the demand for money was highly interest elastic; failure to distinguish between the short- and long-run marginal propensity to save led to overestimating the long-run saving rate, thereby fostering concern with stagnation, and to underestimating the short-run propensity, thereby exaggerating the short-run multiplier. Interest rates were supposed to affect, at best, the demand for long-lived fixed investments, and the interest elasticity was deemed to be low. Thus, shocks were believed to produce a large response. Finally, investment demand was seen as capriciously controlled by "animal spirits," thus providing an important source of shocks. All this justified calling for very active stabilization policies. Furthermore, since the very circumstances which produce a large response to demand shocks also produce a large response to *fiscal* and a small response to *monetary* actions, there was a tendency to focus on fiscal policy as the main tool to keep the economy at near full employment.

C. *The Phillips Curve*

In the two decades following *The General Theory*, there were a number of developments of the Keynesian system including dynamization of the model, the stress on taxes versus expenditures and the balanced budget multiplier, and the first attempts at estimating the critical parameters through econometric techniques and models. But for present purposes, the most important one was the uncovering of a "stable" statistical relation between the rate of change of wages and the rate of unemployment, which has since come to be known as the Phillips curve. This relation, and its generalization by Richard Lipsey to allow for the effect of recent inflation, won wide acceptance even before an analytical underpinning could be provided for it, in part because it could account for the "puzzling" experience of 1954 and 1958, when wages kept rising despite the substantial rise in unemployment. It also served to dispose of the rather sterile "cost push" – "demand pull" controversy.

In the following years, a good deal of attention went into developing theoretical foundations for the Phillips curve, in particular along the lines of search models (for example, Edmund Phelps et al.). This approach served to shed a new light on the nature of unemployment by tracing it in the first place to labor turnover and search time rather than to lack of jobs as such: in a sense unemployment is all frictional—at least in de-

veloped countries. At the same time it clarified how the availability of more jobs tends to reduce unemployment by increasing vacancies and thus reducing search time.

Acceptance of the Phillips curve relation implied some significant changes in the Keynesian framework which partly escaped notice until the subsequent monetarists' attacks. Since the rate of change of wages decreased smoothly with the rate of unemployment, there was no longer a unique Full Employment but rather a whole family of possible equilibrium rates, each associated with a different rate of inflation (and requiring, presumably, a different long-run growth of money). It also impaired the notion of a stable underemployment equilibrium. A fall in demand could still cause an initial rise in unemployment but this rise, by reducing the growth of wages, would eventually raise the real money supply, tending to return unemployment to the equilibrium rate consistent with the given long-run growth of money.

But at the practical level it did not lessen the case for counteracting lasting demand disturbances through stabilization policies rather than by relying on the slow process of wage adjustment to do the job, at the cost of protracted unemployment and instability of prices. Indeed, the realm of stabilization policies appeared to expand in the sense that the stabilization authority had the power of choosing the unemployment rate around which employment was to be stabilized, though it then had to accept the associated inflation. Finally, the dependence of wage changes also on past inflation forced recognition of a distinction between the short- and the long-run Phillips curve, the latter exhibiting the long-run equilibrium rate of inflation implied by a *maintained* unemployment rate. The fact that the long-run tradeoff between unemployment and inflation was necessarily less favorable than the short-run one, opened up new vistas of "enjoy-it-now, pay-later" policies, and even resulted in an entertaining literature on the political business cycle and how to stay in the saddle by riding the Phillips curve (see for example, Ray Fair, William Nordhaus).

II. The Monetarists' Attack

A. The Stabilizing Power of the Hicksian Mechanism

The monetarists' attack on Keynesianism was directed from the very beginning not at the Keynesian framework as such, but at whether it really implied a need for stabilization. It rested on a radically different empirical assessment of the value of the parameters controlling the stabilizing power of the Hicksian mechanism and of the magnitude and duration of response to shocks, given a stable money supply. And this different assessment in turn was felt to justify a radical downgrading of the *practical relevance* of the Keynesian framework as distinguished from its *analytical validity*.

Liquidity preference was a fine contribution to monetary theory but in practice the responsiveness of the demand for money, and hence of velocity, to interest rates, far from being unmanageably large, was so small that according to a well-known paper by Milton Friedman (1969), it could not even be detected empirically. On the other hand, the effect of interest rates on aggregate demand was large and by no means limited to the traditional fixed investments but quite pervasive. The difficulty of detecting it empirically resulted from focusing on a narrow range of measured market rates and from the fact that while the aggregate could be counted on to respond, the response of individual components might not be stable. Finally, Friedman's celebrated contribution to the theory of the consumption function (1957) (and my own work on the life cycle hypothesis with Richard Brumberg and others, reviewed by the author, 1975) implied a very high short-run marginal propensity to save in response to transient disturbances to income and hence a small short-run multiplier.

All this justified the conclusion that (i) though demand shocks might qualitatively work along the lines described by Keynes, quantitatively the Hicks mechanism is so strong that their impact would be *small* and *transient*, provided the stock of money was kept on a steady growth path; (ii) fiscal policy actions, like other demand shocks, would have *minor* and *transitory* effects on demand, while changes in money would produce *large* and *permanent* effects on money income; and, therefore, (iii) the observed instability of the economy, which was anyway proving moderate as the postwar period unfolded, was most likely the result of the unstable growth of money, be it due to misguided endeavors to stabilize income or to the pursuit of other targets, which were either irrelevant or, in the case of balance of payments goals, should have been made irrelevant by abandoning fixed exchanges.

B. The Demise of Wage Rigidity and the Vertical Phillips Curve

But the most serious challenge came in Friedman's 1968 Presidential Address, building on ideas independently put forth also by Phelps (1968). Its basic message was that, despite appearances, wages were in reality perfectly flexible and there was accordingly *no* involuntary unemployment. The evidence to the contrary, including the Phillips curve, was but a statistical illusion resulting from failure to differentiate between price changes and *unexpected* price changes.

Friedman starts out by reviving the Keynesian notion that, at any point of time, there exists a unique full-employment rate which he labels the "natural rate." An unanticipated fall in demand in Friedman's competitive world leads firms to reduce prices and also output and employment along the short-run marginal cost curve—unless the nominal wage declines together with prices. But workers, failing to judge correctly the current and prospective fall in prices, misinterpret the reduction of nominal wages as a cut in *real* wages. Hence, assuming a positively sloped supply function, they reduce the supply of labor. As a result, the effective real wage rises to the point where the resulting decline in the demand for labor matches the reduced supply. Thus, output falls not because of the decline in demand, but because of the entirely voluntary reduction in the supply of labor, in response to erroneous perceptions. Furthermore, the fall in employment can only be temporary, as expectations must soon catch up with the facts, at least in the absence of new shocks. The very same mechanism works in the case of an increase in demand, so that the responsiveness of wages and prices is the same on either side of the natural rate.

The upshot is that Friedman's model also implies a Phillips-type relation between inflation, employment or unemployment, and past inflation,—provided the latter variable is interpreted as a reasonable proxy for expected inflation. But it turns the standard explanation on its head: instead of (excess) employment causing inflation, it is (the unexpected component of) the rate of inflation that causes excess employment.

One very basic implication of Friedman's model is that the coefficient of price expectations should be precisely unity. This specification implies that whatever the shape of the short-run Phillips curve—a shape determined by the relation between expected and actual price changes, and by the elasticity of labor supply with respect to the perceived real wage—the long-run curve *must be vertical*.

Friedman's novel twist provided a fresh prop for the claim that stabilization policies are not really needed, for, with wages flexible, except possibly for transient distortions, the Hicksian mechanism receives powerful reinforcement from changes in the real money supply. Similarly, the fact that full employment was a razor edge provided new support for the claim that stabilization policies were bound to prove destabilizing.

C. The Macro Rational Expectations Revolution

But the death blow to the already badly battered Keynesian position was to come only shortly thereafter by incorporating into Friedman's model the so-called rational expectation hypothesis, or *REH*. Put very roughly, this hypothesis, originally due to John Muth, states that rational economic agents will endeavor to form expectations of relevant future variables by making the most efficient use of all information

provided by past history. It is a fundamental and fruitful contribution that has already found many important applications, for example, in connection with speculative markets, and as a basis for some thoughtful criticism by Robert Lucas (1976) of certain features of econometric models. What I am concerned with here is only its application to macro-economics, or *MREH*, associated with such authors as Lucas (1972), Thomas Sargent (1976), and Sargent and Neil Wallace (1976).

The basic ingredient of *MREH* is the postulate that the workers of Friedman's model hold rational expectations, which turns out to have a number of remarkable implications: (i) errors of price expectations, which are the only source of departure from the natural state, cannot be avoided but they can only be short-lived and random. In particular, there cannot be persistent unemployment above the natural rate for this would imply high serial correlation between the successive errors of expectation, which is inconsistent with rational expectations; (ii) any attempts to stabilize the economy by means of stated monetary or fiscal rules are bound to be totally ineffective because their effect will be fully discounted in rational expectations; (iii) nor can the government successfully pursue *ad hoc* measures to offset shocks. The private sector is already taking care of any anticipated shock; therefore government policy could conceivably help only if the government information was better than that of the public, which is impossible, by the very definition of rational expectations. Under these conditions, *ad hoc* stabilization policies are most likely to produce instead further destabilizing shocks.

These are clearly remarkable conclusions, and a major *re*discovery—for it had all been said 40 years ago by Keynes in a well-known passage of *The General Theory*:

> If, indeed, labour were always in a position to take action (and were to do so), whenever there was less than full employment, to reduce its money demands by concerted action to whatever point was required to make money so abundant rela-

tively to the wage-unit that the rate of interest would fall to a level compatible with full employment, we should, in effect, have monetary management by the Trade Unions, aimed at full employment, instead of by the banking systems.
[p. 267]

The only novelty is that *MREH* replaces Keynes' opening "if" with a "since."

If one accepts this little amendment, the case against stabilization policies is complete. The economy is inherently pretty stable—except possibly for the effect of government messing around. And to the extent that there is a small residual instability, it is beyond the power of human beings, let alone the government, to alleviate it.

III. How Valid Is the Monetarist Case?

A. *The Monetarist Model of Wage Price Behavior*

In setting out the counterattack it is convenient to start with the monetarists' model of price and wage behavior. Here one must distinguish between the model as such and a specific implication of that model, namely that the long-run Phillips curve is vertical, or, in substance, that, in the long run, money is neutral. That conclusion, by now, does not meet serious objection from nonmonetarists, at least as a first approximation.

But the proposition that other things equal, and given time enough, the economy will eventually adjust to any indefinitely maintained stock of money, or *n*th derivative thereof, can be derived from a variety of models and, in any event, is of very little practical relevance, as I will argue below. What is unacceptable, because inconsistent with both micro and macro evidence, is the specific monetarist model set out above and its implication that all unemployment is a voluntary, fleeting response to transitory misperceptions.

One may usefully begin with a criticism of the Macro Rational Expectations model and why Keynes' "if" should not be replaced by "since." At the logical level, Benjamin Friedman has called attention to the omission from *MREH* of an explicit learning model, and has suggested that, as a result, it can only be interpreted as a description not of short-run but of long-run equilibrium in which no agent would wish to recontract. But then the implications of *MREH* are clearly far from startling, and their policy relevance is almost nil. At the institutional level, Stanley Fischer has shown that the mere recognition of long-term contracts is sufficient to generate wage rigidity and a substantial scope for stabilization policies. But the most glaring flaw of *MREH* is its inconsistency with the evidence: if it were valid, deviations of unemployment from the natural rate would be small and transitory—in which case *The General Theory* would not have been written and neither would this paper. Sargent (1976) has attempted to remedy this fatal flaw by hypothesizing that the persistent and large fluctuations in unemployment reflect merely corresponding swings in the natural rate itself. In other words, what happened to the United States in the 1930's was a severe attack of contagious laziness! I can only say that, despite Sargent's ingenuity, neither I nor, I expect, most others at least of the nonmonetarists' persuasion are quite ready yet to turn over the field of economic fluctuations to the social psychologist!

Equally serious objections apply to Friedman's modeling of the commodity market as a perfectly competitive one—so that the real wage rate is continuously equated to the *short-run* marginal product of labor—and to his treatment of labor as a homogenous commodity traded in an auction market, so that, at the going wage, there never is any excess demand by firms or excess supply by workers. The inadequacies of this model as a useful formalization of present day Western economies are so numerous that only a few of the major ones can be mentioned here.

Friedman's view of unemployment as a voluntary reduction in labor supply could at best provide an explanation of variations in labor force—and then only under the questionable assumption that the supply function has a significantly positive slope—but cannot readily account for changes in unemployment. Furthermore, it cannot be reconciled with the well-known fact that *rising* unemployment is accompanied by a fall, not by a *rise* in quits, nor with the role played by temporary layoffs to which Martin Feldstein has recently called attention. Again, his competitive model of the commodity market, accepted also in *The General Theory*, implies that changes in real wages, adjusted for long-run productivity trend, should be significantly negatively correlated with cyclical changes in employment and output and with changes in money wages. But as early as 1938, John Dunlop showed that this conclusion was rejected by some eighty years of British experience and his results have received some support in more recent tests of Ronald Bodkin for the United States and Canada. Similar tests of my own, using quarterly data, provide striking confirmation that for the last two decades from the end of the Korean War until 1973, the association of trend adjusted real compensations of the private nonfarm sector with either employment or the change in nominal compensation is prevailingly positive and very significantly so.[1]

This evidence can, instead, be accounted for by the oligopolistic pricing model—according to which price is determined by *long-run* mini-

mum average cost up to a mark-up reflecting entry-preventing considerations (see the author, 1958)—coupled with some lags in the adjustment of prices to costs. This model implies that firms respond to a change in demand by endeavoring to adjust output and employment, without significant changes in prices relative to wages; and the resulting changes in available jobs have their initial impact not on wages but rather on unemployment by way of layoffs and recalls and through changes in the level of vacancies, and hence on the length of average search time.

If, in the process, vacancies rise above a critical level, or "natural rate," firms will endeavor to reduce them by outbidding each other, thereby raising the rate of change of wages. Thus, as long as jobs and vacancies remain above, and unemployment remains below, some critical level which might be labeled the "noninflationary rate" (see the author and Lucas Papademos, 1975), wages and prices will tend to accelerate. If, on the other hand, jobs fall below, and unemployment rises above, the noninflationary rate, firms finding that vacancies are less than optimal —in the limit the unemployed queuing outside the gate will fill them instantly—will have an incentive to reduce their relative wage offer. But in this case, in which too much labor is looking for too few jobs, the trend toward a sustained decline in the rate of growth of wages is likely to be even weaker than the corresponding acceleration when too many jobs are bidding for too few people. The main reason is the nonhomogeneity of labor. By far the largest and more valuable source of labor supply to a firm consists of those already employed who are not readily interchangeable with the unemployed and, in contrast with them, are concerned with protecting their earnings and not with reestablishing full employment. For these reasons, and because the first to quit are likely to be the best workers, a reduction of the labor force can, within limits, be accomplished more economically, not by reducing wages to generate enough quits, but by firing or, when possible, by layoffs which insure access to a trained labor force when demand recovers. More generally, the inducement to

---

[1] Thus, in a logarithmic regression of private nonfarm hourly compensation deflated by the private nonfarm deflator on output per man-hour, time, and private nonfarm employment, after correcting for first-order serial correlation, the latter variable has a coefficient of .17 and a *t*-ratio of 5. Similar though less significant results were found for manufacturing. If employment is replaced by the change in nominal compensation, its coefficient is .40 with a *t*-ratio of 6.5. Finally, if the change in compensation is replaced by the change in price, despite the negative bias from error of measurement of price, the coefficient of this variable is only $-.09$ with an entirely insignificant *t*-ratio of .7. The period after 1973 has been omitted from the tests as irrelevant for our purposes, since the inflation was driven primarily by an exogenous price shock rather than by excess demand. As a result of the shock, prices, and to some extent wages, rose rapidly while employment and real wages fell. Thus, the addition of the last two years tends to increase spuriously the positive association between real wages and employment, and to decrease that between real wages and the change in nominal wages or prices.

The Monetary Mechanism   9

reduce relative wages to eliminate the excess supply is moderated by the effect that such a reduction would have on quits and costly turnover, even when the resulting vacancies can be readily filled from the ranks of the unemployed. Equally relevant are the consequences in terms of loss of morale and good will, in part for reasons which have been elaborated by the literature on implicit contracts (see Robert Gordon). Thus, while there will be some tendency for the rate of change of wages to fall, the more so the larger the unemployment—at least in an economy like the United States where there are no overpowering centralized unions—that tendency is severely damped.

And whether, given an unemployment rate significantly and persistently above the noninflationary level, the rate of change of wages would, eventually, tend to turn negative and decline without bound or whether it would tend to an asymptote is a question that I doubt the empirical evidence will ever answer. The one experiment we have had—the Great Depression—suggests the answer is negative, and while I admit that, for a variety of reasons, that evidence is muddied, I hope that we will never have the opportunity for a second, clean experiment.

In any event, what is really important for practical purposes is not the long-run equilibrium relation as such, but the speed with which it is approached. Both the model sketched out and the empirical evidence suggest that the process of acceleration or deceleration of wages when unemployment differs from the noninflationary rate will have more nearly the character of a crawl than of a gallop. It will suffice to recall in this connection that there was excess demand pressure in the United States at least from 1965 to mid-1970, and during that period the growth of inflation was from some 1.5 to only about 5.5 percent per year. And the response to the excess supply pressure from mid-1970 to early 1973, and from late 1974 to date was equally sluggish.

B. *The Power of Self-Stabilizing Mechanisms: The Evidence from Econometric Models*

There remains to consider the monetarists' initial criticism of Keynesianism, to wit, that even without high wage flexibility, the system's response to demand shocks is small and short-lived, thanks to the power of the Hicksian mechanism. Here it must be acknowledged that every one of the monetarists' criticisms of early, simpleminded Keynesianism has proved in considerable measure correct.

With regard to the interest elasticity of demand for money, post-Keynesian developments in the theory of money, and in particular, the theoretical contributions of William Baumol, James Tobin, Merton Miller, and Daniel Orr, point to a modest value of around one-half to one-third, and empirical studies (see for example, Stephen Goldfeld) are largely consistent with this prediction (at least until 1975!). Similarly, the dependence of consumption on long-run, or life cycle, income and on wealth, together with the high marginal tax rates of the postwar period, especially the corporate tax, and leakages through imports, lead to a rather low estimate of the multiplier.

Last but not least, both theoretical and empirical work, reflected in part in econometric models, have largely vindicated the monetarist contention that interest effects on demand are pervasive and substantial. Thus, in the construction and estimation of the MIT-Penn-Social Science Research Council *(MPS)* econometric model of the United States, we found evidence of effects, at least modest, on nearly every component of aggregate demand. One response to money supply changes that is especially important in the *MPS*, if somewhat controversial, is via interest rates on the market value of all assets and thus on consumption.

There is, therefore, substantial agreement that in the United States the Hicksian mechanism is fairly effective in limiting the effect of shocks, and that the response of wages and prices to excess demand or supply will also work *gradually* toward eliminating largely, if not totally, any effect on employment. But in the view of nonmonetarists, the evidence overwhelmingly supports the conclusion that the *interim* response is still of significant magnitude and of considerable duration, basically because the wheels of the offsetting mechanism grind slowly. To be sure, the first link of the mechanism, the rise in short-term rates, gets promptly into play and heftily, given the low money demand elasticity; but most expenditures depend on long-term rates, which generally respond but gradually, and the demand response is generally also gradual. Furthermore, while this response is building up, multiplier and accelerator mechanisms work toward amplifying the shock. Finally, the classical mechanism—the change in real money supply through prices—has an even longer lag because of the sluggish response of wages to excess demand.

These interferences are supported by simulations with econometric models like the *MPS*. Isolating, first, the working of the Hicksian mechanism by holding prices constant, we find that a 1 percent demand shock, say a rise in real exports, produces an impact effect on aggregate output which is barely more than 1 percent, rises to a peak of only about 2 percent a year later, and then declines slowly toward a level somewhat over 1.5 percent.

Taking into account the wage price mechanism hardly changes the picture for the first year because of its inertia. Thereafter, however, it becomes increasingly effective so that a year later the real response is back at the impact level, and by the end of the third year the shock has been fully offset (thereafter output oscillates around zero in a damped fashion). Money income, on the other hand, reaches a peak of over 2.5, and then only by the middle of the second year. It declines thereafter, and tends eventually to oscillate around a *positive* value because normally, a demand shock requires eventually a change in interest rates and hence in velocity and money income.

These results, which are broadly confirmed by other econometric models, certainly do not support the view of a highly unstable economy in which fiscal policy has powerful and everlasting effects. But neither do they support the monetarist view of a highly stable economy in which shocks hardly make a ripple and the effects of fiscal policy are puny and fast vanishing.

C. The Monetarist Evidence and the St. Louis Quandary

Monetarists, however, have generally been inclined to question this evidence. They coun-

tered at first with tests bearing on the stability of velocity and the insignificance of the multiplier, which, however, as indicated in my criticism with Albert Ando (1965), must be regarded as close to worthless. More recently, several authors at the Federal Reserve Bank of St. Louis (Leonall Andersen, Keith Carlson, Jerry Lee Jordan) have suggested that instead of deriving multipliers from the analytical or numerical solution of an econometric model involving a large number of equations, any one of which may be questioned, they should be estimated directly through "reduced form" equations by relating the change in income to current and lagged changes in some appropriate measure of the money supply and of fiscal impulses.

The results of the original test, using the current and but four lagged values of M^1 and of high Employment Federal Expenditure as measures of monetary and fiscal impulses, turned out to be such as to fill a monetarist's heart with joy. The contribution of money, not only current but also lagged, was large and the coefficients implied a not unreasonable effect of the order of magnitude of the velocity of circulation, though somewhat higher. On the other hand, the estimated coefficients of the fiscal variables seemed to support fully the monetarists' claim that their impact was both small and fleeting: the effect peaked in but two quarters and was only around one, and disappeared totally by the fourth quarter following the change.

These results were immediately attacked on the ground that the authors had used the wrong measure of monetary and fiscal actions, and it was shown that the outcome was somewhat sensitive to alternative measures; however, the basic nature of the results did not change, at least qualitatively. In particular, the outcome does not differ materially, at least for the original period up to 1969, if one replaces high employment outlays with a variable that might be deemed more suitable, like government expenditure on goods and services, plus exports.

These results must be acknowledged as disturbing for nonmonetarists, for there is little question that movements in government purchases and exports are a major source of demand disturbances; if econometric model estimates of the response to demand disturbances are roughly valid, how can they be so grossly inconsistent with the reduced form estimates?

Attempts at reconciling the two have taken several directions, which are reviewed in an article coauthored with Ando (1976). Our main conclusion, based on simulation techniques, is that when income is subject to substantial shocks from many sources other than monetary and fiscal, so that these variables account for only a moderate portion of the variations in income (in the United States, it has been of the order of one-half to two-thirds), then the St. Louis reduced form method yields highly unstable and unreliable estimates of the true structure of the system generating the data.

The crucial role of unreliability and instability has since been confirmed in more recent work of Daniel O'Neill in his forthcoming thesis. He shows in the first place that different methods of estimation yield widely different estimates, including many which clearly overstate the expenditure and understate the money multipliers. He further points out that, given the unreliability of the estimates resulting from multicollinearity and large residual variance, the relevant question to ask is not whether these estimates differ from those obtained by structural estimation, but whether the *difference is statistically significant*; that is, larger than could be reasonably accounted for by sampling fluctuations.

I have carried out this standard statistical test using as true response coefficients those generated by the *MPS* model quoted earlier.[2] I find that, at least when the test is based on the largest possible sample—the entire post-Korean period up to the last two very disturbed years—the difference is totally insignificant when estimation is in level form (F is less than one) and is still not significant at the 5 percent level, when in

first differences.

This test resolves the puzzle by showing that there really is no puzzle: the two alternative estimates of the expenditure multipliers are not inconsistent, given the margin of error of the estimates. It implies that one should accept whichever of the two estimates is produced by a more reliable and stable method, and is generally more sensible. To me, those criteria call, without question, for adopting the econometric model estimates. But should there be still some lingering doubt about this choice, I am happy to be able to report the results of one final test which I believe should dispose of the reduced form estimates—at least for a while. Suppose the St. Louis estimates of the expenditure multiplier are closer to God's truth than the estimates derived through econometric models. Then it should be the case that if one uses their coefficients to forecast income beyond the period of fit, these forecasts should be appreciably better than those obtained from a forecasting equation in which the coefficients of the expenditure variable are set equal to those obtained from econometric models.

I have carried out this test, comparing a reduced form equation fitted to the period originally used at St. Louis, terminating in 1969 (but reestimated with the lastest revised data) with an equation in which the coefficients of government expenditure plus exports were constrained to be those estimated from the *MPS*, used in the above F-test. The results are clear cut: the errors using the reduced form coefficient are not smaller but on the average substantially *larger* than those using *MPS* multipliers. For the first four years, terminating at the end of 1973, the St. Louis equation produces errors which are distinctly larger in eight quarters, and smaller in but three, and its squared error is one-third larger. For the last two years of turmoil, both equations perform miserably, though even here the *MPS* coefficients perform just a bit better. I have repeated this test with equations estimated through the first half of the postwar period, and the results are, if anything, even more one-sided.

The moral of the story is pretty clear. First,

[2]For the purpose of the test, coefficients were scaled down by one-third to allow for certain major biases in measured government expenditure for present purposes (mainly the treatment of military procurement on a delivery rather than work progress basis, and the inclusion of direct military expenditure abroad).

reduced form equations relying on just two exogenous variables are very unreliable for the purpose of estimating structure, nor are they particularly accurate for forecasting, though per dollar of research expenditure they are surprisingly good. Second, if the St. Louis people want to go on using this method and wish to secure the best possible forecast, then they should ask the *MPS* or any other large econometric model what coefficients they should use for government expenditure, rather than trying to estimate them by their unreliable method.

From the theory and evidence reviewed, we must then conclude that opting for a constant rate of growth of the nominal money supply can result in a stable economy only in the absence of significant exogenous shocks. But obviously the economy has been and will continue to be exposed to many significant shocks, coming from such things as war and peace, and other large changes in government expenditure, foreign trade, agriculture, technological progress, population shifts, and what not. The clearest evidence on the importance of such shocks is provided by our postwar record with its six recessions.

IV. The Record of Stabilization Policies: Stabilizing or Destabilizing

A. *Was Postwar Instability Due to Unstable Money Growth?*

At this point, of course, monetarists will object that, over the postwar period, we have *not* had a constant money growth policy and will hint that the observed instability can largely be traced to the instability of money. The only way of meeting this objection squarely would be, of course, to rerun history with a good computer capable of calculating 3 percent at the helm of the Fed.

A more feasible, if less conclusive approach might be to look for some extended periods in which the money supply grew fairly smoothly and see how the economy fared. Combing through our post-Korean War history, I have been able to find just two stretches of several years in which the growth of the money stock was relatively stable, whether one chooses to

measure stability in terms of percentage deviations from a constant growth or of dispersion of four-quarter changes. It may surprise some that one such stretch occurred quite recently and consists of the period of nearly four years beginning in the first quarter of 1971 (see the author and Papademos, 1976). During this period, the average growth was quite large, some 7 percent, but it was relatively smooth, generally well within the 6 to 8 percent band. The average deviation from the mean is about .75 percent. The other such period lasted from the beginning of 1953 to the first half of 1957, again a stretch of roughly four years. In sharp contrast to the most recent period, the average growth here is quite modest, only about 2 percent; but again, most four-quarter changes fell well within a band of two percentage points, and the average deviation is again .7. By contrast, during the remaining 13-year stretch from mid-1957 to the end of 1970, the variability of money growth was roughly twice as large if measured by the average deviation of four quarter changes, and some five times larger if measured by the percentage deviation of the money stock from a constant growth trend.

How did the economy fare in the two periods of relatively stable money growth? It is common knowledge that the period from 1971 to 1974, or from 1972 to 1975 if we want to allow a one-year lag for money to do its trick, was distinctly the most unstable in our recent history, marked by sharp fluctuations in output and wild gyrations of the rate of change of prices. As a result, the average deviation of the four-quarter changes in output was 3.3 percent, more than twice as large as in the period of less stable money growth. But the first stretch was also marked by well above average instability, with the contraction of 1954, the sharp recovery of 1955, and the new contraction in 1958, the sharpest in postwar history except for the present one. The variability of output is again 50 percent larger than in the middle period.

To be sure, in the recent episode serious exogenous shocks played a major role in the development of prices and possibly output, although the same is not so readily apparent for the period 1953 to 1958. But, in any event, such extenuating circumstances are quite irrelevant to my point; for I am not suggesting that the stability of money was the major cause of economic instability—or at any rate, not yet! All I am arguing is that (i) there is no basis for the monetarists' suggestion that our postwar instability can be traced to monetary instability—our most unstable periods have coincided with periods of relative monetary stability; and (ii) stability of the money supply is not enough to give us a stable economy, precisely because there are exogenous disturbances.

Finally, let me mention that I have actually made an attempt at rerunning history to see whether a stable money supply would stabilize the economy, though in a way that I readily acknowledge is much inferior to the real thing, namely through a simulation with the *MPS*. The experiment, carried out in cooperation with Papademos, covered the relatively quiet period from the beginning of 1959 to the introduction of price-wage controls in the middle of 1971. If one eliminates all major sources of shocks, for example, by smoothing federal government expenditures, we found, as did Otto Eckstein in an earlier experiment, that a stable money growth of 3 percent per year does stabilize the economy, as expected. But when we allowed for all the historical shocks, the result was that with a constant money growth the economy was far from stable—in fact, it was distinctly less stable than actual experience, by a factor of 50 percent.

B. *The Overall Effectiveness of Postwar Stabilization Policies*

But even granted that a smooth money supply will not produce a very stable world and that there is therefore room for stabilization policies, monetarists will still argue that we should nonetheless eschew such policies. They claim, first, that allowing for unpredictably variable lags and unforeseeable future shocks, we do not know enough to successfully design stabilization policies, and second, that the government would surely be incapable of choosing the appropriate

policies or be politically willing to provide timely enforcement. Thus, in practice, stabilization policies will result in destabilizing the economy much of the time.

This view is supported by two arguments, one logical and one empirical. The logical argument is the one developed in Friedman's Presidential Address (1968). An attempt at stabilizing the economy at full employment is bound to be destabilizing because the full employment or natural rate is not known with certainty and is subject to shifts in time; and if we aim for the incorrect rate, the result must perforce be explosive inflation or deflation. By contrast, with a constant money supply policy, the economy will automatically hunt for, and eventually discover, that shifty natural rate, wherever it may be hiding.

This argument, I submit, is nothing but a debating ploy. It rests on the preposterous assumption that the only alternative to a constant money growth is the pursuit of a very precise unemployment target which will be adhered to indefinitely no matter what, and that if the target is off in the second decimal place, galloping inflation is around the corner. In reality, all that is necessary to pursue stabilization policies is a rough target range that includes the warranted rate, itself a range and not a razor edge; and, of course, responsible supporters of stabilization policies have long been aware of the fact that the target range needs to be adjusted in time on the basis of forseeable shifts in the warranted range, as well as in the light of emerging evidence that the current target is not consistent with price stability. It is precisely for this reason that I, as well as many other nonmonetarists, would side with monetarists in strenuous opposition to recent proposals for a target unemployment rate rigidly fixed by statute (although there is nothing wrong with Congress committing itself and the country to work toward the eventual achievement of some target unemployment rate through *structural* changes rather than aggregate demand policies).

Clearly, even the continuous updating of targets cannot guarantee that errors can be avoided altogether or even that they will be promptly recognized; and while errors persist, they will result in some inflationary (or deflationary) pressures. But the growing inflation to which Friedman refers is, to repeat, a crawl not a gallop. One may usefully recall in this connection the experience of 1965–70 referred to earlier, with the further remark that the existence of excess employment was quite generally recognized at the time, and failure to eliminate it resulted overwhelmingly from political considerations and not from a wrong diagnosis.[3]

There remains then only the empirical issue: have stabilization policies worked in the past and will they work in the future? Monetarists think the answer is negative and suggest, as we have seen, that misguided attempts at stabilization, especially through monetary policies, are responsible for much of the observed instability. The main piece of evidence in support of this contention is the Great Depression, an episode well documented through the painstaking work of Friedman and Anna Schwartz, although still the object of dispute (see, for example, Peter Temin). But in any event, that episode while it may attest to the power of money, is irrelevant for present purposes since the contraction of the money supply was certainly not part of a comprehensive stabilization program in the post-Keynesian sense.

When we come to the relevant postwar period, the problem of establishing the success or failure of stabilization policies is an extremely taxing one. Many attempts have been made at developing precise objective tests, but in my view, none of these is of much value, even though I am guilty of having contributed to them in one of my

[3] Friedman's logical argument against stabilization policies and in favor of a constant money growth rule is, I submit, much like arguing to a man from St. Paul wishing to go to New Orleans on important business that he would be a fool to drive and should instead get himself a tub and drift down the Mississippi: that way he can be pretty sure that the current will eventually get him to his destination; whereas, if he drives, he might make a wrong turn and, before he notices he will be going further and further away from his destination and pretty soon he may end up in Alaska, where he will surely catch pneumonia and he may never get to New Orleans!

worst papers (1964). Even the most ingenious test, that suggested by Victor Argy, and relying on a comparison of the variability of income with that of the velocity of circulation, turns out to be valid only under highly unrealistic restrictive assumptions.

Dennis Starleaf and Richard Floyd have proposed testing the effectiveness of stabilization by comparing the stability of money growth with that of income growth, much as I have done above for the United States, except that they apply their test to a cross section of industrialized countries. They found that for a sample of 13 countries, the association was distinctly positive. But this test is again of little value. For while a negative association for a given country, such as suggested by my $U.S.$ test, does provide some weak indication that monetary activism helped rather than hindered, the finding of a positive association across countries proves absolutely nothing. It can be readily shown, in fact, that, to the extent that differential variability of income reflects differences in the character of the shocks—a most likely circumstance for their sample—successful stabilization also implies a positive correlation between the variability of income and that of money.

But though the search for unambiguous quantitative tests has so far yielded a meager crop, there exists a different kind of evidence in favor of Keynesian stabilization policies which is impressive, even if hard to quantify. To quote one of the founding fathers of business cycle analysis, Arthur Burns, writing in 1959, "Since 1937 we have had five recessions, the longest of which lasted only 13 months. There is no parallel for such a sequence of mild—or such a sequence of brief—contractions, at least during the past hundred years in our country" (p. 2). By now we can add to that list the recessions of 1961 and 1970.

There is, furthermore, evidence that very similar conclusions hold for other industrialized countries which have made use of stabilization policies; at any rate that was the prevailing view among participants to an international conference held in 1967 on the subject, "Is the busi-

The Monetary Mechanism   **15**

ness cycle obsolete?'' (see Martin Bronfenbrenner, editor). No one seemed to question the greater postwar stability of all Western economies—nor is this surprising when one recalls that around that time business cycle specialists felt so threatened by the new-found stability that they were arguing for redefining business cycles as fluctuations in the *rate of growth* rather than in the *level* of output.

It was recognized that the reduced severity of fluctuations might in part reflect structural changes in the economy and the effect of stronger built-in stabilizers, inspired, of course, by the Keynesian analysis. Furthermore, the greater stability in the United States, and in other industrialized countries, are obviously not independent events. Still, at least as of the time of that conference, there seemed to be little question and some evidence that part of the credit for the greater stability should go to the conscious and on balance, successful endeavor at stabilizing the economy.

V. The Case of Supply Shocks and the 1974–76 Episode

A. *Was the 1974 Depression Due to Errors of Commission or Omission?*

In pointing out our relative postwar stability and the qualified success of stabilization policies, I have carefully defined the postwar period as ending somewhere in 1973. What has happened since that has so tarnished the reputation of economists? In facing this problem, the first question that needs to be raised is whether the recent combination of unprecedented rates of inflation as well as unemployment must be traced to crimes of commission or omission. Did our monetary and fiscal stabilization policies misfire, or did we instead fail to use them?

We may begin by establishing one point that has been blurred by monetarists' blanket indictments of recent monetary policy: the virulent explosion that raised the four-quarter rate of inflation from about 4 percent in 1972 to 6.5 percent by the third quarter of 1973, to 11.5 percent in 1974 with a peak quarterly rate of 13.5, can in no way be traced to an excessive, or

to a disorderly, growth of the money supply. As already mentioned, the average rate of money growth from the beginning of 1970 to the second half of 1974 was close to 7 percent. To be sure, this was a high rate and could be expected sooner or later to generate an undesirably high inflation —but how high? Under any reasonable assumption one cannot arrive at a figure much above 6 percent. This might explain what happened up to the fall of 1973, but not from the third quarter of 1973 to the end of 1974, which is the really troublesome period. Similarly, as was indicated above, the growth of money was reasonably smooth over this period, smoother than at any other time in the postwar period, staying within a 2 percent band. Hence, the debacle of 1974 can just not be traced to an erratic behavior of money resulting from a misguided attempt at stabilization.

Should one then conclude that the catastrophe resulted from too slavish an adherence to a stable growth rate, forsaking the opportunity to use monetary policy to stabilize the economy? In one sense, the answer to this question must in my view be in the affirmative. There is ample ground for holding that the rapid contraction that set in toward the end of 1974, on the heels of a slow decline in the previous three quarters, and which drove unemployment to its 9 percent peak, was largely the result of the astronomic rise in interest rates around the middle of the year. That rise in turn was the unavoidable result of the Fed's stubborn refusal to accommodate, to an adequate extent, the exogenous inflationary shock due to oil, by letting the money supply growth exceed the 6 percent rate announced at the beginning of the year. And this despite repeated warnings about that unavoidable result (see, for example, the author 1974).

Monetarists have suggested that the sharp recession was not the result of too slow a monetary growth throughout the year, but instead of the deceleration that took place in the last half of 1974, and early 1975. But this explanation just does not stand up to the facts. The fall in the quarterly growth of money in the third and fourth quarters was puny, especially on the basis of revised figures now available: from 5.7 percent in the second to 4.3 and 4.1—hardly much larger than the error of estimate for quarterly rates! To be sure, in the first quarter of 1975 the growth fell to .6 percent. But, by then, the violent contraction was well on its way—between September 1974 and February 1975, industrial production fell at an annual rate of 25 percent. Furthermore, by the next quarter, monetary growth had resumed heftily. There is thus no way the monetarist proposition can square with these facts unless their long and variable lags are so variable that they sometimes turn into substantial leads. But even then, by anybody's model, a one-quarter dip in the growth of money could not have had a perceptible effect.

B. What Macro Stabilization Policies Can Accomplish, and How

But recognizing that the adherence to a stable money growth path through much of 1974 bears a major responsibility for the sharp contraction does not per se establish that the policy was mistaken. The reason is that the shock that hit the system in 1973–74 was not the usual type of demand shock which we have gradually learned to cope with, more or less adequately. It was, instead, a supply or price shock, coming from a cumulation of causes, largely external. This poses an altogether different stabilization problem. In particular, in the case of demand shocks, there exists in principle an ideal policy which avoids all social costs, namely to offset completely the shock thus, at the same time, stabilizing employment and the price level. There may be disagreement as to whether this target can be achieved and how, but not about the target itself.

But in the case of supply shocks, there is no miracle cure—there is no macro policy which can both maintain a stable price level and keep employment at its natural rate. To maintain stable prices in the face of the exogenous price shock, say a rise in import prices, would require a fall in all domestic output prices; but we know of no macro policy by which domestic prices can be made to fall except by creating enough slack,

thus putting downward pressure on wages. And the amount of slack would have to be substantial in view of the sluggishness of wages in the face of unemployment. If we do not offset the exogenous shock completely, then the initial burst, even if activated by an entirely transient rise in some prices, such as a once and for all deterioration in the terms of trade, will give rise to further increases, as nominal wages rise in a vain attempt at preserving real wages; this secondary reaction too can only be cut short by creating slack. In short, once a price shock hits, there is no way of returning to the initial equilibrium except after a painful period of both above equilibrium unemployment and inflation.

There are, of course, in principle, policies other than aggregate demand management to which we might turn, and which are enticing in view of the unpleasant alternatives offered by demand management. But so far such policies, at least those of the wage-price control variety, have proved disappointing. The design of better alternatives is probably the greatest challenge presently confronting those interested in stabilization. However, these policies fall outside my present concern. Within the realm of aggregate demand management, the only choice open to society is the cruel one between alternative feasible paths of inflation and associated paths of unemployment, and the best the macroeconomist can offer is policies designed to approximate the chosen path.

In light of the above, we may ask: is it conceivable that a constant rate of growth of the money supply will provide a satisfactory response to price shocks in the sense of giving rise to an unemployment-inflation path to which the country would object least?

C. The Monetarist Prescription: Or, Constant Money Growth Once More

The monetarists are inclined to answer this question affirmatively, if not in terms of the country's preferences, at least in terms of the preferences they think it should have. This is evidenced by their staunch support of a continuation of the 6 percent or so rate of growth through

1974, 1975, and 1976.

Their reasoning seems to go along the following lines. The natural rate hypothesis implies that the rate of inflation can change only when employment deviates from the natural rate. Now suppose we start from the natural rate and some corresponding steady rate of inflation, which without loss of generality can be assumed as zero. Let there be an exogenous shock which initially lifts the rate of inflation, say, to 10 percent. If the Central Bank, by accommodating this price rise, keeps employment at the natural rate, the new rate of 10 percent will also be maintained and will in fact continue forever, as long as the money supply accommodates it. The only way to eliminate inflation is to increase unemployment enough, above the natural rate and for a long enough time, so that the cumulated reduction of inflation takes us back to zero. There will of course be many possible unemployment paths that will accomplish this. So the next question is: Which is the least undesirable?

The monetarist answer seems to be—and here I confess that attribution becomes difficult —that it does not make much difference because, to a first approximation, the cumulated amount of unemployment needed to unwind inflation is independent of the path. If we take more unemployment early, we need to take less later, and conversely. But then it follows immediately that the specific path of unemployment that would be generated by a constant money growth is, if not better, at least as good as any other. Corollary: a constant growth of money is a satisfactory answer to supply shocks just as it is to demand shocks—as well as, one may suspect, to any other conceivable illness, indisposition, or disorder.

D. *Why Constant Money Growth Cannot Be the Answer*

This reasoning is admirably simple and elegant, but it suffers from several flaws. The first one is a confusion between the price level and its rate of change. With an unchanged constant growth of the nominal money stock, the system will settle back into equilibrium not when the rate of inflation is back to zero but only when, in addition, the price level itself is back to its initial level. This means that when inflation has finally returned back to the desired original rate, unemployment cannot also be back to the original level but will instead remain above it as long as is necessary to generate enough deflation to offset the earlier cumulated inflation. I doubt that this solution would find many supporters and for a good reason; it amounts to requiring that none of the burden of the price shock should fall on the holder of long-term money fixed contracts— such as debts—and that all other sectors of society should shoulder entirely whatever cost is necessary to insure this result. But if, as seems to be fairly universally agreed, the social target is instead to return the system to the original rate of inflation—zero in our example—then the growth of the money supply cannot be kept constant. Between the time the shock hits and the time inflation has returned to the long-run level, there must be an additional increase in money supply by as much as the price level or by the cumulant of inflation over the path.

A second problem with the monetarists' argument is that it implies a rather special preference function that depends only on cumulated unemployment. And, last but not least, it requires the heroic assumption that the Phillips curve be not only vertical in the long run but also linear in the short run, an assumption that does not seem consistent with empirically estimated curves. Dropping this last assumption has the effect that, for any given social preference, there will be in general a unique optimal path. Clearly, for this path to be precisely that generated by a constant money growth, would require a miracle—or some sleight of the invisible hand!

Actually, there are grounds for holding that the unemployment path generated by a constant money growth, even if temporarily raised to take care of the first flaw, could not possibly be close to an optimal. This conclusion is based on an analysis of optimal paths, relying on the type of linear welfare function that appears to underlie the monetarists' argument, and which is also a straightforward generalization of Okun's famous "economic discomfort index." That index (which according to Michael Lovell appears to have some empirical support) is the sum of unemployment and inflation. The index used in my analysis is a weighted average of the cumulated unemployment and cumulated inflation over the path. The weights express the relative social concern for inflation versus unemployment.

Using this index, it has been shown in a forthcoming thesis of Papademos that, in general, the optimum policy calls for raising unemployment at once to a certain critical level and keeping it there until inflation has substantially abated. The critical level depends on the nature of the Phillips curve and the relative weights, but does not depend significantly on the initial shock—as long as it is appreciable. To provide an idea of the order of magnitudes involved, if one relies on the estimate of the Phillips curve reported in my joint paper with Papademos (1975), which is fairly close to vertical and uses Okun's weights, one finds that (i) at the present time, the noninflationary rate of unemployment corresponding to a 2 percent rate of inflation can be estimated at 5.6 percent, and (ii) the optimal response to a large exogenous price shock consists in increasing unemployment from 5.6 to only about 7 percent. That level is to be maintained until inflation falls somewhat below 4 percent; it should then be reduced slowly until inflation gets to 2.5 (which is estimated to take a couple of years), and rapidly thereafter. If, on the other hand, society were to rate inflation twice as costly as unemployment, the initial unemployment rate becomes just over 8 percent, though the path to final equilibrium is then shorter. These results seem intuitively sensible and quantitatively reasonable, providing further justification for the assumed welfare function, with its appealing property of summarizing preferences into a single readily understandable number.

One important implication of the nature of the optimum path described above is that a constant money growth could not possibly be optimal while inflation is being squeezed out of the system, regardless of the relative weights attached to unemployment and inflation. It would tend

to be prevailingly too small for some initial period and too large thereafter.

One must thus conclude that the case for a constant money growth is no more tenable in the case of supply shocks than it is in the case of demand shocks.

VI. Conclusion

To summarize, the monetarists have made a valid and most valuable contribution in establishing that our economy is far less unstable than the early Keynesians pictured it and in rehabilitating the role of money as a determinant of aggregate demand. They are wrong, however, in going as far as asserting that the economy is sufficiently shockproof that stabilization policies are not needed. They have also made an important contribution in pointing out that such policies might in fact prove destabilizing. This criticism has had a salutary effect on reassessing what stabilization policies can and should do, and on trimming down fine-tuning ambitions. But their contention that postwar fluctuations resulted from an unstable money growth or that stabilization policies decreased rather than increased stability just does not stand up to an impartial examination of the postwar record of the United States and other industrialized countries. Up to 1974, these policies have helped to keep the economy reasonable stable by historical standards, even though one can certainly point to some occasional failures.

The serious deterioration in economic stability since 1973 must be attributed in the first place to the novel nature of the shocks that hit us, namely, supply shocks. Even the best possible aggregate demand management cannot offset such shocks without a lot of unemployment together with a lot of inflation. But, in addition, demand management was far from the best. This failure must be attributed in good measure to the fact that we had little experience or even an adequate conceptual framework to deal with such shocks; but at least from my reading of the record, it was also the result of failure to use stabilization policies, including too slavish adherence to the monetarists' constant money growth presciption.

We must, therefore, categorically reject the monetarist appeal to turn back the clock forty years by discarding the basic message of *The General Theory*. We should instead concentrate our efforts in an endeavor to make stabilization policies even more effective in the future than they have been in the past.

REFERENCES

L. C. Andersen and K. M. Carlson, "A Monetarist Model for Economic Stabilization," *Fed. Reserve Bank St. Louis Rev.*, Apr. 1970, *52*, 7–25.

―――― and J. L. Jordan, "Monetary and Fiscal Action: A Test of Their Relative Importance in Economic Stabilization," *Fed. Reserve Bank St. Louis Rev.*, Nov. 1968, *50*, 11–23.

V. Argy, "Rules, Discretion in Monetary Management, and Short-Term Stability," *J. Money, Credit, Banking*, Feb. 1971, *3*, 102–22.

W. J. Baumol, "The Transactions Demand for Cash: An Inventory Theoretic Approach," *Quart. J. Econ.*, Nov. 1952, *66*, 545–56.

R. G. Bodkin, "Real Wages and Cyclical Variations in Employment: A Reexamination of the Evidence," *Can. J. Econ.*, Aug. 1969, *2*, 353–74.

Martin Bronfenbrenner, *Is the Business Cycle Obsolete?*, New York 1969.

A. F. Burns, "Progress Towards Economic Stability," *Amer. Econ. Rev.*, Mar. 1960, *50*, 1–19.

J. T. Dunlop, "The Movement of Real and Money Wage Rates," *Econ. J.*, Sept. 1938, *48*, 413–34.

O. Eckstein and R. Brinner, "The Inflation Process in the United States," in Otto Eckstein, ed., *Parameters and Policies in the U.S. Economy*, Amsterdam 1976.

R. C. Fair, "On Controlling the Economy to Win Elections," unpub. paper, Cowles Foundation 1975.

M. S. Feldstein, "Temporary Layoffs in the Theory of Unemployment," *J. Polit. Econ.*, Oct. 1976, *84*, 937–57.

S. Fischer, "Long-term Contracts, Rational Expectations and the Optimal Money Supply Rule," *J. Polit. Econ.*, forthcoming.

B. M. Friedman, "Rational Expectations Are Really Adaptive After All," unpub. paper, Harvard Univ. 1975.

Milton Friedman, *A Theory of the Consumption Function*, Princeton 1957.

―――― , "The Role of Monetary Policy," *Amer. Econ. Rev.*, Mar. 1968, *58*, 1–17.

―――― , "The Demand for Money: Some Theoretical and Empirical Results," in his *The Optimum Quantity of Money, and Other Essays*, Chicago 1969.

―――― and A. Schwartz, *A Monetary History of the United States 1867–1960*, Princeton 1963.

S. Goldfeld, "The Demand for Money Revisited," *Brookings Papers*, Washington 1973, *3*, 577–646.

R. J. Gordon, "Recent Developments in the Theory of Inflation and Unemployment," *J. Monet. Econ.*, Apr. 1976, *2*, 185–219.

J. R. Hicks, "Mr. Keynes and the "Classics"; A Suggested Interpretation," *Econometrica*, Apr. 1937, *5*, 147–59.

John Maynard Keynes, *The General Theory of Employment, Interest and Money*, New York 1935.

R. G. Lipsey, "The Relation Between Unemployment and the Rate of Change of Money Wage Rates in the United Kingdom, 1862–1957: A Further Analysis," *Economica*, Feb. 1960, *27*, 1–31.

M. Lovell, "Why Was the Consumer Feeling So Sad?," *Brookings Papers*, Washington 1975, *2*, 473–79.

R. E. Lucas, Jr., "Econometric Policy Evaluation: A Critique," *J. Monet. Econ.*, suppl. series, 1976, *1*, 19–46.

―――― , "Expectations and the Neutrality of Money," *J. Econ. Theory*, Apr. 1972, *4*, 103–24.

M. Miller and D. Orr, "A Model of the Demand for Money by Firms," *Quart. J. Econ.*, Aug. 1966, *80*, 413–35.

F. Modigliani, "Liquidity Preference and the Theory of Interest and Money," *Econo-*

metrica, Jan. 1944, *12*, 45–88.

———, "New Development on the Oligopoly Front," *J. Polit. Econ.*, June 1958, *66*, 215–33.

———, "The Monetary Mechanism and Its Interaction with Real Phenomena," *Rev. Econ. Statist.*, Feb. 1963, *45*, 79–107.

———, " Some Empirical Tests of Monetary Management and of Rules versus Discretion," *J. Polit. Econ.*, June 1964, *72*, 211–45.

———, "The 1974 Report of the President's Council of Economic Advisers: A Critique of Past and Prospective Policies," *Amer. Econ. Rev.*, Sept. 1974, *64*, 544–77.

———, "The Life Cycle Hypothesis of Saving Twenty Years Later," in Michael Parkin, ed., *Contemporary Issues in Economics*, Manchester 1975.

——— **and A. Ando,** "The Relative Stability of Monetary Velocity and the Investment Multiplier," *Amer. Econ. Rev.*, Sept. 1965, *55*, 693–728.

——— **and** ———, "Impacts of Fiscal Actions on Aggregate Income and the Monetarist Controversy: Theory and Evidence," in Jerome L. Stein, ed., *Monetarism*, Amsterdam 1976.

——— **and R. Brumberg,** "Utility Analysis and the Consumption Function: Interpretation of Cross-Section Data," in Kenneth Kurihara, ed., *Post-Keynesian Economics*, New Brunswick 1954.

——— **and L. Papademos,** "Targets for Monetary Policy in the Coming Years," *Brookings Papers*, Washington 1975, *1*, 141–65.

——— **and** ———, "Monetary Policy for the Coming Quarters: The Conflicting Views," *New Eng. Econ. Rev.*, Mar./Apr. 1976, 2–35.

J. F. Muth, "Rational Expectations and the Theory of Price Movements," *Econometrica*, July 1961, *29*, 315–35.

W. D. Nordhaus, "The Political Business Cycle," *Rev. Econ. Stud.*, Apr. 1975, *42*, 169–90.

A. M. Okun, "Inflation: Its Mechanics and Welfare Costs," *Brookings Papers*, Washington 1975, *2*, 351–90.

D. O'Neill, "Directly Estimated Multipliers of Monetary and Fiscal Policy," doctoral thesis in progress, M.I.T.

L. Papademos, "Optimal Aggregate Employment Policy and Other Essays," doctoral thesis in progress, M.I.T.

Edmond S. Phelps, "Money-Wage Dynamics and Labor-Market Equilibrium," *J. Polit. Econ.*, July/Aug. 1968, *76*, 678–711.

——— **et al.,** *Microeconomic Foundations of Employment and Inflation Theory*, New York 1970.

A. W. Phillips, "The Relation Between Unemployment and the Rate of Change of Money Wage Rates in the United Kingdom, 1861–1957," *Economica*, Nov. 1958, *25*, 283–99.

T. J. Sargent, "A Classical Macroeconomic Model for the United States," *J. Polit. Econ.*, Apr. 1976, *84*, 207–37.

——— **and N. Wallace,** " 'Rational' Expectations, the Optimal Monetary Instrument, and the Optimal Money Supply Rule," *J. Polit. Econ.*, Apr. 1975, *83*, 241–57.

D. Starleaf and R. Floyd, "Some Evidence with Respect to the Efficiency of Friedman's Monetary Policy Proposals," *J. Money, Credit, Banking*, Aug. 1972, *4*, 713–22.

Peter Temin, *Did Monetary Forces Cause the Great Depression?*, New York 1976.

James Tobin, *Essays in Economics: Vol. 1, Macroeconomics*, Chicago 1971.

Reprinted from

THE AMERICAN ECONOMIC REVIEW

© The American Economic Association

The Monetary Mechanism   21

Errata

Page 9, column 2, paragraph 2, lines 2 and 3: "values of M^1 and of high Employment Federal Expenditure" should read "values of $M1$ and of High Employment Federal Expenditure."

Page 16, column 2, paragraph 3, line 5: "to an optimal" should read "to optimal."

LIQUIDITY PREFERENCE AND THE THEORY OF INTEREST AND MONEY

By Franco Modigliani

PART I

1. INTRODUCTION

THE AIM OF this paper is to reconsider critically some of the most important old and recent theories of the rate of interest and money and to formulate, eventually, a more general theory that will take into account the vital contributions of each analysis as well as the part played by different basic hypotheses.

The analysis will proceed according to the following plan:

I. We start out by briefly re-examining the Keynesian theory. In so doing our principal aim is to determine what is the part played in the Keynesian system by the "liquidity preference," on the one hand, and by the very special assumptions about the supply of labor, on the other. This will permit us to distinguish those results that are due to a real improvement of analysis from conclusions that depend on the difference of basic assumptions.

II. We then proceed to consider the properties of systems in which one or both Keynesian hypotheses are abandoned. We thus check our previous results and test the logical consistency of the "classical" theory of money and the dichotomy of real and monetary economics.

III. From this analysis will gradually emerge our general theory of the rate of interest and money; and we can proceed to use this theory to test critically some recent "Keynesian" theories and more especially those formulated by J. R. Hicks in *Value and Capital*[1] and by A. P. Lerner in several articles.

IV. Finally, to make clear the conclusions that follow from our theory, we take issue in the controversial question as to whether the rate of interest is determined by "real" or by monetary factors.

In order to simplify the task, our analysis proceeds in general, under "static" assumptions; this does not mean that we neglect time but only that we assume the Hicksian (total) "elasticity of expectation" to be always unity. In Hicks's own words this means that "a change in current prices will change expected prices in the same direction and in the same proportion."[2] As shown by Oscar Lange, this implies that we assume the "expectation functions," connecting expected with present prices, to be homogeneous of the first degree.[3]

[1] J. R. Hicks, *Value and Capital*, Oxford University Press, 1939, 331 pp.

[2] *Ibid.*, p. 205.

[3] Cf. O. Lange, "Say's Law: a Restatement and Criticism" in *Studies in Mathematical Economics and Econometrics*, edited by Lange, McIntyre, and Yntema, The University of Chicago Press, 1942, pp. 67–68.

Since all the theories we examine or formulate in this paper are concerned with the determinants of equilibrium and not with the explanation of business cycles, this simplification, although it is serious in some respects, does not seem unwarranted.

2. THREE ALTERNATIVE MACROSTATIC SYSTEMS

As a first step in the analysis, we must set up a system of equations describing the relation between the variables to be analyzed. In doing this we are at once confronted with a difficult choice between rigor and convenience; the only rigorous procedure is to set up a complete "Walrasian" system and to determine the equilibrium prices and quantities of each good: but this system is cumbersome and not well suited to an essentially literary exposition such as we intend to develop here. The alternative is to work with a reduced system: we must then be satisfied with the rather vague notions of "physical output," "investment," "price level," etc. In what follows we have chosen, in principle, the second alternative, but we shall check our conclusions with a more general system whenever necessary.

The equations of our system are:

$$(1) \qquad M = L(r, Y),$$
$$(2) \qquad I = I(r, Y),$$
$$(3) \qquad S = S(r, Y),$$
$$(4) \qquad S = I,$$
$$(5) \qquad Y \equiv PX,$$
$$(6) \qquad X = X(N),$$
$$(7) \qquad W = X'(N)P.$$

The symbols have the following meaning: Y, money income; M, quantity of money in the system (regarded as given); r, rate of interest; S and I, saving and investment respectively, all measured in money; P, price level; N, aggregate employment; W, money wage rate; X, an index of physical output.[4] We may also define C, consumption measured in money, by the following identity:

$$(8) \qquad C \equiv Y - I.$$

Identity (5) can be regarded as defining money income. There are

[4] This system is partly taken from earlier writings on the subject. See especially O. Lange, "The Rate of Interest and the Optimum Propensity to Consume," *Economica*, Vol. 5 (N. S.), February, 1938, pp. 12–32, and J. R. Hicks, "Mr. Keynes and the 'Classics'; A Suggested Interpretation," ECONOMETRICA, Vol. 5, April, 1937, pp. 147–159.

so far 8 unknowns and only 7 equations; we lack the equation relating the wage rate and the supply of labor. This equation takes a substantially different form in the "Keynesian" system as compared with the "classical" systems.

In the classical systems the suppliers of labor (as well as the suppliers of all other commodities) are supposed to behave "rationally." In the same way as the supply of any commodity depends on the relative price of the commodity so the supply of labor is taken to depend not on the money wage rate, but on the real wage rate. Under the classical hypothesis, therefore, the last equation of the system takes the form:

(9a) $N = F\left(\dfrac{W}{P}\right)$; or, in the inverse form: $W = F^{-1}(N)P.$

The function F is a continuous function, although not necessarily monotonically increasing.

The Keynesian assumptions concerning the supply-of-labor schedule are quite different. In the Keynesian system, within certain limits to be specified presently, the supply of labor is assumed to be perfectly elastic at the historically ruling wage rate, say w_0. The limits mentioned above are given by equation (9a). For every value of W and P the corresponding value of N from (9a) gives the maximum amount of labor obtainable in the market. As long as the demand is less than this, the wage rate remains fixed as w_0. But as soon as all those who wanted to be employed at the ruling real wage rate w_0/P have found employment, wages become flexible upward. The supply of labor will not increase unless the money wage rate rises relative to the price level.

In order to write the last equation of the "Keynesian" form of our system, we must express this rather complicated hypothesis in functional form. Taking (9a) as a starting point, we may write:

(9) $W = \alpha w_0 + \beta F^{-1}(N)P,$

where α and β are functions of N, W, P, characterized by the following properties:

(10)
$$\alpha = 1, \quad \beta = 0, \quad \text{for} \quad N \leq N_0,$$
$$\alpha = 0, \quad \beta = 1, \quad \text{for} \quad N > N_0,$$

where N_0 is said to be "full employment." Equations and inequalities (10) thus state that, unless there is "full employment" $(N = N_0)$, the wage rate is not really a variable of the system but a datum, a result of "history" or of "economic policy" or of both. Equation (9) then reduces to $W = w_0$. But after "full employment" has been reached at wage rate w_0, the supply of labor ceases to be perfectly elastic: W becomes a variable to be determined by the system and (9) becomes a "genuine" equation. We should add that, even in the "Keynesian" system, it is admitted that the wage rate will begin to be flexible downward before employment has reached the zero level: but in order not to complicate equation (9) still further we can, without serious harm, leave the hypothesis in its most stringent form.

For generality we may also use equation (9) as it now stands, as the "supply of labor" function of the "classical" theory. But instead of conditions (10) we have the identities (for all values of N)

$$(11) \qquad \alpha \equiv 0, \qquad \beta \equiv 1.$$

Some remarks are also necessary concerning the "demand for money" equation. According to the "quantity theory of money," the demand for money does not depend on the rate of interest but varies directly with money income. Under this hypothesis equation (1) reduces to

$$(1a) \qquad M = kY.$$

By properly combining the equations and conditions written above, we obtain three different systems which we will analyze in turn.

I. A "Keynesian" system consisting of equations (1) to (7) and (9) and conditions (10).

II. A "crude classical" system consisting of equations (1a), (2) to (7), and (9), and identities (11).

III. A "generalized classical" system consisting of the equations listed under II but with (1a) replaced by (1).

3. A RECONSIDERATION OF THE KEYNESIAN THEORY

In reconsidering the Keynesian system we shall essentially follow the lines suggested by J. R. Hicks in his fundamental paper, "Mr. Keynes and the 'Classics.'"[5] Our main task will be to clarify and develop his arguments, taking into account later theoretical developments.

Close consideration of the Keynesian system of equations [equations (1) to (7) and (9) to (10)] reveals that the first 4 equations contain only 4 unknowns and form a determinate system: the system of monetary equilibrium. We therefore begin by discussing its equations and its solution.

4. THE TRANSACTION DEMAND FOR MONEY

In a free capitalistic economy, money serves two purposes: (a) it is a medium of exchange, (b) it is a form of holding assets. There are accordingly two sources of demand for money: the transaction demand for money and the demand for money as an asset. This is the fundamental proposition on which the theory of the rate of interest and

[5] ECONOMETRICA, Vol. 5, April, 1937, pp. 147–159.

money rests; it is therefore necessary to analyze closely each source of demand and the factors that determine it.

The transaction demand for money is closely connected with the concept of the income period. We may define the income period as the (typical) time interval elapsing between the dates at which members of the community are paid for services rendered. We shall assume for the moment that this income period is approximately the same for every individual and that it coincides with the expenditure period.[6]

Each individual begins the income period with a certain income arising out of direct services rendered or out of property and with assets (physical and nonphysical) having a certain market value. In his endeavor to reach the highest level of satisfaction he is confronted with two sets of decisions: (a) he must decide what part of his income he will spend on consumption and what part he will save, (b) he must determine how to dispose of his assets.

The first set of decisions presents no special difficulty of analysis. On the basis of his tastes, his income, and market prices he will make a certain plan of expenditure to be carried out in the course of the income period. The amount of money that is necessary for individuals to carry out their expenditure plans is the *transaction demand for money by consumers*, as of the beginning of the period. The average transaction demand, on the other hand, depends on the rate at which expenditure takes place within the period.[7]

The difference between the individual's money income and the amount he decides to spend in the fashion discussed above is the money value of his savings (dissavings) for the income period. It represents the net increment in the value of his assets.

5. THE DEMAND FOR MONEY AS AN ASSET

Having made his consumption-saving plan, the individual has to make decisions concerning the assets he owns. These assets, let us note, consist of property carried over from the preceding income period *plus current savings*.

There are essentially three forms in which people can keep their assets: (a) money, (b) securities,[8] and (c) physical assets.

---

[6] This means, for instance, that people are required by custom or contract to pay within the income period for what they have consumed in the period (rent, grocery bill, etc.) or else must rely on "consumers' credit."

[7] Thus if expenditure should proceed at an approximately even rate, it would be one-half the initial demand.

[8] Under the name of securities we include both fixed-income-bearing certificates and common stocks or equities. From the strictly economic point of view, common stocks should perhaps be considered as a form of holding physical assets. For institutional reasons, however, equities have very special properties which make them in many respects more similar to bonds than to physical assets.

We shall for the moment eliminate the third alternative by distinguishing between entrepreneurial and nonentrepreneurial decisions. We consider as entrepreneurs individuals who hold assets in physical form; decisions concerning the acquisition or disposal of physical assets will accordingly be treated as entrepreneurial decisions and will be analyzed in connection with the schedule of the propensity to invest [equation (3)]. An individual's decision to acquire directly physical assets (say a house) or to reinvest profits in his enterprise can be split into two separate decisions, a decision to lend (to himself) and a decision to increase his entrepreneurial risk by borrowing (from himself).

We are therefore concerned here exclusively with decisions concerning nonphysical assets and with those factors that influence the choice between the first two alternatives. Our problem is to determine whether there is any reason for individuals to wish to hold some or all of their assets in the form of money and thus to demand money over and above the quantity they need for transactions.

In this respect there is little to add to the exhaustive treatment that this subject has received in recent literature.[9]

There are two properties that all assets, whether physical or not, share in different degrees: liquidity and risk. Following a criterion particularly stressed by Jacob Marschak, we shall define liquidity of an asset in terms of the perfection of the market in which it is traded. An asset is liquid if this market is perfect, i.e., an individual's decision to buy or sell does not affect the price finitely; it is illiquid in the opposite case. It is riskless if the price at which it sells is constant or practically so; it is risky if the price fluctuates widely.

Securities clearly share with money the property of being highly liquid assets. Where there is an organized market, securities will not be significantly inferior to money in this respect. They have, however, two clear drawbacks in comparison with cash:

(a) They are not a medium of exchange. Assets generally accrue in the form of money through savings, and a separate transaction is necessary to transform them into securities. This transaction involves both subjective and objective costs.

(b) They are more risky than money since their market price is not constant. Even the "safest" type of securities, on which the risk of default can be neglected, fluctuates in price as the rate of interest moves. There are, it is true, some types of loans for which this last risk can be neglected, namely very-short-term loans. Let us assume, for the sake

[9] See, for instance, J. R. Hicks, *Value and Capital*, Chapters XIII and XIV and *passim;* J. M. Keynes, *The General Theory of Employment, Interest and Money*, New York, Harcourt, Brace and Company, 1936, 403 pp.; Mabel Timlin, *Keynesian Economics*, University of Toronto Press, 1942, Chapters V and VI; etc.

of precision, that the money market is open only on the first day of the income period; then the shortest type of loans will be those that mature at the end of said period. These types of assets will not be subject to the risk mentioned under (b) since, by assumption, the rate of interest cannot change while they are outstanding.[10]

It is just for this type of assets, however, that the disadvantage mentioned under (a), namely the cost of investment, weighs more heavily: for the yield they promise for the very short duration of the loan can only be small, so that even a moderate cost is sufficient to wipe it out. If, as is likely, the cost of investment does not rise in proportion to the amount invested, then short loans may be an interesting investment for large sums, but not so for small investors. Thus, if this were the only possible form of investment, we should expect that any fall in the rate of interest, not accompanied by a corresponding fall in the cost of investing, would induce a growing number of potential investors to keep their assets in the form of money, rather than securities; that is to say, we should expect a fall in the rate of interest to increase the demand for money as an asset.

In this respect, securities of longer maturity would appear to be superior, since the yield to be gathered by holding them until maturity is larger, while the cost of acquiring them need not be different. But as the importance of the cost element decreases, the importance of the risk element grows. As is well known, a given change in the rate of interest will affect most the present value of those bonds whose maturity is furthest away. If the only reason for owning assets were to earn the income they produce, these price fluctuations would not be so important. For, as long as the owner is in a position to hold the asset until maturity, there would be only a potential loss, a loss of better opportunities. There can be little doubt, however, that for a large part of the community the main reason for holding assets is as a reserve against contingencies. A form of assets whose value is not certain must be, *ceteris paribus*, inferior to one whose value is certain, namely money.

This very fact, besides, gives an additional reason why bonds of longer maturity should be a less safe form of holding assets. For there is much less certainty about faraway income periods than there is about the near future and the possibility that one will have to realize the assets before their maturity, if any, increases accordingly; while, on the other hand, it becomes increasingly difficult to make reliable forecasts about the level of the rate of interest and the future market value of the assets.

[10] Even if this assumption were relaxed, the possible fluctuations in the rate of interest would be negligible and the extent to which they would affect the present value of the securities mentioned above could be disregarded.

Securities, on the other hand, are clearly superior to money in that they yield an income. The ruling rate of interest measures the remuneration to be obtained by accepting the drawbacks and assuming the risks that are characteristic of securities as compared with money. Or, to look at it from another point of view, it measures the cost of holding money instead of securities in terms of forgone income. Thus a fall in the rate of interest has, in any event, the effect of making cash cheaper and hence more attractive as a form of holding assets.

In addition, several other reasons can be mentioned that cause a low rate of interest to discourage the holding of securities. In the first place, the risk element involved in holding securities becomes more pronounced when the rate of interest is low, for a smaller fall in the capital value of the asset is sufficient to wipe out the income already earned by holding the asset. Thus, for instance, the smaller the rate of interest, the smaller is the *percentage change* in the rate itself necessary to absorb the yield obtained by holding the asset a given length of time. Again, it has been pointed out by some authors that, as the rate of interest becomes lower, there is some ground to expect that possible movements will be predominantly in the direction of an increase and therefore unfavorable to the holders of securities.

In conclusion then, the lower the rate of interest, the larger will be the number of owners of assets who will prefer to hold these assets in the form of money for the income period; the demand for money to hold (as distinguished from money to spend, previously considered) or demand for money as an asset is a decreasing function of the rate of interest. Denoting this demand by D_a, we can write

$$D_a = D_a(r)$$

for the schedule of demand for money to hold.

What can we say about the characteristics of this function? It must clearly be a monotonically decreasing function of the rate of interest; in addition, however, it must have, in the author's opinion, two important properties:

In the first place, there must be some value of r, say r', such that $D_a(r) = 0$ for $r \geq r'$. For there must be, for every individual, some minimum net yield per income period that will induce him to part entirely with money as an asset. Hence, if he can find some type of securities such that by holding them for a given number of income periods he expects to obtain a net yield equal to or larger than the minimum, his demand for money to hold will fall to zero.[11]

[11] Let i_0 denote the minimum yield (per income period) at which an individual is ready to hold no assets in the form of money during the period. We may also assume, without being unrealistic, that this minimum yield is the same for each

Since this is true for every individual, there must also be some system of interest rates which is sufficient to reduce the aggregate demand to zero.

The second characteristic is more peculiar. Since securities are an "inferior" way of holding assets, it is generally recognized that there must be some minimum rate of interest, say r'', at which nobody will be willing to hold nonphysical assets except in the form of money. When this level is reached, the demand for money to hold becomes "absolute" and the rate of interest cannot fall any lower. Hence, $D_a'(r) = \infty$ for $r \gtreqless r''$.

6. THE DEMAND FOR MONEY: CONCLUSION

We have so far discussed the demand for money as an asset and the transaction demand for money by individuals; to complete the analysis we must consider the transaction demand by firms. In principle, the same considerations apply here as were stated in connection with individuals' transaction demand. Firms, as well as individuals, have an institutional expenditure-receipt pattern and, given this pattern, the average demand depends on the volume of transactions. We must however ever recognize that, in the case of firms, generalizations are less meaningful since their expenditure and receipt flows are generally less certain and uniform than for individuals.

Then, too, we must admit that we may have oversimplified the consumers' transaction demand by assuming that individuals have a rigorously defined plan of expenditure at the beginning of the income period. It may very well be that under more realistic conditions they will de-

---

income period. Suppose that the securities which, in his opinion, present the best opportunity are expected by him to produce a net yield (including capital appreciation) i_0', i_1', $\cdots$, i_n' in periods $1, 2, \cdots, n$. He will be induced to invest provided there is some value of n for which

$$(1 + i_0')(1 + i_1') \cdots (1 + i_n') \geqq (1 + i_0)^n.$$

From M. Timlin's treatment of this subject (*Keynesian Economics*, Chapter III) it would appear that marginal holders should expect any security to yield the same net income, at least during the current period. This however is correct only if the expectations of all dealers about the future short rates of interest agree with the market expectation as shown by the forward rates established in the market. [The forward rate for the nth income period ahead can always be found by comparing the price of riskless securities maturing n periods ahead with those maturing $(n+1)$ periods ahead.] But if an individual believes this forward rate to be too high he may acquire the security at once even though he may expect that it will yield in the current period less than some other security. For, assuming that he is right, he will be able to realize his capital gain as soon as the market recognizes its error and there is no telling when this will occur. If he should wait until the next income period and hold for the current one the asset that promises to pay a higher yield, he may lose his chance of making the expected capital gain.

sire to carry some cash above the amount they plan to spend as a reserve and to avoid ending the period with a zero cash balance. This however does not substantially affect our argument. All we are interested in establishing is that, within an institutional framework, there must be for any given volume (value) of transactions a certain amount of money that is necessary to carry them out. This amount clearly depends on such institutional factors as the length of the income period and the prevailing customs as to the settlement of current purchases by firms and must therefore be substantially independent of the level of the rate of interest. The level of the rate of interest influences decisions concerning the disposition of assets, and *money needed to carry out transactions planned for the coming income period is not an asset.* In particular, there must be some level of the rate of interest that is sufficient to reduce to zero the demand for money to hold, and hence the total demand to its minimum institutional level which depends on the volume of transactions. As the rate of interest rises above this level, the demand for money will be substantially unaffected and will depend exclusively on the level of money income.

On the basis of these considerations we may, in a first approximation, split the total demand for money into two parts: the demand for money to hold, $D_a(r)$, and the demand for money to spend or for transactions, $D_T(Y)$; and write

$$(12) \qquad L(r, Y) = D_a(r) + D_T(Y) = M.$$

This is not really necessary for our argument, but is very useful since it will constantly remind us of the two sources of demand for money and it will permit us to analyze more conveniently the part played by each variable.

With this in mind we shall find it useful to consider the functioning of the money market in which decisions concerning the disposition of nonphysical assets are carried out.

7. THE MONEY MARKET AND THE SHORT-RUN EQUILIBRIUM OF THE RATE OF INTEREST

There are two ways of looking at this market: (a) in terms of flows (savings and net borrowing) and (b) in terms of stocks. It is from this latter point of view that we shall consider it at this moment.

The supply in this market consists of the stock that is not needed for transactions. On the basis of our first approximation (12), this supply, denoted by S_a, will be

$$S_a = M - D_T(Y),$$

and is determined for any value of the money income and the fixed supply of money.

A position of equilibrium in the money market is reached when a system of interest rates is established at which dealers are willing to hold for the income period all the available supply. Or, from a different angle, the system of interest rates is determined by the price (in terms of forgone income) that dealers are willing to pay to hold assets in the form of money for the coming income period.

This can easily be translated into the usual Marshallian supply and demand apparatus, provided we replace the system of interest rates by a single rate r, as shown in Figure 1.

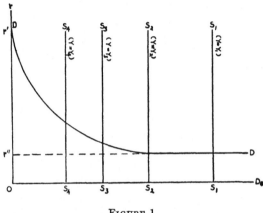

FIGURE 1

DD is the demand curve for money to hold, sloping downward and to the right (when the price, the rate of interest, rises, the demand falls, as in the case of ordinary commodities). The vertical lines are various supply curves corresponding to different values of Y and the fixed value of M. As the income increases, the supply falls: hence

$$Y_4 > Y_3 > Y_2 > \cdots .$$

Since a fall in supply causes a rise in price, the graph shows clearly that equation (1) gives r as an increasing function of Y.

The characteristics of the D_a function described above are shown in in the graph. We noted that, for $r \geq r'$ the demand falls to zero; hence the graph of DD joins the vertical axis and coincides with it.

On the other hand, when the rate of interest falls to the level r'', the demand for money to hold becomes infinitely elastic. Any increase in the supply of money to hold now fails to affect the rate of interest, for the owners of the extra supply will either desire to hold this in the form of cash; or else they will find some owners of securities, who, being just indifferent as to holding cash or securities, will be willing to sell without any necessity for bidding up the price of securities (lowering the rate of interest). Thus, in Figure 1, when the interest rate r'' is reached, the graph of DD becomes parallel to the D_a axis; the income corresponding to r'' cannot be more than Y_2; but if income should fall below Y_2 it would not change the interest rate.[12] This situation that plays such an important role in Keynes's *General Theory* will be referred to as the "Keynesian case."

In the diagram we have assumed that there is a single rate of interest r, instead of a whole system of rates for loans of different duration. While it may be assumed that in principle all the rates tend to move in the same direction, we must bear in mind that the extent to which a change in the supply of money changes the rates on loans of different maturities depends on the character of interest expectations.

A change in the supply will necessarily affect the short rates (unless the short rate has already reached its minimum). But the extent to which it will affect longer rates depends on the relation between the current spot rate and expected future rates.

To denote the relationship between current and expected rates we may again use the Hicksian elasticity of expectation. If this elasticity is unity, expected short rates move in the same direction and in the same proportion as the spot rate; if it is less than unity, a given percentage change in short rates leads to a smaller percentage change in expected rates; and vice versa for elasticity larger than one.

If the expectations about future short rates are based predominantly on the current shorter rates, then the elasticity of expectation tends toward one and the whole system of rates moves in close conformity. But if dealers have rigid expectations based on different elements, the elasticity of expectation will be low and a change in short rates will affect longer rates only to the extent that some of the discount rates, which determine the present value of the assets, are changed.

In practice we may expect that this elasticity will be larger than zero and smaller than one and that it will be larger for the rates expected in the near future.[13]

To the extent that this is true there will be two reasons why rates on loans of shorter maturity should move in closer agreement with the very short rate: (a) because they are more affected by a change in the current short rate, (b) because the other future short rates (of which they are an average) are more influenced by such a change.

[12] From equation (1) we obtain $dr/dY = -L_Y/L_r$, where the subscripts denote partial derivatives. Hence $dr/dY = 0$ if $|L_r| = \infty$.

[13] Denoting by $r_1, r_2, \cdots, r_n$ the short rate of interest anticipated for periods $1, 2, \cdots, n$, we may expect that

$$\frac{\partial r_1}{\partial r_0} > \frac{\partial r_2}{\partial r_0} > \cdots > \frac{\partial r_n}{\partial r_0}.$$

These necessary qualifications do not alter our previous conclusions concerning the determination of equilibrium in the money market. The equilibrium system of interest rates is determined in each period by the condition that the supply of money to hold, which (given M) depends on the transaction demand for money and hence on income, be equal to the demand for money to hold. We may therefore proceed to draw the graph of equation (1), $M = L(r, Y)$. This is the LL curve of Figure 3. Any point on this curve shows the equilibrium value of r corresponding to a value of Y and the fixed value of M: it shows therefore positions of possible equilibrium in the money market. We must prove next that only one point on this curve is consistent with the long-run equilibrium of the system.

8. SAVING, INVESTMENT, AND THE *IS* FUNCTION

The first part of our system yields a second relationship between interest and income. Making use of equations (2) and (3) and the equilibrium condition (4) we obtain: $I(r, Y) = S(r, Y)$. In order to gain some idea of the shape of this curve we may again make use of a graphical method illustrated in Figure 2.

Figure 2-B is the graph of equation (3). Since $\partial S/\partial r$ is usually considered small and of unknown sign we have simplified the drawing by eliminating r. This curve describes the relationship between money income and the proportion of it that people choose not to consume. Its position depends on the value of the fixed money wage rate w_0: given the wage rate, to any level of money income there corresponds a certain real income and price level and, therefore, a certain level of money saving. In this diagram Y_2 denotes the highest money income that can be reached with the money wage rate w_0, and A is the full employment relationship between saving and income.

The straight line beginning at A gives the relationship between money income and money saving once full employment has been reached and the second part of condition (10) replaces the first.[14] We have then what is usually called inflation: real income cannot change but money income can rise to any level. As all prices rise simultaneously the amount of real income saved is unchanged while its money value rises in the same proportion as the price level and money income.[15] The dotted curved line, on the other hand, gives a potential

[14] This line is the continuation of the radius vector from the origin to A.

[15] This is strictly correct only if inflation does not provoke any permanent redistribution of income; or if the redistribution does not affect the aggregate propensity to save. Since wages rise with prices we can exclude redistributions from working class to nonworking class. But we cannot exclude redistribution from fixed-income receivers (especially owners of securities) to profits. It is difficult to say whether this will change sensibly the aggregate propensity to save; it is probably a good approximation to assume that the effect will be negligible.

relation between S and I if it were possible to raise the real income above the full employment level.

Figure 2-A is the graph of equation (2). Each curve in this graph shows the amount of investment that would be undertaken at different levels of the rate of interest and for a fixed value of the income. To larger values of Y correspond investment curves higher and to the right.

Since the vertical scale is the same in both Figure 2-A and Figure 2-B, we may use the following method to find the shape of $S(Y) = I(r, Y)$: For any value of Y, say Y_1, the corresponding amount of saving, S_1, can be read from the SS curve. But in equilibrium $S = I$, hence we can draw a line parallel to the Y axis at height S_1 and prolong it until it inter-

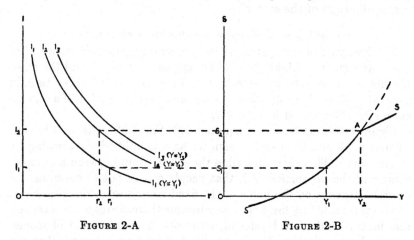

FIGURE 2-A   FIGURE 2-B

sects the investment curve of Figure 2-A corresponding to the income Y_1. We may thus find the rate of interest r_1 that corresponds to the given income Y_1.

The character of the relationship between r and Y that emerges from this diagram cannot be established a priori as in the case of the LL curve discussed before. For, as Y increases, S in Figure 2-B increases too, but the corresponding value of r in Figure 2-A may increase or decrease. It all depends on the way the change in income affects the position of the investment curves. If the increase in income tends to raise the desire to save more than the desire to invest, the rate of interest will fall; in the opposite case it will rise.[16] This last possibility is, in our opinion, unlikely to occur, but it may materialize when entrepreneurs are highly optimistic and the existing equipment is already working at capacity.

[16] From $S(r, Y) = I(r, Y)$ we obtain $dr/dY = (S_Y - I_Y)/(I_r - S_r)$, where the subscripts denote partial derivatives. Since $I_r - S_r$ may be expected to be negative, we have $dr/dY \gtreqless 0$ as $S_Y \gtreqless I_Y$.

The relationship between r and Y emerging from equations (2) and (3) and the equilibrium condition (4) is shown as the IS curve of Figure 3. In the normal case it will slope downward and to the right as in this diagram, but it is conceivable that, at least in a certain range, it may slope upward to the right. In this case $S_Y < I_Y$ and it is usually assumed that the equilibrium of the system will be unstable (and neutral if $S_Y = I_Y$). We shall see, however, that, with inelastic money supply, the negative slope of the IS curve is a sufficient but not necessary condition for stability.

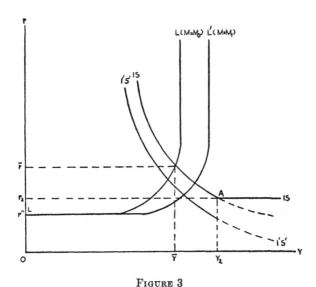

FIGURE 3

The IS curve must also have another important property. In Figure 3, A denotes the equilibrium relationship between full-employment income (Y_2) and rate of interest (r_2). Money income cannot rise above the full-employment level denoted by Y_2 except through inflation, i.e., if wages and prices rise in the same proportion as income. As the stage of inflationary prices and wage increases is reached, the "real" value of investment that it pays to undertake at any interest rate is unchanged since yields and costs change in the same proportion.[17] The

[17] Following the example of Mr. Keynes we may define the marginal efficiency of an asset as the discount rate that makes the sum of the expected marginal discounted yields equal to the marginal cost of the asset. The expected yields need not all be equal since they depend on the expected net physical yield as well as on expected future prices; and neither is necessarily constant in time. But the expected physical yield does not depend on prices; and, owing to our "static assumption" of unit elasticity of expectation, expected prices change in the same proportion as present prices. Therefore the summation of the yields changes in

money value of profitable investments, on the other hand, rises proportionally to prices and money income. As we have seen above, the same will be true of money savings. It follows that inflationary increases in income raise saving and investment in the same proportion and must therefore leave the equilibrium value of the rate of interest unchanged at the full-employment level r_2. It is for this reason that in Figure 3, to the right of A, the IS curve becomes parallel to the income axis. The dotted curved line beyond A is again the hypothetical relationship between r and Y if it were possible to raise real income above the full-employment level (and if the wage rate should remain unchanged at the level w_0).

9. THE MONEY MARKET AND THE DETERMINANTS OF MONETARY EQUILIBRIUM

We may now finally proceed to consider the process by which the equilibrium of the system is established. For this purpose we must once more revert to the money market which we must, this time, consider in terms of flows rather than in terms of stocks.

In Section 5 we have seen that the rate of interest is established in the money market by the condition that supply of and demand for the stock of money to hold must be equal. This condition is sufficient to determine a position of short-run equilibrium, i.e., a position of equilibrium for the income period. We must now consider under what conditions this level of the rate of interest will also represent a position of long-run equilibrium. As in the textbook analysis of demand and supply, a position of long-run equilibrium is characterized by the fact that neither price nor quantity (demanded and supplied) tend to change any further. In the present case a position of long-run equilibrium will be reached only when the rate of interest does not tend to change from one income period to the other and this in turn is possible only if the stock of money to hold remains constant in time.

Now in each income period people increase their assets by current savings; the money thus saved, since it is not needed for transactions, constitutes an increase in the supply of money to hold. Borrowing, on the other hand, automatically decreases the supply of money to hold by taking cash out of the money market and putting it into active circulation again, through expenditure on investments. If net saving exceeds net borrowing then, on balance, the supply of money to hold

---

the same proportion as marginal cost and so does the aggregate value of investments having marginal efficiency equal to or larger than r_2. Under unit elasticity of expectation a given change in all present prices does not modify entrepreneurs' production plans.

will increase above the level of the previous period, say $D_{a \cdot 0}$. But at the old rate of interest (r_0) people will not want to hold the extra supply; they will therefore try to purchase securities and thus will lower the rate of interest. If, on the other hand, at the interest rate r_0 borrowers desire to borrow in the period more than the current amount of money savings, they must induce dealers in the money market to reduce the demand for money as an asset below the previous level $D_{a \cdot 0}$; and this is possible only if the rate of interest rises. There are then three possibilities. (The subscripts 0 and 1 denote quantities in periods zero and one, respectively.)

(1) $S_1 > I_1$: then $D_{a \cdot 1} > D_{a \cdot 0}$ and the rate of interest falls.

(2) $S_1 = I_1$: here $D_{a \cdot 1} = D_{a \cdot 0}$ and the rate of interest is unchanged.

(3) $S_1 < I_1$: then $D_{a \cdot 1} < D_{a \cdot 0}$ and the rate of interest rises.

Recalling our definition of long-run equilibrium, we see at once that only situation (2) satisfies it. In equilibrium then, both demand for and supply of the stock of money to hold and demand for and supply of the flow of saving must be equal.[17a] In addition, however, it is necessary that the flows of saving and of borrowing be themselves constant in time. This is possible only if two conditions hold: (a) The borrowing that occurs must be equal to the amount of investment that entrepreneurs wish to undertake at the given rate of interest and income level. The relationship between I_1, r_1, and Y_1 must be described by a point on the corresponding curve of Figure 2-A. (b) The income (and the rate of interest) must be as large as is required to induce people to go on saving an amount S_1. The relationship between Y_1, S_1, and r_1 must be described by a point lying on the curve of Figure 2-B. But if conditions (a) and (b) are satisfied the relationship between Y and r will be described by a point lying on the IS curve of Figure 3. Thus a position of full equilibrium must be represented by a point lying at the same time on the LL curve (denoting equilibrium between demand for and supply of the stock of money to hold) and on the IS curve (denoting equality and constancy in time of the inflow and outflow of cash in the money market); hence it must be given by the intersection of these two curves.

This is shown in Figure 3 where the equilibrium values of r and Y, thus determined, are denoted by $\bar{r}$ and $\bar{Y}$. Analytically this corresponds to the simultaneous solution of the two relationships between the income and the rate of interest obtained from equations (1), (2), (3), and (4): $M = L(r, Y)$ and $S(r, Y) = I(r, Y)$.

[17a] The classical example of the level of water in a reservoir fits this case perfectly. The rate of interest, like the level of the water, can be constant only if inflow and outflow are equal.

10. A DYNAMIC MODEL OF THE KEYNESIAN THEORY AND
THE STABILITY OF EQUILIBRIUM

So far our analysis has apparently been "timeless"[18] since it was based on the system of equations of Section 2, in which time does not appear explicitly. A close examination of the last sections, and especially Sections 7 and 9, will reveal, however, that dynamic elements have gradually slipped into our analysis, thanks to the device of "long- and short-run equilibrium," the oldest and simplest device of developing a dynamic theory with a static apparatus. Actually the criterion that distinguishes short- from long-run equilibrium is essentially a dynamic one: namely, the length of time that is required for certain decisions to be carried out, or, more generally, for certain causes to show their effects.

In our case, the equilibrium of the "money market" is a condition of short-run equilibrium (that determines the rate of interest for each period) because it is the result of decisions that can be carried into effect immediately. The condition saving = investment, on the other hand, is a condition of long-run equilibrium because the equality of *ex ante* saving and investment cannot be brought about instantaneously. This is a different way of stating the familiar proposition that the multiplier takes time to work out its full effect. This well-known fact is in turn explained essentially by the existence of a fundamental time lag: the lag between the time when income is earned and the time when it becomes available for expenditure. In the economic systems in which we live, people are usually paid for services already rendered. The income earned (or produced) in a period is the value of services rendered which will be paid for at the end of the normal income period; while the income available for expenditure represents payment for services rendered in the previous period. Decisions as to spending and saving can refer only to the disposable income, and are essentially motivated by it, even though income earned may have some influence.

This explains why the graph of the *IS* curve, unlike the *LL* curve, describes not instantaneous relationships but only possible positions of long-run equilibrium. When the two curves intersect we have a position of full equilibrium since both short- and long-run conditions are satisfied.

It will therefore be useful at this point to give explicit recognition to the dynamic elements that form the basis of our approach. This is the purpose of the following system of difference equations which may be considered as the simplest dynamic model of our theory.

---

[18] The word "timeless" has been used here to avoid confusion since the word "static" has already been used to denote the assumption of homogeneity of the first degree of the "expectations functions."

$$(2.1) \qquad\qquad M = L(r_t, Y_{d \cdot t}),$$

$$(2.2) \qquad\qquad I_t = I(r_t, Y_{d \cdot t}),$$

$$(2.3) \qquad\qquad S_t = S(r_t, Y_{d \cdot t}),$$

$$(2.4) \qquad\qquad Y_{d \cdot t} = C_t + S_t,$$

$$(2.5) \qquad\qquad Y_t = C_t + I_t,$$

$$(2.6) \qquad\qquad Y_{d \cdot t} = Y_{t-1}.$$

In this system Y denotes income earned and Y_d income disposable. This is a new variable to which corresponds the new equation (2.6). The remaining equations of the system are unchanged.

By repeated substitution the system reduces to the two equations

$$Y_t = Y_{t-1} - S_t + I_t = Y_{t-1} - S(Y_{t-1}, r_t) + I(Y_{t-1}, r_t),$$
$$M = L(r_t, Y_{t-1}).$$

Solving the second equation for r_t and substituting in the first, we obtain a single equation of the form: $Y_t = f(Y_{t-1})$ which determines the time path of the income. By similar procedure we obtain the time sequence of the other variables.

If the system is stable, each variable approaches some definite value which it will maintain in time until there occurs some change in the form of the functional relationship or in some parameter (M or w_0). Equation (2.1) is again the "equation of the money market" that determines the value of r for any period; but we have a position of long-run equilibrium only when $r_t = r_{t-1}$. And this implies $Y_t = Y_{d \cdot t} = Y_{t-1}$ and therefore $S_t = I_t$.

The importance of this system is not limited to the fact that it defines rigorously concepts that were loosely used in our previous analysis. It serves also another important purpose: namely it permits us to determine the conditions of stability for the system.

Following the usual method, we proceed to expand equations (2.1) to (2.3) by Taylor series around the equilibrium values neglecting all terms of degree higher than one. We then obtain:

$$0 = L_r \dot{r}_t + L_Y \dot{Y}_{t-1} + \cdots,$$
$$I_t = I(\bar{r}, \bar{Y}) + I_r \dot{r}_t + I_Y \dot{Y}_{t-1} + \cdots,$$
$$S_t = S(\bar{r}, \bar{Y}) + S_r \dot{r}_t + I_Y \dot{Y}_{t-1}.$$

Subscripts denote partial derivatives taken around the equilibrium values ($\bar{r}$, $\bar{Y}$) and $r_t = \dot{r}_t - \bar{r}$, $\dot{Y}_t = Y_t - \bar{Y}$. By making use of (4) and (5) and by repeated substitution we obtain the following linear difference equation with constant coefficients:

$$\dot{Y}_t = \dot{Y}_{t-1} \left[1 + \frac{L_Y}{L_r} (S_r - I_r) + I_Y - S_Y \right].$$

The solution of this equation takes the form: $\dot{Y} = \kappa\lambda^t$ or $Y = (Y_0 - \overline{Y})\lambda^t$, since $\dot{Y}_0 = Y_0 - \overline{Y} = \kappa$. Y_0 is determined by the initial conditions and

$$\lambda = 1 + \frac{L_Y}{L_r}(S_r - I_r) + I_Y - S_Y.$$

The stability condition is $|\lambda| < 1$; in the present case this reduces to

$$(2.7) \qquad -\frac{L_Y}{L_r} - \frac{r}{S_r - I_r} < \frac{I_Y - S_Y}{S_r - I_r} < -\frac{L_Y}{L_r}.$$

Since the middle term is the slope of the IS curve and the right-hand term is the slope of the LL curve, the right-hand condition has a very clear graphical meaning. Stability requires that the slope of the IS curve be algebraically smaller than the slope of the LL curve. The slope of the LL curve cannot be negative ($L_Y > 0$, $L_r \geq 0$). Also general economic considerations suggest that $S_r - I_r > 0$. Hence this condition is necessarily satisfied if $I_Y - S_Y < 0$, i.e., when the IS curve falls from left to right. But this is not necessary. Stability is also possible when the IS curve rises in the neighborhood of the equilibrium point as long as it cuts the LL curve from its concave toward its convex side.[19]

If the stability conditions are satisfied, the variables approach their equilibrium values, which are the same as those obtained by solving the static system of Section 2. In the opposite case they diverge more and more from these values in a process of cumulative contraction or expansion. In the same way, a change in some of the data will lead to a new stable equilibrium if the new functions satisfy the conditions written above.

It is interesting to note that, as long as the money supply is inelastic, the system must always have at least one stable solution since eventually the LL curve becomes perpendicular to the horizontal axis and hence its slope must become larger then the slope of the IS curve.

11. THE DETERMINANTS OF REAL EQUILIBRIUM

It is now time to consider the role of the second part of the system in the determination of equilibrium. Equations (5), (6), and (7) *explain* the forces that determine the real variables of the system: physical output, employment, real wage rate.[20]

---

[19] It is only as $L_r \to \infty$ (demand for money to hold infinitely elastic, LL curve parallel to the horizontal axis) that the condition $I_Y - S_Y < 0$ becomes necessary for equilibrium. This holds equally if the supply of money is infinitely elastic for this has the same effect as $L_r = \infty$.

[20] The price level is also necessary to determine the real wage rate, given the money wage rate W.

The most important of these equations is (7), which states the conditions of equilibrium in the production of goods whether for consumption or for investment.[21] Production will be extended up to the point at which the given and fixed money wage rate w_0 is equal to the marginal net product of labor, or, if we prefer, up to the point at which price equals marginal labor cost.[22] This assumes that the only variable factor is labor and the quantity of equipment is fixed; a condition that is approximately satisfied in the case we are considering. Eliminating equation (5) by substitution into (7) we can reduce this part of the system to two equations in the two unknowns X and N, where X' is used for dX/dN:

$$W_0 = X'(N)\frac{Y}{X}, \qquad X = X(N).$$

Since the money income is determined exclusively by the *monetary* part of the system, the price level depends only on the amount of output. If, at any given price level, the fixed wage is less than the marginal product of labor, the forces of competition lead to an expansion of employment and output which forces prices down. This lowers the marginal product of labor until it becomes equal to the wage rate. If the wage rate exceeded the marginal product of labor, output and employment would contract, which would force prices up. We see clearly from Figure 3 that the amount of employment thus determined will, in general, not be "full employment"; that is, unless the LL curve intersects the IS curve at (Y_2, r_2) or to the right of it.

12. UNDEREMPLOYMENT EQUILIBRIUM AND LIQUIDITY PREFERENCE

This last result deserves closer consideration. It is usually considered as one of the most important achievements of the Keynesian theory that it explains the consistency of economic equilibrium with the presence of involuntary unemployment. It is, however, not sufficiently recognized that, except in a limiting case to be considered later, this result is due entirely to the assumption of "rigid wages"[23] and not to the Keynesian liquidity preference. Systems with rigid wages share the common property that the equilibrium value of the "real" variables is determined essentially by monetary conditions rather than by "real" factors (e.g., quantity and efficiency of existing equipment, relative

[21] The equilibrium price of each type of physical asset is found by capitalizing a series of expected marginal yields at the current rate of interest. The expected yields of the marginal unit need not be equal in each period.

[22] This is a sufficient condition under assumption of perfect competition; the modifications necessary in the case of monopolies cannot be considered here.

[23] The expression "rigid wages" refers to the infinite elasticity of the supply curve of labor when the level of employment is below "full."

preference for earning and leisure, etc.). The monetary conditions are sufficient to determine money income and, under fixed wages and given technical conditions, to each money income there corresponds a definite equilibrium level of employment. This equilibrium level does not tend to coincide with full employment except by mere chance, since there is no economic mechanism that insures this coincidence. There may be unemployment in the sense that more people would be willing to work at the current real wage rate than are actually employed; but in a free capitalistic economy production is guided by prices and not by desires and since the money wage rate is rigid, this desire fails to be translated into an economic stimulus.

In order to show more clearly that wage rigidities and not liquidity preference explain underemployment equilibrium we may consider the results to be obtained by giving up the liquidity-preference theory and assuming instead the crudest quantity-of-money theory while keeping the assumption of rigid wages. This can be done by merely replacing equation (1) of our system by the equation

(1a) $M = kY.$

Since M and k are constant this equation is sufficient to determine money income. Equations (5), (6), and (7) determine directly physical output and employment as we saw in Section 10. Once more there is no reason to expect that the level of employment thus determined will be "full employment"; and yet the system will be in equilibrium since there will be no tendency for income, employment, and output to change.

It is very interesting to see what part is played under these conditions by equations (2) and (3), the saving and investment equations that have been so much stressed by all the Keynesians. Since the income is determined by equation (1a), equation (2) reduces to an "orthodox" supply-of-saving schedule, giving saving as a function of the rate of interest. For the same reason, equation (3) reduces to a demand-for-saving schedule. Both schedules can be represented in a Marshallian supply and demand diagram as is done in Figure 4. The intersection of these curves, i.e., the equilibrium condition, demand = supply, determines the level of the rate of interest.

Finally let us notice that, in this system also, the rate of interest depends on the quantity of money, or more exactly on the ratio M/W. A change in M (W constant) raises real income and shifts both the SS and II curves to the right. The net result will be a fall in the rate of interest, if the increase in income raises the desire to save more than the desire to invest (normal case); a rise, in the opposite case.

In spite of these significant similarities between the present system and the Keynesian system, in which we recognize the existence of liquidity demand for money, there remains one very important difference; this difference is to be found in the role played by the rate of interest in the determination of equilibrium. In both cases the level of employment depends on the quantity of "active" money. But in the Keynesian system this depends on the rate of interest and consequently also on the propensities to save and invest. In the present case the quantity of active money is fixed and independent of the rate of interest. Hence the propensities to save and invest are not a part of the mechanism determining employment; they merely determine the amount of resources devoted to the improvement of the means of production.

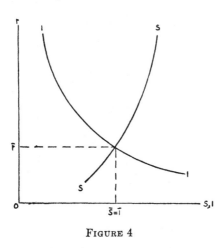

FIGURE 4

We now proceed to consider the determinants of equilibrium in a system in which we do away not only with the liquidity-preference theory but also with the assumption of rigid wages.

13. THE LOGICAL CONSISTENCY OF THE QUANTITY THEORY OF MONEY AND THE DICHOTOMY OF MONETARY AND REAL ECONOMICS

In order to discuss the quantity theory of money we substitute equation (1a) for (1) and replace conditions (10) by the identities (11).

It was shown in Section 8 that a given change in prices will change income, investment, and saving in the same proportion. Consequently, after Y in equations (2) and (3) is replaced by the expression given in (5), the saving and investment equations may be written in the form

$$(3.2) \qquad \frac{I}{W} = I\left(r, \frac{P}{W}X\right),$$

$$(3.3) \qquad \frac{S}{W} = S\left(r, \frac{P}{W}X\right).$$

Next we divide both members of equations (4) and (5) by W obtaining

(3.4)
$$\frac{S}{W} = \frac{I}{W},$$

(3.5)
$$\frac{Y}{W} \equiv \frac{P}{W} X,$$

(3.6)
$$X = X(N),$$

(3.7)
$$\frac{W}{P} = X'(N),$$

(3.9)
$$N = F\left(\frac{W}{P}\right),$$

$$\left[(3.8) \qquad \frac{Y}{W} \equiv \frac{I}{W} + \frac{C}{W}\right].$$

Equations (3.2) to (3.7) and (3.9) form a system of 7 equations in the 7 unknowns I/W, S/W, P/W, Y/W, r, X, N. These unknowns are therefore determined. Next we can write equation (1a) in the form $M = kPX = Wk(P/W)X$. But since P/W and X have already been determined, this equation determines the money wage rate and hence the price level, money income, etc. This is essentially the "classical" procedure, and we can only repeat the classical conclusions to the effect that the real part of the system, namely, employment, *interest rate*, output, or real income, do not depend on the quantity of money. The quantity of money has no other function than to determine the price level.

This result does not, of course, depend on any special feature of our system. It will always follow, provided all the supply and demand functions for commodities[24] and labor are homogeneous of the zero degree; and since we are proceeding under "static" assumptions, all the supply and demand functions must be homogeneous of zero degree, if people behave rationally.[25]

This conclusion, which is very old indeed, has some interest since it has been recently challenged by Oscar Lange. Of all the recent attacks against the traditional dichotomy of monetary and real economics, Lange's criticism is by far the most serious because it maintains that "the traditional procedure of the theory of money involves a

[24] "Commodities" are, in this context, all goods except money.
[25] For a proof of this statement see O. Lange, "Say's Law: A Restatement and Criticism," *op. cit.*, pp. 67 and 68. Professor Lange shows that the homogeneity of first degree of all expectation functions is a sufficient condition for all demand and supply equations for "commodities" to be homogeneous of zero degree.

[logical] contradiction."[26] We propose to show, however, that, while Lange's criticism of Say's law cannot be questioned, it does not invalidate the logical consistency of the procedure of the quantity theory of money.

According to Lange, Say's law implies that the amount of cash people desire to hold is always identically equal to the quantity in existence: denoting by D_n and S_n the demand and supply of money respectively, we can write this as $S_n \equiv D_n$. Lange then states that "a proportional change of all prices does not induce a substitution between different commodities"[27] and concludes that "the demand and supply functions of commodities are, *when Say's law holds*, homogeneous of zero degree."[28] But the homogeneity of the supply and demand functions for commodities does not depend on Say's law: it depends on the assumption of rationality and the homogeneity of the expectation functions. Since a proportional change in all prices does not change the price ratios it also does not change the marginal rate of substitution, and therefore does not induce a substitution between different commodities.

Let us now consider a system in which there are n goods ($n-1$ commodities and money). As is well known, there are only $n-1$ prices to be determined, the price of money being unity, and $n-1$ independent supply and demand equations, for one follows from the rest. Since the supply and demand functions for commodities are homogeneous of zero degree, the quantities demanded of the $n-1$ commodities are functions of the $n-2$ price ratios p_i/p_{n-1} ($i=1, 2, \cdots, n-2$), where p_{n-1} is chosen arbitrarily.[29] At the same time the demand and supply function to be eliminated is also arbitrary; we may, if we choose, eliminate one of the $n-1$ referring to commodities; we are then left with $n-2$ equations for commodities to determine the $n-2$ price ratios. Hence the price ratios are determined. To determine the actual prices we use the demand and supply equation for money as was done above. In Lange's system this is written:

$$k \sum_{i=1}^{n} p_i S_i = M, \quad \text{or also} \quad k p_{n-1} \sum_{i=1}^{n} \frac{p_i}{p_{n-1}} S_i = M,$$

where S_i denotes the equilibrium quantity supplied and demanded of the ith commodity. Since k is a constant this equation determines p_{n-1} and consequently all other prices.

As long as Say's law is not assumed, this procedure is perfectly legitimate; and we cannot escape the classical conclusion that money

[26] *Ibid.*, p. 65.
[27] *Ibid.*, p. 63.
[28] *Ibid.*, p. 63. Italics ours.
[29] In our own system p_{n-1} was arbitrarily chosen as the wage rate.

is "neutral," just a "veil." If, however, Say's law holds, the demand and supply of money are identically equal. The nth equation is therefore not a genuine equation. Thus we have only $n-2$ independent equations to determine $n-1$ prices: the system is not determinate. In Lange's own formulation, the nth equation degenerates into the identity

$$kp_{n-1} \sum_{i=1}^{n} \frac{p_i}{p_{n-1}} S_i \equiv M,$$

which is satisfied by any value of p_{n-1} whatever; the price level is thus indeterminate.[30]

Hence one of Lange's conclusions, namely that "Say's law precludes any monetary theory,"[31] is perfectly justified. But Lange goes on to draw a conclusion which does not follow, namely that "the traditional procedure of the theory of money involves a contradiction. Either Say's law is assumed and money prices are indeterminate, or money prices are made determinate—but then *Say's law and hence the neutrality of money* must be abandoned."[32] But the traditional theory of money is not based on Say's law. The necessary condition for money to be neutral is that the $n-1$ "real" demand and supply equations be homogeneous of order zero and this homogeneity does not "disappear when Say's law is abandoned."[33] Under "static" assumptions money is neutral even without assuming Say's law, if only people are assumed to behave "rationally"; this is all that the classical theory assumes and needs to assume.[34]

The most serious charge against the classical dichotomy can thus be dismissed, as long as we maintain our "static" assumptions.

14. LIQUIDITY PREFERENCE AND THE DETERMINANTS OF THE RATE OF INTEREST UNDER THE ASSUMPTION OF FLEXIBLE WAGES[35]

With this in mind we may now proceed to analyze our third system consisting of equations (1) to (7), (9), and identities (11). In this system we recognize that there are two sources of demand for money,

[30] Then k changes in inverse proportion to p_{n-1} instead of being a constant.

[31] O. Lange, *op. cit.*, p. 66.

[32] *Ibid.*, p. 65. Italics ours.

[33] *Ibid.*, p. 66.

[34] Lange's result seems due to a failure to distinguish between necessary and sufficient conditions. Say's law is a sufficient condition for the neutrality of money but not a necessary one. Lange asks me to inform the reader that he agrees with my conclusion. This conclusion, however, does not invalidate his result that under Say's law the money prices are indeterminate.

[35] The expression "flexible wages" is used here and in the following pages for brevity in place of the more exact expression "homogeneity of zero degree of the supply-of-labor function."

the transaction demand and the liquidity demand. But, as in the case just analyzed, we make no restrictive assumptions as to the supply-of-labor equation. The suppliers of labor as well as the suppliers of all other commodities are supposed to behave "rationally." It follows that the only difference between the present case and the case just considered is in equation (1). As in the previous case, the last 7 equations form a determinate system which is sufficient to determine the 7 unknowns it contains, namely *the "real" variables of the system and the rate of interest.*

By use of equation (5) or (3.5) equation (1) takes the form

$$(3.1) \qquad M = L\left(r, \, W\frac{P}{W}X\right).$$

Since r and P/W are already determined, this equation determines the 8th unknown of the system, the wage rate: and therefore also the price level, money, income, etc.[36]

We thus reach the conclusion that under "static" assumptions and "flexible" wages, *the rate of interest and the level of employment do not depend on the quantity of money.*

Two questions arise at once: (a) what determines the rate of interest and (b) what part do the rate of interest and liquidity demand for money play in the determination of equilibrium.

Strictly speaking, the rate of interest is determined by all the equations of a Walrasian system *except the supply-of-and-demand-for-money equation.* But it is clear that in the first approximation of partial-equilibrium analysis, the determination of the rate of interest must be associated with equations (3.2) and (3.3), the saving and investment schedules. To explain the level of the rate of interest we could use once more Figure 4, changing the variables measured on the horizontal axis from S or I into S/W or I/W. We must add at once, however, that these two schedules should in no way be confused with the schedules of supply of and demand for savings (or supply of and demand for securities) used in the textbook explanation of the determination of the rate of interest.

Equation (3.3) only tells us what part of their real income people wish to devote to increasing their assets rather than to consumption, at different levels of the rate of interest.

In a similar fashion equation (3.2) shows that by devoting output worth I/W to the improvement of the means of production, it is possible to increase real income by an amount $(I/W)(1+r)$ per unit of time. The value of r depends on the given technical conditions, on the

[36] Except in the Keynesian case considered later (Section 16).

quantity I/W and $(P/W)X$ according to the relation expressed by equation (3.2). This shows clearly the fundamental factors that determine the rate of interest. The given technical conditions, expressed by the production function [equation (3.6)], together with *tastes* of people for earning and leisure, expressed by the supply-of-labor function [equation (3.9)], give the level of real income that can be reached.[37] The saving schedule, equation (3.3), tells us what part of this income the community desires to save. The technical conditions (inventions, quantity of capital already in existence, etc.) expressed by the marginal-efficiency-of-investment function (3.2), determine the marginal efficiency of the amount of investment that the giving up of consumption permits undertaking: this is the equilibrium rate of interest.

Let us now examine what part is played by liquidity preference in the present system. On the basis of the given rate of interest determined in the fashion discussed above, people decide what quantity of money they want to hold as an asset. Hence, provided the liquidity demand is finite, the rate of interest, together with the supply of money, determines the quantity of active money and therefore the price level. Thus under "flexible" wages, *the desire to hold assets in liquid form does not determine the rate of interest, but determines the price level*. It follows that any factor that influences the demand for money as an asset, either directly or through the rate of interest, will have a repercussion on the price level, unless it is counteracted by an appropriate change in the quantity of money. This will in particular be the case with changes in the propensities to save and to invest.

15. LIQUIDITY PREFERENCE UNDER RIGID AND FLEXIBLE WAGES—AN EXAMPLE

In order to see clearly the different implications of the liquidity-preference theory under different hypotheses as to the supply of labor we may briefly consider the effects of a shift in the investment schedule [equation (2) or (3.2)].

Suppose that the system is in equilibrium at money income Y_0: the flow of investments is I_0, and its marginal efficiency, r_0, is the equilibrium rate of interest. Now let us assume that for some reason the rate of investment that seems profitable at any level of the rate of interest falls. In particular the marginal efficiency of the rate of investment I_0 falls to the level $r_1 < r_0$. In order for the system to reach a new position of equilibrium, it is necessary that the rate of interest fall to this level. Except under special circumstances, to be considered later, as

---

[37] Under flexible wages there is, of course, always full employment under the conditions mentioned in Section 16.

the rate of interest falls, the demand for money as an asset rises, and a certain amount of current money savings remains in the *money market* to satisfy the increased demand. If the supply of money is not properly increased, this, in turn, implies a fall in money income.

Under the conditions of our last model (flexible wages) the fall is brought about by an all-around reduction in wages and prices. The price level reaches its new equilibrium position when the supply has been increased sufficiently to satisfy the liquidity demand for money associated with the interest rate r_1.[38] The net effect of the shift is then to depress the interest rate, the money income, and money wages without affecting the real variables of the system, employment, output, real wage rate.[39]

But if money wages are rigid downward, the reduction in money income, made necessary by the fall in the rate of interest, becomes a reduction in real income and employment as well. The effect of the shift in the investment schedule is now to start a typical process of contraction so frequently described in Keynesian literature. As producers of investment goods make losses, they have no other choice than to dismiss workers, even though their physical productivity is unchanged. This, in turn, reduces the demand for consumption goods and causes unemployment to spread to this sector. Real income falls along with money income (the price level is likely to fall to a smaller extent). The fall in money income increases the supply of money to hold; the fall in real income decreases saving and raises its marginal efficiency above the level r_1.[40] This double set of reactions leads finally to a new equilibrium, with a smaller money and real income, less employment, higher real wages (since the price level falls) and a rate of interest somewhere below r_0 and above the new "full employment interest" r_1.[41] In terms of our graphic apparatus, a decreased marginal efficiency of capital (or increased propensity to save), shifts the IS curve to the left, as shown by the curve $I'S'$, and lowers interest rate and income, money as well as real income.

[38] The rate of interest must necessarily fall to the level r_1, for the real income and therefore the amount of real savings will be unchanged, and the marginal efficiency of this amount of real savings is r_1, by hypothesis.

[39] The real wage rate clearly cannot fall. If the real wage rate had fallen, entrepreneurs would try to expand employment while the supply of labor would, if anything, contract. If it had risen, the opposite situation would occur, and neither of these situations is compatible with equilibrium.

[40] Except if the IS curve is not monotonic decreasing, in which case the process of contraction will be more pronounced.

[41] If there was no full employment in the initial situation, then r_1 is simply the rate of interest that would maintain the old level of employment. This conclusion is also subject to the qualification mentioned in footnote 40.

16. TWO LIMITING CASES: (A) THE KEYNESIAN CASE

There is one case in which the Keynesian theory of liquidity preference is sufficient by itself to explain the existence of underemployment
equilibrium without starting out with the assumption of rigid wages.
We have seen (Section 5) that, since securities are inferior to money as
a form of holding assets, there must be some positive level of the rate
of interest (previously denoted by r'') at which the demand for money
becomes infinitely elastic or practically so. We have the Keynesian
case when the "full-employment equilibrium rate of interest" is less
than r''. Whenever this situation materializes, the very mechanism
that tends to bring about full-employment equilibrium in a system
with "flexible" wages breaks down, since there is no possible level of
the money wage rate and price level that can establish full-employment
equilibrium.

From the analytical point of view the situation is characterized by
the fact that we must add to our system a new equation, namely $r = r''$.
The system is therefore overdetermined since we have 9 equations to
determine only 8 unknowns.

Equations (3.2) and (3.3) are sufficient to determine the value of the
real income (since r is already determined). But this value will in general not be consistent with the value of the real income determined by
the last four equations. More workers would be willing to work at the
ruling real wage rate than are employed, but efforts at reducing real
wages and increasing employment are bound to fail. For any fall in
wages and prices increases the supply of money to hold but cannot
lower the rate of interest below the level r'' since the demand for money
as an asset is infinitely elastic. As Keynes would say, labor as a whole
will not be able to fix its own real wage rate.

It appears clearly that, in this case, equilibrium is determined by
those very factors that are stressed in the typical Keynesian analysis.
In particular, real income and employment is determined by the position and shape of the saving and investment function, and changes in
the propensity to invest or to save change real income without affecting
the interest rate.

The price level on the other hand is in neutral equilibrium (at least
for a certain range of values). It will tend to fall indefinitely as long as
workers attempt to lower money wages in an effort to increase employment; and it can only find a resting place if and when money wages become rigid.

In this case the Keynesian analysis clearly departs from the classical
lines and it leads to conclusions that could scarcely have been reached
by following the traditional line of approach.

Whether the situation we have characterized as the "Keynesian case" is typical of some or all modern economic systems is a factual question which we cannot attempt to answer here. It is beyond doubt however that its interest is not purely theoretical.[42]

(B) THE CLASSICAL CASE

We have the classical case when the equilibrium rate of interest is sufficiently high to make the demand for money to hold zero or negligible. Graphically, the *IS* curve of Figure 3 intersects the *LL* curve in the range in which *LL* is perpendicular to the income axis. Under these conditions changes in the rate of interest (except possibly if they are of considerable size) tend to leave the demand for money unchanged or practically so; $L_r = 0$ or negligible and $M = L(Y)$. The properties of a system satisfying this condition have already been sufficiently analyzed in Sections 11 and 12.[43]

17. PRELIMINARY CONCLUSIONS

This brings to an end the first part of our analysis which aimed principally at distinguishing, as far as possible, to what extent the results of the Keynesian analysis are due to a more refined theoretical approach (liquidity preference) and to what extent to the assumption of rigid wages. We may summarize the results of our inquiry in the following propositions:

I. The liquidity-preference theory is not necessary to explain under-

---

[42] In the *General Theory* Keynes explicitly recognizes that the situation described as the "Keynesian case" does not seem, so far, normally to prevail in any economic system. This situation, on the other hand, certainly plays an important part in some phases of the business cycle, when a great feeling of uncertainty and the anticipation of price reductions increase the attractiveness of liquidity and, at the same time, decreases the propensity to invest. Besides, it may also soon become a normal feature of some economies if there should come to prevail a real scarcity of investment outlets that are profitable at rates of interest higher than the institutional minimum. Modifying a well-known statement of Hicks we can say that the Keynesian case is either the Economics of Depression or the Economics of Abundance. (Hicks's original statement: "The General Theory of Employment is the Economics of Depression" is found in "Mr. Keynes and the 'Classics,'" *op. cit.*, p. 155.)

[43] To what extent the "classical case" is met in practice is again a factual question. In our opinion a moderately high rate of interest is sufficient to make it unattractive to hold assets in the form of cash and therefore to induce members of the community to limit their holdings to the amount necessary for transactions (which is determined by the institutional set-up). It is perhaps not unreasonable to expect that under normal conditions a "pure" rate of interest (i.e., net of default risk) in the neighborhood of 5 per cent might be sufficient to reduce the demand for money to hold to negligible proportions.

employment equilibrium; it is sufficient only in a limiting case: the "Keynesian case." In the general case it is neither necessary nor sufficient; it can explain this phenomenon only with the additional assumption of rigid wages.

II. The liquidity-preference theory is neither necessary nor sufficient to explain the dependence of the rate of interest on the quantity of money. This dependence is explained only by the assumption of rigid wages.

III. The result of the liquidity-preference theory is that the quantity of active money depends not only on the total quantity of money but also on the rate of interest and therefore also on the form and position of the propensities to save and to invest. Hence in a system with flexible wages the rate of interest and the propensities to save and to invest are part of the mechanism that determines the price level. And in a system with rigid wages they are part of the mechanism that determines the level of employment and real income.

We proceed now to make use of our results for two purposes: (a) To examine critically some of the theories that have their logical foundation in the Keynesian analysis. (b) To state some general conclusions about the determinants of the rate of interest.

PART II

18. GENERAL REMARKS ABOUT THE ASSUMPTION OF WAGE RIGIDITY IN THE KEYNESIAN THEORIES

In the *General Theory* Keynes does of course recognize the fundamental importance of the relation between money wages and the quantity of money as is shown by his device of the wage units. This very fact, on the other hand, has had the effect of obscuring the part played by wage rigidities in the determination of economic equilibrium. This can be clearly seen in a large body of literature based on the Keynesian analysis, and will be illustrated with a few examples.

(A) Let us first consider the role of investment.

The statement that unemployment is caused by lack of investment, or that a fall in the propensity to invest or an increase in the propensity to save will decrease employment, has become today almost a commonplace.

As we have seen, however, lack of investment is sufficient to explain underemployment equilibrium only in the "Keynesian case," a situation that is the exception and not the rule.

It is true that a reduced level of employment and a reduced level of investment go together, but this is not, in general, the result of causal relationship. It is true instead that the low level of investment and employment are both the effect of the same cause, namely a basic maladjustment between the quantity of money and the wage rate. It is the fact that money wages are too high relative to the quantity of money that explains why it is unprofitable to expand employment to the "full employment" level. Now to each level of employment and income corresponds a certain distribution of the employment between the production of consumption and investment goods determined by the saving pattern of the community. Hence, when the over-all level of employment is low there will be a reduced level of investment as well as a reduced level of consumption. And the level of investment is low because employment is low and not the other way around.

What is required to improve the situation is an increase in the quantity of money (and not necessarily in the propensity to invest); then employment will increase in every field of production including investment. Again, it is true that, in general, a fall in the propensity to invest (the propensity to save being constant) tends to decrease employment (and that an increase in the same propensity has the opposite effect), but this occurs only because it decreases (or increases) the quantity of money available for transactions relative to the money wage rate and therefore makes it profitable to expand employment. Exactly the same result could be obtained by deflating (or inflating) the quantity of money directly. That a change in the marginal efficiency of investment has no direct influence on aggregate employment can be clearly seen in the "classical case" when the demand for money to hold is zero or negligible. In this case the change mentioned above does not affect employment, but only the rate of interest and therefore, at most, the distribution of the unchanged amount of employment between consumption and investment.

In conclusion, then, the statement that unemployment is caused by lack of investment assumes implicitly that every possible economic system works under the special conditions of the "Keynesian case"; and this is clearly unwarranted. In general the reduced level of employment is not a cause, but just a symptom of unemployment, which in turn is due to essentially monetary disturbances.

This formulation is not only more correct but carries also important implications about the concrete form of economic policies necessary to relieve unemployment.

(B) Another typical result of understressing the assumption of rigid wages is to be found in connection with the concepts of a "natural rate of interest" and of "cumulative inflation" and "deflation" of Wicksellian analysis.[44]

[44] See J. Marschak, "Wicksell's Two Interest Rates," *Social Research*, Vol. 8, November, 1941, pp. 469–478.

This "natural rate" is the equilibrium (and therefore full-employment) interest rate of a system with flexible wages and not of a Keynesian system with rigid wages. Under "flexible" wages, as we know, the equilibrium rate of interest does not depend on the quantity of money. But, because of the time required for a new position of equilibrium to be reached when some of the conditions change, it will depend on the rate of change of M. Thus the money authority will be able to keep r below (or above) its equilibrium value by increasing (or decreasing) the quantity of money without limit; we thus get a process of cumulative inflation or deflation. Under Keynesian assumptions this ceases to be true; but only because wages are assumed rigid and in this condition, as we have seen, it is in general possible to change the rate of interest with a finite change in the quantity of money.[45]

(C) As a last example, we may quote Lange's "optimum propensity to consume."[46] This concept, outside of its theoretical interest, is only of practical importance if for some reason, money wages and money supply are absolutely inelastic. In general all that is required to increase employment is to expand the quantity of money (or at worst reduce wages) without any necessity for interfering with the propensity to consume.[47]

19. LERNER'S THEORY OF THE RATE OF INTEREST

We proceed now to consider the typically "Keynesian" theory of the rate of interest and money due to A. P. Lerner. We choose Lerner's theory, because its extremism and its clear-cut formulation permit of a useful criticism.

[45] The case is more complicated if the relation between Y and r described by the IS curve is not monotonic decreasing in the relevant range. It might then appear that an attempt of the money authority at reducing the interest rate will result in a fall in income and employment. This is the result reached by Marschak. Actually as the money authority expands the quantity of money by open-market policy it finds that the rate of interest eventually rises along with income and employment instead of falling. If the money authority insists on keeping the interest rate at the planned level it will have to go on expanding the quantity of money. This will either push the system to some new equilibrium if the planned rate is equal to or larger than the full-employment rate, or it will cause inflation if the planned rate is below this level. But in no event will an initial attempt at lowering r by open-market policy lead to a contraction of income.

[46] Oscar Lange, "The Rate of Interest and the Optimum Propensity to Consume," *Economica*, Vol. 5 (N. S)., February, 1938, pp. 12–32.

[47] If the demand for money is infinitely elastic the propensity to consume plays an important role in the determination of employment. In this case the optimum level of consumption C' would clearly be $C' = Y' - I(r'', Y')$, where Y' is full-employment income and r'' the critical level of the rate of interest for which $L_r = \infty$.

The substance of Lerner's argument, as far as we can make out, is this: The "classical theory" that saving and investment determine the rate of interest must be rejected: saving and investment, being identically equal, cannot determine interest. This is instead determined by the quantity of money according to a demand-for-money function, say $M = f(r)$.[48]

The first argument is clearly unimportant since it is based on definitions. If one accepts the Keynesian definitions then, of course, actual (or *ex post*) saving and investment are identical; and clearly the *ex post* identity, saving $\equiv$ investment, cannot determine either the rate of interest or income. This however does not prove that the propensities to save and to invest are irrelevant to the determination of interest.

We know on the contrary, that, under assumption of flexible wages, neither of Lerner's arguments holds. In this case the rate of interest is independent of the quantity of money and, except in limiting cases, is determined only by the propensities to save and to invest [equations (3.2) and (3.3)].

Let us stress, in order to avoid misunderstandings, that we perfectly agree with Lerner and with all the Keynesians that saving and lending are the result of two independent decisions; our equation (3.3) is a saving schedule and not a schedule of supply of loanable funds. However we cannot agree with Lerner that to treat saving as a "demand-for-securities schedule" is, without qualifications, a serious blunder, or that the classical analysis as to the effect of shifts in the desire to invest or to save is right by pure chance. We must remember that saving and lending coincide when the demand for money to hold is zero or constant. The quantity theory of money starts out with the assumption that the demand for money to hold is identically zero: $D_a'(r) \equiv 0$ or $M = L(Y)$. Now this assumption is unsatisfactory for a general theory, but may be fully justified under certain conditions.

We know that, when the equilibrium rate of interest is sufficiently high, the demand for money to hold does become zero, even if it is not assumed to be identically zero. And, under historically realized conditions, the equilibrium rate of interest may be sufficiently high to make the demand for money to hold so negligible and so scarcely affected by observed changes in the interest rate that this demand can, safely, be neglected. Interest becomes a factor of secondary importance and can

---

[48] See especially, "Alternative Formulations of the Theory of Interest," *Economic Journal*, Vol. 48, June, 1938, pp. 211–230; and "Interest Theory—Supply and Demand for Loans or Supply and Demand for Cash?" This latter paper has been recently made available to me by Mr. Lerner in manuscript form; it is to be published in the *Review of Economic Statistics*. The present criticism is also the result of a long personal discussion and correspondence.

be dropped along with many others which certainly do influence the demand for money but are not sufficiently relevant to warrant separate consideration. Under these conditions, the assumption $M = L(Y)$ will give a satisfactory approximation to economic reality.[49] Under changed historical conditions this assumption is no longer justified and it becomes necessary to take into account new factors to avoid oversimplifications.[50]

When we recognize that the demand for money to hold need not be zero (and as long as it is finite), saving and lending coincide only when the demand for money to hold is constant, that is to say, in equilibrium. The equality of money savings and lending becomes an equilibrium condition which, under flexible wages, *determines the price level, not the rate of interest*. And this in turn may explain the traditional lack of attention to the demand for money to hold in connection with the theory of interest.

Thus Lerner's theory cannot explain the rate of interest in a system with "flexible" wages. Let us then see whether it holds within the limits of his (tacit) assumption of rigid wages. We will agree at once that under this assumption the rate of interest depends on the quantity of money, but this is true only in a very special sense. If we look at our "Keynesian" model we find that we have 7 equations in 7 unknowns and two arbitrary quantities or "parameters," M and W_0. The solution of the system gives each of the 7 variables as functions of these arbitrary parameters: $\bar{r} = r(M, W)$, $\overline{Y} = Y(M, W)$, $\overline{N} = N(M, W)$, etc. On the basis of previous considerations these can be written:

$$(5.1) \qquad \bar{r} = r\left(\frac{M}{W}\right), \qquad\qquad (5.2) \qquad \overline{Y} = Y\left(\frac{M}{W}\right), \text{ etc.}$$

If this is the sense in which Lerner states that r is a function of M, his statement is formally correct. But in the first place it is not very helpful for understanding the determinants of the rate of interest. In a system with rigid wages practically every economic variable depends on the quantity of money (and the money wage). The rate of interest depends on M as much as the price of shoes or employment in ice-

[49] The fact that hoarding and unemployment have always developed in certain phases of the business cycle is not an objection to that. For these are features for a theory of business cycles to explain. Here we are only comparing static theories.

[50] Thus for example, the outcome of a certain physical experiment may be influenced, to a slight extent, by changes in humidity. Then, if the experiment is carried out in a place in which the observed variations in humidity are not sufficient to affect the outcome sensibly, it is perfectly justifiable to neglect it. If the same experiment were conducted somewhere else, where humidity is known to be highly unstable, precautions should be taken in interpreting the results.

cream manufacturing. In the second place it has nothing to do with Keynes's liquidity preference: r depends on M even if we neglect the liquidity demand for money (see Section 11). Hence if Lerner's equation, $M = f(r)$, corresponds to our equation (5.1), then it is not a demand-for-money schedule, but an empirical relationship obtained by previous solution of a system of equations of which the demand for money itself is one. And his approach certainly throws no light on the determinants of the rate of interest.

The only alternative is to consider Lerner's equation as a true demand for money corresponding to our equation (1): $M = L(r, Y)$. But why has the second variable been omitted? The answer is clear; by concentrating attention on the liquidity preference and the demand for money to hold, sight has been lost of the demand for money to spend. Thus we go from one extreme to the other; instead of neglecting the influence of the rate of interest as in the "quantity theory," we neglect the part played by income in determining the demand for money. The results of this unjustified omission are serious in many respects. The most serious is that it leads to the conclusion (reached by Lerner) that saving and investment play no part in the determination of the rate of interest.[51] Figure 3 shows on the contrary that equations (2) and (3) play as vital a role as the demand-for-money equation. It is clear also that changes in the propensity to save or to invest or in the wage rate, lead directly to changes in the interest rate.

To defend his point Lerner is forced to say that changes in these propensities affect the rate of interest *because* they change the demand for money, i.e., because they shift the graph of $M = f(r)$.[52] But this is true and by definition only if Lerner identifies $M = f(r)$ with our equation (5.1). Since this equation is obtained by previously solving the whole system, it contains the relevant parameters of the functions which determine the rate of interest. A change in any of these parameters changes or shifts the function $r = r(M/W)$ accordingly. But, as we

[51] In "Alternative Formulations of the Theory of Interest," Lerner writes: "For the first, easy step [from the classical to the modern theory of interest] is the insinuation of Liquidity Preference as a junior partner in the old established one-man firm in the business of interest-determination, and the second . . . step is to put Saving-Investment, the senior partner, to sleep, as a preliminary to kicking him out" (*op. cit.*, p. 221).

[52] That this is Lerner's point of view may be seen for instance in the following passage from a letter written to me in June, 1943. Discussing the effects of an increase in the propensity to invest in the "classical case" (demand for money to hold equal zero) he writes: "Even in that case there must be a fall in income which decreases the need for cash which lowers the rate of interest so that the investors have a signal that they should increase investment, but an infinitesimal decrease in employment is sufficient to bring about any necessary fall in the rate of interest. . . ."

have already seen, equation (5.1) cannot possibly help us in understanding the determinants of the rate of interest.[53]

Another consequence of Lerner's formulation is that it leads to the
conclusion that the interest rate can always be lowered by increasing
the quantity of money, at least to the point where the demand becomes
infinitely elastic; while the truth is that no finite change in the quantity
of money can hold the interest rate below the full-employment level.[54]

Let us finally note that Lerner's theory is not fully satisfactory even
in the "Keynesian case." It is true that in this case saving and investment do not determine the rate of interest, but it is equally clear that
the rate of interest does not depend on the quantity of money.

In conclusion, to say that the rate of interest is determined by the
schedule $M = f(r)$ is useless and confusing if this schedule is arrived at
by previous solution of the entire system; it is an unwarranted simplification, full of serious consequences, if this function is treated as an
ordinary demand function. And the statement that the propensity to
save and invest plays no part in determining the rate of interest is true
only in a limiting case: the Keynesian case.

20. HICKS'S THEORY—THE RATE OF INTEREST AND THE COST OF INVESTING IN SECURITIES

In *Value and Capital* Hicks has developed what is probably the most
daring attempt at reducing the rate of interest to a purely monetary
phenomenon.

In Hicks's own words the rate of interest is explained by the "imperfect moneyness" of securities. "The imperfect moneyness of those bills
which are not money is due to their lack of general acceptability: it is
this lack of general acceptability which causes the trouble of investing
in them"[55] and it is this trouble, namely "the trouble of making transactions [i.e., of purchasing securities] which explains the short rate of
interest."[56] And these same factors also explain the long rate since the
long rate is some average of the short rates plus a premium to cover
the risk of (unanticipated) movements in the future short rates.[57]

Thus the rate of interest is explained by the fact that securities are
not a medium of exchange and is determined essentially by the cost of

[53] To give another example, we can solve the system to obtain, say, the equilibrium output of shoes (Q) as a function of the quantity of money: $Q = f(M, W)$
or $M = F(Q, W)$. But to say that a change in tastes changes the output *because* it
shifts this function is formally correct but perfectly useless as a tool of analysis.

[54] Proper qualifications must be made for the case in which the IS curve is not
monotonic decreasing.

[55] *Value and Capital*, p. 166.

[56] *Ibid.*, p. 165.

[57] *Ibid.*, Chapter XI.

making loan transactions. This is certainly an unusual theory of interest and an astonishing one, to say the least; it appears irreconcilable with the theory we have developed throughout this paper.

Hicks's theory finds its origin in an attempt to answer a question posed by the Keynesian analysis. The reason that induces people to hold assets in the form of cash rather than securities is that the value of even the safest type of securities is not certain: it is subject to changes due to movements in the rate of interest. Now, as we have seen, this risk decreases as the duration of the loan transaction becomes shorter: and it disappears entirely on loans that last only one "Hicksian week" (or one income period in our model) since by hypothesis the rate of interest cannot change. There must then be some other reason to stop people from holding all of their assets in the form of securities and thus reducing their demand for "money to hold" to zero; this reason can only be the cost of investing in this riskless type of loans. This is Hicks's starting point: and so far there seems to be no difference from our own approach as developed in Section 5. But from these correct premises Hicks draws the wrong conclusion: namely *that it is the cost of investing that explains the rate of interest.* To say that the cost of investing is necessary to explain *why* the demand for money to hold is not always zero and to say that it *explains* the rate of interest are quite different statements. There is a logical gap between the two. Thus, for example, from the correct premise that the cost of automobiles in New York cannot fall to zero because they have to be transported from Detroit, there does not logically follow the conclusion that the cost of cars in New York is explained or determined by the cost of transporting them.

There is a different way of explaining the rate of interest, which is not less satisfactory for the fact of being obvious: namely that for certain categories of people (entrepreneurs as well as spendthrifts) it is worth while to pay a premium to obtain spot cash against a promise to pay cash in the future. This is the course we have followed: and it is clearly all that is necessary to explain the existence of the rate of interest. The cost of investing continues to play an important part in our theory: (a) it explains why the demand for money to hold is not identically zero; (b) it explains why the rate of interest can never fall below a certain level in a free capitalistic economy; and hence it explains the pecularities of the Keynesian case. But it is clear that it is not necessary to explain the rate of interest.

Our next task is to show that the cost of investing is also not sufficient to explain the nature of interest. To this end we must disprove Hicks's statement that if people were to be "paid in the form of bills . . . there would be no cost of investment and therefore . . . no reason for the bills to fall to a discount,"[58] i.e., no rate of interest. It is easy to show that, even if "bills" were to be used as medium of exchange, there would be no reason for the rate of interest to fall to zero.

Let us consider first the case of a "stationary state." It is well known that the stationary state is characterized by the fact that the rate of change of the quantity of capital is zero; the marginal efficiency of the existing quantity of capital is equal to the rate of interest, say r_0, that makes net saving equal to zero.[59] Now it is theoretically conceivable that, in this state, securities might replace money as a medium of exchange;[60] their purchasing power would be objectively determined by their discounted value since, by hypothesis, the future rate of interest is known and constant. Their aggregate value would also be constant but, since individual savings need not be zero, there would be a net flow from dissavers to savers. Under these conditions it is clear that securities would continue to yield the rate of interest r_0, even though they would be performing the function of a medium of exchange. Thus, as far as the stationary state goes, Hicks's conclusion does not follow: the interest rate would be zero only in the special case $r_0 = 0$.

Next let us consider an expanding economy, in which the net level of saving and investment is not zero, and let us assume again that it is technically possible for securities to be accepted as a medium of exchange.[61]

In this economy, if there is to be no inflation, it is necessary that the rate of money investment be not larger than the rate of (ex ante) saving. Now there are two possibilities:

(a) There exists some mechanism by which the net increase in outstanding securities cannot exceed net savings. Then the competition of borrowers to obtain loans will automatically determine the level of the rate of interest.

(b) There is no limitation as to the issuance of new securities per unit of time. Then, of course, the rate of interest would be zero, since there would be no necessity for borrowers to compete. But the result would clearly be a situation of unending and progressive inflation. In the first case the stability of the quantity of active money and therefore of the price level is assured by the fact that savers would increase their "hoards" of securities-money, at a rate equal to the net increase in the value of outstanding securities. But in the second case there is nothing

---

[58] *Ibid.*, p. 165.

[59] For a more detailed description of the conditions that give rise to a stationary state see, for instance, M. Timlin, *Keynesian Economics*, Chapter IV.

[60] See, for instance, *ibid.*, p. 53.

[61] This would require that all people agree at all times on the present value of every security.

to stop the price level from rising indefinitely, except if it so happens that the "full employment" rate of interest is zero or negative.[62]

We may therefore safely conclude that the rate of interest is not explained by the fact that securities are not money. Once we recognize this, the complicated and confusing Hicksian theory about the imperfect moneyness of securities becomes unnecessary and should, in our opinion, be abandoned.

To say that different assets share in different degrees the quality of "moneyness" either has no meaning or it is based on a confusion between liquidity and the properties of a medium of exchange. It is true that different assets have different degrees of liquidity, since the liquidity depends on the perfection of the market in which a good is traded. And it is also true that money is probably, under normal conditions, the most liquid of all assets. But the property of money is that it is accepted (freely or by force of law) as a medium of exchange: and liquidity does not make money out of something that is not money. Whatever one's definition of liquidity, to say that a government bond, a speculative share, a house, are money in different degrees, can at best generate unnecessary confusion. It is true that money and securities are close substitutes, but this connection is to be found elsewhere than in degrees of moneyness; it depends on the fact that both money and securities are alternative forms of holding assets in nonphysical form. Securities are thus close substitutes for money, but not for money as a medium of exchange, only for money as an asset.

Having shown that the cost of investment neither explains nor determines the rate of interest, we will agree with Hicks that "the level of that [short] rate of interest measures the trouble involved in investing funds . . . to the marginal lender."[63] One cannot disagree with this statement any more than with the statement that the price of butter measures the marginal utility of butter to each member of the community.[64] Both statements are either tautologies or definitions of rational behavior. They are tautologies if they mean that all those who found it convenient to perform a certain transaction have done so. They are definitions of rational economic behavior if they state the conditions under which economic agents will maximize their satisfac-

[62] We are well aware of the fact that the excess of money investment over (*ex ante*) saving does not lead to inflation, unless there is full employment to begin with, or until full employment is reached. It remains true however that, except in the case mentioned in the text, a zero rate of interest must eventually lead to inflation.

[63] *Op. cit.*, p. 165.

[64] More exactly: the ratio of the price of butter to that of any other commodity measures the ratio of their respective marginal utilities.

tion.[65] But it is clear that whether these statements are tautologies or definitions they are not sufficient to explain either the price of butter or the level of the rate of interest.

To conclude then we agree with Hicks that the rate of interest is at least equal to the cost of investing to the marginal lender, but this statement is not very helpful for understanding the rate of interest. But the Hicksian theory that the rate of interest is determined or simply explained by the imperfect moneyness of securities must be discarded as faulty.

21. SAVING AND INVESTMENT OR SUPPLY OF AND DEMAND FOR CASH?—CONCLUSIONS

It will now be useful, in concluding this paper, to restate in brief form the general theory of interest and money that emerges from our analysis.

We believe that the best way of achieving this aim is to show how, by means of our theory, we can answer the controversial question that has caused so much discussion in recent economic literature.

Is the rate of interest determined by the demand for and supply of cash? Or is it determined by those "real factors," psychological and technological, that can be subsumed under the concepts of propensity to save and marginal efficiency of investment?

We consider it to be a distinct advantage of our theory that we can answer both questions affirmatively. We do not have to choose between these two alternatives any more than between the following two: Is the price of fish determined by the daily demand and the daily supply; or is it determined by the average yearly demand and the cost of fishing?

Since we have maintained throughout this paper that, in general, saving and lending are independent decisions, we must clearly agree that the "daily" rate of interest is determined by the demand for and supply of money to hold (or, for that matter, by demand for and supply of loanable funds).[66] It is this very principle that has formed the base of our analysis of the money market (Section 7). But we cannot stop at this recognition and think that this is sufficient for a general theory of the rate of interest.

To come back to our example, it is certainly true that the daily price

[65] If anything, Hicks's statement is less illuminating, since there is, at least theoretically, the possibility that the rate of interest may exceed the cost of lending idle funds to the marginal lender: it is this very possibility that gives rise to the "classical case."

[66] In this respect we have nothing to add to the arguments developed by Hicks in Chapter XII of *Value and Capital*. There are enough equations to determine all the prices on each Monday and it makes no difference which equation is eliminated.

of fish is entirely explained by the daily catch of fish. But if we want to understand why the daily price fluctuates around a certain level and not around a level ten times as high, we must look for something more fundamental than the good or bad luck of the fishermen on a particular day. We shall then discover that the number of fishermen and the amount of equipment used does not change daily but is determined by the condition that the average returns, through good and bad days, must be sufficiently high to make the occupation of fishing (and investment in fishing equipment) as attractive as alternative ones.

What is obviously true for the price of fish must also hold for the price of loans. The statement that the "daily" rate is determined by the "daily" demand for and supply of money (or, more exactly, of money to hold) does not greatly advance us in the understanding of the true determinants of the rate of interest. This theory by itself is insufficient to explain, for instance, why in countries well-equipped and of great saving capacity, like England or the United States, the system of rates of interest fluctuates around low levels (2 or 3 per cent for the pure long rate and much less for short rates); while it fluctuates around much higher levels (5 or 6 per cent or more for the long rate) in countries poor in savings or rich but scarcely developed. Is that because in the last-mentioned countries the supply of cash is insufficient? Clearly not. The explanation for this difference can only run in terms of those more fundamental factors, technological and psychological, that are included in the propensity to save and the marginal efficiency of investment.

As we have shown in our model the equality of demand and supply of loanable funds is the equilibrium condition for the week (or for our income period) and determines the equilibrium rate of interest (or system of rates) for the week. It corresponds to the short-run equilibrium condition of the Marshallian demand and supply analysis: price equals marginal cost. But the stock of money to hold (the supply) tends itself to change and thus push the "daily" rate toward the level at which the flow of money saving equals the flow of money investment. The condition, (ex ante) saving = (ex ante) investment, corresponds to the long-run Marshallian condition (under perfect competition): price = average cost including rent.

The first condition is satisfied even in the short period since it is the result of decisions that can be carried out instantaneously (see Section 5). The second is a long-run condition and therefore may actually never be satisfied: but it is necessary to explain the level toward which the weekly rate tends (even though this level may never be reached since the long-run equilibrium rate of interest itself changes).

Thus, to complete our theory, we must be able to explain what determines the level of long-run equilibrium. At this point we find that our answer is not unique since it depends on the assumptions concerning the form of the supply-of-labor schedule.

I. As long as wages are flexible, the long-run equilibrium rate of interest is determined exclusively by real factors, that is to say, essentially by the propensity to save and the marginal efficiency of investment. The condition, money saving = money investment, determines the price level and not the rate of interest.

II. If wages are rigid it is still true that the long-run equilibrium rate of interest is determined by the propensities to save and to invest but the situation is now more complicated; for these propensities depend also on money income and therefore on the quantity of active money which in turn depends itself on the level of the rate of interest. Thus, unless wages are perfectly flexible or the supply of money is always so adjusted as to assure the maintenance of full employment, the long-run equilibrium rate of interest depends also on the quantity of money and it is determined, together with money income, by equations (1), (2), and (3) of our model. We want however to stress again that the dependence of the rate of interest on the quantity of money does not depend on liquidity preference. In a system with rigid wages not only interest but also almost every economic variable depends on the quantity of money.

III. Finally our theory of the rate of interest becomes even less uniform when we take into account the "Keynesian case." In this case clearly the long-run equilibrium rate of interest is the rate which makes the demand for money to hold infinitely elastic. The economic theorist here is forced to recognize that under certain conditions the rate of interest is determined exclusively by institutional factors.

Bard College of Columbia University

Postscript

I want to take the opportunity offered by this reprinting to warn the reader that the latter part of section 13, beginning with the second paragraph on page 160, contains several errors which vitiate the argument—though the main conclusion can be salvaged. These errors and their implications were first pointed out by D. Patinkin, in "Relative prices, Say's Law and the Demand for Money," *Econometrica,* April 1948, and elaborated in *Money Interest and Prices,* Row, Peterson, 1956, appendix to Chapter 8. While it is not possible in this postscript to provide a rigorous restatement, we offer a brief sketch of the correct formulation.

In the first place, in line with the model used throughout the rest of the paper, one must add to the $n - 1$ commodities and money mentioned on page 161, an $n + 1$ good, namely bonds, a good whose quantity may be positive (credits) or negative (debts). Also, when credits and debts are taken into account, the homogeneity of zero degree in prices of the *individual* demand functions for commodities no longer logically follows from rational behavior. Nor can homogeneity be introduced as a plausible, ad hoc, behavior assumption.

On the other hand it can be verified that, provided (a) the given money supply consists entirely of bank money which is offset by the debt of the private sector to the banking system, and (b) all existing bonds represent claims on, or liabilities to, the private sector (including banks), then *aggregate* private real wealth will be invariant under a proportional change of all prices (no Pigou effect exists). Under these conditions it is both permissible and justifiable to postulate that (c) the *market* demand for each commodity is homogeneous of zero degree and the *market* demand for money is homogeneous of first degree, in all commodity prices. Indeed (c) is then equivalent to assuming that the aggregate demand for each commodity and for money is unaffected by a mere redistribution of wealth. Such an assumption does not seem unreasonable, at least as a convenient first approximation. (It follows of course from assumptions (a) to (c) that the net demand for bonds by household and banks combined is not homogeneous in prices, as can be verified from the budget equation of individuals plus banks).

Under assumptions (a) to (c) the argument in the rest of the paper remains valid. That the bond market is, at times, not given explicit treatment, is accounted for by the fact that, through the so-called Walras Law, one of the markets is necessarily cleared when the remaining ones are cleared, and hence need not be explicitly exhibited.

January 1960.

Errata

Page 63, 6 lines from the bottom: "$S_t = S(\bar{r}, \bar{Y}) + S_r \dot{r}_t + I_Y \dot{Y}_{t-1}$" should read "$S_t = S(\bar{r}, \bar{Y}) + S_r \dot{r}_t + S_Y \dot{Y}_{t-1}$."

Page 63, 4 lines from the bottom: "$r_t = \dot{r}_t - \bar{r}$" should read "$\dot{r}_t = r_t - \bar{r}$."

Page 64, equation (2.7): the term "$-\dfrac{r}{S_r - I_r}$" should read "$-\dfrac{2}{S_r - I_r}$."

Page 64, line 10: "$L_r \geqq 0$" should read "$L_r \leqq 0$."

Page 77, paragraph 2, line 9: "expand" should read "contract."

"Postscript"

Page 183, line 3: "the second paragraph on page 160" should read "the third paragraph on page 68."

Reprinted from
THE REVIEW OF ECONOMICS AND STATISTICS
Published by Harvard University
Copyright, 1963, by the President and Fellows of Harvard College
Vol. XLV, No. 1, February 1963

THE MONETARY MECHANISM AND ITS INTERACTION WITH REAL PHENOMENA

Franco Modigliani, *Massachusetts Institute of Technology*

THIS paper traces the major developments of lasting value in our understanding of the monetary mechanism and its role in the economy which have occurred since the early forties, when the process of digesting the General Theory [11] and integrating it with the earlier streams of thinking had been more or less completed. I consider here primarily the state of monetary thought as of about the mid-fifties, leaving to another time consideration of the evolution that has occurred since.

The middle of the 1950's provides, in my view, a useful landmark in reviewing the evolution of monetary and macroeconomic theory, since the developments that occurred up to that time are, on the whole, rather different in purpose and approach from those that have occurred later. The development in the first-mentioned period seems to me to consist largely of refinements, clarifications, and developments of the basic framework, which had already been laid out by the early forties. The most significant contributions in the more recent period, on the other hand, have tended to approach monetary issues in terms of the theory of asset management and portfolio decisions, exploiting concurrent advances in the theory of saving, in managerial economics and, most importantly, in the theory of choice under uncertainty. These developments, on the whole, have not led to any major revision or rejection of the positions reached by the mid-fifties, but have rather been concerned with providing a better understanding of the determinants of the demand for money and its relation with the demand and supply for various other assets, physical as well as financial, by final transactors and by "financial intermediaries."

This paper is, in essence, a summary of a longer and more rigorous statement which I expect to complete later, and which, together with an exploration of the developments since the 1950's, will be published elsewhere when completed. Because it is in the nature of a summary, I have frequently found it necessary to sacrifice rigor and to omit nearly all of the proofs and many of the references.

The material is divided into six major sections. The first is a brief comparison of a basic model of money and the economy which I believe would have been widely accepted about 1944, with a corresponding model as of the middle of the 1950's. The following sections, then, examine in some detail the implications of the mid-fifties model for the relationship to crucial variables in the economy, and for major lines of monetary and fiscal policy.

I

The Mid-50's Model and Its Relation to the 1944 Model

I hope I may be permitted the liberty of using the macroeconomic model presented in my 1944 article, "Liquidity Preference and the Theory of Interest in Money" [13], as a representation of where monetary economists thought money stood in relation to the economy at about that period. This model is reproduced in Table 1 (with very minor modifications of notation), together with a revised version labeled the "Mid-50's model." This is essentially the model that I would have used had I been writing a comparable article at that time (and did actually use in my class lectures, cf. [15]).

While no systematic attempt is made here at justifying in detail the equations of the model, a task which was substantially performed in the 1944 paper, in this section we will review the main differences as well as similarities between the original and the revised model.

The two models are basically identical in spirit: they both treat the economy at a highly aggregative level in terms of four goods and corresponding markets. Two of the goods are physical commodities, labor and real output,

[79]

and two are money-fixed claims, money and bonds. For the sake of concreteness, real output is visualized as consisting of a single homogeneous commodity which, in the mid-fifty model, I choose to label the MM (read mum). This output can be either used for current consumption (C) and thereby disappears, or can be instead devoted to investment (I), thereby becoming part of the capital stock (K). Thus, X, C, I, S are measured in MM/time, and K in MM's. Similarly, labor (N) is measured in man-hours/time. The two money-fixed claims on the other hand are measured in units of money assumed to be the dollar, and bonds are to be regarded as one-period loans or claims to future (next-period) money. The amount of bonds held by a transactor may be positive or negative; in the latter case it represents the transactor's debt.

Corresponding to the four commodities there are three independent prices or terms of trade with money: the price of output — or general price level — P ($\$/MM$); the price of labor, W ($\$/man-hour$); and the price of a dollar, next period, $(1/1 + r)$, where r is the rate of interest. In addition, both models, at least at the outset, assume:

A.1: certainty
A.2: absence of money illusion (which is an implication of rational behavior)
A.3: unit elasticity of price expectations (and independence of interest rate expectations from current prices)

The main differences between the two models can be summarized under five headings:

1. *Explicit reliance on a general equilibrium formulation.* The mid-fifty model is explicitly structured in terms of markets, one for each

TABLE 1.

COMPARISON OF 1944 WITH MID-50's MODEL
DEFINITIONS AND CLASSIFICATION OF VARIABLES

I. *Endogenous variables*
   (a) *Flow variables:* (1) X, Real income; (2) C, Real consumption; (3) I, Real investment; (4) S, Real saving; (5) X^d, Real aggregate demand; (6) N, Employment (man-hours per unit of time); (7) N', Labor supply; (8) Y, Money income
   (b) *Price variables:* (9) P, Price of output; (10) W, Price of labor (wage rate); (11) r, Rate of interest
   (c) *Money market variables:* (12) M^d, Demand for money by private sector; (13) B^p, Demand for bonds by non-bank private sector; (14) B^b, Demand for bonds by banks; (15) M^b, Supply of bank money
II. *"Initial conditions":* K_o, Real stock of capital; v_o^j, Net worth of jth household; $V_o = \sum_j v_o^j$, Aggregate net worth of private sector; $[V_o] = (v_o^1, v_o^2, \ldots v_o^j, \ldots)$.
III. *Other parameters:* W_o, Rigid money wage rate; N', "Full employment" labor supply; M, Money supply; M^*, Supply of government money; M^{*p}, Government money outside banks; $M^{*b} = M^* - M^{*p}$, Government money held by banks; G, Supply of government bonds.

MODEL I (1944)

(3) $PS = S(r, Y)$
(2) $PI = I(r, Y)$
(6) $X = X(N)$
(7) $X_N(N) = W/P$
$W = a W_o + (1 - a) F^{-1}(N) \times P$
(9) $a = \begin{cases} 1, \text{if } N < N' \\ 0, \text{otherwise} \end{cases}$
(4) $PS = PI$
(8) $PC = Y - PS$
(5) $Y = PX$
(1) $M = L(r, Y)$

MODEL II (mid-50's)

(1) $C = C(X, NW/P, r, [V_o/P])$
(2) $I = I(r, X, K_o)$
(3) $X^d \equiv C + I$
(4a) $X = X(N, K_o)$ or (4b) $X = s(P/W, K_o)$
(5a) $X_N(N, K_o) = W/P$ or (5b) $N = n^d(W/P, K_o)$
(6) $\begin{cases} N' = n^s(W/P), \text{ if } n^d(W_o/P, K_o) > n^s(W_o/P) \\ W = W_o \quad \text{ if } n^d(W_o/P, K_o) \leq n^s(W_o/P) \end{cases}$
(7) $X^d = X$
(8) $N' = N$
(9) $S \equiv X - C$
(M.1) $Y \equiv PX$
(M.2) $M^d = L(r, Y, P, [V_o]) = PL(r, Y/P, [V_o/P])$
(M.3) $M^d = M$
(M.4) $M = M^p + M^{*p}$
(M.5) $M^b = B^b + M^{*b}$
(M.6) $B^p = B(r, X, N, P, W, [K_o], [G_o + M_o^*])$
(M.7) $B^p + B^b = G$

MEMOS

(i) $B_o^p + B_o^b = G_o$
(ii) $M_o = M_o^b + M_o^{*p} = B_o^b + M_o^*$
(iii) $M_o + B_o^p = G_o + M_o^*$
(iv) $V_o = PK_o + M_o + B_o^p = PK_o + G_o + M_o^*$
(v) $K_1 = K_o + I$

commodity, with each market in turn described by (a) supply conditions, (b) demand conditions, and (c) clearing of market or equilibrium conditions, of which one is redundant (Walras' law).

The main advantage of the general equilibrium framework is that it insures a systematic and, at least initially, symmetrical treatment of all markets.[1] For the commodity market, the demand conditions are described by equations (1) to (3); the supply conditions by (4b) and the clearing conditions by (7). In the labor market the supply is given by (6), to be reviewed more closely below; the demand by (5); and market clearing by (8). The remaining two markets are described under the next heading, 2.

2. *Explicit treatment of the bond market and more precise formulation of the relation between the demand and supply of money and bonds and the banking system.* In the 1944 model, the money market was described very summarily by a single equation (I.1) and the bond market was omitted altogether. In the mid-1950's model, the money market is again described by a demand (M.2), a supply (M.4), and a clearing of market equation (M.3). Furthermore, two sources of money supply to the private sector are recognized: bank money (M^b) and government money (M^{*p}). The bond market is described by the last three equations. (M.5) is a streamlined consolidated balance sheet of the banking system (including the central bank, if any); the left-hand side is the liability side or bank money supply, which must be equal to the asset side consisting of government money (M^{*b}) and bank credit (B^b) which can also be regarded as the banking system demand for bonds. (M.6) gives the *net* demand for bonds by the public, the difference between lending (gross demand) and borrowing (gross supply). (M.7) is the clearing of market condition; the left-hand side is the aggregate net demand by the private sector and the right-

[1] Without the benefit of this crutch, in my 1944 paper I was led in the formal model of section 2, to drop any explicit reference to the bond market — implicitly treated as the redundant one — which, in turn, caused some unfortunate and unnecessary misunderstandings [9]. More seriously, I forgot altogether the existence of this commodity in the analysis of section 13, which resulted in some outright wrong statements, as was shown later by Patinkin [20], [21].

hand side is the *net* supply of bonds to the private sector, which would be zero in the absence of government debt, and is otherwise equal to this debt, G.

While the bond market is thus given explicit treatment, it is still permissible to treat this market as the redundant one and we shall find it convenient to do so. Furthermore, for the purpose of this paper, we shall regard the two components of the money supply and hence their sum M as exogenously determined by the government or through the monetary authority's control over the banking system, or both, without concerning ourselves with the many possible institutional devices through which this control can be exercised. Under these conditions it is found that the last four equations, (M.4) to (M.7) describing the banking system and the bond market can be disregarded, so long as one is interested in the functioning of the rest of the system. This is because the first twelve equations, consisting of the nine "real equations" (1) to (9) and the three monetary equations (M.1) to (M.3), form a determined subsystem in the first twelve variables listed at the top of Table 1, namely the eight flow variables, the three price variables, and the demand for money. The analysis that follows, therefore, is primarily concerned with this subsystem.

3. *Improvements in the consumption and investment function and in particular more adequate recognition of the role of stocks.* Since the mid-forties the consumption function has received a great deal of attention at both the theoretical and the empirical levels. Many of the contributions, and notably the "permanent income" hypothesis of Friedman [7] and the "life cycle hypothesis" of Modigliani, Brumberg and Ando [14] [16] [1], have de-emphasized the role of current income and emphasized the role of other variables, particularly long-term income expectations and wealth. The consumption function (1) is sufficiently general to be consistent both with the original simple-minded Keynesian version and with the more recent but still controversial formulations. In particular, it is consistent with the life-cycle hypothesis according to which aggregate consumption can be approximated by a linear homogeneous function of aggregate labor in-

come $\dfrac{NW}{P}$ and net worth (V_o/P), with coefficients depending in principle on the rate of return on capital (r) [1].

Similarly, the investment function, or investment component of aggregate demand (2) can be shown to be consistent with a wide variety of approaches and hypotheses, such as the crude acceleration principle, the so-called "flexible accelerator" or gradual adjustment hypothesis, or even the more traditional formulation relying upon the production function and the marginal productivity of capital. Every one of these approaches implies that investment demand must be an increasing function of the level of output and a decreasing (or at least nonincreasing) function of the initial stock of capital and of the cost of capital.

4. *Correction of the faulty formulation of the homogeneity properties of the consumption, investment, and demand for money functions.* The new formulation of equations (1) and (2) and of (M.2) implies that the real demand for consumption, investment, and money is homogeneous of zero degree in money income, wealth, and prices, or the corresponding money demand is homogeneous of first degree in the same three variables. This property is an implication of the assumption of rational behavior. In the 1944 model I had intended to make this same assumption but in fact did not formulate it properly; I assumed instead that the three money demands were homogeneous of first degree in *money income alone.* This formulation leads to the incorrect implication that a change in money income has the same effect on money consumption whether due to a change in real income with prices constant, or to a change in prices with real income constant; and similarly for the other two variables. This error in turn led to a peculiar and objectionable property of the model, to wit that the first four equations of the model form a closed subsystem in the four variables (PX) (or Y), PS, PI and r, involving in particular M as a parameter. This dichotomization implies that the equilibrium values of the rate of interest and the money flow variables are independent of the real variables of the system, and in particular of the form of the production function

and of the level at which the rigid money wage W_o is set. This ceases to be true once the consumption and investment function are properly [2] formulated as in Model II. In particular, as shown below, for a given production function (including in it the initial stock of capital), and given M, an increase in W_o will normally tend to result in an increase of r, as well as of P, money income, investment and consumption, and in a fall in employment, real income and the other real flows.[3]

5. *Use of a more convenient and effective device for expressing the hypothesis of wage rigidity.* This device embodied in equation (6) relies on the notion of a "potential" supply function $n^s(W/P)$, expressing the maximum supply of labor available at each real wage. By combining this function with the demand function we can determine the excess supply (or demand) at any real wage. The hypothesis of wage rigidity then states that the money wage will not be bid below the rigid level W_o, even if there is an excess supply at this level. This hypothesis is formalized in equation (6). In fact, this equation together with (5b) and (8) simultaneously implies that W and N are determined by the intersection of the demand function (5b) and the potential supply function, if this intersection determines a value of W larger than W_o; otherwise $W = W_o$ and the level of employment is determined by the demand function alone. The difference between this level of employment and the potential supply at W_o is then "involuntary unemployment" in the Keynesian sense. Note finally that equation (6) can also be used to formalize the classical assumption of wage flexibility by merely setting W_o equal to zero or, at any rate,

[2] By "properly," I do not of course mean empirically correct but merely consistent with the hypothesis I intended to formalize.

[3] I might add, in partial defense of my 1944 construction and for solace to those who may have accepted it, that, if the production function is given and if W_o is treated as an unchangeable parameter, then the system *does* imply the existence of a unique relation between money consumption or investment, and money income; but then it implies also a unique relation between these variables and r, so that even under the stated conditions equation (I.1) and (I.2) could not be regarded as behavior equations but, at best, as reduced forms. Furthermore, the functional form of these reduced forms would shift around with changes in W_o or the form of the production function. Thus, even though in many cases my original system leads to "correct" inferences, it is an unreliable tool of analysis.

sufficiently low to insure that the first line will apply in the relevant range.

From this brief review it should be apparent that most of the differences between the 1944 and the mid-fifties model are matters of elegance, clarity, and minor improvements — with the main exception of the correction of the error under (4) above. Even the explicit recognition of the role of stocks examined under (3) is not crucial, if we regard the model as focusing on the determinants of short-run equilibrium, since, in general, stocks are initial conditions which can be treated as given parameters. An exception to this statement must be made with respect to the inclusion of wealth in the consumption function, for, in the presence of a government debt fixed in money terms, real wealth, V_o/P, cannot be regarded as a given initial condition. As will presently be shown, the resulting "wealth effect" has interesting logical implications, although it is of practical relevance *only* under the assumption of wage and price flexibility, an assumption which has little, if any, empirical substance.

The remaining sections of the paper are devoted to examining various implications of the model, focusing in part on issues which have been prominently debated in the period under review. In the two sections immediately following, the analysis rests entirely on the mid-fifties model discussed so far. Then, in sections IV and V, this model will be broadened and amended to allow explicitly for the role of government and for certain imperfections in the capital market. Finally, in the concluding section VI, I endeavor to summarize the results with special reference to the importance of money and monetary factors as a determinant of the real variables.

II

Implications of the Model Under Price Flexibility — Homogeneity, Dichotomy, Neutrality, and the Role of the Supply and Demand for Money

We proceed first to a summary of some implications of the model within the classical framework of price and wage flexibility. Its main justification is the hope of disposing for good of a controversy, connected with the names of Pigou and Patinkin, which has

plagued the profession, draining the resources into what strikes me as a largely barren endeavor.

In essence, the Patinkin controversy revolves around two main issues concerning the properties of an economic system relying on a token money as medium of payment, namely (1) the neutrality of money and (2) the validity of the dichotomy of monetary and real economics. It will be useful to define more precisely the nature of these issues and their implications.

Neutrality. Money is said to be neutral if the equilibrium value of the real variables of the system — in our model the flow variables, X, C, I, N, S, the price ratio P/W, and r — is independent of the money supply M. If money is neutral, then at most M can affect the actual level of prices, or terms of trade between current commodities and money — P and W in our model. A special case of neutrality is where, in addition, prices are proportional to M, the so-called "quantity theory of money." [4]

Dichotomy. This issue can be defined in many alternative ways, as is apparent from Patinkin [21] where many possible meanings of the word are considered and carefully divided into good ones (valid) and bad ones (invalid). The problem I am concerned with here might be defined in terms of certain mathematical properties of systems of simultaneous relations or, instead, in terms of the substantive economic issues involved.

If we take the first approach, we may say that the dichotomy holds if the system of simultaneous relations purporting to describe the functioning of the economy has the following property: the entire set of relations can be "dichotomized" into two subsets, one of which, containing the relations describing the functioning of all markets except the money and bond market, forms a determinate subsystem of the entire system and is therefore sufficient to determine all the real variables of the system. Obviously, if the dichotomy in the above sense holds, then the equilibrium value of the real variables is independent of the money supply — i.e., dichotomy implies neutrality. But in ad-

---

[4] This definition of the quantity theory of money is obviously quite different from the one adopted by Friedman in [6] and is, I believe, more consistent with generally accepted terminology.

dition these equilibrium values are also independent *of the form of the demand-for-money equation*. This last implication is, of course, the significant one from the economic point of view, for it justifies separating the study of the functioning of a free market economy into a "monetary" and a "real" branch. In particular, when concerned with the real variables we need pay no attention to monetary habits and institutions (although the converse need not be true).

This then suggests an alternative and probably more fruitful definition of dichotomy, namely, as a warranted separation of monetary and real economics (or value theory). Specifically, we can say that the dichotomy holds if the equilibrium value of the real variables of the system is *independent of both the supply and the demand for money*. Note that in this second sense it is quite possible for the dichotomy to hold in the long but not in the short run (or, conceivably, vice versa).

Of course, to the extent that the equilibrium of the system (whether in the short or in the long run) can be identified with the solution of a system of simultaneous relations, dichotomy in the first sense implies dichotomy in the second. But our second definition is broader and is a proposition about the real world, even though in passing judgment about its validity we may have to rely on the mathematical properties of certain formal descriptions thereof. Note finally that, in terms of our second definition, we can meaningfully say that the dichotomy is "approximately" valid, in the sense that it provides a good first approximation to observed phenomena.

In terms of these definitions, Patinkin's basic contention can be summarized as follows: in an economy relying on a token money as a medium of exchange, the dichotomy does not hold, but under certain conditions money will be neutral. In particular the following two assumptions, in addition to assumptions A.1 to A.3 above, are generally sufficient for the neutrality to hold (cf. [21], especially chapters IV, VIII, and Mathematical Appendix 4).

A.4, Concerning the functioning of markets: absence of price rigidity in any market

A.5, Concerning tastes: the market demand and supply for each commodity is in-variant under a redistribution of wealth among transactors [5]

It is found that Patinkin's contention is basically unwarranted, although no attempt at rigorous proof is possible here. Furthermore, while the argument runs in terms of the aggregative model of Section I, it holds as well if we recognize the existence of many different commodities and kinds of labor. Specifically, the following propositions can be established (for a closed economy).

(1) *If the money supply consists entirely of bank money and there is no government debt,*[6] *the dichotomy is valid.*[7] Basically the reason is that under these conditions, and assumptions A.1 to A.5, all the demand and supply equations for commodities are homogeneous of zero degree in the prices, P and W, and hence can be expressed as functions of their ratio, W/P. This holds in particular for the consumption function (1). In fact, A.5 implies that wealth affects consumption only through its aggregate value V_o/P. But V_o/P in turn can be replaced by the initial stock of physical capital K_o, since the money component of aggregate net worth is exactly offset by the indebtedness to the banking system (cf. Memo iv in Table 1). Thus P appears in the consumption function only in the form W/P.[8] It can be readily verified that

---

[5] Patinkin has been especially concerned with what may be called "neutrality in principle," i.e., neutrality with respect to a "neutral" change in the money supply, which is defined as one that leaves undisturbed the relative distribution of cash balances. For this type of neutrality, Patinkin does not need assumption A.5. However, as will be apparent from (2) and (3) below, when neutrality does not hold with assumption A.5, "neutrality in principle" does not hold either.

[6] By government debt is meant here any claim (positive or negative) of the private sector (including banks) on the government, whether interest bearing or not. Hence, the assumption of no government debt implies that M^{*b}, M^{*b} and G are all zero, which, using (M.4), (M.5) and (M.7), in turn implies $M = M^b = B^b = -B^p$. In other words, the money supply consists entirely of what Gurley and Shaw call "inside money" (cf. [8] p. 73).

[7] This conclusion, which was stated in my 1960 Postscript to [13], has recently been acknowledged by Patinkin [19] in his very useful review of Gurley and Shaw [8], which also contains some of the results summarized under (3) below.

[8] Note that the consumption demand — as well as labor supply — of *individual* households will generally not be homogeneous of zero degree in prices. Indeed changes in the price level affect *individual* wealth by determining the real value of money fixed claims and debts. However, since *aggregate* wealth is unaffected, such changes only result in

under these conditions the first nine equations of the model form a determined subsystem in all the real variables including the price ratio W/P. This subsystem is therefore sufficient to determine these variables without any reference to the supply of money or to the demand for money equation (M.2). The only role of the monetary part is to determine the price level P, and hence finally also W. Furthermore, if assumption A.5 is extended to the demand for money, then it also turns out that P is strictly proportional to M so that the quantity theory also holds.

It may be useful to try to state in plain English the major forces determining equilibrium in the system described by Model II under the stated assumptions. This mechanism can be summarized roughly as follows:

i. Given the production function, including the initial stock of capital, and hence consumers net worth, and given the preferences for current and future consumption as compared with leisure, there is a unique real-wage rate W/P that clears the labor market, and leads in turn to a unique level of output X: this corresponds to the simultaneous solutions of the four equations (4) to (6) and (8) in the four variables, P/W, N, N^s and X.

ii. For given X, preferences for current versus later consumption (including in later consumption planned bequests) and the terms of trade between them, represented by r, determine the size of current consumption C and the desired carry-over of resources, $S = X - C$. It is the function of the rate of interest to insure that investors will be induced to add to the stock of capital an amount I equal to the desired carry-over S. These forces are described by the remaining five real equations of the system, (1) to (3), (7) and (9), and complete the determinants of the real variables.

iii. Given the real solution, the price level together with certain institutional factors (such as length of the income period, synchronization of receipt and expenditure, transaction costs, etc.) determine the demand for money arising from transaction requirements and, possibly, also on asset account. There is then a unique price level that equates the demand to the

a redistribution of wealth between households, which by A.5 does not affect *aggregate* demands and supplies.

exogenous supply M. This same price level also induces the private sector to issue, on balance, enough claims against itself to satisfy the banking system demand for bonds, which banks pay with M.[9]

The determination of the price level can be exhibited graphically as in Figure 1, in terms

FIGURE 1

THE ROLE OF THE SUPPLY OF MONEY IN THE DETERMINATION OF THE PRICE LEVEL AND THE RATE OF INTEREST: THE CASE OF PURE BANK MONEY

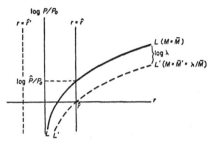

of the coordinates of the point of intersection of two curves in the (r,P) plane. (Actually, on the ordinate it is convenient to plot the logarithm of P/P_o, where P_o may be thought of as the previously ruling price.) One of these curves is the graph of the line $r = \hat{r}$, perpendicular to the r axis, stating that the rate of interest must be at the level $\hat{r}$ that clears the commodity market and which is determined by the real part of the system. The other, denoted by LL, is the graph of the equation that must be satisfied in order for the money market to be cleared, namely: $P \times L(r, \hat{X}, K_o) = \overline{M}$. Treating $\overline{M}$ as a given parameter and $\hat{X}$ as already determined by the real part of the system, this equation can be looked upon as a relation between the two variables r and P. Its graph shows, in effect, the be-

[9] It is apparent from the above that even in a system relying entirely on "inside money" the determinancy of the price level can be established without reference, explicit or implicit, to Gurley and Shaw "portfolio balance" or "diversification" mechanism ([8], especially Chap. V). Indeed that mechanism is intimately related to their very objectionable treatment of firms as separate and self-contained entities. In our model the net worth of firms is treated as a component of households' wealth.

havior of the so-called income velocity of circulation (more precisely its logarithm) as a function of the interest rate, except for a proportionality factor, $\overline{M}/X$. It can be expected to rise from left to right, since a priori considerations abundantly supported by empirical evidence (see, e.g., [12], [29], [2], [30]) suggest that, as r rises, velocity rises, the real demand for money falls (since X is given) and hence P must rise to reduce the real supply. The position of LL depends, of course, on the money supply $\overline{M}$. A change in this supply from $\overline{M}$ to say $\overline{M}'$ would shift it parallel to itself by a distance log $(\overline{M}'/\overline{M})$.

While the general shape of the LL graph is clear within the empirically observed range of variation of r, there may be some doubts as to its behavior for extreme values. For instance, as r grows indefinitely the graph may rise indefinitely or may instead approach some asymptote. Similarly, there is some question as to whether r can ever be bid down to zero. But whatever views one might hold about the possibility of a zero interest rate, one thing is certain, namely that in perfect markets, and as long as money has negligible storage costs, the money market can never be cleared with a negative r. For, even if banks were prepared to lend at a negative rate, everybody would wish to borrow "infinitely large" amounts and hold the money so borrowed to earn the premium now paid to borrowers. Hence the demand for money (as well as the supply of bonds) must become infinite at rates more than negligibly negative; and for any finite supply of money $\overline{M}$ there would be an excess demand for money and the money market would not be cleared. This means that the locus of LL lies entirely in the half plane to the right of a line perpendicular to the abscissa and coinciding with the ordinate axis, or possibly negligibly to the left of it, on account of the storage cost of money, if any.

As can be seen from the figure, if the money authority is concerned with maintaining a constant price level, then it should set the money supply at a level such that the corresponding LL curve intersects the other curve on the r axis, where log $(P/P_o) = 0$ or $P = P_o$. If we visualize the mechanism of price deter-

mination as one in which prices stay put at some given level as long as at that level the market is cleared, and rise (or fall) if at that level there is an excess demand (or an excess supply), then the task of the money authority in maintaining a stable price level can be stated in a somewhat different and not uninteresting form. That is, instead of enforcing directly the money supply $\overline{M}*'$ of Figure 1, it may endeavor, through appropriate devices, to enforce the rate of interest $r' = \hat{r}$ and then let the money supply seek its own level in response to the demand generated by the initial price level P and the given value of r. If it succeeds in picking and enforcing a rate r' equal to the natural rate $\hat{r}$, then the money supply will be precisely $\overline{M}'$ as we can see from the figure. Of course, if r' is set too low there will be excess demand which will raise P and cause an expansion in M, and this process will tend to continue as long as r' is enforced — this is simply the familiar Wicksellian cumulative process of inflation. Conversely, if r' is set too high there will be cumulative deflation and contraction in M. The only way of stopping the cumulative inflation is either to raise r' to the right level or to clamp down on the money supply letting r seek its equilibrium level, at $\hat{r}$.

The above analysis is subject to one important qualification, namely that the two equations graphed in the figure may fail to possess a solution. This failure is bound to occur if $\hat{r}$, the value of r that is consistent with clearing the commodity market, is negative; and there is nothing impossible in principle about $\hat{r}$ being negative, whatever might be the factual relevance of this possibility. Under these conditions the value of r that clears the commodity market cannot clear the money market, and conversely. In graphical terms, if $\hat{r}$ is negative, then the line $r = \hat{r}$ lies to the left of the ordinate, and therefore cannot have a point of intersection with LL which must lie entirely to its right.

This possibility, which is, of course, the "Keynesian case," or liquidity trap, might occur even with $\hat{r}$ positive, if sufficiently small.

but is bound to occur if $\hat{r}$ is negative. The economic system, then, does not possess a resting point except through wage rigidity, or appropriate interferences with the market process, including devices for making money sufficiently expensive to store.

In summary, with pure bank money the classical conclusions about neutrality and dichotomy are valid, and so is the Keynesian contention that a market system may not possess a position of equilibrium.

(2) *If the money supply consists entirely of government money and there is no other form of national debt,*[10] *then money is neutral but the dichotomy does not hold,* i.e., the equilibrium value of the real variables is independent of the *supply* but not of the *demand* for money. This is the assumption underlying Patinkin's analysis and his conclusion stands in this case.

The dichotomy breaks down because the variable V_o/P now can be expressed at $K_o + M/P$, and hence P appears in the consumption function (1) separately and not merely in the form of a price ratio W/P. Thus, the first nine equations of the system now involve 10 unknowns and cannot be solved separately. However, this subsystem can be solved for the nine real variables in terms of M/P, the "real money supply." In particular, let $r(M/P)$ and $X(M/P)$ be the solution for r and X. By inserting this solution into the clearing condition for the money market one obtains

$$\frac{M}{P} = L(r(M/P),\ X(M/P),\ K_o + \frac{M}{P})$$

This equation in the single variable M/P yields a solution, say $(\hat{M/P})$, which in turn can be used to obtain the solution for all the remaining real variables. This solution implies that the *real* money supply and all the real variables are independent of the *nominal* money supply. In other words, money is neutral in that a change in M merely changes P in proportion $(P = \dfrac{M}{(\hat{M/P})})$ but leaves the equilibrium value of the real variables unchanged. Yet these equilibrium values are not invariant under a shift in the *demand function* for money expressed by L, for in general a change in this function would give rise to a different solution for M/P, and, hence, for the real variables.

(3) *In the presence of national debt or with a mixed money supply, neither the dichotomy nor the neutrality holds.* This conclusion can be shown to follow from the previous two. Just how a change in the money supply or in the demand for money will affect the real variables of the system depends on which component of the supply is changed and on the relative size of the components and of the national debt. As an illustration, consider the empirically most relevant case where the money supply consists entirely of bank money and the national debt is positive. Then an increase in the money supply, by increasing P and reducing real wealth, will tend to increase saving and reduce the rate of interest to the extent necessary to produce a matching increment in investment. But different conclusions would hold under other assumptions, which need not be analyzed in this summary.

The results summarized under (1) to (3) above are helpful in assessing the theoretical and empirical relevance of explicitly recognizing the dependence of consumption on wealth, to which attention was first called by the well-known contributions of Scitovsky and Pigou [27], [22], [23]. From (1) above it is apparent that this recognition has no significant implication unless there exists in the economy some net money fixed claims on (or to) the government,[11] whether in the form of money or in the form of interest-bearing debt. However, when such claims do exist, as is usually the case, then the wealth effect has significant implications. In particular, a system satisfying assumptions A.1 to A.5 will generally possess a position of full employment equilibrium, contrary to Keynes' conclusion. This is because V_o/P now includes a component which is inversely related to the price level P. Thus, by making W, and hence P, sufficiently small, it is generally possible to make real wealth and consumption so large and the rate of saving and investment so small that the commodity market can be cleared with a positive rate of interest, consistent with the clearing of the money market. In terms of Figure 1,

[10] In the terminology of Gurley and Shaw, the money supply consists entirely of "outside" money (cf. [8] pp. 72–73).

[11] Or foreigners, if we consider an open economy.

the value of r clearing the commodity market is no longer a constant $\hat{r}$ but, instead, a decreasing function of P, i.e., a curve falling from left to right. At least for sufficiently low P this curve may be expected to lie to the right of the ordinate axis and to intersect there the LL curve.

This conclusion is not without interest from the standpoint of the history of economic controversies. But it does not imply by any means that one can rely on the Pigou-Scitovsky effect mechanism as a practical stabilization device, and that, if only wages were sufficiently flexible, a market economy could never be plagued by lack of effective demand. For one thing, the conclusion is valid only so long as we assume that redistributional effects can be neglected, and that the elasticity of price expectation is no larger than unity. Furthermore, in depressed situations in which a system without a government-money fixed liability would have no solution under wage flexibility, the size of deflation required to re-establish full employment might well be such as to produce even more damage than widespread unemployment. Thus, even if the cure could be counted on not to kill the patient — which is doubtful — there would be a great deal to be said for a less gruesome remedy such as fiscal policy.

Another implication of the wealth effect is that under the conditions of case (3), which are empirically by far the most relevant, the convenient classical proposition that "money is but a veil" is not warranted. But to keep the role of the wealth effect in proper perspective, it should be noted that the same conclusion would hold even in the absence of this effect as soon as we drop any of the heroic assumptions A.1 to A.5. In short, while there is really no ground for holding that in the "real world" money is ever strictly neutral, the lack of neutrality is due only in negligible portion to the Pigou-Scitovsky effect. Indeed, within the range of variation of prices characterizing a normal healthy economy, that wealth effect is likely to be so negligible that, were it not for other forces, especially wage-price rigidities, money would be very nearly neutral. In particular, interest rates would be nearly un-

affected by monetary policy, and prices would respond roughly in proportion to the money supply. Since in the long (and even not so long) run, rigidities can be neglected, I would conclude that neutrality and the quantity theory — in the sense of a stable relation between the money supply and the value of output at any given interest rate — is a good long-run approximation, subject, however, to the stricture that in the long run monetary institutions may gradually change. In the case of really rapid inflation, the Pigou effect may be a little less negligible but still of secondary importance in comparison with the redistributional effect. Furthermore, given a large change in M, the proposition that the price level will change roughly in proportion is likely to provide a good approximation, once the change in M has come to an end. Thus, the significance of the wealth effect appears to be primarily technical, but its empirical relevance would seem to be small, at least under normal conditions.

III

Implications of the Model Under Wage Rigidity

A. *The Strict Keynesian Version.* As already noted, wage rigidity can be said to exist if the wage rate W will not be bid below some level W_o even though at this wage rate there is an excess supply of labor; and the rigidity is "effective" if the market clearing value of W is less than W_o. The implications of wage rigidity will be examined first in terms of what may be called the "strict Keynesian version" of the model, which assumes pure bank money and no national debt (and thus no Pigou effect) and competitive behavior in the commodity and the capital markets and on the demand side of the labor market.

Under these assumptions in the absence of wage rigidity the dichotomy holds and the real system (1) to (9) would possess a solution for all the real variables. Let $\hat{X}, \hat{N}, \hat{r}$, and (P/W) denote this solution for the corresponding variables and let us label it the "full employment" solution. With wage rigidity, however, the dichotomy breaks down, for though P does not appear separately in (1), W appears separately in (6), and thus the nine real equations contain ten unknowns. The equilibrium value of the real variables depends then on the money supply M, as well as on the rigid wage W_o, and more specifically on their ratio M/W_o.

This conclusion, and its implications, can be illustrated by the simple graphical apparatus of Figure 2, if we are prepared to make a few

FIGURE 2

WAGE RIGIDITY AND MONETARY POLICY

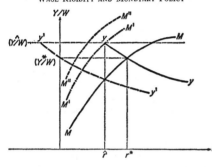

convenient simplifying assumptions. In particular, suppose that, to a first approximation, the demand for money can be treated as homogeneous of first degree in money income and not significantly affected by wealth, i.e., $M^d = L(r,Y) = YL^*(r)$. Then in order for the money market to be cleared we must have $YL^*(r) = M$, which implies

(k.1) $$Y/W = \frac{M/W}{L^*(r)}.$$

Taking M and W as given parameters, this is a relation between Y/W (income in wage units) and r, shown in Figure 2 as the MM curve. (Note that the Keynesian device of using labor as the numeraire is a very natural one since the rigid wage provides a stable unit of measurement.) This curve can again be regarded as the graph of income velocity as a function of interest rates, except for a proportionality factor, M/W. Thus, a change in the ratio M/W will cause the curve to shift up or down in proportion to the change.

Next, from the real part of the system one can derive a second relation between these same variables which must be satisfied for the commodity and labor markets to be cleared.

For this purpose we first derive from (4b) a relation between P/W and X, which represents in essence the Marshallian short-run supply function for commodities (short run, because K_o is fixed). By means of this relation and (5b), consumption demand given by (1) can be expressed in terms of X and r only, say, $C = C^*(X,r)$. Substituting this result and (2) into (3) and (7) one obtains an expression of the form

$$C^*(X,r) + I\ (X,r) = X$$

(the initial condition K_o being subsumed in the functional form), which can be solved for X in terms of r, say

(k.2) $$X = x(r).$$

For any given value of r this relation yields that level of output for which the sum of the corresponding consumption and investment demands just equal output, and the commodity market is cleared. Finally, by multiplying X by the corresponding supply price P/W, we arrive at the desired relation between $Y/W = (P/W)\ X$ and r, say

(k.3) $$Y/W = y(r).$$

It is represented in Figure 2 by the yy curve and is shown only for values of $Y/W \leq (\hat{Y/W})$, since for larger values there would be an excess demand for labor, i.e., the labor market would not be cleared (nor could the rigidity be effective).

Since the assumption of competition in the commodity markets precludes the possibility of a falling short-run supply function — i.e., P/W must be a nondecreasing function of X — the slope of the function $y(r)$ depends on that of the function $x(r)$. This slope referred to the r axis in turn can be shown to be given by the expression $(C_r^* + I_r)\ \dfrac{1}{1 - C_z^* - I_z}$. Here C_z^* and I_z denote respectively the marginal propensity to consume and invest with respect to changes in real income, and C_r^* and I_r are the corresponding propensities with respect to changes in r. The first factor $(C_r^* + I_r)$ can be taken to be negative since C_r^* is negative and I_r, whatever its sign, is most unlikely to outweigh it. The second factor is a generalization of the conventional multiplier, sometimes called the "supermultiplier," and is generally assumed to be positive. If so, X, and hence Y/W will be a declining function of r as shown in the figure. It should be observed, however, that, contrary to a common view, there is really nothing impossible or unstable about the supermultiplier being negative (or zero) in some regions and the graph of yy rising from left to right (or being parallel to the ordinate).

The intersection of MM and yy gives the equilibrium values, say $(Y\overset{*}{/}W)$ and r^*, and these values clearly depend on M/W_o which controls the position of MM. The equilibrium value of real income X^*, can then be obtained by substituting r^* into (k.2), $(P/W)^*$ from X^* and the supply function and so on; and they must all be functions of M/W_0.

In our graph the equilibrium position is one of less than "full employment." Full employment could be reached only with a larger money supply in wage units which would shift up the MM curve to a position where it intersects the yy curve at the full employment point $[\hat{r},(Y\overset{\wedge}{/}W)]$. The money supply required to reach this position can be seen from (k.1) to be $(M\overset{\wedge}{/}W) = (Y\overset{\wedge}{/}W) L^* (\hat{r})$. Under wage flexibility the adjustment would of course occur through the market process as unemployment would cause W to fall, and hence M/W to rise, until the labor market is cleared. But under wage rigidity it can only come about by an expansion of the *nominal* money supply to the level $M' = (M\overset{\wedge}{/}W) \times W_o$. This expansion can be achieved by the monetary authority either by directly enforcing the correct money supply M' or by picking and enforcing the correct rate of interest $\hat{r}$, and letting the money supply seek its appropriate level M'. (Both processes may, of course, go on simultaneously.) Note that in the present model both monetary expansion and money wage reductions act only through shifts in the MM curve and lead to the same value of Y/W and r, and to differences only in money prices and income. This "Keynesian" result depends, however, on our having assumed away a "Pigou-Scitovsky" effect, by supposing G to be zero.

We need still to consider what would happen if the initial money supply were such that the MM curve passes above the full employment point, as is the case for the curve $M''M''$ in Figure 2. Here, of course, if wages are only rigid downward, the classical mechanism takes over; the rate of interest being initially too low, there is excess demand in the commodity market which bids up prices and wages; the rise in wages eventually reduces the effective money supply M/W, shifting down the MM curve, until it intersects the yy curve at the full employment point. The process just described corresponds to what is usually called "demand-pull" inflation.

Oversimplified as our model is, it brings into sharp focus the predicament of the money authority in a system with rigid wages, namely, to continuously pick and enforce the correct monetary policy (the money supply M', or the interest rate $\hat{r}$, or both) under inadequate knowledge of the relevant portion of the MM and yy curves and their shift through time. Also the consequences of errors are asymmetric. If it follows a more "loose" policy, it generates demand-pull inflation or price rises which, under wage rigidity, are largely irreversible. If it follows a "tighter" policy it engenders unemployment and not merely deflation — presumably a somewhat lesser evil as long as contained within limits. In reality the problem is further complicated by the fact that the monetary authority may be expected to pursue the double goal of full employment *and* price stability. Unfortunately, these two objectives will be inconsistent with each other if the exogenously determined wage rate is such that, when combined with the full employment price-wage ratio (P/W), it implies a full employment price level, $\hat{P} = (P/W) \times W_o$, higher than the historically received one. This is of course the "cost push" case. If the monetary authority pursues full employment it cannot prevent a rise in prices; while if it refuses to go along and expand the money supply enough to insure full employment at the given wage, it will certainly cause unemployment, while it may not even succeed in preventing some rise in prices.

The dilemma is even more dramatic if the wage rate is controlled by a mechanism whereby money wages tend to rise at a rate depending on the level of unemployment, and this rate of change is larger than the "rate of increase of productivity" (the rate at which $P/\hat{W}$ falls) at rates of unemployment larger than what might be regarded as unavoidable frictional unemployment (see, e.g., [26]). According to some views this is *the* predicament of our times, but I don't propose here to assess this claim or, even less, to propose remedies.

In concluding this section it is well to call attention to two types of situation where to reach and maintain full employment is beyond the power of the monetary authority. One is the well-known case where the full employment rate of interest $\hat{r}$ is negative (or possibly very close to zero), represented in Figure 2 by the curve $y'y'$. It corresponds to a situation where, in an economy with flexible wages, there would be no set of prices and interest rate capable of simultaneously clearing all markets. The system can have a solution only if wages are rigid and unemployment is allowed to develop, permitting the elimination of the excess supply that would otherwise arise at any positive rate of interest. In fact, the fall in employment is accompanied by a reduction in *supply X*. To be sure, this fall tends to reduce also the *demand*, but only to a smaller extent, as consumption, at least, is kept up by initial wealth and the expectation that the fall in income is but transitory in nature. (In Keynesian terms, the marginal propensity to consume is less than 1.) Thus, at some sufficiently low level of employment and output, the excess supply tends to disappear, and the system finds a resting point. A very aggressive monetary policy might at best bring output close to the ordinate of the point at which the $y'y'$ curve cuts the vertical axis.[12] Only fiscal policy can get the system back to full employment (cf. section IV).

The other case where monetary (as well as fiscal) policy is powerless is the case of "real wage rigidity." Here, because of union pressure, legislation, minimum subsistence levels, or otherwise, the real wage cannot be reduced

[12] Even the most aggressive monetary policy can at best force r to zero, and cannot force the money supply above the demand arising at this interest rate and the price level corresponding to the given wage rate and the level of output $X = x(0)$. To make monetary policy more effective would require very special devices such as making money sufficiently expensive to store.

below some level, say $(W/P)^m$, and this level exceeds the marginal product of labor corresponding to the given production function (including the stock of capital) and full employment of labor. (Full employment in this connection might be defined in terms of some standard labor force participation and work week, or in terms of the potential supply available at the fixed real wage.) There will then be an effective ceiling on output, X and on Y/W, below the full employment ceiling exhibited in Figure 2. Any attempt to expand employment beyond that ceiling, through expansion of the money supply (or fiscal policy), will only succeed in increasing prices and wages without increasing output and employment. The situation just described frequently takes the form of a "balance of payments problem." The attempt to expand employment and income increases imports, forcing a devaluation, or equivalent measures, which increase the price of imports, and lead finally to a rise in money wages and prices. This type of situation, which some hold to be common in underdeveloped economies, can be remedied only if the wage rigidity can be broken or productivity increased through technological progress and capital accumulation, provided this does not immediately result in a commensurate rise in the rigid real wage.

B. Modifications of the Keynesian Model: Imperfections in the Commodity Market and Wealth Effects. The assumption of a competitive commodity market, which justifies the rising supply function of the previous section, may be replaced by an alternative one, possibly more realistic and certainly more convenient. It is the assumption that prices tend to represent a roughly constant markup on unit labor cost, possibly reflecting the prevalence of market imperfections of the oligopolistic type. An alternative formulation of this same hypothesis is that labor income WN is a fairly stable share of total income PX, at least in the neighborhood of full employment, X [31]. Indeed, a constant markup on unit labor cost means:

$$P = (1 + m)\,(WN/X),$$

where m is the markup.

This equation in turn implies:

$$WN = \frac{1}{1+m} (PX) ,$$

where $1/(1+m)$ is the constant share of labor income in total income. The empirical evidence seems, on the whole, to support such a stability, at any rate in the medium run. To be sure, as output fluctuates below, and up to, full employment the share of profits in income tends to fluctuate with output. But total property income is the sum of profits, interest, and rent income, and the share of the latter two components moves in the opposite direction, imparting stability to the share of total property income and hence also of labor income.

Suppose further that in the short run N is approximately proportional to X, i.e., that the elasticity of output with respect to labor input is close to 1. This hypothesis does not seem to be grossly inconsistent with the empirical evidence, at least in the neighborhood of full employment. (It is, however, inconsistent with the assumption that the real wage is equal to the marginal product of labor, for then the elasticity of X with respect to N would be equal to the labor share of income, which is well below unity.) Under this further assumption N/X can be approximated by a constant, say, n, and consequently P/W becomes itself a constant or

(4.i) $P/W = (1+m)n \equiv \pi,$

an equation that replaces the original (4b). The parameter π is of course a constant only at a given point of time. It may be expected to fall over time as productivity, X/N, rises through technical progress and the accumulation of capital, and hence labor input per unit of output, n, falls. If (4.i) holds, then the demand for labor is no longer given by (5) but directly by solving the production function (4a) for N in terms of X and K_0. Finally we may wish to recognize that, in the short run, the labor supply may be rather inelastic with respect to the real wage rate, and hence may be adequately approximated by a constant, say N^l. Then equation (6) is replaced by

(6.i) $\begin{cases} N^s = N^l \text{ if } n^d(X, K_0) \geqq N^l \\ W = W_0 \text{ if } n^d(X, K_0) < N^l \end{cases}$

These various modifications do not change the count of equations or unknowns of Model II. However, the resulting system — call it II.i — is somewhat easier to see through. For, so long as W is rigid at W_0, P itself can be regarded as given exogenously (since it is proportional to W_0). Hence, instead of solving the system for Y/W in terms of r, we can solve it for Y/P. But Y/P is X and hence its solution in terms of r is simply (k.2). Similarly, equation (k.1) can be rewritten as $Y/P = (M/P)/L(r)$ and Figure 2 can be redrawn with the more conventional and convenient variable Y/P measured on the ordinate, and the money supply stated in "real" terms, M/P.

The implications of this model are roughly the same as those discussed in the previous section, but easier to comprehend and expose. In particular, the price level P may be regarded as determined by the rigid wage (together with labor productivity and the constant mark-up) provided that the money supply is no larger than what is required to transact a full employment income at the price level corresponding to W_0. But if the money supply is larger, so that the first line of equation (6.i) holds, then P is determined by the money supply, $P^* = M/L(r, \hat{Y}/P)$, and the wage rate is determined by P and hence, indirectly, again by M.

The implications of the model are also not appreciably affected if one recognizes the existence of a money-fixed government debt, G. In terms of the graphical analysis of Figure 2, the main effect of G is found to be that equation (k.2) must be changed to

(k.2′) $X = Y/P = x(r, G/P).$

Accordingly, the graph of this equation — the yy curve — is not independent of the value of P and hence of W_0. In particular, a fall in W_0, by reducing P and increasing real wealth and consumption, would require a smaller rate of investment and hence a larger value of r to clear the commodity market for any given X. It tends therefore to shift the yy curve to the right. The full employment level of Y/P might also be affected, via the labor supply, but presumably not significantly, at least for reasonable changes in P. Similarly the money market clearing condition becomes (k.1') $L(r,Y/P,G/P) = M/P.$

Hence, the position of MM depends not only upon the real money supply M/P but also directly on P and hence W_o. Given M/P, a fall in W_o and P should tend to increase the demand for money, i.e., reduce velocity for any given r, shifting MM downward.

The main implication is that monetary expansion and money wage cuts need not have a symmetrical effect on output and the other real variables, since the equilibrium value of these variables, while still a function of M and W, no longer depends merely on their ratio. Pure monetary expansion still affects the equilibrium by shifting up the MM curve. But a wage cut of the same proportion would shift up MM somewhat less (because of the wealth effect on the demand for money), and would also shift yy to the right. If, as seems likely, the wealth effect on the commodity market is larger than that on the demand for money, a wage cut will tend to result in a somewhat larger increase in X than would monetary expansion. But the difference may be expected to be altogether negligible: a priori considerations as well as empirical estimates [1] suggest that the shift in either curve from the wealth effect is likely to be minor, for reasonable changes in W_o and reasonable assumptions about the ratio of G to aggregate net worth — say, 0 to 20 per cent. In part, this is due to the fact that the change in wealth resulting from the "deflation" is likely initially to affect consumption only moderately, the rest of the effect being spread in time.

Note, finally, that because wage deflation tends to shift the yy curve to the right — provided it does not generate expectations of further fall in prices — it could conceivably lead to an expansion of employment even in situations where monetary policy as such is powerless. Hence, across-the-board wage cuts might appear to provide a possible alternative to fiscal policy. But, as already noted at the end of section II, this view has little practical merit. For even if we wave aside the problem of enforcing an over-all wage cut, this approach provides at best a weak and unreliable tool, inconsistent with the maintenance of a stable price level.

IV

The Role of Government Monetary and Fiscal Operations

The essential implications of government fiscal operations can be formalized by the addition of two equations to Model II and certain modifications in some of the remaining ones.

The main modifications are the introduction of total tax receipts and other fiscal parameters in the consumption function and possibly in some other equations such as (2), (4), and (5); the addition of government purchases of goods F to the definition of aggregate demand (3), and the purchases of labor services, F_n, to the demand for labor on the right-hand side of (8); and the addition of the government stock of capital, K_o^g in (2), (4) and (5). The two additional equations are: (i) a tax collection equation, which may be considered as part of the real system, of the general form

(10) $T = t(X, V_o/P, P, [\tau]),$

where T denotes tax receipts net of transfer payments measured in real terms (i.e., measured in MM's) and $[\tau]$ denotes the relevant set of tax parameters; (ii) the government budget identity, to be added to the monetary set,

(M.8) $PF + WF_n - PT = \Delta G + \Delta M^*$

The left-hand side is the budget deficit in money terms, denoted hereafter by D. On the right-hand side, M^* may be usefully defined as "net government money" or the difference between the amount of money issued by the government (if any) and the amount of bank-created money held by the government. It is also convenient for present purposes to replace (M.4) and (M.5) by the single equation

(M.4g) $M = B^b + M^*,$

while dropping the variable M^b.

After these additions and modifications, the set of equations (1) to (10) plus (M.1) to (M.3) turns out again to form a closed subsystem in the original variables plus T, but involving now a new set of "fiscal policy parameters," to wit, F, F_n, and $[\tau]$. Hence in examining the implications of the "government model," it is permissible to concentrate on this subset and to disregard again the bond market and the other monetary relations. However, some of these relations and in particular (M.4g) and (M.8) are useful to clarify the relations between monetary and fiscal policy, which are essentially linked through debt management. In particular, from these two equations we can derive the relation

$$\Delta M = (\Delta B^b - \Delta G) + D.$$

This relation serves to make clear that, in principle, through appropriate monetary and debt management, monetary and fiscal policies can be made entirely independent of each other. That is, a given deficit (or surplus) D can be made consistent with any change in M through appropriate changes in B^b, the amount of credit extended by the banking system to the rest of the economy, or in G, the amount of government debt held by the private sector. It is for this reason that, in our model, we can continue to treat the money supply M as exogenously given even in the presence of government fiscal operations. And we define monetary policy as the control of the money supply and not merely of the amount of bank credit.

The role of fiscal policy and its relation to monetary policy can again be analyzed through a graphical apparatus analogous to that of Figure 2 and set out in Figure 3.

FIGURE 3

MONETARY VERSUS FISCAL POLICY

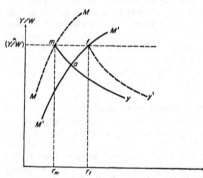

The money market clearing conditions are basically unchanged and so is the nature and interpretation of the MM curve. Its position is again controlled by the real money supply M/W and possibly also to a minor extent directly by W, through the wealth effect. As for the commodity market, through a series of substitutions of the type described earlier and a few suitable simplifications and approximations — such as neglecting direct government purchases of labor — we can obtain a condition stating the equality of demand and supply in this market of the form:

(g) $$C^*(X, r, G/W, T, [\tau]) + I^*(X, r, [\tau]) + F = X.$$

If we further use (10) to eliminate T, the above equation can be solved for X in terms of r and fiscal parameters. From this solution in turn we can derive the relation

(k.3g) $$Y/W \equiv (P/W)X$$
$$= (P/W)x^*(r, F, [\tau], G_0/W), X \le \hat{X}.$$

For given values of the fiscal policy "parameters," F and $[\tau]$, this equation can be looked at as a relation between Y/W and r, represented in our graph by the yy curve. Its position in the plane depends of course on fiscal policy, and this dependence can be conveniently approximated by a series of fiscal "multipliers" describing the upward (or downward) shift of the curve in terms of the change in Y (given r) per unit change in the indicated parameter. The formulae below, obtained by total differentiation of equation (g), above, or (10) or both, provide a sample of such multipliers' effect on real income X. The effect on Y/W can be obtained by multiplying these formulae by P/W, (if P/W can be taken as a given parameter). The symbol C_T^* denotes here the marginal effect on consumption of an increase in tax payments (usually assumed to equal the marginal propensity to consume with respect to income, C_x^* with sign reversed) and t_x is the marginal change in tax receipts per unit change in income before taxes.

(i) Effect of unit change in expenditure, F:

$$\frac{dX}{dF} = 1/(1 - C_x^* - C_T^* t_x - I_x^*)$$

(ii) Effect of an increase in tax payments T or, equivalently, of a decrease in deficit D, expenditure constant (under the approximation that consumption depends only on the tax liability and not on the specific form of taxes):

$$\frac{dX}{dT}\Big|_{F \text{ constant}} = C_T^*/(1 - C_x^* - I_x^*)$$

(iii) Effect of an increase in deficit, through increased expenditure, tax schedules unchanged:

$$\frac{dX}{dD} = 1/[1 - C_x^* - I_x^* - (1 + C_x^*)t_x]\ ^{13}$$

(iv) Effect of an increase in expenditure matched by an equal increase in taxes (balanced budget multiplier):

$$\frac{dX}{dF}\Big|\, dT = dF = (1 + C_T^*)/(1 - C_I^* - C_x^*)\ ^{14}$$

If the relevant marginal effects are roughly independent of the magnitude of X (and T), then a given fiscal change would shift the yy curve parallel to itself; however, this need not be the case in general. If one drops the assumption that P/W is independent of X, then each of the above expressions must be multiplied by $(1 + E)(P/W)$ where E is the elasticity of P/W with respect to X, which may also vary with X.

This analysis of how various possible fiscal operations shift the curve up or down must, however, be qualified in one important way: it is strictly valid only so long as the shifted curve remains below the full employment ceiling Y/W. In principle, this ceiling might itself respond to fiscal policy, though the responsiveness is likely to be slight in the short run and may be ignored for present purposes. Once the shifted curve bumps against the ceiling, further changes in the fiscal variable will obviously have zero multiplier effects (in real terms); and to see how they affect the economy one needs a very different kind of analysis, much along the traditional lines of public finance.

But before taking up this point, one may review the more or less conventional analysis as to the relation between fiscal and monetary policy as stabilization devices. Suppose that, for an initially given set of policies, the MM curve and the yy curve can be represented by the two solid curves of Figure 3, intersecting at point a, below full employment. This situation

may be visualized as one actually prevailing, or as the one that would tend to come about under a *status quo* policy. There are then two "pure" policies and very many mixed policies that might be used to shift equilibrium to (or at least toward) the full employment ceiling. One is pure monetary policy, which would consist in expanding the money supply or enforcing a lower interest rate or both, shifting the MM curve to the position $M'M'$ and establishing full employment at m. Pure fiscal policy on the other hand would consist in manipulating taxes or expenditure or both, shifting the yy curve to the position $y'y'$ and reaching full employment at f.

Wherein lies the difference between position m and f, aside from the difference in r, and in the income velocity of circulation, which can be picked up from the graph? Since, by assumption, both are full employment positions, output X and employment N will be the same. The difference consists therefore in the utilization of output as between private consumption, public consumption, and capital formation.

1. Suppose, first, that fiscal policy took the form of increased expenditure, tax structure constant. Then, at least to a first approximation, consumption C will be the same at m and f, and the difference will be found in the utilization of $X - C$. Clearly, f will involve a smaller amount of *private* capital formation, I, and a larger use of X by the government. *Total* capital formation will depend further on the way F is divided between F^c (government capital formation) and $F - F^c$ (expenditure on current account).

2. If, on the other hand, the shift in yy is brought about entirely by personal tax reductions, F constant, then higher consumption replaces a portion of private capital formation which is repressed through the higher interest rate (higher and lower here always mean relative to m and not to a).

3. Finally, tax reductions might partly take the form of "investment incentives." Then consumption is likely to expand somewhat less and investment to contract somewhat less than in case 2. However, some reduction in investment relative to m is still almost sure to occur. In fact, a reduction in taxes, no matter what its form, always increases income net

---

[13] This expression could be negative, even though $1 - C_x^*$ $- I_x^*$ is positive, if $dX/dF)t_x > 1$ in which case an increase in F will increase T by a larger amount, reducing the deficit. Then an increase in D can be obtained only by reducing F, and hence X.

[14] This multiplier is usually stated to be unity, but this conclusion is seen to hold only under the special assumptions $C_T^* = -C_x^*, I_x^* = 0$.

of taxes — disposable income at f is higher than at m. For I to be as high as at m, the tax inducement to invest, which increases yields permitting the higher interest rate at f, would have to induce larger saving out of a given disposable income, and sufficiently so to offset the increased disposable income. This is a most unlikely outcome, especially if one believes that a higher rate of interest is more likely to reduce than to increase saving. Thus, paradoxically, reliance on tax inducements to invest instead of on monetary policy to stimulate demand is likely to generate a *lower* rate of investment.[15] In addition, it will tend to produce higher yields on investment and higher market interest rates. In general, one may conclude that the main differential effect of using tax incentives instead of monetary policy to stimulate investment, when either method could be effective, is to produce higher yields which are in turn consistent with higher market interest rates. This difference might be desirable in the context of certain balance of payments problems which are, however, beyond the scope of the present "closed economy" model.

The conclusion to be drawn from this brief analysis is that, in so far as full employment could be maintained by purely monetary devices — i.e., where the initial yy curve lies entirely sufficiently within the positive quadrant — the choice between monetary policy and various types of fiscal policy to achieve the appropriate level of aggregate demand must be based on traditional considerations. These are: the relative merits of private versus public consumption in choosing between C and $F - F^c$; the relative "social" yield of private versus government capital formation in choosing between I and F^c; and finally, on "intergeneration" comparisons in choosing between total current "consumption" $C + F - F^c$, on the one hand, and total capital formation $I + F^c$ on the other. As I have argued in some detail in [18],

[15] Some might question the empirical relevance of this conclusion on the ground that I am ignoring here the corporate form, and that tax inducement to corporations might increase corporate saving and thus total saving and private investment. Basically, my position on this point is that corporate saving, except possibly in the very short run, is a substitute for, and not an addition to, saving out of conventional disposable income. This conclusion follows readily from the M-B-A consumption function in combination with the argument set forth in [17].

by pushing capital formation at the expense of consumption we increase the stock of capital and real income available to the community in the future, at the expense of the current generation. I have also argued that a neutral policy might be regarded as one that makes the current generation pay for the government services it is currently receiving, and that such a policy requires, by and large, collecting currently in taxes an amount equal to $F - F^c$. Lower taxes make future generations pay for the services enjoyed by the current generation, while higher taxes, in essence, make the current generations pay for services enjoyed by future generations.

There remain to consider briefly two cases. The first, when we start out from a position of full employment, requires very little additional comment. Here, an increase in government expenditure must clearly be justified on grounds other than maintenance of full employment. If the increased expenditure is not accompanied by higher taxes, then consumption will be unchanged and hence the whole increase in F must come from a reduction in I, as the government taps private saving that would otherwise have gone into capital formation. This is the standard case on which rests the "classical" argument that deficit financing shifts the burden to "future generations" (cf. [3] and the references cited there, and [18]). Since the reduction in I and expansion of government borrowing will tend to be accompanied by higher interest rates, an appropriate restrictive monetary policy will be called for. In terms of Figure 3, this situation could be represented as a shift of the commodity market curve from yy to $y'y'$. It requires a shift of the money curve from MM to $M'M'$, in order to offset the higher velocity of circulation accompanying the higher interest rate.

If the increased expenditure is accompanied by a matching increase in taxes there will still be some shift to the right of the yy curve, as consumption will tend to fall by less than taxes (the multiplier effect of a balanced budget). Hence, again, private capital formation I will have to be restricted somewhat through a higher interest rate and a tighter monetary policy. The maintenance of private investments would, in the short run, require instead an appropriate budget surplus put at the disposal of investors, to offset the reduced private saving.

There is, second, the "Keynesian" case where the yy curve crosses over to the second quadrant. Here (aside from the rather impractical monetary cures mentioned earlier) fiscal policy is the only remedy, at least to the extent necessary to shift the yy curve to a position where it can make contact with monetary policy. Even in this situation a case can be made in principle for favoring government capital formation over other ways of stimulating demand, since, as I have argued in [18], there will otherwise be a "burden" on future generations, although, in any event, the burden will be small in relation to the benefits accruing to the current generation.

This analysis of the *modus operandi* of monetary and fiscal policies and their implications suggests, at least to me, that the case for a currently balanced budget, and hence for relying on monetary rather than on fiscal policy as a first line of defense in counteracting shifts in the forces controlling aggregate demand, is somewhat stronger than might have appeared some time ago. However, the choice of a proper mix involves many more aspects than those we can develop here, including considerations of reliability of the tools and of feasibility in a given concrete institutional setting. In particular, exclusive reliance on monetary policy, whenever this policy could, in principle, do the job, might require swings in the money supply and interest rates of a size that might prove unsettling to the working of the economy. (See, however, the argument of the next section.) These considerations support a policy of built-in stabilizers with reasonably high marginal tax take t_x, (which, remember, includes transfers). Such stabilizers tend to moderate the swings in time in the position of the yy curve resulting from shifts in the investment or consumption function or both, thus reducing the burden imposed on monetary policy. On the same grounds, a good case can be made for some countercyclical variation in expenditure and tax parameters, although at least from present evidence one might have reservations about the suitability of tax cuts announced to be but temporary (cf. [18] section IX). But there still remains a prima-facie case for balancing

the budget over a suitable span of time (cyclically balanced budget) in so far as this is consistent with full employment, unless a convincing case can be made for discriminating between generations.

V

Imperfections in the Capital Markets — the Availability Doctrine

The models on which we have relied so far assume, at least implicitly, a well-functioning competitive capital market in which investments are limited and brought into line with saving through the mechanism of the rate of interest or cost of capital. In such a model there exists a single short-run equilibrium rate of interest which measures both the return to lenders and the cost to borrowers, and also equals (or at least is not less than) the internal marginal rate of return to all units.[16] There is also no need to give separate treatment to financial intermediaries: all loans may be regarded as extended directly from the lending or surplus units to the final borrowers needing funds to finance their expenditure.

That this assumption is unrealistic probably no one would have disputed seriously. It was, however, the merit of the availability doctrine, advanced in the postwar period, that it made a convincing case for the proposition that disregard of certain institutional imperfections of the capital market leads to an unsatisfactory and seriously distorted view of the *modus operandi* of monetary policy and its consequences (see, e.g., [24] [25] [4] [28]). Actually, the promoters of this doctrine seem to have been largely motivated by a specific issue of monetary policy: the advisability of abandoning the policy of pegging the yield of government securities, which in turn made it impossible to maintain close control over the money supply. They were primarily interested in establishing that, even if one accepted the then-prevailing view that aggregate demand was very inelastic with respect to interest rates (i.e., the elasticity

[16] Note that even if we wished to recognize the existence of a plurality of maturities, under our present assumption of certainty, the current return — interest plus capital gain — would be the same on all maturities and equal to *the* short rate.

of our $y(r)$ function was close to zero), abandonment of that policy and re-establishment of effective limitations on the quantity of money would not result in a sharp rise in interest rates, consequent collapse of the price of government securities, and soaring cost of servicing the national debt. To support this contention, they advanced a number of arguments, varying considerably in generality and persuasiveness. Here we shall be concerned primarily with one argument which seems to have the greatest validity and general applicability: the proposition that interest rates charged to borrowers by financial intermediaries are largely controlled by institutional forces and slow to adjust at best; and that the demand for funds is accordingly limited not by the borrowers' willingness to borrow at the given rate but by lenders' willingness to lend — or, more precisely, by the funds available to them to be rationed out among the would-be borrowers.

The implications of this proposition can be grasped most easily by considering one limiting case. Suppose the task of making credit available to units in need of financing requires specialized knowledge and organization and is therefore carried out exclusively by specialized institutions which we may label financial intermediaries. That is, surplus units, whose wealth exceeds their holding of physical assets and who carry the balance of their wealth in the form of claims on other units, do not lend directly to the deficit units, but instead lend to, or acquire claims on, the intermediaries. The intermediaries in turn lend to the final debtors of the economy at some rate, say r', which, at least in the short run, may be taken as institutionally given, and adjusts at best only slowly to market conditions, as indicated below. Let us also assume initially that the rate r' is such that the flow of net demand for credit from intermediaries (gross borrowing less repayments) exceeds the net flow of funds acquired by them and that the two are brought into equality by rationing the available supply among the potential borrowers. The rate r' in turn also controls the rate intermediaries pay to their creditors or depositors, say r_{in}.

Under these conditions the flow of borrowing and borrowers' demand for commodities is limited not by the cost of borrowing r' but by the flow of funds made available to intermediaries by primary lenders. Also the single rate r of the perfect market model, measuring simultaneously (i) the return to primary lenders, (ii) the cost to final borrowers, (iii) the internal marginal rate of return from investments, and (iv) the opportunity cost of holding money, is replaced by a plurality of rates. Accordingly, the demand for money can no longer be regarded as a function of the rate of interest r, but will depend instead on the opportunity cost which will vary between r_{in} for lending units and the internal rate for rationed units. Unfortunately, the internal rate is no longer obtainable from market quotations, nor is it otherwise directly observable.

Some measure, however, or index of prevailing internal rates might be derived from the investment function, equation (2) of our model. Suppose we solve this equation to express r as a function of I and X:

$$(3a) \qquad r_s = R(I,X), \frac{dr_s}{\partial I} < 0, \frac{dr_s}{\partial X} > 0$$

Under perfect markets this function would give the internal rate corresponding to the given value of I and X. The same would be true under rationing, if rationing were "efficient," i.e., if the flow of investment were allocated among units in the very same way in which it would be distributed through the price mechanism under perfect markets. Since rationing cannot be perfectly efficient, the opportunity cost will presumably vary from unit to unit, but r_s might still provide a reasonable indicator of prevailing internal rates. Accordingly, the demand for money might be approximated by replacing in equation (M.2) the variable r with the variables r_{in} and r_s, or also r' and r_s on the ground that r_{in} is itself a function of r'. The same substitution must of course be made in equation (1).

Except for these modifications of equations (1) and (M.2) and the re-interpretation of (3), or its equivalent (3.a), as defining the index r_s, our original system of equations (1) to (M.3) of Model II can still be used to formalize the functioning of an economy with capital rationing of the type described. Furthermore, if we treat r' and r_{in} as exogenously given, these equations still form a determined system in the twelve original endogenous variables (except that r is replaced by r_s).

The working of this system can again be clarified by a graphical analysis of the type of Figure 2, and exhibited in Figure 4. Specifi-

FIGURE 4

SOME IMPLICATIONS OF THE "AVAILABILITY DOCTRINE"

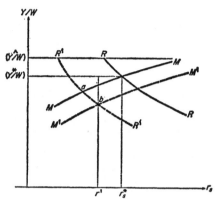

cally, from the first nine equations in ten endogenous variables we can derive again a relation between X and r_s, which it is now convenient to write as $r_s = R\ (X)$. This equation expresses the relation between the index of internal rates and the level of output when the commodity and labor markets are cleared at the corresponding level of output, which means in particular that the rate of investment equals the rate of saving. Stated differently and somewhat less precisely, it shows the internal marginal rate of return prevailing when the level of aggregate demand is X and the flow of resources available for investment is equal to the rate of saving prevailing at this level of output. Since to each value of X there corresponds a value of P/W we can also obtain a corresponding equilibrium relation between r_s and Y/W, which is shown in Figure 4 as the RR curve. This curve is shown as falling from left to right on the same grounds on which the yy curve was drawn with a negative slope in Figures 2 and 3; a larger income makes possible a larger rate of investment which in turn implies a lower marginal rate of return.

As for the money market, by assuming as a convenient approximation either that P/W can be treated as a constant and $G = 0$, or that M^d is homogeneous of first degree in money income and not significantly affected by wealth, we can write the market clearing condition as: $L(Y/W, r', r_s) = M/W$. For given values of M/W and r', this condition yields a second relation between Y/W and r_s, shown again as the MM curve. The general shape of this curve must be similar to that of the corresponding MM curve of Figure 2; however, its elasticity with respect to the variable on the abscissa must be smaller, since r_s is only one of the rates affecting the velocity of circulation while the other, r', is constant by assumption. The intersection of the two curves yields the equilibrium value of Y/W and r_s, say $(Y/W)^*$ and r_s^*, from which the equilibrium value of X and other variables can be inferred. The assumed value of the parameter r' is also shown in the figure. Under certain assumptions, the gap between r' and r_s can be taken as an indicator of the size of the rationing gap (or fringe of unsatisfied borrowers), the size of the demand for credit unsatisfied at the lending rate r'.

It is apparent from our figure that the workings of a model with capital rationing of the type considered are not radically different from those of the original Model II. In particular, if we start from a position of full employment equilibrium, an upward or downward shift in the position of the RR curve, reflecting, e.g., an improvement or deterioration of investment opportunities, would lead, respectively, to "inflation" or unemployment, unless offset by appropriate changes in the money supply. Also, in a situation of less than full employment equilibrium, such as the one assumed in our figure, unemployment could be cured by an appropriate monetary expansion. However, under capital rationing this outcome could come about without any change in the lending rate r'.

The mechanics of this operation are not difficult to trace out. The expansion of the money supply is initially accomplished by a relaxation of rationing by banks and a consequent expansion of lending. However, as income expands in response to the direct increase in investment and the induced expansion of consumption, the higher rate of investment can be sustained without further monetary expansion through the increased flow of saving, which in part results also in an increased flow of credit available from intermediaries.

Similarly, an increase in W, M constant would tend to result in higher prices and a fall in the rate of real investment and income, partly moderated by a rise in the velocity of circulation under the influence of the increase in r_s. In terms of our figure, the MM curve shifts down and $(Y/W)^*$ falls as the rise in Y, induced by the higher r_s, is proportionally smaller than the increase in W.

While r' may be taken as given in the short run, it may be expected to adjust gradually over time, tending toward some normal relation to r_s^*. But because this adjustment is a slow one, we may infer that even if r_s^* swings sharply and rapidly over time in response to cyclical and other forces, r' will tend to fluctuate over a much smaller range. Thus, the capital rationing mechanism provides a plausible way of reconciling moderate fluctuations in market rates with a widely shifting and interest-inelastic investment schedule.

We must, however, stop to consider what might be expected to happen if, as the result of a rapid decline in investment opportunities, the RR curve were to shift downward to a position such as $R'R'$ in our figure. This new curve intersects MM at a, but this intersection could not possibly describe a position of equilibrium. It implies in fact an equilibrium value of r_s smaller than r' which is impossible since, clearly, for every borrower the internal rate must be no less than r'. What is involved here is that at a, with the lending rate r' borrowers are unwilling to borrow all that the intermediaries would have available to lend and the rate of investment is less than the rate of saving, so that income must fall.

In order to exhibit the new equilibrium position, let us assume at first that the rationing gap can dwindle to zero, intermediaries being willing to lend to anybody prepared to pay r', and that under these conditions r_s can be as low as r'. Then, as far as the commodity market is concerned, equilibrium could be reached at b, where the perpendicular through r' intersects $R'R'$. At this point, in fact, r_s equals r' and the commodity market is cleared, since b is on the $R'R'$ curve. (In other words income at b is such that the rate of investment demand at r' equals the rate of saving.)

What happens to the money market condition? As intermediaries are unable to lend all the funds they receive, they accumulate cash balances, reducing the supply of money outside intermediaries, which is the relevant measure of M, and causing the MM curve to shift down to the point where it also intersects the $R'R'$ curve at b. This is, however, only one possible outcome; the other possibility is that the banking system will be unable to maintain the money supply at the initial level as the flow of debt repayment exceeds the flow of credit demanded at r'. Thus the fall in M in the hands of the public may occur in part through intermediaries' accumulation and in part through a reduction of total money supply. Of course, the untapped lending power of both banks and intermediaries may gradually put downward pressure on r' leading to a rise in X, a reactivation of idle intermediaries' balances or an expansion in bank money, or both.

Insofar as lending institutions may not be willing to lend to all borrowers prepared to pay the rate r', a "minimal" rationing gap must exist in the new equilibrium position; hence the equilibrium point may tend to fall somewhat below and to the right of (b) on the $R'R'$ curve, and correspondingly the MM curve must shift down further till it goes through this point.

It appears from the above analysis that the recognition of the role of intermediaries and market imperfections in the guise of sluggish lending rates and of direct rationing rather than price rationing has certain significant implications. First, it helps to account for fluctuations in market lending rates which appear rather modest in relation to likely cyclical swings in the return from investment. Second, it implies that monetary policy may affect aggregate demand without appreciably affecting lending rates, at least in the short run. Third, it suggests that monetary policy — understood now as the control over the power of banks to create money rather than over the actual money supply — may break down under less stringent conditions than those of the original Keynesian case. Because of sticky lending rates monetary policy may become powerless even when the value of r_s corresponding to a full employment output is well above zero.

The model we have used can be considerably enriched by relaxing various oversimplifications. For instance, one can allow for a class of "prime borrowers," who are able to borrow directly from the public as well as from intermediaries and banks in a roughly competitive market, at a rate r_p, which, in contrast to r', will tend to be sensitive to variations in the internal rate r_s. While these refinements must be passed by here, it is worthwhile to review briefly the relevance of the imperfections described to the problem which provided the original motivation for the availability doctrine, namely, the consequences of pegging or dropping the peg on government securities. This task can be accomplished by merely adding borrowing by the government (a "prime" borrower) to the model we have discussed, and hence a stock of government securities. In addition, we must take into account some institutional features of the American monetary system, and notably that the money supply is controlled by the "Central Bank" through the size of its demand liabilities.

Clearly, under perfect capital markets the yield on government securities, r_g, must coincide with the rate of interest r. Any attempt on the part of the Central Bank to impose a lower yield could only result in its having to acquire the outstanding stock with a corresponding increase in its liabilities and in the potential money supply. Consider now the situation under the imperfect market model. Here government bonds can be held either by primary lenders or by banks or by intermediaries. Since primary lenders have the choice of holding either governments or claims on intermediaries, their demand for governments, at a given point of time (when their total portfolio can be assumed as given), must be an increasing function of r_g and a decreasing function of r_{in}. Similarly, the demand of intermediaries and banks must be an increasing function of r_g and a decreasing function of r'. Hence, treating r_{in} as a function of r', the total demand for governments might be written as

$$G^d = G(r', r_g).$$

(This function might well include additional variables, such as the size of the rationing gap. However, the simplest formulation above is adequate for present purposes. Note also that the demand depends on initial conditions subsumed in the functional form.) Hence, clearing of market requires $G(r', r_g) = G$. With r' exogenously given, this condition yields the equilibrium value of r_g. In general one might expect $r_g < r' < r_s$, implying that market imperfections of the type under consideration tend to reduce the cost of government borrowing.

To examine the consequence of pegging and unpegging in a context similar to that in which the issue was debated, let us suppose we start from an initial position of full employment equilibrium with the yield on governments at r_g^o. Suppose next that there occurs an upward shift in RR, leading in turn to some rise in r'. Then if the money supply were kept unchanged (or somewhat decreased to offset the rise in velocity) the equilibrium value of r_g would also rise. Suppose, however, the Central Bank tried to peg r_g at the initial level r_g^o. As under perfect market conditions, this pegging could only be accomplished at the cost of permitting an expansion in the money supply, since at r_g^o there would arise an excess supply of government bonds which the Central Bank would be forced to acquire. The expansion in M would, of course, result in an expansion of lending and of aggregate demand, which under full employment would imply inflationary price increases.

Consider next the consequence of dropping the peg and putting an end to monetary expansion. Under perfect market conditions this would result in all rates and yields including r_g moving to that rate $\hat{r}$ which limits real investment demand to the full employment flow of saving; $\hat{r}$ is of course the same as the full employment rate $\hat{r}_s$, given by the intersection of the shifted RR curve with the full employment line $Y/W = (Y/W)$. Especially if investment demand, and hence the RR curve, is very inelastic, the upward shift in RR would result in a large increase in $\hat{r}_s$, implying a correspondingly sharp increase in r_g. But, with market imperfections of the type considered, r_g is controlled by r' and r_{in} and not directly (or at least not significantly) by r_s. Hence, so long as r' does not respond much, at least initially, to the shift in RR and the main effect of the shift is to increase the rationing gap, $\hat{r}_g$ will not be appreciably higher than r_g^o. Hence dropping the pegging policy will not result in sharp change in r_g, at all commensurate to the shift in $\hat{r}_s$, as claimed by the supporters of the availability doctrine. Actually, this conclusion may be considered as a special case of a more general result: because r_g is tied to r', and not directly to r_s^*, rationing not only tends to reduce on the average the cost of government borrowing but also tends to reduce the amplitude of fluctuations in r_g, as compared with what they would be under perfect market conditions.

VI

Some Concluding Remarks: The Role of the Money Supply and the False Dichotomy Between Quantity Theory and Income-Expenditure Theory

By way of conclusion and partial summary of this survey I propose to examine in this section what are the implications of the analysis for the critical question: how important is the role of monetary factors, and particularly of the money supply, as a determinant of the level of money income, output, and prices? Interest in this long-standing issue has been rekindled by a number of recent writings, and particularly by a challenging contribution of Friedman and Meiselman [5] in which the authors suggest that prevailing views in this matter readily fall into two opposing camps. One camp, which may be identified with the quantity theorists, holds that the quantity of money "is a key factor in understanding and even more controlling economic change"; and presumably from this view it is but a short and unavoidable step to accept Friedman's recommendation that discretionary monetary management be replaced by the simple rule of expanding the money supply at a constant rate. The other camp holds that "the stock of money matters little" and is supposed to consist of those embracing the "income-expenditure theory." From the test carried out by Friedman and Meiselman to assess the relative merits of the two points of view, it turns out that the "income-expenditure theory" is operationally defined as the hypothesis that current measured consumption is a linear function of measured disposable income, plus corporate saving, plus corporate profit inventory valuation adjustment, plus a couple of further adjustments.[17]

It should be readily apparent that the view of the monetary mechanism which emerges from this survey — and which I like to think is widely shared at the present time, at least in its broad outline — cannot possibly be forced into either of these camps. Nor is this surprising. In the first place the "income-expenditure theory" as operationally defined above is in no way inconsistent with the quantity theory, at least as defined by Friedman himself, as the hypothesis of stable demand for money (cf. [6], especially page 16). And in the second place both accepting and rejecting either of these theories is perfectly consistent with a wide range of views about the importance of the money supply as a determinant of income, including at one end the view that it is the key factor and, at the other end, the view that it matters not at all.

We suggest that the Friedman and Meiselman analysis, as well as many of the arguments over the importance of money, suffer from a failure to distinguish clearly between endogenous and exogenous forces and between structural relations and "reduced forms."

To make this point clear let us take as a starting point the model underlying the analysis of section IV. It consists of a system of thirteen equations in as many endogenous variables which will, in general, admit of a solution for all the endogenous variables in terms of exogenous variables and the param-

[17] The test actually carried out by Friedman and Meiselman consists in correlating consumption, C, with "offset to saving," A, which is the sum of investment, government deficit, and net exports. But these two variables will be linearly related if and only if C is a linear function $C + A$, which, using well-known accounting identities and definitions, can be readily shown to be equal to the sum of disposable income, corporate savings, corporate inventory valuation adjustment, excess of wage accruals over wage disbursements, and statistical discrepancy (cf. [5], appendix A). We are not aware of any author's having advanced such a formulation of the consumption function and Friedman and Meiselman unfortunately have not provided the reader with any specific reference.

eters of the structural equations. Consider in particular the solution for income Y. So long as wage rigidity holds, we can write this solution as

(i) $Y = f(M, F, [\tau]; W, [p])$

where F and $[\tau]$ are fiscal policy parameters and $[p]$ is the set of relevant parameters of the structural equations, reflecting technology, tastes and initial conditions. Alternative points of view about the importance of money and the real cleavage of opinions can be profitably stated and clarified in terms of the properties of the "reduced form" function f of equation (i) implied by the underlying set of structural relations.[18]

To say that output and prices are totally unaffected by monetary factors means that f does not include M among its arguments. We shall refer to this point of view as the "effective demand only" theory abbreviated as EDO. Clearly, for EDO to be valid the system of equations obtained after deleting (M.2) and (M.3) should contain a determinate subsystem involving P, X, and Y. Furthermore, this subsystem must not involve r; for if it did its solution would also determine uniquely the demand for money (cf. equation M.2) and the value so determined would in general not be equal to the supply; in other words the entire system would then be inconsistent. Among the implications of this result the following are relevant for present purposes.

First, EDO is not equivalent to what is usually called the "theory of effective demand" — the assertion that the level of output is determined by the effective demand for it and not by the productive capacity of the economy. That proposition is hardly more than a truism, even if a fruitful one — just like the proposition that a change in effective demand can affect income only through a change in M or in the velocity of circulation, or both. The essence of EDO is the proposition that effective demand is *totally unaffected by the supply of money either directly or indirectly*.

Second, EDO is perfectly consistent with the quantity theory, as it requires no special assumptions about the demand for money ex-

cept that it should not be a function of X and P only.

Third, EDO bears no relation whatever to the "income-expenditure theory" tested by Friedman and Meiselman. For it requires no special assumption about the form of the consumption function or its stability, except that consumption should not depend on the rate of return from assets. It is true that the "elementary model" frequently used for introducing students to Keynes relies on a linear consumption function, say $C = c_o + cY$, and exogenously given investment, I. This model falls under EDO, but because of the assumption about I and not about the consumption function.

The implications of EDO can be conveniently visualized in terms of Figures 2 and 3. Since the commodity market equations now determine a unique value of Y, say Y^*, totally unrelated to the value of r, the yy curve degenerates to straight line parallel to the abscissa and at a distance Y^*/W_o above it. Of course, the value of Y^* and hence the position of yy depends on parameters of the commodity market equations and on fiscal parameters and this dependence is in fact described by the reduced form f.[19] For instance, in the "elementary classroom model" we have

$$Y^* = (c_o + I)/(1 - c) = f(c_o, c, I)$$

if the government is excluded, and a somewhat more complex expression involving fiscal parameters if the government is included. The intersection of yy and MM determines the rate of interest, which therefore depends on the money supply and is in fact the only variable that monetary policy can affect (cf. [6], p. 17).

Our analysis leads us to reject the EDO theory and hence to the conclusion that M appears as an argument of the reduced form f. For it accepts the view that, in general, an increase in M will result in an increase in effective demand, basically by way of increasing investment demand. This increase in turn may come about partly because the expansion of M will initially tend to reduce the cost of capital (though this reduction may be only

[18] The idea of relying on the reduced form f for contrasting alternative points of view was first suggested to the author by Albert K. Ando.

[19] It might be noted in passing that the EDO model runs into some logical difficulties if the yy curve were to be above the full employment line — i.e., if effective demand were to exceed full employment output.

transitional) and partly because it permits a relaxation of rationing and a larger flow of investment expenditure, financed initially through newly created money and subsequently through the larger flow of money saving.

Consider next the view that income is completely determined by monetary forces, i.e., by the demand for and supply of money, independently of conditions in the "commodity" markets. We shall label this point of view the "money only" theory and abbreviate it as MO. Clearly, for MO to be valid, equations (M.2) and (M.3) must form a *determinate* subsystem involving Y, and M^d. But a two-equation system can be determined only if it contains no more than two unknowns. It follows that a necessary and sufficient condition for the MO theory to be valid is that the demand for money should be a function of Y and Y only, or say $M^d = L(Y)$. Thus, MO is not equivalent to the quantity theory but only to a very special form of it; and it is perfectly consistent with the view that consumption is a linear function of current income and current income only. In fact, it requires no special assumption about any of the other equations of the system, except that r must appear somewhere in these equations.[20]

By equating demand and supply one finds: $M = L(Y)$, implying

(ii) $$Y = L^{-1}(M),$$

where L^{-1} is the inverse of the function L. Comparing this result with (i) we see that under MO the function f is simply L^{-1}, the inverse of the demand function for money. Accordingly, stability of the demand for money implies stability of the function f.

In terms of our figures 2 or 3, MO implies that the MM curve degenerates to a straight line parallel to the abscissa and at a height $(Y/W) = \dfrac{L^{-1}(M)}{W}$. With income already determined by the monetary part, the only function left for the commodity market curve yy is to determine the rate of interest at the point where it crosses the above line. Thus changes

[20] If r were to appear nowhere in the remaining 11 equations these would also form a determinate subsystem in 11 unknowns (the original thirteen minus M^d and r), and its solution for Y would generally be inconsistent with the solution generated by (M.2) and (M.3).

in the commodity market, and in particular in the consumption and investment function, or in fiscal parameters do not affect income at all, but only the rate of interest.[21]

One special case of the MO theory is the "elementary model" frequently used for introducing students to the quantity theory, which takes the form $L(Y) = (1/V)Y$, where the constant V is the velocity of circulation. Then equation (i) becomes $Y = VM$. Under the further assumption that (1) V is in fact constant in time, at least up to a stochastic component which is both unpredictable and uncorrelated with any of the remaining variables of the system; (2) full employment output grows at an approximately constant rate g; and (3) it is desired to make money income grow at a rate which is consistent with the maintenance of full employment, provided prices are stable; one is finally led to the Friedman rule that monetary management should consist exclusively in expanding the money supply at g per cent per year.[22]

Our analysis rejects MO because it acknowledges that the demand for money depends *also* on the rate of interest or, more generally, on the rate of return obtainable by exchanging money for other assets. This dependence, which even Friedman accepts in principle, is amply supported by empirical evidence. To admit that r enters in (ii) — or somewhat loosely that the velocity of circulation depends on r — may appear to require no more than a minor amendment to the MO theory. For, it may be argued, equations (M.2) and (M.3) still imply a relation between income and the

[21] It will be noted that the MO theory as stated is only a theory of the determinants of money income; in order to derive from it propositions about P and X one needs some theory of the relation between these three variables which can only be derived from other equations of the system. In so far as this relation can be established without reference to the "commodity demand equations" (1) and (2), as is true for instance in our own model II (cf. equation 4.b), it can still be said that the level of income is independent of the state of effective demand. And this conclusion remains valid under the somewhat more general demand for money equation $M^d = L(P,X)$.

[22] This policy prescription can be shown to be valid under somewhat more general assumptions than those stated in the text. In particular, if the demand for money can be approximated by the form $L(P,X) = KPX^a$, as Friedman has suggested, then the required expansion of the money supply is $\dot{M}/M = a\,\dot{X}/X = ag$.

money supply, namely $M = L(r,Y)$. In particular suppose for the sake of argument that $L(r,Y)$ is homogeneous in Y and can therefore be written as $L^*(r)Y$. Then solving the above equation for Y we can write

(iii) $Y = V(r)M,$

so that Y is still proportional to M, except that the proportionality factor depends on r. Or, in other words, Y is still controllable through M except that M must be adjusted to offset changes in velocity.

This line of argument however is worthless. For equation (iii) in contrast to (i) is not a reduced form equation; it contains the endogenous variable r which like all other variables is a function of all parameters, including M. Thus whether and to what extent a change in M affects Y depends on its effect on r and $V(r)$, and this effect cannot possibly be inferred from (iii) alone. It depends on what relation exists between Y and r, a relation that can only be derived through the commodity markets and is embodied in the yy curve of Figures 2 and 3. It is only through this relation — which is well defined if EDO does not hold — that we can eliminate r from (iii) and obtain a solution for Y in terms M and other parameters. This solution is, of course, simply the reduced form f.

Because our analysis implies that M appears as an argument of the function f, it agrees with Friedman and Meiselman that the money supply is an important factor in understanding and even in controlling the level of income. But because it also implies that the function f is not merely the inverse of a stable demand function for money but rather the result of a complex interaction of monetary and real forces it leads equally to rejection of the view that the money supply is the only device for controlling Y, that it is always an adequate device, and most of all that it is in any meaningful sense the "cause" of economic instability.

The usefulness of M as a stabilization device depends critically on the nature and form of f. Suppose we fix the value of the fiscal parameters at some stated level, and consider the set of values of Y achievable by varying M (for given W_o). This set may not include the full employment value $(\hat{Y}/W)$. In terms of Figures 2 and 3 this will happen whenever the yy curve intersects the full employment line sufficiently far to the left — the so-called liquidity trap. There will then be a ceiling to Y/W short of $\hat{Y}/W$, either because r and Y approach some asymptote, or because beyond a point the money authority loses the power of expanding the money supply. We suggest that the real cleavage of expert opinion is not at all between those who hold the MO doctrine and those holding the EDO doctrine but rather revolves around whether $\hat{Y}$ is achievable by monetary policy nearly all of the time, only some of the time, or hardly ever. We are inclined toward the first-mentioned view, at least for reasonable values of the fiscal parameters — say values implying an approximately balanced budget in the neighborhood of full employment. But we are ready to admit that this view is debatable and that, in any event, the past is not necessarily a good guide to the future.

In so far as $\hat{Y}$ is achievable by monetary policy, if a larger or smaller value of Y is allowed to develop one might be justified in saying that the accompanying unemployment or price rise results from an inadequate or excessive money supply. But this is quite different from saying that therefore the behavior of the money supply is the *cause* of instability. In the first place, because money is not the only possible tool for stabilization and not necessarily the best (cf. section IV), failure to avoid fluctuations could be attributed to fiscal policy as well as to inadequacies in the money supply. Second, and much more important, recognition that the relation between Y and M embodied in the function f depends not only on the demand for money but also on the remaining equations of the system has widespread implications. If f were simply the inverse of the demand for money equation, as asserted by MO, and if one also accepted the various other assumptions that justify the Friedman rule, then it would indeed follow that departures of Y from its stable path could be attributed only to autonomous departure of the money supply from the growth path implied by the rule. But this conclusion becomes invalid, even if the demand for money is quite stable, once we recognize that the function f will shift around under the impact of shifts in the demand functions for commodities. Such shifts will cause deviations of Y from the desired path even though M is on the path. Even if these deviations could be offset by appropriate changes in M, we cannot say that M is the cause of instability any more than we can say that the fact that headache can be avoided by taking aspirin makes aspirin the cause of

headaches. The cause of the instability lies in these shifts and not in autonomous changes in M. On the contrary such changes are necessary if the shifts in the commodity markets are to be effectively offset. Thus, just because this analysis agrees with Friedman's on the importance of money and on the stability of the demand for money it leads to a categorical rejection of the notion of entrusting the control of the money supply to his simple mechanical rule.

BIBLIOGRAPHY

1. Ando, A. K. and Modigliani, F., "The 'Life Cycle' Hypothesis of Saving: Aggregative Implications and Tests," *American Economic Review*, Mar. 1963, pp. 55–84.
2. Bronfenbrenner, M. and Mayer, T., "Liquidity Functions in the American Economy," *Econometrica*, Oct. 1960.
3. Buchanan, J. M., *Public Principles of the Public Debt*, Irwin, 1958.
4. Fforde, J. S., "The Monetary Controversy in the U.S.A.," *Oxford Economic Papers*, Oct. 1951.
5. Friedman, M. and Meiselman, D., "The Relative Stability of Monetary Velocity and the Investment Multiplier in the United States, 1897–1958," in *Stabilization Policies* (in press, 1963), Prentice-Hall for the Commission on Money and Credit.
6. Friedman, M., ed., *Studies in the Quantity Theory of Money*, University of Chicago Press, 1956.
7. Friedman, M., *A Theory of the Consumption Function*, Princeton University Press, for National Bureau of Economic Research, 1957.
8. Gurley, J. G. and Shaw, E. S., *Money in a Theory of Finance*, Brookings, 1960.
9. Hahn, F., "The Rate of Interest and General Equilibrium Analysis," *Economic Journal*, Mar. 1955, pp. 52–66.
10. Kareken, J. H., "Lenders' Preferences, Credit Rationing and the Effectiveness of Monetary Policy," *Review of Economics and Statistics*, Aug. 1957, pp. 292–302.
11. Keynes, J. M., *The General Theory of Employment, Interest and Money*, Harcourt, Brace, 1935.
12. Latané, H. A., "Income Velocity and Interest Rates: A Pragmatic Approach," *Review of Economics and Statistics*, Nov. 1960, pp. 445–449.
13. Modigliani, F., "Liquidity Preference and the Theory of Interest and Money," *Econometrica*, Jan. 1944, pp. 45–88; reprinted in *Readings in Monetary Theory*, and in *The Critics of Keynes*, ed. by H. Hazlitt, pp. 131–184, with a 1960 postscript.
14. Modigliani, F., and Brumberg, R., "Utility Analysis and the Consumption Function: An Interpretation of Cross-Section Data," in *Post Keynesian*

Economics, ed., K. Kurihara, Rutgers University Press, 1954, pp. 388–436.
15. Modigliani, F., *Lecture Notes on Monetary Theory*, Carnegie Institute of Technology, Spring Term, 1955 (dittoed).
16. Modigliani, F. and Ando, A. K., "The 'Permanent Income' and the 'Life Cycle' Hypothesis of Saving Behavior: Comparison and Tests," in *Consumption and Saving*, ed. by Friend and Jones, University of Pennsylvania Press, 1960, Vol. 2, pp. 49–174.
17. Modigliani, F. and Miller, M. H., "Dividend Policy, Growth, and the Valuation of Shares," *Journal of Business*, Oct. 1961, pp. 411–433.
18. Modigliani, F., "Long Run Implications of Alternative Fiscal Policies and the Burden of the National Debt," *Economic Journal*, Dec. 1961, pp. 411–433.
19. Patinkin, D., "Financial Intermediaries and the Logical Structure of Monetary Theory, A Review Article," *American Economic Review*, Mar. 1961, pp. 95–116.
20. Patinkin, D., "Relative Prices, Say's Law and the Demand for Money," *Econometrica*, Apr. 1948.
21. Patinkin, D., *Money, Interest and Prices*, Row-Petersen, 1956.
22. Pigou, A. C., "The Classical Stationary State," *Economic Journal*, 1948, pp. 343–351.
23. Pigou, A. C., "Economic Progress in a Stable Environment," *Economica*, N. S. 1947, pp. 180–190; reprinted in *Readings in Monetary Theory*.
24. Roosa, R. V., "Interest Rates and the Central Bank," in *Money, Trade and Economic Growth*: In Honor of John H. Williams, New York, Macmillan, 1951.
25. Roosa, R. V., "The Revival of Monetary Policy," *Review of Economics and Statistics*, Feb. 1951, pp. 29–37.
26. Samuelson, P. and Solow, R., "Analytical Aspects of Anti-Inflation Policy," *American Economic Review*, May 1959, pp. 177–194.
27. Scitovsky, T., "Capital, Accumulation, Employment and Price Rigidity," *Review of Economic Studies*, Vol. VIII, pp. 69–88.

28. Smith, W., "On the Effectiveness of Monetary Policy," *American Economic Review*, Sept. 1956, V. 46, No. 4.

29. Stedry, A. C., "A Note on Interest Rates and the Demand for Money," *Review of Economics and Statistics*, Aug. 1959.

30. Teigen, R. L., "Demand and Supply Functions for Money in the United States: Some Structural Estimates," doctoral dissertation, M.I.T., 1962.

31. Weintraub, S., *A General Theory of the Price Level, Output, Income Distribution and Economic Growth*, Philadelphia, 1959.

Errata

Page 80, equation 5a: "$X_N(N, K_0 = W/P$" should read "$X_N(N, K_0) = W/P$."

Page 85, figure 1: label on broken curve, "$L'(M = \overline{M}' = \lambda/\overline{M})$" should read "$L'(M = \overline{M}' = \lambda\overline{M})$."

Page 86, column 2, line 9: "money supply $\overline{M}*'$" should read "money supply $\overline{M}'$."

Page 89, column 2, 5 lines from the bottom: "$C\ddagger$" and "I_r" should be interchanged.

Page 95, column 1, footnote 13, line 2: "$dX/dF)t_x > 1$" should read "$(dX/dF)t_x > 1$."

rate of interest (see, for example, p. 168). Since the *General Theory* the term "liquidity preference" has come to be used to refer to the hypothesis or theory that the aggregate quantity of money demanded by the economy will, *ceteris paribus*, tend to be smaller the higher the rate of interest.

Keynes's analysis of the systematic and intimate relation between the demand for money and interest rates and its implications is generally acknowledged to be one of his major contributions to economics. It is one of the two main pillars on which the edifice of the *General Theory* rests, the other being the hypothesis that in a contemporary monetary economy, money prices and especially money wages tend to be rigid in the downward direction (see "Liquidity preference, monetary theory and monetary management," below).

The demand for money

Pre-Keynesian theories. Information about the history of theories of the demand for money may be found elsewhere [*see especially* MONEY, *articles on* QUANTITY THEORY *and* VELOCITY OF CIRCULATION; *see also* Marget 1938 *and* Patinkin 1956, pp. 373–472]. It will suffice to recall here that although monetary theorists had long recognized that money is a "store of value" as well as a "medium of exchange," prevailing theories of the demand for money before the *General Theory* tended to stress the role of money as a medium of exchange and the "transaction demand." The two major, broadly accepted formulations before the *General Theory* were that of Irving Fisher and that of the Cambridge school. Fisher (1911) started from the now well-known identity called Fisher's equation of exchange: $MV \equiv PT$, where M is the quantity of money in circulation, T is the volume of transactions, P is the price level, and V is the "transaction velocity of circulation." This equation is also frequently restated as $MV_y \equiv PX \equiv Y$, where X is "real income," Y is money income, and V_y is the "income velocity of circulation." From these identities Fisher derived his theory by hypothesizing (1) that at a given point of time V can be taken as constant (or at least as largely independent of M) and (2) that V tends to change, at best, very slowly over time, being largely determined by institutional and technological factors with a high degree of inertia. The major factors of this kind include the frequency of receipts and disbursements (intimately related in turn to the so-called income period, which is the length of the interval between the dates at which various types of income, such as wages, salaries, and dividends, are typically paid), the degree of synchronization of

LIQUIDITY PREFERENCE

"Liquidity preference" is a term that was coined by John Maynard Keynes in *The General Theory of Employment, Interest and Money* to denote the functional relation between the quantity of money demanded and the variables determining it (1936, p. 166). He also used this term, or such variants of it as "liquidity preference function" and "liquidity function," to denote more narrowly the relation between the quantity of money demanded and the receipts and expenditures, prevailing financial arrangements, the rapidity of transportation, and so on. [*See* MONEY, *article on* VELOCITY OF CIRCULATION*.*]

By contrast, the so-called Cambridge school tried to put the explanation of the demand for money into the more familiar format of value theory, i.e., in terms of a demand-for-money equation, $M^d = kY$, an exogenously given supply of money, M, and a clearing-of-market equation, $M^d = M$, implying $M = kY$ (see, e.g., Pigou 1917; Marshall 1923). By comparing this equation with Fisher's equation above, one can readily see that $k = 1/V_y$, i.e., that k is the reciprocal of the velocity of circulation. Indeed, in analyzing the determinants of k and the reasons for its hypothesized stability, the Cambridge school tended to stress largely the same forces on which Fisher's theory rests.

The Fisher and Cambridge models are generally regarded as providing the definitive basis for the so-called "quantity theory of money," a view of very old standing according to which the price level, P, tends to be directly proportional to M. In order for this relationship to follow logically from these models, not only must M not affect V (or k), as those models imply, but also one must suppose that money is "neutral" in the wider sense that it does not affect any of the "real" variables of the system—inputs, outputs, and relative prices, including interest rates. Under this assumption, which, as shown below (see "The significance of liquidity theory under wage flexibility"), might provide a reasonable approximation under conditions of perfect wage and price flexibility, real income, X, may be taken as fixed at the "full employment" level, say $\bar{X}$. From either the Fisher or the Cambridge equation it then follows that

$$P = \left(\frac{V_y}{\bar{X}}\right) M = \left(\frac{1}{k\bar{X}}\right) M,$$

that is, the price level is proportional to the quantity of money, M.

It should be acknowledged that some of the writers in the Cambridge tradition did at times suggest that the demand for money might depend on wealth and that they did make some occasional references to the possible influence of interest rates (see, for example, Pigou [1917] 1951, p. 166; Lavington 1921, p. 30; Marshall 1923, chapter 4; for still earlier references, see Eshag 1963, pp. 13–14). But they failed to explore systematically the effect of interest rates on the demand for money and the implications of this effect. This failure is even more conspicuous in Fisher. He makes no mention of interest rates in his list of

factors affecting velocity, and although he makes fleeting mention of the "waste of interest" involved in holding money (1911, p. 152), one finds no reference to this passage in the index under the rubric "interest rates."

Two authors who anticipated Keynes in giving adequate recognition to the role of interest rates are Walras, in 1899, and Schlesinger, in 1914 (see Patinkin 1956, notes C and D), but their contributions were largely overlooked at the time. The most significant pre-Keynesian analysis of liquidity preference is generally acknowledged to be that of Hicks (1935), which, however, preceded the *General Theory* by but one year and was partly inspired by Keynes's earlier work, *A Treatise on Money*, published in 1930. This contribution to monetary theory, which in some respects has turned out to be even more influential for further developments than that of Keynes, will be touched upon below.

Keynes's theory. In chapters 13 and 15 of the *General Theory*, Keynes distinguished three "motives" for holding money. The first, the "transaction motive"—sometimes broken down into an income motive and a business motive—corresponds quite closely to the motives stressed by Fisher and the Cambridge school. Like his predecessors, Keynes did not regard transaction balances as being significantly affected by interest rates. The second motive is the "precautionary motive." Under this heading Keynes included balances not earmarked for some definite expenditure in the near future but held instead to "provide for contingencies requiring sudden expenditure and for unforeseen opportunities of advantageous purchases" (1936, p. 196). But why should these balances be kept in the form of idle cash instead of being invested in some kind of readily marketable securities, to be converted into cash if and when the contingency arises? The reason is that the market value of a debt instrument (or "bond"), if it is liquidated before its maturity, is uncertain, even if there is absolutely no risk of default. It depends on the market rate of interest prevailing at the future time of liquidation for loans having a duration equal to the remaining life of the bond: the higher this rate, the lower the market value. This uncertainty about the realization value of a bond would not by itself make bonds inferior to cash as a store of ready purchasing power if the sum of the uncertain liquidation value and the cash interest earned could be counted on to exceed the amount initially invested. However, there can be no such assurance, since between the times of purchase and liquidation interest rates could rise sufficiently to produce a capital loss in excess of the interest earned. Keynes suggested in particular that the likelihood of a net loss would be larger the smaller the yield of the bond originally acquired. This is because the smaller the yield, the smaller the rise in the rate of interest (in absolute as well as in percentage terms) that will produce a capital loss sufficient to wipe out the accrued interest earned. Furthermore, Keynes suggested that if the current rate is low by historical standards, it will usually be regarded as more likely to rise than to fall. He concluded that the lower the current rate, r, the stronger the incentive to hold precautionary reserves in the form of cash instead of securities. Therefore the (real) demand to hold money for precautionary reasons will tend to be inversely related to r. At the same time, somewhat surprisingly, Keynes did not appear to regard precautionary balances as very sensitive to r. Accordingly, much of the time he lumped together the demand for transaction and for precautionary reasons and regarded the sum, which he labeled M_1, as primarily controlled by—or a function of—current income. Thus, in his notation $M_1 = L_1(Y)$, where the function L_1 denotes the demand for money resulting from the transaction and precautionary motives.

The third and remaining source of demand for money is the speculative motive, a rather complex mechanism that Keynes had partly anticipated in *A Treatise on Money* (1930). In essence, speculative balances are balances held in cash rather than invested in (long-term) bonds, not just because of the risk that interest rates might rise but rather because of a definite expectation that the price of long-term bonds is likely to fall, and at a rate that more than offsets the interest earned by holding them. A person entertaining such an expectation would prefer to hold cash yielding nothing rather than invest it in what he regards as overpriced long-term bonds that would yield him a negative return. Since the price of long-term bonds varies inversely with long-term interest rates, we may equally well characterize speculative balances as those held by persons who regard the current long-term rate as untenably low and about to rise sufficiently rapidly.

The real significance of the speculative motive is that it may significantly impair, or even thwart altogether, efforts of the central bank to reduce long-term interest rates to the extent necessary to maintain investment at the level consistent with full utilization of resources (see "Liquidity preference, monetary theory, and monetary management," below). Normally, the central bank can expect to enforce lower long-term interest rates, or higher prices of long-term bonds, by buying such

bonds with newly created money. Suppose, however, that a large portion of the market holds definite views about the minimum maintainable level of the long-term rate and hence the maximum maintainable level of bond prices. If, then, the bank attempts to bid up the price of bonds to that maximum or beyond, it will find the public prepared to dump a large portion of its long-term bond holding. The bank will therefore have very little success in lowering the long-term rate, even though it is prepared to acquire a large volume of bonds and to expand the money supply correspondingly. What happens in this situation is that the increase in the money supply is absorbed, not by an increased transaction demand, but by an offsetting increase in the speculative demand, with a resulting fall in the velocity of circulation. In other words, the expansion in M, instead of achieving the desired expansion in income, Y, that would occur if V_y, the velocity of circulation, remained constant, tends to generate an offsetting change in V_y, with little effect on Y. A situation of this type has come to be known in the Keynesian literature as a "liquidity trap."

Keynes denoted speculative balances by M_2 and wrote the demand function for such balances as $M_2 = L_2(r)$, where L_2 is a decreasing function of r (1936, p. 199). This formulation—that M_2 increases as r falls—is somewhat misleading, since presumably M_2 should depend not on r as such but only on r in relation to the prevailing market expectations about the maintainable rate, say r^e. Nor can r^e be supposed to stay constant through time or to be uniquely related to r itself. Keynes's formulation might be defended as a useful "short run" approximation: at a given point in time, r^e can be taken as a constant or, at least, as changing more slowly than r. Hence, a fall in r would necessarily imply a fall *relative* to r^e and thus a rise in M_2 (*ibid.*, pp. 201–202). Under this interpretation, however, one should be aware that L_2 may be subject to significant shifts through time as a result of shifts in market expectations.

The sum of the transaction and precautionary demand, M_1, and the speculative demand, M_2, is the total demand for money proposed by Keynes: $M = M_1 + M_2 = L_1(Y) + L_2(r)$ (*ibid.*, p. 199). The Keynesian literature has tended to de-emphasize the sharp distinction between the three motives for holding money and to write the demand for money in the more general form $M = L(r, Y)$. There has also been a tendency to minimize the role of interest expectations, r^e, and to associate the liquidity trap with a low *absolute* level of the interest rate. The implied relation between M and r for a

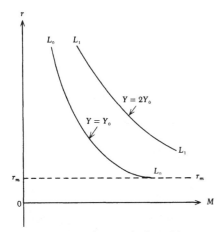

Figure 1 — Relation between the demand for money and the interest rate

given value of Y, say Y_0, is shown in Figure 1 by the curve labeled $L_0 L_0$. (The choice of coordinates is dictated by the economists' peculiar convention, popularized by Marshall, of representing demand curves with the quantity demanded measured on the abscissa and the price on the ordinate.) The quantity of money demanded increases continuously as r falls, until, for some sufficiently low value, r_m, the liquidity trap is reached and the curve becomes horizontal (the demand becomes infinitely elastic). Alternatively, the demand curve might be drawn to approach the level r_m asymptotically. Just how low r_m may be depends somewhat on "institutional" factors and on whether r is understood to be the long-term or the short-term rate. But we can, with complete generality, place a lower bound on r_m: in a monetary economy, r_m can never be more negative than the (marginal) cost of storing money. In particular, when money is an intangible, the cost of storing it (at least in the form of bank deposits) is essentially zero, and therefore r_m cannot be (significantly) negative. Indeed, a negative r can be regarded as a premium paid by the lender to the borrower for carrying money over; for example, a short-term rate of -2 per cent per period means that the lender is willing to pay $100 to receive only $98 at the end of the period. If the cost of storing is less than 2 per cent, everybody would wish to borrow indefinitely large amounts, since by merely holding the money one would earn the excess of 2 per cent over storage costs. This implies in particular that with a zero

(marginal) storage cost, at a negative rate of interest the demand for money must become indefinitely large—or, equivalently, that no matter how large the quantity of money, r can never be negative. Hence, the demand curve must tend to approach a horizontal asymptote, $r = r_m$ (or possibly reach it from above for some finite M and become discontinuous). Furthermore, r_m cannot be lower than zero (quite generally, it cannot be more negative than the marginal cost of storing money), although it may well be higher, as in Figure 1.

The curve labeled $L_1 L_1$ illustrates the effect on the demand for money of increasing Y, say from Y_0 to $2Y_0$ in Figure 1. Clearly, the demand for money must be greater at any given rate r; that is, LL must shift to the right. The relation between $L_0 L_0$ and $L_1 L_1$ becomes especially simple if the demand function $L(r, Y)$ takes a more specialized form, which was suggested, for example, by Pigou (1917) and tested by Latané (1954; 1960) and which has been gaining favor in recent writings—namely, $M = k(r)Y = Y/V(r)$. This formulation provides an obvious bridge between Keynes's original formulation and the received Fisher and Cambridge models. It implies that for a given r the fraction k (or the velocity of circulation, V) will be constant but that k will tend to fall (or V to rise) as the rate of interest rises. In terms of Figure 1, it implies that $L_1 L_1$ is obtainable from $L_0 L_0$ by multiplying by 2 the abscissa value of $L_0 L_0$ corresponding to any given r. More generally, it implies that the LL curve corresponding to any given Y is simply the graph of $k(r)$, up to a proportionality factor, Y. Similarly, the graph of $V(r)$,

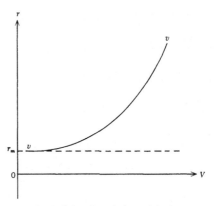

Figure 2 — Velocity of circulation and the interest rate

the velocity of circulation as a function of the interest rate, is the graph of the reciprocal of L_0L_0 up to a proportionality factor, $1/Y_0$. The general shape of the graph of $V(r)$ is shown by the vv curve of Figure 2.

Post-Keynesian developments. As indicated earlier, post-Keynesian developments of liquidity theory were inspired not only by Keynes's *General Theory* but at least as much by two germinal ideas advanced by Hicks (1935). Hicks's first suggestion was that the major reason why transactors hold money balances having little or no yield when they could invest them in a large number of income-yielding assets, some at least not significantly less safe than money, is to be found in the costs and the "bother" of the transactions necessary to move from money into earning assets and back to money (p. 19).

The portfolio approach. Hicks's second suggestion was that the theory of the demand for money must be developed out of a more general theory of the allocation of wealth among various assets. This theory, Hicks suggested, should be analogous to the standard theory of consumers' choice, except that the object of choice, instead of being consumption flows, would be the various stocks appearing on the asset and liability side of the balance sheet, and prices would be replaced by expected yields. He saw this substitution as presenting a real challenge, since yields in contrast to prices would have to be recognized as uncertain, and this uncertainty in turn would have important implications for the nature of choices.

Both ideas have been extensively pursued with the help of the emergence of the theory of choice under uncertainty [see DECISION MAKING, *article on* ECONOMIC ASPECTS]. At present the major differences of view between monetary theorists (and they are not very major) seem related to the relative importance assigned to each of Hicks's two ideas.

Among those who have pursued the portfolio, or wealth, approach, the formulation of Friedman (1956), developed in numerous writings, has been particularly influential [see MONEY, *article on* QUANTITY THEORY]. Friedman views the demand for money as being determined by wealth (broadly understood as the present value of expected net future receipts from all sources), by the distribution of wealth between human and nonhuman (i.e., marketable) wealth, by the expected yield of all major types of assets that are alternatives to money as ways of holding wealth, and by the "utility attached to the services rendered by money" relative to other assets—namely, bonds, equities,

and physical commodities. By combining this theory with his suggestion (1957) for ways of approximating wealth (or, more precisely, "permanent income," which is, however, essentially proportional to wealth as defined above) Friedman has endeavored to cast his theory in testable form and actually to test it (1959). He has concluded that his model fits the facts well, in that the demand for money increases with wealth and more than in proportion, although he can find little evidence that interest rates in fact play a significant role.

Other authors have been more concerned with developing and refining theoretical aspects of the Keynes–Hicks approach (see the very useful survey provided by Johnson 1962). Among their attempts, especially worth noting are the recent contribution of Turvey (1960) and the elegant formulation of the theory of choice between money and bonds of various maturities developed by Tobin (1958) along the lines of the modern theory of portfolio selection.

Transaction costs and the Neo-Fisherian approach. The portfolio approach suffers from one major inadequacy. As long as there exist any interest-bearing obligations that are issued by creditworthy borrowers and are of sufficiently short maturity—for example, redeemable on demand or on very short notice—it is impossible to explain why any portion of the portfolio should be held in the form of money, yielding less or nothing at all—except by explicit analysis of the role of transaction costs.

Even Keynes's stricture that, for sufficiently low interest rates, money may dominate bonds because of the uncertainty of the realization value cannot apply to short maturities or demand loans. These instruments dominate money in every possible dimension: they are equally safe, they yield an income, and they can be converted into the medium of exchange, if and when it is needed, at face value. Why, then, should anyone hold money, except for the very instant he receives a payment or is about to make one? The necessary and sufficient condition, as Hicks rightly pointed out, is that out-of-pocket costs and the effort required in moving from cash to bonds and back to cash exceed the yield. At first sight these transaction costs may appear too trivial to account for any substantial holding of cash, let alone for the observed cash holdings. (Aggregate cash holdings of U.S. consumers at the end of 1963 were estimated to represent slightly less than two months' income.) But this casual impression is misleading. It is well known, for instance, from the theory of optimum inventory holdings that transaction costs do account for a substantial portion of inventories held by business (which in the United States amount to some three months' sales). This parallel between business inventories and cash holdings is not fortuitous, for in many respects the holding of a stock of cash by transactors is closely analogous to the holding of a stock of goods by business. In fact, Allais (1947, chapter 8a) and Baumol (1952) pioneered in showing that the holding of cash balances could be analyzed by a straightforward application of the so-called lot-size formula of inventory theory: in order to avoid incurring too frequently the costs involved in transforming securities into cash, it pays to secure cash in a bulk or "lot" that will take care of expenditure requirements for a certain length of time, even though interest will be forgone on the amount withdrawn. Similarly, if a transactor is receiving money in a more or less continuous trickle, it will pay to accumulate a "lot" before investing it. The size of the lot, and hence the average cash balance held relative to the rate of outpayments (or receipts), which corresponds to the Cambridge k or to the reciprocal of the velocity of circulation, will be positively associated with the size of transaction costs and inversely associated with the rate of interest. Tobin (1956) refined and improved on this analysis, applying it more specifically to the consumer receiving his income in bulk at income-payment dates and spending it gradually over the income period.

Although these contributions are to be regarded as illustrative rather than as aimed at deriving an exact demand equation for money, they do point up one very fundamental principle. The amount that can be earned by investing an amount of cash, m, that will not be needed to meet expenditures for some span of time, t, in a security yielding r per cent per year, is approximately $m(tr - c)$, where c is the brokerage fee, if any, per dollar of investment. The investment will not be worthwhile unless this product exceeds the lump-sum cost of the two-way transaction, including both the out-of-pocket and the bother costs. To illustrate the order of magnitudes involved, suppose that a person earns $12,000 a year, paid monthly; he then receives $1,000 once a month. Suppose he spends these receipts at an even rate. He might then consider keeping half the sum for current expenditure and investing the remaining half, or $500, which he will not need until the first half is exhausted—that is, for half a month. Suppose the yield of a 15-day security, net of commissions, is 3 per cent per year; then all he stands to earn

from the transaction is $500 × .03/24, or a mere 62.5 cents. If the two-way transaction cost and bother exceeds this, he will invest none of the monthly receipts and thus will end up holding, on this account, an average cash balance of $500, or 1/24 of his (annual) income. Note that if he were paid twice as frequently—that is, $500 every two weeks—it would a fortiori not pay him to bother, and he would be holding an average cash balance of $250, or 1/48 of his income.

The conclusion to be drawn from these illustrations can be summarized as follows: In a money-using economy, transactors are paid in money and in turn must pay in money; lack of synchronization between receipts and payments gives rise to pools of money that will not be needed for some length of time. Given the rate of return and the cost and effort of transactions, it will not pay to invest such pools unless the product of their size and the length of the "idle" time exceeds some critical threshold level. Thus, the basic reason for holding idle cash balances is not that they provide a useful service but simply that it does not pay to shed them. Obviously, given the rate of interest, the extent to which it does not pay to shed idle money, and thus the average cash balance held, will depend on such institutional-technological factors as (a) transaction costs—the higher the cost, the smaller the incentive to shed; (b) the size and nature of the transactor's business —large transactors may be confronted with pools so large that it pays to shed them even for very short periods, and they may also have an incentive to set themselves up so as to minimize marginal transaction costs; and (c) the frequency of income payment and settlement dates—the greater the frequency, the smaller the average cash balance. But these are, by and large, precisely the factors emphasized by Fisher in explaining the determinants of the velocity of circulation. The new element is the recognition that given all these factors, the average cash balance demanded will tend to fall with the rate of interest, which provides the incentive to shed.

How does the Keynesian liquidity trap fit into this model? The first point to be noted is that Keynes's theory of the speculative demand suffers from his excessive concentration on long-term bonds as the alternative to cash, to the neglect of short-term instruments. The proposition that people will flee from long-term bonds when the price of those bonds is deemed to be untenably high seems valid enough, but the obvious abode for the funds accruing from moving out of long-term bonds should be short-term ones, not cash.

However, a massive endeavor to move from long-term into short-term instruments will unavoidably depress short-term rates, perhaps to such an extent that for many investors the investment will no longer be worth the effort. Thus, they may eventually end up holding cash, but because of the low level of short-term rates, not directly in response to the low level of long-term rates. In short, the central bank's endeavor to depress long-term rates by buying bonds and increasing the money supply can always be counted on to depress short-term rates. However, it may not be very successful in depressing long-term rates to the desired extent, except insofar as a persistent low level of the short-term rate may eventually persuade the public that the long-term rate is really not unreasonably low. A good example of such a development is provided by the United States in the late 1930s. Because of a sizable monetary expansion after 1932, by 1939–1940 the short-term rate on government bills had been driven down very nearly to zero (below 2/10 of 1 per cent), but the long-term rate on high-grade bonds was still hovering around 3 per cent (down from about 4.7 per cent in 1929). In this sense the Keynesian liquidity trap must still be acknowledged as a possible serious hindrance to the effectiveness of monetary policy. And in any event, the proposition that no market rate—long or short—can ever be negative retains its validity.

The theory that emerges from the preceding discussion emphasizes the flow of transactions (and therefore income rather than wealth) and interest rates, especially the short rate and the rate on savings deposits, as the main arguments of the demand function for money. It further suggests that the parameters of this function are largely determined by the forces emphasized by Fisher and should therefore tend to change at best slowly through time. Because the model represents an obvious blend of the motives emphasized by Fisher and by Keynes and Hicks, we have referred to it as the Neo-Fisherian approach (although this terminology is not in general use).

Although the contrast between the "portfolio" approach and the "transaction" approach has deliberately been emphasized here, it is well to recognize that the difference between these two models is minor—largely a matter of relative emphasis—both in principle and in terms of practical implications. In particular, these models concur in the conclusion that the demand for money should be "homogeneous of first degree in current prices"—that is, that a change in the price level, other things being equal, should give rise to a propor-

tional change in the demand for money while leaving unaffected "real demand" (demand measured in terms of purchasing power over commodities).

Empirical verification. Since the appearance of the *General Theory*, considerable effort has been devoted to assessing empirically the responsiveness of the demand for money to variations in interest rates and more generally to estimating demand functions for money and testing their stability (see, for the United States, Johnson 1962, pp. 354–357).

These investigations have tended to confirm that the demand for money is positively and closely associated with income or wealth or both and that a change in the price level tends to result in a proportional change in demand. They have also overwhelmingly tended to confirm that this demand is significantly responsive to changes in interest rates in the direction hypothesized by Keynes. The only significant exception in this regard is Friedman's results, cited in the section "The portfolio approach," above. His contrary conclusions, however, have been criticized for being very much dependent on the specific definition of money he uses (which includes means of payment and some, but not all, savings deposits), on the specific period chosen for his tests, and on his statistical techniques. They have also been criticized because his model, although it apparently fits the period from the second half of the last century to the late 1940s quite well, is not able to account for the very significant rise in velocity that has occurred since the beginning of the 1950s, concomitantly with the marked rise in interest rates. In particular, Meltzer (1963) and Brunner and Meltzer (1964), who otherwise fully sympathize with Friedman's basic theory, have found marked and significant interest-rate effects, whether one uses as additional variables income, or permanent income, or a measure of nonhuman wealth. The major novelty in their results is the strong showing of the nonhuman wealth variable as compared with current income, although these results contrast with those reported by other investigators using a different measure of wealth (e.g., Bronfenbrenner & Mayer 1960). On the whole, it seems fair to say that at the moment the evidence is not adequate for the fine discrimination between the wealth and the neo-Fisherian formulations of the demand for money.

Liquidity preference, monetary theory, and monetary management

The Keynesian revolution. As suggested earlier, the two major analytical contributions of the *Gen-*

eral Theory are the hypotheses of liquidity preference and of wage rigidity. The systematic analysis of the implications of these two highly fruitful hypotheses and their interaction was made more powerful and incisive by a third novelty, which is primarily methodological. This is the development of "aggregative analysis," or what has since come to be known as macroeconomic analysis. Economists had long before been used to analyzing economic variables as reflecting the interaction of simultaneous relations, and the notion of equilibrium was used precisely to denote the value of the variables simultaneously satisfying all the relevant relations. However, before the *General Theory* this method of analysis was generally applied in so-called "partial equilibrium analysis," that is, the study of some portion of the economy—say, the market for a particular commodity or a group of interrelated commodities. The method had also been applied with some success, largely by Walras, to the economy as a whole in "general equilibrium analysis," which formally recognizes the interactions of all possible markets, treating the economy as a very large scale closed system of simultaneous equations. The novelty of aggregative analysis consists in lumping together a large number of commodities having common characteristics for the problem at hand and treating the aggregate as a single commodity. This approach makes possible the approximation of the whole economy with a small system of simultaneous relations, and, by permitting closer scrutiny and understanding of the interactions, it has proved to be highly fruitful.

Analysts of Keynes's work have correctly pointed out that none of these basic ingredients of the *General Theory*—liquidity preference, wage rigidity, or the aggregative approach—was entirely new. We have documented this point above with respect to liquidity preference. The novelty consisted in the masterly way in which the ingredients were blended, which enabled Keynes to provide an analytical explanation of the phenomenon of unemployment and its possible persistence in an advanced capitalistic economy and to shed new light on the role and limitations of monetary and fiscal policy in controlling the level of employment and prices. It is this achievement, and its enormous impact on economics, that has since come to be known as the Keynesian revolution.

The rest of this section, relying largely on aggregative analysis, endeavors to sketch out the role of liquidity preference, first under the classical assumptions of perfect wage and price flexibility and then in combination with the empirically far more relevant hypothesis of downward wage rigid-

ity. Our focus is primarily on the significance of liquidity preference as seen *today*, some thirty years after the appearance of the *General Theory*, rather than on summarizing or criticizing Keynes's original formulation. Accordingly, in what follows, the post-Keynesian elaborations are freely drawn upon.

The basic model. In Keynes's *General Theory* and, more particularly, in later endeavors by other authors to formalize its message (e.g., Hicks 1937; Lange 1938; Modigliani 1944; 1963; Patinkin 1956), the whole economy is reduced (explicitly or implicitly) to four aggregates: aggregate output, X; labor, N; money, M; and bonds, B. For each of these aggregate commodities there is a "market" characterized by supply conditions, demand conditions, and the "clearing-of-market" or equilibrium requirement that demand must equal supply. Demand and supply, in turn, are controlled by three prices or terms of trade between each commodity and money: P, the price of output (the "price level"); W, the price of labor (the "wage rate"); and $1 + r$, the number of dollars obtainable next period by lending a dollar today, where r is the rate of interest. To understand the mechanism determining the level of economic activity in a given short interval and the role of liquidity preference, we must examine the structure of the four markets and their interaction.

The demand for output in the commodity market, usually referred to in the literature as "aggregate demand" and denoted here by X^d, is a central construct of Keynesian analysis. It has given rise to a voluminous literature, both theoretical and empirical, which can be summarized here very briefly, since it is covered in other articles [*see in particular* INCOME AND EMPLOYMENT THEORY; CONSUMPTION FUNCTION; INVESTMENT, *article on* THE AGGREGATE INVESTMENT FUNCTION]. Two sources of demand are distinguished: current consumption, C, and investment demand, I—i.e., demand for current output destined to increase the stock of productive capital. Thus, $X^d = C + I$. Theoretical considerations, and the empirical evidence, suggest that consumption in turn is primarily controlled by (*a*) the level of real income and that, disregarding for the moment the fiscal activity of the government sector, can be equated with aggregate output, X; (*b*) net real private wealth, A; and possibly (*c*) the rate of interest, r. This can be formalized by means of the "consumption function," $C = \mathcal{C}(X, A, r)$. Investment demand can be taken to be positively associated with aggregate output and negatively associated with the rate of interest and the pre-existing stock of capital, K_0; thus,

$I = \mathcal{I}(r_0, X, K_0)$. Finally, net private real wealth, A, the sum of all privately held assets minus private debt, can be expressed as $A = K_0 + G/P$; that is, it consists of the stock of capital plus the money value of the outstanding government debt, G, deflated by the price level, P, to express it in terms of purchasing power over output.

The four equations given above can be conveniently reduced to a single one by first substituting for A in the consumption function and then substituting this function and the investment function into the definition of aggregate demand:

$$(1) \quad X^d = \mathcal{C}\left(X, K_0 + \frac{G}{P}, r\right) + \mathcal{I}(r_0, X, K_0).$$

Next, we observe that in equilibrium, aggregate demand X^d must equal aggregate supply, or

$$(2) \qquad X = X^d.$$

We use this property to replace X with X^d in the right hand side of (1). The resulting equation contains X^d on both sides of the equality. We can, however, "solve" the equation explicitly for X^d, obtaining finally an expression of the form

$$(1') \qquad X^d = D\left(r, K_0, \frac{G}{P}\right),$$

which will be referred to hereafter as the aggregate demand relation. Note that aggregate demand, X^d, may be expected to be negatively associated with r. This is because an increase in r will reduce investment demand directly, and this reduction, in turn, will reduce aggregate demand even further by means of its depressing effect on consumption demand, which depends on total output—this is the so-called multiplier effect [see CONSUMPTION FUNCTION]. Insofar as investment demand itself depends on output, X^d may in fact not decrease continuously as r rises, but this complication will be ignored here.

To complete the description of the output market, we also need an "aggregate supply function." Aggregate supply, X, may be expected to be positively associated with (a) the price, P, at which firms can sell their output relative to the wage rate, W, they must pay, or P/W, and (b) with the pre-existing capital stock, K_0 (on the convenient approximation that the increment in the stock of capital resulting from current investment will not become productive until the next period); thus,

$$(3) \qquad X = S\left(\frac{P}{W}, K_0\right).$$

In the labor market, the aggregate demand for labor, N, can be inferred from the so-called aggregate production function, relating output, X, to the input of labor and the stock of capital, K_0. This function implies that N can be expressed in terms of X and K_0, say, $N = F(X, K_0)$. It is, however, more convenient to replace X in this equation with the right-hand side of (3), thus obtaining the "labor demand" equation

$$(4) \qquad N = \mathfrak{N}\left(\frac{P}{W}, K_0\right).$$

The description of the supply side of the labor market is a somewhat more complex task, for it is here that we must formalize the Keynesian notion of "downward wage rigidity." In its broadest sense, this term connotes the absence of "wage flexibility," of a state of affairs in which money wages fall promptly whenever the supply of labor exceeds the demand for it and keep falling as long as the excess supply persists. In a narrower definition, it means that the current money wage will not be bid below some floor level, W_0 (reflecting the past history of the system), no matter how large the excess supply of labor—though it can be freely bid up in response to excess demand for labor. For present purposes, we shall rely on this narrower version, which we label "absolute" rigidity, because it is more readily formalized. However, the conclusion of the analysis below would not change qualitatively if the wage rate had some tendency to fall for sufficiently large unemployment and falling prices, as long as the reaction was sluggish and unsystematic. There can be little doubt that wage rigidity in this sense is, and has been for some time, a feature of free market economies.

To formalize the hypothesis of absolute wage rigidity we need to introduce the notion of a "potential supply of labor function," say, $\mathcal{E}(W/P)$, which gives the level of employment "desired," or labor force available, at any given real wage, W/P. Now, let E denote the actual level of employment. Then absolute wage rigidity can be expressed as follows:

$$(a) \ W = W_0, \qquad \text{if } \mathfrak{N}\left(\frac{P}{W_0}, K_0\right) < \mathcal{E}\left(\frac{W_0}{P}\right),$$

$$(5)$$

$$(b) \ E = \mathcal{E}\left(\frac{W}{P}\right), \quad \text{if } \mathfrak{N}\left(\frac{P}{W_0}, K_0\right) \geq \mathcal{E}\left(\frac{W_0}{P}\right),$$

$$(6) \qquad E = N.$$

Line (a) of (5) states in essence that if at the rigid wage W_0 the demand for labor falls short of the potential supply, then the actual wage rate will coincide with W_0. Employment, being equal to the *demand* for labor as stated by (6), will then fall short of the potential supply, and the difference will represent the so-called involuntary unemployment. If, however, at W_0 the demand exceeds the potential supply, then line (b) of (5) becomes applicable: the floor level loses its relevance, and the actual wage will have to rise enough to equate the demand with the potential supply. This formulation of wage rigidity has the advantage that it can encompass wage flexibility as a limiting case, in which we assign to W_0 a value so small that the relevant portion of (5) will necessarily be line (b).

In the money market, the demand, M^d, can be expressed as $M^d = L(PX, PA, r)$, where L is, of course, the liquidity preference function that (in recognition of the two major points of view summarized in the section "Post-Keynesian developments" of liquidity preference) is written as a function of both money income (PX) and wealth (PA). By expressing A in terms of its components, K_0 and G, and using the property that a change in the price level should tend to give rise to a proportional change in the demand for money, the preceding equation can be rewritten as

$$M^d = PL(X, K_0 + G/P, r).$$

However, for the purpose of the graphical analysis that is developed below, we shall frequently find it convenient to rely on the specialized version $M^d = PX/V(r)$, where $V(r)$, it will be recalled, denotes the velocity of circulation as a function of the rate of interest. As to the supply side, unless otherwise specified, it will be assumed that money is created by the banking system in the process of purchasing debt instruments (bonds) issued either by the private sector or by the government, and that the total supply of money, M, is exogenously determined through central bank policy. Since in equilibrium we must have $M^d = M$, the description of the money market can be reduced to a single equation obtained by replacing M^d with M in the above equations:

$$(7) \qquad M = PL(X, K_0 + \frac{G}{P}, r),$$

or

$$(7') \qquad M = \frac{PX}{V(r)}.$$

Equations (1) to (7) involve seven endogenous variables: X^d, X, N, E, P, W, r. They therefore form a closed system whose solution describes the short-run equilibrium of the economy. This solution also depends, of course, on the parameters of the various equations, on initial conditions, such as K_0 and G, and on policy variables, of which in the present case there is but one, the money supply, M. The demand and supply for the remaining commodity,

namely, bonds, B, are not explicitly displayed in the system because, by a well-known principle called Walras's law, it can be shown that the demand and supply for one commodity out of the set of all commodities are necessarily equal when all other markets are "cleared" (that is, when demand equals supply); we choose the bond market as the redundant one (Modigliani 1963).

With the help of this system we can now focus on the role of monetary forces, in particular that of liquidity preference, in the determination of equilibrium, beginning with the classical assumption of wage flexibility.

Wage flexibility. As already noted, under the assumption of wage flexibility the labor supply conditions are fully described by line (b) of equation (5). But this equation, together with that for labor demand, equation (4), and the equilibrium condition (6), turns out to involve only three variables: N, E, and P/W (or its reciprocal, the real wage). They therefore form a closed subsystem which can be solved independently of the rest. This solution yields the equilibrium real wage, $W\hat{/}P$ (where "$\hat{\ }$" denotes an equilibrium value), and employment, $\hat{N}$ (which is also "full employment" since it coincides with the labor supply). From (3) we can then infer the equilibrium or full-employment level of output, $\hat{X}$.

At this point it becomes useful to distinguish two possible cases, the one in which there is no national debt and the one in which there is.

No national debt. Referring back to the aggregate demand relation (1'), we observe that if G is zero, then the third argument of the aggregate demand function is necessarily zero, no matter what value P may take: in other words, *aggregate demand does not depend on the price level*. (This important implication, it should be noted, depends critically on the approximation implicit in the formulation of the consumption function, that aggregate consumption, C, depends only on *aggregate* net wealth, not on its distribution between households. Changes in the price level will of course affect the demand of individual consumers by causing redistributions of wealth between creditors and debtors, but our aggregative assumption implies that such redistributions will affect only the distribution of consumption between households, without affecting the total.) Since K_0 is a given initial condition, it can be seen that the right-hand side of (1') contains only one variable, r. It follows that from (1') we can infer the equilibrium value of r, $\hat{r}$, which makes the aggregate demand, X^d, equal to the aggregate supply, $\hat{X}$. Next, substituting $\hat{r}$ and $\hat{X}$ into the money-market equation

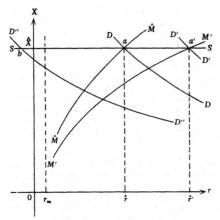

Figure 3 — Equilibrium under wage flexibility

(7), we can determine the price level $\hat{P}$ that equates the demand for money with the given supply (provided such a value of P exists; see below). Finally, from $\hat{P}$ and the equilibrium real wage, $\mathrm{W}/\hat{P}$, we can infer the equilibrium money wage, $\hat{W}$.

The nature of the solution can be clarified by means of Figure 3, in which X is measured on the ordinate and r on the abscissa. The horizontal line labeled SS, cutting the ordinate at $\hat{X}$, represents the aggregate supply consistent with full employment —that is, with the clearing of the labor market. It is a horizontal line because, as should be apparent from the derivation above, the value of $\hat{X}$ does not explicitly depend on r. The curve labeled DD is the graph of the aggregate demand relation (1'), which is shown falling from left to right for the reasons stated earlier. Equilibrium in the commodity (and labor) market is thus represented by the point of intersection of the demand and supply curves, namely, point a, with coordinates $(\hat{X},\hat{r})$.

There remains to be shown the role of money and the money market in the determination of equilibrium. For this we refer back to equation (7') and note that for a given value of M/P this equation expresses a relation between the two variables X and r. It is therefore amenable to graphical representation in our figure. Indeed, the shape of this graph can be readily inferred by solving (7') for X to obtain $X = V(r)(M/P)$. Given M/P, the graph of this equation is simply that of $V(r)$, already shown in Figure 2, except for a proportionality fac-

tor and for the fact that the axes are interchanged, r now being measured on the abscissa instead of the ordinate. The result is a curve such as $M'M'$, which represents the locus of (7') for an arbitrarily chosen value of the "real" money supply, $(M/P)'$. It rises from left to right because, as r increases and transactors are induced to economize on their cash holdings, the velocity of circulation increases, and thus a given "real" money supply is capable of financing a larger and larger volume of transactions, X.

It should be readily apparent that the curve corresponding to·some other value of M/P, say, a value m times larger, can be obtained from the $M'M'$ curve by multiplying by the factor m the ordinate of the $M'M'$ curve corresponding to any given value of r. It follows that provided $\hat{r}$ (the abscissa of point a) is to the right of r_m there will be some unique value of M/P, say, $M/\hat{P}$, such that the corresponding MM curve will go through the point of intersection, a, of the other two curves. This unique curve is represented by $\hat{M}\hat{M}$ in the figure. Thus, with a real money supply $M/\hat{P}$, the money market as well as the commodity and labor markets will all be simultaneously cleared with the output $\hat{X}$ and the rate of interest $\hat{r}$. But this in turn means that, given the actual money supply M, the price level must tend to the equilibrium level $\hat{P}$, such that $M/\hat{P} = (M/\hat{P})$, or $\hat{P} = M/(M/\hat{P})$. Similarly, $\hat{W} = \hat{P}(W/\hat{P})$, where $(W/\hat{P})$ is the full-employment equilibrium real wage. A higher value of W and P would make the money supply inadequate to transact the full-employment income, unless the rate of interest were higher than $\hat{r}$. But a higher r would reduce the aggregate demand below the full-employment supply. This in turn would cause unemployment which, with flexible wages, would lead to a fall of W and hence of P to the equilibrium levels $\hat{W}$ and $\hat{P}$; the converse would be true for values of P and W below the equilibrium levels.

There are three main implications of this analysis to which attention must be called:

(a) Provided $\hat{r} > r_m$, the only economic effect of M is to determine the price level $\hat{P}$; furthermore, it is apparent from the derivation of the last paragraph that $\hat{P}$ is proportional to M, so that, in this sense, the quantity theory of money holds.

(b) The equilibrium value of P corresponding to a given M depends, not only on full-employment output $\hat{X}$, which controls the position of SS, and on slowly changing institutional factors determining the shape of $V(r)$, but also on r. As can be seen from Figure 3, the larger $\hat{r}$ is, the smaller will be the equilibrium real money supply. But $\hat{r}$, for a given $\hat{X}$, is in turn associated with the position of the aggregate demand relation, DD. A rise in the aggregate demand relation—reflecting an increase in consumption or investment demand or both at each level of income and of the interest rate—will result in an upward shift of the DD curve, and this in turn will move to the right the point of intersection, a, of aggregate demand and supply, increasing its r coordinate. Such a shift is illustrated by the curve $D'D'$ intersecting SS at a'. If in the face of such a shift the central bank does not force an appropriate contraction in M, excess demand will arise in the commodity and labor markets that will force up wages and prices up. This will reduce the real money supply, lowering the MM curve, until a value of P is reached such that MM coincides with $M'M'$. If the price rise is to be avoided, the central bank must enforce an appropriate reduction in M (in the same proportion in which prices would rise otherwise). We deduce that once liquidity preference is recognized, if the monetary authority is concerned with maintaining the stability of the price level over time—as it must be if a monetary economy is to work smoothly—it must actively manage the money supply, enforcing a (relatively) larger money supply, and a smaller value of r, when demand tends to be slack and a relatively smaller supply, and higher r, when demand tends to be more active.

(c) Suppose, however, that in some period demand is slack and the DD curve is so depressed that it intersects SS at a value of r smaller than r_m, as illustrated by $D''D''$ intersecting SS at b in Figure 3. It is then apparent that there can be no possible value of M/P such that the corresponding MM curve will go through b, since regardless of the value of M/P, every MM curve must lie entirely to the right of r_m. In this situation, sometimes referred to as "the Keynesian case" or "the special Keynesian case," the economic system will not have any equilibrium solution (a set of prices and interest rates that can simultaneously equate all demands and supplies). If prices and wages are flexible, they will both tend to fall indefinitely under the pressure of excess supplies. But this fall, which under normal conditions would re-establish equilibrium by shifting MM up, can now never prove sufficient. By the same token, monetary policy also breaks down: there is no feasible expansion of the money supply sufficient to eliminate the excess supply of goods and labor.

Thus, from liquidity preference Keynes was able to derive the important and novel result that under certain conditions an economy using a token money

may simply break down, having no maintainable position of equilibrium (except through government fiscal policy or wage rigidity, which will be discussed below).

Positive national debt. The government debt, G, may consist of interest-bearing instruments (government bonds) or government fiat money or both, circulating along with or instead of the money created by the banking system. In any case, if G is positive, it is apparent from equation (1') that aggregate demand depends not only on r but also on P. In terms of Figure 3, equation (1') must now be represented by a *family* of curves, one for each value of P. For the sake of illustration, suppose that the curve DD in the figure corresponds to the received price level, P_0. It can readily be established that to a different value of P, say, $P_1 < P_0$, there will correspond a new DD curve higher and to the right, such as $D'D'$. This is because a fall in P will increase the real value of the government debt held by the public and hence the real net worth of the private sector. This in turn will tend to increase consumption demand, and hence total demand, for any given r. Conversely, a rise in P will shift DD downward and to the left.

This dependence of aggregate demand on P when G is not zero has come to be known in the literature as the "real-balance effect," and also as the "Pigou effect" because Pigou called attention to it in a very influential work (1947). However, the point had been made earlier by others, in particular by Scitovsky (1940). The main implication of the real-balance effect is that even with flexible wages the system *will* in general have a position of full-employment equilibrium. In other words, it rules out the possibility of the "Keynesian case" discussed above. To illustrate this point, suppose that corresponding to the received price, P_0, the aggregate demand function had the position $D''D''$ in the figure, which could not possibly intersect an MM curve on SS. Since the position of DD now *depends* on P, as P falls under the pressure of excess supply the DD curve will keep shifting to the right at the same time that MM shifts upward. Except under very special *ad hoc* assumptions, MM and DD will eventually intersect on SS at some point to the right of r_m.

This demonstration that, provided G is positive, a system with flexible wages will possess a position of full-employment equilibrium, contrary to Keynes's conclusion, has been seized upon by some of Keynes's critics as disposing of one of his most significant and novel results. They have concluded that underemployment equilibrium can arise only from wage–price rigidities. This view must be regarded as unwarranted, mainly for the following reasons: (*a*) Keynes's conclusion stands when $G = 0$. (*b*) Even when $G > 0$, the conclusion that a full-employment solution would exist is valid only under the assumption, implicit in the model, that falling prices do not generate perverse expectations of further falls, which would reduce demand. Furthermore, it ignores the likelihood that a violent deflation, which might be necessary to produce a sufficient increase in the real value of the national debt, would severely disrupt a monetary economy by producing wholesale debtors' insolvency. In view of these considerations, Pigou's demonstration has little practical relevance, as Pigou himself acknowledged ([1947] 1951, p. 251). Even if full employment could be re-established by sufficient deflation of prices and wages, it would be preferable to avoid this outcome by relying on the kind of fiscal policy devices, discussed in the next section, that one would have to fall back on when $G = 0$. To look at the matter in a slightly different light, wage and price rigidity, instead of hindering the working of a monetary economy, may provide it with a degree of price stability that in the long run contributes to its smooth working, even though this rigidity makes the task of successful monetary management more challenging.

Downward wage rigidity. The working of the system when the level of the rigid wage W_0 is sufficiently high to be at least potentially effective can be illustrated by Figure 4, which is a simple variant of Figure 3. For this purpose it is convenient to

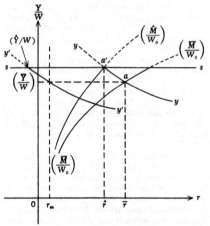

Figure 4 — Equilibrium with a rigid wage level (W₀)

introduce a new symbol to denote money income, Y, which is related to other variables of the system by the identity

(8) $$Y \equiv PX.$$

Also, for the sake of exposition we deal formally with the case $G = 0$, with some occasional reference to the (rather minor) modifications called for if this restriction is discarded.

We recall that with $G = 0$ the right-hand side of (1') contains only the variable r. From (1'), (2), and (3) we can then derive a relation between Y/W and r. Here Y/W is income measured in what Keynes called wage units (that is, income measured in terms of labor as a *numéraire*). We first solve equation (3) for P/W in terms of X and write the solution as

(3') $$P/W = \mathcal{P}(X),$$

a "Marshallian" short-run supply function indicating the price—in terms of the cost of labor—needed to call forth a given supply, X. Next, using (1') and (2), we can express X as a function of r. It follows that Y/W can itself be expressed as a function of r—say, $Y/W \equiv X(P/W) = X\mathcal{P}(X) = y(r)$. This equation is an obvious variant of the aggregate-demand relation (1'), shown as DD in Figure 3, except that output is expressed in wage units. Accordingly, its graph, shown by the yy curve of Figure 4, bears a close relation to that of DD in Figure 3, from which it differs only by the factor P/W. In particular, yy must fall from left to right if DD does, since P/W is an increasing function of X. The horizontal line ss again represents "full-employment output" in wage units, $(P/W)\hat{X}$, where P/W and $\hat{X}$ can be inferred from the solution of the system under flexible wages. The portion of yy above ss has been dashed to indicate that it can never be "effective," since real income there exceeds the full-employment level.

The curve rising from left to right and labeled $\bar{M}/W_0$ is again derived from the money market equation (7'), on the assumption that the given money supply is $\bar{M}$. First solve (7') for PX, obtaining $PX = V(r)M$. Next replace M with $\bar{M}$ and divide both sides by W_0. This yields $Y/W_0 = V(r)(\bar{M}/W_0)$. Its graph must look like that of MM in Figure 3, for it is again the graph of $V(r)$ up to a proportionality factor M/W_0 (instead of M/P, as in Figure 3). It shows the level of income (in wage units) that can be transacted at each level of r, given the money supply in wage units.

If the yy curve and the money-market curve intersect in their effective range—below or on ss—as in Figure 4, then the coordinates of their point of intersection, labeled a, show the equilibrium value of income, $\bar{Y}/W$, and of the rate of interest, $\bar{r}$. If this intersection does not fall on ss, then the equilibrium is one of less than full employment. It is a position of *equilibrium* despite the presence of unemployment because, under wage rigidity, the excess supply of labor does not lead to any further adjustment (at least in the short run). By contrast, if wages were flexible, the excess supply would bid down W which, with $\bar{M}$ given, would raise $\bar{M}/W$, shifting the MM curve upward and moving its point of intersection with yy upward and to the left until it coincided with the full-employment point, a' in the figure. (If G is assumed to be positive, the fall in W will also tend to shift yy upward, moving a' to the right.)

Even under wage rigidity, output and employment could be increased by increasing the money supply, which, with W given at W_0, would raise M/W and hence the MM curve. In fact, provided that a' is to the right of r_m, there is an ideal money supply, $\hat{M}$, that produces an MM curve that intersects yy at a'. Alternatively, the goal of optimal monetary policy might be visualized as that of enforcing the rate of interest that would generate an aggregate demand equal to full-employment output, supplying whatever quantity of money is needed to enforce that rate. In terms of Figure 4, the rate of interest called for is, of course, $\hat{r}$ (which is the r coordinate of a'), and the corresponding quantity of money is again $\hat{M}$.

This analysis should help to show how the interaction of liquidity preference and wage rigidity makes the task of economic stabilization through monetary policy a highly complex and difficult one. In the absence of wage–price rigidities the concern of monetary policy would be reduced to the maintenance of price stability. And in the absence of liquidity preference the velocity of circulation could be counted upon to be sufficiently stable to make this task a relatively easy one. In a stationary economy it would call essentially for a stable money supply, whereas in an expanding economy it would call for a money supply that keeps pace with the growth of full-employment output, a growth that also appears to be characterized by a fair degree of stability.

But under wage rigidity, monetary policy has the double task of trying to achieve both price stability and full employment. Furthermore, because liquidity preference causes the velocity of circulation to vary with interest rates, the money supply needed to reach these goals will vary, relative to full-employment output, with variations in aggregate demand conditions. In terms of Figure 4,

a rise in consumption or investment demand relative to income will shift the yy curve to the right; a corresponding fall will shift it to the left. These shifts have to be countered by contrary adjustments of the money supply relative to the level of full-employment output. Furthermore, failure to adjust the money supply properly will tend to have asymmetrical consequences. An excessive money supply will still give rise to increases in prices that could have been avoided and that are largely irreversible. But too small a money supply will result in an insufficient aggregate demand that, aside from deflationary effects on the price level, will result in the waste and social scourge of unemployment.

Note also that the central bank's control over the price level is at best partial and largely unidirectional. The price level is anchored to the wage rate, which monetary policy can readily push up by being too expansive but which it can hardly hope to force down, except possibly through the painful and wasteful route of prolonged and widespread unemployment. Furthermore, if the minimum money wage—the W_0 of equation (5)—tends to be pushed up even before full employment is reached, whether through powerful unions or through partial bottlenecks or both, and if the rise tends to exceed the rate of increase of productivity, then monetary (as well as fiscal) policy will be faced with the unsavory choice between "creeping inflation" and chronic unemployment. Whether this dilemma is in fact a serious and real one revolves around the issue of the determinants of the over-all level of money wages, an issue that the Keynesian analysis has opened up but that is still far from settled. [*See* INFLATION AND DEFLATION; *see also* Phillips 1958.]

One other implication of the Keynesian framework, which can be only touched upon in this survey dealing primarily with monetary aspects, is that fiscal policy provides an alternative approach to the control of aggregate demand for economic stabilization [*see* FISCAL POLICY]. Fiscal policy can be accommodated in our macroeconomic model by adding government expenditure on goods and services as a component of aggregate demand in equation (1'), making consumption (and possibly investment) depend on taxes as well as on income produced, and adding an equation relating tax collection to income and tax rates. Without attempting to pursue this line here we may indicate that, in terms of Figure 4, fiscal policy—defined as policy concerned with the level of government expenditure and taxation—will affect the position and shape of the aggregate demand relation yy. An

The Monetary Mechanism 111

increase in expenditure will shift it upward and to the right; an increase in tax rates will shift it in the opposite direction. Thus, given a position of less than full employment equilibrium such as *a* in Figure 4, output and employment could be raised toward or up to the full-employment level by increased government expenditure, tax reductions, or both, which would shift the *yy* curve to the right.

The possibility of affecting equilibrium output and employment through fiscal tools becomes of critical importance in the special "Keynesian case," in which the aggregate demand is so depressed that the *yy* curve intersects *ss* to the left of the minimum achievable interest rate, r_m. In this case (illustrated by the curve *y'y'* in Figure 4) full employment, as we have seen, is beyond the reach of monetary policy, for no money curve can have points to the left of r_m. Fiscal policy is then the only effective tool of stabilization policy, at least until the *yy* curve has been shifted rightward enough to cut *ss* to the right of r_m.

Beyond this point—and, more generally, whenever the intersection of *yy* and *ss* is to the right of r_m—either fiscal or monetary tools can be used in the pursuit of full employment and price stability. Of course, both tools can be used simultaneously and in coordinated fashion. This should be clear from the fact that, in terms of Figure 4, fiscal policy acts basically on *yy* whereas monetary policy acts basically on the money curve. (The graphical apparatus of Figure 4 was chosen to illustrate the working of the system partly because of its convenience in isolating the *modus operandi* of monetary and fiscal policy.)

There is a substantial literature concerned with the analysis of the relative advantages and shortcomings of monetary and fiscal policy in terms of such criteria as reliability, response delays, ease of implementation, and reversibility (for monetary policy, see Johnson 1962, pp. 365–377; for fiscal policy see, e.g., Keiser 1964, part 5), effects on long-run economic growth (e.g., Smith 1957; Modigliani 1961), and, more recently, differential impact on the balance of payments (e.g., Mundell 1962). Because of the complexity of the problem it is not surprising that there have been substantial differences in points of view between economists favoring the use of one tool, or of some specific mix, and those favoring others. These differences can be traced in part to differences in the subjective valuation of different goals. But in part they revolve around disagreement about the empirical importance of the "Keynesian case" in which monetary policy becomes powerless to maintain or reestablish full employment, either because it is

ineffective in reducing interest rates any further (at least in the short run) or because the achievable reduction in interest rates is insufficient to induce the required expansion in investment and aggregate demand.

Liquidity preference, that is, the proposition that the demand for money is systematically and significantly affected by interest rates, has proved to be a major, lasting contribution to economic analysis, well supported by empirical evidence. From an analytical point of view its great significance lies in the implication that under certain conditions— the "special Keynesian case"—even an economy with flexible wages and prices might not possess a stable full-employment equilibrium. But beyond this fundamental theoretical contribution, the dramatic impact of the *General Theory* on economic theory and policy can be traced to its insightful analysis of the role of liquidity preference in a world of widespread wage and price rigidities. This analysis has led to a new understanding and fundamental reappraisal of the role of money and of the tasks and limitations of monetary and fiscal policy.

With downward wage rigidity (and even ignoring international trade) money cannot be regarded, even in first approximation, as "neutral," a mere veil having no effect on the economy other than the determination of the price level, except possibly when the money supply is excessive. Under conditions of less than full employment due to lack of demand, and barring the special Keynesian case, monetary policy plays a crucial role in the determination of income and employment. In the special Keynesian case, on the other hand, monetary policy breaks down, since it is incapable, at least in the short run, of affecting either output or prices.

FRANCO MODIGLIANI

BIBLIOGRAPHY

ALLAIS, MAURICE 1947 *Économie & intérêt: Présentation nouvelle des problèmes fondamentaux relatifs au rôle économique du taux de l'intérêt et de leurs solutions.* 2 vols. Paris: Librairie des Publications Officielles.

BAUMOL, WILLIAM J. 1952 The Transactions Demand for Cash: An Inventory Theoretic Approach. *Quarterly Journal of Economics* 66:545–556.

BRONFENBRENNER, MARTIN; and HOLZMAN, FRANKLYN D. 1963 Survey of Inflation Theory. *American Economic Review* 53:593–661.

BRONFENBRENNER, MARTIN; and MAYER, THOMAS 1960 Liquidity Functions in the American Economy. *Econometrica* 28:810–834.

BRUNNER, K.; and MELTZER, ALLAN H. 1964 Some Further Investigations of Demand and Supply Functions for Money. *Journal of Finance* 19:240–283.

ESHAG, EPRIME 1963 *From Marshall to Keynes: An Essay on the Monetary Theory of the Cambridge School.* Oxford: Blackwell.

FISHER, IRVING (1911) 1920 *The Purchasing Power of Money: Its Determination and Relation to Credit, Interest and Crises.* New ed., rev. New York: Macmillan.

FRIEDMAN, MILTON (editor) 1956 *Studies in the Quantity Theory of Money.* Univ. of Chicago Press. → See especially pages 5–21, "The Quantity Theory of Money—A Restatement," by Friedman.

FRIEDMAN, MILTON 1957 *A Theory of the Consumption Function.* National Bureau of Economic Research, General Series, No. 63. Princeton Univ. Press.

FRIEDMAN, MILTON 1959 The Demand for Money: Some Theoretical and Empirical Results. *Journal of Political Economy* 67:327–351.

HICKS, JOHN R. (1935) 1951 A Suggestion for Simplifying the Theory of Money. Pages 13–32 in American Economic Association, *Readings in Monetary Theory.* Philadelphia: Blakiston.

HICKS, JOHN R. 1937 Mr. Keynes and the "Classics": A Suggested Interpretation. *Econometrica* 5:147–159.

JOHNSON, H. G. 1962 Monetary Theory and Policy. *American Economic Review* 52:335–384.

KEISER, NORMAN F. 1964 *Macroeconomics, Fiscal Policy, and Economic Growth.* New York: Wiley.

KEYNES, JOHN MAYNARD (1930) 1958–1960 *A Treatise on Money.* 2 vols. London: Macmillan. → Volume 1: *The Pure Theory of Money.* Volume 2: *The Applied Theory of Money.*

KEYNES, JOHN MAYNARD 1936 *The General Theory of Employment, Interest and Money.* London: Macmillan. → A paperback edition was published in 1965 by Harcourt.

LANGE, OSKAR 1938 The Rate of Interest and the Optimum Propensity to Consume. *Economica* New Series 5:12–32.

LATANÉ, HENRY A. 1954 Cash Balances and the Interest Rate: A Pragmatic Approach. *Review of Economics and Statistics* 36:456–460.

LATANÉ, HENRY A. 1960 Income Velocity and Interest Rates: A Pragmatic Approach. *Review of Economics and Statistics* 42:445–449.

LAVINGTON, FREDERICK 1921 *The English Capital Market.* London: Methuen.

MARGET, ARTHUR W. 1938 *The Theory of Prices: A Re-examination of the Central Problems of Monetary Theory.* Vol. 1. Englewood Cliffs, N.J.: Prentice-Hall.

MARSHALL, ALFRED 1923 *Money, Credit and Commerce.* London: Macmillan.

MELTZER, ALLAN H. 1963 The Demand for Money: The Evidence From the Time Series. *Journal of Political Economy* 71:219–246.

MODIGLIANI, FRANCO (1944) 1951 Liquidity Preference and the Theory of Interest and Money. Pages 186–239 in American Economic Association, *Readings in Monetary Theory.* New York: Blakiston. → First published in Volume 12 of *Econometrica.*

MODIGLIANI, FRANCO 1961 Long Run Implications of Alternative Fiscal Policies and the Burden of the National Debt. *Economic Journal* 71:730–755.

MODIGLIANI, FRANCO 1963 The Monetary Mechanism and Its Interaction With Real Phenomena. *Review of Economics and Statistics* 45 (Supplement):79–107.

MUNDELL, ROBERT A. 1962 The Appropriate Use of Monetary and Fiscal Policy for Internal and External Stability. International Monetary Fund, *Staff Papers* 9:70–77.

PATINKIN, DON (1956) 1965 *Money, Interest, and Prices: An Integration of Monetary and Value Theory.* 2d ed. New York: Harper.

PHILLIPS, A. W. 1958 The Relation Between Unemployment and the Rate of Change of Money Wage Rates in the United Kingdom: 1861–1957. *Economica* New Series 25:283–299.

PIGOU, A. C. (1917) 1951 The Value of Money. Pages 162–183 in American Economic Association, *Readings in Monetary Theory.* Philadelphia: Blakiston.

PIGOU, A. C. (1947) 1951 Economic Progress in a Stable Environment. Pages 241–251 in American Economic Association, *Readings in Monetary Theory.* Philadelphia: Blakiston. → First published in Volume 14 of *Economica* New Series.

PIGOU, A. C. 1950 *Keynes's General Theory: A Retrospective View.* London: Macmillan.

SCITOVSKY, TIBOR 1940 Capital Accumulation, Employment and Price Rigidity. *Review of Economic Studies* 8:69–88.

SMITH, WARREN L. 1957 Monetary–Fiscal Policy and Economic Growth. *Quarterly Journal of Economics* 71:36–55.

TOBIN, JAMES 1956 The Interest-elasticity of Transactions Demand for Cash. *Review of Economics and Statistics* 38:241–247.

TOBIN, JAMES 1958 Liquidity Preference as Behavior Towards Risk. *Review of Economic Studies* 25, no. 2: 65–86.

TURVEY, RALPH (1960) 1961 *Interest Rates and Asset Prices.* New York: Macmillan.

The Monetary Mechanism

9 The Channels of Monetary Policy in the Federal Reserve—MIT—University of Pennsylvania Econometric Model of the United States

F. MODIGLIANI
Massachusetts Institute of Technology

I. Introduction[1]

The purpose of this paper is to provide a survey of the basic structure of the Federal Reserve – MIT – University of Pennsylvania (FMP) model, 1972 vintage, focusing on the channels through which the major tools of monetary policy affect aggregate real output, the price level and thus, finally, money income. We also endeavour to contrast these channels with those relevant for the transmission of fiscal policy, though the emphasis is on the monetary mechanism.

The presentation is divided into two parts. In section II we examine the major markets for both tangibles and intangibles that are explicitly modelled in the FMP model, tracing the path of causation from the money and short-term securities markets through other financial markets to the components of aggregate demand, aggregate output, employment, wages, and prices, with various feedbacks to the money and financial markets. It is shown that the channels of monetary policy include, in addition to fairly conventional ones such as the impact of interest rates on fixed business investment and on residential construction, some less conventional ones by way of consumers' expenditures on both durables and non-durables and services and by way of state and local government expenditure. In section III we examine by means of policy simulations of the model the path of response of *aggregate* output to a change in monetary policy, resulting from the simultaneous contribution of these channels, their interaction, and their interaction with the system multiplier. We are concerned both with the short run (the first three years) and the very long run.

As will become apparent in the next section, the model is basically structured along neo-Keynesian lines. Thus output is controlled by aggregate demand, and the money supply affects real aggregate demand (almost) exclusively by way of interest rates, and affects the price level only through its effect on aggregate real demand

[1] The model presented here is the result of a team under the direction of the author, Albert Ando and, initially, Frank de Leeuw, and included at various times Robert Rasche, Edward Gramlich, Charles Bischoff, Gordon Sparks, Harold Shapiro, Richard Sutch, Dwight Jaffee, Jared Enzler, and John Kalchbrenner. I also wish to thank my research assistant, Mr Lucas Papademos, for his help and valuable suggestions in preparing this paper. The research was supported by a grant of the Board of Governors of the Federal Reserve System to the Social Science Research Council.

in relation to the capacity of the economy. Nonetheless, as shown in section III, in the longest run the response of the economy to both monetary and fiscal policy is very much consistent with the views advanced by Friedman and the monetarists. In particular, the money supply does *not* affect real output, or real interest rates (money is neutral) but only the price level; and a change in real government expenditure, money supply (and tax rates) constant, does *not* affect real output but only its composition, as the expansion in government expenditure tends to displace an equal amount of private demand.

However, these monetarist results hold only in the very long run, which is of little relevance in framing stabilization policies. In the 'short run' both monetary and fiscal policies have powerful effects, first on real output and, more gradually, on prices, with the relative size of the two effects dependent on the degree of slack in the economy. Finally, it is shown that the least conventional channel of monetary policy – that via consumption – increases substantially both the magnitude and the speed of response of the system to the monetary tools while, at least for some initial conditions, it tends to reduce the response to fiscal policy.

II. Structure of the Model and the Channels of Monetary and Fiscal Policy

1. The Approach

In providing a description of the major markets and their interaction it is useful to begin from the money and short-term securities market in which the impact of monetary policy is first felt. We then proceed to the other financial markets, to the commodity markets covering the components of aggregate output and determining, with fiscal policy, aggregate income and disposable income, and finally to the labour market and the determinants of prices and wages.

Figure 9.1 illustrates the links between markets and the direction of causality. In this diagram every symbol denotes a variable. Those encased in rectangular boxes are exogenous (or normally exogenous) policy variables; other exogenous and predetermined variables are encased in a triangle; and endogenous variables are encircled. A line joining two variables indicates a causal association, with the arrow indicating the direction of causality. If the influence occurs with a long (distributed) lag, the joining line is shown as a broken one.

2. The Money and Short-term Market

This market, which is described in more detail in Modigliani, Rasche, and Cooper [14], consists of a money supply and a money demand equation. The supply equation, derived from the maximization of bank profits in the presence of a stochastic deposits flow and commercial loan demand, expresses the supply of demand deposits by banks as an increasing function of unborrowed bank reserves, $UR\$$, of reserve requirements, RR, of the short-term market rate, i_S, and, transiently, of the change of commercial loans, $CL\$$, and as a decreasing function of the discount rate, i_D. The response of supply to any of the variables is not simultaneous, but still fairly fast. The demand equation, based on the neo-Fisherian formulation – that is, on the transaction demand type of models of Baumol [3], Tobin [19], Miller and Orr [13] – expresses the demand for demand deposits as an increasing function of money *GNP*, $X\$$, (with unit elasticity) and a decreasing function of the rates of return on the two instruments deemed to be the closest substitute for money holding, namely, the short rate and the rate on saving deposits, i_{SD}. The two

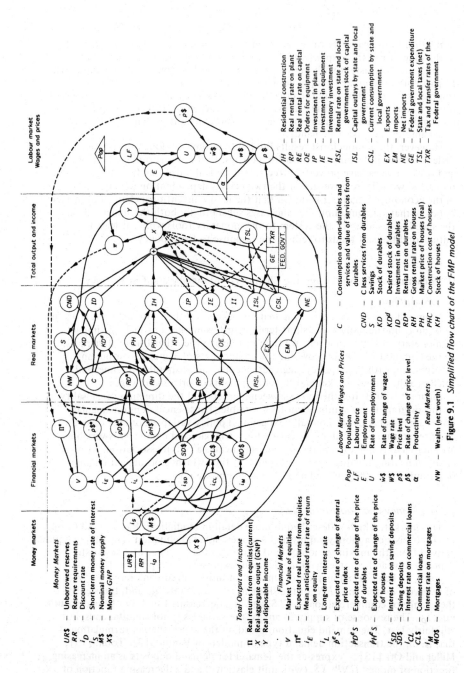

Figure 9.1 Simplified flow chart of the FMP model

Column headers across top: Money markets | Financial markets | Real markets | Total output and income | Labour market Wages and prices

Money Markets

URS$ – Unborrowed reserves
RR – Reserve requirements
i_D – Discount rate
i_S – Short-term money rate of interest
M$ – Nominal money supply
X$ – Money GNP

Total Output and Income

π – Real returns from equities (current)
X – Real aggregate output (GNP)
Y – Real disposable income

Financial Markets

V – Market Value of equities
Π^e – Expected real returns from equities
i_E – Mean anticipated real rate of return on equity
i_L – Long-term interest rate
$\dot{p}^e$$ – Expected rate of change of general price index
$\dot{p}D^e$$ – Expected rate of change of the price of durables
$\dot{p}_H^e$$ – Expected rate of change of the price of houses
i_{SD}
SD$ – Interest rate on saving deposits
Saving deposits
i_{CL}
CL$ – Interest rate on commercial loans
Commercial loans
i_M
MO$ – Interest rate on mortgages
Mortgages

Labour Market Wages and Prices

Pop – Population
LF – Labour force
E – Employment
U – Rate of unemployment
$\dot{w}$$ – Rate of change of wages
W$ – Wage rate
$\dot{p}$$ – Rate of change of price level
P$ – Price level
α – Productivity

Real Markets

NW – Wealth (net worth)

C – Consumption on non-durables and services and value of services from durables
CND – C less services from durables
S – Savings
KD – Stock of durables
KD^d – Desired stock of durables
ID – Investment in durables
RD* – Rental rate on durables
PH – Market price of houses (real)
RH – Gross rental rate on houses
PHC – Construction cost of houses
KH – Stock of houses

IH – Residential construction
RP – Real rental rate on plant
RE – Real rental rate on capital
OE – Orders for equipment
IP – Investment in plant
IE – Investment in equipment
II – Inventory investment
RSL – Rental rate on state and local government stock of capital
ISL – Capital outlays by state and local government
CSL – Current consumption by state and local government
EX – Exports
EM – Imports
NE – Net imports
GE – Federal government expenditure
TSL – State and local taxes (net)
TXR – Tax and transfer rates of the Federal government

FED. GOVT.

rates contribute roughly equally to the long-run elasticity of demand which is estimated at about −0.4. This figure is fully consistent with the transactions model, which implies an elasticity appreciably smaller than zero but larger than −0.5. The adjustment of demand to changes in the arguments is comparatively slow, some 20% per quarter.

By solving the money demand and supply equations simultaneously for the two variables $M\$$ and i_s, we can express each variable in terms of all the other arguments of both the demand and supply equations. This is the 'reduced form' represented in the extreme left of Figure 9.1.

3. Other Financial Markets

The model focuses on five main financial instruments and corresponding markets, in addition to the money and short-term market. These fall into two groups:

(i)   Instruments for which the public as well as intermediaries appear on both sides of the market. These include long-term bonds and corporate equities besides money and short-term debt.

(ii)   Instruments for which one side of the market includes only intermediaries − to wit, commercial loans and saving deposits and, to a first approximation, mortgages.

Note that, as usual, with six instruments there are only five independent markets to be cleared in the model; the market for short-term debt is implicitly treated as redundant.

3.1 Long-term securities

In the long-term market, equilibrium requires that the expected 'one-period' holding yield should equal the short-term rate, except possibly for a risk premium. This condition in turn implies that the long-term rate must be an average of the current and future expected short-term rates over the life of the bond. We hypothesize that the short rate expected at t to rule τ periods later, $_t i_s^e(\tau)$, can be thought of as the sum of an expected real short rate, $_t r_s^e(\tau)$, and an expected rate of inflation, $_t \dot{p}\$^e(\tau)$, and that both expectations can be approximated closely by a weighted average of past real rates and rates of inflation. (Strictly speaking, we need only to make this assumption for $_t r_s^e(t+1)$ and $_t \dot{p}\$^e(t+1)$ and to postulate that expectations are 'rational' (cf. Modigliani and Shiller [17]). It then readily follows that, aside from a risk premium, the long rate, $(i_L(t))$ is a weighted average of the current and past values of i_s and $\dot{p}\$$.

This hypothesis fits the data remarkably well. The weights of the lagged values of i_s sum to approximately unity (as required by the model), of which just less than one-quarter applies to the current rate and the rest is distributed over a substantial spread of years. As for the risk premium, it could in principle depend on the relative supplies of longs and shorts; we have, however, been unable to detect this effect empirically, casting doubts on the effectiveness of debt maturity management as a stabilization device. We do find, however, that the premium is positive and tends to rise with the recent variability of short rates − a plausible measure of uncertainty about future rates.

All this is summarized in our diagram by indicating that i_s and $\dot{p}\$$ determine the long rate i_L, though with a long distributed lag.

3.2 Equity market

We can only provide here a rather streamlined and simplified account of our attempts at modelling this rather complex market. Disregarding for present purposes complications introduced by special growth opportunities, we can think of the market basket of equities as a claim to the stream of profits – of indefinite duration – produced by the assets currently held by the corporate sector. Denote by $\tilde{\Pi}^*(t)$ the average annual value of this stream anticipated by the market (a random variable) and by $\Pi^e(t)$ its mathematical expectation at date t. We can then express the market value of stock V as resulting from the capitalization of $\Pi^e(t)$ at some appropriate rate i_E, or

$$V(t) = \Pi^e(t)/i_E \qquad (9.1)$$

(Equivalently, one may think of i_E as the market price of expected profits or, under some further reasonable assumptions, as a close approximation to the expected rate of return, given the market value $V(t)$.) In order to clear the equity market the capitalization rate i_E must equal the real long rate, $(i_L - \dot{p}\$^e)$, plus an appropriate risk premium, say Z, or

$$i_E = (i_L - \dot{p}\$^e) + Z \qquad (9.2)$$

One might arrive at (9.2) by postulating a demand equation for equity, representing some fraction f of net worth, NW,

$$V^d = f(i_E - i_L + \dot{p}\$^e, z)NW \qquad (9.3)$$

where z (possibly a vector) denotes variables controlling the required risk premium – for example, investors' risk preferences and the covariance of $\tilde{\Pi}^*(t)$ with the anticipated return from total wealth. By equating the demand (V^d) with the supply (V) and solving for i_E, we obtain an expression like (9.2), with $Z = F(z, V/NW)$; this derivation brings out explicitly the fact that, in principle, the composition of wealth should be among the variables controlling the risk premium.

Estimation of (9.2) involves three major problems: (*i*) finding a suitable approximation to Π^e from which in turn we can derive an operational measure of i_E; (*ii*) finding an approximation to $\dot{p}\$^e$; and (*iii*) determining the components of Z. To solve the first problem, one might rely on current profits, or some average of current and past profits. We have relied primarily on dividends on the ground that, under the prevailing practice of dividend stabilization, Π^e may be expected to be proportional to dividends, the proportionality factor being the reciprocal of the target payout ratio. However, since dividends tend to lag far behind profits, we actually use a weighted average of dividends and current profit; the weights were estimated from the data in the process of estimating (9.2), and are heavily concentrated on the dividend component. This approximation to Π^e is denoted by Π^c. Problem (*ii*) is handled by using a distributed lag of past $\dot{p}\$$ which comes into play when the rate of inflation has consistently exceeded a threshold level. As for the third problem, we have had but limited success. We have found little evidence that the premium depends on the composition of wealth, V/NW; the only variable which appears associated with the observed risk premium Z is a very long-run average of the rate of unemployment, which is presumably associated with uncertainty or dispersion in $\tilde{\Pi}^*(t)$, the anticipated level of average profits.

Once we have estimated equation (9.2), in operating the model we use this equation to compute the capitalization rate, and equation (9.1) to compute the market value of equity, with Π^e replaced by Π^c. Accordingly Figure 9.1 shows the capitalization rate as determined by the long rate and the expected rate of inflation, and the market value of equity determined by the capitalization rate and expected real returns from equities. (The dependence on the rate of unemployment is omitted so as not to clog the diagram.) Finally, expected real equity returns are accounted for by corporate profits with a long distributed lag (reflecting the nature of the relation between dividends and profits).

A number of authors have reported at various times evidence that the market value of equity may tend to rise (and hence i_E to fall) with the rate of change of the money supply, ($M\$$). We have also found some, though by no means clear-cut, evidence of such an effect. We can find no sound reason why, given current dividends and profits, $M\$$ should have an effect on expected profits, or why, given the long rate and the expected rate of inflation, it should affect the required rate of return, i_E. Consequently, we have omitted $M\$$ in the main variant of the model though we do have an alternative version of the stock market equation including $M\$$ which we have used occasionally for simulations. In this version, there would also be in Figure 9.1 a direct link from $M\$$ to i_E and hence V, constituting also the only effect of $M\$$ not going though the short-term market rate.

3.3 Mortgage market

This is discussed briefly below in connection with the housing sector, section 4.2. For a fuller description, *see* Jaffee [10].

3.4 Commercial loans

This market requires only a brief description since it does not play a crucial role in the present version (for more details, *see* Jaffee [9]). Briefly, the 'supply' of loans in the short run takes the form of a rate (i_{CL}) quoted by banks; and the quantity is determined by the demand side. The quoted i_{CL} adjusts fairly quickly (50 per cent per quarter) to an equilibrium rate which is an increasing function of opportunity cost, measured by i_L, and of the proportion of assets tied up in loans. In addition, there are transient effects. Because the market is highly oligopolistic, banks tend to look for a common signal; there is strong evidence that changes in the discount rate provide such a function.

As for the demand side, the basic idea is that in the long run firms rely on commercial loans (CL) to finance a certain portion of their various tangible and intangible assets: most of the inventories (II) and net receivables (assumed proportional to sales) and smaller portions of their fixed capital, plant (IP), and equipment (IE). The remainder is to be covered by long-term sources, debt or equity. The proportion financed by CL is a decreasing function of the spread ($i_{CL} - i_S$) and ($i_{CL} - i_L$). However, since long-term capital is to be raised only for 'permanent' needs, and since it takes time to raise it, there is an additional transient demand associated with the rate of change of all assets.

This explains the set of arrows leading to the variables $CL\$$ and i_{CL} in the graph. (For simplicity, the effects on commercial loans of investment expenditure are subsumed under the effect of real GNP). It will be seen that there is but one arrow leading from the variables of this market to other sectors, namely the arrow from $CL\$$ to ($M\$$, i_S); indeed, in the present version of the model the only feedback is that changes in commercial loans tend to increase the money supply, providing a mechanism by which money demand directly generates money supply, at least transiently. We had hoped to find some effect of commercial loan rationing on aggregate demand. Actually, we have found evidence of rationing and even a way of measuring this variable (cf. Jaffee and Modigliani [8] and Jaffee [9]); but, unfortunately, we have not been able to find significant quantitative evidence of the effect of rationing on any component of demand — perhaps because tighter rationing does not significantly affect larger firms, which account for the bulk of expenditure and may also provide financing for smaller ones.

3.5 Saving deposits

This sector actually consists of four distinct intermediaries including insurance companies (cf. Modigliani [16] and Slovin [18]), but for the present purpose it can be summarized into a single market.

Again, the 'supply' of deposits takes the form of a rate (i_{SD}) quoted by the depository intermediaries; this rate depends on the return on the assets on which they invest, basically the mortgage rate (i_M) (plus i_{CL} for commercial banks) and on the rates of competing assets, i_L and i_S. The adjustment tends to be very gradual but is speeded along if deposits grow less fast than the portfolio of loans to their customers (e.g. mortgages for saving and loan, and mortgages plus commercial loans for commercial banks). Finally the adjustment may be constrained by rate ceilings. The actual level of deposits is determined by demand equations in which the equilibrium demand is a fraction of net worth (NW) depending on relations between the rate offered on the asset and the rate on competing money fixed assets (i_S, i_L), and, because of transaction demand, on the ratio of real disposable income to wealth. However, the adjustment is quite slow, particularly for that portion of the growth of wealth that arises from capital gains rather than from current saving. This market has two main feedbacks. Firstly, the rate on savings plays an important role in the demand for money. The interaction between the two markets ensures that in the long run the rates on saving deposits and on short-term money will tend to maintain a stable relationship to each other and contributes to making the demand for money more interest-elastic in the long than in the short term. The other feedback is through the inflow of saving deposits funds, controlling the supply by intermediaries, or mortgage funds, which in turn affect construction, as indicated below.

4. Real Markets – the Components of Aggregate Demand

4.1 Plant and equipment

Monetary policy has long been recognized, at least in principle, to have an impact on investment in plant and equipment and residential construction. For equipment, *IE*, the main feature that distinguishes our formulation from that of most preceding models is that we explicitly rely on the hypothesis of a putty-clay technology (cf. Bischoff [4] and Ando *et al.* [2]). Since, under these conditions, existing equipment cannot be modified in response to variations in relative prices, changes in the cost of capital affect (gross) investment only through the capital intensity of the desired gross current addition to capacity, ΔX^c; that is, $I_t = \hat{k}_t \Delta X^c_t$, and $\hat{k}_t = k(RE_t)$, where $\hat{k}$ is the cost-minimizing capital/output ratio and RE is the current real rental rate. Since we assumed a Cobb-Douglas production function (which we find to be not inconsistent with the evidence), we can write

$$k(RE) = \frac{p\$}{q\$} \frac{1-e^{-(RE)\hat{T}}}{RE} \simeq \frac{p}{q} \cdot \frac{A}{RE} \qquad (9.4)$$

where $p\$$ and $q\$$ denote, respectively, the price of output and of capital goods, and T is the optimum economic life of equipment (which depends on the rate of technological progress and on the real rental rate). The approximation relies on the consideration that, under reasonable assumptions, $\hat{T}$ turns out to be large (in the order of 15 years) implying that $e^{-(RE)T}$ is small, and to be very insensitive to variations in the cost of capital. The real rental rate (RE) is the sum of the depreciation rate (taken as exogenous) and the real cost of capital, which should be measured by the mean anticipated real rate of return on equity (i_E). As we have already seen, one possible approximation to i_E is given by Π^c/V, that is, by approximating the non-observable Π^e by Π^c. It is also apparent from (9.2) that, if the risk premium Z could be assumed constant, i_E could also be approximated by the real rate ($i_L - \dot p\$^e$), up to a constant. Since neither assumption is valid we have actually used a weighted average of these two alternative approximations; the weights were estimated from the data and it is found that i_L accounts for nearly two-thirds of the total.

To assess the effect on investment of a change in the long-term interest rate (i_L) we first note that, by assumption, the long-run elasticity of investment with respect to RE is unity. However, i_L represents but one portion of RE, the other portions being represented by i_E and by depreciation. Taking account of the effect of i_L on i_E, and also of the effect of various tax provisions (corporate profit, depreciation allowances, investment credit), it is found that the overall steady-state elasticity of investment with respect to i_L, in the normal range of variation of i_L, is of the order of 0.7–0.8. However, one would not expect an instantaneous response of investment. We estimate an Almon distributed lag response pattern and find that the response builds up gradually to its long-run level, as one would expect for a putty-clay technology. It begins only with a one-quarter lag; after one year, it reaches 75% of the steady-state effect, and the full response takes roughly six quarters. (By contrast, with the conventional putty-putty technology the response of investment would initially overshoot the long-run level.)

The other major variable determining investment in equipment is the desired gross addition to capacity, which we approximate by a distributed lag on total output, X. Finally, it should be mentioned that in the model the equipment function does not generate investment directly but rather orders for equipment, OE. These, in turn, generate deliveries, and hence investment expenditure, with a distributed lag whose average length is itself variable and an increasing function of the ratio of unfilled orders to capacity (approximated by sales).

The model for investment in plant (IP) is basically the same as that for investment in equipment. The results are also analogous, with the exception that for investment in plant there is evidence of some degree of *ex post* substitution, as the response of investment to a change in RP, the rental rate, involves some overshooting.

In line with the above, our diagram shows both IE and IP as determined by the two components of the cost of capital, ($i_L - \dot p\$^e$) and i_E, through RE and RP on the financial side, by aggregate output on the real side, and by tax provisions, in every case with long distributed lags.

4.2 Residential construction

Here we rely on a rather different model (described in more detail in Kalchbrenner [11]) of the putty-putty variety, on the ground that residential capital produces an output of services without any significant labour input — hence there can be no question of *ex post* fixed labour-capital coefficients. Basically, we assumed that the rate of new construction depends upon the profitability of building houses which, in turn, depends upon the relation between the market price of existing houses (PH) and the construction cost (PHC); that is,

$$IH = f(PH/PHC) \qquad (9.5)$$

The price of existing houses is obtained in turn by capitalizing the 'net return' at a required rate of return, measured by a weighted average of the long-term interest rate and the rate on mortgages. The net return to the owner is the gross rental rate (RH) less taxes and depreciation and plus the expected appreciation of the property. Thus

$$PH\$ = \frac{RH\$ - PH\$(\delta_H + \tau_H - \dot{PH\$}^e)}{w_1 i_L + w_2 i_M}$$ (9.6)

where δ_H and τ_H are the depreciation and tax rates respectively, and $\dot{PH\$}^e (= \Delta PH\$^e / PH\$)$ denotes the expected percentage capital appreciation. Solving for $PH (= PH\$ / P\$)$ gives

$$PH = RH/RH^*$$ (9.7)

where

$$RH^* = w_1 i_L + w_2 i_M + \delta_H + \tau_H - \dot{PH\$}^e$$ (9.8)

can be thought of as the 'required' gross rate of return. Finally, the gross rental rate (RH) is derived by equating the demand for housing space (KH^d) with the existing stock (KH). The main arguments of the demand equation are RH, 'permanent income' (approximated by consumption, C) and net worth (NW); that is,

$$KH^d = g(RH, C, NW).$$ (9.9)

Equating to KH and solving for RH yields

$$RH = F(KH, C, NW)$$ (9.10)

By substitution into (9.5) and (9.7) we obtain the investment equation in reduced form:

$$IH = f\left(\frac{F(KH, C, NW)}{RH^* PHC}\right)$$ (9.11)

To understand the implications of the model and of the estimated parameters with regard to the elasticity of construction with respect to interest rates, one must distinguish between the short and the long run. If we start from an equilibrium situation with $IH = \delta_H KH$, so that the stock of housing is constant, and the 'required' gross rate of return is lowered, then initially the real price of houses rises (since RH is constant) and this increases residential construction by more than replacement, increasing the housing stock; however, as the stock increases the rental rate and real price decline, reducing investment again until a new steady state is reached. The long-run elasticity of the stock, and hence investment, can be expressed as

$$\eta_{IH,RH^*} = \frac{\eta_{g,RH}\ \eta_{f,PH/PHC}}{\eta_{g,RH} + \eta_{f,PH/PHC}}$$ (9.12)

where g is the demand function defined in (9.9) and f is the supply function defined in (9.5). Our current estimates of these critical elasticities are respectively 1.27 and 0.95, so that η_{IH,RH^*} is around 0.55. The response to the weighted average interest rate is somewhat smaller, since this average is but a portion of RH^* (cf. (9.8)) — however, this portion turns out to be rather close to unity since δ_H is quite small for houses and is also partly offset by the expected appreciation term, and because of special tax provisions for home ownership (which we have omitted from discussion). Thus the long-run elasticity with respect to i_L is not far from 0.5. In the short run, however, while the stock is building up to the new steady state, the response of investment to changes in i_L is considerably larger. It should be largest at the very beginning, except for the fact that our model allows for a gradual response of *PH* to *RH** and of *IH* to *PH/PHC*. As a result, the impact elasticity is 0.75 and, if the change in *RH** is maintained, the response continues to grow to a peak of about 1.3 in the third quarter. These figures again must be scaled down somewhat to make them apply to i_L rather than *RH**.

In addition to the more or less traditional mechanism outlined, the model allows for two further channels of influence of monetary policy on construction activity. Firstly, the demand for housing, and hence investment, depends also on wealth; this in turn is significantly affected by monetary policy, along lines discussed below in relation to consumption. Secondly, we have found some evidence of transient effects on residential construction from credit rationing in the mortgage market. It is hypothesized that the mortgage market is not instantaneously cleared by the mortgage rate; as a result, investment is affected by the inflow of intermediaries' funds to the mortgage market, measured specifically by the change in their outstanding mortgage commitments. This mechanism can make a significant contribution under two circumstances. Firstly, because the rate of interest on saving deposits adjusts slowly, a rapid rise in market rates can transiently reduce the inflow of saving deposits. Secondly, if ceilings on this rate keep it at a low level relative to market rates, intermediaries will be able to attract an abnormally low flow of saving deposits (so-called disintermediation). In either case, the adverse effect on the inflow of deposits tends to reduce their supply of mortgage funds, increasing rationing.

The model described was intended to apply both to one-to-four family dwellings, which are primarily owner-occupied, and to multiple family dwellings, with proper adjustment for tax treatment. Unfortunately, in the case of multiple family units we were unable to identify the effect of the cost of capital via required returns.

4.3 Consumers' expenditure

This is a sector on which monetary policy is usually assumed to have no direct impact or, at best, only a modest one via consumers' purchases of durables. The situation is quite different for our model.

We begin by defining consumption (*C*) as expenditure on non-durables and services plus the value of services from durables. This latter quantity is measured by *RD.KD*, where *KD* denotes the stock of durables and $RD = PD(i_L + \delta_D)$ is the rental rate (*PD* denotes the price of durables and δ_D is their depreciation rate). The life cycle model suggests that *C* should depend on wealth (*NW*) and on after-tax labour income (*see* Ando and Modigliani [1]). Because it is difficult to estimate this quantity for the US we have been forced, regretfully, to replace labour income by disposable income, *Y* (but with taxes treated on an accrual rather than cash basis). This makes *C* a function of *NW* and *Y* as shown in the flow chart. The most satisfactory results are obtained with a long (twelve quarters) distributed lag on disposable income and a short (four quarters) lag on wealth. The latter variable makes a highly significant contribution, with *t*-ratios as high as 8, though the weights decline rapidly, the first two coefficients accounting for some 80% of the sum. This sum amounts to 0.053, a figure of substantial magnitude and one which accords reasonably well with both *a priori* expectations and previous results of annual models.

As is apparent from Figure 9.1, the presence of *NW* in the consumption function implies a direct channel of influence from monetary policy to consumption; it goes from the money market to the short-term rate, to the long-term interest rate, to the required rate of return on equities, to the market value of shares, and hence to wealth. (In principle, there should also be effects through at least two other components of net worth, namely, the value of land and the value of houses; however, at the moment we cannot measure these effects for the want of usable estimates of the relevant prices.) To assess the quantitative effect, we may note that the elasticity of the rate of return on equities with respect to the long rate (the rate of change of prices constant) is about unity, that of the market value of shares with respect to the equity yield is precisely unity, and finally, that share holdings are presently about one-third of aggregate net worth. Thus the elasticity of C with respect to i_L is approximately

$$\eta_{C,i_L} \simeq (0.33)(0.05)\frac{NW}{C} \simeq 0.08 \qquad (9.13)$$

since NW is roughly five times greater than consumption, Thus, a 10% increase in the long rate would initially reduce consumption by nearly 1%. The resulting impact on aggregate output is quite large and of the same order of magnitude as that resulting from the response of the components of gross investment, when account is taken of the much larger magnitude of consumption. Furthermore, it is relatively fast. Of course, a given change in the long rate would require, in the short run, a much larger change in the short rate.

Some critics of the model, even though willing to accept the general approach to the consumption function, have expressed disbelief that consumption could possibly respond so strongly and promptly to the corporate stock component of wealth. This is for two reasons. Firstly, the ownership of stock is heavily concentrated in the upper percentiles of the distribution of wealth or income, where the marginal propensity to consume should be relatively low. Secondly, as Duesenberry [7] has asserted, one should expect a relatively long response time for capital gains on stock, in part because the holder must tend to think of them as partly transient. A rebuttal of some of these criticisms has been provided elsewhere (Modigliani [15]); however, we do see some merit in the hypothesis that the response to changes in V may be slower than that to the rest of NW. We have tested the hypothesis by allowing different lags for the two components and find that the most convincing results are obtained by replacing the four-quarter distributed lag on NW with an eight-quarter lag on V and a zero lag on $(NW-V)$ — though, interestingly, the improvement in fit is negligible, and the weights decline rather rapidly. This alternative specification is about to be adopted in the model, but the results of simulations quoted later rest on the older version.

Consumption is not a component of aggregate demand in terms of conventional national income accounting. What we need is consumers' expenditure; this is obtained by subtracting from C the imputed rent on KD and adding gross purchases of, or investment in, durables (ID).

To account for ID, we start, much as in the case of housing, from a long-run demand for the stock in terms of income and the rental rate: $KD^d = f(C,RD^*)$, and $RD^* = PD(i_L + \delta_D - PD\$^e)$. Investment in durables then serves to make up, gradually, any discrepancy between KD^d and the initial stock.

Note that, in contrast to the case of residential construction, we assume here that the supply is infinitely elastic at the price PD (which, like the general price level $p\$$, is determined basically by an oligopolistic mark-up on minimum average cost; *see* p. 254). This is because the depreciation rate for durables, estimated at 0.22 per year, is some ten times larger than that for residential structures; as a result, realistic fluctuations in desired net additions to the stock require but moderate fluctuations in gross investment (ID) which, we can suppose, can generally be accommodated within the existing productive capacity. This assumption would not be tenable in housing, where a rise in residential investment is assumed to require a rise in the price of housing, both to ration output and to attract additional capacity.

The long-run elasticity of KD with respect to RD^* implied by the estimated parameters is just above 0.5, which is not unreasonable though perhaps a little low. However, the elasticity with respect to i_L is a good deal lower because the high value of δ_D implies that i_L is only a small portion of RD^*, around one-sixth or one-seventh. Accordingly, the elasticity with respect to i_L turns out to be only around 0.08. Once again this measures the long-run response for both KD and ID, from steady state to steady state; initially, the response of ID is larger in order to bring the stock to the new equilibrium level. Because of the gradual response of the demand for stock to the rental rate, the elasticity with respect to the latter starts at about 0.3, and reaches a peak of around 0.9 in four to six quarters. To calculate the elasticity ($\eta_{ID,iL}$) these figures need to be multiplied by about 0.15. In addition, a change in i_L can affect KD^d and ID by way of net worth and consumption but this is a rather small effect. On the whole, we find that the channels via durables make a contribution that is not altogether negligible, though smaller than for all other components studied so far.

4.4 Inventory investment

The role of this last component of private expenditure is seen as that of bringing the stock (KI) to the appropriate cost minimizing level ($\widehat{KI}$) in relation to sales for goods made to stock, and in relation to new orders for goods made to order. To avoid extensive disaggregation we approximate the first type of goods by aggregate consumers' expenditure. For goods made to order, we distinguish between equipment and federal government defence procurement. The first component is modelled according to the standard stock adjustment framework, with investment a function of current and past sales, determining $\widehat{KI}$, and of the initial stock. Current sales are both a determinant of desired stock and a measure of drain, possibly in part unintentional; hence its sign is uncertain *a priori* and our estimate turns out to be negative. The component related to goods made to order is accounted for by a distributed lag on orders; orders for equipment are generated by the corresponding investment equation, and those for defence are taken as exogenous.

In addition, we hypothesize that inventory investment might be affected by financial conditions in two ways: the optimum inventory/sales ratio should respond to the real short rate, $i_s - \dot{p}\$^e$; and investment in inventories might respond to changes in credit rationing. To our great disappointment, we have been unable to uncover evidence for either effect. In the case of interest rates, the failure may reflect the fact that the wide swings of this volatile component are dominated by accelerator effects. In the case of credit rationing, we suspect identification difficulties in that inventory variations are largely financed by commercial loans and thus rationing tends to be tightest when inventory investment is high. Though our search has not ended, inventory investment is currently the only component of private domestic demand (besides investment in multiple dwellings) which is not directly affected by monetary policy.

4.5 State and local government expenditure

This sector is treated as endogenous and is modelled somewhat like the household sector. Current expenditure is controlled by 'needs', measured by urban population, say, by resources available in the guise of the tax base, measured by consumption, and by grants-in-aid by the federal government. For capital expenditure, we rely on a putty-putty framework with the optimum long-run stock of capital ($\overline{KSL}$) depending on the factors above plus the rental rate, which is of the usual form, $RSL = PDSL\,(\delta_{DSL} + i_{SL})$. The rate i_{SL} differs from i_L because of the tax exemption feature of state and local bonds; it is determined in a market which need not be discussed here except to note that i_{SL} is very closely linked to i_L, to which it is very nearly proportional, with a short adjustment lag. In the expression for the rental rate there is no adjustment for the expected rate of inflation; this is because we have found no evidence so far to support this hypothesis. Fortunately, this failure is more plausible for this sector than for any other.

The contribution of the cost of capital (rental rate) to the explanation of construction expenditure is quite significant (the t-ratio for the sum of weights is around 6) and the implied long-run elasticity of the stock (KSL) (and hence also of investment, in the stationary state) with respect to the rental rate turns out to be fairly high, of the order of 0.7. Because the depreciation rate is estimated to be small, only 1.75% per year, the interest rate is the dominant component of the rental rate and the long-run elasticity of the stock (and investment) with respect to i_{SL} and hence the long rate is only a little lower. Investment brings the stock gradually to the long-run equilibrium level, though the estimated speed of adjustment, less than 2% per year, is rather implausibly low. Because the adjustment is so slow, the initial response of investment to changes in the rental rate is negligible (around 0.03) and it rises only gradually, reaching a peak after eight quarters. The peak elasticity would be 1.4 in the absence of growth but declines rapidly with the rate of growth since depreciation is so small; given the current relation between ISL and KSL it is around 0.3–0.4. It would thus appear that this particular channel, which is a rather unorthodox one, is quantitatively of some importance, though, not surprisingly, it is very sluggish.[1]

4.6 Federal government expenditure on goods and services

This item is taken as exogenous. The federal government is represented by the box in the lower right-hand corner of Figure 9.1. Taxes and transfer rates are also taken as exogenous. On the other hand, state and local (net) taxes (TSL) are endogenous and basically determined by current consumption and capital outlays by state and local governments.

---

[1] In the version of the model used in the simulations reported in section III the construction expenditure equation includes, in addition, a five-quarter distributed lag of the difference between the change in the short-term rate and in the municipal rate. This term, which was meant to measure the impact of tight markets on capital expenditure via credit rationing and related phenomena, is actually statistically not very significant (the sum of weights has a t-ratio just over 2) but turns out to have some weird implications for the response to certain types of monetary policies. Specifically, the impact elasticity on ISL of a change in i_S is not far from 0.1. This is not *per se* a large figure. However, it must be remembered that in our model, because of the gradual adjustment of the demand for money, the impact elasticity of i_S with respect to M is quite high (close to 30). Hence a change in M by 1% in a given quarter (or an annual rate of 4%, which is not altogether unrealistic) implies an increase in ISL of some 3% in the same quarter, which seems highly questionable. The term has, therefore, been eliminated in the current version. Its presence in the version used in section III tends to produce some overstatement of the first quarter response of GNP and some distortion in its composition; however, this effect does not seem to be too serious and in any event tends to wash out rapidly.

4.7 Foreign trade

This component is modelled along conventional lines. Exports are at present exogenous, and imports are basically a function of real aggregate output, the rate of utilization of capacity, and relative prices.

4.8 Summary of final demand sectors

In summary, we find that monetary policy has a direct impact on all components of final demand except five. These exceptions comprise

(i)   Sectors which are by assumption exogenous: the only one in our model is federal government expenditure on goods and services, and some transfers.

(ii)   Sectors for which we would not *a priori* expect a significant impact of monetary policy: these consist of state and local government expenditure on current account, and the net foreign trade balance (as long as the system operates under fixed exchange rates).

(iii)   Sectors for which we had expected, but could not empirically establish, a measurable impact of monetary policy. These include construction of multiple family dwellings and inventory investment. Since, at least in the first case, we cannot accept the empirical result as conclusive, we suspect our model may understate the effects of monetary policy, but hopefully not to a significant extent.

Of those components that are affected by interest rates, the one with the highest long-run elasticity seems to be investment in plant and equipment (η is just less than unity), one-to-four family residential construction ($\eta = 0.55$), followed by expenditure on consumers' durables and other consumption (η around 0.08), and finally by state and local government investment. However, because of the putty-clay nature of equipment and, partially, plant and their relatively slow response, it is the residential construction component that turns out to exhibit both the peak response ($\eta = 1.3$) and the fastest peak response (three quarters). In terms of peak response size, investment in plant ranks next, followed by equipment, durables and consumption. But in terms of speed it is consumption that ranks second (one year) followed by equipment and durables (six quarters) and plant.

Finally, if we assess the contribution to aggregate output *through* each sector, by weighting the elasticities by the share of the sector in GNP, investment in equipment ranks highest but, surprisingly, it is almost tied by consumers' expenditures, followed by housing, plant, and consumers' durables. Considering that consumption is also the fastest to respond and the second to reach peak, we see a picture emerging in which consumption, through the wealth effect, plays a major role in transmitting the initial impulse of monetary policy. It will soon be seen that this picture is supported by simulation results.

5. Aggregate Output and Income

The sum of the demand components determines GNP as indicated in Figure 9.1, which in turn feeds back on various components of the demand for output and also, together with tax rates and transfers, determines corporate profits; this latter feeds into the market value of equities and disposable income, which feeds into consumption and, through saving, into net worth.

6. Labour Market, Wages, and Prices

To close the model we need to account for the behaviour of prices whose level and rate of change affect many sectors. The relevant mechanism is sketched out

in the right-hand portion of the flow chart under the heading of labour market.[1]
Firstly, the price level (p\$) is determined by an oligopolistic mark-up on long-run
minimum average cost; its main component is unit labour cost determined by the
wage rate (w\$) and long-run productivity, α. The mark-up is assumed constant
except for a cyclical component measured by the ratio of unfilled orders to sales.
This model clearly implies that the real wage (w) is basically determined by employers; this is in our view a good approximation in a nearly closed economy (such as
the US) or in an open economy under a floating exchange rate, though it is almost
certainly inappropriate for an open economy under a fixed exchange rate regime.

Finally, the wage rate is determined by a fairly conventional Phillips mechanism:
that is, $\dot{w}$\$ is a function of the rate of unemployment (u) and of the rate of change
of prices, $\dot{p}$\$. Because the coefficient of $\dot{p}$\$ is a good deal less than unity, there is
a stable, non-vertical, long-run trade-off locus between u and $\dot{p}$\$. We have done
substantial work on a much more ambitious model, distinguishing between unionized
and non-unionized labour, and allowing for such factors as overtime and the number
of workers whose contract is negotiated in the given quarter. However, since these
refinements, though of interest *per se*, did not significantly improve the fit, we are
at present retaining the standard model.

The price level together with real aggregate output gives the value of GNP in
current prices, which feeds into the money demand equations. Finally, $\dot{p}$\$ contri-
butes to the determination of real interest rates by influencing expectations about
the future rate of change of various prices.

7. The Channels of Fiscal Policy

Although this paper concentrates on the channels of monetary policy, the flow
chart also provides a summary view of the channels of fiscal policy. These are fairly
conventional. Expenditure affects real aggregate output directly through federal
government expenditure. In addition, because state and local expenditure is endogenous, it also affects this component of demand through transfers (grants-in-aid)
to these entities. Taxes and transfers affect output mostly through disposable
income, but can also affect individual components through excise taxes and sub-
sidies as well as through various tax incentives. Figure 9.1 shows only two of these
effects – that on housing, through various concessions to home owners, and that
on investment in equipment through investment credit – which are particularly
important in the US.

III. System Response to Selected Policy Instruments

1. Methodology

Having examined the individual channels through which monetary and fiscal
policy tools affect aggregate demand, we proceed to provide some indications of
how the system as a whole responds to the standard monetary tools, focusing on
the magnitude and timing of the response and the contribution of the newer
channels appearing in our model.

We measure aggregate demand by gross national product both in constant prices
(*GNP*) and in current prices (*GNP*\$). The response is computed by the method of
comparative dynamic simulations inside the historical period. That is, we first

[1] A further description of this sector is given in De Menil and Enzler [6].

simulate the model with the policy variables on their historical path. We refer to this simulation as the 'historical' or 'control' run and denote the GNP so computed by GNP^c. Next, we run a second simulation with one or more policy variables changed in some specified way. We refer to this second simulation as a 'policy' run and label $GNP^* - GNP^c$ the 'response path'. When the policy variable has the same dimension as GNP, we usually divide the above difference by the change in the policy variable and refer to the result as a policy multiplier.

We examine the response to three monetary policy variables: the money supply, unborrowed reserves, and the short-term interest rate. In addition, we present the response of GNP to a change in government purchases of goods. This response, when expressed per $ billion of exogenous change, is essentially the 'expenditure multiplier'. It measures the response to any 'exogenous' change in expenditure – i.e. a change not brought about by a change in income – and results from the consumption multiplier, the accelerator, and their interaction. This multiplier is of interest not merely because it measures the effect of a change in government expenditure on goods, but also because the response to any other policy variable is profoundly affected by this multiplier. Indeed, this response can be looked upon as the superimposition of two effects: a direct effect of the policy variable on one or more components of aggregate demand plus the multiplier response to this direct effect.

Unfortunately, the 'multiplier' turns out to be an ill-defined concept, for it depends on what assumptions are made as to which monetary variable is exogenous. One possible assumption is that the exogenous monetary policy variable is the short-term interest rate, the Central Bank supplying whatever amount of monetary base is required to maintain the short-term rate on its historical path. An alternative assumption is to take the money supply as given. Clearly, this is the notion that is most relevant in analysing the response to a once-and-for-all change in the money supply (or unborrowed reserves) and it is therefore used in all the simulations reported below.

Since our system contains a number of essential non-linearities, the response is in general not independent of initial conditions – that is, the state of the system at the beginning of the policy simulations – or of the actual path of the exogenous variables over the period of the policy experiment. Because of limitations of space, we focus our attention on a single policy experiment generally starting in the near past, around the beginning of 1967. We recall here that 1967 is a year in which unemployment was already quite low, and which was followed by expansionary fiscal and monetary policies which further increased the inflationary pressures in the economy. To assess the sensitivity of our results to the specific initial and historical conditions we shall report, for comparison, selected results of a policy simulation beginning around 1962, a period of considerable slack in the economy followed by a very gradual expansion of aggregate demand, reduction of unemployment, and reasonably stable prices until 1965. The comparison helps to assess whether the above described difference in initial conditions produces differential effects that are *a priori* credible and 'sensible'.

In section 3 we examine the GNP response for the first twelve quarters following the change in the policy variable. Of course, the response generally continues well beyond three years. The cut-off is determined, in part, by the fact that at the time the simulations were run we did not have reliable data much beyond three years and, in part, by the consideration that one would seldom be concerned with the response to a policy change very far into the future. However, from the long-run properties of the system it is possible to establish, without recourse to simulation, what the 'longest-run' response will be. By this term, we mean the limit to which the response tends if a limit exists or, which is equivalent, if the system is dynamically stable. We start out in section 2 below by considering these long-run responses, showing that they are quite 'classical' and consistent with many of the monetarists' contentions. However, comparison with the results reported in section 3 will show that these responses, which apply to the proverbial long-run in which we are all dead, have very little relation to what occurs immediately following the policy change and for many quarters thereafter.

2. Long-run Response to Policy Variables

2.1 Change in government expenditure

The initial effect of a rise in federal expenditure in our model is, of course, to raise GNP directly and indirectly via the multiplier and accelerator. Yet one can readily show that in the 'longest run' the real multiplier, given the nominal money supply, $M\$$, must be zero. This is because as long as the multiplier is positive, prices must keep rising faster than in the base simulation (because of lower unemployment) and money GNP, $GNP\$$, must therefore be higher. But since by construction, $M\$$ is the same in the two simulations, interest rates must stay higher, which in turn gradually 'crowds out' investment as well as consumption (through the wealth effect) until GNP falls back to the original track. Thus, in the longest run the response of real GNP is zero. The only effect of the additional government expenditure is to displace an equal amount of other expenditure through higher interest rates, and to raise the general price level, $p\$$, and $GNP\$$ to an extent that depends both on the rise in i_s needed to displace the other expenditure and on the responsiveness of velocity to changes in interest rates.

2.2 Change in money supply

The initial effect of a rise in $M\$$ by $dM\$$ is, of course, to lower interest rates, thereby increasing investment and consumption, and hence GNP. Yet one can readily establish, by a reasoning analogous to that under 2.1 above, that in the longest run the response of GNP must tend to zero – that is, that money is neutral. Similarly, $GNP\$$ must tend to rise by $dM\$$ times the velocity of circulation computed at the value of the interest rate prevailing for the base simulation. This in turn implies that the percentage change in $p\$$ must tend to $dM\$/M\$$, i.e. that the quantity theory holds.

2.3 Change in unborrowed reserves

In the longest run the effect is that of a change in the quantity of money equal to the change in reserves, divided by reserve requirements. Hence, again there are no real effects but only a change in $p\$$ and $GNP\$$ proportional to the change in $M\$$.

2.4 Change in the short-term interest rate

In this case it is not possible to give a definite and general answer as to the longest-run response of the system. This is basically for the reason stressed by Friedman and the monetarists. If the Central Bank insists on pegging the rate of interest at any given level, the money supply needed to enforce this policy, as well as the price level, may eventually have to rise (or fall) at an indefinitely high rate. (However, for *our* model this conclusion holds only on the assumption that the government does not take appropriate stabilization measures – a qualification that the monetarists are likely to disregard.)

This outcome depends on the fact that in the longest run our model tends to exhibit the characteristics of so-called 'neo-classical' growth models. As in these models there exists — at least if we assume tax revenue approximately homogeneous of first degree in money income, and government expenditure proportional to income — a unique 'natural real rate of interest' that is consistent with the model moving along a golden age growth path, with the natural rate of growth determined by technological progress and population growth. The natural real rate of interest is determined by the production function, the parameters of the consumption function, the natural rate of growth, and fiscal policy in the sense of the ratio of government deficit (or surplus) to GNP. Together with this real rate there is a 'natural' money rate which equals the real rate plus the rate of change of prices, determined in turn by the rate of growth of the money supply (which must also be assumed constant on the golden age path).

Suppose we take such a growth path as our control run and consider the effect of lowering the money rate by di_S, letting $M\$$ change as necessary to produce this rate. The only way the system can get back on the growth path with the lower rate being enforced is for the expected rate of change of prices to *decrease* permanently by an amount di_S, so as to leave the real rate unchanged. But the system will not respond in this way; on the contrary, the fall in i_S, being initially a fall in the real rate, will stimulate investment and consumption which, by decreasing unemployment, will actually cause the rate of inflation to rise. As a result, the real rate falls even further, causing more and more pressure on unemployment and, hence, a faster and faster rate of growth of $\dot{p}\$$ (and $M\$$). In other words, if the money rate is fixed and money supply is endogenously determined so as to support that rate, then the system is dynamically unstable. These are, of course, the kind of considerations which lead monetarists to conclude that the Central Bank should never take as its target the enforcement of a given money interest rate; our model would support this conclusion only if the words 'for ever' were inserted after 'enforcement'. But it does not imply that the Bank should not have a temporary interest rate target, provided the target is appropriately changed in the light of the circumstances; this point will become especially clear when, in the next section, we examine the short-run response to a change in i_S.

3. Short-run Response to Policy Variables

3.1 Graphical presentation

Figures 9.2–9.6 show the response of total output for a period of three years following a step change in the indicated policy variable. In each graph the shaded columns in the left-hand portion of the diagram show the response for real GNP, while those on the right give the same information for money GNP. Because the distinction between money and real interest rates and the resulting explicit recognition of the role of price expectations is a relatively novel feature of our econometric model, we have also endeavoured to provide some information about the specific contribution of this mechanism to the overall GNP response. To this end, the shaded columns drawn from the horizontal *downward* show the response of the full system including the price expectational mechanism, while the shaded columns *above* the horizontal exhibit the response of a system in which that mechanism is suppressed. This suppression was accomplished by taking in each relevant equation the rate of change of price term — which is our operational measure of $\dot{p}\$^{e}$ and is subtracted from the money rate to yield the real rate — as exogenously given at its historical value, instead of calculating it endogenously from the history of prices generated by the simulation. Note that, since in the relevant equations $\dot{p}\$^e$ is assumed to be zero (or at any rate a constant), as long as the prevailing rate of inflation remains below a threshold value (estimated empirically at 1.5% per year), the response shown in the upper part of the graph represents also the full system response under conditions of stable prices.

The other major novel feature of our model is the wealth effect on consumption. In order to provide information about the role of this mechanism we have also computed the response after suppressing the effect of the (real) interest rate on consumption through the value of the corporate equity component of net worth. This suppression is accomplished by the simple device of severing the connection between interest rates and the rate i_E at which expected profits are capitalized. That rate is instead taken as exogenous (i.e. at its historical value). Of course, this is not equivalent to taking wealth as exogenous, since wealth contains many assets beyond equity in corporate enterprises; indeed, as noted earlier, in recent years that component has amounted to only about one-third of the total. Nor is it strictly equivalent to taking the market value of equity as exogenous. For that value is obtained by capitalizing dividends and we continue to treat dividends as endogenous; thus any policy change which affects GNP will still affect wealth by changing the flow of dividends via both real and price effects. The response excluding wealth effects is shown in each graph by means of the unshaded columns adjoining the shaded ones.

Finally, in order to assess the role of initial conditions, we also show in Figures 9.2–9.4 the results of a simulation beginning in the first quarter of 1962. These results are represented by dashed vertical lines to the left of the two columns.

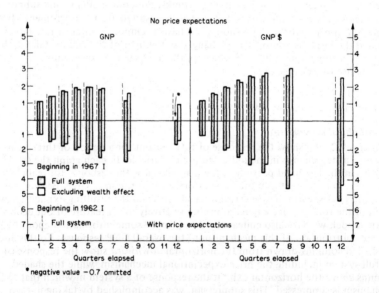

Figure 9.2 *Expenditure multipliers (based on $10 million change in exports)*

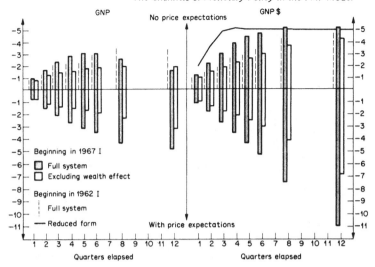

Figure 9.3   *Response of GNP to an exogenous change in
the stock of demand deposits (based on $2
billion decrease spread evenly over two quarters)*

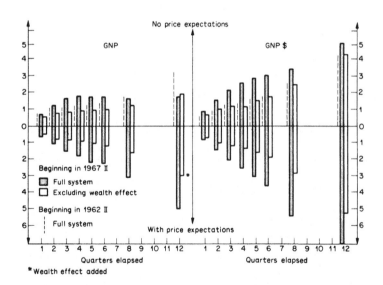

Figure 9.4   *Response of GNP to an exogenous change in
the stock of demand deposits (based on $2
billion increase spread evenly over two quarters)*

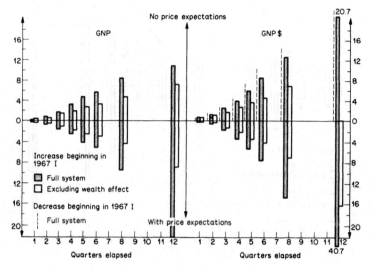

Figure 9.5 *Response of GNP to a $0.5 billion change in unborrowed reserves*

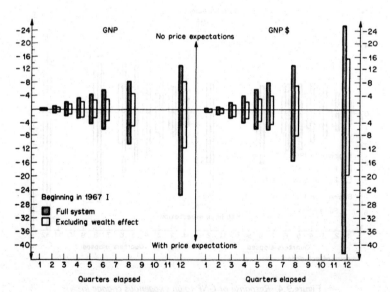

Figure 9.6 *Response of GNP to a change of 0.5 in the Treasury bill rate*

It is hoped that with the help of this introduction the figures are largely self-explanatory. We shall, therefore, limit ourselves to brief comments.

3.2 The multiplier (Figure 9.2)

The highlights of the results may be easily summarized. When the price-expectational mechanism is absent, the *GNP* multiplier reaches a maximum of about 2 by the fifth quarter. It then declines as the rise in *GNP$* generates higher interest rates which 'crowd out' investment and consumption; it crosses zero roughly after three years. The *GNP$* multiplier, as expected, reaches a somewhat higher and later peak, but it still turns around before the end of two years.

The price expectational mechanism makes relatively little difference for the first four to six quarters, but thereafter it considerably amplifies both multipliers. The peak value of the *GNP* multiplier is now about 3 and is reached after three years. The reason of course is that, at least for a while, the higher interest rates are offset by more bullish price expectations, which reduce *pro tantum* the 'real' rate. Nonetheless, the multiplier finally reaches a peak and begins to decline rapidly, for, with the money supply given, eventually the increase in interest rates exceeds the increase in the expected rate of change of prices. In view of the low unemployment in the simulation period, the *GNP$* multiplier gets quite high; it reaches 6 by the end of our simulation and is still rising, though presumably it is not far from its peak.

The multiplier for the simulation beginning in 1962 is a little higher and reaches a peak a little later because, through the curvilinearity of the Phillips curve, the multiplier effect on the rate of change of prices is lower in the early, slack period, and this permits more growth in *GNP*. On the whole, this conclusion is qualitatively sensible; expenditure multipliers on real GNP are larger when there is more slack. Indeed, in the limit, if we started out with the labour force already at a very high rate of utilization, one would expect the real multiplier to dwindle toward zero as, say, the additional government expenditure would rapidly have to displace other components of expenditure. The difference shown in the graph is perhaps smaller than one might expect; but it should be remembered that in 1967 I the rate of unemployment was still at 4.2% as compared with 5.5% in 1962.

Finally, comparison of the shaded and unshaded columns shows that, as long as price expectational effects are not operating, the wealth effect, though initially negligible, eventually *reduces* the multiplier and appreciably accelerates its decline. This is to be expected as the rise in interest rates tends to reduce the equity component of wealth, choking off consumption. This effect does not begin immediately because initially the effect of rising rates is more than offset by rising dividends and profits. However, with elastic price expectations the wealth effect tends to *increase* the multiplier response, since the expectation of rising prices initially lowers the real rate, though the money rate rises, and thus increases the equity component of wealth.

3.3 Response to a change in the money supply (Figures 9.3 and 9.4)

The effects of a fall in *M$* (Figure 9.3) and that of a rise (Figure 9.4) are shown separately because they turn out to be rather different. The asymmetry can be traced to the fact that the long rate depends not only on the current short rate and its past but also the on risk premium which is an increasing function of the variability of the short-term rate. As a result, a *reduction* in *M$* will raise i_L through two mechanisms: by raising the short rate and by increasing its variability and, hence, the risk premium. On the other hand, in the case of an *expansion* of *M$* the first mechanism will make for a lower i_L but the second will again make for an increased

i_L. Hence a rise in $M\$$ tends to cause a fall in i_L which is both slower and starts smaller than the rise resulting from a fall in $M\$$.[1]

We may call attention to the following major implications of Figures 9.3 and 9.4:

(i)   The wealth effect increases and appreciably speeds up the response; indeed, in quarters three to eight it accounts for roughly half of the total.

(ii)   When the economy has more slack the response of money GNP is somewhat smaller throughout the first three years, because prices rise less; but for the same reason, the response of real GNP is larger, at least after a while.

(iii)   The contraction in *GNP* generated by a reduction in $M\$$ reaches a peak which is over 50% larger than the expansion generated by an equal rise in $M\$$. For *GNP$* the response to expansion is merely much slower, but it eventually reaches the same plateau. The notion that monetary policy is more powerful and faster-acting in reducing than in expanding activity is of course a very old one, though our model accounts for this by a mechanism somewhat different from that traditionally visualized ('You can lead a horse to water but you cannot make it drink'.) On the whole, we feel that the mechanism in our model resulting from the asymmetric response of i_L to a rise as against a fall in i_S is a credible one, though its magnitude could be overestimated.

(iv)   One significant feature of the *GNP$* response to a fall in $M\$$ is that it bears a reasonable similarity to the response implied by the coefficients of the so-called 'reduced form' equations of the Federal Reserve Bank of St. Louis, i.e. the co-efficients obtained by regressing the change in *GNP$* on a distributed lag of past changes in $M\$$. This statement can be verified by comparing the histogram in the right portion of Figure 9.3 with the solid curve plotted in the upper quadrant which graphs the response implied by a recent estimate of the reduced form coefficients. The resemblance is in a sense encouraging, but we are inclined to play it down. For one thing, in the reduced form, $M\$$ is defined as currency plus demand deposits whereas in our simulations it includes only demand deposits. Hence our response should be larger. In addition, the response implied by our model is substantially difference depending on whether $M\$$ is increased or decreased and on the initial conditions, including whether prices are stable or rising rapidly in the base run, so

---

[1] The results shown in Figures 9.3 and 9.4 were obtained from a simulation in which demand deposits ($M\$$) were changed by $1 billion in 1967 I and by another $1 billion in 1967 II. The choice of this particular pattern was dictated by two considerations. On the one hand, we wanted the change in $M\$$ to be sufficiently large not to distort the calculated multipliers by rounding errors. On the other hand, we wanted to avoid a large sudden jump in $M\$$ which, for reasons discussed above, would produce a sharp transient change in the short rate and hence increase the 'risk premium' component of the long-rate equation. Since the stock of demand deposits in 1967 was around $140 billion, an increase of $2 billion in a single quarter would have represented an annual rate of increase of some 6% over and above the historical growth which was already of the order of 4%. By smoothing the $2 billion increase over two quarters we halved the annual rate of increase in $M\$$ over the period in which the additional demand deposits were injected. The histograms in the figures show the effect of the change in demand deposits on GNP beginning with the quarter of the *second* of the two increments, namely 1967 II, per $ billion change in the money supply. It should be noted that this response differs in some respects from the response in the quarter of the first injection; in particular in that quarter the induced change in the short rate is roughly twice as large.

that the expectational mechanism operates. The similarity is close for only one of the simulations: when M$ is reduced and the price expectational mechanism is not operative. Last but not least, there is reason to suppose that the reduced form method tends to yield a significantly upward biased estimate of the response to an *exogenous* change in M$ (*see* Modigliani [15], Epilogue). It is, nonetheless, suggestive that, if the wealth effect is excluded, the response implied by the model bears consistently much less resemblance to the reduced form estimates.

3.4 Response to a change in unborrowed reserves (Figure 9.5)

Figure 9.5 shows the response to an increase in UR$. In addition, in the simulation we have tied the discount rate (i_D) to i_S, by taking the spread between them exogenous at the historical level. If i_D were kept constant, then the initial fall in i_S would induce a fall in borrowing, partly offsetting the expansion of UR$. The following points are worth noting.

(i)   The response is much slower than in Figures 9.3 and 9.4, as the lag between a change in UR$ and a change in M$ — which is long in the US because of the relatively low degree of concentration in banking — is superimposed on the lag from M$ to GNP and $\dot{p}$$.

(ii)   The change of some $21 billion in GNP$ by the end of three years is not overlarge considering that under US reserve requirements a change in UR$ by $0.5 billion should eventually lead to a rise in M$ of some $3.5 billion, which, with the interest rates prevailing during the simulation period, would result in the longest-run in a rise in M$ of the order of $20 billion.

(iii)   The response of GNP$ to a *decrease* in UR$ is shown by the vertical dashed lines. It is seen that it is again larger and faster than the response to an increase, but now the difference is minor. This is because the response of both M$ and i_S is both gradual and smooth and hence does not significantly increase the variability component of the risk premium in i_L.

3.5 Response to a change in the short rate (Figure 9.6)

The response here is quite gradual, as the change in i_S is only gradually communicated to i_L, and there are further lags before this latter effect gets fully communicated to the commodity markets. However, by the end of the simulation the effect is quite large (and is still growing), which is not surprising in the light of the comments in section 2 above.

4. The Contribution of Individual Components in the Overall Response to a Change in the Money Supply

Figures 9.7 and 9.8 show the paths of response to a change in M$ of the short and the long rate and of the individual components of demand.

The movement of the interest rates is shown in Figure 9.7, right-hand scale. Since we are specifically dealing with a decline in M$ the expected response here is a rise. As one would expect, in view of the gradual adjustment in the demand for money, the short rate initially overshoots considerably the equilibrium level. If income were constant, it would fall back to this level by the second quarter and remain there. But since income is actually falling, i_S itself continues to fall, though quite gently. Eventually, however, it falls below the original level. Somewhat surprisingly, this turnaround (which the monetarists have stressed) requires only about six quarters. The long rate, which lags much behind, overshoots much less and does not fall below the initial level until the end of the simulation. (This is in sharp contrast to a decline in *exogenous expenditure*, when both rates fell monotonically over the same period.)

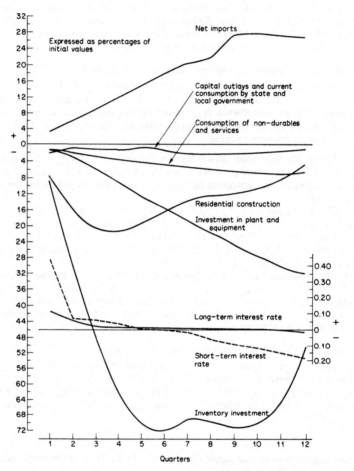

Figure 9.7 *Response of the components of GNP and of interest rates to a $2 billion decrease in the stock of demand deposits (percentage of initial values)*

The other curves in Figure 9.7 exhibit the change in *GNP* and its components, each relative to its level in the base period (measured along the left-hand scale). This change is essentially the elasticity of response to M$,$\eta$, up to a proportionality factor (namely, the relative change in M$, which is some 7.5 per thousand).

The response, it should be recalled, reflects both the direct impact of the movement of the long rate and the indirect effect of the multiplier and accelerator. For *GNP*,η builds up from about one-sixth in the first quarter to about unity after three years. Aside from inventories, the behaviour of which reflects entirely the accelerator, the component responding fastest is residential construction. Construction, however, is also the first to retrace its course, as i_L starts falling again and the decline in *GNP* decelerates. In the case of investment in plant and equipment, because of the much longer lag involved, the response builds up slowly though it eventually becomes the largest. For consumption all we can see from this graph is that the responsiveness is consistently rather low, lower than for *GNP* as a whole. Imports is the only one of the remaining components which exhibits a large response. The response is in fact surprisingly high; it seems to reflect the effect of the rate of capacity utilization, quite large in this period.[1]

The component part chart (Figure 9.8) presents the same information from a different angle. Instead of focusing on the elasticity of response it focuses on the actual contribution of each component to the total *GNP* response; this contribution is the relative response of Figure 9.6 multiplied by the size of the component. Because the contribution of imports is consistently negative, and to avoid lines crossing each other, the origin for measuring the first component, consumers' expenditure, is not the horizontal axis but the ordinate of the import component.

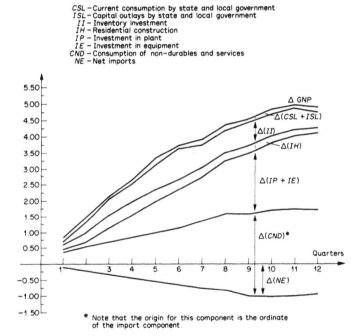

CSL – Current consumption by state and local government
ISL – Capital outlays by state and local government
II – Inventory investment
IH – Residential construction
IP – Investment in plant
IE – Investment in equipment
CND – Consumption of non-durables and services
NE – Net imports

* Note that the origin for this component is the ordinate of the import component

Figure 9.8 *Response of the components of GNP to a $2 billion decrease in the stock of demand deposits ($ billion) — signs inverted*

---

[1] The relatively large response of state and local government expenditure in the first quarter can be traced to the problem reported in footnote 1, p. 252.

It is apparent that consumption is the most important contributor, as the low response elasticity is outweighed by the large size. Also, because of the relatively fast response to interest rates, its role appears especially important in the early transmission; in the first quarter, for example, it provides 60% of the total and the share declines only moderately thereafter. Nor is this result attributable to the feedback of *GNP* on consumption. Indeed, in the case of the multiplier response of Figure 9.2 the share of consumption starts around 40% and gradually rises to 80%. On the other hand, plant and equipment investment, despite its size, contributes rather little in the first two or three quarters, during which it is overshadowed by residential construction, but by the third year its contribution grows to nearly 50%, rivalling that of consumption. Construction instead dwindles in relative and even in absolute importance.

IV. Concluding Remarks

On the whole, the qualitative and quantitative results of section III appear consistent with the picture of the individual channels of monetary policy which emerged from the analysis in section II. They also seem eminently sensible and credible. In addition, these results (as well as others relating to the movements of components in current prices) are also vaguely consistent with the results of reduced form estimates for individual components (for example, those of Meiselman and Simpson [12]). All this suggests that, despite the negative attitude of some monetarists, it may be possible to chart the channels through which monetary policy works as a rule and on the average, account being taken of initial conditions and the effects of non-linearities and variable lags.

Needless to say, these results are rather preliminary and much remains to be done, especially in checking the apparent critical role of consumption in the transmission process. Comparison with similar analysis for other countries with both similar and different structures may be especially helpful. For the moment we can at least hope to have made some contribution towards an understanding of the *modus operandi* of monetary policy.

References — Chapter 9

[1] ANDO, A. and MODIGLIANI, F. 'The 'Life Cycle' Hypothesis of Saving: Aggregate Implications and Tests', *American Economic Review*, 1963, vol. 53, no. 1, part 1, pp. 55—84; and 1964, vol. 54, no. 2, part 1, pp. 111—13.

[2] ANDO, A., MODIGLIANI, F., RASCHE, R., and TURNOVSKY, S. 'On the Role of Expectations of Price and Technological Change in an Investment Function', *International Economic Review*, 1974, vol. 15, no. 2.

[3] BAUMOL, W. 'The Transactions Demand for Cash: An Inventory Theoretic Approach', *Quarterly Journal of Economics*, 1952, vol. 56, no. 4, pp. 545—56.

[4] BISCHOFF, C. W. 'A Study of Distributed Lags and Business Fixed Investment', Unpublished Ph.D. Dissertation (Massachusetts Institute of Technology, 1968).

[5] BISCHOFF, C. W. 'The Effect of Alternative Lag Distributions', Chapter III, pp. 61—130, in FROMM, G. (Ed.) *Tax Incentives and Capital Spending* (The Brookings Institution and North-Holland, 1971).

[6] DE MENIL, G. and ENZLER, J. J. 'Prices and Wages in the FR-MIT-PENN Econometric Model', pp. 277—308, in ECKSTEIN, O. (Ed.) *The Econometrics of Price Determination* (Board of Governors of the Federal Reserve System and Social Science Research Council, 1972).

[7] DUESENBERRY, J. S. Discussion, pp. 86—92, to MODIGLIANI, FRANCO, 'Monetary Policy

and Consumption: Linkages via Interest Rate and Wealth Effects in the FMP Model', in *Consumer Spending and Monetary Policy: The Linkages*, The Federal Reserve Bank of Boston Monetary Conference Series No.5 (The Federal Reserve Bank of Boston, June 1971).

[8] JAFFEE, D. M. and MODIGLIANI, F. 'A Theory and Test of Credit Rationing', *American Economic Review*, 1969, vol. 59, no. 5, pp. 850–72.

[9] JAFFEE, D. M. *Credit Rationing and the Commercial Loan Market* (John Wiley and Sons, 1971).

[10] JAFFEE, D. M. 'An Econometric Model of the Mortgage Market', Chapter 5, pp. 139–208, in GRAMLICH, E. M. and JAFFEE, D. M. (Eds) *Savings Deposits, Mortgages, and Housing* (D. C. Heath and Co., 1972).

[11] KALCHBRENNER, J. G. 'A Model of the Housing Sector', Chapter 6, pp. 209–34, in GRAMLICH, E. M. and JAFFEE, D. M. (Eds) *Savings Deposits, Mortgages, and Housing* (D. C. Heath and Co., 1972).

[12] MEISELMAN, D. I. and SIMPSON, T. D. 'Monetary Policy and Consumers' Expenditure: The Historical Evidence', pp. 229–78, in *Consumer Spending and Monetary Policy: The Linkages*, The Federal Reserve Bank of Boston Monetary Conference Series No. 5. (The Federal Reserve Bank of Boston, June 1971).

[13] MILLER, M. H. and ORR, D. 'A Model of the Demand for Money by Firms', *Quarterly Journal of Economics*, 1966, vol. 80, no. 3, pp. 413–35.

[14] MODIGLIANI, F., RASCHE, R., and COOPER, J. P. 'Central Bank Policy, the Money Supply, and the Short-term Rate of Interest', *Journal of Money, Credit and Banking*, 1970, vol. 2, no. 2, pp. 168–218.

[15] MODIGLIANI, F. 'Monetary Policy and Consumption: Linkages via Interest Rate and Wealth Effects in the FMP Model', pp. 9–84, in *Consumer Spending and Monetary Policy: The Linkages*, The Federal Reserve Bank of Boston Monetary Conference Series No.5. (The Federal Reserve Bank of Boston, June 1971).

[16] MODIGLIANI, F. 'The Dynamics of Portfolio Adjustment and the Flow of Savings Through Financial Intermediaries', Chapter 3, pp. 63–102, in GRAMLICH, E. M. and JAFFEE, D. M. (Eds) *Savings Deposits, Mortgages, and Housing* (D. C. Heath and Co., 1972).

[17] MODIGLIANI, F. and SHILLER, R. J. 'Inflation, Rational Expectations and the Term Structure of Interest Rates', *Economica*, 1973, vol. XL, no. 157, pp. 12–43.

[18] SOLVIN, M. B. 'Deposit Rate Setting at Financial Institutions', Chapter 4, pp. 103–38, in GRAMLICH, E. M. and JAFFEE, D. M. (Eds) *Savings Deposits, Mortgages, and Housing* (D. C. Heath and Co., 1972).

[19] TOBIN, J. 'The Interest-elasticity of Transactions Demand for Cash', *Review of Economics and Statistics*, 1956, vol. 38, no. 3, pp. 241–47.

Errata

Page 242: variable "*PHC*," which is circled, should have an arrow leading to it from the variable "*p$*."

Page 256, section 2.2, line 7: "*dM$/MS*" should read "*dM$/M$*."

Page 261, 5 lines from the bottom: "but also the on risk" should read "but also on the risk."

Chapter 1

IMPACTS OF FISCAL ACTIONS ON AGGREGATE INCOME AND THE MONETARIST CONTROVERSY: THEORY AND EVIDENCE*

Franco MODIGLIANI and Albert ANDO

with the assistance of J. GIANGRANDE

1. The Issues

After many years of sharp and sometimes acrimonious controversy between the monetarists and their sympathizers on the one hand, and the "non-monetarists" on the other, over the effects of monetary and fiscal actions on aggregate income, some consensus seems finally emerging at least over what to disagree about: the main significant area of remaining disagreement seems to be over the *short- and medium-run* impact of *pure macro fiscal actions* on *aggregate money income*. The monetarists (hereafter the "m"s) hold, in Friedman's words that it "is certain to be temporary and likely to be minor" (1972), while the non-monetarists (the "n-m"s) hold that it must be substantial – at least for a good many quarters. Since our purpose here is to contribute to a clarification of the issues, it is well to start by spelling out the operational meaning of the four italicized expressions.

(i) By a *macro fiscal action* we mean an exogenous action of the treasury changing expenditure or receipts, that is, specifically: (a) a change in the quantum of goods and services purchased by the (federal) government (G), or (b) a change in the rate of taxation and transfers. The term thus excludes many other events which affect current dollar receipts and expenditures, such as increases in outlays due to changes in the price level, or a change in tax receipts due to changes in real and/or money income. For the "n-m"s, these events should have no significant causal effects on real or money income.

* The contribution of Ando and Giangrande, and the cost of computations necessary to the preparation of this paper was supported by the National Science Foundation grant GS-32383X to the University of Pennsylvania.

To conserve space, our discussion will focus on one specific macro fiscal action, namely a maintained change in G; however, the results can be readily generalized to the case of tax changes.

(ii) By *pure* we mean that the fiscal action does not give rise to a change in the money supply. Operationally, we define the *impact* of the fiscal action as the difference between the path of money income ($X\$$) of two economies which are identical in all other respects (initial conditions, policy variables, other exogenous variables) except for the fiscal action. The impact of the fiscal action on any variable Z, t quarters after the stimulus, will be denoted by $\Delta * Z_t \equiv Z_t' - Z_t$ when Z_t' and Z_t are, respectively, the values of Z in the economy subject to the shock and in the comparison economy. Of course, the behavior of $\Delta * Z_t$ will in general not be independent of the date at which the experiment is performed.

Fivm the point of view of tying the fiscal with the monetary policy, the most suitable definition of money aggregate would be the monetary base: however, for practical purposes, we find it more convenient to use M_1. This should not make a major difference, and may even be more suitable when account is taken of the interest elasticity of demand for currency, which, together with fractional reserve, would tend to make M_1 respond to the demand for it, for a given base. In other words, taking M_1 as given should strengthen the monetarist case.

(iii) By *short- and medium-run* we mean a period of two to three years. To be sure, this span is arbitrary but it is chosen in the light of two considerations. First, many "n-m"s, and certainly the authors, would agree that, *given time enough* (and provided the system is stable), as increase in real government expenditure is likely to crowd out entirely some other component of expenditure, with the result that the initial increase in income will, eventually, largely disappear, at least in real terms [cf. Modigliani (1971), Ando (1974)]. And they would also agree that the same conclusion holds for the increase in income resulting, initially, from the rise in consumption consequent upon a reduction in taxes. Insofar as money income is concerned, we would expect to find some permanent effect, since the crowding out of other components is achieved largely through a rise in prices and in the entire family of interest rates, which must increase velocity, and, hence, increase money income, given M_1 However, this effect would probably be small and is even somewhat uncertain as it depends on the extent to which private net worth consists of money fixed outside debt. Thus, there is no significant disagreement on the proposition that, by the time a new "long-run equilibrium" is reached, the macro fiscal actions will have no significant effect, at least on real income. However, in the "n-m"s view, this long-run equilibrium outcome will require a very long time (if not forever); it is, therefore, hardly more than a *curiosum* which tells us nothing about the response in the span relevant to the design of policy – say the first one to three years. For the "n-m"s in this initial span, the response will rise to a sizeable peak and will remain consistently positive. By contrast, many monetarists seem to take quite seriously the implications of the St. Louis reduced form estimates implying that the response reaches a puny peak by the second quarter, and disappears altogether by the end of two years. Hence, the real controversial issue concerns what happens in the first three to, say, twelve quarters.

(iv) Finally we want to concentrate on $X\$$, again to focus on points of maximum difference. The "n-m"s have always recognized that, if M_1 is constant, G will crowd out some investment so that the impact of G on X will, at some point, decline, and this might even occur in short order. However, since the crowding out arises from an increase in interest rates, there must initially be a rise in $X\$$. This would come about in part from a rise in prices, though only in part, since prices could not rise unless there was an expansion of X and employment. But because the "n-m"s (and perhaps even "m"s) hold that prices are sluggish – especially downward – even if the effect on X should be shortlived, the effect on $X\$$ must be fairly lasting. Thus if the St. Louis coefficients were estimates of effects in real terms the "n-m"s might conceivably accept them as an outside possibility. But an unreconcilable disagreement arises over the implied impact on $X\$$.

In what follows, we propose to make one more attempt at reaching some consensus that pure fiscal actions do have an appreciable effect on money income (i.e., multipliers well above unity) in the short and medium run. To this end we will start by reviewing "n-m"s, and some "m"s, hypotheses about the individual links and their interaction and the empirical evidence supporting these hypotheses. Next we will endeavor to show why the empirical evidence provided by the St. Louis type reduced forms is grossly unreliable and/or irrelevant.

2. The Non-Monetarists Model and Empirical Evidence

We find it convenient to use the structure of the MPS model to illustrate the "n-m" position both for the sake of concreteness and because it facilitates the task of mustering the supporting empirical evidence. To be sure, not all of the "constituents" for whom we purport to speak would agree with every detail of our formulation, but we do believe that they would broadly agree with its essence, at least qualitatively.

Before examining the response of $X\$$ to G implied by the MPS, it is useful to review some of the earlier models, in part, because this helps to set the MPS structure in perspective and, in part, to show how the difference between monetarists and non-monetarists has narrowed down in time, in part, no doubt, through learning from monetarists' contributions.

2.1. The Earliest Keynesian Model

In the earliest text-book version, the multiplier was given by the well-known formula

$$\frac{\mathrm{d}X\$}{\mathrm{d}G} \equiv \frac{\Delta * X\$}{\Delta * G} = \frac{1}{1 - c(1 - \tau)}, \tag{1}$$

where c is the m.p.c. and τ the marginal tax rate. $\Delta * X\$$ denotes the limiting value taken by $\Delta * X\$_t$ when (if ever) it has stopped changing. The common-sense of (1) is that income must rise enough to provide extra saving equal to the increase in the government deficit ($\Delta * G - \tau\Delta * X\$$). Allowing for a gradual response of C to X, some time would be required for this rise to occur, but, once reached, it would be maintained. This result would, of course, be applicable only if: (i) the interest rate, rather than M_1, were kept constant ("permissive monetary policy"), and (ii) there were no response of P to X (so that $\Delta * X = \Delta * X\$$), which could make sense, at best, if there was plenty of slack in the economy.

2.2. The IS–LM Paradigm

If M_1, rather than r, is kept constant, but the other assumptions are maintained, one obtains the classic formula

$$\frac{\Delta * X\$}{\Delta * G} = \frac{1}{1 - c(1 - \tau) + H}, \qquad H = \frac{I_r L_y}{L_r}, \tag{2}$$

which epitomizes the Hicksian rendition of the General Theory: income must rise to the point where the increase in saving offsets the higher deficit minus the fall in investment crowded out by $\Delta * G$. Because the response of I to r would be gradual, the equilibrium position (2) could be reached only after a substantial stretch of time. On the other hand, the gradual response of the demand for money to r, might speed up the process, by causing some initial overshooting of r [cf. Tucker (1968)].

2.3. Wealth Effects

Formulae (1) and (2) still neglect the effect of wealth (W) in the consumption function. As shown in Modigliani (1971), once we allow for W, formula (1) would have to be changed to

$$\frac{\Delta * X\$}{\Delta * G} = \frac{1}{\tau},$$ (3)

that is, income would have to rise enough to make the deficit disappear; for, as long as there was a deficit, W and C, and hence X, would continue to rise. Note that equation (3) had already been derived by Christ (1968) without allowing for W, but that was under the assumption that the deficit was entirely financed by money creation.

Similarly, one can readily establish that, allowing for wealth effects, (2) is changed to

$$\frac{\Delta * X\$}{\Delta * G} = \frac{1}{\tau + H},^1$$ (4)

i.e., income must rise enough so that the incremental budget deficit equals the displaced investment. But the attainment of this equilibrium level would require a very long time (especially since the increase in r will have a negative impact on W). Hence a long-run equilibrium formula like (4) is already of rather questionable relevance for an analysis of short-run response. This conclusion is reinforced by the consideration that once we take into account the effect of ΔG on investment, we must also allow for acceleration effects on all durable goods – plant, equipment, housing consumers durables. These effects, being transient (if the system is stable), are almost sure to result in over-shooting and may dominate the initial response.

2.4. Wage–Price Effects

Yet even formula (4) is not the relevant one for it still ignores the effect of the rise in G on wages and prices. The "n-m"'s by and large accept the view that ceteris paribus, the rate of change of money wages, and hence of prices, is larger if unemployment is lower (which is consistent both with the view that the longest-run Phillips curve is vertical and that it is not). It then follows, as pointed out,

---

[1] This formula ignores the effect of the interest on the debt and tax revenue therefrom, which is quantitatively small but introduces some further complications.

e.g., in Modigliani (1971) and Ando (1974), that, in the longest run (and provided the system is stable), $\Delta * X$ must approach zero. For, as long as it is positive, prices must rise faster than they would have in the absence of $\Delta * G$, causing $\Delta * P$, and hence $\Delta * r$, to be positive. This in turn, would keep reducing all interest elastic components of aggregate demand, such as investment and consumption (via W). Thus, in the end $\Delta * G$ must "crowd out" an equal amount of other components of demand, or

$$\frac{\Delta * X}{\Delta * G} = 0. \tag{5a}$$

On the other hand, as noted earlier, we would expect $\Delta * G$ to cause a *permanent* increase in $X\$$ – in the sense that the effect would hold in the new long-run equilibrium – because the increase in r, needed to produce the crowding out, produces a permanent increase in velocity. The permanent effect is given by

$$\frac{\Delta * X\$}{\Delta * G} = X\$ \ \frac{1}{P}\frac{\Delta * P}{\Delta * G} = \frac{1}{H}, \tag{5b}$$

where H is defined in (2), except that I_r must now be thought of as measuring the responsiveness to r of all components of (real) private demand, and not just of investment. Even this conclusion should be readily acceptable to monetarists since it was clearly stated by Friedman (1972), though in the specific context of a pure tax increase: ". . . the lowered interest rate resulting from the federal government absorbing a smaller share of annual saving will reduce velocity; the transition to the lower velocity reduces spending for a given money stock. . ." The only puzzling thing about the above passage is that the acknowledgment of a once and for all reduction in $X\$$ for a given M was used to support the statement quoted earlier that "any net decrease in spending from these sources is certain to be *temporary*".[2] (Italics supplied).

But we must emphasize once more that, at least according to the parameter estimates of the MPS model, the limiting position described by (5a) and (5b) is relevant, at best, in the proverbial Keynesian long run.[3]

---

[2] The only way to reconcile the two passages is to suppose that Friedman is confusing the effect of the tax on expenditure with its rate of change. The rate of change of expenditure will be negative only temporarily, namely in the period of "transition to the lower velocity", but, at the end of the transition, the level will stay permanently lower.

[3] In addition, (5a) and (5b) are only approximately valid for they do not take into account all relevant effects. For instance (5b) neglects the possibility that a portion of private wealth might take the form of net money fixed assets: allowing for this possibility would add to the denominator a term consisting of the elasticity of private demand with respect to private wealth times the share of wealth represented by money fixed claims – thus reducing the permanent effect. Similarly, one should allow

2.5. The Short- and Medium-Run Response

As is apparent from the above, in our view, none of the multiplier formulae just reviewed is of much relevance for the problem on hand, which is the response in the first two or three years. However, they help to call attention to the various mechanisms that contribute to shape the short-run response of money income. They can be summarized as follows:

(i) *The direct effect of G*, which, being a component of X, must contribute at least $1 (per dollar), in the opening quarters.

(ii) *The induced consumption effect* which results from the increase in net of tax income: all the leading hypotheses maintain, and the evidence confirms, that, in an uncertain world, the response of consumption (to be distinguished from consumer expenditure) to a change in income is quite gradual, especially if income includes profits. The permanent income hypothesis leads to a Koyck type distributed lag of indefinite length. In the MPS, relying on the life cycle hypothesis, the distributed lag extends over a finite but substantial period – the past three years. Thus, if the consumption multiplier were the only mechanism at work, we would expect the response to continue to build up for a substantial period tending according to (1), to a limiting value of about 1.5 (since $c \simeq 0.66$ and $\tau \simeq 0.5$). Note also that mechanism (i) and (ii) will be reduced by the marginal propensity to import, estimated at somewhat over 0.10 in the MPS.

(iii) *The accelerator mechanism*: the timing here is more difficult to judge on *a priori* ground, but one would expect the build-up of durable goods, including consumers' durables, to service the larger demand, to occur gradually, except in the case of inventories and possibly consumers durables. On the other hand, if the system is stable, this effect must, at some point, reverse itself.

(iv) *The price effect* which will make $\Delta * X\$$ larger than $\Delta * X$. It must be remembered, in this connection, that, in order to make our analysis conform with the St. Louis approach, we must define $\Delta * X\$$ as the change in the value of *GNP* and not the value of the change, i.e., $\Delta *(X\$) = P \cdot \Delta *(X) + X \cdot \Delta * P$. As P rises, the second term can make a large contribution relative to the first. Just how fast this

Footnote 3 continued
for the fact that the displacement of investment by government expenditure would tend to reduce the capital–labor ratio, and hence X, at least as conventionally measured. Taking this effect into account would tend to make $\Delta * X/\Delta * G$ negative and to increase the price response given in (5b).

effect builds up clearly depends on the extent of slack in the economy. The evidence suggests that there are significant lags in the response of wages to unemployment, of prices to wages, and finally of wages to prices; indeed it is this kind of lag that accounts for the stagflation of 1970–1971 and of today. Accordingly the increase in P should tend to occur gradually, but to become important within the span with which we are concerned, particularly if the rate of employment is high to begin with.

(v) *The wealth effect* which tends to increase consumption through the higher level of wealth resulting from a larger flow of saving. However, one should expect this effect to contribute negligibly over the run with which we are concerned.

(vi) *The Hicksian crowding out effect* which starts with the rise in interest rates resulting from the rise in $X\$$, in the face of an unchanged supply of money. The beginning of this process may be related, in monetarist style, to the additional borrowing by the government to finance the incremental deficit. However, it must be remembered that the extra borrowing is matched by an equal flow of incremental saving; hence, the reason for the rise in r must finally be traced to the need to induce the public to transact a larger volume of business with the same cash balance. This strain, and consequent rise in r, increases as the secondary effects listed above contribute to expand $X\$$. The initial impact of the strains in the money market falls on the short rate which may rise fairly fast, since the available evidence suggests that the demand for money adjusts slowly to r; but the adjustment of the long rates may be expected to be a good deal more sluggish (since they reflect expectations of many future short rates). Finally the rise in the long rates will adversely affect private demand. The channels through which this effect occurs in the MPS are quite varied, as the monetarists prescribe. There are a dozen interest rates and capitalization rates for money fixed as well as equity streams, and every endogenous component of demand responds to at least one rate, except state and local government purchase of services, and (regretfully) inventories. However, the response takes time, though the speed varies for different components.

(vii) *The Pigou–Patinkin "outside debt" effect.* The rise in prices will also have an adverse effect on consumption insofar as money fixed public debt constitutes a significant portion of net worth – which is not the case for the U.S. In part, for this reason, this effect, which is crucial in Patinkin's analysis, is likely to contribute only to a minor extent, at least in the medium run.

On the whole, the evidence suggests that the main contractive mechanism, (vi) tends to work more slowly than the major expansive ones, (i), (ii), (iii). Hence one would expect the response to grow for at least the first few quarters; somewhat later, real output will turn down (if the system is stable) through the combined effect of the accelerator and higher interest rates, and it is hard to say a priori which would play the larger role (nor would this be independent of initial conditions); on the other hand, $\Delta * P$, and hence $\Delta * X\$$, should continue to rise after X peaks through the term $X\Delta * P$, and should remain substantial even when $\Delta * X$ dwindles to zero or first turns negative (something one would hardly expect much before two to three years).

In the light of the above, one should find hardly surprising the results presented in figure 1. Figure 1a shows the response of money GNP ($X\$$) and of real GNP (X) and its components to a maintained change in government expenditure on goods (GG) implied by the MPS. Figure 1b shows the response of interest rates and prices. The data are obtained from a simulation in which G was increased by 1 billion in 1958.1 (M_1 constant). In figure 1a, the top Δ-curve represents

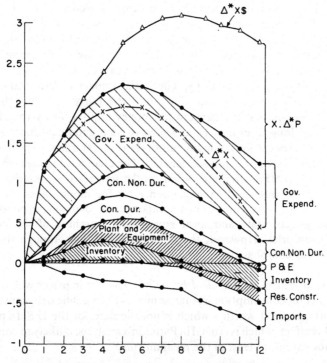

FIGURE 1a. Response of money GNP ($X\$$) and real GNP (X) and its components to a one billion maintained change in GG (government purchase of goods), based on MPS – initial conditions of 1958.1.

$\Delta * X\$$; $\Delta * X$ is represented by the X-curve which is also the sum of the individual real components. Some of these components are positive and they cumulate to the upper dotted curve; some are negative and they cumulate to the bottom dotted curve. The X-curve is the algebraic sum of the positive and negative components and thus falls inside the upper dotted curve. Finally, the distance between the X-curve and the Δ-curve measures the price effect.

A few points are worth noting about the chart. First, the peak response, in real terms – X-curve – is reached fairly early, in about 5 quarters. It is around 2, a figure similar to that reported for other models. This is larger than can be accounted for by equation (2), because of the accelerator mechanism. The role of this mechanism can be inferred also from the rise in the investment components, which are also the first to peak: inventory in quarter 4, consumers durables in 5, and equipment in 6. This suggests that the major mechanism causing the early end of the expansion is the accelerator. However, there is little doubt that the Hicksian crowding out mechanism also begins to work early contributing to the fall of investment, and is important in pushing the response down after the peak. This can be seen, e.g., from the fact that several investment components turn negative (i.e., fall below what they would have been without $\Delta * GG$) when the X response is still quite positive; this happens for residential construction as early

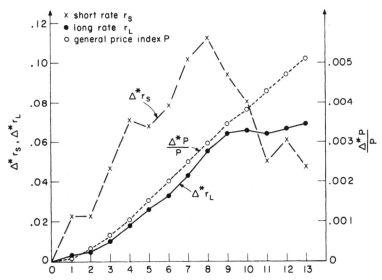

FIGURE 1b. Response of selected intensive variables to a one billion maintained change in GG (government purchase of goods), based on MPS – initial conditions of 1958.1.

as quarter 7, for equipment in quarter 11 and consumers durables in 12. Finally, the price effect, $X \cdot \Delta * P$, behaves pretty much as expected: $\Delta * P$ grows slowly at first but it continues to rise well after X has peaked; thus $\Delta * X\$$ reaches its peak some three quarters later than $\Delta * X$ (in quarter 8), and by the end of three years, it is still substantial, though by then $\Delta * X$ is close to zero.

It should be stressed that, especially because of the price effect, according to the MPS, both the $\Delta * X\$$ and the $\Delta * X$ path can vary substantially, depending on initial conditions. Indeed in a simulation in which the GG shock was applied in 1966.1, the response is found to be explosive. Nonetheless, the results reported in the chart are fairly typical of those obtained at least in the years preceding the Vietnam war.

Having thus established why it is impossible to make any sense of response patterns of the type implied by the St. Louis estimates, we must proceed to review some of the mechanisms most commonly advanced by monetarists, or their interpreters, to account for a very small and purely fleeting response even of $X\$$.

3. Some Monetarists Mechanisms and Their Weaknesses

3.1. The Role of Wealth in the Demand for Money

Some monetarists might claim that in our reasoning we have failed to take into account the role of wealth in the demand for money and that, if we had, our conclusions would be radically different. Indeed the increase in wealth generated by the deficit, and its financing through public debt, must lead to a prompt rise in the demand for money. Since M_1 is constant, the result must be an increase in interest rates which will greatly speed up the crowding out effect. Indeed, Blinder and Solow, in a well-known paper (1973, p. 330), have concluded that if Lw is large enough "fiscal policy does not work" and as a result of ΔGG, "income falls cumulative and without limit". We propose to argue that this monetarist conclusion must be rejected for three reasons: (i) even if W enters the demand for money, $\Delta * X$ must still be positive for a good while, and this holds a fortiori for $\Delta * X\$$; (ii) theory suggests that, with well-functioning capital markets as in the U.S. in the postwar period, W should *not* enter the demand for money; and (iii) empirical evidence supports this theoretical conclusion. We will take up these points in turn.

(i) Clearly r cannot rise unless W rises; but W cannot rise unless saving increases, which requires a rise in X! Put a little differently, if the deficit induced by GG immediately displaces an equal amount of I, W would remain constant and, therefore, r would not rise and could not displace I. Thus we must first have a rise in X; then the gradual accumulation of W can raise r and begin to affect I; there is absolutely no reason why this process should work any faster than the Hicksian one; and, certainly once the rise in X has caused higher prices, $\Delta * X\$$ can be counted upon to be positive for quite a while. The contrary conclusion reached by Solow and Blinder is due in our view to many shortcomings of their analysis which have been partly pointed out in Ando (1974). But, for present purposes, their critical shortcoming is that, in the model used to establish the above mentioned conclusion, they have neglected price effects, and, more seriously, they have failed to recognize that wealth includes not only the public debt but also the stock of capital. In addition, they define the multiplier quite unusually as the limiting value taken by $\Delta * (X)$ when the deficit vanishes, rather than when $\Delta * X$ ceases to change. The latter condition, in turn, requires that $\Delta * W$ should also be stationary, and not that the deficit be zero. Had they avoided these shortcomings, they would have found that, under their assumption of slack resources and given P, dX/dG does have a finite value which is a generalization of (4), namely

$$\frac{\Delta * X}{\Delta * G} = \frac{1}{\tau + H + (S/C_w)(1 - c)(1 - \tau)}, \quad S = \frac{I_r L_w}{L_r} > 0. \quad (6)$$

This formula is obtained by making use of the condition that, in the limit, the rate of saving in the economy experiencing the increase in G must return to the same as in the comparison economy. Note that (6) implies that the final effect of $\Delta * G$ is to permanently increase the deficit and reduce the rate of investment. The right-hand side of (6) must be smaller than that of (4) (as long as $c < 1$), so that the L_w does imply a smaller multiplier; nonetheless (6) must be clearly positive.

(ii) In an appendix to Ando and Modigliani (1974), Ando and Shell have established that, with well-functioning markets, and in the presence of a short-term asset involving no risk of principal, the demand for money must depend only on the short-term rate and the volume of transactions (as well as on transaction costs), but must be independent of either wealth or $\dot{P}$. In the MPS, the money demand equation does not contain wealth because we could find no evidence that it had a significant effect; the Ando–Shell results support this specification.[4]

---

[4] The measures of transaction used in the MPS model – *GNP* for demand deposits and consumers' expenditure for currency – do not explicitly take into account transactions on wealth account. In the course of estimating the money sector, we did initially include one variable providing at least a partial measure for such transactions [see Modigliani, Rasche and Cooper (1970)]. This variable was, however, dropped in the final version incorporated in the model because its effect was quantitatively too small to justify the effort of endogenizing it. But we could not find evidence that the wealth transaction effect could be effectively proxied by wealth itself, a result confirmed by the Goldfeld study cited in (iii) below.

(iii) Finally the hypothesis that wealth has no effect on money demand in the U.S. has been confirmed by the exhaustive empirical study of Goldfeld (1973). It is true that Goldfeld finds some mild evidence for an effect of the rate of change of wealth (which he interprets as related to transactions in assets generated by saving). However, extrapolation tests uniformly show that the inclusion of this variable worsens the extrapolation. In any event, this effect could not significantly affect any of our quantitative conclusions, especially since it is, at best, transient.

3.2. The Effect of the Increase in Debt on r, via the Composition of Wealth

Another mechanism claimed by the monetarist and not mentioned by us is the portfolio composition effect: the financing of the deficit raises the ratio of debt instruments to other components of wealth, raising r and thus contributing directly to the crowding out. This argument has been examined with some care and rejected in Ando (1974), to which the reader is referred. It will suffice here to summarize his conclusions:
(i) The issue of debt cannot affect the short-term rate, which, in view of the Ando–Shell argument, depends only on M_1 and $X\$$.
(ii) Hence, if the extra deficit is entirely financed by short-term debt, the resulting increase in the supply of shorts and of sure assets relative to the other components of wealth, will tend to *lower* long-term rates and the required rate of return on equity. This effect, of course, contributes to promoting rather than displacing investment.
(iii) Only if the deficit were primarily financed by long-term debt, the effect of the new issue could conceivably be that of raising the required return on capital, though the effect is uncertain.
(iv) Given the existence in the U.S. of a very large short-term market and its extensive use by the government, we can conclude that even this argument is inconclusive and could not be empirically important. Indeed, in the MPS model, this composition of wealth mechanism is ignored because, much as we tried, we could not find a measurable effect.

3.3. Conclusions

We must conclude that none of the monetarists' arguments reviewed provides cause for questioning the "n-m"s results reported in section 2, either qualitatively or quantitatively. The only remaining problem is: how then can we account for the St. Louis results? It is to this last topic that we now turn.

4. The Unreliability of the Reduced Form Approach

The St. Louis approach has been frequently criticized because of the specific choice of independent variables. We shall largely bypass this issue here because we do not regard it as the crucial one; if the method is basically unreliable, the choice of variables is irrelevant.[5] Hereafter we find it convenient to measure fiscal action, as in figure 1, by government purchases except that we now lump together expenditures on goods and services (G); but no great significance should be attached to this specific choice, other than that of convenience. Indeed, if one runs a "reduced form" (RF) regression using as independent variables ΔM_1 and $\Delta G\$$, one obtains coefficients that look very much like those obtained with other measures of fiscal policy, such as the full employment deficit. This can be seen from the X-curve in figure 2a, which shows the RF coefficients of ΔG current and lagged up to seven quarters estimated over the period 1958.1–1969.4 by a third-degree Almon polynomial – a typical St. Louis specification. It is apparent that the response path, $\Delta * X\$_t$ (the cumulant of the coefficients in the graph) reaches its peak already in the second quarter, and it is quite shallow, but 1.2. It then declines steadily and is practically down to zero by the last quarter. Indeed $\Delta * X\$_8 / \Delta * G\$$ amounts to only 0.38, as shown in the legend. It is also apparent that these coefficients bear little relation to those implied by the $\Delta * X\$$ path produced by the MPS simulation reported in figure 1a, which are shown in figure 2a by the Δ-curve. Figure 2b shows RF coefficients of ΔM_1 current and lagged. The X-curve gives again the ΔM_1 coefficients of the RF estimated on actual data, and the Δ-curve those implied by a simulation of the MPS model in which M_1 was changed by one billion (spread over two quarters), beginning in 1962.1.[6] Again, there is little similarity between the two curves, except that in this case, the RF estimates imply a distinctly larger and faster response.

What should one make of the striking discrepancy between the MPS response and that implied by the RF estimates? Must one conclude that the theory advanced in section 2 is all wrong, and the empirical evidence underlying it is, somehow, irrelevant? In Modigliani (1971), it was suggested that the answer should be negative and the hypothesis was advanced that the discrepancy

---

[5] This a somewhat different position from that set forth in Modigliani (1971); the shift reflects, in part, the result of research done in preparation for this paper, reported below.

[6] The reason for choosing a simulation with 1962 initial conditions is that for the MPS, the $\Delta * X\$ / \Delta * M$ path is much more dependent on initial conditions than the $\Delta * X\$ / \Delta G$ path. The pattern produced by the 1962 simulation is more typical of those obtained up to the late sixties, than that obtained in 1958, which is rather more sluggish. The reason for spreading the increase over two quarters is set out in Modigliani (1971, pp. 46–47).

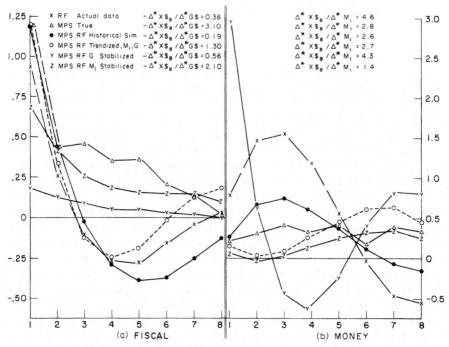

FIGURE 2. True response and reduced form estimates for the MPS model.

results from the fact that, for a system as complex as the U.S. economy, the St. Louis reduced form approach is a very unreliable method of estimating the true response path of $X\$$ to changes in monetary or fiscal aggregates.

4.1. A Test of Reliability Based on Simulation

The above hypothesis was supported by means of a simulation experiment which was labeled, perhaps somewhat inappropriately, a Monte Carlo experiment. Since there has been a good deal of misunderstanding concerning the nature and implications of this test, especially among monetarists, it may be appropriate to review it here. Basically the experiment was designed to test how well the mechanism built inside a fairly complex "black box" having at least some vague similarity to the U.S. economy, could be estimated by applying the St. Louis RF method to the output generated by the black box. The black box chosen for this experiment was the MPS model, and the output was the time series of dollar GNP ($X\$$), of $G\$$ and of demand deposits (MD) generated by a dynamic simulation for the period 1958.1 to 1969.4, using as inputs the historical value of G, and of the treasury bills rate, RTB, as well as of the other policy and exogenous variables. By regressing the value of $\Delta X\$$ so obtained on the current and lagged values of $\Delta MD\$$ and $\Delta G\$$, we can test whether the coefficients of a St. Louis type RF can provide a reasonably close estimate of the "true" response path of $X\$$ to changes in $G\$$ and $MD\$$ which is built into the black box that generated the data, namely the MPS model. The true path is, of course, known with certainty, from the structure of the MPS model and could be conveniently inferred from policy simulations such as those underlying figure 1. It was found that the response of $X\$$ to $G\$$ estimated by the RF bore no recognizable relation to the true response of the MPS model which had generated the data (though it showed some mild similarity to the estimates obtained by applying RF to the historical data).

4.2. Some Replications of the Simulation Test

Figures 2 and 3 report the results of a number of replications of the simulation experiment just described. The first, reported in figure 2, is again based on the MPS and involves only relatively minor variations: (1) to improve the comparability with the St. Louis exercises, the simulation of MPS was carried out taking M_1 rather than RTB as the historically given monetary policy variable, and (ii) in the reduced form, the monetary variable was also M_1 rather than demand deposits.[7]

The coefficients of the reduced form estimated from the output of this simulation, again for the period 1958.1–1969.4, are shown by the black-dot-curve, in figure 2a for government expenditure, and in figure 2b for M_1. This curve is labeled "historical" in the legend, because, in the simulation, all policy and exogenous variables are assigned their historical values, as in the Modigliani (1971) experiment. The true typical MPS response, of which the RF coefficients are supposed to be an estimate, is shown in each figure by Δ-curve. It is apparent from figure 2a that there is, again, little recognizable relation between the true response and the RF estimate of this response, e.g., the estimated response reaches a shallow peak in the second quarter and by the eighth quarter is close to zero, in fact even closer to zero than for the RF estimated from actual data – the X-curve. In the case

[7] In addition, the version of the MPS used for this paper differs slightly from that used in Modigliani (1971). For present purposes, the only significant difference is in the equation accounting for the market value of corporate shares, a component of net worth. The old equation was found to have unacceptable long-run implications and was re-estimated imposing some constraints on the coefficients. For the current equation, see MPS (1973).

of M_1 – figure 2b – the discrepancy between true and estimated response is less striking, though the RF clearly tends to overestimate the early response.

Layton (1972), in the course of pursuing a systematic analysis of the extent and possible sources of bias in RF estimates, replicated the simulation experiment outlined above for three other U.S. models differing widely, in terms of size, complexity, period of estimation, and model structure. These are:

(1) The model by Moroney and Mason [M–M (1971)] – an eight-equation, linear model, with parameters estimated over the period 1953.3–1965.4. It is fairly monetarist in inspiration, with all variables in current prices and the monetary variable consisting of the unborrowed monetary base. For the RF experiment, the output was obtained from a simulation of the model from 1954.1 to 1969.4, and the RF coefficients were estimated by regression for 1958.1–1969.4.
(2) The Kuh–Schmalensee (K–S) model, with 42 behavioral equations, highly non-linear and estimated over the period 1959.1–1969.4. The RF coefficients were estimated by the same method and the same period used for M–M. The money variable is unborrowed reserves.
(3) The well-known Brookings model, probably the largest in existence. The inputs for the RF estimates were obtained from various sources described in Layton, and the sample period was 1953.4–1962.4. Also, because of the nature of the available information, the dependent variable was ΔX rather than $\Delta X\$$ and the fiscal variable ΔG rather than $\Delta G\$$.

The results of these tests are summarized in figure 3, taken directly from Layton (except for labelling). Part I of each figure reports the coefficients of the fiscal variable, and part II those of the monetary variable. The true response of the model is shown by the histogram: for the M–M model which is linear, it was computed analytically, for the other two models from simulations. The total response at the end of nine quarters (the cumulant of the coefficients) or $\Delta^* X\$_9$ in our notation, is shown next to the legend. It is worth noting first the broad similarity in the fiscal multipliers implied by the three models and the MPS. Thus by the end of one year the value falls within a range of 0.5, between 2.15 and 2.65; by the end of two years the range is even narrower, between 2.5 and 2.8. On the other hand, the money multipliers cannot be readily compared because of the different monetary aggregates used for the different models.

The dashed curve in figures 3a and 3b and both curves in figure 3c, labelled "historical" in the legend, exhibit the results of the replication of Modigliani's test for each model. Specifically, they show the response as estimated by RF from the output of a simulation in which all policy and exogenous variables appearing in each model assumed their historical value. In the case of figure 3c, two historical RF estimates are reported, one based on a nine quarter lag (light solid line) and the other on 13 (heavy line).

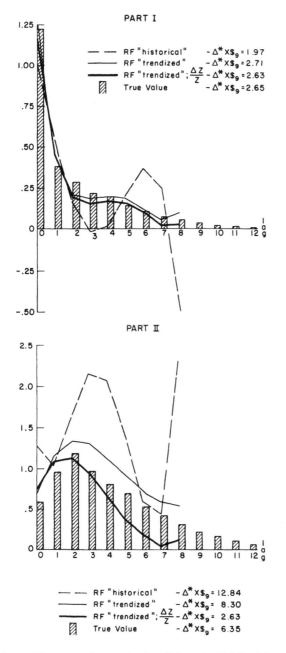

FIGURE 3a. The true and several reduced form implied fiscal (part I) and monetary (part II) multipliers of the Moroney–Mason model – nine quarters.

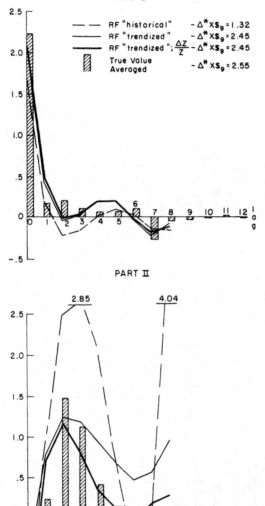

FIGURE 3b. The true and several reduced form implied fiscal (part I) and monetary (part II) multipliers of the Kuh–Schmalensee model – nine quarters.

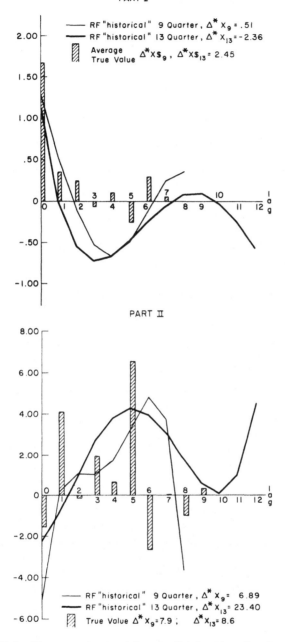

FIGURE 3c. The true and reduced form implied fiscal (part I) and monetary (part II) multipliers of the Brookings model.

It is seen that in every case the RF estimates of the fiscal response tend to underestimate substantially the true response. Thus by the end of the first year the cumulated response estimated by RF is between one half and three quarters of the true response. By the end of the second year, when as already noted, the true response scatters narrowly around $2\frac{3}{4}$, the RF estimate range all the way from nearly 2 for the M–M model, having but two exogenous variables, down to 0.5 and 0.2 for the large-scale Brookings and MPS model. In the case of the money multipliers in part II of each chart, the RF estimates are again generally rather poor; indeed in the case of the K–S model, they are outright wild. Furthermore, they overestimate substantially the true response from the very beginning (with some exceptions for the Brookings model).

4.3. An Objection to the Simulation Experiment

Layton's results just reported are also relevant in answering one plausible criticism that has been levied against Modigliani's simulation experiment. The argument runs as follows.[8] Suppose the true response of the U.S. economy to the monetary and fiscal variables were that implied by the St. Louis RF. The MPS model must then be badly misspecified, in view of the wide discrepancy between these RF estimates and the response implied by the model. To be sure, the model does manage to track reasonably well the historical path of the U.S. economy over the period of the experiment, but this can be accounted for by the consideration that it was estimated over this same period and that with enough ingenuity, and use of degrees of freedom, one can always manage to reproduce a finite set of observations, no matter how false one's model. At the same time, the very fact that the model tracks closely, implies that the output of the simulation used to estimate the RF is *close to the historical path*. It then follows that the RF estimates based on this simulation *must* give rise to coefficients which are close to those of the historical RF and hence very different from the model's response. The discrepancy between the model response and the RF estimate, it is concluded, results from this mechanism and not from any inherent shortcoming of the RF method.

We have never found this argument very convincing since in a ten year dynamic simulation, the MPS model does not track that well. This is especially true of first differences which are always hard to track, especially for the MPS which was designed to account for the level of, rather than the change in, variables. Hence it is pretty far from the mark to assert that the simulation output is simply the historical path.

In any event, Layton's results provide more direct evidence counter to this

---

[8] The argument that follows has been advanced on several occasions in both oral and written communications, including one by Keith M. Carlson.

argument. We may note, in fact, that two of his models, the M–M and K–S, were estimated just like the MPS over a period which includes the years 1958–1969 which were used to estimate the RF coefficients of figure 3, as well as the RF based on actual data. The argument reported above would then imply that the RF estimates of M–M, K–S and MPS should be close to each other and close to those obtained from actual data. In fact, as in apparent from the charts and from the summary of the results reported earlier, one finds that the three RF are quite different from each other and, except possibly for the MPS, also quite different from the RF based on actual data. Finally the RF estimates are also uniformly very poor estimates of true response paths of each of the three models which are broadly similar to each other. We can conclude, therefore, that the "plausible" argument summarized at the beginning of this paragraph can, in fact, not provide an explanation for the fact that RF based on the models' output provides poor estimates of the models' true response.

What then could account for the poor performance of RF? Modigliani (1971, p. 72) called attention to "severe danger of bias in reduced forms" and listed two likely sources:

(i)   the presence of correlation between the policy variables included in the RF regression and other policy and exogenous variables which affect $X\$$ but are omitted in the RF;

(ii) in the case of the M_1 coefficients, the likelihood that, at least at times during the period, "the variable directly controlled by the monetary authority was unborrowed, or free reserves or interest rates", M_1 being then an endogenous variable.

More recently, several authors, notably Goldfeld and Blinder (1972), have called attention to another source of difficulties, to wit:

(iii) the reduced form coefficients will be biased insofar as, over the period of estimation, the policy variables included in the RF have been maneuvered for the purpose of economic stabilization.

In the rest of this section, we endeavor to provide evidence that each of these sources of bias does, in fact, play an important role in distorting the RF estimates over the period of observation. In addition, evidence will be adduced that the RF estimates are plagued not only by bias but also by marked unreliability.

4.4. The Effect of Correlation Between the Included Independent Variables and Omitted Exogenous Variables

Layton (1972) designed and carried out a rather ingenious test to ascertain the role of the correlation between the included policy variables and the omitted exogenous variables, in biasing the RF estimates. It consisted in *eliminating* the correlation by *replacing*, in the stimulation of the models, the historical value of the omitted exogenous variables either by a constant equal to the mean value of the variable (for intensive type variables), or by a time trend fitted to the data (for the extensive variables). It is clear that with this transformation, the first difference of every exogenous variable is basically a constant and hence cannot be correlated with the policy variables, which were kept on their historical path. Unfortunately, the available budget forced Layton to limit the experiment to the two smaller models – the M–M having but two exogenous variables and the K–S having 33.

The RF coefficients estimated on the output of the simulation just described are shown by the light solid curve in figures 3a and 3b. The result, at least for the fiscal variable, is rather dramatic; for both models, the downward bias in the cumulated response disappears and the shape of the RF coefficients fit very closely the true response.

For the monetary variables on the other hand, the fit, while greatly improved, is still not very close and still tends to overestimate the response, especially in the case of K–S. Layton conjectured that this could be due, in part, to the fact that the method described above might not have totally eliminated the correlation. This is because his trends were exponential, and hence the arithmetic increments would still exhibit a positive time trend which would be present also in the included policy variables. To eliminate this last source of correlation, he proceeded to re-estimate the RF coefficients with all variables expressed as percentage changes, $\Delta Z/Z$. The resulting coefficients (multiplied by the mean values of the variable to which they refer to make them comparable with the other estimates), are shown by the heavy solid curve in figures 3a and 3b. For the fiscal variables, there is hardly any change from the previous results; for the monetary variable there is a fair improvement for K–S but less for M–M, as the overestimation is replaced by underestimation.

These results suggest that, at least for the fiscal variable, the correlation with the excluded exogenous variables is a major and, perhaps *the* major source of distortion in the RF coefficients. However, before accepting this conclusion, we must review the results of a replication of Layton's experiment, conducted with MPS. In this experiment, the correlation between included and excluded variables, was eliminated not by changing the *exogenous* variables, à la Layton, but by replacing the historical values of the *policy variables* by exponential time trends fitted to the actual values, plus a randomly drawn additive component. This component was designed to have a substantial serial correlation (0.8), and a variance equal to some chosen multiple, *m*, of the variance of the residuals around trend. Clearly these concocted policy variables could not be *systematically* correlated with the excluded exogenous variables which were kept on their historical paths. The serial correlation and a sufficiently large variance were designed to insure enough lasting variation in the policy variables to affect significantly aggregate output.

In figure 2, the o-curve shows the RF estimates for the simulation in which m was assigned a rather large value, namely 9. Somewhat to our surprise, these estimates are seen to bear again very little resemblance to the true structure, and look a lot more like those of the RF based on actual data, even though the simulated path is now quite a bit different from the actual one. Not less surprising, in another simulation with $m = 4$ (and hence a weaker signal), the pattern of the fiscal coefficients (not shown in figure 2) turns out to have the same general J-shape, but the underestimation is distinctly smaller, the total response after nine quarters amounting to 2.7. On the other hand, the M coefficients are quite non-sensical, starting negative and cumulating to -0.68! The implications of these results, which at first sight seem inconsistent with Layton's, will be taken up in section 4.7 below.

4.5. The Effect of the Monetary Policy Variable Being Different from M_1

To test the relevance of this source of bias suggested by Modigliani (1971) a simulation was run in which the fiscal variables had the same value as in the experiment last described, but RTB was replaced by its trend, M_1 being then computed from the model. The result was that the M_1 coefficients assumed a much more plausible shape, and the total 9 quarter response rose from -0.68 to 2.48! Clearly, this can be an important source of RF bias, even if the choice of interest rates as the control variable occurs only some of the time.

4.6. The Effect of the Policy Variables Being Actively Used for Stabilization

As shown by Goldfeld and Blinder one would expect that, if a policy variable is actively used to stabilize X, then RF coefficients will underestimate the true response to that variable and, likely, overestimate the response to other policy variables included in RF. To test the importance of this effect in the simulation last described, the fiscal variable G consisting of trend plus random error was replaced by a different series designed to stabilize unemployment (U); this series was arrived at by a combination of informal simple proportional and derivative stabilization rules and some judgment. The chosen G maintained unemployment between 3.5 and 4.5%, whereas in the absence of stabilization the fluctuation over the simulation period had been between 3 and 7%. The RF estimates based on this simulation are shown in figure 2 by the Y-curve. As expected, the coefficients of the fiscal variable heavily underestimate the true response, those of M_1 substantially overestimate it, and neither bear resemblance to the true response.

Finally, the Z-curve in figure 2 shows the results of a simulation in which the fiscal variable is trend plus random error with $m = 9$ (as in the first experiment described), while M_1 was used to stabilize U; because stabilization by M_1 alone is somewhat harder to accomplish, we only succeeded in keeping U between 3.5 and 5.5%. The response to M now has a strange shape: it is appreciably lower than the o-curve based on a comparable simulation in which neither M nor G were used to stabilize U, and as expected, generally underestimates the true response. The clear conclusion is that the Goldfeld–Blinder effect could be quite important.

4.7. Overall Unreliability of RF as a Short-Cut to Estimating Structure

In summary, all the experiments point to the unavoidable conclusion that the RF is a very unreliable method for estimating structure. A glance at figure 2 is sufficient to establish that RF can yield widely different estimates of the structure of the model generating the data. As it turns out, in the experiments we have performed, none of the RF estimates comes even close to reproducing the response of $X\$$ to G built into the MPS model, and all of them underestimate substantially the response at least beyond the second quarter. This underestimation, however, is happenchance and we have no doubt that, by conducting a few more simulations, we could come up with some RF estimates looking similar to the structure or even overestimating the true response.

The reason why Layton was able to come pretty close to the true structure by merely eliminating the correlation between included and excluded variables, is to be found primarily in the nature of his technique and, to a minor extent, in the fact, that the response he was trying to reproduce came from models having much simpler structure than MPS – let alone the U.S. economy! Having turned the rate of change of the exogenous variables into a constant in his simulation, the system was exclusively driven by the two included policy variables. Since in addition M–M is linear, Layton's method was bound to reproduce very nearly its structure. Failure to reproduce it exactly would only come from forcing the response to be described by a low-order polynomial of 9 terms. This conclusion is confirmed by the fact that his RF correlation (R^2) was 0.99. For the non-linear K–S model, another possible source of distortion is that the response varies with initial conditions. This factor was apparently not important as R^2 was again 0.99. For the MPS experiment, on the other hand $X\$$ was buffeted around by the exogenous variables kept on their historical path. Accordingly, R^2 is almost universally between 0.45 and 0.65, a range quite comparable to that obtained with historical data. (For our historical RF, R^2 is 0.57.) The unreliability is hardly surprising when so much of the movement in $X\$$ comes from excluded variables.

We conclude that the RF is both a severely biased and quite unreliable method of estimating the response of a complex economy to fiscal and monetary action. This is unfortunate because it really looked like a brilliant short-cut. As it turns out, it has only served to mislead students of macro economics, and to waste efforts in rationalizing its numerical results.

We can only conclude in the same vein in which we concluded our exchange with Friedman and Meiselman many years ago – there are no viable alternatives to the painstaking task of looking inside the black box. When this is done, one cannot fail to conclude that the effects of macro fiscal actions are certain to be long-lasting and likely to be substantial.

Bibliography

Ando, A., 1974, Some aspects of stabilization policies, the monetarist controversy and the MPS model, International Economic Review 15, pp. 541–571.

Ando, A. and F. Modigliani, 1974, Some reflection on describing structures of financial sectors, With an appendix by Ando and Shell, in: The Brookings model: Perspective and recent developments (North-Holland, Amsterdam).

Blinder, S. and R. M. Solow, 1973, Does fiscal policy matter? Journal of Public Economics 2, pp. 319–337.

Christ, C., 1968, A simple macroeconomic model with a government budget restraint, Journal of Political Economy 76, pp. 53–67.

Friedman, M., 1972, Comments on the critics, Journal of Political Economy 80, pp. 906–950.

Goldfeld, S. M., 1973, The demand for money revisited, Brookings Papers on Economic Activity 3, pp. 577–637.

Goldfeld, S. M. and A. S. Blinder, 1972, Some implications of endogenous stabilization policy, Brookings Papers on Economic Activity 3, pp. 585–640.

Layton, D. H., 1972, An analysis of the bias in the reduced form technique of estimating structural properties of economic systems, Master Thesis (M.I.T., Cambridge, Mass.).

Modigliani, F., 1971, Monetary policy and consumption, in: Consumer spending and monetary policy: The linkages (Federal Reserve Bank, Boston, Mass.).

Modigliani, F., R. Rasche and J. P. Cooper, 1970, Central bank policy, the money supply, and the short-term rate of interest, Journal of Money, Credit and Banking 2, pp. 166–218.

MPS, 1973, Quarterly econometric model equations (obtainable from: EFA, University of Pennsylvania, Philadelphia, Penn.).

Stein, J. L., 1976, Inside the monetarist black box, Chapter 3 of this volume.

Tucker, D., 1968, Credit rationing, interest rate lags, and monetary policy speed, Quarterly Journal of Economics 82, pp. 54–84.

PART II
The Demand and Supply of Money and Other Deposits

FRANCO MODIGLIANI, ROBERT
RASCHE, and J. PHILIP COOPER

Central Bank Policy, the Money Supply, and the Short-Term Rate of Interest

I. INTRODUCTION*

The purpose of this paper is to examine the mechanism by which central bank actions are transmitted through financial markets. In particular, we focus on the impact of these actions on interest rates and the money supply. As such, this study is only a portion of a larger project, currently underway, to study the impacts of monetary and fiscal policies on "ultimate goals" of stabilization policies, for example, income, employment, and price levels. A primary objective of this broader study is to examine the dynamics of various policy actions. Consequently, we have attempted a thorough investigation of the lag structure of our hypotheses. In addition, we have employed a number of refined statistical procedures in the attempt to purify our estimates of various biases. Ultimately we shall attempt to validate these various techniques through extensive simulation analysis.

In Part II we review the theory of the demand for money, and present estimates of two demand functions, one for currency outside banks and the other for publicly-held demand deposits at commercial banks. For the purposes of our broader model we feel that it is necessary to disaggregate currency, the quantity of which is determined by the demand of the public, from demand

* The authors wish to thank all their colleagues in the FRB-MIT Econometric Model Project for their helpful criticism during the course of this research. Financial support was provided by the Board of Governors of the Federal Reserve System through the Social Science Research Council.

FRANCO MODIGLIANI *is professor of economics and management at the Massachusetts Institute of Technology.* ROBERT RASCHE *is assistant professor of economics at the University of Pennsylvania.* J. PHILLIP COOPER *is an instructor in business economics and finance in the Graduate School of Business at the University of Chicago.*

deposits, whose behavior results from the interaction of the demand of the public sector and the portfolio adjustment process of the commercial banking sector. In Part III we present a theory of the supply of demand deposits based on the demand of the banking sector for earning assets. Finally, in Part IV we examine these equations as a model of short-term interest rate determination, and present the results of alternative estimation techniques and simulation analysis.

II. The Demand for Money

1. The Basic Hypothesis

Our point of departure in specifying the demand for money is the "Neo-Fisherian" model [7]. According to this hypothesis, the demand for money is basically related to the flow of transactions and arises from a lack of synchronization between receipts and payments, coupled with the transactions costs involved in exchanging money for short-term assets. In this model, the ratio of money demand to transactions, the Cambridge K or the reciprocal of "velocity," is controlled by the interest obtainable on short-term assets relative to transactions costs. Assuming that real transactions costs per real dollar have not significantly and systematically changed over the period of observation and neglecting for the moment transactions on asset account, we are led to a demand equation of the Pigou-Latane [14, 15] form

$$M = K(i)Y. \qquad \frac{\delta K}{\delta i} < 0 \qquad (2.1)$$

Here M denotes money demanded, i stands for a vector of available returns on short-term assets, and Y denotes a broad measure of the flow of transactions, such as GNP in current dollars.

We must, however, think of (2.1) as representing the "long-run" demand equation which need not be satisfied instantaneously because we expect that time is required for the public to respond to changes in interest rates as well as to adjust cash balances to the optimum level. To stress this point, we rewrite (2.1) as

$$M^* = K(i)Y \qquad (2.2)$$

where M^* is the demand for money corresponding to "indefinitely" maintained values for i and Y.

We next hypothesize that the actual demand for money M adjusts gradually toward the equilibrium level given by (2.2).[1] This gradual adjustment hypothesis can be approximated either by the "arithmetic" form

$$\Delta M = \gamma(M^* - M_{-1}) = \gamma(K(i)Y - M_{-1}) \tag{2.3'}$$

or by the "logarithmic" form

$$\Delta m = \gamma'(m^* - m_{-1}) = \gamma'(k(i) + y - m_{-1}), \tag{2.3''}$$

where lower case letters denote the logarithm of the corresponding capital letters. Equations (2.3') and (2.3") are roughly equivalent to each other and both can be directly estimated, once we specify the functional form and arguments of $K(i)$ or $k(i)$.

2. Relation of the Basic Hypothesis to the Friedman and Allais Models

Before we present the evidence that equation (2.3), with the appropriate specification for $K(i)$ or $k(i)$, fits the data for the United States in the postwar period remarkably well, it is useful to point out the consistency of our hypothesis with the so-called "permanent income" model of Friedman [8], with the Brunner-Meltzer Model [4], and with the model recently advanced by Allais [1].

To establish the relation to Friedman's model, we first solve (2.3') for M to obtain

$$M_t = \gamma K_t Y_t + (1 - \gamma)M_{t-1}, \text{ where } K_t \equiv K(i_t). \tag{2.4}$$

Recursively substituting for the lagged value of M yields

$$M_t = \gamma \sum_{\tau=0}^{\infty} (1 - \gamma)^\tau K_{t-\tau} Y_{t-\tau}. \tag{2.5}$$

If we now follow Friedman in neglecting the effect of interest rates on the demand for money (even though this specification is shown below to be inconsistent with the evidence),[2] then K_t can be taken as a constant K, and (2.5) becomes

$$M_t = \gamma K \sum_{\tau=0}^{\infty} (1 - \gamma)^\tau Y_{t-\tau}.$$

[1] Another study which distinguishes short-run and long-run demand for money is Chow [5]. This study, however, involves quite different assumptions about the origin of the demand for money.
[2] See also Laidler [13] for evidence on the effect of interest rates within the framework of the Friedman model.

The summation on the right-hand side is readily recognized as an exponentially weighted average of past income, entirely analogous to Friedman's "permanent income." There are, to be sure, some differences in specification, since (2.5) implies an average of past *aggregate money income*, whereas Friedman averages *per capita real income* and then multiplies it by permanent prices and population. But these are rather minor differences, especially with a sluggish series like income. Furthermore, as will soon be apparent, our empirical estimate of γ based on quarterly data turns out to imply a weighting factor for annual data which is not very different from that used by Friedman to construct his "permanent income."

The relation of our model to the Brunner and Meltzer generalization of the Friedman model can be most conveniently established by starting from the approximation (2.3″) and expressing $k(i)$ as a linear function of the logarithm of i. Again solving the equation recursively for m, one can readily establish that our hypothesis implies that m_t can be expressed as an exponentially weighted average of past incomes and of the short-term rates that appear as arguments of k, except that the average is now of the geometric rather than of the arithmetic variety. Since the weighted average of past incomes can again be identified as a variant of Friedman's "permanent income", the main difference between our formulation and that of Brunner and Meltzer reduces to the fact that they measure the return on money substitutes by the current long-term interest rate, whereas our model implies an exponentially weighted average of current and past short-term rates. Even this difference in specification can be largely reconciled in the light of recent results suggesting that long-term interest rates are closely related to a weighted average of past short-term rates (though the weighting structure is not strictly of the monotonically declining form implied by (2.3″) [17]).

Allais' basic proposition is that the velocity of circulation is an exponentially weighted average of past changes in money income. Solving (2.3″) for m, subtracting y from both sides of the equation and rearranging terms, we obtain

$$
\begin{aligned}
m_t - y_t &= \gamma'k_t + (1 - \gamma')(m_{t-1} - y_t) \\
&= \gamma'k_t + (1 - \gamma')(m_{t-1} - y_{t-1}) - (1 - \gamma')(y_t - y_{t-1}).
\end{aligned} \tag{2.6}
$$

Remembering the definition of velocity $V \equiv Y/M$ or $v = y - m$, (2.6) can be rewritten as

$$
v_t = -\gamma k_t + (1 - \gamma')\Delta y_t + (1 - \gamma')v_{t-1}
$$

or, substituting recursively,

$$
v_t = (1 - \gamma') \sum_{\tau=0}^{\infty} (1 - \gamma')^\tau \Delta y_{t-\tau} - \gamma' \sum_{\tau=0}^{\infty} (1 - \gamma')^\tau k_{t-\tau}. \tag{2.6'}
$$

Treating k_t as a constant instead of a function of interest rates, the second term reduces to a constant. Thus (2.3) is seen to imply that velocity is a weighted average of past rates of change in Y, though again the detailed specifications of Allais' weighted average differ somewhat from those implied by (2.3″).[3]

3. The Demand for Demand Deposits

The basic hypothesis (2.3) has been applied to demand deposits and currency with somewhat different specifications of the independent variables. For demand deposits, denoted by Md (or md in log form), the vector i should include rates on those instruments that, in the given institutional setting, are the closest alternatives to holding demand deposits unneeded for very short time intervals (which themselves may be partly random). Since our demand equation includes households as well as firms, we need to consider the relevant instruments for each. In the case of large firms and wealthy households, the relevant substitute may be taken as a short-term market instrument like treasury bills or commercial paper and, more recently, certificates of deposit. In the case of other households, the closest substitute can be taken as savings deposits, and the relevant rate is therefore the rate offered on this instrument, which we denote by r_s.

The first two rows of Table 1 show the results of the test of hypothesis (2.3) in each of its two variants, (2.3′) and (2.3″). In both cases, the dependent variable was taken as M/Y (or its log, $m - y$), the reciprocal of velocity. For (2.3′) we have approximated $K(i)$ linearly in the two rates, and thus, the equation estimated has the form

$$M/Y = \gamma(a_0 - a_1 i - a_2 r_s) + (1 - \gamma)\frac{M_{-1}}{Y} + u$$

$$= a_0{}' - a_1{}' i - a_2{}' r_s + a_3{}' \frac{M_{-1}}{Y} + u, \tag{2.7′}$$

which is derived by dividing both sides of (2.4) by Y. This form was deemed to yield more reliable estimates of the structural coefficients by making the error component u more nearly homoscedastic, and by reducing the collinearity among all the "independent" variables which would have resulted from the trend-like behavior of both M and Y. In the case of (2.3″), the form estimated is that given by the first equality of equation (2.6), but with $k(i)$ specified to be linear in the logarithms, i.e.,

---

[3] The difference in specifications would seem to become important only when rates of change of income are subject to wide fluctuations in time, i.e., essentially in the case of hyperinflation. In such situations, the more complex specification of Allais has obvious merits, while his neglect of interest rates on money fixed assets becomes totally unimportant.

TABLE 1

DEMAND DEPOSIT ESTIMATES: 1955,I–1966,IV

Row	Form	1 i	2 r_s	3 MD_{-1}/Y	4 $N°P/Y$	5 $r_{cd}-r_s$	6 STK/Y	7 Const.	8 n_i (S.R.)	9 w_s (S.R.)	10 n_i (L.R.)	11 w_s (L.R.)	12 Total L.R. Interest Elast.	13 ρ	14 σ_e	15 R^2	16 $d-w$	17 Relative Error (%)	18 σ_u	19 Relative Error (%)
1	Ratio	-.00214 (-6.04)	-.00411 (-2.50)	.8414 (18.4)	—	—	—	.0536 (3.57)	.03	.05	.18	.32	.50	.58	.00090	.999	2.01	.41	.00110	.52
2	Log	-.0180 (-4.32)	-.0163 (-1.20)	.9259 (28.2)	—	—	—	-.0733 (-2.03)	.018	.016	.24	.22	.46	.52	.0047	.999	1.84	.47	.0055	.55
3	Ratio	-.00212 (-5.44)	-.00428 (-2.08)	.8330 (10.6)	.0046 (.12)	—	—	.0542 (3.48)	.03	.05	.18	.30	.48	.58	.00091	.999	2.01	.41	.00112	.52
4	Ratio	-.0021 (-5.70)	-.0048 (-2.48)	.8163 (13.9)	—	-.0006 (-.65)	—	.0610 (3.30)	.03	.06	.16	.26	.42	.60	.00091	.999	2.04	.41	.00113	.52
5	Ratio	-.00218 (-6.23)	-.0039 (-2.40)	.856 (18.8)	—	—	.00005 (1.44)	.0486 (3.24)	.03	.05	.19	.33	.52	.56	.00089	.999	2.09	.40	.00108	.51
6	Ratio	-.0047	-.0098	.658	-.0298	—	—	.127	.07	.12	.20	.35	.55	.68	.00132	—	1.68	.59	.00187	.88

$$m - y = \gamma'(\alpha_0 + \alpha_1 \log i - \alpha_2 \log r_s) + (1 - \gamma')(m_{-1} - y) + u'$$
$$= \alpha_0' - \alpha_1' \log i - \alpha_2' \log r_s - \alpha_3'(m_{-1} - y) + u'. \qquad (2.7'')$$

The last seven columns of Table 1 provide measures of goodness of fit based on various characteristics of the estimated error component. Since there was evidence of significant serial correlation in the error term, both equations have been estimated using the autoregressive transformation. Column 13 shows the estimated value of the autoregression coefficient, i.e., of the coefficient of the equation

$$u_t = \rho u_{t-1} + \epsilon_t.$$

The next three columns show the standard deviation of the error term ϵ of the above equation, R^2, and the Durbin-Watson measure of serial correlation. Column 17 provides an estimate of the relative or percentage error. For the logarithmic form, this figure is the same as that of column 14, while for the ratio form we have estimated the relative error by dividing the figure of column 14 by the mean value of the dependent variable, M/Y (which is .221 for the period of observation). It should be noted that these statistics are not an adequate measure of the explanatory power of the hypothesis per se, since ϵ only measures the error in any quarter given u_{-1}, the actual error in the quarter before. Since this error can only be known after the quarter has elapsed, ϵ can best be characterized as a measure of the "one-period" forecast error.

A more useful measure of how well the hypothesis explains the phenomenon under investigation is provided by the standard deviation of the error term u, which is given in columns 18 and 19. It can be verified readily that σ_u depends on σ_ϵ, as well as the serial correlation of the ϵ: if the ϵ's are serially independent, then $\sigma_u = \sigma_\epsilon/\sqrt{1 - \rho^2}$. Note that when the equation does not involve the lagged dependent variable, u can be looked upon as measuring the error of a "dynamic" simulation, in which the computed value of the dependent variable is computed entirely from the values of the independent variables. When the independent variables include the lagged dependent variable, however, the error of a dynamic simulation is more complex, being also an increasing function of the coefficient of the lagged dependent variable.

It is apparent that there is little difference between the fit of the two variants of our hypothesis. For (2.3') the relative "one-period" error is only four-tenths of one per cent, implying an error in Md of about half a billion dollars (since the mean value of Md in the period is some 120 billion dollars). For (2.3'') the one-period error is somewhat higher, but the difference in terms of the u error is less pronounced because of the lower serial correlation. However, the two forms do have somewhat different implications about the role of interest rates. In both cases the coefficient of the bill rate is highly significant, but (2.3′) implies a short-run elasticity almost twice as high (cf. column 8). The difference is even more pronounced in the case of the savings deposit rate, with (2.3′) implying an elasticity about three times as high (column 9). Closer examination reveals that these differences can be traced in large measure to differences in the coefficient of the variable M_{-1}/Y, which is an estimate of $(1 - \gamma)$. Equation (2.3″) implies a speed of adjustment of less than 8 per cent per quarter, while (2.3′) yields an estimate of 16 per cent. If we use these estimates of γ and γ' to compute the long-run elasticities (columns 10, 11, and 12), we find that the two versions have similar implications. In particular, the long-run elasticity of demand with respect to a simultaneous change in both rates is substantial, around one-half. This estimate implies, for example, that an increase in both rates from three to four per cent would eventually increase velocity by some 15 per cent. However, (2.3′) assigns a relatively larger role to the savings deposit rate r_s and, even more important, it implies a considerably faster response.

On the whole, we are inclined to question the reliability of the estimates provided by the logarithmic version (2.3″). A speed of adjustment of less than 10 per cent per quarter seems hardly credible. Even the estimate implied by (2.3′), 16 per cent per quarter, or roughly half the full effect within the first year, may appear on the low side; but it is not altogether unreasonable when one recalls that the delay we are measuring reflects in part the time it takes for the public to change the effort devoted to economizing money in response to changes in interest rates. Since (2.3′) seems to fit the data slightly better, we are inclined to conclude that this version provides a better approximation to the money demand mechanism over the sample period and shall rely on it in what follows. Some caution is required in that the linear approximation to $K(i)$ may become poor for values of i very much outside the range of observation, say, 1 to 6 per cent. This is especially true at the low end, for a linear form is incapable of capturing significant liquidity trap effects.

4. Refinements of the Basic Hypothesis

A number of tests have been carried out to assess the empirical significance of certain refinements of the basic hypothesis (2.3) which have been proposed by various authors. Since these tests were not very successful, we shall review them very briefly.

i. Real Income Effects.—Several authors have suggested that the proportionality factor K of equation (2.1) might be systematically affected by real per capita income. In particular, Friedman [7] has maintained, partly on the strength of his own empirical analysis, that money is a luxury, the demand for which rises proportionately faster than real income. This would imply a positive elasticity of K with respect to real per capita income. On the other hand, the inventory-theoretic analysis of Baumol, Tobin, and others (3, 20) suggests that there should be some economies of scale in cash holdings, implying that the elasticity of K with respect to real income should be negative, possibly as low as $-.5$. Others, such as Ando and Modigliani [2] have suggested that both effects might well be present, but to a minor and largely offsetting extent, resulting in no significant net effect. These hypotheses can be most easily tested for version (2.7″) by adding the logarithm of real per capita income to the set of independent variables listed; its coefficient should be positive under the "luxury" hypothesis and negative if there are significant economies of scale. It should be noted, however, that the finding of a significant coefficient for this variable could not be unambiguously interpreted as supporting either position because, over the period, real per capita income is basically a secular trend and hence the variable could proxy for other slowly-changing forces, such as changes in transaction costs, payment habits, and the like. In practice, the problem of interpretation did not arise because the coefficient of the variable, though negative as implied by the economy of scale hypothesis, is quite small ($-.05$) and its t-ratio was less than one.[4] A similar test was repeated for version (2.7′) by adding to the independent variables the *reciprocal* of real per capita income; its coefficient should thus be negative to be consistent with Friedman's hypothesis. The outcome reported in row 3 confirms the above results, in that the coefficient of the variable is positive but totally insignificant, while the remaining coefficients are basically unchanged. These results can also be interpreted as indicating absence of significant trend-like forces acting on the demand for money.

ii. The Effect of Transactions on Wealth Account.—These were neglected in the basic hypothesis (2.2), which would be justified insofar as the ratio of transactions on wealth account to transactions on GNP account remains roughly stable.[5] Such stability is plausible in view of the well-known stability in the wealth-income ratio, yet it cannot be taken for granted. Unfortunately, it is very hard to get a measure of transactions on wealth account. As a crude approximation, we have tried the ratio of the value of stock transactions on all exchanges[6] to current dollar GNP. According to the model, the coefficient of such a variable should be positive since transactions on wealth account should increase the demand for money relative to income, or equivalently, reduce income velocity. The results are reported in Table 1, row 5. The variable turned out to have the expected positive coefficient, but the implied elasticity of Md with respect to this variable, was negligible. It was therefore decided to let this small systematic effect be impounded in the error term.

[4] In order to allow a larger range of variation for the variable and thus increase the efficiency of the test, the period of fit was extended back to the beginning of 1950. The remaining coefficients are affected only moderately, tending to closer agreement with those of row 2.
[5] Rewrite (2.2) as (2.2′), $M = K(i)(aY + bW) = K(i)[(a + b)(W/Y)]Y$. If W/Y is a constant, (2.2′) is indistinguishable from (2.2).
[6] This series was obtained from SEC date.

iii. Effect of Certificates of Deposit.—As noted earlier, this instrument is likely to be a relevant substitute for money in large transactors. Accordingly, the rate on certificates of deposit deserves testing. There is one difficulty—certificates of deposit did not become a significant factor until around 1962–63. To get around this difficulty, we use as an additional variable r_{CD}^*, defined as the spread between the certificates of deposit rate, and r_s when this spread is positive, and otherwise zero.[7] As can be seen from the results reported in row 4, the coefficient of this variable has the anticipated negative sign, but it is statistically insignificant and the implied effect on Md is rather negligible.

iv. Effects of the Rate of Change of i.—One might conceive that the rate of change of i could exert some influence on Md by way of expectation effects. If short-run interest expectations are prevailingly regressive, then a rise in i might be regarded as providing an exceptionally favorable opportunity to invest short-term balances and thus would have a negative effect on (Md/Y). If, on the other hand, short-term expectations were prevailingly extrapolative—as some recent evidence might suggest (see, e.g., Modigliani-Sutch [17])—then Δi should have a positive sign in (2.7') and (2.7'').[8] Tests of the rate-of-change hypothesis were limited to the bill rate (there being little ground for expectational effects in the case of a sluggish rate like r_s) and did not prove very conclusive. The coefficient of Δi is generally negative, but is not significant and is not robust with respect to minor changes in specifications. However, some further light on the role of Δi can be garnered from the test reported immediately below.

v. Stock Adjustment Delay Versus Learning and Expectational Effects.—In the equations of the forms (2.7') and (2.7''), which underlie the tests presented so far, the coefficient γ is meant to reflect two types of delay which, in principle, are distinguishable. The first type of delay is the usual stock adjustment, reflecting the time it takes for the public to adjust the cash balance to the *desired* level. A second source of delay might be expected to reflect the time it takes for the desired cash balance, or more precisely, for the desired ratio of money to transactions to respond to changes in interest rates. An attempt at estimating separately the two types of lags can be made by relying on the Allais version of the basic hypothesis displayed in (2.6'). In this equation the lagged dependent variable has been replaced by distributed lags on the "independent" variables. The first distributed lag in Δy can be associated with the gradual adjustment, hence the weighting structure should be of the Koyck type, declining steadily, roughly at an exponential rate (cf. Figure 1(A)). Once we

---

[7] Before 1962 this variable was assigned a value of zero.

[8] The gradual adjustment model has the somewhat uncomfortable implication that a one-time change in the money supply, with income constant, would initially be accommodated by an overshooting of the short-term rate to a level below the long-run equilibrium value [22]. This feature would be attenuated if the initial fall in the rate induces a temporary increase in money holdings, as implied by a negative coefficient for the rate of change of i.

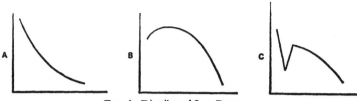

FIG. 1. Distributed Lag Patterns.

express $k_{t-\tau}$ in terms of $i_{t-\tau}$ and $r_{s(t-\tau)}$, the second term can be broken down into two weighted averages of past values of i and r_s, respectively. In the case of r_s, all weights should be negative; but if it takes time for the desired cash balance to adjust to this rate, as seems reasonable, then the peak response should correspond to somewhat lagged values of r_s. In other words, the lag distribution should exhibit the humped pattern shown in Figure 1(B). In the case of i this learning delay should be less pronounced or even absent, since we should expect i to affect primarily large transactors who in turn should respond faster. However, in this case we must also take into account the rate-of-change effect discussed in section iv. Extrapolative expectations implying a positive sign for Δi would lead to a more pronounced humped pattern (since the coefficient of the current rate would be pushed toward zero and that of the lagged rate would become more negative); on the other hand, a negative sign for Δi would give rise to the jagged pattern shown in Figure 1(C).

An attempt has been made to estimate the separate weighting structures for each of the three variables by relying on the Almon technique. In view of the appreciable serial correlation of the error of (2.7″), the error term of the equation was assumed to satisfy a second-order autoregressive scheme.

The results presented in Table 2 must be taken with considerable caution in view of the large number of parameters estimated (12) and the considerable number of further choices open to the investigator (degrees of each polynomial, length of lags). It is nonetheless encouraging that the results conform rather well to the implications of the neo-Fisherian model set out above, and illustrated in Figure 1. It is also apparent that the weighting structure for the bill rate exhibits the jagged pattern of Figure 1(C), providing some support for the hypothesis of short-run regressivity in expectations and in its "stabilizing" implications. Note, however, that both the estimated long-run elasticities and the speed of adjustment are a good deal lower than those implied by the ratio form of row 1 of Table 1.

In conclusion, the above battery of tests suggests that the demand for money may be affected by variables other than those appearing in (2.7′), but only to a minor extent, and that the effect of past values of the independent variables may be somewhat more complex than the Koyck type of distributed lag structure implied by (2.7′). Nevertheless, pragmatic considerations have led us to adopt (2.7') for the present as an operationally acceptable approximation to the demand for money to be used in the model.[9] It should be noted, however, that the estimates of the coefficients on this equation presented in row 1 were estimated by least squares, a method that is likely to lead to significant "simultaneous equation" bias in view of a second relation connecting the short-term rate to the stock of money via the money supply mechanism. We shall come back to this question in Part IV after we have developed our model of the money supply. We note here that this bias is likely to cause an underestimation of the elasticity of demand, particularly with respect to the short rate i, and probably also of the speed of adjustment.

5. Demand for Currency

Here we again rely on a model of type (2.3), but we replace Y by consumers' expenditure, C, on the ground that the use of currency (Mc) largely arises out of such transactions. However, we should expect interest rates, especially i, to be less important in this case. In carrying out the test we have to face one special difficulty. At the end of World War II the currency-deposit ratio was unusually high by historical standards, a phenomenon widely held to be related to (1) black market operations under price controls and rationing and (2) the hoarding of U.S. currency in foreign countries. These unusual sources of demand were presumably gradually eliminated over the early postwar years. Accordingly, we would expect the model which we fit over the years 1955–66 to underestimate the currency-deposit ratio when extrapolated back into the Korean War years.

The results of the estimation are presented in Table 3 for both the linear (row 1) and logarithmic (row 2) forms of our specification. It should be noted that in both of these equations the only interest rate which appears is r_s; in each case we tried the treasury bill rate as an additional regressor, but its coefficient was always small and insignificant. Again, the 'fits' are quite close and the results are on the whole sensible. The estimated speed of adjustment in both equations is remarkably close to that which we found when we estimated the demand for demand deposits in the linear form and which we regard as more reasonable than that produced by the logarithmic form for Md. The elasticities with respect to r_s are of the same order of magnitude as those of demand deposits, but the total interest elasticity of currency demand is considerably lower than that of demand deposits, since i has no significant contribution in this case. A characteristic of both results in Table 3 is the very high serial correlation as indicated by estimated autoregression coefficient ρ in excess of 0.7. In this respect the logarithmic form is superior to the linear one.

---

[9] We have added to (2.7') the real income variable, despite its negligible contribution on the ground that this variable already appears elsewhere in the complete system.

TABLE 2

Demand Deposit Estimates: Distributed Lag Form, 1952,I–1965,IV*

	t-0	t-1	t-2	t-3	t-4	t-5	t-6	t-7	t-8	t-9	z
$ln(Y) - ln(Y_{-1})$	-.916 (14.86)	-.838 (9.39)	-.722 (6.41)	-.582 (4.79)	-.431 (3.57)	-.284 (2.51)	-.153 (1.60)	-.054 (.88)	.00		-3.981
$ln(i)$	-.0245 (4.27)	-.0138 (2.44)	-.0223 (5.06)	-.0239 (4.89)	-.0206 (4.17)	-.0143 (2.93)	-.0071 (1.38)	-.0009 (.18)	.0021 (.56)	.00	-.1252
$ln(r_s)$	-.0147 (.39)	-.0543 (1.59)	-.0457 (2.46)	-.0376 (4.28)	-.0300 (3.24)	-.0230 (1.74)	-.0165 (1.11)	-.0105 (.79)	-.0050 (.59)	.00	-.2372

Const. -1.104 (-26.68) $\bar{R}$ .999 σ_e .00419 d-w 2.07 ρ_1 1.52 ρ_2 -.56

* NOTE: Δy = 3rd degree polynomial over period t to t-8; constrained to zero at t-8.
$ln(i)$ = 3rd degree polynomial over period t-1 to t-9; constrained to zero at t-9.
$ln(r_s)$ = 2nd degree polynomial over period t-1 to t-9; constrained to zero at t-9.

TABLE 3

Currency Demand Estimates: 1955,I–1966,IV

Row	Form	1 r_e	2 M_{-1}/C	3 Const.	4 w_e (S.R.)	5 w_e (L.R.)	6 ρ	7 σ_e	8 R^2	9 $d - w$	10 σ_u
1	Ratio	-.0014 (-1.89)	.8369 (13.60)	.0190 (2.57)	.04	.25	.78	.00031	.999	2.42	.00058
2	Log	-.0395 (-2.09)	.8324 (14.70)	.3590 (3.01)	.04	.24	.71	.0034	.999	2.31	.0050

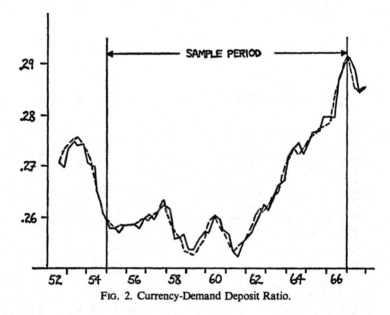

FIG. 2. Currency-Demand Deposit Ratio.

In Figure 2 we have graphed the actual currency-deposit ratio and that computed from the linear forms in Tables 1 and 3. This ratio, which is frequently supposed to be rather stable, has actually exhibited a surprising amount of variation in the postwar period, falling from over 30 per cent at the end of the war down to a low point just over 25 per cent in the mid-fifties, and rising back up to over 29 per cent by the end of 1966. These movements have in part a cyclical character, with the currency-deposit ratio tending to rise in expansions (1951–53, 1955–57, 1959–60, and 1962–66) and to fall during contractions. It is apparent that our model accounts fairly well for the observed movements, though, of course, it would systematically underestimate the level of the ratio in the early postwar years. In particular, it catches rather well all major turning points. The swings in the ratio, and, in particular, its cyclical features are accounted for in our model by (1) movements in interest rates; since demand deposits are more interest-elastic than currency, a rise in interest rates tends to raise the ratio, (2) movements of the market i relative to the more sluggish rate r_s ; since Md responds much more to i than does Mc, cyclical swings in short-term market rates cause similar procyclical swings in the currency ratio, and (3) the fact that C is less cyclically variable than Y, which tends to moderate the cyclical tendency resultings from (1) and (2).

6. Refinements of the Currency Demand Model

i. Real Income Effects.—As in the case of demand deposits, it is conceivable that the ratio Mc/C could be affected, either way, by an increase in real per capita permanent income. We thought this variable could well be approximated by real consumption per capita, but this measure did not contribute significantly when added to the specifications in Table 3.

ii. Effects of the Spread of Credit Cards.—We hypothesize that credit cards are at least in part a currency-saving device, and hence that an increase in credit card credit outstanding relative to consumption would reduce Mc/C. Furthermore, we expected that the ratio of credit outstanding to consumption would show a very marked rising trend over the postwar period. Unfortunately, there is no entirely satisfactory measure of credit card credit outstanding by itself. The closest approximation we could secure is represented by the series "charge accounts plus service credit."

To our surprise this series rose appreciably faster than consumption up to the mid-fifties but has had amazingly little trend since. It is therefore not surprising that when this variable was added, it had a totally insignificant coefficient. We interpret this result not as a rejection of the hypothesis that credit cards are a currency-saving device, but rather as an indication that this effect cannot be measured with these data.

III. THE MONEY SUPPLY MECHANISM

1. The Basic Approach

The total money supply in the model consists of the sum of currency and demand deposits. The supply of currency in our framework is entirely controlled by the demand for currency (see Part II, section 5). Therefore, to understand the total money outstanding, we must understand the determinants of the stock of demand deposits, namely, the interaction of the central bank, the commercial banking sector, and the public demand. Also, since in the present American system the bulk of demand deposits is created by the member banks and the behavior of their deposits in turn largely controls the total (at least in the short run), in the rest of this section we deal explicitly with this component.

Our approach to the supply of deposits by member banks differs somewhat in spirit, as well as in operational details, from the most recent empirical studies which endeavor to handle the problem by focusing on the "demand" for excess reserves and for borrowing from the Federal Reserve.[10]

We start instead from the notion that to account for the supply of demand deposits we need to understand the forces controlling banks' demand for earning assets. Furthermore, in developing the short-run dynamics of the supply equation, we assign a crucial role to the behavior of commercial loans. This role, which has already been recognized by other authors (e.g., Gold-

[10] For example, see Meigs [16], Orr and Mellon [18], Goldfeld [9], Goldfeld and Kane [10], Hester and Pierce [11], and DeLeeuw [6].

feld [9]), arises from the fact that, in the case of commercial loans as distinguished from most other assets, the initiative lies largely with the customers rather than with the bank. More specifically, we hypothesize that, in the face of an upsurge in commercial loan demand, banks will endeavor to accommodate this demand because of the importance of their commercial loan customers as a source of deposits as well as other business. On the other hand, in the face of a decline in demand, there is rather little they can do to prevent borrowers from reducing their indebtedness.

Thus, in the short run, fluctuations in the volume of commercial loans will tend to reflect variations in customers' demand. Given enough time, these variations will give rise to movements in the opposite direction in the portfolio of other assets and/or to actions designed to control the volume of commercial loans; but, since these actions require time, within a period as short as one quarter we should expect changes in the level of commercial loans to give rise to significant changes in the same direction in the level of total assets and of demand deposits, even though this may require corresponding short-run changes in borrowings and opposite changes in excess reserves.

2. Determinants of Investment Portfolio for a Single Bank

In order to derive formally our money supply hypothesis, it is convenient to start out from the condensed balance sheet of a member bank set out in Table 4, which also serves to introduce the needed notation. We add the following definitional identities:

Unborrowed reserves $RU \equiv R - B^*$ (3.1)

Free reserves $FR = S - B^* \equiv (R - B^*) - (R - S) \equiv RU - RR$ (3.2)

These identities in turn imply:

$$FR = D(1 - \delta) + T(1 - \tau) - CL - I + CA \qquad (3.3)$$

Proceeding along lines analogous to those suggested by, for example, Mellon and Orr [18] or Tobin [21], we visualize the bank as holding anticipations as to the level of deposits, both demand and time, and as to the volume of commercial loan demand that will prevail over the coming "decision" period, but realizing that these anticipations are subject to error. This notion can be formalized by assuming that the bank regards the above three variables as random variables $\tilde{D}$, $\tilde{T}$, and $\widetilde{CL}$ subject to a known (subjective) probability distribution. Let the $\bar{D}$, $\bar{T}$, $\overline{CL}$ denote the mathematical expectations of the three random variables and define

$$\tilde{x}_D \equiv \tilde{D} - \bar{D}, \quad \tilde{x}_T \equiv \tilde{T} - \bar{T}, \quad \tilde{x}_{CL} \equiv \widetilde{CL} - \overline{CL}. \qquad (3.4)$$

The problem of the bank can now be formalized as that of choosing the most profitable level of its investment portfolio I. To a given choice of I, there will correspond an uncertain outcome in terms of free reserves, since that outcome depends on the realization of the three random variables, $\tilde{D}$, $\tilde{T}$, and $\widetilde{CL}$. By means of (3.3) and (3.4) the relation between $\widetilde{FR}$, the chosen I, and the three random variables can be expressed as follows:[11]

$$\widetilde{FR} = \tilde{D}(1 - \delta) + \tilde{T}(1 - \tau) - \widetilde{CL} - I + CA$$

$$= [\overline{D}(1 - \delta) + \overline{T}(1 - \tau) - \overline{CL} - I + CA] \qquad (3.5)$$

$$+ [\tilde{x}_D(1 - \delta) + \tilde{x}_T(1 - \tau) - \tilde{x}_{CL}] = \overline{FR} + \tilde{x}$$

where

$$\overline{FR} \equiv \epsilon[FR] = \overline{D}(1 - \delta) + \overline{T}(1 - \tau) - \overline{CL} - I + CA \qquad (3.6)$$

and

$$\tilde{x} \equiv [\tilde{x}_D(1 - \delta) + \tilde{x}_T(1 - \tau) - \tilde{x}_{CL}] \qquad (3.6')$$

The assumed probability distribution for variables D, T, and CL implies a probability distribution for the variable x, which we shall denote by $\phi(x)\,dx$; the corresponding cumulative distribution will be denoted by $\Phi(x)$. (Note that there is no reason why the three components of x are independently distributed; on the contrary, if the volume of loans affects the volume of deposits as it is usually assumed, $\tilde{x}_D$ and $\tilde{x}_{CL}$ will be positively correlated. Similarly, $\tilde{x}_D$ and $\tilde{x}_T$ may be negatively correlated.) Clearly, the probability distribution $\phi(x)$ will be different for different banks. In particular, we should expect that its dispersion, as measured by the standard deviation, would tend to grow with the size of the bank as measured, for example, by its deposits, though presumably less than in proportion because of the operation of the "law of large numbers." This in turn means that the slope of $\Phi(x)$ may be expected to be smaller, the larger the bank, at least in the neighborhood of $x = 0$.

Equation (3.6) brings out the fact that, for given anticipations about D, T, and CL, the mathematical expectation of free reserves is controlled by the decision variable I (which, in the short run, is also the only decision variable on the reasonable assumption that the net capital account, CA, can be regarded as given).

[11] Recent changes (September, 1968) in the method of calculating required reserves will alter the form of this decision problem somewhat. More important, though, the method of arriving at an aggregate money supply (see below) requires modification to accommodate the new system.

We note in particular that (3.6) implies $(d\overline{FR})/dI = -1$, i.e., an increase in I reduces the expected value of free reserves by an equal amount.[12]

We assume that the bank endeavors to choose I so as to maximize expected returns from its portfolio. Since this implies that a bank will not normally plan to simultaneously borrow and hold surplus reserves, we can identify negative free reserves with borrowing and will denote by r the cost of borrowed funds. Similarly, positive free reserves may be identified with surplus reserves and the return thereon will be denoted by r_s (which may, of course, be zero). Finally, we denote by i_{CL} and i, respectively the return on commercial loans and on I. Under these conditions, expected profits can be expressed as follows:

$$\text{Expected profits } P = K + r_{cL} \overline{CL} + iI + r \int_{-\infty}^{-\overline{FR}} (\overline{FR} + \tilde{x})d\Phi(\tilde{x})$$

$$+ r_s \int_{-\overline{FR}}^{\infty} (\overline{FR} + \tilde{x})d\Phi(\tilde{x}) = K + i_{cL}\overline{CL} + iI \qquad (3.7)$$

$$+ r_s \overline{FR} + (r - r_s) \int_{-\infty}^{-\overline{FR}} (\overline{FR} + \tilde{x})d\Phi(\tilde{x})$$

In the expression following the first equality sign, K denotes those components of profits which are independent of portfolio composition (operating costs, interest on time and demand deposits, etc.); the next two terms represent the expected returns from commercial loans and the investment portfolio;[13] the first integral term is the expected cost of borrowing if the realization of the random variable $\tilde{x}$ is sufficiently small to make borrowing necessary; finally, the second integral is expected return from surplus reserves if positive free reserves should arise. By adding and subtracting $r_s \int_{-\infty}^{-\overline{FR}} (\overline{FR} + \tilde{x}) d\Phi(\tilde{x})$ and by rearranging terms, one also readily derives the expression on the right of the second equality. The result is an expression for profits in terms of the two variables I and $\overline{FR}$, which in turn are tied to each other through equation (3.6). To find the optimum level of I, we therefore need to differentiate (3.7) totally, with respect to I, taking into account (3.6). This yields the first-order maximum condition

[12] The validity of this conclusion depends on the tacit assumption that the bank we are dealing with is but a small component of the banking system and that therefore it will not anticipate that the acquisition or sale of assets will significantly affect its own deposits. It might not be a good approximation for a heavily concentrated banking system such as exists in other countries; and even in the U.S., it may not hold in special cases, such as certain acquisitions of newly-issued government securities.

[13] For expository convenience, we assume that i is independent of the size of portfolio I, i.e., that the average and marginal rate of return coincide. Dropping this assumption would not affect any conclusion, except that in (3.8) and later equations i should be interpreted as the marginal rate of return of funds allocated to I.

$$\frac{dP}{dI} = i + r_s \frac{d\overline{FR}}{dI} + (r - r_s) \int_{-\infty}^{-\overline{FR}} \frac{d\overline{FR}}{dI} d\Phi(\tilde{x})$$

$$= i - r_s - (r - r_s)\Phi(-\overline{FR}) = 0. \tag{3.8}$$

Here $\Phi(-\overline{FR})$ is the probability that $\tilde{x}$ will not exceed $-\overline{FR}$ or, equivalently, the probability of FR being negative. As one should expect, this probability rises as I increases, and hence $\overline{FR}$ falls.

Let us at this point use a subscript j to characterize a specific bank j. Then condition (3.8) can be rewritten as

$$\widehat{FR}_j = -\Phi_j^{-1}\left(\frac{i - r_s}{r - r_s}\right) \tag{3.8'}$$

where $\widehat{FR}_j$ is the profit-maximizing value of $\overline{FR}$ for bank j, and Φ_j^{-1} is the inverse of the cumulated distribution $\Phi_j(x)$. The determination of $\widehat{FR}_j$ and its relation to $\Phi(x)$ is shown graphically in Figures 3a and 3b. Clearly, Φ_j^{-1} is a monotonically non-decreasing function of its argument and its slope (at least in the relevant neighborhood) may be expected to be larger, the larger the size of the bank. Substituting now from (3.8') into (3.6) and solving for I, we finally obtain

$$\hat{I}_j = \overline{D}_j(1 - \delta) + \overline{T}_j(1 - \tau) - \overline{CL}_j + CA_j + \Phi_j^{-1}\left(\frac{i - r_s}{r - r_s}\right), \tag{3.9}$$

which expresses, for bank j, the profit-maximizing value of the size of its investment portfolio $\hat{I}_j$, in terms of its expectations $[\overline{D}_j, \overline{T}_j, \overline{CL}_j, \Phi(x)]$ and the rates i, r and r_s.

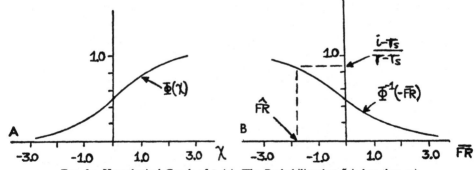

FIG. 3a. Hypothetical Graph of $\Phi(x)$ (The Probability that $\tilde{x}$ is less than x.)
FIG. 3b. Graph of $\Phi^{-1}(-\overline{FR})$ (The Probability that x is less than $-FR$, i.e. that FR is Negative for Given $\overline{FR}$) and Determination of $\widehat{FR}$, Given $(L - r_s)/r - r_s)$.

Note that for finite maximizing values $(\widehat{FR}_j, \widehat{I}_j)$ to exist, it must be assumed that markets and/or institutional forces ensure that $0 < (i - r_S) < (r - r_S)$; under these conditions, we find

$$\frac{\partial \widehat{I}_j}{\partial i} = -\frac{\partial \widehat{FR}_j}{\partial i} > 0; \qquad \frac{\partial \widehat{I}_j}{\partial r} = -\frac{\partial \widehat{FR}_j}{\partial r} < 0.$$

3. Investment Portfolio and the Supply of Deposits for the Aggregate Banking System

Equation (3.9) exhibits the investment portfolio decision of an individual bank. It is clear, however, that if all banks face the same rates (and assuming for the present that they are subject to the same reserve requirements), we can describe the aggregate demand for investments by the banking system as a whole by simply summing (3.9) over all member banks, obtaining

$$\hat{I} = \bar{D}(1 - \delta) + \bar{T}(1 - \tau) - \overline{CL} + CA - \widehat{FR} \qquad (3.10)$$

where $\bar{D} = \Sigma \bar{D}_j$ is the aggregate expectation of deposits and similarly for the remaining variables. In particular,

$$\widehat{FR} = \Sigma FR_j = -\Sigma \Phi_j^{-1}\left(\frac{i - r_S}{r - r_S}\right) = -\psi\left(\frac{i - r_S}{r - r_S}\right) \qquad (3.11)$$

where ψ still exhibits the properties of Φ_j^{-1}.

Equation (3.10) assumes that aggregate investment is entirely determined by beginning-of-period anticipations. A somewhat more general formulation is to assume that banks are willing and able to adjust, in part, their portfolios to errors of anticipations which emerge during the period itself and, at the same time, to allow for the possibility that a portfolio adjustment to bring free reserves to the optimum level $\widehat{FR}$ might occur only gradually in time. To take into account these two possibilities, we rewrite (3.10) in the form

$$I = \bar{D}(1 - \delta) + m_D(1 - \delta)(D - \bar{D}) + \bar{T}(1 - \tau)$$

$$+ m_T(1 - \tau)(T - \bar{T}) - \overline{CL} - m_{CL}(CL - \overline{CL})$$

$$- [n_F\widehat{FR} + (1 - n_F)FR_{-1}] + CA + \epsilon. \qquad (3.12)$$

Here D is the actual level of deposits, and hence $(D - \bar{D})$ is the error of anticipation; this holds similarly for T and CL. The reaction coefficients m_D, m_T, and m_{CL} measure the extent to which the investment portfolio responds (on the average) to errors of anticipations emerging within the decision period.

They may thus be expected to be positive but to fall short of unity for two reasons. First, banks may be unable to adjust the portfolio fully on short notice; but, in addition, they may not find it worthwhile to respond fully to the extent that the difference between the realization and the expectation may be deemed to be in the nature of transient fluctuations. For this second reason, the three coefficients might well have different values. In particular, m_T might be larger than the remaining two because of the lower volatility of time deposits. Finally, the coefficient n_F measures the speed with which banks plan to adjust their portfolio (on the average) to meet the free reserve target. For the sake of completeness the right-hand side of (3.12) should also contain a stochastic error term reflecting variations around the average response. For convenience of exposition, however, such error terms will be omitted until we have arrived at the formulation which is best suited for empirical testing and estimation.

In (3.12) the expected values $\bar{D}$, $\bar{T}$, and $\overline{CL}$ are not directly observable. Hence, if we are to test and estimate our model, we must approximate these non-observable anticipations in terms of observables. The most elementary and commonly used expectation model is the "static" hypothesis

$$\bar{Z} = Z_{-1} \quad \text{for} \quad Z = D, T, \text{ or } CL.$$

In the present instance, however, it seems more reasonable to suppose that banks do endeavor to anticipate change and have enough information to do so with some success on the average. This hypothesis can be formulated in the form

$$\bar{Z} = Z_{-1} + m_Z'(Z - Z_{-1}) \quad \text{or} \quad (Z - \bar{Z}) = (1 - m_z')(Z - Z_{-1}),$$

$$Z = D, T, \text{ or } CL. \tag{3.13}$$

Here again m_Z' may be expected to lie between zero and unity, being closer to unity for those variables which are more accurately forecasted. On a priori grounds, one would conjecture that, of the three components, changes in D would probably be the hardest to predict and those in T the easiest, implying $m_D' < m_{CL}' < m_T'$.

Substituting (3.13) into (3.12), rearranging terms, and making use of identity (3.3) we deduce

$$\Delta I = n_D(1 - \delta)\Delta D + n_T(1 - \tau)\Delta T - n_{CL}\Delta CL - n_F(\widehat{FR} - FR_{-1})$$

$$+ \Delta CA \tag{3.14}$$

$$\text{where} \quad n_Z = 1 - (1 - m_Z)(1 - m_Z'); \quad Z = D, T, CL.$$

These coefficients, it will be noted, measure the extent to which the investment portfolio responds to changes in D, T, and CL within the decision period. They should fall between an upper limit of unity if the changes are fully predicted ($m_{z'} = 1$) or banks are able and willing to adjust perfectly to forecast error ($m_z = 1$), and a lower limit of zero if banks are on the average totally unsuccessful in predicting change ($m_{z'} = 0$) and equally unable to adjust to forecast error ($m_z = 0$). On a priori grounds, we might expect $n_T > n_{CL} > n_D$, with n_D itself rather close to zero.

Equation (3.14) expresses the change in I in terms of changes in D, T, and CL. For the purpose of the present paper, we may regard T and CL as exogenously given though they are endogenous to the entire FRB-MIT model. D, however, cannot be treated similarly, since our task is precisely that of accounting for D. The apparent impasse can be resolved by observing that, for the system as a whole, there is a second relation between I and D that can be inferred from the balance sheet identity of Table 4 after summing over all banks in the system, namely

$$\Delta D = \Delta RU + \Delta CL + \Delta I - \Delta T - \Delta CA. \tag{3.15}$$

This second equation is seen to relate the money supply explicitly to central bank policy by way of unborrowed reserves, RU. By solving (3.14) and (3.15) simultaneously for I and D, we can thus express D and I in terms of the policy variable RU, the "exogenous variables," T and CL, and of $\widehat{FR}$, which in turn depends on the relevant rates. In particular, the solution for the money supply D can be expressed as

$$\Delta D = \frac{1}{(1 - n_D) + \delta n_D} [\Delta RU + (1 - n_{CL})\Delta CL \\ - (1 - n_T + \tau n_T)\Delta T - n_F(\widehat{FR} - FR_{-1})]. \tag{3.16}$$

TABLE 4

STANDARDIZED BANK BALANCE SHEET

Assets		Liabilities	
Reserves Total	R	Demand Deposits	D
Required	RR	Federal Government	Dg
against demand deposits	δD	All others	Dp
against time deposits	τT	Time Deposits	T
Surplus (excess reserves	S	Borrowing (from FRB	B^*
and loans in Federal		and Federal Funds	
Funds Market)		Market)	
Commercial Loans	CL	Miscellaneous Liabilities	$CA + MA$
Other Investments	I	and Capital	
Miscellaneous Assets	MA		

Equation (3.16) is a key result and deserves close scrutiny and interpretation. To this end, it is helpful to consider two limiting cases. Suppose first that the system is able to forecast perfectly or to adjust fully to any forecast error, so that $n_D = n_T = n_{CL} = n_F = 1$. Since, under this assumption, $FR_{-1} = \widehat{FR}_{-1}$, (3.16) reduces to the well-known formula

$$\Delta D = \frac{\Delta RU - \tau \Delta T - \Delta FR}{\delta} \quad \text{implying also}$$

$$D = \frac{RU - \tau T - FR}{\delta},$$

(3.16′)

i.e., the change (level) of deposits is equal to the change (level) of reserves available to support demand deposits, divided by the required reserve ratio. This is a generalization of the elementary textbook "equilibrium" (or monopoly bank) formula, $D = RU/\delta$, which allows for reserve requirements against time deposits and for an "optimum" level of free reserves. Suppose, at the opposite extreme, that banks are totally unable to forecast and adjust to forecast error, so that $n_D = n_T = n_{CL} = 0$. Then (3.16) reduces to

$$\Delta D = \Delta RU - n_F(\widehat{FR} - FR_{-1}) + \Delta CL - \Delta T \qquad (3.16'')$$

If we put ΔCL, ΔT and $\widehat{FR}$ equal to zero, $n_F = 1$, and disregard borrowing so that FR equals excess reserves (3.16″), together with the second half of identity (3.2) in differenced form, describes analytically the textbook version of the step-by-step expansion of deposits; that is, it implies that a given increment in RU will generate an expansion of D through time, which asymptotically approaches the equilibrium value given by (3.16′), with the disequilibrium gap after t periods proportional to $(1 - \delta)^t$. The two additional terms in CL and T in (3.16″) come from the fact that, if all changes come as a surprise and banks do not adjust at all to errors, then an expansion of loans will produce an equal expansion of deposits while a shift from demand to time deposits will reduce D and increase T by equal amounts.

The expansion of D implied by (3.16) is, of course, somewhere in between these limiting cases. The adjustment is gradual, but at a rate faster than implied by (3.16″). The key reason for a less than instantaneous response, even if $n_F \simeq 1$, is that n_D is likely to be close to zero. If so, the adjustment of any one bank tends to create surprises and thus throw other banks out of adjustment, thereby causing delays in the complete adjustment of the entire system. This delay will tend to be greater the less concentrated the banking system. For a monopoly bank, one might well expect a speedy adjustment, though even here the difficulty of forecasting ΔRU, ΔCL, and ΔT suggests that all the adjustment coefficients would still be less than one.

4. Target-Free Reserves, the Cost of Borrowing and the Return from Lending

Before we can test and estimate (3.16) we must express $\widehat{FR}$ in terms of interest rates. To this end we can rely on equation (3.11), but we need to establish an appropriate parametric representation for the function and an appropriate empirical counterpart for the rates i, r_s, and r, that appear as arguments of that function. We shall deal first with this second issue.

Insofar as i is concerned, since the relevant decision period is presumably rather short, for example, of the order of the averaging period for reserve requirements (one to two weeks), the choice at the margin can be visualized as between free reserves and short-term market instruments; hence, a rate such as the three-month treasury bill rate seems a reasonable choice (one might prefer returns on bills of even shorter maturity except for the difficulty of obtaining equally reliable data).

The problem of the remaining two rates is considerably more complex. Since no interest is received on excess reserves, one might be inclined to set r_s at zero, and to equate r with the discount rate, hereafter denoted by d. Under these conditions, (3.8) would reduce to $\widehat{FR} = -\psi(i/d)$. In reality, the identification of r with d is subject to serious objection. For one thing, it would imply that whenever the bill rate exceeds the discount rate, a rather frequent occurrence in recent years, free reserves would tend to become indefinitely small. The point is that d is a very biased measure of the true opportunity cost of making up reserve deficiencies because, in the present American system, borrowing at the window is a "privilege" subject to many constraints. Accordingly, there is ample reason to suppose that the true opportunity cost of borrowing at the window is generally higher than d, and the more so the larger the volume (and average duration) of outstanding borrowing. This hypothesis is strongly supported by the evidence of recent years which shows that as borrowings grow, the rate of the Federal Funds market in which banks can borrow freely tends to be bid up to a growing premium over the discount rate. Equally serious objections can be raised against taking r_s as zero. Indeed, since positive free reserves include loans in the Federal Funds market as well as excess reserves in the conventional definition, it would appear that r_s itself must be related to the Federal Funds rate.

The above considerations suggest that a really adequate analysis of the determinants of FR would require explicit treatment of other markets, notably the Federal Funds market. Unfortunately, this line of approach would take us far afield. We shall rely instead on a shortcut which makes no explicit reference to the Federal Funds market, though it is in fact derivable from a fuller analysis of that market.

First, it is shown in Appendix A, by an explicit analysis of demand and supply in the Federal Funds market, that the equilibrium conditions in that market imply a relation between the rate r, the discount rate d, and the level of free reserves, say

$$r = R(d, FR),$$ (3.17)

with the properties $R_d \geq 0$, $R_{FR} \leq 0$, and R_d probably less than, but close to, unity.

Second, we suggest that (3.11) can be approximated as follows:

$$\widehat{FR} = -\psi\left(1 + \frac{i - r}{r - r_s}\right) \simeq F(i,r) \simeq f(i - r)$$ (3.11')

The approximation is supported by the consideration that $r - r_s$ should tend to remain relatively constant, reflecting basically costs associated with transacting in the Federal Funds market (see also Appendix A). From (3.9), we can also infer that

$$F_i \simeq f' \simeq \frac{\partial FR}{\partial i} < 0, \qquad F_r \simeq -f' \simeq \frac{\partial FR}{\partial r} > 0.$$

The two equations (3.11') and (3.17) involve three endogenous variables—$\widehat{FR}$, r, and FR— in addition to the two exogenous variables d and i; to close the system we need one additional equation. This equation can be derived from the deposit supply equation (3.16) by restating it in terms of free reserves, relying on the identity (3.2) and the definition of required reserves. First, from the second equation in (3.2) (neglecting for the moment the possibility of changes in reserve requirements) we infer

$$\Delta FR = \Delta RU - \Delta RR = \Delta RU - \delta\Delta D - \tau\Delta T.$$

Substituting now for ΔD from (3.16) and solving for FR, the result can be expressed as

$$FR = \mu\widehat{FR} + \left\{(1 - \mu)FR_{-1} + \frac{\mu}{n_F}\left[(1 - n_D)\frac{1 - \delta}{\delta}\Delta RU\right.\right.$$
$$\left.\left. - (1 - n_{CL})\Delta CL + n_T^*\Delta T\right]\right\},$$ (3.18)

where

$$\mu = \frac{\delta n_F}{(1 - n_D) + \delta n_D};$$
$$\cdot n_T^* = (1 - n_T) + \tau(n_T - n_D) - \frac{\tau}{\delta}(1 - n_D).$$ (3.18')

We note here for later reference that μ, and hence the coefficients of all variables except that of ΔT, should fall between zero and unity. In the case of ΔT, the sign of the coefficient implied by the model cannot be established a priori, since $n_T{}^*$ could be negative if n_T is sufficiently greater than n_D, that is, if I responds more to time deposit than to demand deposit changes within the period—whether because T is easier to forecast or because of greater response to forecast errors.[14]

We could at this point endeavor to estimate the parameters of the three equations listed above and think of the supply of deposits as generated by the simultaneous solution of this system plus the identity

$$D = \frac{RU - \tau T - FR}{\delta}. \qquad (3.19)$$

We shall not pursue this approach because it presents some serious difficulties.[15] We shall proceed instead to derive and estimate directly a free reserve equation representing the "reduced" form of the above "structural" system. That is, we can conceptually solve the system to yield reduced forms relating each of the three endogenous variables, $\widehat{FR}$, FR, and r, to the exogenous variables. In particular, if we denote by Q the linear combination of variables appearing inside the curly brackets in the right-hand side of (3.18), the solution can be expressed as

$$FR = g(i, d, Q). \qquad (3.20)$$

or to a linear approximation as:

$$FR = a_0 + a_1 i + a_2 d + a_3 Q = a_0 + a_1 i + a_2 d + a_3(1 - \mu)FR_{-1}$$
$$+ a_3 \frac{\mu}{n_F}\left[(1 - n_D)\left(\frac{1 - \delta}{\delta}\Delta RU\right) - (1 - n_{CL})\Delta CL + n_T{}^*\Delta T\right]. \qquad (3.21)$$

[14] This conclusion is at first sight surprising, for given RU and bank assets, an increase in T can only come from a shift from demand deposits into time deposits and such a shift releases reserves by an amount $(\delta - \tau)\Delta T$. But this inference is valid only if the shift is totally unanticipated, and there is no response to forecast errors, i.e., if $n_D = n_T = 0$. Indeed, it can be verified that under these conditions the coefficient of ΔT in (3.18) is precisely $(\delta - \tau)$. When the shift is at least partially anticipated and/or errors corrected, the situation is more complex because assets do respond to the shift. The outcome depends then on the comparative responsiveness of I to changes in T and D. Specifically, from the definition of $n_T{}^*$, we can infer that

$$n_T{}^* \gtrless 0 \quad \text{as} \quad \frac{1 - n_T}{1 - n_D} \gtrless \frac{\tau(1 - \delta)}{\delta(1 - \tau)} \simeq \frac{\tau}{\delta}:$$

[15] The main difficulty is that $\widehat{FR}$ and r are not directly observable. The first problem can be easily handled by substituting for FR in (3.18) from equation (3.11'). The variable r poses a more serious difficulty; for the more recent years, it could be measured by the observed Federal Funds rate, but even this approach breaks down for earlier years when prevailing conventions prevented banks from ever bidding the Federal Funds rate above the discount rate.

Furthermore, by relying on the model's specifications about the properties of the partial derivatives of the equations (3.11′) and (3.17), we can derive inferences about the sign of and relation between the parameters a_1, a_2, and a_3. In particular, it can be shown that these specifications imply:

$$a_1 < 0, \qquad a_2 > 0 \qquad 0 < a_3 \leq 1$$

and also $|a_1| > |a_2|$ i.e. an increase in i tends to reduce free reserves by more than an equal change in d.[16] A word of caution, however, should be entered concerning the appropriateness of the linear approximations (3.21) to the function g of (3.20). The considerations set forth in formulating the equation (3.11′) and deriving (3.17) in Appendix A suggest that $\widehat{FR}$, and thus FR, are definitely not linear functions of i and d in the large. In particular, the relation between FR and i, for given d (and Q) is likely to exhibit the shape represented in Figure 4. Accordingly, the linear approximation (3.21), also exhibited in the figure, can only be valid as long as the spread $(i - d)$ remains within reasonable limits. This condition was probably roughly satisfied over the period of observation; since the spread has generally remained inside 100 basis points, a range within which the linear approximation should prove bearable.[17] However, the empirical results reported below should be regarded as valid only within a range of spreads of the indicated magnitude.

Subject to the above qualifications, we could proceed to estimate equation (3.21′). Unfortunately, before we can do so, we must face one more hurdle.

[16] The system (3.11′), (3.17) and (3.18) can be reduced by substitution to: $FR - \mu F(i, R[d,FR]) - Q = 0$. By implicit differentiation, we find:

$$a_3 \approx \frac{\delta FR}{\delta Q} = \frac{1}{1 - \mu F_r R_{FR}}$$

$$a_1 \approx \frac{\delta FR}{\delta i} = F_i \left(\frac{\delta FR}{\delta Q} \right) = \mu F_i a_3$$

$$a_2 \approx \frac{\delta FR}{\delta d} = \mu F_r R_d \left(\frac{\delta FR}{\delta Q} \right) = \mu F_r R_d a_3$$

Therefore:

$$0 < \frac{\delta FR}{\delta Q} < 1, \quad \frac{\delta FR}{\delta i} < 0, \quad \frac{\delta FR}{\delta d} > 0 \quad \text{and} \quad \left| \frac{\delta FR}{\delta i} \right| > \left| \frac{\delta FR}{\delta d} \right|$$

It is sufficient for the last inequality that $-F_r \approx F_i \approx f'$ and that R_d does not exceed unity, a condition which seems likely to hold, as shown in the Appendix.

[17] This inference seems reasonable, at least in the case of a positive spread; it is conceivable, however, that on the negative side the non-linearity may become pronounced well before a spread of 100 points is reached. However, since there have been very few occasions in which d has persistently exceeded i by more than fifty basis points, it is very hard to detect the non-linearity empirically, though some efforts in that direction are still in course.

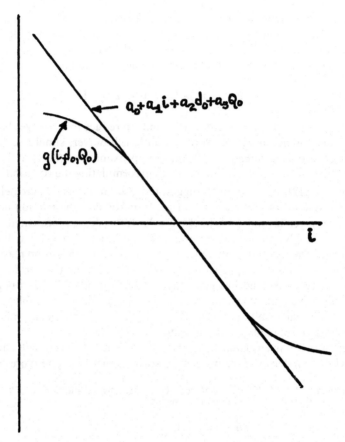

$$a_0 + a_1 i + a_2 d_0 + a_3 Q_0$$

$$g(i, d_0, Q_0)$$

$$i$$

FIG. 4. The Relationship between Desired Free Reserves and the Bill Rate, for Fixed Discount Rate.

Equation (3.21′) applies directly to a "decision period." In practice, however, because of data availability and convenience of analysis, as well as the fact that the decision period is best regarded as a theoretical rather than an operational construct, the time unit we wish to employ will not coincide with the "decision period." In our specific case, for example, the time unit for the entire MIT-FRB model is a calendar quarter, which presumably extends over several decision periods. We must therefore stop to inquire how our analysis can be extended to cover an arbitrary time period.

5. Generalization to a Unit Period Including a Number of Decision Periods

The method by which our results can be generalized depends somewhat on the specific definition of the variables. For our present purpose, we wish to define all stock variables as relating to the end of the period, and therefore all increments as relating to the change in stock between the beginning and the end of the chosen unit period.

Then let $Z(t)$, $Z = FR, RU, CL, T$ denote the stock of each variable at the end of unit period t and $\Delta Z(t)$ the change in stock in the course of unit period t. Similarly, let $\Delta Z(t, \tau)$ denote the change in the course of the τth decision period of period t, and let the number of decision periods within the unit period be m (which, we assume, can be represented by an integer). We propose to show that from (3.21'), we can, under appropriate conditions, derive an approximation in terms of $Z(t)$ and $\Delta Z(t)$. To this end, we first use (3.21) recursively to substitute m times for the lagged dependent variable. The result can be expressed as

$$
\begin{aligned}
FR(t) = \sum_{\tau=1}^{m} [a_3(1 - \mu)]^{m-\tau} &\left(a_0 + a_1 i(t, \tau) + a_2 d(t, \tau) \right. \\
&+ \frac{a_3 \mu}{n_F} \left[(1 - n_D) \frac{1 - \delta}{\delta} \Delta RU(t, \tau) - (1 - n_{CL}) \Delta CL(t, \tau) \right. \\
&\left. \left. + n_T{}^* \Delta T(t, \tau) \right] \right) + [a_3(1 - \mu)]^m FR(t - 1).
\end{aligned} \tag{3.22}
$$

The interpretation of $i(t, \tau)$ and $d(t, \tau)$ is evident from the context. Now, on the condition that RU, CL, and T grow relatively smoothly within each period, we can use the approximation

$$
Z(t, \tau) = \frac{\Delta Z(t),}{m} \qquad \tau = 1, \cdots, m, \qquad Z = FR, RU, CL, T \tag{3.22'}
$$

Similarly, on the condition that i and d remain reasonably constant within each period, we can approximate $i(t, \tau)$ by the mean value of i in period t, say, $i(t)$, and similarly for d. With these approximations, we deduce the following basic hypothesis to be tested empirically:

$$
\begin{aligned}
FR(t) = A_0 + A_1 i(t) + A_2 d(t) + B_1[(1 - \delta)\Delta RU] \\
+ B_2(\delta\Delta CL) + B_3(\delta\Delta T) + CFR(t - 1).
\end{aligned} \tag{3.23}
$$

The meaning of (3.23) can be more readily understood by rewriting it in the difference form

$$
\begin{aligned}
\Delta FR(t) = C'[A_0' + A_1' i(t) + A_2' d(t) - FR(t - 1)] \\
+ B_1[(1 - \delta)\Delta RU] + B_2(\delta\Delta CL) + B_3(\delta\Delta T)
\end{aligned} \tag{3.23'}
$$

whose coefficients are related to those of (3.23) and to the various parameters introduced earlier as follows:

$$C' = 1 - C = 1 - [a_3(1 - \mu)]^m$$

$$A_j' = \frac{A_j}{1 - C} = \frac{a_j}{1 - a_3(1 - \mu)} \qquad j = 0, 1, 2$$

$$B_1 = (1 - n_D)B; \qquad B_2 = -(1 - n_{CL})B; \qquad B_3 = n_T{}^*B$$

$$B = \left[\frac{C'}{[1 - a_3(1 - \mu)]}\right]\left[\frac{\mu a_3}{m\delta n_F}\right]$$

According to (3.23′), the change in free reserves in the unit period involves four distinct components: (i) the first term in square brackets results from the adjustment of free reserves toward their equilibrium value $\widehat{FR}$. Indeed, the quantity $A_0' + A_1'i(t) + A_2' d(t)$ can be shown to be an estimate of $\widehat{FR}$, corresponding to the prevailing values of i and d.[18] C' is the proportion of the gap between $FR(t)$ and the initial value $FR(t - 1)$ that is made up within the unit period. It is therefore a measure of the speed of adjustment toward equilibrium. This speed is seen to be an increasing function of μ; and from (3.18′) in turn, we see that μ is an increasing function of n_F, the speed of portfolio adjustment at the level of the individual bank, and of n_D, the speed of response to changes in deposits. In addition, C' is seen to increase with m, the number of decision periods per unit period, and thus with the length of the period. But note that while C' should accordingly tend to approach unity as we lengthen the unit period, the approximation (3.22′) becomes less tenable. (ii) The second component reflects the response to a change in unborrowed reserves. This response, measured by B_1, could be as low as zero if n_D were unity, in which case the portfolio would expand enough to absorb ΔRU fully into required reserves. On the other hand, for values of n_D and n_F approaching zero B_1 approaches unity, since the only effect of ΔRU would then

[18] Using the results of footnote 16, we deduce

$$A_1' = \frac{a_1}{1 - a_3(1 - \mu)} \simeq \frac{F_i}{1 - F_r R_{FR}}$$

$$A_2' = \frac{a_2}{1 - a_3(1 - \mu)} \simeq \frac{F_r R_d}{1 - F_r R_{FR}}$$

It can be verified that these two expressions in turn are the partial derivatives of $\partial FR/\partial i$ and $\partial FR/\partial d$ obtained by total differentiation of the system (3.11′), (3.17), and (3.18) for the case where $FR = FR_{-1}$ and all components of Q other than FR_{-1} are zero, so that (3.18) reduces to $FR = \widehat{FR}$.

be to increase D by an equal amount and hence to increase FR by $(1 - \delta)RU$. (iii) The third component is the response to a change in CL and its coefficient should again fall between zero and -1. However, we should expect $|B_2| < B_1$ on the ground that n_{CL} is likely to exceed n_D.[19] (iv) Finally, the last term is the response to a change in time deposits, and its coefficient B_3 is of uncertain sign for reasons expounded earlier.

It should be recognized that since μ depends on the reserve ratio δ, in principle all the coefficients (3.23) should vary in time if δ changes, even if all other behavior coefficients were stable. It can be verified, however, that variations in δ of the order of magnitude observed in the relevant post-war period should be expected to have rather minor effects on the coefficients. It would therefore appear that they can be treated as constant to a good approximation.[20]

6. Final Specification of the Hypothesis and Operational Definition of Variables

Equation (3.24) below completes our operational formulation of the money supply hypothesis[21]

$$FR = A_0 - A_1 i(\bar{D}_{-1}) + A_2 d(\bar{D}_{-1}) + A_3 FR_{-1} + A_4(1 - \delta)\Delta RU$$
$$- A_5\delta\Delta CL + A_6\delta\Delta T + A_7(RL). \tag{3.24}$$

The second modification is the addition of the last term, $A_7(RL)$, which will be called the "reserve release term." This term originates from the consideration that there are two distinct ways in which the central bank can change the amount of demand deposits that can be supported by unborrowed reserves: (i) by changing directly RU through open market purchases (although RU can also change through inflow or outflow of currency); (ii) by changing the required reserve ratio against either demand or time deposits. If we denote by $\Delta\delta$ and $\Delta\tau$, respectively, the difference between the required ratios in the current and the previous period, it is clear that the change in δ and τ is equivalent to an increase in RU amounting to:

---

[19] One might also be inclined to think that C should be smaller than B_1 on the ground that there should be a larger response to an initial condition such as $FR(t - 1)$ than to a variable changing within the period, such as RU. This relation, however, need not hold if n_D were sufficiently larger than n_F. This can be verified by considering the limiting case $n_D = 1, 0 < n_F < 1$. We then find $B_1 = 0 < C = [\mu_3(1 - n_F)]^m$.

[20] Note that dependence of B_j on δ is entirely due to the factor C'/δ since the remaining factor $\mu a_3/n_F m[1 - a_3(1 - \mu)]$ can be shown to be independent of μ (and hence of δ) along the lines of footnote 18. Now both numerator and denominator of the former factor increase with δ and therefore B_j should be relatively insensitive to variations in δ. Since the coefficients A_1 and A_2 are also functions of C' but do not contain the δ in the denominator, we might have scaled $i(t)$ and $d(t)$ in (3.23) by δ. This has indeed been tested in our attempt to find the most stable form of the coefficients, but it made very little empirical difference.

[21] The current time subscript t is now understood.

$$RL = -[\Delta\delta D_{-1} + \Delta\tau T_{-1}].$$

Indeed, RL, like RU, measures the change that would occur in free reserves if all other bank assets and liabilities (except D itself) were unchanged. The only difference is that, under the assumed conditions, a change in RU must be accompanied by an equal change in D; and, hence, in the final analysis FR would change only by $(1 - \delta)\Delta RU$, whereas in the case of changes in reserve requirements, D would be unchanged and FR would change by the full RL.

The above considerations suggest that the effect of changes in reserve requirements could be handled by simply adding RL to $(1 - \delta)\Delta RU$ and treating the sum as a single variable whose cóefficient should be A_4. This approach, however, is not quite consistent with the derivation of (3.24); for, as we have seen, the coefficients of the three increments are related in part to the ease with which banks can foresee such changes and respond to them if unforeseen. From this point of view, reserve releases generated by changes in reserve requirements may be rather different from those generated by addition to unborrowed reserves. In particular, changes in RU basically affect individual banks through changes in deposits, and their effect is not distinguishable from that of any other source of deposit changes. Thus the predictability of, and response to, changes in RU is unlikely to differ appreciably from that of deposit changes in general, as summarized in the coefficient n_D. On the other hand, legal reserve releases occur in one shot, and there can be little question about their permanence (furthermore, each bank can anticipate the response of the rest of the system). We should therefore expect that, even if their occurrence is not easier to forecast, the response to them would be faster; this means that A_7 can be expressed as $(1 - n_{RL})A$ with $n_{RL} > n_D$, implying $A_7 < A_4$.

Strictly speaking, this conclusion applies only to reserve releases through changes in reserve requirements. In the present American system, however, reserve releases occur not only through changes in legal reserve requirements but also, to some extent, through shifts in deposits between classes of banks or between types of deposits subject to different reserve requirements. Such shifts, which occur continuously and more or less haphazardly, might best be lumped together with RU rather than with RL. Since such releases are typically quite small and because of the difficulty of separating the contribution of the source of changes in δ and τ, we have actually included under RL all changes regardless of source. (These releases are quantitatively very unimportant in those quarters for which there were *legal* reserve releases.)

For the empirical test reported below, FR and RU (which are subject to considerable short-run variability) have been defined as the daily average value in the two months surrounding the end of each quarter. Similarly, FR_{-1} is the same average for the preceding quarter. CL, on the other hand, is the end of quarter stock of commercial and industrial loans. Ideally, it should include only commercial loans at member banks, but considerations of data availability as well as consistency with the rest of the FRB-MIT model have led us to approximate this quantity by commercial loans at all commercial banks. Finally, all monetary variables are measured in billions of dollars and interest rates in percentage points.

7. *Empirical Results*

Row 1 of Table 5 exhibits the parameters of equation (3.24) estimated by ordinary least squares after "normalization" by dividing both sides by the scale variable $\bar{D}_{-1}$. We note immediately that the estimated coefficient of T is only slightly positive, which we have seen to be consistent with the model. Its value is, in fact, well within the range implied by the model.[22] It is, however, of quite negligible magnitude, implying that a $1 billion change in time deposits would increase free reserves by only $4 million—insignificantly different from zero. It seems, therefore, preferable to drop this variable of little empirical relevance, especially since a few other tests relying on other methods of estimation pointed consistently in the same direction. When this is done, one obtains the estimates exhibited in row 2. These results, on the whole, are quite favorable to the hypothesis. All the coefficients have the sign implied and have fairly significant t-ratios despite the large number of variables—(six plus the seasonal dummies and constant)—and the substantial collinearity among several of them (e.g., the bill rate and the discount rate). The standard error (adjusting roughly for the scale variable whose mean value is 105 billion) is about 80 million, equivalent to just over half a billion when expressed in terms of money supply (since $\delta \simeq .15$).

Before taking a closer look at individual coefficients and their consistency with our model, we should like to touch briefly on some refinements of the basic hypothesis which, on the whole, did not prove too worthwhile.

i. Timing of the Legal Reserve Release.—While changes in unborrowed reserves should tend to occur randomly through the quarter, legal reserve releases generally occur in bulk at a specified date and typically with advance warning ranging from a couple of weeks up. Under these conditions, one should expect that the extent to which banks can take advantage of the release by the end of the quarter would depend on the timing of the release. A release occurring, say, very close to the end of the quarter, should largely show up in free reserves at the end of that quarter, while a release occurring at the very beginning might be largely used up and leave little trace in free reserves. With this thought, we added to the variables of row 2 an additional variable measuring the timing, θRT where θ is the proportion of the quarter elapsed before a

---

[22] One can establish that, given the prevailing values of δ and τ over the period of observation, our model would be consistent with a coefficient of the time deposit variable at least as low as $-.3$, as compared with the estimated value of .03.

legal change in reserve requirements becomes effective. Experimentation included using the announcement dates in lieu of effective dates and constraining the proportion of RL left in FR when legal changes occur at the end of a quarter to unity. These constraints were implemented by setting $A_7 = 1$ and adding in terms of the form $(\Theta - 1)RL$ or $(e^{\Theta-1} - 1)RL$ which vanish when $\Theta = 1$ and are expected to be negative otherwise for positive RL. While these trials yield coefficients with the appropriate signs, in no case did they improve the fit significantly. Note that Θ was set at .5 whenever no legal changes in reserve requirements occurred.

ii. Growing Aversion to Borrowing.—The recent study of the discount window by Bernard Schull [19] reports some evidence that, from 1955 to date, banks have shown increasing reluctance to make use of the window, whether as a result of the way the window was administered or for other reasons. As a crude test of this hypothesis, we have added a linear time trend and the results are shown in row 4. It is seen that the trend has the anticipated positive sign. It can be interpreted as implying that the constant term of the free reserves equation has increased at the rate of .000029 × 105 = .003 or some 3 million per quarter. This is quite negligible relative to quarterly changes but over a ten-year period it amounts to a sizable 120 million; however, as one can see from the t ratio, the estimate of the coefficient is very unreliable and the variable adds negligibly to the explanation (indeed, after adjustment for degrees of freedom, the standard error rises). For this reason, and furthermore, because one would always hesitate in extrapolating mechanically a time trend, we feel that omission of the variable is likely to yield on the whole a more reliable estimate of the money supply mechanism.

Having thus been led back to row 2 as providing the most reliable estimate of the coefficients of our model, we may proceed to a closer inspection of their magnitude and the reaction between them in the light of our model. Specifically, from row 2 and equation (3.24) we can infer the following equilibrium demand for free reserves:

$$FR = A_0\bar{D}_{-1} - \bar{D}_{-1}\left\{\frac{.00122i - .00144d}{1 - .705}\right\}$$

$$\simeq A_0\bar{D}_{-1} + .54d - .46i = A_0\bar{D}_{-1} - .54(i - d) + .082i$$

where we have assigned to $\bar{D}$ the value 110, roughly its mean value for the 60's, and the constant A_0 is left unspecified because it varies seasonally. Now the coefficient of the spread is of a credible order implying a reduction of free reserves of 540 millions per 100 basis points of spread. But contrary to our expectations, the coefficient of the bill rate is less than that of the discount rate in absolute value, though the difference is quite small and not significantly different from zero. The interpretation of the remaining coefficients of row 2 is straightforward. They imply that only about one-third of an increase in unborrowed reserves is utilized for the expansion of assets and deposits within the same quarter while the remaining two-thirds goes temporarily to swell free reserves. In the case of reserves provided by a legal reserve release, the response is, as expected, somewhat faster, as only some forty per cent remain unused by the end of the quarter. The contribution of the commercial loan term is seen to be highly significant and quantitatively impressive; the coefficient implies that $n_{CL} > n_D$, as expected. But even so, it suggests that only around one-half of the increase in commercial loans is offset within the period by liquidation of other assets while the remaining one-half shows up as an increase in demand deposits.

On the whole, these coefficients imply a rather slow speed of adjustment, reflecting, according to our model, error of forecast plus failure to adjust to errors; but it should always be recalled that these errors of forecast result in part from the fact that as individual banks adjust to their errors they change the deposits of other banks contributing to their error. That the result is a rather slow adjustment to "disturbances"—changes in reserves and in commercial loans—is confirmed by the coefficient of the lagged dependent variable. As can be seen from (3.23), this coefficient equals $[a_3(1 - \mu)]^m$ where

$$\mu = \frac{\delta n_F}{(1 - n_D) + \delta n_D}, \qquad 0 \le a_3 \le 1,$$

and m is the number of "decision periods per unit time." Thus, for $n_F = 1$, even assuming that n_D is very close to zero as seems plausible, $[a_3(1 - \mu)]$ cannot exceed $(1 - \delta)$ or roughly .85. Since our estimate of A_3 is .7, the implied value of m would be in the order of 2 to 3. This is rather low since on a priori ground we should have expected a figure closer to 6 (implying a two-week decision period). However, if we allow n_F to range below unity, implying a less than immediate adjustment of actual to target reserves, more plausible values for m are implied. The presence of a_3, of course, acts in the other direction.

In assessing these results, we observe that two coefficients do not quite check with the implications of the model, namely the coefficient of i which is too low relative to that of d, and the coefficient of the lagged dependent variable that seems somewhat too high. These coefficients are precisely those that are most subject to least squares bias. Furthermore, the direction of this bias is such that the result could produce the observed inconsistencies with the theoretical model. This is most easily seen in the case of coefficient of the lagged dependent variable; it is well known that if the true error component of the equation has positive serial correlation, a most likely situation when dealing with quarterly data, the ordinary least squares estimate of that coefficient is upward biased. In the case of the bill rate, on the other hand, the bias may be expected to come from the simultaneity problem already mentioned in connection with the demand equation: This simultaneity may be expected to lead to a positive correlation between the error component and short-term market yield as measured by the bill rate, which would impart an upward bias to our estimate, pushing it toward zero. Before we can pass final judgement on the consistency of our model with the data, we therefore need to consider procedures for minimizing the bias in the estimates and the results obtained from following such procedures. This is the task to which we turn in Part IV. In the process, we shall also be able to assess how well our money demand and supply mechanisms together account for the behavior of demand deposits and short-term interest rates.

IV. System Estimation: The Determination of the Rate of Interest and the Stock of Money

1. The Closed System

In this section we consider a complete submodel of interest rate and money supply determination which encompasses the theory and empirical results presented in the preceding pages. For reference we have reproduced in Table 6, lines 1 and 2, the empirically estimated equations reported in row 3 of Table 1 and row 2 of Table 5, and in Table 6, line 3, the reserve identity (3.19). If D, the stock of member bank demand deposits could be identified with Md, the stock of demand deposits held by the public, then the above three equations could be regarded as a closed system of simultaneous equations in the three variables: free reserves, the treasury bill rate, and the stock demand deposits, with all other variables exogenous. In fact, Md and D differ in a number of respects. First, not all demand deposits, relevant to the determination of the legal reserve requirements of member banks, reflect the public's demand for money balances. Sizeable deposits are held by the U.S. Treasury in tax and loan accounts at commercial banks. Such deposits clearly do not reflect the public's demand for transactions balances and are excluded from the demand deposit adjusted concept which we have used in the empirical results presented in Part II. Second, not all banks are members of the Federal Reserve System, and therefore there is a discrepancy between privately held demand balances subject to reserve requirements and total privately held deposits. Finally, we have used a seasonally adjusted series for the demand deposit adjusted concept, while our deposits subject to reserve requirement are not seasonally adjusted.[23] These three problems have been subsumed in the identities presented in lines 4 and 5 of Table 6. Identity (4) is derived from the definition of the ratio S,

[23] In addition, the current definition of demand deposits adjusted includes foreign bank balances held at Federal Reserve banks. The behavior of these balances, as well as foreign-owned balances at commercial banks, is presumably sensitive to developments in both foreign and U.S. capital markets. Unfortunately, this introduces a measurement error into the concept for balances demanded. It also adds another residual factor in the demand-supply identity.

TABLE 5
FREE RESERVE ESTIMATES

Row	Sample Period	1	2	3	4	5	6	7	8	9	10	11	12	13	14	15	16	17
			A_0			A_1	A_3	A_5	A_4	A_6	A_9	\multicolumn 2 A_7		Time	ρ	R^2	σ_u	$d-w$
		Const.	S_1	S_3	S_4	$-i$	d	$\frac{FR_{-1}}{D_{-1}}$	$\frac{(1-\theta)\Delta RU}{D_{-1}}$	$\frac{-\delta\Delta CL}{D_{-1}}$	$\frac{\delta\Delta T}{D_{-1}}$	$\frac{-RL}{D_{-1}}$	$\frac{X\cdot RL}{D_{-1}}$					
1	1955–66	.00100 (1.07)	−.00198 (−3.13)	−.00231 (−4.08)	−.00210 (−2.10)	.00125 (2.34)	.00144 (2.38)	.692 (10.2)	.639 (7.93)	.508 (5.09)	.0284 (.24)	.381 (3.94)	—	—	—	.952	.000792	2.07
2	1955–66	.00100 (1.08)	−.00204 (−3.53)	−.00237 (−4.84)	−.00223 (−2.67)	.00122 (2.39)	.00144 (2.41)	.705 (16.0)	.646 (8.13)	.502 (5.23)	—	.394 (5.00)	—	—	—	.952	.000782	2.09
3_A*	1954–66	.00120 (1.13)	−.00219 (−3.31)	−.00249 (−4.29)	−.00267 (−2.78)	.00108 (1.95)	.00129 (1.46)	.712 (14.2)	.664 (7.08)	.485 (4.45)	—	4.59 (3.15)	.00557 (.024)	—	—	.945	.00089	1.92
3_B*	1954–66	.00107 (.839)	−.00225 (−2.82)	−.00230 (−3.41)	−.00308 (−2.68)	.00022 (.356)	.00045 (.597)	.768 (13.2)	.701 (6.24)	.393 (3.05)	—	1.0	.809 (5.08)	—	—	.913	.00107	2.04
4	1955–66	.00091 (.97)	−.00192 (−3.25)	−.00230 (−4.59)	−.00185 (−1.94)	.00169 (2.27)	.00143 (2.40)	.612 (5.53)	.604 (6.49)	.531 (5.21)	—	.347 (3.63)	—	.00003 (.87)	—	.953	.000785	1.99
5†	1955–66	.00172 (1.73)	−.00290 (−4.45)	−.00267 (−5.02)	−.00366 (−4.34)	.00126 (2.24)	.00145 (2.21)	.700 (14.4)	.649 (7.37)	.511 (3.99)	—	.348 (3.92)	—	—	—	.942	.000962	2.39
6	1955–66	.00268	−.00205	−.00233	−.00219	.00158	.00133	.648	.657	.512	—	.346	—	—	.227	—	.000931	2.07

* For Row 3_A, $X = \theta$; For Row 3_B, $X = (\theta - 1)$.
† Data for CL in this test were seasonally adjusted.

TABLE 6

1. $Md = -.0021iY - .0043r_sY + .0542Y + .0046(N \cdot P) + .833Md_{-1}$

2. $FR = (.001 - .00204S_2 - .00237S_3 - .00223S_4)\bar{D}_{-1} - .00122i\bar{D}_{-1} + .00144d\bar{D}_{-1} + .646(1 - \delta)\Delta RU - .502\delta\Delta CL + .394RL + .705FR_{-1}$

3. $D = \dfrac{RU - \tau T - FR}{\delta}$

4. $Md^{NB} = SD - Mg$

5. $Md = JsMD^{NB}$

of total demand deposits at all commercial banks to total member bank deposits D, both seasonally unadjusted

$$S \equiv (MD^{NB} + Mg)/D \tag{4.1}$$

where Md^{ns} is private deposits not seasonally adjusted and Mg is U.S. Treasury deposits at all commercial banks. Once we have calculated S for all time periods from (4.1), we treat it as an exogenous variable to our subsystem.[24] Identity (5) reflects the seasonal adjustments which have been made in the official series. The seasonal factor Js, which varies slightly from year to year, is also treated as an exogenous variable in our system.

The system 1 to 5 is represented in a flow chart in Figure 5 with arrows indicating the causal flow among the endogenous variables. This diagram clearly indicates the major sources of exogenous influences upon the sector: (1) gross national product through the demand side of the market; (2) the instruments of monetary policy, unborrowed reserves, the discount rate, and reserve requirements through the supply side; and (3) time deposits and commercial loans which are exogenous to our submodel.

2. Stimulation of the Least Squares Estimates

In preceding sections we have reported on the properties, statistical and economic, of the component equations of our system. We now wish to examine the behavior of the equations considered as a system with the aid of the closing identities given in Table 6. We are particularly interested in establishing how well our model can account for the observed behavior of the stock of demand deposits and the treasury bill rate, both within the period of observation and in extrapolation.

Our vehicle for this investigation is the so-called dynamic simulation technique. In this procedure a set of initial conditions, including lagged dependent variables and the contemporaneous exogenous variables, are supplied to the

[24] In the context of the larger FRB-MIT Econometric Model we have endogenized this variable. Its behavior over the sample period can be accurately replicated by seasonal variables and a secular trend.

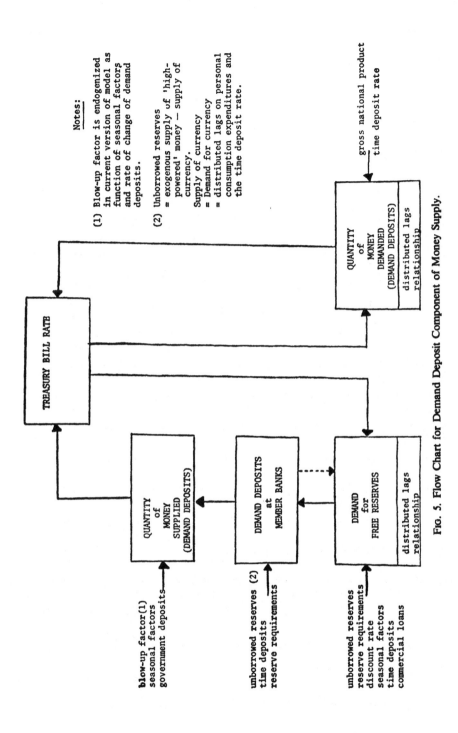

Notes:

(1) Blow-up factor is endogenized in current version of model as function of seasonal factors and rate of change of demand deposits.

(2) Unborrowed reserves = exogenous supply of 'high-powered' money — supply of currency.

Supply of currency = Demand for currency = distributed lags on personal consumption expenditures and the time deposit rate.

TREASURY BILL RATE

QUANTITY of MONEY DEMANDED (DEMAND DEPOSITS) distributed lags relationship

gross national product
time deposit rate

QUANTITY of MONEY SUPPLIED (DEMAND DEPOSITS)

blow-up factor(1)
seasonal factors
government deposits

DEMAND DEPOSITS at MEMBER BANKS

unborrowed reserves (2)
time deposits
reserve requirements

DEMAND for FREE RESERVES distributed lags relationship

unborrowed reserves
reserve requirements
discount rate
seasonal factors
time deposits
commercial loans

Fig. 5. Flow Chart for Demand Deposit Component of Money Supply.

model. Solution values are determined for the first-period endogenous variables. The initial conditions are then updated in time, using the contemporaneous exogenous variables and the first-period solution values for the lagged endogenous variables, and a second-period solution is generated. This procedure is repeated for subsequent periods.[25]

With this procedure the simulated errors will differ from the single equation estimation errors for two reasons. First, in the simulation procedure the equations are evaluated as a system, so endogenous variables which appear on the right-hand side of structural specifications assume their simulated, not historical values. Second, the procedure of using the *lagged simulated* values, rather than the *lagged historical* values of the endogenous variables implies that the simulation errors are generated in part as weighted averages of the past errors.

The period chosen for the simulation analysis was 1955(I)–1968(I), which includes the entire sample period for the estimation plus *five* post-sample quarters. The results are presented graphically in Figures 6a to 6c, which compare actual and simulated values. Table 7 presents some summary statistics.

From Figure 6a it can be seen that the computed value of demand deposits tracks the long run behavior of the series well, at least within the period of observation ending in 1966(I). The root-mean-square error is .89 million, well below one per cent. There are clearly some periods in which the errors are consistently sizeable, most noticeably in 1959. However, because the errors are highly serially correlated, the computed values tend to grow and decline with the actual, even in this period. In the remaining periods in which the money supply declined mildly—1957(IV), 1962(I)–1962(III), and 1966(I)–1966(IV)—the computed value either declined or at least leveled off. Unfortunately, the results of the extrapolation are not too encouraging since in the last three quarters the computed value completely misses the sharp rise of the actual series.

Figure 6b shows the results for free reserves, a variable that, in contrast to demand deposits, exhibits little long-run trend but has sharp cyclical fluctuations. Our simulation again tracks these fluctuations rather well. However, the simulation errors of Figure 6b provide little new information since it can be verified that the errors are roughly proportional to those of 6a with the proportionality factor averaging around −7.5.[26] Nevertheless, Figure 6b is

---

[25] It should be noted that these are exact or deterministic simulations. The stochastic disturbance terms of the estimated specifications have been set identically equal to zero.

[26] Indeed, if we note by $U(Md)_t$ and $U(FR)_t$ the simulation error in Md and in FR, respectively, in a given quarter t, then from Table 6 one can infer that:

$$U(Md)_t = -\left(\frac{Js}{\delta}\right)_t = u(FR)_t \simeq -7.5u\ (FR)_t$$

Since the quantity Js/δ has tended to remain reasonably stable in the medium run, though exhibiting a mildly rising trend averaging around 7.5.

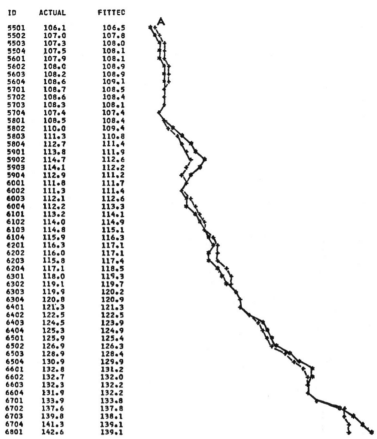

ID	ACTUAL	FITTED
5501	106.1	106.5
5502	107.0	107.8
5503	107.3	108.0
5504	107.5	108.1
5601	107.9	108.1
5602	108.0	108.9
5603	108.2	108.9
5604	108.6	109.1
5701	108.7	108.5
5702	108.6	108.4
5703	108.3	108.1
5704	107.4	107.4
5801	108.5	108.4
5802	110.0	109.4
5803	111.3	110.8
5804	112.7	111.4
5901	113.8	111.9
5902	114.7	112.6
5903	114.1	112.2
5904	112.9	111.2
6001	111.8	111.7
6002	111.3	111.4
6003	112.1	112.6
6004	112.2	113.3
6101	113.2	114.1
6102	114.0	114.9
6103	114.8	115.1
6104	115.9	116.3
6201	116.3	117.1
6202	116.0	117.1
6203	115.8	117.4
6204	117.1	118.5
6301	118.0	119.3
6302	119.1	119.7
6303	119.9	120.2
6304	120.8	120.9
6401	121.3	121.3
6402	122.5	122.5
6403	124.5	123.9
6404	125.3	124.9
6501	125.9	125.4
6502	126.9	126.3
6503	128.9	128.4
6504	130.9	129.9
6601	132.8	131.2
6602	132.7	132.0
6603	132.3	132.2
6604	131.9	132.2
6701	133.9	133.8
6702	137.6	137.8
6703	139.8	138.1
6704	141.3	139.1
6801	142.6	139.1

FIG. 6a. Plot of Actual (*) and Fitted (+) Values.

useful to bring into perspective the complexity of the task of tracing short-run fluctuations in free reserves which constitute the endogenous component of the stock of deposits.

Table 7 reports the standard deviations of the simulation errors for both *Md* and *FR* and compares them with the single equation errors of the money supply (or free reserve) equation. It appears that within the period of observation the simulation error is some 80 per cent larger than the money demand error and some 60 per cent larger than the supply equation error. The amplification is thus substantial but not altogether surprising. The simulation error reflects not only the interaction of the single equation errors but also the substitution of the lagged dependent variable with the simulated value. This substitution is likely to be the primary contributor to the substantial serial correlation of the simulation errors which is apparent in Figure 6.

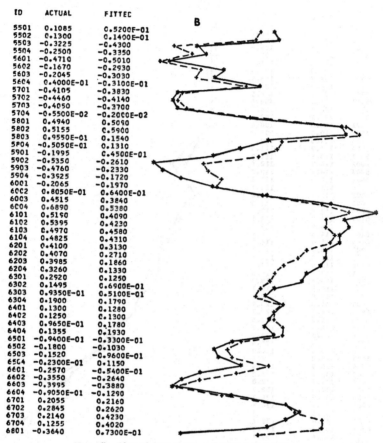

ID	ACTUAL	FITTED
5501	0.1085	0.5200E-01
5502	0.1300	0.1400E-01
5503	-0.3225	-0.4300
5504	-0.2500	-0.3350
5601	-0.4710	-0.5010
5602	-0.1670	-0.2930
5603	-0.2045	-0.3030
5604	0.4000E-01	-0.3100E-01
5701	-0.4105	-0.3830
5702	-0.4460	-0.4140
5703	-0.4050	-0.3700
5704	-0.5500E-02	-0.2000E-02
5801	0.4940	0.5090
5802	0.5155	0.5900
5803	0.9550E-01	0.1540
5804	-0.5050E-01	0.1310
5901	-0.1995	0.4500E-01
5902	-0.5350	-0.2610
5903	-0.4760	-0.2330
5904	-0.3925	-0.1720
6001	-0.2065	-0.1970
6002	0.8050E-01	0.6400E-01
6003	0.4515	0.3840
6004	0.6890	0.5380
6101	0.5190	0.4090
6102	0.5395	0.4230
6103	0.4970	0.4580
6104	0.4825	0.4310
6201	0.4100	0.3130
6202	0.4070	0.2710
6203	0.3985	0.1860
6204	0.3260	0.1330
6301	0.2920	0.1250
6302	0.1495	0.6900E-01
6303	0.9350E-01	0.5100E-01
6304	0.1900	0.1790
6401	0.1300	0.1280
6402	0.1250	0.1300
6403	0.9650E-01	0.1780
6404	0.1355	0.1930
6501	-0.9400E-01	-0.3300E-01
6502	-0.1800	-0.1030
6503	-0.1520	-0.9600E-01
6504	-0.2300E-01	0.1150
6601	-0.2570	-0.5400E-01
6602	-0.3550	-0.2640
6603	-0.3995	-0.3880
6604	-0.9050E-01	-0.1290
6701	0.2055	0.2160
6702	0.2845	0.2620
6703	0.2140	0.4230
6704	0.1255	0.4020
6801	-0.3640	0.7300E-01

FIG. 6b. Plot of Actual (*) and Fitted (+) Values.

The table also confirms the sizeable deterioration of the fit in the extrapolation. This appears to be related to the poor performance of the supply function. The single equation error of this equation rises by nearly 30 per cent, while the fit of the money demand equation does not worsen appreciably.

Turning to Figure 6c, we see that the model also succeeds in accounting for the broad features of behavior of the treasury bill rate. The root-mean-squared error is 33 basis points. The peaks of 1957, 1959–60, and 1966, and the sharp troughs of 1958 and 1967 are predicted with approximately correct amplitude and timing. The most disturbing feature of this simulation is the intracycle behavior of the simulation errors. These can be roughly characterized as cyclical with high frequency and low amplitude—a "spiking" effect. It is apparent from the graph that this feature can be largely traced to a similar "spiking" of the simulated series which exhibits sharp short-run fluctuations that find no

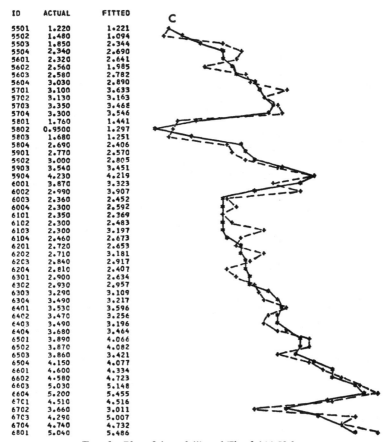

ID	ACTUAL	FITTED
5501	1.220	1.221
5502	1.480	1.094
5503	1.850	2.344
5504	2.340	2.690
5601	2.320	2.641
5602	2.560	1.985
5603	2.580	2.782
5604	3.030	2.890
5701	3.100	3.633
5702	3.130	3.163
5703	3.350	3.468
5704	3.300	3.546
5801	1.760	1.441
5802	0.9500	1.297
5803	1.680	1.251
5804	2.690	2.406
5901	2.770	2.570
5902	3.000	2.805
5903	3.540	3.451
5904	4.230	4.219
6001	3.870	3.323
6002	2.990	3.907
6003	2.360	2.452
6004	2.300	2.592
6101	2.350	2.369
6102	2.300	2.483
6103	2.300	3.197
6104	2.460	2.673
6201	2.720	2.653
6202	2.710	3.181
6203	2.840	2.917
6204	2.810	2.407
6301	2.900	2.634
6302	2.930	2.957
6303	3.290	3.109
6304	3.490	3.217
6401	3.530	3.596
6402	3.470	3.256
6403	3.490	3.196
6404	3.680	3.464
6501	3.890	4.066
6502	3.870	4.082
6503	3.860	3.421
6504	4.150	4.077
6601	4.600	4.334
6602	4.580	4.723
6603	5.030	5.148
6604	5.200	5.455
6701	4.510	4.516
6702	3.660	3.011
6703	4.290	5.007
6704	4.740	4.732
6801	5.040	5.486

FIG. 6c. Plot of Actual (*) and Fitted (+) Values.

counterpart in the actual series. One might conjecture that this failure reflects an underestimation of the short-run elasticity of both demand and supply with respect to the treasury bill rate, resulting from simultaneous equation bias. By underestimating these elasticities we would be led to overestimate the variation in the treasury bill rate necessary to accommodate short-run shifts of the demand or supply schedule (arising for example from movements of Y or RU or from the error component).

In the next section we report the results obtained by an alternative estimating procedure designed to avoid the simultaneous equation bias.

3. An Alternative Estimation Technique

The object of our alternative estimation procedure was to replace the endogenous variables, current and lagged, on the right-hand side of our specifica-

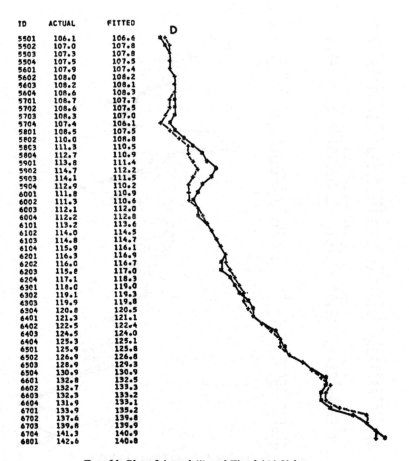

ID	ACTUAL	FITTED
5501	106.1	106.6
5502	107.0	107.8
5503	107.3	107.8
5504	107.5	107.5
5601	107.9	107.4
5602	108.0	108.2
5603	108.2	108.1
5604	108.6	108.3
5701	108.7	107.7
5702	108.6	107.5
5703	108.3	107.0
5704	107.4	106.1
5801	108.5	107.5
5802	110.0	108.8
5803	111.3	110.5
5804	112.7	110.9
5901	113.8	111.4
5902	114.7	112.2
5903	114.1	111.5
5904	112.9	110.2
6001	111.8	110.9
6002	111.3	110.6
6003	112.1	112.0
6004	112.2	112.8
6101	113.2	113.6
6102	114.0	114.5
6103	114.8	114.7
6104	115.9	116.1
6201	116.3	116.9
6202	116.0	116.7
6203	115.8	117.0
6204	117.1	118.3
6301	118.0	119.0
6302	119.1	119.3
6303	119.9	119.8
6304	120.8	120.5
6401	121.3	121.1
6402	122.5	122.4
6403	124.5	124.0
6404	125.3	125.1
6501	125.9	125.8
6502	126.9	126.8
6503	128.9	129.3
6504	130.9	130.9
6601	132.8	132.5
6602	132.7	133.3
6603	132.3	133.2
6604	131.9	133.1
6701	133.9	135.2
6702	137.6	139.8
6703	139.8	139.9
6704	141.3	140.9
6801	142.6	140.8

FIG. 6d. Plot of Actual (*) and Fitted (+) Values.

tions with instrumental variables which are functions of only exogenous variables.[27] Our instrumental variables were obtained from the dynamic simulations described above. The solution values, generated by this simulation procedure, are functions of the ordinary least squares parameter estimates, the exogenous variables and the (pre-sample period) initial conditions of the endogenous variables. Both the demand and supply equation were re-estimated with a correction for serial correlation, using the instruments for the current and lagged

[27] The standard two-stage squares technique (TSLS) uses a first stage estimation of the reduced form to obtain instrumental variables. This procedure breaks down in our case since (1) a large number of variables are required in the first stage estimation when the errors of the structural equations are serially correlated and (2) we expect substantial variation of the reduced form coefficients over time arising from the non-linearities in the structural specifications.

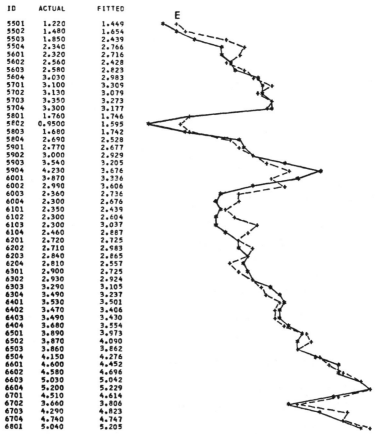

ID	ACTUAL	FITTED
5501	1.220	1.449
5502	1.480	1.654
5503	1.850	2.439
5504	2.340	2.766
5601	2.320	2.716
5602	2.560	2.428
5603	2.580	2.823
5604	3.030	2.983
5701	3.100	3.309
5702	3.130	3.079
5703	3.350	3.273
5704	3.300	3.177
5801	1.760	1.746
5802	0.9500	1.595
5803	1.680	1.742
5804	2.690	2.528
5901	2.770	2.677
5902	3.000	2.929
5903	3.540	3.205
5904	4.230	3.676
6001	3.870	3.336
6002	2.990	3.606
6003	2.360	2.736
6004	2.300	2.676
6101	2.350	2.439
6102	2.300	2.604
6103	2.300	3.037
6104	2.460	2.887
6201	2.720	2.725
6202	2.710	2.983
6203	2.840	2.865
6204	2.810	2.557
6301	2.900	2.725
6302	2.930	2.924
6303	3.290	3.105
6304	3.490	3.237
6401	3.530	3.501
6402	3.470	3.406
6403	3.490	3.430
6404	3.680	3.554
6501	3.890	3.973
6502	3.870	4.090
6503	3.860	3.862
6504	4.150	4.276
6601	4.600	4.452
6602	4.580	4.696
6603	5.030	5.042
6604	5.200	5.229
6701	4.510	4.614
6702	3.660	3.806
6703	4.290	4.823
6704	4.740	4.747
6801	5.040	5.205

Fig. 6e. Plot of Actual (*) and Fitted (+) Values.

TABLE 7

ROOT MEAN SQUARE ERRORS OF SINGLE EQUATIONS AND DYNAMIC SIMULATIONS

	SINGLE EQUATOIN		DYNAMIC SIMULATION	
	Sample	Sample and Extrapolation	Sample	Sample and Extrapolation
Md	.49	.506	.888	1.048
FR	.072	.092	.117	.135
i	—	—	.331	.347

B. Two-Stage Estimates:

	SINGLE EQUATION		DYNAMIC SIMULATION	
	Sample	Sample and Extrapolation	Sample	Sample and Extrapolation
Md	.734	.757	1.014	1.066
FR	.072	.091	.135	.139
i	—	—	.287	.285

endogenous variables on the right-hand side. This procedure is not consistent[28] but it may reduce some of the biases of the ordinary least squares coefficient estimates.

The results of this estimation technique applied to the money demand equation $(2.7')$[29] and the free reserve equation (3.24) are reported in the last row of Tables 1 and 5 respectively. In both cases the standard deviation of the residual error increases, but this is as expected since, if there is least squares bias, then that method will underestimate the variance of the true structural error. It is significant, however, that for both equations the estimates of the coefficients of the endogenous variable have moved in the direction we anticipated.

In the first equation, the coefficient of i, and thus the short-run elasticity of the bill rate, has more than doubled in absolute value. Similarly, the speed of adjustment of actual demand deposits to target levels has doubled as the coefficient of the lagged variable Md_{-1}/Y falls. Yet the relationship between the coefficients of i and r has been maintained as the coefficient of r_a also increased considerably in absolute value. The long-run elasticities do not change appreciably because of the offsetting effects of the preceding two changes.

Turning to the second equation, we note again that the estimated coefficient of the treasury bill rate has increased by nearly one-third and now, as suggested by our model, exceeds that of the discount rate. Similarly the coefficient of lagged free reserves falls somewhat, implying a faster speed of adjustment.

4. Simulation Results with the Alternative Estimates

The results obtained in a dynamic simulation test based on the alternative coefficient estimates are reported in Figures 6d and 6e and in the last three rows of Table 7. The results for the money supply are rather disappointing since the root-mean-square error, instead of improving, grows from .89 to 1.01 billion. However, a comparison of Figures 6a and 6d reveals that the entire deterioration can be traced to an even larger underestimation in the troublesome period, 1958–59. From the middle of 1960, and including the extrapolation period, the new simulation tracks better, though not by a large margin. In the case of the bill rate the improvement is more clear cut and uni-

---

[28] This method is similar to the type of *full information* estimators discussed in Klein [12], pp. 66–70. It differs in that Klein assumes that the simulation is performed using structural coefficients which were obtained from a consistent estimation procedure such as TSLS. In .this non-linear case, our procedure is subject to the same uncertainties regarding consistency as the methods which Klein discusses. In addition, the method is unlikely to be consistent because there is a high probability that the simulation errors (the actual value of the endogenous variable—solution value) will be correlated with the exogenous variables. This latter problem arises only since we are using a two-stage, least-squares computational design rather than the more general instrumental variable framework. See McCarthy, University of Pennsylvania discussion paper 125 (mimeo).

[29] This equation was estimated normalized on the bill rate i. Errors in variables considerations led to making the variable with the larger relative error variance the dependent variable.

form. For the period of fit the root-mean-square error improves from 33 to 29 basis points. The spiking phenomenon is generally reduced, though this improvement seems to have been achieved at the cost of missing the extreme fluctuations registered by the actual series in 1958(II) and 1959(IV). Finally, the two-stage estimate performs distinctly better in the extrapolation test. In contrast to the experience with the least-square estimates, the performance of every one of our variables in the extrapolation period is not appreciably different from that in the period of observation. This supports the view that the two-stage procedure provides more reliable estimates of the underlying structure.

5. Some Remarks on the Problem of Specifying the Exogenous Policy Variables

In our estimation, as well as in the simulation tests, we have relied on the assumption that unborrowed reserves, reserve requirements, and the discount rate can be regarded as policy variables exogenously set by the Federal Reserve and hence uncorrelated with the error terms of the structural equations. As is well known, this specification is subject to serious questions. In setting these variables the Fed can be expected to be influenced by the behavior of other variables including the money supply and the bill rate, which by our hypothesis are affected by the error term. In particular, in certain periods the Fed could have set an interest target and used open market operations (and possibly other tools) to keep the bill rate pegged at the desired level. In this case the bill rate should be taken as exogenous for estimation purposes and unborrowed reserves (or other policy variables) as endogenous. Similarly, in such periods simulation tests treating the bill rate as endogenous lose their value.

There are grounds for holding that such a situation may have prevailed during the early 1960's when, because of balance of payment considerations, the Fed seems to have been primarily concerned with maintaining in the short run a stable or slowly rising treasury bill rate. This may explain why in this period, in Figure 6e as well as in Figure 6c the movements of the simulated value of the bill rate seem to bear little relation to the relatively minor movements that actually occurred in this variable.

Since at present we cannot tell with confidence which variables should be treated as endogenous at different times, nor do we have powerful techniques for estimating parameters when certain variables are endogenous at one time and exogenous at others, there is little we can do at the moment except be aware of possible biases, test what difference alternative specifications would make, and make proper allowances in assessing the result of simulation tests of goodness-of-fit. Of course, for purposes of policy simulation, given estimates of the coefficients, one can readily treat as exogenous the bill rate or the money supply as long as some policy variable is correspondingly endogenized.

6. Conclusion

In this paper we have formulated, estimated, and tested a structural model of the money supply and short-term interest rates in the present U.S. economy. These variables are seen as resulting from the interaction of the demand for money by the public and the supply of money which reflects the behavior of the Federal Reserve setting certain policy variables, the behavior of the commercial banks in managing their assets and liabilities in response to fluctuations in their reserves and the demand for commercial loans, and the behavior of the U.S. treasury cash balance reflecting fiscal and debt management operations. The coefficients have been estimated both by least squares and by an alternative two-stage procedure. The results provide support for our model in that the estimated coefficients, especially those derived from the two-stage experiment, are in agreement with the a priori specifications, and the model accounts rather well for the behavior of the variables it purports to explain.

Needless to say, both the model and the methods of estimation and testing need refinement and improvement. Furthermore, the specifications may need to be modified in the light of institutional changes and emerging financial innovations.[30] Nonetheless, we feel that the results presented in this paper are sufficiently encouraging to justify their use in the present form as a component of the FRB-MIT model.

APPENDIX: RELATION OF THE MODEL IN THE TEXT TO THE FEDERAL FUNDS MARKET

We propose to exhibit here the derivation of equation (3.17) of the text from an explicit model of the Federal Funds Market. To this end, we identify the borrowing rate r with the Federal Funds rate—which we regard as appropriate as long as there are no extraneous constraints on the behavior of the Federal Funds rate.

Next, we can visualize the supply of loans in our market as coming from banks which end up with a reserve surplus for the period and the demand as coming from banks which end up with a reserve shortage and thus have to borrow. Denote by S the aggregate surplus (and free reserves) of all banks with a surplus and by B^* the aggregate borrowings of the banks with negative free reserves. We can then express aggregate free reserves as:

[30] In particular, we are currently working on further tests for the effects on both the demand and supply specifications of the emergence of the CD market and of changes in the method of computing required reserves. Eventually, we shall have to consider what effects the activity in the Eurodollar market in 1969 had on our structure.

$$FR = S - B^* \qquad (1)$$

Now S and B^* will vary with FR and the relation that may be expected to hold, on the average, among the three variables is sketched in Figure 7. In this figure, S is measured on the ordinate from the origin up while B^* is measured from the origin down. When FR is zero, some banks will have positive free reserves, and their aggregate reserve position S is represented by point b on the ordinate; this aggregate will be just balanced by the aggregate negative position B^* of the remaining banks, shown by b'. As FR rises, we may expect a growing proportion of banks to have positive free reserves and a declining number to have a negative position. Accordingly, B^* may be expected to decline and approach asymptotically zero (or at least some small positive number as shown by the curve $b'c'$ graphed in the southeast quadrant. By the same token, in view of (1), S will approach asymptotically FR (i.e., the dotted 45-degree line with equation $S + FR$) as shown by curve bc. Conversely, as FR declines, S will approach zero as shown by ab, and B^* will approach the 45-degree line, as shown by $a'b'$. All this can be summarized by the fundamental relation:

$$S = S(FR), \qquad 0 < S' < 1 \qquad (2a)$$

$$B^* = S(FR) - FR = B^*(FR), \qquad 0 > B^{*\prime} > -1 \qquad (2b)$$

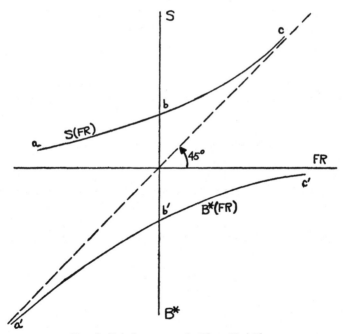

FIG. 7. Relation among the Three Variables.

The supply of loans in the Federal Funds market, FFL, can now be expressed as the difference between the aggregate surplus S and that part of the surplus that banks choose to hold in the form of excess reserves E, i.e.:

$$FFL = S - E \tag{3}$$

But as suggested in the text, the portion of S kept in the form of E may be expected to depend on the return from lending, namely the rate r, or

$$E = \eta(S, r), \qquad 0 \le \eta_S \le 1, \qquad \eta_r \le 0. \tag{4}$$

Furthermore, making use of (2) to express S in terms of FR, we can also write:

$$E = E(FR, r), \qquad E_{FR} = \eta_S S' \ge 0, \qquad E_r = \eta_r \le 0.$$

The supply function for Federal Funds can now be finally expressed as

$$FFL = S - E(FR, r) = l(FR, r), \qquad 0 \le l_{FR} = S'(1 - \eta_S) \le 1; \tag{a}$$
$$l_r = -\eta_r \ge 0.$$

Similarly, the demand for borrowing in the market will be $FFB = B^* - B$, where B is borrowing at the window. Considerations similar to those used in deriving (4) suggest that FFB should be an increasing function of B^*, and a decreasing function of $r - d$, the spread between the cost of securing Federal Funds and that of obtaining funds at the window, or:

$$FFB = b^*(B^*, r, d), \qquad 0 < b_{B^*}^* \le 1, \qquad b_r^* \le 0, \qquad b_d^* \ge 0 \tag{5}$$

The relation between FFB and r for given B^* might be expected to look somewhat like curve bb in Figure 8. The distance between the curve and the horizontal line of height B^* equals borrowing at the window B. When r falls below d, the use of Federal Funds is cheaper even in terms of cash cost; the use of B would tend to be limited to smaller banks and/or possibly, seasonal needs. As r rises above d, B rises and FFB shrinks, though eventually limitations on the use of the window would cause B to flatten out. Changes in B^* should lead to roughly parallel shifts in the curve, except for the fact that FFB can never become negative. This means that b_{B^*} should be positive and generally close to, but not higher than, unity in the relevant range indicated in (5) above. Note also that since FFB should depend basically on the spread $r - d$, we can infer that $b_r^* \simeq -b_d^*$. Now, making use of (1) and (2), we can express B^* as a function of FR, $B^* = S(FR) - FR$, and therefore, substituting in (5), we can write:

$$FFB = b(FR, r, d), \quad \text{with} \quad b_r = b_r^* \le 0,$$
$$b_d = b_d^* \ge 0, \qquad b_{FR} = -b_{B^*}^*(1 - S') < 0 \tag{b}$$

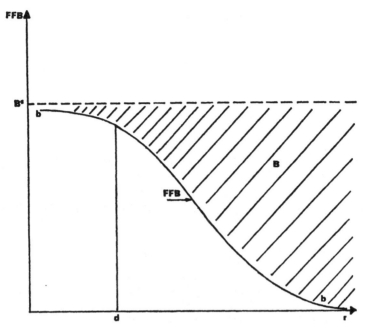

FIG. 8. Relation between *FFB* and *r*.

The description of the market can now be completed by the market-clearing condition:

$$FFB = FFL. \tag{c}$$

Substituting in (c) from (b) and (a), we find that equilibrium implies

$$b(FR, r, d) = l(FR, r), \tag{6}$$

an equation which can be solved for r in terms of FR and to yield $r = R(FR, d)$, which is equation (3.17) in the text. The properties of R_{FR} and R_d can be inferred by the differentiation of (6) and the properties of the functions l and b, stated in (a) and (b) above. We find:

$$R_{FR} = \frac{b_{FR} - l_{FR}}{l_r - b_r} < 0, \qquad R_d = \frac{b_d}{l_r - b_r} > 0.$$

Furthermore, if, as suggested above, $b_d \simeq -b_r$, we can also infer that R_d is less than unity.

The above analysis is also useful in clarifying the relation between (3.11) and the approximation (3.11′) in the text. Equation (3.11) involves not only r

but also the return from lending r_s. But this variable in turn can be expressed as an average of r and r_E, the return on excess reserves weighted by the proportion of S kept in each form, or

$$r_S = r_E(E/S) + (r - c)(FFL/S) = (r - c)(FFL/S)$$
$$= (r - c)\frac{l(FR, r)}{S(FR)} . \quad (7)$$

Here c is an approximation to transaction costs in the Federal Funds market, and the second equality follows since, under present arrangements, $r_E = 0$. Once more, r_S can be eliminated from (3.11) by using the last equality in (7). The resulting expression is analogous to (3.11'), except that in the approximation we have dropped the variable FR from the list of arguments of F.

LITERATURE CITED

1. ALLAIS, M. F. C. "A Restatement of the Quantity Theory of Money," *American Economic Review* (December, 1966), 1123–57.

2. ANDO, A. and FRANCO MODIGLIANI. "Velocity and the Investment Multiplier," *American Economic Review* (September, 1965), 693–728.

3. BAUMOL, W. J. "The Transactions Demand for Cash," *Quarterly Journal of Economics* (November, 1952), 545–54.

4. BRUNNER, K. and A. H. MELTZER. "Predicting Velocity: Its Implications for Theory and Policy," *Journal of Finance* (May, 1963), 319–54.

5. CHOW, G. "On the Long-Run and Short-Run Demand Function for Money," *Journal of Political Economy* (April, 1966), 111–31.

6. DELEEUW, F. "A Model of Financial Behavior," in J. Duesenberry, et al., ed. *The Brookings Quarterly Econometric Model of the United States.* Rand-McNally, 1965. Pp. 465–530.

7. FRIEDMAN, B. "The Demand for Money: Testing a Neo-Fisherian Approach." Unpublished paper presented at the meeting of the Econometric Society (December, 1966).

8. FRIEDMAN, M. "The Demand for Money: Some Theoretical and Empirical Results," *Journal of Political Economy* (August, 1959), 327–51.

9. GOLDFELD, S. *Commercial Bank Behavior and Economic Activity.* North-Holland, 1966.

10. GOLDFELD, S. and E. KANE. "The Determinants of Member Bank Borrowing," *Journal of Finance* (September, 1966), pp. 499–514.

11. HESTER, D. and J. PIERCE. "Cross-section Analysis and Bank Dynamics," *Journal of Political Economy* (July/August, 1968), Part II, pp. 755–76.

12. KLEIN, L. R. *An Essay on the Theory of Economic Prediction.* Helsinki, 1968.

13. LAIDLER, D. "The Rate of Interest and the Demand for Money—Some Empirical Evidence," *Journal of Political Economy* (December, 1966), 543–55.

14. LATANE, H. A. "Cash Balances and the Interest Rate—A Pragmatic Approach," *Review of Economics and Statistics* (September, 1954), 456–61.

15. ———. "Income Velocity and Interest Rate—A Pragmatic Approach," *Review of Economics and Statistics* (November, 1960), 445–49.

16. MEIGS, A. JAMES. *Free Reserves and the Money Supply*. University of Chicago Press, 1962.

17. MODIGLIANI, F. and R. SUTCH. "Innovation in Interest Rate Policy," *American Economic Review* (May, 1966), 178–97.

18. ORR, D. and W. G. MELLON. "Stochastic Reserve Losses and Bank Credit," *American Economic Review* (September, 1961), 614–23.

19. SCHULL, B. "Report on Research Undertaken in Connection with the System Study." Board of Governors of the Federal Reserve System: Reappraisal of the Federal Reserve Discount Mechanism.

20. TOBIN, J. "The Interest Elasticity of Transactions Demand for Cash," *Review of Economics and Statistics* (August, 1956), 241–47.

21. ———. Unpublished Monetary Theory Manuscript. New Haven: 1959 (mimeographed), chapter viii.

22. TUCKER, D. P. "Income Adjustment to Money-Supply Changes," *American Economic Review* (June, 1966), 431–49.

Errata

Page 172, line 1: "$m - y = \gamma'(\alpha_0 + \alpha_1 \log i - \cdots$" should read "$m - y = \gamma'(\alpha_0 - \alpha_1 \log i - \cdots.$"

Page 184, line 1, last term: "$(r - r_s)\int_{-\infty}^{-FR} \frac{\overline{dFR}}{dl} d\phi(\bar{x})$" should read "$(r - r_s)\int_{-\infty}^{-FR} \frac{\overline{dFR}}{dl} d\phi(\bar{x}).$"

Page 184, last line (below figure 3): "Given $(L - r_s)/r - r_s)$" should read "Given $(i - r_s)/(r - r_s).$"

Page 194, equation (3.22'): "$Z(t, \tau) = \frac{\Delta Z(t)}{m}$" should read "$\Delta Z(t, \tau) = \frac{\Delta Z(t)}{m}.$"

Page 197, line 2: "Indeed, RL, like RU" should read "Indeed, RL, like $\Delta RU.$"

Page 203, section 2 heading: "2. Stimulation of the Least Squares Estimates," should read "2. Simulation of the Least Squares Estimates."

Page 205, footnote 26, line 3: "$U(Md)_t = -\left(\frac{Js}{\delta}\right)_t = u(FR)_t \doteq -7.5u(FR)_t$" should read "$U(Md)_t = -\left(\frac{JsS}{\delta}\right)_t \cdot U(FR)_t \doteq -7.5U(FR)_t.$"

Page 205, footnote 26, line 4: "Since the quantity Js/δ" should read "since the quantity $JsS/\delta.$"

Page 214, line 14: "degree line with equation $S + FR$" should read "degree line with equation $S = FR.$"

3

The Dynamics of Portfolio Adjustment and the Flow of Savings Through Financial Intermediaries

Franco Modigliani

This paper is concerned with the process of accumulation of household claims on the four major intermediaries dealt with in the FMP model. We account for the behavior of quarterly flows, and the stocks outstanding at the end of each quarter, for passbook savings deposits at commercial banks, savings and loan association deposits, mutual savings bank deposits, and life insurance reserves net of policy loans.

The paper is divided into four sections. The first section sets out the general form of the model we intend to test and estimate. This model is then applied to time deposits; to the other two depository institutions; and, with appropriate modifications, to life insurance reserves.

A Model of Long-Run and Short-Run Determinants of Stocks and Flows

The theory of portfolio selection would lead us to expect that, aside from transactions costs, or given time enough for adjustment, the proportion of total net worth allocated to any asset would be a function of (i) the expected rate of return on the asset, (ii) the expected rate of return on competing assets, (iii) the covariance of the rate of return on the asset with every other asset, and (iv) some appropriate measure of risk aversion which might in principle vary with per capita real net worth. If then portfolio adjustments were instantaneous and we could measure explicitly the various expectations referred to above, we would have at all times

$$A_i(t) = \alpha_i(t)V(t) \qquad (3\text{-}1)$$

where $A_i(t)$ and $V(t)$ denote end of quarter values for the ith asset and net worth respectively; and where the long-run proportion α_i is related to the expected rates (r_i^e, r_j^e) and the variance, as in

$$\alpha_i(t) = \alpha_i\{r_i^e(t), [r_j^e(t)], [\sigma_{ij}^e(t)], \dots\} \qquad (3\text{-}1a)$$

63

The quarterly saving flow $S_i(t)$ would then be given by

$$S_i(t) = A_i(t) - A_i(t - 1) = \alpha_i(t)V(t) - A_i(t - 1) \qquad (3\text{-}2)$$

However, even a cursory examination of the behavior of quarterly flows into the four intermediaries under consideration suggests that equations (3-1) and (3-2) are not very useful for quarterly data unless one allows properly for delayed adjustment. To see this, let us rewrite (3-2) as follows [hereafter we drop the subscripts i and t and abbreviate $(t - 1)$ by a subscript -1]:

$$S = \alpha \, \Delta V + V_{-1}(\alpha - \alpha_{-1}) \qquad (3\text{-}3)$$

The first term is the change in A resulting from the growth of wealth and the second is the flow needed to rebalance the initial portfolio in the light of changes in α. But dividing both sides of equation (3-3) by A and using equation (3-1) we can also infer that

$$\frac{S}{A} = \frac{\Delta V}{V} + \frac{V_{-1}}{V} \frac{\Delta \alpha}{\alpha} \simeq \frac{\Delta V}{V} + \gamma \frac{\Delta \alpha}{\alpha}$$

where $\gamma = V_{-1}/V$, or approximately one.

Hence the rate of growth of the asset is approximately the sum of the rate of growth of wealth and the percentage change in α. Over long periods of time the second term would average close to zero and S/A would average close to the rate of growth of wealth. But in the short run even moderate quarterly fluctuations in α should cause S/A to fluctuate fairly widely. In particular, since the long-run growth of wealth has been about 6 percent a year, or 1.5 percent a quarter, a decline in α by as little as 2 percent should lead to negative values of S/A. However, it turns out that even in the short run S/A has remained fairly close to its mean, never exceeding 4 percent per annum nor going below zero for savings and loan deposits and never exceeding 5 percent and going below zero only once for passbook savings. In view of the fact that rates of return on market instruments competing with saving deposits had sustantial short-run changes compared with the sluggish behavior of intermediary rates, we must conclude that α tends to respond very slowly to measured changes in relative rates, unless it is very inelastic with respect to these rates. The results reported in the following section will be seen to support the view of a very slow adjustment process and a fairly high elasticity.

Two basic mechanisms could account for a slow short-run response to variations in relative return. The first is that because of costs of adjustment—both pecuniary and nonpecuniary—A/V moves only gradually toward the desired ratio: we can refer to this source of delay as the *portfolio rebalancing* lag. The second is that the desired ratio might respond only gradually to measured returns, both because of inertia in habits and because the unobservable expected rates r_j^e are likely to be influenced not only by r_j but also by its past values: we can characterize this second source of lags as a *learning-expectational lag* (referred to hereafter, for brevity, as *expectational lag*).

The standard way to allow for gradual adjustments of stocks is through the so-called stock adjustment model, in which the adjustment per unit of time is hypothesized to be a fraction, say g, of the gap between the long-run equilibrium and the beginning-of-period value of the relevant variable. We can write this specification as

$$\Delta A = g(A^* - A_{-1})$$

or, on substitution,

$$S = g(\alpha V - A_{-1}) \tag{3-4}$$

This is the formulation that explicitly or implicitly underlies past empirical studies in which the current flow, or the terminal stock, is regressed on rates of return, wealth or some proxy for it like income, and the lagged stock.

But this formulation does not seem to be consistent with either the rebalancing or the expectational lag. To see its inconsistency with the rebalancing lag, rewrite (3-4) as

$$S = g\alpha \, \Delta V + g(\alpha V_{-1} - A_{-1})$$

We see that it implies an equally slow adjustment in correcting the initial stock imbalance and in the allocation of the fresh flow of wealth. However, since the adjustment lag presumably arises from the cost of shifting from previously held assets into new ones, there is no reason why it should apply to newly accumulated wealth—at least if for the moment we neglect the role capital gains.

To see the inconsistency of equation (3-4) with the notion that the delay is due primarily to the expectational lag, we denote by a^* *the optimum ratio perceived at time* t (as contrasted with α which is the true optimum) and suppose that it can be expressed as

$$a^* = g\alpha + (1 - g)a^*_{-1} \tag{3-5}$$

where $g\alpha$ can be approximated by some function of current and recently observed values of the arguments of (3-1a). One can think of α as the value of a^* generated by (3-5) when its arguments remain constant until a^* adjusts completely. Suppose further that the portfolio adjusts promptly to this currently perceived optimum value, so that

$$A = a^* V \tag{3-6}$$

implying

$$a^* = \frac{A}{V} \equiv a \qquad (3\text{-}7)$$

We can then substitute in equation (3-5) the observable ratio a for the non-observable a^*, obtaining

$$a - a_{-1} = g(\alpha - a_{-1}) \qquad (3\text{-}8)$$

This equation will be recognized as the standard form of the stock adjustment equations but now applied to the portfolio share rather than the actual stock as in (3-4).[1]

By noting that S can be written identically as $a_{-1} \Delta V + (a - a_{-1})V$, it is seen that (3-8) implies that

$$S = a_{-1} \Delta V + gV(\alpha - a_{-1}) \qquad (3\text{-}9)$$

or, also

$$S = g\alpha V - A_{-1} \left[g - \frac{(1 - g)\,\Delta V}{V_{-1}} \right] \qquad (3\text{-}9a)$$

Equation (3-9) shows that S can be expressed as the sum of a fraction a_{-1} of the increment in wealth and a portfolio rebalancing term which is a fraction g of the imbalance $(\alpha - a_{-1})V$. Expression (3-9a) is provided for comparison with the standard formulation (3-4). It shows that, under the pure expectational lag hypothesis (3-5) and (3-6), in a growing system (i.e., $\Delta V > 0$) the coefficient of A_1 is less than g. In fact, if g were small, less than $\Delta V/V$, the coefficient of the lagged dependent variable might even be positive. This may help to explain the generally surprising small "speed of adjustment" reported in past studies—i.e., a coefficient of A_{-1} very close to unity if

---

[1] One interesting property of the version of the model proposed in (3-8) is that, in contrast to the standard formulation (3-4), it allows for the possibility that *all* components of wealth adjust slowly toward their equilibrium value. Or, to put it differently, our hypothesis can be applied consistently to every asset even though it implies a gradual adjustment. It can be readily verified that if wealth has but two components, they both adjust at the same speed. Indeed, it follows from the budget equation that $a_1 + a_2 = 1$ and $\alpha_1 + \alpha_2 = 1$. But then using (3-8) we find:

$$a_2 = 1 - a_1 = 1 - (a_1)_{-1} - g[\alpha_1 - (a_1)_{-1}] = (a_2)_{-1} + g[\alpha_2 - (a_2)_{-1}]$$

which shows that asset 2 also adjusts toward the equilibrium value α_2 at the speed of g per period. By contrast, in the standard stock adjustment formulation (3-4), if one asset adjusts gradually, the other must absorb the slack. The difference arises from the fact that in the expectational model the current flow ΔV is immediately allocated according to the perceived optimum ratios a_i^*, which in turn satisfy the budget constraint

$$\sum_i a_i^* = 1.$$

the dependent variable is $A(t)$, and very close to zero if the dependent variable is $S(t)$. If our hypothesis (3-5) and (3-6) is a good approximation, this coefficient is seen to be a downward biased estimate of g.

Since equations (3-8) and (3-9) are equivalent, either one could be used to test the model and estimate its parameters [on the other hand, form (3-9a) is not a suitable one because the coefficient of A_{-1} is not a constant]. However, form (3-9) has advantages when we take into account the fact that one part of the increase in wealth $V(t)$ does not reflect current saving but rather accrues "in kind" on certain specific assets as a result of capital gains. Empirically, capital gains (which include revaluation of corporate equities reflecting in part the retention of corporate earnings) turn out to be a quite important component of V over the postwar period. On the average, two-thirds of ΔV is accounted for by capital gains and only about one-third by personal saving, though these proportions have fluctuated widely from quarter to quarter because of the volatility of the capital gains component.

It seems unlikely that these capital gains could be promptly liquidated and reallocated between assets, with the fraction a_{-1} allocated to A.[2] A more reasonable approximation is to hypothesize that only some fraction, m, would be reallocated within the period, the remaining fraction $(1 - m)$ remaining in the short run where it first accrued. Accordingly, equation (3-9) should be modified to

$$S = a_{-1}[\Delta V - (1 - m)CG] + g(\alpha - a_{-1})V$$

$$= a_{-1}SP + ma_{-1}CG + g(\alpha - a_{-1})V \qquad (3\text{-}10)$$

where SP denotes personal saving and CG capital gains. This is the main form that we shall estimate in the next section, and shall refer to as version IA.[3] In order to insure that the coefficient of the first term be unity we can

---

[2] It is even less realistic to suppose that, in case of capital losses, other assets would be liquidated in the stated proportions and the proceeds reinvested in the assets where the capital loss accrued.

[3] Equation (3-10) applies to assets on which there are no capital gains, which include those we are concerned with here. For an asset i affected by capital gains one would have to add to the right hand side of (3-10) a term $(1 - m)CG_i$, where CG_i is capital gains on asset i. Equation (3-10) could be generalized further to take into account the fact that the income earned on saving-type deposits is in part credited to the owner's account instead of being paid out in cash. One might hypothesize that, as a result, some fraction of the income earned, say $(1 - n)$, might tend initially to remain in the asset on which it accrued. To allow for this possibility, we could rewrite (3-10) in the more general form

$$S_i = (a_i)_{-1}[\Delta V - (1 - m)CG - (1 - n) \sum_j r_j(A_j)_{-1}]$$

$$+ (1 - n)r_i(A_i)_{-1} + g[\alpha_i - (a_i)_{-1}]V \qquad (3\text{-}10a)$$

where the summation extends over all relevant savings assets and r_j is the return on asset j per unit period (thus for quarterly data r_j would be $\frac{1}{4}$ the annual rate.) Equation (3-10a) transfer it to the left side. To reduce heteroscedasticity of the error term, both sides have been deflated by V. These operations yield the expression

$$\frac{S - a_{-1}SP}{V} = ma_{-1}\frac{CG}{V} + g\alpha - ga_{-1} \tag{3-11}$$

where $g\alpha$ is some function of observed rates of return on A and competing assets (and possibly other variables) appropriate to the asset under consideration. The coefficient m then provides an estimate of the proportion of current capital gains that is currently reallocated and the coefficient of $a(-1)$ an estimate of the speed of adjustment g of equation (3.5). Finally, the long-run equilibrium ratio corresponding to a maintained level of all rates of return can be inferred from the estimate of $g\alpha$ and g, $\hat{\alpha} = g\alpha/g$.

We shall also test a variant of (3-11), version IB, in which $a_{-1}SP$ remains on the right and is allowed to have a coefficient different from unity. This variant is suggested by noticing that the part of the capital gains associated with price changes and even corporate retention may be readily predictable. Thus the proportion of SP allocated to assets on which there are no capital gains, such as saving deposits, may normally be some multiple of $a_{-1}SP$ in order to maintain portfolio balance with respect to the anticipated portion of CG. We should then expect the coefficient of $a_{-1}SP$, say m', to be no less than unity and furthermore

$$m'a_{-1}SP + ma_{-1}CG < a_{-1}\Delta V$$

implying that

$$m'\frac{SP}{\Delta V} + m\frac{CG}{\Delta V} < 1 \tag{3-11a}$$

Since, as we have just noted, $SP/\Delta V$ and $CG/\Delta V$ average around $\frac{1}{3}$ and $\frac{2}{3}$ respectively, we should expect m' and m to satisfy the condition $m' > 1$ and $\frac{1}{3}m' + \frac{2}{3}m < 1$.

Version I relies on the hypothesis embodied in (3-6) or (3-7) that the

---

can be restated in the testable form

$$\frac{S_i - (a_i)_{-1}\Delta V}{V} = -(1 - m)(a_i)_{-1}\frac{CG}{V} + (1 - n)\left\{(a_i)_{-1}\frac{V_{-1}}{V}\left[r_i - \sum_j r_j(a_j)_{-1}\right]\right\} + g\alpha_i - g(a_i)_{-1}$$

and the coefficient of the second term in square brackets (which involves only observables and no unknown parameters) would provide an estimate of $(1 - n)$. Some attempts were made at testing this hypothesis but they yielded unacceptable results presumably because of multicollinearity between the term in square brackets and the lagged dependent variable, $(a_i)_{-1}$. By dropping the variable, its effect would presumably be captured by the coefficient of $(a_i)_{-1}$. Since the dropped term is positive, its omission might tend to bias down the estimated speed of adjustment given by the coefficient of $(a_i)_{-1}$ and might help to explain the very low estimates of g reported below.

portfolio adjusts quite promptly to a slowly adjusting "perceived" optimum ratio. We could instead hypothesize the coexistence of an expectational lag of the (3-5) type with a rebalancing lag applying to the second component of (3-9) which would then take the form

$$S = a^* \, \Delta V + g'(a^* - a_{-1})V_{-1}$$
$$= a_{-1} \, \Delta V + (a^* - a_{-1})[(1 - g') \, \Delta V + g'V] \qquad (3\text{-}12)$$

where g' is the speed of adjustment of the "rebalancing" component $(0 < g' < 1)$. We shall refer to this alternative hypothesis as version II. Equation (3-12) still involves the nonobservable a^* given by equation (3-5). However, at least provided α does not change very rapidly and g' is reasonably large, as one would expect, one can rely on the approximation

$$a^* - a_{-1} \simeq b(\alpha - a_{-1})$$

where b is a function of g and g' which approaches g as g' approaches unity.[4] Substituting in (3-12) we obtain

$$S = a_{-1}\Delta V + (\alpha - a_{-1})\gamma(\Delta V + \gamma'V) \qquad \gamma = b(1 - g'), \qquad \gamma' = g'/(1 - g')$$
$$(3\text{-}13)$$

---

[4] It follows from (3-5) that

(i) $\qquad a^* - a_{-1} = g(\alpha - a_{-1}) + (1 - g)(a^*_{-1} - a_{-1})$

$\qquad\qquad = g(\alpha - a_{-1}) + (1 - g)(a^*_{-1} - a_{-2}) - (1 - g)(a_{-1} - a_{-2})$

Also, from (3-12), by transposing $a_{-1} \, \Delta V$ and dividing by V, we infer that

(ii) $\qquad a - a_{-1} = g^*(a^* - a_{-1}) \qquad g^* = g' + (1 - g')(\Delta V/V)$

Therefore, $a_{-1} - a_{-2} = g^*(a^*_{-1} - a_{-2})$ and substituting in (i) and collecting terms

(iii) $\qquad a^* - a_{-1} = g(\alpha - a_{-1}) + (1 - g)(1 - g^*)(a^*_{-1} - a_{-2})$

From this basic recursive formula, one can in turn infer by appropriate manipulations

$$a^*_{-1} - a_{-2} = g(\alpha_{-1} - a_{-2}) + (1 - g)(1 - g^*)(a^*_{-2} - a_{-3})$$
$$= g(\alpha - a_{-1}) - g(\Delta\alpha - \Delta a_{-1}) + (1 - g)(1 - g^*)(a^*_{-2} - a_{-3})$$

Finally, substituting back into (iii),

$$a^* - a_{-1} = b(\alpha - a_{-1}) + R$$

where $\qquad\qquad b = g\{1 + [(1 + [(1 - g)(1 - g^*)]\}$

and

$$R = -g(1 - g)(1 - g^*)(\Delta\alpha - \Delta a_{-1}) + [(1 - g)(1 - g^*)]^2(a^*_{-2} - a_{-3})$$

should be of second order of magnitude compared with the first term if $\Delta\alpha$ is generally small and g^* is not very small.

70

Transposing $a_{-1}\,\Delta V$ and dividing by V, equation (3-13) is seen to imply

$$a - a_{-1} = (\alpha - a_{-1})\gamma \left[\gamma' + \frac{\Delta V}{V} \right] = (\alpha - a_{-1})bg' \left[1 + \frac{1 - g'}{g'} \frac{\Delta V}{V} \right]$$

(3-13a)

Comparing this expression with (3-8), it appears that replacing the adjustment process (3-7) with (3-12) still leads to a gradual adjustment of a toward α. However, the speed of adjustment—the coefficient of $(\alpha - a_{-1})$—instead of being constant as in (3-5) is now variable and increases with the rate of growth of wealth, except in the limiting case $g' = 1$ when (3-13a) reduces back to (3-8).[5]

Equation (3-13) is nonlinear in the parameter γ'. It can, however, be estimated, in the form

$$\frac{S - a_{-1}\,\Delta V}{\Delta V + \gamma'V} = (\gamma\alpha) - \gamma a_{-1}$$

(3-14)

by scanning over values of γ' for the value yielding the best fit for S.

If ΔV includes in part capital gains, it would seem appropriate to modify (3-12) so as to include in the first-term ΔV only the current accumulation, and to lump the capital gains component with V_{-1} in the second term. It can be verified that (3-13) and (3-14) remain unchanged except that the quantity ΔV is replaced by $\Delta V - CG$.

Application to Saving Flows into Time Deposits (MP)

The time deposits we are concerned with exclude large CDs held by corporations and foreigners (though unfortunately they include those held by state and local government).[6] We therefore expect this asset to compete most directly with money, especially demand deposits; other types of saving deposits; and with other money fixed assets, especially short-term market assets. We expect it to compete much less directly with equities and physical

---

[5] At the same time, this version shares the property of version I, that it could apply simultaneously to every component of wealth. This is because it retains the assumption that the *current* flow ΔV is allocated promptly in accordance to the perceived optimum ratios.

[6] The definition of time deposits differs slightly from Gramlich and Hulett's in Chapter 2. For Gramlich and Hulett, passbook savings deposits included all member commercial banks and is seasonally adjusted. The measure used in this study includes all commercial banks and is not seasonally adjusted.

assets held by households such as durables and houses. Also the asset is nearly risk free, as the risk of default is negligible and the rate of return is quite predictable in the short run in money terms and even in real terms, considering the sluggishness of the rate of change of prices. Accordingly, we can neglect covariance terms or, at least, approximate them as constant over time. This suggests that α might be of the form

$$\alpha = a_0 + a_1(RTP - RMON) + a_2(RTP - RSL) + a_3(RTP - RMS)$$

$$+ a_4(RTP - r_S) + a_5(RTP - r_L) + a_6(RTP - RR) \tag{3-15}$$

where the symbols denote respectively the rate of return on time deposits (RTP), money $RMON$, saving and loan shares (RSL), mutual saving bank deposits (RMS), some index of short-term market rates (r_S), and long-term market rates (r_L), and the rate of return on equities and physical assets (RR). We should expect all the a_is to be positive and the first three or possibly four to be more important than the remaining ones, with the last the least important.

Because no cash interest is earned on money and because returns on demand deposits in the form of bank services are not readily measurable and are unlikely to have changed appreciably, at least until the last couple of years of our sample, we assume $RMON$ to be a constant $\overline{RMON}$ and thus to be impounded in a new constant term a_0'. But then α can be expressed as a linear function of all rates or

$$\alpha = b_0 + b_1 RTP + \sum_{j=2}^{n} b_j R_j \tag{3-15a}$$

where $$b_0 = a_0 - a_1\overline{RMON}$$

$$b_1 = \sum_{j=1}^{n} a_j$$

$$b_j = -a_j$$

$$j = 2, \ldots, n$$

and R_j is now short for the various rates on competing assets. It should be noted that the sum of all the b coefficients, $\sum_1^n b_j$, should provide an estimate of a_1 and, hence, should be positive and measure the extent to which a rise in RTP leads to a shift from money into time deposits.

Unfortunately, because of the high collinearity of all rates, it would be virtually impossible to secure reliable estimates of the coefficients of each rate by standard OLS procedures. In what follows we have tried in a variety of ways to cut down the number of coefficients to be estimated freely—without, however, succeeding altogether in eliminating multicollinearity problems, as will soon become apparent. One step in that direction is to replace the two rates *RSL* and *RMS*—which tend to move quite closely to each other and with *RTP*—with a single composite rate *RA*, representing an average of *RSL* and *RMS* weighted by recent inflows into the two types of institutions.[7]

In chapter appendix Table 3A-1 rows 1 to 6 present the empirical results of tests of model IA with alternative specifications of the arguments of α and illustrate some of the difficulties created by the multicollinearity of the variables.

Row 1 of Table 3A-1 tests the simplest specification, namely the rate on time deposits, *RTP*, and the average rate *RA* at the two competing depository-type institutions. Both variables have the expected sign and are reasonably significant; and the sum of their coefficient is positive as expected. The proportion of capital gains reallocated currently is estimated at about $\frac{1}{4}$ (column 5) which is not unreasonably though somewhat on the high side; the estimated speed of adjustment *g* is .05 or 5 percent per quarter which, though not large, is larger than reported in other studies. Seasonal dummies for the first and fourth quarters have been added because the data for time deposits are not seasonally adjusted. (The dummy for the second quarter has been dropped since in all tests in which it was used it was negligibly small and insignificant). On the whole, then, all the estimated coefficients appear reasonable; unfortunately, the fit is rather poor as can be seen from the last three columns. Column 18 gives the standard error (SE) of the dependent variable $\Delta MP/V$, i.e., the current flow scaled by total wealth. (We do not give the conventional R^2 measure because in different tests, we use different forms of the dependent variable and, hence, the R^2 are not comparable while the SE are.) Column 19 gives the DW statistics measuring serial correlation of the residuals. Column 20 gives the root mean square (RMSE) of the difference between the actual saving flow *S* and the value computed from the estimated equation. Finally, column 21 gives the correlation coefficient between these two variables. It is seen that the *RMSE* is 1.2 billion as compared with a standard deviation of *S* of just over 1.8 billion: the independent variable accounts for not quite 60 percent of the variance. Also the serial correlation is quite high.

In equation (MP-2), Table 3A-1, we go to the opposite extreme, adding to the specifications both the short-term rate measured by the 3-months Treasury bill rate (*RTB*) and the long-term rate measured by Moody's AAA corporate bond rate (*RCB*). We have also allowed for a transient response to the rate of change of *RTP* and *RCB*. These additions result in a very substantial improvement in the fit as the RMSE measure of column 20 falls by

---

[7] See Appendix B for the precise formula.

$\frac{1}{3}$ to .8 billion, and the serial correlation declines. Furthermore, all the interest variables are seen to have the expected sign. But in every other respect, the results are very unsatisfactory. The capital gain effect is improbably small and the long-run properties of the equation are inconsistent with the basic model; not only is the sum of the interest coefficients negative but, in addition, the lagged dependent variable has a positive sign, which is inconsistent with the basic hypothesis of a gradual adjustment of the share of time deposits toward a long-run equilibrium value. The unreliability of these results is also confirmed by the very high standard errors for all coefficients—especially those of the three rates RTP, RA, and RCB—which is a well-known symptom of multicollinearity. This suggested the desirability of reducing drastically the number of rates by dropping either of the two market rates. As between the short and the long rate, we should expect the former to be the more important, especially since even for long-term instruments what should matter most should be the expected short-term holding yield which should be well approximated by the short rate. Accordingly, in equation (MP-3) we include only three rates: RTP, RA, and RTB (the rate of change of RTP was also tested but systematically turned out to be insignificant once RCB was dropped). The fit deteriorates only moderately indicating that the single rate RTB is a good proxy for the entire family of market rates; this variable is seen to contribute a good deal to the explanation as indicated by a t-ratio of over 5, whereas the role of RA is surprisingly insignificant. However, the lagged dependent variable still fails to exhibit the required negative sign.

A possible source of difficulties might be the well-known changes in the nature of the time deposit market which occurred around the early sixties with the introduction of CDs and a variety of other innovations which in part reflected and, in part, stimulated a much more aggressive competition of commercial banks for time deposits. One might expect these institutional changes to result in higher coefficients of all interest rate variables. However, since we are excluding large CDs from our measure of passbook savings deposits, it would appear that the increased competition would be primarily between interest-bearing money-fixed assets and not with money itself. This means that the sum of the coefficient of all variables which is an estimate of a_1 should not have changed significantly. To enforce this specification, we allowed for different values of the coefficient a_2, a_3, a_4, and a_5, beginning with the middle of 1962, by adding to equation (MP-3) the spread $RTP - RA$, and $RTP - RTB$, beginning with third quarter of 1962. Since a change in slope coefficients generally will be accompanied by a change in intercept, we also added a dummy on the constant, JC. Surprisingly, the spread $RTP - RTB$ turns out consistently to have no significant effect. As can be seen from equation (MP-4), even the spread $RTP - RA$ though of the right sign is barely significant, and the improvement in fit is quite marginal, while the estimate of g remains negligible.

In equation (MP-5), we have added a rather different kind of variable to the specification of α. If, as seems plausible, time deposits are a close substitute to money as a temporary abode of purchasing power, then the stock of time deposits might to some extent be controlled, just like the stock of money, by the volume of transactions. Since we are dealing basically with household holdings, we endeavored to approximate transaction requirements by disposable income. In principle, the effect of income should interact with that of interest rates; i.e., the long-run demand equation should take the form

$$MP = \alpha_v V + \alpha_y YD \tag{3-16}$$

or

$$\frac{MP}{V} \equiv \alpha \equiv \alpha_v + \alpha_y \frac{YD}{V} \tag{3-16a}$$

where α_v and α_y should both be functions of relative rates of return. However, not to compound further our multicollinearity problems, we were led to approximate the right side of (3-16a) by simply adding the variable YD/V to the specification (3-15a), with the expectation that the interest rate terms would capture both the effects through α_v and α_y. The coefficient of YD/V should be positive.

The results, reported as equation (MP-5), fully support this formulation. The coefficient of the YD variable (column 15) is positive with a t-ratio of 5; the fit improves considerably; DW rises; and most variables become more significant, notably the post-1962 dummy variable $RTP - RA$. Furthermore, the lagged dependent variable is now negative and indeed indicates a surprisingly large speed of adjustment of 14 percent per quarter. The only serious "casualty" is the rate RA which was already quite insignificant in (MP-4) and now has an insignificant positive sign. Also the capital gain coefficient appears now improbably high while the constant term turns negative. The result for RA suggests that, before the early sixties, time deposits were not very significantly affected by the rates offered by the other depository institution. This conclusion is somewhat hard to accept except for the evidence, to be shown below, that the other depository institutions were also little affected by the rate on time deposits. Row 6, Table 3A-1, shows that dropping the variable RA produces no significant change in fit and yields coefficients generally more in line with a priori expectation except possibly for the constant term, to which we shall return presently. Note that though the equation implies no significant effect of RA before the early sixties, it does indicate a very strong effect thereafter.

The last three rows of Table 3A-1 present some salient results of a test of variant B of the model, in which we allow the coefficient of $a_{-1}SP$ to differ from unity. Row 7 presents a test of the specification of α underlying row 4. The fit is appreciably better and most coefficients are more reasonable; notably the lagged dependent variable has the expected negative sign. But the coefficient of the new variable in column 4 is much too large to satisfy the inequality (3-11a). However, in row 8, where we add the variable YD/V and drop RA (repeating the specification of row 6) we find that the coefficient of column 4 falls a good deal and is only slightly too large—though it has a very large standard error, making the estimate rather unreliable. The interest rate coefficients also seem quite plausible: since the early sixties an increase in RTP by 1 percent (100 basis points) would tend to increase MP and hence the current saving flow by $4.4 \times 10^{-3} \times V$ or, with V presently running at roughly \$3 trillion, by \$1.3 billion. The implied short-run elasticity of demand for the stock is 4.4×10^{-3} (RTP/a) or, with RTP currently at around 4.5 and the share at about .06, just about $\frac{1}{3}$. The corresponding effect for a one percentage point change in RA is \$.75 billion with a cross-elasticity of about .2; for RTB it is \$.15 billion with an elasticity of .05. We also observe that the sum of all rate coefficients, an estimate of the parameter a_1, is positive as hypothesized and amounts to 1.34×10^{-3}. It implies that a rise by 100 basis points in RTP, and in all other rates so as to keep all spreads unchanged, would tend to increase MP \$4 billion presumably through a reduction of cash balances. This implies a short-run elasticity of time deposits of about .1 and also an elasticity of demand for money with respect to RTP of $-.1$, which is not unreasonable when compared with the estimates obtained from most money demand studies. All these elasticities are, however, much higher in the long run, as can be seen by using row 8 of Table 3A-1 to compute the long-run equilibrium demand function. It is seen from equation (3-10) that, provided (3-11a) holds, which is roughly the case, the equilibrium ratio α can be inferred by dividing the coefficients of columns 7 through 15 by the speed of adjustment g, which is the coefficient of column 6 with sign reversed. Thus

$$MP = \alpha V = .64YD + \begin{cases} -.117V + V(.017RTP - .0048RTB) \\ \qquad\qquad\qquad\qquad\qquad\qquad t < 1962{:}3 \\ -.107V + V(.040RTP - .0048RTB - .023RA) \\ \qquad\qquad\qquad\qquad\qquad\qquad t > 1962{:}3 \end{cases}$$

(MP-8a)

Thus, the long-run slopes and elasticities are some nine times larger than the impact ones; in particular, for RTP a change of 100 basis points would increase the share by .04 (from the current .06) the elasticity of demand being roughly 3, while the elasticity with respect to RA is just below 2. These figures do not seem unreasonable, though the implicit long-run elasticity of demand for money with respect to RTP, about .9, does seem on the high side.

The one serious shortcoming of equations (MP-8) and (MP-8a) is the very high positive coefficient of current income YD and the very high negative coefficients of current wealth V which do seem rather unreasonable, if taken at face value. The first thing to observe in this regard is that, in practice, the income and wealth term largely cancel each other since the ratio of income to wealth has fluctuated fairly narrowly around $\frac{1}{5}$. Furthermore there are good reasons to expect this ratio to be roughly preserved under normal conditions.[8] Thus $.64YD/V$ is roughly .13 and when we add to this the constant term $-.117$ or $-.107$ we get a positive number rather close to zero—about .01 in the first and .02 in the second period. This constant measures the equilibrium share of time deposits when all rates are zero; and there is nothing wrong with the share being just about zero under these limiting conditions, for with zero rates, there would be no reason not to hold all money-fixed assets in the form of money. Yet the results obtained for the individual coefficients cannot be rationalized; they would seem to be seriously biased as a result of the high collinearity between the constant and the very stable variable YD/V, compounded by collinearity between the three variables YD/V, a_{-1}, and $a_{-1}SP$, and even $a_{-1}CG/V$. As a result, the coefficients of these five variables are individually not very reliable; and this hypothesis receives some support from the lack of stability of the estimated coefficients of these variables as one changes the detailed specifications of the equation.

There is little one can do about this problem short of expanding the sample through the passage of time or by some other method. One such method has been attempted and underlies the estimates presented in row 9 of Table 3A-1. There are strong a priori reasons for holding that several of the coefficients of the time deposit equation should have the same value for the other two deposit variables. This holds clearly for the spread $RA - RTP$ which should have the same numerical value, though the opposite sign, for the sum of savings and loans and saving banks deposits. It also holds for the capital gains variable (for the proportion of capital gains currently reallocated is not related to any specific asset), and by the same token for the coefficient of $a_{-1}SP$. Finally, one might conjecture, though with less assurance, that even the speed of adjustment should be roughly the same for

---

[8] If income rises, the increase in personal saving will gradually increase net worth. If net worth rises, it stimulates higher consumption and income. These effects are important for the simulation properties of the sector discussed in Chapter 7.

this group of assets. On the basis of these considerations, all the coefficients of equation (MP-8) have been reestimated simultaneously with those of the remaining two assets subject to the constraint that the above five coefficients should be the same (or the same except for sign in the case of $RTP - RA$). Further details of the procedure are best postponed until we have presented our analysis of the other two deposit assets. The results are shown in row 9 while the implications for the long-run equilbrium share α are shown below.

$$\alpha = \frac{MP}{V} = 1.18\,\frac{YD}{V} + \begin{cases} -.234 + .036RTP - .016RTB & t < 1962{:}3 \\ -.211 + .089RTP - .053RA - .016RTB & \\ & t \geq 1962{:}3 \end{cases}$$

(MP-9a)

In some respects, the alternative estimates appear more reasonable, notably that of capital gains and the smaller speed of adjustment. All impact elasticities (except that of RTB) are smaller by about $\frac{1}{3}$; however, because the speed of adjustment is only $\frac{1}{4}$ as large, the implied long-run elasticities are systematically larger. For example, the elasticity with respect to RTP rises from 3.0 to 3.6, and the implied elasticity of demand for money which appeared already high rises further to almost 1.5. Finally, while both the coefficients of Y and the constant are closer to zero, the long-run coefficients rise further, that of income to 1.14 and the constant to $-.225$ and $-.21$ in the first and second period respectively. The sum of the two terms still largely cancels out, leaving on the average a positive value of just .01 and .03; but the individual coefficients appear to have changed in the wrong direction. We have nonetheless adopted equation (MP-9) as our preferred equation, primarily because of its consistency with the equations for the other two saving deposits. But we retain serious qualms about the reliability of the equation with respect to its long-run properties. Clearly, because of multicollinearity and the slow speed of adjustment, these long-run properties are hard to estimate. At the same time, just because of the slow speed, these properties do not exert a controlling influence on saving flows and, hence, these flows might be tracked reasonably well over a reasonable length of time even lacking a solid estimate of the long-run demand.

In the equations of Table 3A-1, including the "final" equation (MP-9), we have omitted the last term of equation (3-15) or (3-15a) involving the rate of return on nonmoney-fixed assets. As indicated earlier, we do not expect the substitution with these assets to be close enough for this term to contribute significantly to the explanation of saving flows. Furthermore, we were unable to construct an operational measure of the expected rate of return which could be made endogenous to the model and be adequate to capture presumably minor effects: even a measure of return on equity, such as the dividend price ratio possibly adjusted for pay-out, did not seem satisfactory, partly, because we are inclined to the view that the downward trend in the relation of this measure to the prevailing rate of return on money-fixed assets is likely to reflect a shift in risk preferences which would be hard to measure separately. One possible approach is to suppose that the real rate of return has tended to remain relatively stable and to infer the expected money rate of return from some measure of the expected rate of changes of prices. Along these lines we endeavored to add to the specification (3-15a) or (3-16a) a proxy for this expected rate, either in the form of an Almon distributed lag or by using the distributed lag suggested by the long-term rate equation. However, the results both for time deposits and for the other saving deposits were uniformly disappointing—this variable was insignificant and frequently the point estimate of its coefficient was positive instead of negative. This result, which we attribute to multicollinearity of the indicated measure with the family of interest rates already included in the equation, led us to abandon hope of capturing the effect of the last term. We shall comment later on some possible biases resulting from this failure.

Finally, some attempts were made to test and estimate the more refined model II, with distinct speed of adjustments for expectations and portfolio rebalancing. These attempts met with little success, for in scanning over alternative values of g' it was found that the RMSE was hardly affected by the choice of g'. To be more precise, for the limiting value $g' = 0$ (which is really inconsistent with the model as it implies no portfolio adjustment) the RMSE was larger than that shown in Table 3-1, which corresponds to $g' = 1$. But for positive values of g', even if quite small, say, beginning with .02 or .03 and up to unity, the RMSE was somewhat larger for model II if we drop the capital gains term, as seems appropriate for small g'. On the other hand, adding that term, the RMSE hardly changed over the entire range of positive g'. A likely explanation for this disappointing result is suggested on page 85. We thus conclude that our data and estimation procedure are not, at present, sufficiently refined to estimate the more ambitious model II and, hence, decide to rely on model I underlying Table 3A-1.

Deposits at Mutual Saving Banks and
Savings and Loan Associations

One could, in principle, apply our model individually to each of these two assets. We did not, however, regard this approach as desirable because these two assets are so similar that one should expect their response to variations in rates on competing assets to be essentially the same. In order to insure this symmetry, we propose to estimate a single demand for the sum of the two assets, denoted hereafter by MS. The distribution of this total between the two components in turn would seem to be controlled not by portfolio theoretic considerations of risk diversification but much more by institutional factors—notably the historical differences in the geographic location of these institutions and the difference in the rate at which these parts of the country have grown. These locational factors, combined with the costs and other disadvantages of distant banking, the resulting imperfection of information, and habit inertia tend to limit the elasticity of substitution, especially in the short run, but even in the longer run. Accordingly, once we have accounted for the behavior of MS, the behavior of each component will be accounted for by a "distribution" equation, incorporating as far as possible the considerations set out above.

Aggregate Savings and Loan Association and Mutual Savings Bank Deposits

One would expect the specification of α to be similar to that applying to time deposits except possibly for a less close substitution with money and short-term market instruments and a closer one with long-term money-fixed claims.

Table 3A-2, rows 1 to 4, reports the results of tests of model IA with alternative specifications of α. Equation (MS-1) tests the very simple specification involving only the own rate RA, RTP, and the long rate measured by RCB. All variables have the expected sign and order of magnitude and high t-ratios, with the conspicuous exception of RTP which is insignificant and has the wrong sign. Also the fit is not very good and the DW quite low. The result for RTP is typical; in every test run this variable is insignificant and mostly with a small positive coefficient. This is illustrated by equation (MS-2) in which we have added the spread $RA - RTP$ beginning with the 1962:3. The coefficient of this variable has the expected positive sign and an order of magnitude similar to that found for time deposits, and adds substantially to the explanatory power as indicated by the statistics of the last four columns. But somewhat surprisingly, it has the effect of reducing the estimated speed of adjustment g of column 6 to an improbably low level of 1 per thousand per quarter, while the coefficient of RTP remains insignificantly positive. This last result appears to corroborate the indication already supplied by our time deposit analysis that, up to the early sixties, the distribution of deposits between time and other deposits was rather insensitive to the spread in rates, but that the situation changed drastically since then. Accordingly, in equation (MS-3), and thereafter, we drop RTP and we test instead the responsiveness to short-term rates as measured by RTB, allowing also for the possibility of a higher elasticity in the more recent period. The results confirm the importance of this variable, especially since the early sixties, and indicate an improvement in fit and in DW. But some other estimates become less reliable and less credible, presumably because of multicollinearity; in particular, the speed of adjustment becomes insignificant and of the wrong sign—a peculiar result that always seems to accompany the elimination of RTP. Also the capital gain coefficient becomes small and not very significant and so does that of RA, though the latter result is not entirely surprising since the coefficient of column 7 relates now only to the earlier period. The coefficient for the second period—the sum of columns 7, 11, and 12—remains instead rather high.

Equation (MS-4) adds the income variable to the specification of α. The sign of this variable cannot be established with confidence from theory, though a negative sign seems more likely, especially in view of the results obtained for time deposits. One might, in fact, conjecture that for a given level of interest rates the total share of wealth invested in all deposit-type assets would be irresponsive or only slightly responsive to transaction requirements. If so, the total of saving deposits might tend to decrease as income rises relative to wealth because, in view of larger transaction requirements, a larger portion·of deposits would take the form of demand deposits. If, in addition, the time deposit component itself tends to respond positively to YD then the remaining deposit-type assets would be expected to decline. As can be seen from equation (MS-4), the estimated coefficient of YD/V is actually negative and rather significant, and the variable helps to improve the fit appreciably and reduce serial correlation. However, the speed of adjustment coefficient has again an insignificantly positive sign, and the sum of all interest coefficients, an estimate of a_1, becomes negative.

In addition to the above tests of model IA, we made a few tests of model IB, in which the coefficient of the variable $a_{-1}SP$ is estimated freely instead of being forced to unity. These tests did not appear too promising as the coefficient of a_{-1} was generally smaller, instead of larger, than one, as called for by the model. It is also rather unstable under alternative specifications and subject to large error of estimation—while at the same time the remaining coefficients are largely unaffected. This is illustrated by equation (MS-5), in which the remaining specifications are the same as in (MS-4). The coefficient in column 4 is only .26 with a standard error 5 times larger, while the other coefficients suffer from the very same shortcomings noted in equation (MS-4).

In particular, the estimated speed of adjustment coefficient is still insignificantly negative.

It thus appears that, as in the case of time deposits, it is difficult to secure reliable estimates of individual coefficients because of multicollinearity between the variables YD/V, the constant, $a_{-1}SP/V$, $a_{-1}CG/V$, and a_{-1} on the one hand, and between the various rates on the other. In view of this problem and our firm a priori belief that the coefficient of a_{-1} must be negative—though presumably not very large in view of the above results—we made some experiments forcing this coefficient to assume negative values between $-.02$ and $-.05$. We were encouraged to find that this resulted in much more reasonable and fairly stable estimates of the other coefficients, while at the same time the fit was hardly affected as long as the assumed value was no larger than .03 or .04. In equation (MS-6) we show the result for an assumed speed, g, of .03 per quarter, a value that was suggested also by some results obtained by shortening the period of fit to the sixties. It is seen that all the coefficients have the hypothesized sign and a sensible order of magnitude, including the estimated coefficient a_1, the sum of all interest rate coefficients, which is $.25 \times 10^{-3}$. This is $\frac{1}{3}$ as large as that for time deposits, which is sensible, and implies a short-run elasticity of money with respect to RA of about .04 (though the corresponding long-run elasticity of over 1 appears actually too large).

While equation (MS-6) appears quite usable, the imposed value for the speed of adjustment is clearly somewhat arbitrary; furthermore, the parameter estimates are not necessarily consistent with those of the time deposit equation. Accordingly, as explained above, we reestimated this equation simultaneously with the time deposit equation, thus forcing the coefficients of columns 4, 5, 6, and 11 to be the same. The result is shown as equation (MS-7). Because the resulting estimate of g (i.e., $-.036$) is quite close to the value assumed in (MS-6), the estimates of the coefficients are little changed. We give below the long-run share equation implied by row 7, Table 3A-2:

$$\frac{MS}{V} = -.32\frac{YD}{V} + \begin{cases} .113 + .027RA - .015RCB - .002RTB \\ \hspace{4cm} t < 1962{:}3 \\ 0.85 + .084RA - .053RTP - .015RCB - .006RTB \\ \hspace{4cm} t \geqslant 1962{:}3 \end{cases}$$

$$\text{(MS-7a)}$$

A comparison of (MS-7) with (MP-9), or of the above with (MP-9a), is instructive and indicates that on the whole the relation between the coefficients is eminently reasonable, making it unnecessary to have recourse to more complex constrained estimation. Incidentally, since the stock of time deposits, of *MS*, and of money all happen to have had roughly the same value around the end of 1969, about \$200 billion, the elasticities of the stock in each equation are proportional to the slope coefficients. We note in particular that the overall elasticity with respect to the own rate is similar though somewhat larger for *MP* as expected; the same holds for the elasticity with respect to *RTB* and for the elasticity of substitution with money. However, the sum of the coefficients of *YD* is substantially positive. This is contrary to our hypothesis and in our view confirms the suspicion that the estimate of this coefficient in the time deposit equation is substantially upward biased. Fortunately, as noted, this need not be fatal to the explanatory power of the equation because it is likely to be offset by a downward biased estimate of the constant term. Some bias in the coefficients may also result from our inability to estimate the effect of the expected rate of change of prices— probably reflecting the difficulty of measuring this variable adequately. In view of the positive correlation between all interest rates and the rate of change of prices over the period of observation, one would expect a downward bias in the coefficient of the own rate and/or an upward bias in the coefficients of other rates. We doubt that this bias is serious enough to create major difficulties in extrapolation since the estimated long-run response to the own rate or to all rates changing simultaneously do not appear obviously small, and also because the correlation between interest rates and the rate of growth of prices may be expected to continue.

Allocation Between Savings and Loan
Association and Mutual Savings Bank Deposits

In order to account for the allocation of *MS* between its two components, we can rely on our basic model I or II, replacing total wealth *V* by the total *MS*. Furthermore, because *MS* can only change by adding to (or withdrawing from) the initial stock but not through capital gains or losses, the capital gain term is identically zero and the distinction between version *A* and *B* disappears.

Since *MS* consists of only two components, once we have determined one component the other can be obtained as a residual. It is immaterial which of the two we choose to explain in the sense that the result would be the same; that is, if we denote by α_1, the function determining the share going into asset 1, then the function determining the other share is simply $\alpha_2 = 1 - \alpha_1$. In what follows we have chosen to deal explicitly with the savings and loan component.

As indicated at the beginning of this section the specification of α should be a relatively simple matter, at least in so far as the rates of return component is concerned, for we should expect only the differential between the two rates, $RSL - RMS$, to matter. However, because of inertia and the time involved in the spreading of information we were led to test a fairly long distributed lag on the spread, and this time with considerable success. In choosing the form of the distributed lag we allowed for the possibility that the response would depend not only on the level of the spread but also on its rate of change. As is well known, under these circumstances the coefficient of the current variable is positive but the coefficient of the variable lagged one is much smaller and may be negative and followed by coefficients either approaching zero monotonically or first rising to positive values and then falling toward zero. This rather complex shape can most conveniently be accommodated within the Almon polynomial distributed lag approach by freeing the co-efficient of the current variable; the rest of the distribution can then usually be adequately described by a second- or third-degree polynomial.

Table 3A-3 equation (MSL-1) shows the results obtained when α is specified to involve only a distributed lag on $RSL - RMS$. These results strongly support the importance of the rate of change effect as the coefficient of the current variable is very significantly positive while the rest of the distribution begins with a very significant negative value and is hump-shaped. The weighting function is approximated by a second-degree polynomial forced to zero at the end; however, very similar results were obtained with a third-degree polynomial as long as the distributed lag was allowed to include a period of around twelve quarters.

Our very simple hypothesis is seen to fit the data rather well as indicated by the high correlation between the actual and computed flow and by a RMSE of less than $100 million. However, the speed of adjustment g is even smaller than those reported in Tables 3A-1 and 3A-2, whereas one might have expected a faster response in view of the similarity of the assets. The long-run equilibrium share, corresponding to an indefinitely maintained level of the spread, can be inferred by dividing by g the sum of the coefficients of the spread shown in column 6, namely $\alpha = .33 + 2.3(RSL - RMS)$. This result seems to imply a somewhat improbably large substitution between the two instruments. Given enough time, a spread of less than 30 basis points in favor of savings and loans, which actually materialized for a great portion of the period, including the terminal quarter, would eventually lead to the whole of MS taking the form of claims on savings and loans. Similarly a spread of half as much in favor of mutual saving banks would lead to these institutions attracting all of MS.

Equation (MSL-1) makes no explicit allowance for the institutional forces mentioned earlier. We should expect those forces, on balance, to have favored the growth of savings and loan associations, though very likely at decreasing rates as the postwar period unfolded. It seemed desirable to make some allowances for these forces not only to improve our understanding of the process but also because failure to do so could bias the spread coefficient: since the share of savings and loan associations grew substantially from about $\frac{1}{2}$ to $\frac{2}{3}$, and at the same time the spread was, for the most part markedly in their favor, equation (MSL-1) could attribute to the spread an effect which was really due to other forces, thus overestimating the substitution.

There are a variety of ways one could try to account for the institutional forces. However, since any adequate procedure would call for variables that could not be readily endogenized in the model, we have fallen back on the less intellectually satisfying, but hopefully practically adequate, device of some simple time trend. Expecting that the forces favoring the relative growth of savings and loan associations were decreasing in importance, we initially tested a quadratic time trend for evidence of negative curvature. It was indeed found that when a linear and square term in time are added to the distributed lag specification, the linear term has a very significant positive coefficient, and the square term an even more significant negative coefficient— while the shape of the lag distribution was basically unchanged. The estimated time trend reached its peak shortly before the end of the period of observation, around early 1966. Since we have no reason to believe that there actually was a reversal of trend thereafter, and the estimated trend was of necessity very flat until the end of the period of observation which is still close to the peak, it appeared appropriate to suspend the time trend at the date of the estimated peak, namely the second quarter of 1966. The results of this specification are shown in equation (MSL-2). One notes immediately a substantial improvement in the fit and a reduction in the serial correlation. The distributed lag retains pretty much of its original shape and significance, but the speed of adjustment increases appreciably to over 7 percent per quarter; as a result, the long-run properties are rather different as can be seen from the following equation for α.

$$
\alpha = \begin{cases}
.48 + 6.4 \times 10^{-3}(TIME) - 6.75 \times 10^{-5}(TIME)^2 + .29(RSL - RMS) \\
\qquad\qquad\qquad\qquad\qquad\quad t \leqslant 43\ (1966:1) \\[2ex]
.63 + .29(RSL - RMS) \qquad\qquad t > 43 \qquad\qquad \text{(MSL-2a)}
\end{cases}
$$

This alternative estimate is seen to attribute a good deal of the observed shift to savings and loan associations to the trend forces, while the estimated long-run coefficient of the spread is only about $\frac{1}{8}$ as large as in equation (MSL-1), though it still is of respectable magnitude (a spread of 100 basis points would cause the institution with the higher rate to increase its share by 29 percent of the total). On the whole, we regard the estimates of row 2 as more reliable, though it is conceivable that this equation may attribute too much to the trend and not enough to the substitution effect.

The last two rows of Table 3A-3 report the results obtained with the more ambitious version II of the model. In row 3, the specification of α is the same as in row 1; while in row 4, we have added the time trend as in row 2. Because we regard the latter specification as more satisfactory, we concentrate our comments on a comparison of (MSL-2) and (MSL-4).

To estimate the parameters of model II, we made use of equation (3-14) and scanned over alternative values of γ' at intervals of .05 for the value minimizing the RMSE. As reported in column 10, that value turned out to be .15, implying a value of g' (the speed of adjustment of the initial portfolio imbalance) of .13 percent per quarter. However, once more the RMSE turned out to be surprisingly insensitive to variation in γ' (or, equivalently, g'). When g' is forced to unity as in row 3, the RMSE is .0796; whereas for the best value of g', the RMSE of row 4 is reduced only to .07915, a rather negligible difference. Taking the point estimate of γ' at face value, we can infer from equation (3-13a) that the overall speed of adjustment instead of being .074 per quarter is

$$.44 \left(.15 + \frac{\Delta MS}{MS} \right) = .066 \left[1 + 7 \frac{\Delta MS}{MS} \right]$$

Since $\Delta MS/MS$ averages around .02 (corresponding to an annual growth rate of about 8 percent), the alternative estimate again implies an average speed of .075. Of course, in row 4, the speed of adjustment is a variable and is faster the larger $\Delta MS/MS$. But since over the period of observation $\Delta MS/MS$ is not only small but fairly stable, it is apparent that the refinement of a variable speed cannot really "buy" very much, and this presumably explains why the RMSE improves so little. It is only if g' is small relative to $\Delta MS/MS$ and the latter quantity is fairly variable that the refinement could make an appreciable difference. It also turns out, not surprisingly, that the long-run share equation α implied by (MSL-4) is almost identical to that implied by (MSL-2), as can be verified by dividing the coefficients of columns 3, 6, 8, and 9 by the coefficient of column 5.

On the whole, we feel that the results in rows 3 and 4 of Table 3A-3 mildly support the reasonable hypothesis that there is both an expectational and an adjustment lag. However, the sophistication appears to add little to the explanation of the phenomenon because of the appreciable speed of portfolio rebalancing and the relative stability of the rate of growth of MS. For this reason we regard the simpler equation, (MSL-2), as adequate for the purpose of the FMP model. The corresponding equation for mutual saving banks is then determined by subtracting savings and loan deposits from total savings deposits.

Life Insurance Reserves

In accounting for the behavior of life insurance reserves (MIS), we find it desirable to rely on a model somewhat different from that developed for the depository-type institutions. This decision is based on a number of factors and primarily on the consideration that saving in the form of life insurance is largely of the contractual type. As a result, one would expect the flow to be little affected by transient fluctuations in income and concommitant magnified fluctuations of personal saving, or by erratic movement of wealth reflecting capital gains and losses. This suggests that the flow of MIS, ΔMIS, should be related to "permanent" income, rather than to either saving, the change in wealth, or wealth itself, and that permanent income might be operationally approximated by consumption as measured in the FMP model.[9]

In formulating the nature of the relation between consumption and the flow and stock of life insurance, we started from the notion that the accumulation of this type of asset should be controlled by the very forces which provide the foundations for the life-cycle hypothesis of saving. As is well known, that model, with certain additional reasonable assumptions, leads to the conclusion that saving and the stock of accumulated wealth are proportional to income, and hence to consumption, with the proportionality factor depending on the growth trend of real income. Applying this proposition to MIS and recalling that the trend growth of income and consumption, say ρ, has been reasonably stable over the postwar period, we write the long-run equilibrium relation as

$$MIS = \alpha PC \qquad (3\text{-}17)$$

where MIS is the stock of life insurance claims in current dollars, C is real consumption, P the price index of consumption, and α should again be a function of the rate of return on life insurance, and on other assets and possibly of other variables, to be specified presently.

Assuming for the moment a stable price level, it also follows from (3-17) that

$$\Delta MIS = \alpha \, \Delta CP = \alpha \rho C_{-1} P \qquad (3\text{-}18)$$

A cursory examination of the data appears to support the usefulness of

---

[9] Consumption is defined as expenditures on nondurables and services plus the imputed consumption (interest plus depreciation) on the stock of consumer durables, measured in current dollars.

hypothesis (3-17) as a point of departure since, up to the mid-sixties, the ratio of *MIS* to *CP* appears to fluctuate quite narrowly around a level of 29 percent, except possibly for a mild declining trend. Since 1965, however, and especially in the last two years, the downward drift is more pronounced, carrying the ratio down to 25.5 percent by the end of 1969. Even these fluctuations are not inconsistent with the hypothesis since they could reflect variations in α. Furthermore, if α and/or P change in time, the long-run relations (3-17) and (3-18) need not hold in the short run for we should, as usual, expect that it will take some time to bring the stock back into its equilibrium relation; and this rebalancing will have to be accompanied by appropriate transient changes in the flow. Accordingly, in formulating a short-run model, we can again visualize the current flow as consisting of two components. A first component reflects the accumulation appropriate to the current level of permanent income or consumption. If prices were constant, this component would be given by the right side of (3-18). However, if the price level is subject to at least partly unforseen changes, it seems appropriate to allow for some lag in the adjustment of contracts by replacing P by the average level of prices over some earlier period, say $\bar{P}$. The second component should reflect the flow necessary to rebalance the stock and for this portion we propose to rely again on the standard stock adjustment formulation. These considerations lead to

$$\Delta MIS = \rho \alpha C_{-1} \bar{P} + g(\alpha C_{-1} P_{-1} - MIS_{-1})$$

For purpose of empirical testing, this can be conveniently restated in the scaled form

$$\frac{\Delta MIS}{P_{-1} C_{-1}} = (\rho + g)\alpha - ga_{-1} - b\frac{P_{-1} - \bar{P}}{P_{-1}} \qquad (3\text{-}19)$$

where $a \equiv MIS/PC$, and $b = \rho\alpha$ can be taken a constant as long as α is not subject to wide fluctuations. We may also note that $(P_{-1} - \bar{P})/P_{-1}$ can be expressed as a weighted sum of the rate of change of prices over the period of averaging: namely

$$\frac{1}{n} \sum_{1}^{n-1} \tau \dot{p}(t - n + \tau) = \frac{n-1}{2}\frac{\sum \tau \dot{p}(t - n + \tau)}{\sum \tau}$$

where $\dot{p}(t)$ is the rate of change of P in period t, and n is the averaging period.

Turning now to the specification of α, we should clearly include among its arguments some measure of the spread between the return on life insurance reserves, say *RI*, and the return on other money-fixed claims, say, *RO*. Unfortunately, there is no readily available explicit information on the rate of return on *MIS*. As an approximation, we propose to use a distributed lag on the mortgage rate *RM* on the ground that mortgages are a major component of life insurance portfolios and the mortgage rate should also provide a good indicator of the return on the rest of the portfolio. Unfortunately, this rate may also be a good measure of the return available on competing long-term assets, *RO*, especially since it is highly correlated also with *RA*, the return on savings and loan and mutual saving bank deposits. The resulting multicollinearity makes it very hard to use *RA*, or some other rate of return on long-term assets like the corporate bond rate (*RCB*), as an explicit measure of *RO*, as will be shown presently. We were thus generally led to approximate $b(RI - RO)$ by

$$b_1 RM + b_2 \sum_1^m w_\tau RM(-\tau)$$

expecting b_2 positive as reflecting primarily *RI*, and b_1 negative as reflecting primarily the return on competing assets.

This formulation is also supported by the consideration that the behavior of *MIS* and ΔMIS are very significantly affected both in the short and in the long run by the behavior of policy loans. The incentive to borrow against accumulated equity should depend again on the relation between the rate of interest charged on such loans, say *RIL*, and the cost of alternative sources of financing, say *RO'*. This consideration suggests adding to the specification of α a term $c(RO' - RIL)$ with $c < 0$. The rate on policy loans, *RIL*, is set by contract and has apparently remained constant at a conventional level throughout the period covered by our data. As for the alternative cost *RO'*, we conjecture that *RM* may again provide a good proxy. Thus the term $c(RO' - RIL)$ can be reduced to $b_3 RM + b_4$, $b_3 < 0$, $b_4 > 0$ and the specification of α to

$$\alpha = c_0 + c_1 RM + c_2 \sum_1^m w_\tau RM(-\tau)$$

with $c_1 = b_1 + b_3 < 0$, $c_2 = b_2 > 0$. Note that while b_1 and b_2 might be roughly equal in absolute value—meaning that in the long run the return on life insurance will tend to match that on alternative money-fixed assets—the coefficient c_1 should exceed c_2 in absolute value because of the policy loan effect. In other words, as long as *RIL* is unresponsive to change in market rates of return, one should expect that a rise of all rates will, on balance, tend to reduce α.

A case can also be made for adding to the specifications of α some measure of the expected rate of change of prices, $\dot{p}^e$. Even though this variable should not affect the attractiveness of *MIS* versus other money-fixed assets, it should reduce it in comparison with physical assets or claims to such; hence, the sign of $\dot{p}^e$ should be negative. But we should hardly expect it to be very important, for, except in the presence of very large and unpredictable variations in prices, there should be very limited substitution between real assets and such a specialized asset as life insurance reserves.

One further factor that should have appreciably affected the attractiveness of life insurance reserves in the postwar period is the marked growth in various retirement schemes including both (i) the increase in Social Security coverage and benefits and (ii) the spread of private pension funds. The first mentioned development should clearly have an adverse effect; the second is more complex for, in so far as private pension funds are managed by life insurance companies, it could even have increased α. However, since non-insured pension funds have grown distinctly faster than the insured ones, on balance the effect is likely to have been unfavorable; and, when coupled with the growth of Social Security, it could partly account for the declining trend of MIS/PC noted earlier. Because noninsured pension funds are not treated separately in the FMP model, we ended up by trying to capture this last factor by merely adding to the specification of α the ratio of Social Security benefits ($OASI$) to consumption.

Inserting all of the above specifications into equation (3-19) we are led to the following hypothesis as a basis for our empirical tests:

$$\frac{\Delta MIS}{\$C_{-1}} = (\rho + g)\left[c_0' + c_1'RM + c_2' \sum_{\tau=1}^{m} w_\tau RM(-\tau) + c_3'\dot{p}^e + c_4 \frac{OASI}{\$C_{-1}}\right]$$
$$-g\frac{MIS_{-1}}{\$C_{-1}} + c_5' \sum_{\tau=1}^{n} v_\tau \dot{p}(-\tau) \tag{3-20}$$

where $\$C$ denotes consumption in current dollars. This equation can be further simplified by combining like terms and consolidating unknown coefficients. Note in this connection that the only operational way of measuring $\dot{p}^e$ is through a distributed lag on past $\dot{p}$, which could not be disentangled from the other distributed lag associated with c_5'. We thus arrive at the following hypothesis which is directly usable for estimation:

$$\frac{\Delta MIS}{\$C_{-1}} = c_0 + c_1RM + c_2 \sum_{\tau=1}^{m} w_\tau RM(-\tau) + c_3 \sum_{\tau=0}^{n} v_\tau \dot{p}(-\tau)$$
$$+ c_4 \frac{OASI}{\$C_{-1}} + c_5 \frac{MIS}{\$C_{-1}} \tag{3-21}$$

The considerations used in deriving this equation imply c_0, $c_2 > 0$, c_1, c_3, c_4, $c_5 < 0$, and also $c_1 + c_2 < 0$.

To this basic hypothesis we also added one further component aimed at improving the specification of the short-run dynamics of policy loans. An examination of the evidence shows that the flow of such loans is subject to very sharp short-run swings. We conjecture that such swings represent a response not only to the behavior of the alternative cost but also to swings in the stringency of credit rationing in all markets, including the mortgage and the commercial loan market. To capture this effect one might rely on some direct measure of credit rationing such as that developed by Jaffee and Modigliani.[10] We do not follow this course because that variable is not included in the FMP model. However, the above-mentioned study suggests that a significant increase in rationing tends to be accompanied by a substantial narrowing of the spread between the commercial loan rate, RCL, and short-term market rates such as the commercial paper rate, RCP. A cursory examination of the available evidence confirms that in every period in which a substantial increase in RCP brought the spread $RCL - RCP$ to well below 100 basis points, the flow of policy loans exhibits a marked transient increase with a lag of no more than one quarter. This phenomenon is strikingly apparent in 1966:1 to 1967:1, 1967:4 to 1968:3 and 1969:1 to 1969:4 and also, on a more moderate scale, in 1959:4 to 1960:2 and 1965:2 and 1965:3 when the spread did not get quite as narrow.

These considerations suggest that the effect of rationing on the flow of policy loans and thus finally on ΔMIS might be captured through a variable coming into play whenever the spread $(RCP - RCL)$ exceeds some threshold value. To see how such a variable might be constructed, we may start from the following hypothesis about the behavior of policy loans (PL):

$$PL/MIS = k^*[(RCP - RCL) - TR] + k_0 \qquad (3\text{-}22)$$

where TR denotes the threshold level,

$$k^* = \begin{cases} k > 0 & \text{if } (RCP - RCL) - TR \text{ is positive} \\ 0 & \text{otherwise} \end{cases}$$

and k_0 stands for the forces affecting policy loans other than spurts of credit rationing. To a first approximation MIS can be taken as proportional to $\$C$ so that we can rewrite (3-22) as

$$PL/\$C_{-1} = K_0 + K^*(RCP - RCL) - (K^*TR) \qquad (3\text{-}22a)$$

[10] "A Theory and Test of Credit Rationing," *American Economic Review* (December 1969).

with K^* proportional to k^*. Since ΔMIS is reduced by an increase in policy loans, we conclude that the rationing effect may be measured by adding to (3-21) a term as follows:

$$c_6 J + c_7[J(\overline{RCP - RCL})]$$

where J is a dummy variable with value 1 when abnormal rationing is in effect and is zero otherwise and $(\overline{RCP - RCL})$ is an average of the spread in the current and previous quarter, to allow for the short lag in response, mentioned earlier. The coefficient c_7 is then an estimate of $-k$ of (3-22), up to a proportionality factor, and thus should be negative, while $(-c_6/c_7)$ should provide an estimate of the threshold level, TR. The term K_0 of (3-22), on the other hand, is supposed to be already covered by the remaining arguments of (3-21). From the observed behavior of policy loans we tentatively concluded that the dummy variable J should take the value 1 whenever a rise in RCP narrowed the current spread to below $-.7$ (70 basis points) and should retain that value as long as $(\overline{RCP - RCL})$ remained in the neighborhood of $-.7$ or below. Under this rule the quarters in which J is 1 roughly coincide with those mentioned at the end of the previous paragraph.[11]

The empirical results are reported in Table 3A-4. In row 1 we test the basic specification (3-21) and the results appear, in most respects, fairly satisfactory. The statistics of columns 10 to 13 suggest that the model accounts quite well for the behavior of the flow ΔMIS as indicated by RMSE, below 100 million and a quite high correlation of ΔMIS, though the residual errors are highly serially correlated. The speed of adjustment in column 2 is again rather small, as for all other assets; though, for reasons stated earlier, this is one asset for which a slow speed is credible. In line with our hypothesis, the current rate RM is very significantly negative, the coefficient of the distributed lag is positive and smaller in absolute value, and the coefficient of $OASI$ is also negative. The sum of weights of $\dot{p}$ also has the expected negative sign, though it is insignificant and numerically smaller than expected by at least $\frac{1}{3}$.[12] Finally, the long-run implications of the equation also appear not unreasonable. From the coefficients of row 1 and equations

---

[11] The simple rule adopted does not encompass the quarters 1960:2 and 1968:3, coming at the tail end of a tight period, even though policy loans were still quite high; but it did not seem worthwhile to develop a more complex rule in order to accommodate these years. In addition, 1969:4 falls outside the period used for estimation.

[12] This coefficient is the sum of c_3' and c_5', both negative, of equation (3-20). Also, as suggested earlier, c_5 alone should be roughly $-\rho\alpha(n - 1)/2$. Since ρ is just about .01, α in the order of .30, and n was assumed at 12, this should amount to .018, or, since $\dot{p}$ is measured as a percentage, $.18 \times 10^{-3}$, as compared with the estimated value of $.04 \times 10^{-3}$.

(3-20) and (3-21), one can readily establish that the implied long-run equilibrium ratio is

$$\alpha = \frac{.024 - 10.7 \times 10^{-4}RM - 4.0 \times 10^{-5}\dot{p} - .012[OASI/\$C_{-1}]}{.045 + \rho}$$

(MIS-1a)

The coefficient of RM and $\dot{p}$ are the sum of the coefficients in columns 3 and 4 and in column 5 respectively. The growth trend of C was just about 1 percent per quarter so we can take ρ as .01 obtaining

$$\alpha \simeq .43 - .020RM - .7 \times 10^{-3}\dot{p} - .22\frac{OASI}{\$C_{-1}}$$

Since, at the beginning of the period (the end of 1954), RM was around 5 percent and $OASI$ some .02 of consumption (and the contribution of $\dot{p}$ is negligible), the implied value of α is around .33 or a little above the observed ratio of about .3. Our results also imply that α has declined since, because each of these variables has increased by just about 300 basis points: RM from 5 to 8 percent, and $OASI/\$C$ also from 2 to 5 percent. These increases imply a decrease in α to about .26, again a little above the actual value in 1969:3 of .255. Note that the implied effect of $OASI$—a decline in the stock of .2 billion per billion increase in the annual flow—is smaller than one might have expected, especially if $OASI$ is supposed to proxy also for the growth of noninsured pension funds. Yet the measured effect is not altogether negligible, and the relevance of the variable is further supported by the finding that its coefficient remains significant even if one adds a time trend while the time trend itself is not significant (and is positive).

In row 2 of Table 3A-4 we have added the rationing proxy and the results appear to support our formulation. The coefficient of column 8, an estimate of c_7 is negative as expected and quite significant as is the estimate of c_6 in column 7. These two coefficients imply a threshold value of $-(1.17/1.87) = -.63$ which is quite close to the assumed threshold value of $-.7$. They further imply that an increase in spread by 10 basis points would reduce the inflow by about $.1 \times 1.2 \times 10^{-3} \times \$C$ or with $\$C$ now running around $600 billion by somewhat over 100 million, a nonnegligible amount compared with recent quarterly inflows of 1 to 1.5 billion. It is also seen that the fit improves appreciably and DW also rises, though it still remains uncomfortably small. On the other hand, the remaining coefficients are affected only to a minor degree; indeed aside from a slightly higher speed of adjustment, the only nonnegligible change is in the shape of the distributed lag on RM which no longer provides a clear indication of a rate of change effect. This change however can be accounted for by the consideration that the rate of change of RM is itself associated with, and hence a proxy for, the rationing effect. In row 1 the coefficients of RM current and lagged, to some extent capture the rationing effect which in row 2 we endeavor to measure by separate variables. On the other hand, the long-run properties of the two equations, which depend in particular on the *sum* of the coefficient c_1 and c_2, are nearly identical, as can be seen from the following equation, which gives the long-run equilibrium ratio implied by row 2

$$\alpha = .42 - .017RM - 1.3 \times 10^{-3}\dot{p} - .27\left(\frac{OASI}{\$C}\right)_{-1}$$

Finally, in row 3 we show the results of an attempt at measuring explicitly the return RO on competing money-fixed assets, by means of the corporate bond rate. To this end, RI was approximated by

$$\sum_{0}^{m} w_\tau RM(-\tau)$$

and RO by $\overline{RCB}$, an average of RCB in the current and previous two quarters. We should expect the first variable to have a positive and the second a negative coefficient.[13] This formulation fits the data about as well as that of row 2, but the coefficient of RCB is positive (though scarcely significant) while the coefficients of the distributed lag on RM start markedly negative; and, though they eventually turn positive, their sum is still quite negative. At the same time, the sum of all interest rate coefficients, an estimate of $c_1 + c_2$, remains approximately the same as in row 1 and 2, i.e., around -10×10^{-4}, so that the long-run implications are also roughly the same. The other major differences are a distinctly slower speed of adjustment and the greater role assigned both to the $OASI$ variable and to the rate of change of prices.

In summary, all the estimated equations tell roughly the same story: MIS and ΔMIS tend to increase with permanent income as measured by consumption and tend to be adversely affected by the overall level of long-term interest rates—a phenomenon that we primarily attribute to the policy loan effect—by the growth of social security benefits and, very mildly, by the rate of growth of prices. In the short run they are also adversely affected by the rate of change of long-term rates and by variations in the availability of credit, again primarily, we conjecture, through their effect on policy loans. Furthermore, this set of variables appears to account quite well for the

---

[13] We also tried to replace $\overline{RCB}$ by RCB but the results are very close to those reported in row 3.

behavior of ΔMIS and MIS in any of the alternative versions tested. On the whole, however, the version of row 2 appears to yield the most reasonable coefficient estimates and, accordingly, has been selected for inclusion in the model though we suspect that it tends to understate the depressing effect of the growth of pension funds and, therefore, probably to overstate the long-run effect of the level of rates, measured by the sum of the mortgage rate coefficients.

Appendix 3A:
The Flow of Savings

Table 3A-1. Time Deposits at Commercial Banks, Estimated Coefficients

(Standard errors are below the coefficients)

(1) Equation	(2) Model	(3) Constant ($\times 10^{-3}$)	(4) $a_{-1}\dfrac{SP}{V}$	(5) $a_{-1}\dfrac{CG}{V}$	(6) a_{-1}	(7) RTP ($\times 10^{-3}$)	(8) ΔRTP ($\times 10^{-3}$)	(9) RA ($\times 10^{-3}$)	(10) RTB ($\times 10^{-3}$)	(11) RCB ($\times 10^{-3}$)
MP-1	IA	2.9 / 1.1	1.0ᵃ / —	.24 / .15	-.050 / .024	1.30 / .33		-.99 / .51		
MP-2	IA	-0.6 / 1.2	1.0ᵃ / —	.016 / .012	.053 / .024	.54 / .37	1.97 / 0.73	-.10 / .75	-.45 / .13	-.19 / .31
MP-3	IA	0.71 / 0.96	1.0ᵃ / —	.035 / .13	.006 / .022	.98 / .27		-.039 / .43	-.494 / .094	
MP-4	IA	-0.20 / 1.15	1.0ᵃ / —	.02 / .13	.036 / .026	.90 / .43		-.38 / .60	-.556 / .095	
MP-5	IA	-18.0 / 3.8	1.0ᵃ / —	.61 / .15	-.141 / .042	1.51 / 0.38		.91 / .56	-.553 / .078	
MP-6	IA	-14.1 / 3.0	1.0ᵃ / —	.50 / .15	-.105 / .037	1.87 / 0.31			-.527 / .078	
MP-7	IB	0.64 / 1.11	10.3 / 3.2	.17 / .13	-.093 / .051	1.12 / 0.41		.29 / .61	-.650 / .094	
MP-8	IB	-13.0 / 4.5	3.2 / 3.6	.51 / .16	-.111 / .042	1.88 / 0.31			-.539 / .086	
MP-9	IB	-8.5 / 2.3	1.4 / 1.6	.175 / .065	-.036 / .023	1.31 / 0.18			-.590 / .061	

Table 3A–1 continued

Equation	(12) ΔRCB (×10⁻³)	(13) (RTP − RA)ᵇ (×10⁻³)	(14) JCᵇ (×10⁻³)	(15) YD/V (×10⁻³)	(16) JS1 (×10⁻³)	(17) JS4 (×10⁻³)	(18) SE (×10⁻³)	(19) DW	(20) RMSE ΔMP $ Billion	(21) R ΔMP
MP-1					.55	−.27	.574	0.82	1.19	.76
					.18	.19				
MP-2	−0.91				.45	−.21	.423	0.94	0.80	.90
	0.49				.17	.16				
MP-3					.56	−.20	.46	0.75	0.92	.85
					.15	.15				
MP-4		1.24	0.38		.64	−.18	.45	1.02	0.86	.88
		1.19	0.78		.15	.15				
MP-5		3.88	2.15	89.9	.56	−.10	.373	1.23	0.75	.91
		1.12	0.74	18.7	.12	.12				
MP-6		2.73	1.25	75.8	.57	−.11	.379	1.23	0.76	.91
		0.88	0.49	16.7	.13	.13				
MP-7		1.14	0.43		.60	−.17	.420	1.01	0.80	.90
		1.10	0.73		.14	.14				
MP-8		2.56	1.14	70.9	.57	−.12	.382	1.22	0.76	.91
		1.04	0.58	22.6	.13	.13				
MP-9		1.93	0.82	42.9	.60	−.15	—	—	0.80	.90
		0.59	0.34	11.3	.10	.10				

ᵃ Constrained to 1.
ᵇ Variable entered beginning with 1962:3. zero until then.

Table 3A-2. Other Savings Deposits, Estimated Coefficients

(Standard errors are below the coefficients)

(1)	(2)	(3)	(4)	(5)	(6)	(7)	(8)	(9)	(10)
Eq.	Model	Constant $(\times 10^{-3})$	$a_{-1}\dfrac{SP}{V}$	$a_{-1}\dfrac{CG}{V}$	a_{-1}	RA $(\times 10^{-3})$	RTP $(\times 10^{-3})$	RCB $(\times 10^{-3})$	RTB $(\times 10^{-3})$
MS-1	IA	2.0	1.0ᵃ	.267	−.071	1.58	.2	−.90	
		0.8	—	.053	.023	0.31	.24	.11	
MS-2	IA	1.39	1.0ᵃ	.143	−.001	0.646	.27	−.815	
		0.76	—	.047	.025	0.034	.20	.091	
MS-3	IA	0.62	1.0ᵃ	.083	.004	0.48		−.32	−.092
			—	.041	.020	0.28		.15	.059
MS-4	IA	3.45	1.0ᵃ	.053	.012	0.23		−.30	−.093
		1.11	—	.040	.019	0.28		.14	.056
MS-5	IB	2.9	0.26	.063	.017	0.25		−.32	−.074
		1.5	1.21	.044	.020	0.28		.14	.064
MS-6	IB	4.1	1.28	.10	−.03	0.71		−.34	−.122
		1.9	1.18	.43	.02	0.20		.15	.063
MS-7	IB	4.1	1.4	.175	−.036	0.99		−.55	−.077
		2.8	1.56	.065	.023	0.43		.27	.12

	(11)	(12)	(13)	(14)	(15)	(16)	(17)	(18)
Eq.	$(RA-RTP)^b$ $(\times 10^{-3})$	$(RA-RTB)^b$ $(\times 10^{-3})$	JC^b $(\times 10^{-3})$	$\dfrac{YD}{V}$ $(\times 10^{-3})$	SE $(\times 10^{-3})$	DW	RMSE ΔMS \$ Billion	R ΔMS
MS-1					.223	0.90	.50	.81
MS-2	2.87		−1.88		.172	1.25	.38	.89
	0.57		0.40					
MS-3	1.60	.296	−1.11		.161	1.53	.362	.91
	0.58	.078	0.41					
MS-4	2.33	.206	−1.41	−11.7	.151	1.82	.335	.92
	0.60	.081	0.40	4.3				
MS-5	2.23	.205	−1.36	−7.5	.152	1.80	.334	.92
	0.63	.081	0.41	8.1				
MS-6	1.55	.223	−0.76	−11.8	.158	1.72	.341	.92
	0.57	.084	0.33	8.2				
MS-7	1.93	.15	−1.0	−11.7			.36	.92
	0.59	.15	0.42	11.7				

ᵃ Constrained to 1.
ᵇ Variable entered beginning with 62.3, zero until then.

Table 3A-3. Savings and Loan Association Deposits, Estimated Coefficients

(Standard errors are below the coefficients)

(1)	(2)	(3)	(4)	(5)	(6)	(7)												
			$a_{-1}\dfrac{\Delta MS}{MS}$			Distributed Lag on $RSL - RMS$ ($\times 10^{-3}$)												
Eq.	Model	Constant		a_{-1}	Σw	0	−1	−2	−3	−4	−5	−6	−7	−8	−9	−10	−11
MSL-1	I	.0032	1.0[a]	−.010	.0229	13.8	−4.7	−2.6	−.8	.6	1.8	2.5	2.9	3.0	2.8	2.2	1.3
		.0020	—	.003		2.3	1.0	0.7	.4	.2	0.2	0.2	0.3	0.3	0.3	0.2	0.1
MSL-2	I	.0355	1.0[a]	−.074	.0213	11.9	−5.0	−2.7	−.9	.7	1.8	2.6	3.1	3.2	2.9	2.3	1.3
		.0150	—	.030		2.4	1.1	0.7	.5	.3	0.3	0.4	0.5	0.5	0.5	0.4	0.2
MSL-3	II	.016	1.0[a]	−.054	.133	8.3	−2.8	−1.6	−.5	.3	1.0	1.4	1.7	1.8	1.6	1.3	0.7
		.012	—	.016		0.4	0.6	0.4	.3	.2	0.1	0.1	0.2	0.2	0.2	0.1	0.1
MSL-4	II	.210	1.0[a]	−.44	.122	7.1	−2.9	−1.6	−.5	.3	1.0	1.5	1.8	1.8	1.7	1.3	0.8
		.085	—	.18		1.4	0.6	0.4	.3	.2	0.2	0.2	0.3	0.3	0.3	0.2	0.1

Table 3A–3 continued

Eq.	(8) $TIME$ ($\times 10^{-3}$)	(9) $(TIME)^2$ ($\times 10^{-3}$)	(10) γ'	(11) SE ($\times 10^{-3}$)	(12) DW	(13) RMSE ΔMSL	(14) R ΔMSL
MSL-1				.72	1.21	.095	.98
MSL-2	0.47 0.19	−.0050[b] .0017		.68	1.37	.0796	.99
MSL-3			.15		1.15	.094	.99
MSL-4	2.9[b] 1.2	−.030[b] .010	.15		1.31	.0791	.99

[a] Constrainted to 1.
[b] The origin for $TIME$ is 1955:1 and the trend is suspended in 1965:4 (i.e., $t = 43$ thereafter).

Table 3A–4. Life Insurance Reserves, Estimated Coefficients

(Standard errors are below the coefficients)

(1)	(2)	(3)	(4) Distributed Lag on RM (×10⁻⁴)											
Equation	Constant	$(MIS/\$C)_{-1}$ RM (×10⁻⁴)	Σw	−1	−2	−3	−4	−5	−6	−7	−8	−9	−10	−11
MIS-1	.0235	−13.2	2.5[b]	.10	.18	.24	.28	.31	.32	.31	.28	.24	.18	.10
	.0031	2.3	2.9	.11	.21	.28	.33	.35	.37	.36	.33	.28	.21	.12
MIS-2	.0238	−7.0	−2.7[d]	−2.6	−1.7	−1.0	−.4	.1	.4	.6	.7	.6	.4	.1
	.0028	2.7	3.2	1.0	0.7	0.4	.3	.4	.4	.4	.4	.4	.5	.8
MIS-3	.0212	−5.8[f]	−8.2[f]	−4.2	−2.9	−1.7	−.8	−.1	.4	.6	.6	.4	.0	−.6
	.0031	1.3		0.9	0.6	0.4	.4	.4	.4	.4	.4	.4	.5	.7

(5)	Distributed Lag on $\dot{p}$ (×10⁻⁵)											
Equation	Σw	0	−1	−2	−3	−4	−5	−6	−7	−8	−9	−10
MIS-1	−4.0[c]	−0.83	−0.71	−0.60	−0.50	−0.40	−.31	−.24	−.17	−.11	−.07	−.03
	7.2	2.0	1.5	1.2	0.9	0.8	.8	.8	.8	.7	.6	.3
MIS-2	−7.4[e]	−1.6	−1.4	−1.2	−1.0	−0.8	−.6	−.4	−.2			
	6.4	1.4	1.2	1.1	0.9	0.7	.5	.4	.2			
MIS-3	−10.8[e]	−2.4	−2.1	−1.8	−1.5	−1.2	−.9	−.6	−.3			
	6.1	1.4	1.2	1.0	0.8	0.7	.5	.3	.2			

Table 3A–4 continued

Equation	(6) $\left(\dfrac{OASI}{\$C}\right)_{-1}$	(7) JR^a ($\times 10^{-3}$)	(8) $JR \times$ $(\overline{RCP} - RCL)$ ($\times 10^{-3}$)	(9) $\overline{RCB}$ ($\times 10^{-4}$)	(10) SE ($\times 10^{-3}$)	(11) DW	(12) RMSE ΔMIS	(13) R ΔMIS
MIS-1	−.0119 .0082				.241	.74	.084	.94
MIS-2	−.0155 .0082	−1.17 0.34	−1.87 0.58		.207	.99	.069	.96
MIS-3	−.025 .012	−1.01 0.38	−1.60 0.63	3.3 2.8	.206	.99	.071	.96

[a] Dummy variable with value one when $(\overline{RCP} - RCL) > -.7$ (60:1, 65:2, 65:3, 66:1, to 67:1, 68:1, 69:1 to 69:3).
[b] Second degree polynomial constrained at both ends.
[c] Second degree polynomial constrained to zero at right end.
[d] Second degree polynomial, unconstrained.
[e] First degree polynomial constrained to zero at right end.
[f] Second degree polynomial unconstrained but including the current value of RM whose coefficient is given in column (3).

Errata

Page 69, footnote 4: second equation from the bottom should read "$b = g[1 + (1 - g)(1 - g*)]$."

Page 76, paragraph 2, line 16: "seriously biased as a result of" should read "contaminated by."

Page 89: last term in equation (3-21) should read "$c_5 \dfrac{MIS_{-1}}{\$C_{-1}}$."

Page 92, 8 lines from the bottom: ".1 $\times$ 1.2 $\times$ 10^{-3} $\times$ \$C" should read ".1 $\times$ 1.9 $\times$ 10^{-3} $\times$ \$C."

PART III
The Term Structure of Interest Rates

INNOVATIONS IN INTEREST RATE POLICY*

By FRANCO MODIGLIANI *and* RICHARD SUTCH
Massachusetts Institute of Technology

This paper is an examination of the success, or we should say lack of success, of the policy launched at the beginning of 1961 by the incoming Kennedy Administration, which has become known as "Operation Twist." This was an attempt to twist the maturity structure of interest rates by raising yields on securities with short term to maturity while simultaneously lowering, or at least holding the line on, long-term rates. Higher short-term rates were expected to contribute significantly toward stemming the outflow of capital and thus helping the United States balance-of-payments problem, while low long-term rates were considered desirable to stimulate the economy by increasing the flow of private investment. We are not concerned, however, with the broad issue of whether Operation Twist contributed to improving the balance of payments while sustaining domestic activity. Our focus is, rather, on Operation Twist per se. We direct ourselves to a review of the techniques used by the government and Federal Reserve to affect the term structure and attempt to assess how far they succeeded in achieving the stated goal of twisting the yield curve.

As far as we can see there were two main actions aimed directly at such a twisting:

1. Federal Reserve open market operations and Treasury debt management operations directed toward shortening the average term to maturity of the outstanding government debt held by the public. An increase in the relative supply of short-term securities was expected to exert upward pressure on short-term rates, while the corresponding decrease in the availability of long-term securities should have tended to lower long-term yields, thus twisting the term structure in the desired direction.

2. Beginning in January, 1962, the successive increases in the struc-

* The authors wish to express their thanks to Charles Bischoff, of Massachusetts Institute of Technology, for his invaluable assistance in the application of the Almon interpolation technique used in this paper. All computations were performed at the Computation Center of the Sloan School of Management, M.I.T., utilizing the "REGRT" regression program written by Robert Hall. The research was supported in part by a grant from the Ford Foundation to the Sloan School of Management for research in business finance, and by National Science Foundation funds. The authors have had the benefit of discussion with several colleagues, and in particular with Professor Eli Shapiro, of Harvard University, and Professor Paul Samuelson, of Massachusetts Institute of Technology.

178

ture of ceiling rates payable on commercial banks' time and saving deposits under Regulation Q. According to the *Economic Report of the President* of January, 1962, this "action was taken to promote competition for saving and to encourage retention of foreign funds by member banks and thus moderate pressures on this country's balance of payments" [3, p. 88, Table 8]. Also under this heading one should include the recent acquiescence by the Federal Reserve Board to the issuance of unsecured notes and debentures by commercial banks.[1]

An examination of the behavior of key short- and long-term rates between early 1961 and the third quarter of 1965, summarized in Table 1, reveals that short-term rates have risen substantially while long-term rates moved relatively little, some moderately up (government bonds, corporate Aaa) others moderately down (municipals, coporate Baa's, mortgage rates). As a result, the spread between rates on long-term government bonds and the bills rate has declined from 150 base points down to 35 base points, while the difference between Aaa corporate bonds and the commercial paper rate shrank from 125 to 12 base points. These figures would seem to provide impressive evidence that Operation Twist was a remarkable success. To make such an interpretation (as has been frequently done) would be much too hasty, for as historical experience has shown, the spread typically tends to close in a period of recovery and rising short-term rates, such as prevailed between 1961 and the present. Indeed, currently prevailing spreads are still appreciably larger than they were at the peak of the previous cycle in 1959 and early 1960, as can be seen from the last row of Table 1, Part B. Thus the closing of the spreads between the turn of 1960 and the present might reflect merely the normal tendency for spreads to close as short-term rates advance. This hunch can be tested by estimating the historical relationship between the spread and short rates with ordinary regression techniques, and then comparing the actual relation between short and long rates with that predicted by the least square regression. Using government securities we estimated the relation between the spread (S) and the Treasury three month bills rate (r) with quarterly data for the period 1952-I to 1961-IV, obtaining

---

[1] Other tools were brought to bear on the problem but were not designed to twist yield curves; rather, they were policies that were intended to change the reaction of the economy to a given yield curve. These can be broadly summarized under two headings: (1) Measures directly aimed at reducing capital exports for a given structure of long- and short-term rates: these measures include primarily (a) the interest equalization tax and (b) the Johnson Administration program of voluntary restraint in bank lending to foreigners and to domestic firms for foreign operations, and in direct foreign investments. (2) Fiscal measures aimed at increasing the rate of domestic long-term investments for a given level of long-term rates: these measures include (a) the Internal Revenue Department's revised depreciation guide lines and (b) the investment credit provisions. An assessment of these policies is beyond the province of this study, which will concentrate only on those techniques designed to change the shape of the yield curve.

$$R_t - r_t \equiv S_t = 2.16 - 0.495r_t = .495(4.37 - r_t)$$
$$(0.17) \quad (0.070)$$
$$S_e = .39$$

Since in the third quarter of 1965 the bill rate was 3.85 percent, this equation would predict a spread between the long rate and the bill rate of 33 points, almost identical with the spread actually prevailing of 35 base points. Very similar negative conclusions about the effectiveness of Operation Twist can be reached by extrapolating the relation between the commercial paper rate and the spread between this rate and Moody's Aaa bond yields, whether the relation is estimated for the postwar period alone or going back to the beginning of the 1920's.

Are we, then, to conclude that Operation Twist was a total failure, at least with respect to the structure of yields on marketable securities— that the changes which occurred since the inception of that operation are not noticeably different from what might have been expected in its absence? Clearly, to draw such a conclusion from the rudimentary evidence presented above would be no more warranted than to infer from the figures of Table 1 that the policy was a howling success. The point of these simple tests is rather to emphasize that the task of assessing the success of the operation is far from trivial and can only be adequately tackled with the help of a theoretically grounded and empirically tested understanding of the basic forces which tend to shape the yield structure and its variations in time. It is, then, to this challenging task that we must turn first.

I. Recent Theoretical Developments in the Analysis of the Maturity Structure

There is by now general agreement that in an ideal world of no transaction costs or taxes, rational behavior and certainty (about future rates), the maturity structure of yields must be controlled by the simple principle that all outstanding instruments, regardless of maturity, must produce identical returns over any given interval of time—where the return is defined as the sum of cash payments plus any increase (or minus any decrease) in the market value of the instrument. This principle in turn implies that at any date t the spread between the yield of an n period bond and the short rate, $S(n, t) = R(n, t) - R(1, t)$, is equal to minus the capital gain from holding the n period instrument. The capital gain in turn is inversely related to the change in yield: $\Delta R(n, t) = R(n-1, t+1) - R(n, t)$. Consequently, $R(n, t)$ can be expressed in terms of the current short rate $R(1, t)$ and the future long rate $R(n-1, t+1)$. Moreover, since $R(n-1, t+1)$ can in turn be expressed in terms of $R(1, t+1)$ and $R(n-2, t+2)$, and so on, recursively, it is readily apparent that $R(n, t)$ can also be expressed in terms of the current and

TABLE 1
Behavior of Some Key Short- and Long-Term Rates from 1960–61 to the Third Quarter of 1965

Year and Quarter	A. Levels (%)								
	Bills Rate	Commercial Paper Rate	Average Rate on Time Deposits	Average Yield on S&L Shares	Long-term Government Bonds	Corporate Bonds (Moody's)		High Grade Municipals	Conventional Mortgage Yields
						Aaa	Baa		
	(1)	(2)	(3)	(4)	(5)	(6)	(7)	(8)	(9)
1960–3	2.36	3.37	2.57	3.86*	3.82	4.31	5.10	3.60	6.25
1961–1	2.35	3.01	2.65	3.90*	3.83	4.27	5.06	3.34	6.05
1965–3	3.85	4.38	4.15†	4.19‡	4.20	4.50	4.89	3.27	5.85§
	B. Changes								
1960–3 to 1965–3	1.49	1.01	1.58†	0.35*·‡	.37	.19	−.21	−.33	−.40§
1961–1 to 1965–3	1.50	1.37	1.50†	0.29*·‡	.36	.23	−.17	−.26	−.20§
1960–1 to 1965–3	−.09	−.31	1.64†	0.35*·‡	−.02	−.05	−.42	−.72	−.45§

* Average for the year.
† Second quarter of 1965.
‡ Average for 1964.
§ Last quarter of 1964.
SOURCES: Columns 1, 2, 5, 6, 7, 8, *Economic Indicators.*
    Column 4, Savings and Loan League.
    Column 3, Frank de Leeuw and the Federal Reserve Bank of St. Louis.
    Column 9, Federal Housing Administration.

future rates for one period loans prevailing in each of the n periods to maturity, $R(1, t)$, $R(1, t+1)$, $\cdots$ $R(1, t+n-1)$, although the precise form of the functional relation will depend on the shape of the stream of cash payments promised by the bond until maturity. Finally, because the return to the lender and the cost to the borrower over any interval will be the same regardless of the maturity of the instrument held or issued, neither would have a special incentive to match the maturity structure of his assets or liabilities to the length of time for which he intends to remain a creditor or debtor.

There is unfortunately much less agreement as to the determinants of the yield structure in the "real" world. The prevailing points of view may be summarized as follows.

1. At one end of the spectrum is the Pure Expectation Hypothesis, which holds that the certainty model provides an adequate approximation to the real world, except that the equality of returns of the certainty world must now be replaced by the equality of "expected" returns, where the expected returns may be thought of as the mean value (or some other analogous measure of central tendency) of the subjective probability distribution of possible returns. In particular, for every n, $R(n, t)$ must equal $R(1, t)$ minus the expected capital gain, determined by the expected change in the n period rate, say $\Delta R^e(n, t)$. For otherwise holders of bonds with lower expected returns would try to sell them, bidding down their price and raising their yield, and to acquire higher yielding instruments, bidding up their price and reducing their yields, until the postulated relation would come to hold.

2. A variant of the expectation hypothesis, of Keynesian inspiration [10] but articulated largely by Hicks [8], which has wide support at the present, may be labeled the Risk Premium Model. It basically accepts the view that yields on various maturities are related to each other by the expectations of future long rates, and hence also short rates, but it calls attention to differences in the degree of uncertainty which attaches to the expected return to be obtained, in the short run, from holding securities of different length. While the return on short-term securities is certain (since the value of the principal is guaranteed by repayment at the end of the period), the return on longer maturities is not guaranteed because of the uncertainty of future rates and hence of the end of period market value of the bond. Furthermore, the uncertainty tends to be greater the longer the maturity, since a given change in the long rate tends to produce a greater variation in terminal value the longer the remaining life to maturity. If, then, investors are prevailingly risk averters, as a good deal of other evidence suggests, one should expect that if the expected return were the same on all maturities, they would tend to prefer the safer short-term instruments. Hence, in order to induce the market to hold the longer-term maturities supplied by long-

term borrowers, the expected return on these maturities must exceed that on shorter-term instruments by an expected risk or liquidity premium. According to this view, the yield curve will tend to rise more than the curve implied by the pure expectation hypothesis because of the increasing risk premium as the term to maturity increases. The size of these risk premiums might be expected to depend on the relative supplies of longer maturities and the strength of investors' risk aversion.

3. Finally, there is the view that might be labeled the Market Segmentation Hypothesis. The proponents of this approach suggest that both lenders and borrowers have definite preferences for instruments of a specific maturity, and for various reasons, partly due to institutional factors and regulations constraining financial intermediaries, will tend to stick to securities of the corresponding maturity, without paying attention to rates of return on other maturities.[2] Hence the rates for different terms to maturity tend to be determined, each in its separate market, by their independent supply and demand schedules. The rates so set might well imply wide differences in the expected return obtainable in the current period, or over some sequence of periods, by investing in different maturities, but such differences, it is argued, would not induce traders to move out of their preferred maturity—or maturity habitat, as we shall call it—except possibly when the discrepancies become extreme and glaring.

In our view, each of the three models has its merits, but also suffers from shortcomings. We propose, therefore, an alternative model which, in essence, blends the previous three, and which we label the Preferred Habitat Theory. This model shares with the Hicksian approach the notion that the yield structure is basically controlled by the principle of the equality of expected returns, but modified by the risk premiums. Yet it differs from it in one fundamental respect. The Hicksian model assumes that all traders are concerned with the short period return and that, therefore, anybody going long is bearing the risk associated with the uncertainty of the short period return from longer-term instruments. But this view would be correct only if we could assume that every lender desires to turn his portfolio back into cash at the end of the short period; i.e., that he has a short habitat (cf. Meiselman [14]). In reality, however, different transactors are likely to have different habitats, as the segmentation theory points out. Suppose that a person has an n period habitat; that is, he has funds which he will not need for n periods and which, therefore, he intends to keep invested in bonds for n periods. If he invests in n period bonds, he will know exactly the outcome of his investments as measured by the terminal value of his wealth (this being only approximately true if he were to invest in a conventional loan and precisely true for a pure n period loan; that is, a loan that was

---

[2] This view has been stressed by a number of authors, in particular Culbertson [3].

issued on a discount basis). If, however, he stays short, his outcome is uncertain, as it will depend on the future course of the short rates in periods 2, 3, . . . , n-1. Furthermore, he is likely to have to incur greater transaction costs. Thus, if he has risk aversion, he will prefer to stay long unless the average of the expected short rates exceeds the long rate by an amount sufficient to cover extra transaction costs and to compensate him for the extra risk of going short. Similarly, if he should invest in maturities longer than n, he would also be exposing himself to risk, this time to the Hicks-Keynesian uncertainty as to the price he can fetch for his not-yet-matured bonds. Thus, risk aversion should not lead investors to prefer to stay short but, instead, should lead them to hedge by staying in their maturity habitat, unless other maturities (longer or shorter) offer an expected premium sufficient to compensate for the risk and cost of moving out of one's habitat. Similar considerations will clearly apply, *mutatis mutandis*, to the borrower's side of the market.

Under this model the rate for a given maturity, n, could differ from the rate implied by the Pure Expectation Hypothesis by positive or negative "risk premiums," reflecting the extent to which the supply of funds with habitat n differs from the aggregate demand for n period loans forthcoming at that rate. If the n period demand exceeded the funds with n period habitat, there would tend to arise a premium in the n period maturity, and conversely.[3] Such premiums or discounts would tend to bring about shifts in funds between different maturity markets, both through the "speculation" of investors tempted out of their natural habitat by the lure of higher expected returns and through "arbitrage" by intermediaries induced to "take a position" by borrowing in the maturity range where the expected return is low, and lending where the expected return is high.

In summary, then, the Habitat Model implies that the spread $S(n, t)$ between the long rate $R(n, t)$ and the short rate $R(1, t)$ should depend primarily on the expected change in the long rate, $\Delta R^e(n, t)$. But it suggests that the spread could also be influenced by the supply of long- and short-term securities by primary borrowers (i.e., by borrowers other than arbitrageurs) relative to the corresponding demand of primary lenders, to an extent reflecting prevailing risk aversion, transaction costs, and facilities for effective arbitrage operations.

These conclusions can be conveniently summarized in the following equations.

Expected current return on an n period bond

$$\equiv R(n, t) + \text{Expected capital gain}$$
$$= R(1, t) + F_t$$

[3] This is only approximately true, for under risk aversion, funds of habitat n would not be indifferent as to where they would move but would tend to spill, preferably into neighboring maturities where the risk would tend to be smaller.

where F_t stands for the net effect of relative supply factors and could in principle be positive or negative. Solving for $R(n, t)$, and taking the Expected Capital Gain as proportional to the expected fall in the long rate, i.e., to $-\Delta R^e(n, t)$, we can also write

(1) $\quad\quad R(n, t) = R(1, t) -$ Expected capital gain $+ F_t$

$\quad\quad\quad\quad = R(1, t) + \beta\Delta R^e(n, t) + F_t$[4]

II. *An Operational Formulation of the Habitat Model*

Before we can test our hypothesis we must recast equation (1) into an operational form suitable for empirical estimation. This entails specifying both a theory of how expectations are formed and a functional form for the summary term "F." For a model of expectations we draw on the highly imaginative approach of Frank de Leeuw [4] who synthesized two currently held views as to the determinants of the expected change in long-term rates.[5]

One widely held hypothesis associated with Keynes [11] holds that the market expects the interest rate to regress toward a "normal" level based on past experience. Modifying slightly De Leeuw's formulation, we approximate this normal level, denoted by $\overline{R}_t$, by some average of the long rates for the past m periods and a constant which could be thought of as a very long-run normal level. Thus:

$$\overline{R}_t = v \sum_{i=1}^{m} \mu_i R_{t-i} + (1 - v)c \quad\quad 0 < v < 1$$

where R_t is used hereafter as a symbol for the long-term rate and the μ_i's are weights adding up to one. Since the recent experience should be more salient we should expect the μ_i's to decline toward zero as i rises from one to m. This regressive hypothesis can thus be formalized as

(2) $\quad \Delta R_t^e = \alpha_1(\overline{R}_t - R_t) = \alpha_1 \left[v \sum_{i=1}^{m} \mu_i R_{t-i} + (1 - v)c - R_t \right]$[6]

where α_1 is a measure of the speed with which R_t is expected to return to $\overline{R}$.

[4] The substitution of $-\beta\Delta R^e(n, t)$ for the expected capital gain should be recognized as an approximation, if β is taken as constant. Strictly speaking, β can be shown to be a function both of the length to maturity n and of $R(n, t)$ (as well as possibly future short rates). However, the dependence on n need not be neglected if we deal with a fixed maturity n; and the effect of $R(n, t)$ can be shown to be sufficiently small to be neglected to a first approximation within the range of variation of $R(n, t)$ prevailing in the period with which we are concerned.

[5] Meiselman [14] and Kessel [9] have also made important contributions in this area, but while their work provides impressive support for the expectations model, their approach is not directly applicable to our problem.

[6] This hypothesis could also be derived by replacing the notion of a normal level with the notion of a normal range (cf., Malkiel [13]).

A quite different hypothesis, advanced by James Duesenberry, suggests that expectations might be extrapolative: "a rise in rates [leading] to an expectation of a further rise and vice versa" ([5], p. 318). De Leeuw suggests that the recent trend in rates might be approximated by the difference between the current rate and some weighted average of recent past rates and accordingly expresses the extrapolative hypothesis as

$$(3) \qquad \Delta R_t^e = \alpha_2 \left(R_t - \sum_{i=1}^{n} \delta_i R_{t-i} \right); \qquad \alpha_2 > 0$$

where n should be appreciably smaller than m and the weights, δ_i, would probably decline rather rapidly.

Now, as De Leeuw rightly points out, it is quite credible that both hypotheses contain an important element of truth—that expectations contain both extrapolative and regressive elements. If so, we can combine the right-hand side of (2) and (3) to obtain

$$(4) \qquad \Delta R_t^e = - aR_t + \sum_{i=1}^{m} b_i R_{t-i} + dc$$

where $a = (\alpha_1 - \alpha_2)$, $b_i = \alpha_1 v \mu_i - \alpha_2 \delta_i$, with δ_i defined to be zero for $i > n$, and $d = \alpha_1(1-v)$. Since the term in the summation now represents the difference of two lag structures, we can no longer expect it to be of a simple geometric form. Indeed, if the extrapolative element is at all significant (i.e., α_2 is not zero or small compared with $\alpha_1 v$) we should find that initially, since δ_i falls faster than μ_i, b_i rises (possibly even from negative values), reaching a peak in the neighborhood of n and then declines back toward zero.

We are ready now to substitute equation (4) into the basic hypothesis (1) which yields

$$R_t = r_t - \beta aR_t + \sum_{i=1}^{m} \beta b_i R_{t-i} + \beta dc + F_t$$

where r_t is used hereafter to denote the short rate $R(1, t)$. As it now stands, this equation involves the current long rate on both sides; but this can be readily handled by solving the equation for R_t, obtaining finally

$$(5) \qquad R_t = A r_t + \sum_{i=1}^{m} B_i R_{t-i} + C + F_t' + \epsilon_t$$

where

$$A = \frac{1}{1 + \beta a}, \quad B_i = \frac{\beta}{1 + \beta a} b_i, \quad C = \frac{\beta dc}{1 + \beta a} \text{ and } \epsilon_t \text{ is the error term.}$$

We note that, since β and a are supposed to be positive, the coefficient A should be positive but distinctly below unity, and that, since the lag coefficients, B_i, are proportional to the b_i of (4), our earlier inferences about the b_i's—which define the lag structure—applies equally to the B_i's.

III. *Estimation of the Model*

If we disregard for the moment the nondescript supply term F', equation (5) contains only observables and is in principle ready for estimation and testing. In so doing, however, we must face two rather difficult problems. Since the distributed lag on the previous long rates should be quite long and not of the familiar exponentially declining type, it poses estimation problems. These De Leeuw solved with an ingenious technique that involved estimation of only a small number of coefficients rather than a separate coefficient for each lagged value of R (an alternative which would undoubtedly lead to severe multicolinearity problems). However, since his writing, an alternative, more powerful and far more flexible technique for estimating lag structures has been developed by Shirley Almon [1] and pursued by Charles Bischoff in work currently in progress at the Massachusetts Institute of Technology. This procedure imposes very little a priori restriction on the lag structure, requiring merely that it can be approximated by a polynomial. Since our formulation suggests that the lag distribution should rise to a single peak and then fall, we concluded that a fourth degree polynomial would be sufficiently flexible to closely reproduce the true structure.

The Almon Interpolation Distribution involves the calculation of Lagrangian interpolation polynomials, which are used to weight a specified number of past values of the variable whose lag is to be estimated. These weighted averages, or Almon variables, are then entered in the ordinary least squares regression equation. For a fourth degree polynomial, five Lagrangian polynomials would be needed to define the structure. However, since we have a priori reasons to believe that the lag structure will taper off to negligible values at some finite distance in the past, we further impose the restriction that the polynomial to be estimated should assume a zero value at a finite lag. This allows us to use only four Lagrangian polynomials and hence also four Almon variables.[7] The four coefficients estimated for these variables in the regression plus

[7] This is a modification of the procedure which Mrs. Almon followed in her paper on lags between capital appropriations and expenditures [1]. She specified that the lag distribution began as well as ended with a zero value, and thus only three Almon variables were necessary to estimate the fourth degree polynomial. For our purposes the requirement that the polynomial pass through zero at t plus one seemed to place an unwarranted restriction on the shape of the distributed lag. Experiments with several alternative restrictions indicated that a free estimation of the head of the distribution yielded more sensible lag structures and closer fits.

the a priori specification of the intercept yield the five points necessary to define a fourth degree polynomial.

However, before we attempt to apply this technique, we must face another difficulty. Equation (5) purports to explain the dependent variable R_t in terms of lagged values of itself. It is well known that in the presence of serial correlation of the error term, ϵ_t, such a procedure will lead to biased estimates of the coefficients [7].

The problem is particularly serious for our present purposes, as it can be shown that if, in fact, Operation Twist was successful, then an equation of the form (5) estimated by ordinary least squares would very likely tend to conceal and understate the true effectiveness.

One way to handle this difficulty would be to estimate (5) using recently developed techniques for consistent estimation of equations which include a lagged dependent variable.[8] However, we propose an alternative approach. As is well known, an equation in the form of (5) implies that R_t can also be expressed as a function only of r_t and a weighted sum of all previous short rates, r_{t-i}. This result can derived by using equation (5) to express R_{t-1} in terms of r_{t-1}, and R_{t-2} to R_{t-m-1}, and so on, recursively. The final result involves only r_{t-j}, with j extending indefinitely into the past, but with the coefficients of the far removed r_{t-j} approaching zero. Hence, to a first approximation R_t can be expressed as an average of a finite and reasonably small number of lagged values of r:

$$(6) \qquad R_t = \alpha + \beta_o r_t + \sum_{i=1}^{m} \beta_i r_{t-i} + \eta_t{}^9$$

This equation is very similar to (5), from which it differs only because the distributed lag on the long rate is replaced by a distributed lag on the short rate. This substitution is in essence equivalent to hypothesizing that the expected long rate R_t^e can be approximated as a weighted average of past short rates rather than past long rates. This is certainly as sensible a hypothesis as De Leeuw's original. Indeed, it is basically an implication of that hypothesis, and conversely. Whether it is more convenient and efficient to approximate the basic model by a long lag on the long rate or on the short rate is, in the last analysis, a purely pragmatic and empirical issue.[10] But even if (6) should fit the data less well than

---

[8] Such a technique would be similar to that suggested by Liviatan [12].

[9] Ideally, one might wish to estimate an infinite lag on r_t. Estimation techniques for the Pascal-Solow lag distribution [15] now being developed by Robert Hall look to be suitable for such a model, but this will have to wait for a later date. It is very unlikely, however, that refined estimation techniques could substantially alter our conclusions. Incidentally, equation (6) can be recognized as simply the first stage of the Liviatan technique as applied to this model (see footnote 8 above).

[10] The only statistically significant difference between (5) and (6) lies in the stochastic properties of the error term hypothesized for the two models. If (5) holds with nonserially correlated error, then (6) will have an error vector which is autoregressive, and conversely.

(5), it has two significant advantages: (1) because it does not involve the lagged dependent variable, an unbiased estimate of its coefficients can be obtained by ordinary regression techniques; and (2) it provides a more reliable tool for testing Operation Twist, free of the bias noted above.

The basic hypothesis (6) was estimated using the Almon technique described above for the forty quarters spanning the pre-Operation Twist period, 1952-I to 1961-IV, with R_t defined as the yield on long-term government bonds (i.e., due or callable in ten years or later) and r_t defined as the three-months Treasury bills rate. Since we are particularly interested in the behavior of the spread, we have found it convenient to subtract r_t from both sides of the equation. This transformation converts the dependent variable into the spread $S_t = R_t - r_t$ without affecting the right-hand side of the equation or its statistical properties except for changing the coefficient of r_t on the right-hand side from β_o to $-(1-\beta_o)$.

Lags of between two and seven years were tested with the most satisfactory results obtained for lags of around four years. The 16-quarter lag produced lower standard errors, smaller serial correlation, and the most sensible lag structure, although the multiple correlation and DW statistics[11] were not very sensitive to the length of lag, at least beyond four years. The result can be summarized as follows, omitting for the moment variables besides the short rate:

$$(7) \qquad S_t = 1.239 - 0.684\, r_t + \sum_{i=1}^{16} \beta_i r_{t-i}$$
$$ (0.028)\ \ (0.030)$$

$$R^2 = .975 \qquad S_e = .093 \qquad DW = 1.42$$

The expression

$$\sum_{i=1}^{16} \beta_i R_{t-i}$$

represents the finite lag. The 16 coefficients of r_{t-i} (the β_i's) are plotted within a band of plus and minus one standard error, in Figure 1.[12]

These results are rather striking. The coefficient of r_t has the predicted sign and order of magnitude, the lag structure has the predicted shape, and its initial rising segment provides impressive support for the hypothesis that expectations involve significant extrapolative as well as the

---

[11] The symbol DW denotes the Durbin-Watson statistic, a measure of the estimated first order serial correlation of the residual error [6].

[12] The actual least squares regression entered four Almon variables, each of which received highly significant coefficients. These coefficients were unscrambled to obtain the lag structure and its standard error plotted in Figure 1. Because there is no unique way of selecting the interpolation polynomials to be used in the estimation of the lag distribution, the presentation of these four coefficients was thought not to be as helpful to the reader as the summary statistics presented.

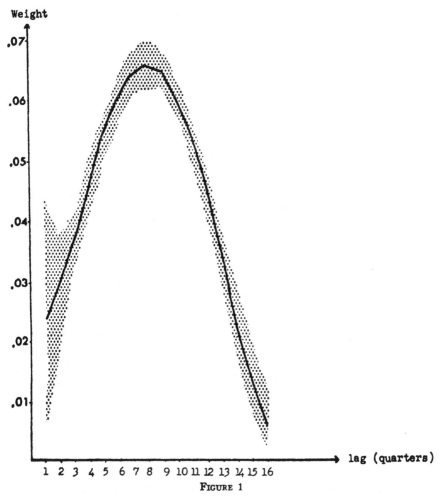

Weight

FIGURE 1

LAG STRUCTURE ON THE SHORT RATE PLUS AND MINUS ONE STANDARD ERROR (EQUATION 7)*
* The coefficients and their standard errors plotted are, from left to right: .0229(.0215), .0293(.0091), .0373(.0054), .0458(.0060), .0536(.0058), .0599(.0048), .0641(.0044), .0656(.0049), .0644(.0055), .0603(.0056), .0537(.0053), .0449(.0051), .0347(.0058), .0239(.0070), .0136(.0074), .0514(.0056).

widely recognized regressive elements. The multiple correlation is quite high and the standard error remarkably low, less than 10 base points. (This, incidentally, is a vast improvement over De Leeuw's original model, which for the same period, even with additional significant variables, has a standard error of 34 base points and a DW of .79.)

There remains to examine whether the small residual error might reflect in some measure supply effects, subsumed under F'_t in equation (5); or more precisely variation in supply conditions for, to some extent, the rather large constant term of (7) may already reflect a risk premium resulting from supply effects. Unfortunately, the measurement of supply-demand effects poses formidable problems, even if we are prepared to limit ourselves to variations in supply, on the assumption that the demand side is not subject to significant variations. The problem arises not only from shortage of data but even more from the statistical and conceptual difficulties of separating the total supply from the relevant primary supply. For this reason, most authors have ended up by measuring supply effects by the composition of the outstanding supply of marketable federal debt outside the Federal Reserve and Government Trust Accounts. De Leeuw in particular tried to test the effect of both the composition and the change in the composition of the debt outstanding in each of four maturity classes. He could find no evidence that the proportion outstanding in the various classes had any effect, but found some evidence that an increase in the proportion of both short (less than one year) and intermediate debt (one to five years) tended to reduce the spread.

We have repeated the tests of De Leeuw and others, and we find that none of the many debt variables we have tested obtains a significant coefficient with the predicted sign.[18] This is somewhat surprising in light of our a priori expectations, but does confirm the findings of most other authors. We must conclude that neither the maturity structure of the government debt nor changes in the maturity structure exert any significant, lasting or transient, influence on the relation between the two rates. This conclusion is supported by lack of positive evidence that these variables affect the spread in the generally supposed direction, and is reinforced by the consideration that the behavior of the spread can be accounted for quite closely without any reference to such variables, implying that their effect, if at all present, could be only of a secondary order of magnitude. This is not to say, of course, that there are no supply-demand effects, but merely that we could find no evidence that operations on the government component of the supply have a noticeable effect on the term structure as defined.

Ironically enough, this finding should be a source of relief to the authorities concerned with debt management because it turns out that,

[18] To illustrate, when we add to (7) the two variables that De Leeuw found to have significant effects in the predicted direction, namely, the change in the proportion of short-term debt, $\Delta[D_S/D_T]$, and the change in the proportion of intermediate debt, $\Delta[D_I/D_T]$, we find

$$S_t = 1.233 - 0.709r_t + \sum_{i=1}^{16} \beta_i r_{t-i} + 0.93 \, \Delta\left[\frac{D_S}{D_T}\right] - 0.97 \, \Delta\left[\frac{D_I}{D_T}\right]$$
$$(0.061) \quad (0.040) \qquad\qquad\qquad (1.20) \qquad\qquad (1.49)$$

The variables D_S and D_I were calculated with an elaborate averaging technique by the flow-of-funds section of the Federal Reserve Board, who generously made them available to us. We have also tried using the proportion of short and long debt, the changes in these proportions, the average length to maturity of publicly-held debt, and other such variables, and in no case were significant supply effects in evidence. This leads us to suspect that the significant coefficients that De Leeuw found in his original studies must be a spurious result.

with a very few and fleeting exceptions, the combined result of Federal Reserve-Treasury debt management since the last quarter of 1961 was to lengthen steadily the maturity of the debt held by the public, reversing a previous trend. While in the first quarter of 1960 the average maturity stood at 4.3 years, the lowest figure on record until that time, by the second quarter of 1965 it stood at 5.7 years. Thus, if lengthening the maturity had the usually supposed effect of increasing the spread, then debt management would have pretty consistently worked toward defeating the goal of Operation Twist.

IV. *Testing the Effects of Operation Twist*

Since equation (7) has sound theoretical underpinnings, as well as strong empirical support, it should provide a sensible basis for a test of the effectiveness of Operation Twist. To this end we extrapolated this equation from the first quarter of 1962 to 1965-II, and the result is graphed as a dashed curve in the top panel of Figure 2. It is apparent that, through the middle of 1964, there is very little evidence that these policies produced an appreciable effect on the term structure. With but a couple of exceptions, the error is within ten base points, or less than the standard error; beginning with the second quarter of 1962, however, the spread is consistently smaller than the computed value and, beginning with 1964-IV, the difference becomes impressive, four to six times the standard error. Thus the best that could be said on the basis of (7) is that the twist policy was slightly to moderately successful.

Since our results indicate that this success is not attributable to debt management by the Treasury or the Federal Reserve, we must consider whether the only other major tool applied might be responsible for what twisting took place. That was, as we noted, the successive increases in the ceiling rates on time deposits under Regulation Q. Particularly noteworthy is the fact that the major increases in the ceiling rate came precisely at the beginning of 1962 and again in the last quarter of 1964. But while the coincidence of dates is suggestive, it is at best circumstantial evidence. To put our case on a solid footing, we must specify the mechanism by which an increase in the ceilings on interest payable to savings deposits could be expected to affect the spread, and then look for direct evidence that this mechanism was actually at work in the period under consideration.

To see what light the Habitat Theory can shed on the nature of the mechanism, we note once more that the rather large constant term in (7) suggests that during the postwar period the expected return from long-term bonds tended to exceed the short rate by a positive premium. According to the Habitat model the prevalence of such a positive premium would indicate a systematic tendency for the primary supply of

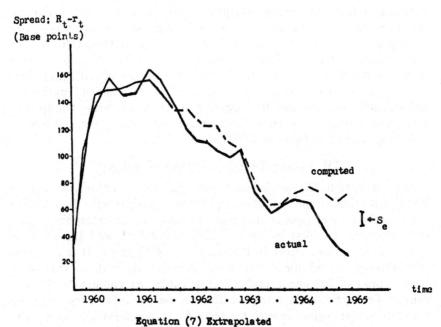

Equation (7) Extrapolated

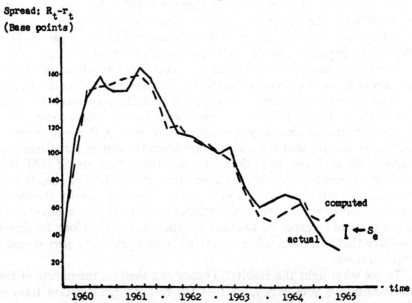

Equation (8) Actual and Fitted Values

FIGURE 2

funds to exceed the primary demand in the short market and to fall short of the primary demand in the long market. We have further seen that under these conditions the size of the premium on longs would depend, among other things, on the "facilities for effective arbitrage operations." In particular, we should expect that any significant impediment to arbitrage, such as a curtailment of the ability of a certain class of would-be arbitrageurs to attract short-term funds with a rate as high as they would otherwise be prepared to pay, would tend to raise the premium. Among such potential arbitrageurs one presumably would include commercial banks, hence the Regulation Q ceiling on time deposit rates (if sufficiently low to be effective) would be a force creating an artificially large premium. Thus, we would presume that increases in the ceiling rate would tend to reduce the spread by allowing banks to arbitrage away part of this premium.

This theoretical formulation suggests that to measure the effect of Regulation Q we need to introduce a variable which (1) should treat the successive lifting of the ceilings, not as positive forces contributing to twist, but rather as the removal of an interference with normal arbitrage operations; and (2) should play the largest role when other short-term rates are very close to or above ceiling; while it should cease to have effect once the ceiling is sufficiently above these rates. Beyond that level, changes in the ceiling should no longer affect the spread. Thus we define a variable, Q, as follows:

$$Q_t = r_t - (q_t - a) \qquad \text{if positive, zero otherwise}$$

where q_t is the ceiling rate under Regulation Q and $(r_t + a)$ is a threshold level such that any higher ceiling would be irrelevant at time t. Just how high the gap, a, should be is hard to guess a priori, and depends in a large measure upon what rate is used for r_t. Since we are dealing with the market for government securities it seems sensible to use the treasury bills rate itself for r_t. For a we assumed somewhat arbitrarily a value of one hundred base points.[14]

When we fit our regression model, including the variable Q, for the entire period from 1952 to mid-1965, we find that the coefficient of the variable Q has the expected positive sign, although it is on the borderline of statistical significance.[15] It is also rather small, as it implies that when r_t equals the ceiling, the premium is only ten base points higher than it would be in the absence of an effective ceiling. The marginal

[14] We use the ceiling rate q_t rather than the average rate actually offered by banks because q_t is the policy variable whose effect we wish to estimate. See also footnote 15.

[15] Nearly identical results are obtained if Q is entered with a one-quarter lag, raising the possibility that a short distributed lag on Q might improve the results, although we have not investigated this approach. It was also found that if the threshold level, a, was chosen to be 50 base points rather than 100, the same qualitative results were obtained.

statistical significance and the small magnitude of the coefficient estimated for Q raises the possibility that other events in the period after 1961 are causing a spurious effect. One such major development, and one that could have affected the ability of commercial banks to attract short-term funds, was the introduction in 1961 of negotiable Time Certificates of Deposit (CD's). To be sure, the spectacular growth of this instrument after 1962 could not have occurred had not the ceiling been raised that year, so that banks could offer CD's at rates competitive with other short-term instruments. Nonetheless, the CD must be regarded as a true financial innovation which could have enhanced the capacity of banks to arbitrage even if Regulation Q had never existed.

To test the effect, if any, of this innovation, one could rely on the dummy variable technique, adding to (7) a variable taking the value one after 1962 and zero everywhere else. This would allow the constant term of the equation (which is a measure of the risk premium) to assume two values: one value for pre-1962 and a second, lower value (the sum of the constant term and the coefficient of the dummy variable) after 1962.

When we entered into the regression such a dummy—denoted by Z in the equation below—its coefficient has the expected negative sign and is significant in relation to its standard error:

$$(8) \qquad S_t = 1.278 - 0.695 r_t + \sum_{i=1}^{16} \alpha_i r_{t-i} - 0.124 Z^{16}$$
$$(0.064) \quad (0.031) \qquad\qquad (0.043)$$

$$R^2 = 0.964 \qquad S_e = 0.103 \qquad DW = 1.02$$

Actual and computed values for this equation are shown in panel 2 of Figure 2.

When Q is added along with Z in a similar regression, the coefficient of Q not only loses its statistical significance but actually becomes negative. This result is confirmed by rerunning (7) with Q but not Z for the period before 1962, thereby excluding the CD years altogether. The coefficient of Q is again negative. This outcome suggests that the successive increases in the ceiling contributed to twist solely by permitting

---

[16] The use of a dummy variable in (8) may appear less than satisfactory, failing to bring out the fact that the contribution of the newly introduced CD's depends on whether the ceiling rate is sufficiently high to enable banks to offer rates competitive with other short-term instruments. With these considerations in mind, we had actually defined the variable Z to take (1) the value 1 only when the ceiling q_t exceeds r_t by at least 50 base points, a gap which we assumed to be sufficiently large to give banks the needed elbow room; (2) the value zero when r_t equals the ceiling, by which time banks would likely lose nearly all power of attracting CD funds; and (3) to decrease linearly between these limits as $(q_t - r_t)$ shrinks from 50 base points to zero. As it turns out, however, from 1962 to 1965-II the ceiling was consistently kept at least 50 base points above r_t. (Note in this connection that for the last quarter of 1964 the ceiling was taken as 4.25, a simple average of the 4 percent rate ruling up to November 24 and the 4.5 rate ruling thereafter.) Therefore, the variable defined above always has the value one, and is undistinguishable from an ordinary dummy. But in extrapolating (8) beyond the period of observation, care should be taken if r_t gets too close to the ceiling, as it has done very recently.

the invention of CD's—for which Operation Twist cannot properly claim credit—to exercise its maximum effect, some twelve base points according to the estimate of equation (8).[17] It should be acknowledged, however, that our results do not effectively enable us to ascertain whether the coefficient of the dummy variable Z measures just the effect of CD's, as intended, or whether it also picks up other, yet unspecified effects of Operation Twist, including possibly psychological effects modifying expectations.

In concluding, we wish to emphasize that the results we have reported represent but the preliminary findings of a continuing study of the determinants of the maturity structure of interest rates. We can indicate, however, that these results are broadly supported by a similar study of the behavior of the spread in the corporate market between the yield on Aaa rated bonds and the commercial paper rate, both for the postwar period and for the longer span beginning with the inception of the Federal Reserve System. At this stage we feel that the following conclusions can be advanced with considerable confidence.

1. The expectation model can account remarkably well for the relation between short- and long-term rates in the United States. Furthermore, the prevailing expectations of long-term rates involve a blending of extrapolation of very recent changes and regression toward a long-term normal level.

2. There is no evidence that the maturity structure of the federal debt, or changes in this structure, exert a significant, lasting or transient, influence on the relation between the two rates.

3. The spread between long and short rates in the government market since the inception of Operation Twist was on the average some twelve base points below what one might infer from the pre-Operation Twist relation. This discrepancy seems to be largely attributable to the successive increase in the ceiling rate under Regulation Q which enabled the newly invented CD's to exercise their maximum influence.

4. Any effects, direct or indirect, of Operation Twist in narrowing the spread which further study might establish, are most unlikely to exceed some ten to twenty base points—a reduction that can be considered moderate at best.

[17] Note that if Z is interpreted along the lines of footnote 16, then for the initial period 1962-I to 1963-II when r_t remained below the old ceiling rate of 3 percent, the introduction of CD's would have contributed some to the closing of the spread even if the ceiling had not been raised. Thus for this initial span the contribution of the increase in ceiling as such must be estimated at somewhat less than 12 points, although how much less it is not really possible to say with confidence.

REFERENCES

1. S. Almon, "The Distributed Lag Between Capital Appropriations and Expenditures," *Econometrica*, Jan., 1965.

2. *Brookings Quarterly Econometric Model of the United States Economy*, J. Duesenberry, G. Fromm, L. Klein, E. Kuh, eds. (Rand McNally and North Holland, 1965).
3. J. Culbertson, "The Term Structure of Interest Rates," *Q.J.E.*, Nov., 1957.
4. F. de Leeuw, "A Model of Financial Behavior," Chap. 13 in [2].
5. J. Duesenberry, *Business Cycles and Economic Growth* (McGraw-Hill, 1958).
6. J. Durbin and G. Watson, "Testing for Serial Correlation in Least Squares Regression, II," *Biometrika*, June, 1951.
7. Z. Griliches, "A Note on Serial Correlation Bias in Estimates of Distributed Lags," *Econometrica*, Jan., 1961.
8. J. Hicks, *Value and Capital* (Oxford Univ. Press, 1939).
9. R. Kessel, *The Cyclical Behavior of the Term Structure of Interest Rates* (N.B.E.R., Occasional Paper 91, 1965).
10. J. Keynes, *A Treatise on Money*, Vol. II (Harcourt, Brace and Co., 1930).
11. ———, *The General Theory of Employment, Interest and Money* (Harcourt, Brace and Co., 1936).
12. N. Liviatan, "Consistent Estimation of Distributed Lags," *Int. Econ. Rev.* Jan., 1963.
13. B. Malkiel, "Expectations, Bond Prices and the Term Structure of Interest Rates," *Q.J.E.*, May, 1962.
14. D. Meiselman, *The Term Structure of Interest Rates* (Prentice-Hall, 1962).
15. R. Solow, "On a Family of Lag Distributions," *Econometrica*, Apr., 1960.

Errata

Page 184: footnote 3 should be shifted to the end of the paragraph in which it appears.

DEBT MANAGEMENT AND THE TERM STRUCTURE OF INTEREST RATES: AN EMPIRICAL ANALYSIS OF RECENT EXPERIENCE

FRANCO MODIGLIANI AND RICHARD SUTCH*
Massachusetts Institute of Technology

THE purpose of this paper is two-fold. We first wish to analyze theoretically the manner in which the yield structure of interest rates ought to be affected by changes in the relative maturity composition of the national debt. Second, we propose to use this theoretical model to estimate empirically the magnitude of such effects. Accordingly, in Part I we outline the Preferred Habitat Theory of the term structure and its implications for the effect of conventional debt management.[1] In Part II we present a sampling of the results from a battery of tests designed to uncover and estimate the effect of debt management during the postwar period on the maturity spectrum of yields on U.S. Treasury securities. Finally, in Part III we summarize and attempt to interpret our results.

* The authors would like to extend their thanks to Peter Buck for his assistance in preparing this paper and to Charles Bischoff, who generously made available his considerable experience in applying the Almon distributed lag estimator, without which their task would have been immeasurably more difficult.

The results reported here are part of a larger investigation which is supported in part by a grant from the Ford Foundation to the Sloan School of Management for Research in Finance, and in part by a grant from the Committee on Economic Stabilization of the Social Science Research Council.

All computations were performed at the Computation Center of the Sloan School of Management, Massachusetts Institute of Technology.

[1] The Preferred Habitat Theory was first set forth by the authors in a previously published paper (Modigliani and Sutch, 1966), and will be developed more fully in a forthcoming paper which will also present extensive empirical tests of the model.

I. THE HABITAT THEORY AND THE DETERMINATIONS OF EXPECTATIONS

In developing a theoretical framework for analyzing the effects of debt management on the maturity structure of interest rates, we rely primarily on the Preferred Habitat Theory, which was first set forth in Modigliani and Sutch (1966). The habitat theory is basically an adaptation of the expectational theory of the structure of interest rates under certainty to a world in which (1) future rates are in fact uncertain; (2) transactors, both final wealth holders and final borrowers, have definite preferences as to the length of time they want to keep their funds invested or for which they require financing (that is, they have a preferred maturity habitat); and (3) both types of transactors generally exhibit risk aversion, and hence, other things equal, would prefer to match maturities in their portfolios to their habitat so as to be sure of the return or cost. In addition to final transactors, the model also recognizes the existence of arbitragers, or intermediaries, prepared simultaneously to borrow and lend in different maturities when the differences in expected returns provide sufficient inducement to compensate for the risk involved in the operation.

The classical, or "expectation," theory of the yield structure relies on the obvious proposition that under rational behavior, perfect markets, certainty, and

569

287

negligible transaction costs, all debt instruments outstanding must have identical total returns over any given holding period, independently of their final maturity. The total returns consist of cash income (coupon payments) plus capital gains or losses due to changes in the market value of the security. One can readily derive several implications of this principle: (1) At any point in time the yield of an instrument having m periods to maturity is uniquely related to the one-period yield that is expected to prevail in each of the following m periods. (2) For long-term bonds having a market value close to par and with realistic interest rates, the relation between the yield and the future short rates can be closely approximated by a simple average of these m future short rates. (3) If the future course of the short rate were known with certainty and with negligible transaction costs, there would be a unique maturity structure of interest rates, both current and future, consistent with rational market behavior. Finally, both borrowers and lenders, regardless of habitat, would be totally indifferent as to the maturity structure of their assets or liabilities.

But we recognize that future short rates are uncertain and suggest that the expectation of them can be reasonably described by a probability distribution of possible rates. It follows that the only way that a transactor with an m-period habitat can acquire certainty of return or cost is for him to invest or borrow only through m-period instruments. Going shorter would expose him to uncertainty concerning the borrowing or lending terms prevailing for the balance of the period; going longer would expose him to uncertainty about the market value of the unexpired instrument at the time of its intended liquidation.

If transactors were indifferent to risk, then the theory implies that the m-period rate would be simply an average of the mean expected short rates over the m future periods. Arbitrage would reinforce this tendency, although the presence of substantial transaction costs would weaken it. On the other hand, when transactors are risk averse, they will prefer to invest in maturities matching their habitat unless the return expected from dealing elsewhere were sufficiently attractive to induce them to assume the risk.

If the demand for funds by those with an m-period habitat exceeds the quantity of m-period funds which lenders are willing to supply at the interest rate which equates the expected holding yields of all instruments, then the m-period rate must rise sufficiently to move some borrowers elsewhere and/or to attract additional funds from other habitats and from arbitragers, until demand and supply are brought into equilibrium. The amount by which the market-clearing m-period rate exceeds the rate which equates the yields is the "risk" premium that attaches to that maturity. Similarly, if the demand fell short of supply, the maturity would command a negative risk premium, or safety discount.

For present purposes, it is useful to exploit another implication of the pure expectations theory. The equality of yields over any holding period, and in particular over the current unit period, implies that the difference, or spread, between the cash return on an m-period bond and the "one-period" rate must be such as to offset the change in the market value of the bond in the course of the period. If the bond initially sells at par, then the cash return is the same as the bond "yield," and the increase in market value will be approximately proportional to the *decrease* in market yield in the course of the period. We have, therefore,

$$R(m) - r = \text{capital appreciation}$$
$$= \gamma \Delta R(m), \quad (1)$$

where $R(m)$ is the bond yield, r the short rate, and γ a proportionality factor (which in general depends itself on m as well as $R[m]$). The above formula can be shown to remain a good approximation even if the bond does not sell at par, but in its neighborhood, and $R(m)$ is defined as the average yield to maturity rather than the current period cash return.

Once we drop the assumption of certainty and no transaction costs, the change in yield in the course of one period, and hence the capital gain, becomes a random variable, and the symbol $\Delta R(m)$ should be thought of as a measure of central tendency of the probability distribution for expected changes in $R(m)$. The presence of uncertainty and transaction costs leads us to reformulate (1) as follows:

$$R(m) - r = \gamma \Delta R(m) + P(m), \quad (2)$$

where the last term, $P(m)$ is the difference between the premium commanded by an m-period loan and the premium prevailing in the short-term market.

According to the liquidity preference or Hicksian theory (Hicks, 1939) of interest rates, in which all lenders are implicitly assumed to have prevailingly short habitats and borrowers prevailingly long habitats, $P(m)$ should tend to rise more or less continuously with m. The habitat theory, on the other hand, asserts that there is little we can say a priori about the behavior of $P(m)$ except on the basis of definite knowledge of prevailing habitats of both lenders and

borrowers, for which we have in fact not much usable information. One may venture the guess that $P(m)$ may tend to be positive for most m, on the hunch that in the short market the supply of funds is likely to exceed the demand. However, there is no reason why it should be monotonically rising with m, and indeed it would be a rather surprising coincidence if it were so. However, $P(m)$ should be a smooth function of m, on the double grounds that habitats may not be sharply defined and that, in any event, the spillover from any maturity because of risk premium would tend to move preferably to nearby maturities. Thus if $P(m)$ were appreciably positive for a given m, we should expect it to be positive in the neighborhood of m.

From the above account we can readily infer the implications of the habitat theory concerning the effect of debt management aimed at changing the maturity composition of the outstanding supply. Clearly, an increase in the aggregate supply of debt of maturity m, matched by a decline in other maturities and not accompanied by a corresponding change in the distribution of lenders' habitats, must tend to increase the premium at maturity m and in its neighborhood relative to all other maturities and especially to those where the supply decreased. This conclusion applies to a reshuffling of the maturity composition of the national debt, provided again it is not accompanied by an offsetting movement in age composition of other primary debt. In applying these inferences to $P(m)$ of equation (2), it must be remembered that it measures the difference between the premiums for maturity m and maturity 1. Thus an increase in the supply of debt of maturity 1 drawn uniformly from other maturities should *decrease* $P(m)$ for all m greater than 1, though the effect should be most marked for long maturities and decrease toward zero as m approaches 1. A similar increase in the supply of some maturity m longer than 1 should increase P for that m and neighboring maturities, whether longer or shorter; and the effect should tend to dwindle into insignificance as we move away from m, in either direction.

In order to carry out empirical tests of the effect of debt management on the premium component of equation (2), we need somehow to measure or approximate $\Delta R(m)$, the *expected* change in the long rate, a variable which is not directly observable. This is in principle a difficult problem which has long defied a satisfactory solution. However, elsewhere we have presented (Modigliani and Sutch, 1966) an operational hypothesis of the major forces controlling the expectation of changes in the long rate and indicated how it can be empirically estimated and tested. We demonstrated that the model is remarkably effective in explaining the spread between the short and the long rate in the market for U.S. Treasury securities during the postwar period.[2] Since the rationale of our model, which is essentially an adaptation of the approach first suggested by Frank de Leeuw (1965), has already been explained in Modigliani and Sutch (1966), we shall only briefly summarize it here.

Our model of expectations basically rests on the hypothesis that the change in $R(m)$ expected at any given date is determined by the course of interest rates over the recent past. The effect of the past history of rates on the current expectation can be expressed by a linear

[2] We have also tested the model over a much longer span of time, using Moody's Aaa Corporate Bond yield and the commercial paper rate. We found equally impressive explanatory power and an amazing stability through time.

function or moving average of past rates, that is,

$$\gamma \Delta R(m)_t \simeq a + \sum_{i=0}^{n} \beta_i R_{t-i}. \quad (3)$$

The shape of the lag structure, the β_i's, reflects the way in which past experience is extrapolated. Empirically, the weighting structure is found to resemble an inverted U. This shape has the reasonable implication that the most recent trend is expected to continue for a while, but gradually the expected rates will tend to move back toward a long-run normal level which is related to an average level of rates over some past horizon.

The past rates entering in the moving average could either be long- or short-term rates, since the model itself implies that the long rate can finally be expressed as an average of short rates. Statistical considerations related to unbiased estimation as well as the criteria of goodness of fit have led us to select short rather than long rates as the component of the moving average. Making use of this specification and substituting (3) into (2), one obtains

$$R(m)_t - r_t$$

$$= a + \sum_{i=0}^{n} \beta_i r_{t-i} + P(m)_t + \eta,$$

where η is the stochastic error component. Note that we can transfer the short rate from the left- to the right-hand side of the equation without affecting the coefficient estimates or the statistical properties of the regression model. Thus

$$R_t = r_t + \sum_{i=0}^{n} \beta_i r_{t-i} + a + P_t + \eta_t$$

$$= \beta_0' r_t + \sum_{i=1}^{n} \beta_i r_{t-i} + a + P + \eta.$$

where

$$\beta_0' = 1 + \beta_0 .$$

If we initially neglect the premium component P_t by treating it as a constant plus a random component which can be merged with the error term, then all variables appearing in the equation are directly observable; their coefficients can in principle be estimated and tested for significance and a priori plausibility. The only remaining problem relates to the estimation of the coefficients of the weighted average, which contains a substantial number of terms. Reliance on standard least-square methods would lead to serious problems, both through loss of degrees of freedom and, more seriously, due to multicolinearity between the various rates appearing in the distributed lag. Fortunately, these problems can be handled quite effectively by relying on the Lagrangian interpolation technique recently adapted by Shirley Almon (1965).[3] This technique estimates the coefficients of the distributed lag as points lying on a polynomial of specified degree which is restrained to fall to zero at some point in the past, corresponding to the end point of the moving average. For our problem it was decided that a fourth-degree polynomial would be flexible enough to fit closely any a priori acceptable lag structure. With such a specification, the Almon technique requires estimating only four coefficients, the coefficients of four Almon variables, each of which is a certain

[3] The Almon-Lagrange estimator was developed by Shirley Almon and is described in her paper on the lag between appropriations and expenditures (1965). In this paper we employ a slight modification of her technique, which is described more fully in our previously cited paper. We are indebted to Charles Bischoff for the Massachusetts Institute of Technology for his assistance and advice in employing this estimator.

linear function of the n past observations.

When we employ this technique to estimate the model using fifty-seven quarterly observations from the first quarter of 1952 to the first quarter of 1966, we obtain:

$$R_t = \underset{(0.063)}{1.491} + \underset{(0.036)}{0.259} \; r_t \tag{4}$$

$$+ \sum_{i=1}^{16} \beta_i r_{t-i},$$

$$R^2 = .959, \; \bar{S}_e = .128.[4]$$

The long-term rate R in this equation is the average yield on long-term securities of the U.S. government, and r, the short-term rate, is the average market yield on three-month Treasury bills.[5] The term

$$\sum_{i=1}^{16} \beta_i r_{t-i}$$

represents the distributed lag. A finite lag of sixteen terms proved optimal, in terms of the standard error of estimate. The lag structure has been plotted in Figure 1 within a band of plus and minus one standard error.

[4] The R^2 is not corrected for degrees of freedom, but $\bar{S}_e$, the standard error of estimate, has been corrected for the loss of six degrees of freedom, including four used by the Almon estimator.

[5] The data are averages over each quarter of the monthly averages reported in the *Federal Reserve Bulletin* and are expressed in percentage terms. The bill rate, however, has been converted to a bond yield equivalent from the published bank discount basis. The equation, therefore, is not identical to equation (7) of our previous paper. The equation in the text also differs in that the period of fit includes seventeen additional observations, and has the long rate as the dependent variable, while that in the *American Economic Review* article used the spread between the long and short rates as the left-hand variable. However, since the current short rate is included among the independent variables, this switch, as we mentioned, does not affect the estimated coefficients of the least-squares estimation. One need only subtract 1.0 from the coefficient of the contemporaneous short rate to obtain the corresponding coefficient for the equation in spread form.

It is apparent from the multiple correlation coefficient and the standard error of estimate that equation (4) fits the data remarkably well. The unexplained residual error has a standard deviation of barely thirteen basis points, representing merely 3.5 per cent of the mean value of the long rate. The closeness of the fit can also be verified from Figure 2, in which we have graphed as a solid line the actual course of the spread between the long rate and the bill rate, together with the value computed from equation (4) (plotted with +'s).

An examination of the residuals of equation (4), charted at the bottom of

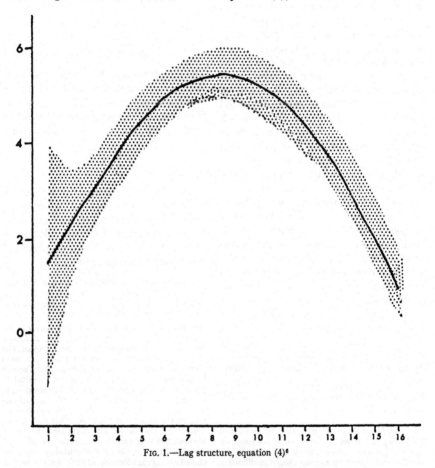

Fig. 1.—Lag structure, equation (4)[6]

[6] The coefficients plotted and their standard errors are as follows, from left to right:

.014 (.027), .022 (.012), .030 (.007), .038 (.007),
.004 (.007), .049 (.006), .053 (.005), .055 (.005),
.054 (.006), .052 (.006), .049 (.006), .043 (.005),
.036 (.006), .028 (.007), .019 (.007), .010 (.006).

the graph on a magnified scale, indicates that the error term, though small, exhibits pronounced serial correlation,[7] suggesting the influence of some further systematic and slowly changing forces affecting the spread. In terms of our model, these residuals would reflect in part the influence of variables other than the past history of rates on the market's expectations of the future of the long rate and, additionally, forces leading to variations in the size of the risk premium differential between the long and the short market. Such forces could include variations in the maturity structure of the outstanding supply brought about by changes in the age composition of the government debt.

A test of this hypothesis is the central task of this paper and will be pursued systematically in Part II. Before embarking on this analysis, we should be

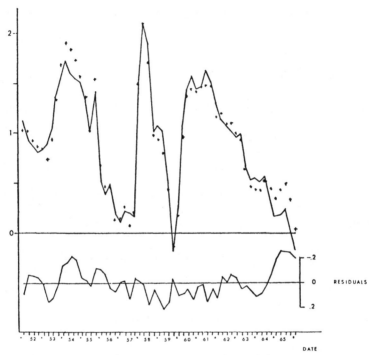

Fig. 2.—Actual and predicted values of spread between long- and short-term rates

part the influence of variables other than the past history of rates on the market's expectations of the future of the long rate and, additionally, forces leading to variations in the size of the risk premium differential between the long and the short market. Such forces could include variations in the maturity structure of the government debt.

[7] That is, they are not randomly distributed through time. Instead, a strong continuity is reflected in a low Durbin-Watson statistic of 0.582.

aware of the fact that the extremely close fit obtained in equation (4) already sets a significant limit on the likely quantitative impact of debt management, at least on the very long rate. With the unexplained error in (4) below thirteen basis points, it would seem that changes in the age composition of the debt of the size experienced in the period of observation could not have affected the spread by more than a few basis points!

The Term Structure of Interest Rates   **293**

II. EMPIRICAL TESTS OF POSTWAR EXPERIENCE

The proposition that the fiscal-monetary authority has at least some power to affect the yield structure by changing the age composition of the outstanding debt is one that appears to be broadly accepted at the present time.[8] Indeed, this conclusion which we have derived from the habitat theory is equally implied by other widely accepted theories of the term structure. In particular, the Hicksian expectation-cum-liquidity-preference model (Hicks, 1939), which currently is probably the most widely accepted, implies that lengthening of the outstanding debt should tend to increase the spread between the short and longer rate.

A number of studies in recent years have endeavored to substantiate this conclusion empirically and to provide quantitative estimates of the effects, which might provide a guide to policy makers.[9]

Several of these studies have found some evidence in support of the conclusion, but, as far as we can see, even where favorable evidence has turned up, it has been fairly tenuous, and the authors have generally not been inclined to claim that it was very conclusive.[10]

A number of tests on the effect of the maturity structure of the debt on the relation between the long- and short-term rates were conducted by the present authors in connection with the analysis reported in Modigliani and Sutch (1966). As mentioned (p. 191), the results on the whole were surprisingly negative, al-though space prevented us from presenting the detailed tests substantiating this conclusion. In the present paper we begin by reviewing those results, together with those from a number of additional tests conducted since. We then proceed to examine the outcome of an extensive investigation on the entire yield spectrum by focusing on the behavior of yields for several selected maturities.

The basic approach we follow consists of adding to equations of type (4) various relevant measures of the maturity composition of the publicly held marketable debt issued by the federal government, and examining whether these variables appear to produce effects both quantitatively and statistically significant and in accord with what our theoretical framework would lead us to expect.

It should be stressed immediately that this approach has rather serious shortcomings. Our model suggests that debt management should affect the yield structure through its effect on the age composition of the *total* outstanding supply of primary securities, which includes the debt of federal, state, local, and foreign governments, as well as domestic and foreign private issues. Because other debt instruments might not be perfect substitutes for the federal debt, the yield curve for government securities might additionally be *directly* influenced by the specific composition of

[8] There are, of course, exceptions to this statement. For instance, Meiselman (1962) appears to be rather skeptical about the extent to which the yield structure will be affected by changes in the age composition of the outstanding issues.

[9] Some idea of the approaches employed and the conclusions reached can be found in Okun (1963), Wallace (1964), de Leeuw (1965), and Scott (1965).

[10] One possible exception is Scott (1965), whose analysis based on monthly observations for 1952–59 concludes that the average length to maturity of the marketable debt has a significant positive effect on the spread between the long and the short rate. His estimated effect is 3.5 basis points for an increase in the average maturity of one month. The relevant coefficient in his equation has a *t*-ratio of close to four. As will appear below, our model, which allows explicitly for the effect of expectations and fits the data substantially better than his equation, leads to results which are at odds with this conclusion.

the federal debt, though one would expect this influence to be secondary. Unfortunately, there seems to be no satisfactory way at present to compute reliable measures of the age composition of primary debt other than that of the federal government. The approach we are forced to use assumes implicitly that the age composition of the federal debt is a satisfactory proxy for the total. This is

of preferred habitats of lenders and of private borrowers, but again we have not been able to devise any operational solution to this problem. Over the fifteen-year period covered, such shifts might have been appreciable, though we have no specific reason for suspecting that such was the case. In any event, this consideration also suggests that results relating to the effect of short-run *changes*

TABLE 1

DEBT EFFECTS ON THE RELATION BETWEEN THE YIELD ON LONG-TERM
GOVERNMENT SECURITIES AND THE TREASURY BILL RATE

VARIABLE	COEFFICIENT AND ITS STANDARD ERROR ON	
	Level	Change
(1) Average length to maturity (years)......	−0.048 (0.042)	−0.098 (0.076)
(2) Proportion of short....................	0.178 (0.385)	1.715 (0.777)*
(3) Proportion of intermediate I...........	1.164 (0.334)*	−0.714 (1.048)
(4) Proportion of intermediate II..........	−1.415 (0.323)*	−2.694 (1.186)*
(5) Proportion of long....................	0.215 (1.440)	−1.535 (2.722)
(6) Proportion of short I..................	−1.283 (0.866)	−1.241 (0.739)
(7) Proportion of short II.................	0.432 (0.386)	2.204 (0.605)*
(8) Ratio of long to short I...............	0.160 (0.136)	0.173 (0.134)

* Coefficient is more than twice its standard error.

clearly a tenuous assumption, even though in the period under study the federal debt represented a very large (but declining) proportion of the total. On the other hand, for the purpose of measuring short-run changes in the age composition, reliance on the federal debt may be less objectionable since there is some evidence that the composition of the non-federal debt is reasonably stable in the short run.

It would also be desirable in our tests to find ways of controlling for the possible effect of changes in the distribution

in supply may be more reliable than those relating to levels.

Table 1 presents the results of a number of tests, each of which consists of introducing a presumably relevant measure of the age composition of the federal debt into equation (4). The results presented are the estimated coefficients of the debt variables, and, in parentheses beneath them, their standard errors. For each variable we report in the first column the effect of the level and in the second column the effect of its rate of change, as measured by the first difference. We do not present the coefficient estimates of the expectational variables of equation (4), since in no case does the introduction of a debt variable materially alter the point estimates or their significance. All results presented were based on ordinary least-squares regressions containing fifty-three quarterly observations spanning the period from the second quarter of 1952 to the second quarter of 1965, the last date for which a number of our debt variables are available.

As a check, every test presented has been repeated for a shorter period terminating with the last quarter of 1961. This was done to test the stability in time of any of the results, and also because of a number of developments in the capital markets dating from early 1962 which conceivably might have altered the expectational relationship or produced spurious resuts.[11] The regressions have also been repeated for both periods with seasonal dummy variables to control for any spurious effect that a seasonal pattern in the debt composition might otherwise introduce. Generally, we found very similar results for all these variations. Accordingly, we do not report the coefficient estimates for the shorter period or those with seasonals separately, but we shall mention any instances in which the results not presented are significantly at odds with those in the tables.

The first test we applied was to introduce the most commonly used measure of the maturity composition of the debt, namely, the average length to maturity. The measure we have employed differs from the published data in that the debt to which it refers includes only marketable debt in the hands of the public, rather than all outstanding debt.[12]

A lengthening of the average maturity should presumably tend to increase the long rate relative to the short one, and hence the coefficient of this variable should be positive, and so should be the coefficient of its change. In fact, both coefficients are *negative*, though not large relative to their standard error. This is clearly a rather surprising result.

It may be objected that the average age to maturity is not a very sensible summary measure for our purpose. This measure will be equally affected when a just-maturing issue is replaced by a two-year issue, as when a forty-year issue is swapped for a forty-two-year one. Yet many would hold that the first transaction would have a considerably larger effect on the yield structure than the second. This shortcoming may be especially pronounced for the more recent period when the Treasury has been relying on advance refunding techniques, which will tend to lengthen the average maturity, although operating primarily within the relatively long end of the spectrum.[13]

An alternative, and for our purpose

---

[11] Among these developments we might mention the launching of "Operation Twist"—the purported attempt to use available policy instruments to raise short rates relative to long rates and thus twist the entire term structure—the rapid expansion of the volume of negotiable certificates of deposit (the CD) since 1961, and also the more active manipulation of the maximum interest rate ceiling on time deposits by the Federal Reserve under "Regulation Q." For a discussion of the effect of Operation Twist and the influence of Regulation Q and the CD on the term structure, see Modigliani and Sutch (1966).

[12] The difference is the amount of debt which is held by the Federal Reserve Banks and in federal government trust accounts. The measure, which can be computed from published data in the *Treasury Bulletin*, was made available to us through the research staff of the Board of Governors of the Federal Reserve System.

[13] These and other objections to the use of the average length to maturity are spelled out in Malkiel (1962) and Luckett (1965).

more useful, measure of age composition may be provided by the proportion of the total volume of outstanding debt accounted for by issues falling within a specified maturity range—for example, the proportion of the total debt that will mature in one year or less. A difficulty with such a measure is that it will be subject to erratic jumps when an issue crosses the boundary line between maturity classes. It would not be reasonable, of course, to expect significant changes in yield patterns from one month to the next simply because a single issue crosses some conventional boundary.

These problems can be overcome by computing a weighted average in such a way that it gives a specific issue larger and larger fractional weights as it approaches the maturity class, full weight while it is within the boundaries, and then declining weights as it moves out of and away from the maturity range. Four such weighted averages have been computed by the Flow of Funds Section of the Federal Reserve and generously made available to us. The first series consists of the "proportion of short debt," which is defined to include all securities maturing within one year plus proportions of those maturing between one and two years, the proportions declining linearly from 100 per cent for one-year maturities to zero for two-year maturities. A second series, labeled "intermediate I" debt, consists of all issues maturing in two to four years plus that proportion of securities maturing in one to two years which is not included in the "short" class, plus a fraction of those maturing in four to six years, again declining from 100 per cent to zero. A third class defined as "intermediate II" debt includes all maturities between six and eight years and proportions of those aged from four to six and eight to twelve. Finally, the

proportion of long debt is defined as all maturities over twelve years with proportions of those between eight and twelve.

These variables have been entered into the basic equation both singly and in various combinations as proportions of the total outstanding debt, as changes in those proportions, as percentage changes, and the like. Rows (2)–(5) of Table 1 give the coefficients and the respective standard errors for eight of these variables, when each is entered separately.

The habitat theory suggests that the most relevant of these variables should be the proportion of short debt— row (2)—and the proportion of long debt—row (5). An increase in the proportion of short debt should tend to reduce the yield differential, or spread, while an increase in the proportion of long debt should increase it. Hence the coefficient of the first of these variables should have a negative sign, and the same should be true for its rate of change. Instead, the estimated coefficient for this variable is seen to be *positive*, though of negligible magnitude, and the coefficient of the rate of change is also positive and *not* so negligible. The proportion of long debt has the expected positive sign but is quite insignificant and of negligible magnitude. It implies that if the proportion of long debt is increased by 1 per cent of the total debt outstanding—roughly equivalent to $1.5 billion for the period under review—the spread would increase by a mere two-tenths of one basis point! Even more disappointing is the fact that the change in the proportion of long debt has a negative coefficient.

Looking at the four coefficients in rows (3) and (4) of Table 1, we find somewhat larger entries, three of them with t-ratios in excess of two. But these coefficient estimates make little sense. It is difficult to imagine why debt in the intermediate class I—basically the one-to-five-year range—should have much of an effect on the spread between the very long- and the short-term rate. Furthermore, since the range of maturity in question is rather close to the short end of the spectrum, if anything we should expect an increase in the supply in this range to tend to *reduce* the spread. Instead, the sign of the coefficient is *positive*, and though the rate of change has a negative sign, it is totally insignificant. If one were prepared to rationalize this positive coefficient on the ground that an increase in supply in any class other than the shortest should increase the spread, then one should expect an even stronger positive effect for the proportion of intermediate debt II—basically, the five-to-ten-year range. But instead this coefficient is perversely negative. Thus, with the coefficients of the two presumably most relevant variables negligible, or having the "wrong" sign, and the other coefficients making little sense, the only possible conclusion one seems justified in drawing is that, so far as these tests are concerned, there is absolutely no evidence to support the predicted effect of the age composition of outstanding debt on the spread.

We have carried out quite a few additional tests, using several of the variables in Table 1 simultaneously, for example, the level and rate of change in the same class, the level in different classes, and other combinations. In no case do we find the coefficient of the two theoretically most relevant variables significant and with the right sign, or a sensible pattern for the other coefficients.

It was this battery of tests that supported the negative report in our earlier paper. These no doubt disturbing con-clusions have been criticized by our discussants, who have looked for possible shortcomings in the design of our tests. In particular, Malkiel (1966) suggested that our "short-term" class included too wide a spectrum of maturities. He would predict that it is the relative supply of "very short term issues" that would exert the greatest influence on the short rate and hence on the spread. He mentions in particular the fact that "the relative supply of short term securities did increase in the early part of the [Operation Twist] period" as evidence of implementation of that operation.

Since this criticism has a priori plausibility, and it seemed conceivable that significant changes might have occurred over time in the age distribution within our "short-term" class, we have proceeded to construct a series of very short-term debt, which we have defined as that portion of the short-term debt which matures within three months. This enables us to break down the short-term debt into two subclasses which we label, respectively, "short I" and "short II." The percentage distribution of outstanding debt between these two classes, as well as the remaining three classes defined earlier, is exhibited in Figure 3, on which we shall comment soon.

On a priori grounds, one should expect that an increase in the proportion of either short I or short II debt should tend to reduce the spread; but if Malkiel's conjecture is correct, short I should have a distinctly more powerful effect. An empirical test of these propositions is provided in rows (6) and (7) of Table 1. The results on the whole appear favorable to the hypothesis, though they are disappointingly shaky. The coefficient of the very short-term debt is negative, and so is that of its rate of change; but neither coefficient exceeds by much its standard error. And quantitatively, the effects are again quite small. An increase in the proportion of short I debt by 1 per cent of the total debt would reduce the spread by barely over one basis point. Or, to increase the spread by ten

rity should be more affected by the supply of debt in that maturity range, one might infer that the *spread* between the long and short rate would be most responsive to a variable that measures the relative change between the two matu-

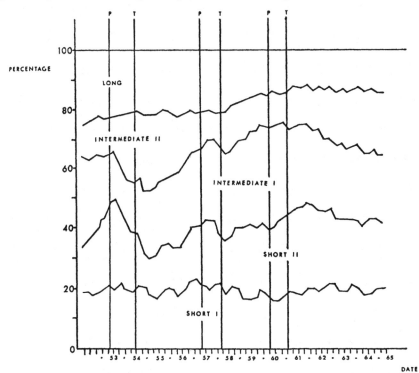

FIG. 3.—Percentage distribution of U.S. government marketable debt by maturity class

basis points would require increasing the volume of very short debt by some 50 per cent above its current standing. The coefficient of the proportion of short II, on the other hand, turns up with the wrong sign and appears insignificantly small.[14]

In row (8) of Table 1 we present the results of a test which one might expect to be more powerful than those presented so far. Since the yield in any given matu-

rity classes, such as the ratio of the proportion of long to the proportion of

[14] This positive sign might be spurious if there were a tendency for the proportion of Short I and II to move against each other—a distinct possibility which would also bias toward zero the coefficient of Short I debt. When both variables are used simultaneously to control for this possibility, the coefficient of Short I remains essentially unchanged at −1.29 (though the standard error falls somewhat, to 0.68), while the coefficient of Short II becomes essentially zero (0.09, with a standard error of 0.30). Again, the result is in the right direction, but far from impressive.

very short debt. Unfortunately, even this test fails to produce any solid evidence of significant supply effects. While the coefficient has the expected positive sign, it is again rather small, both absolutely and in relation to the standard error.[15]

The failure of the very short debt variable to produce significant results is disappointing but might be dismissed by pointing to the striking stability in the postwar period of the proportion of this debt to the total volume in the hands of the public. In Figure 3 we plot cumulatively the percentage composition of the

TABLE 2

MEANS AND STANDARD DEVIATIONS OF FIVE
COMPONENTS OF MARKETABLE DEBT
1962–65

Component	Mean	Standard Deviation
Proportion of short I........	.1954	.018
Proportion of short II.......	.2183	.049
Proportion of intermediate I..	.2501	.047
Proportion of intermediate II	.1565	.046
Proportion of long.........	.1797	.041

debt for our five maturity classes. It is evident that the short I debt has much less variability than any of the other components. The proportion ranges from a low of 15.7 per cent in the fourth quarter of 1960 to a maximum of 24.0 per cent in the second quarter of 1957. It is also worth noting that it showed hardly any increase in the Operation Twist period. In the first quarter of 1962 it stood at 20.2, and a year later it reached a peak

[15] In the second quarter of 1965, the proportion of Short I debt was 20.4 per cent of the total, while the long-term debt accounted for 14.2 per cent. If the government had moved 1 per cent of the total debt from the short to the long end, the coefficients estimated would imply that the spread would have widened about three basis points the first quarter and then, with no further changes, would have fallen back to about 1.5 points above the previous level.

of 21.3 per cent. Thereafter, it declined, though negligibly. Thus, even in terms of this measure, there is little evidence that the debt-management tool was ever seriously employed in the pursuit of Operation Twist.

The other components of the debt, on the other hand, show a good deal more variation, as can be verified from Figure 3 and from the summary statistics in Table 2. On the whole, the fact that these tests fail to uncover any significant effect of debt variables on the spread between the long and the short rate cannot be brushed off as merely resulting from absence of movements in the composition of the debt. Nor can it be argued that we are unable to uncover evidence because of a strong contracyclical debt-management policy, a possibility envisaged by Smith (1966). If the Treasury were to increase "liquidity" by shortening the average length to maturity in recessions, when short rates are typically low and the spread large, we might find a shortening of maturities associated with high spreads, even though the real effect was to prevent them from being even higher than they actually were. Also marked on Figure 3 are the business cycle peaks and troughs of the National Bureau of Economic Research (NBER), and we can see little evidence of a contracyclical policy in any of the three contraction periods. Both the proportions of short I and short II actually fell between third quarter 1953 and third quarter 1954. The 1958 recession saw the proportion of short I plus short II debt fall from 42.7 per cent of the total national debt to 38.8 per cent. The proportion of very short debt did increase between the fourth quarter of 1957 and the first quarter of 1958; however, every other quarter of that contraction showed a decline in the proportion of short I. Moreover, the average length to maturity increased from 60.6 months to 64.8 months between the NBER peak in July, 1957, and the end of the contraction in April of the next year. Again, in the last recession, the average length of the publicly held debt was increased, this time by 2.5 months, although in this case the proportion of combined short I and II did increase.

On the whole, these results appear rather negative, even if not unqualifiedly so. But before we attempt to draw conclusions, we propose to review the findings of some further tests, utilizing a body of data which includes twelve specific points on the yield curve for government securities. The attempt is worthwhile for at least two reasons:

1. The average yield on long-term government bonds, which we examined above, is not a rate defined for any given maturity, but is rather an average of all bonds over 10, 12, or 15 years, depending on the period. Conceivably, the changing maturity composition of the long-term average itself is obscuring the effect of debt operations on the yield curve.

2. It may be that the effect of debt management is more readily ascertainable on the intermediate maturities.

Morgan Guaranty Trust Company, one of the largest dealers in government securities, keeps daily records of their own transactions in Treasury issues. From these data they prepare each month a plot of the average yield to maturity over the month for every issue by its length to maturity. A smooth curve is drawn through the points, and rates are read from this curve for one, two, three, up to twelve years to maturity. Morgan has very generously made these data available to us, and we have used them to prepare quarterly averages for the period from 1952 through 1965. In our tests, we have generally made use of the data for each of the twelve individual maturities; however, to save space, we limit ourselves to giving results for only four selected maturities—2, 4, 8, and 12 years. Because of the remarkable "continuity" in all of the results we have found, the interested reader can, to a very good approximation, estimate the results for the missing maturities by interpolating between those given.

As in the case of the long rate, we can deduce from the habitat theory that the spread between each of these yields and the short rate should again be related to the expected capital appreciation and hence be an increasing function of the expected change in the yield. By again relying on the notion that the expected change in yield is systematically related to the past history of rates, we are led to the hypothesis that for each maturity—aside from variables affecting the risk premium—the spread can be accounted for by the current short rate and a moving average of past short rates. This implies, finally, that the rate itself should be explainable by an equation of type (4) up to an error component reflecting other forces impinging on expectations as well as forces affecting the size of the risk premium (or discount) for that maturity. This hypothesis is well supported by the Morgan data, as indicated by the following results obtained for the period 1952 I to 1966 I.

$$R(2)_t = \begin{array}{c} 0.409 \\ (0.114) \end{array} + \begin{array}{c} 0.852 \ r_t \\ (0.066) \end{array}$$

$$+ \sum_{i=1}^{16} \beta_i r_{t-i} \qquad \begin{array}{c} R^2 = .943 \\ \bar{S}_e = .232 \end{array} ; \qquad (5-2)$$

$$R(4)_t = \begin{array}{c} 0.726 \\ (0.114) \end{array} + \begin{array}{c} 0.661 \ r_t \\ (0.066) \end{array}$$

$$+ \sum_{i=1}^{16} \beta_i r_{t-i} \qquad \begin{array}{c} R^2 = .931 \\ \bar{S}_e = .233 \end{array} ; \qquad (5-4)$$

$$R(8)_t = 1.064 + 0.465 \, r_t$$
$$(0.085) \quad (0.050)$$

$$+ \sum_{i=1}^{16} \beta_i r_{t-i} \qquad \begin{array}{l} R^2 = .949 \\ \bar{S}_e = .174 \end{array} ; \qquad (5\text{--}8)$$

$$R(12)_t = 1.234 + 0.368 \, r_t$$
$$(0.072) \quad (0.042)$$

$$+ \sum_{i=1}^{16} \beta_i r_{t-i} \qquad \begin{array}{l} R^2 = .958 \\ \bar{S}_e = .146 \end{array} . \qquad (5\text{--}12)$$

In each case, it is found that the length of the distributed lag that yields the most satisfactory result is on the order of sixteen quarters. Accordingly, this is the length used in estimating the lag structures plotted in Figure 4.[16] Our concern

[16] It should be noted that this finding, as well as the striking similarity of the weighting structures, is by no means accidental. It can be shown that this is precisely what one should find if (1) the relation between various rates is in fact controlled by expectations about future rates; (2) expectations of future rates are based on an extrapolation of past history, according to a stable pattern measured by the weighting structure; and (3) expectations are consistent in the sense that if the expectations held at date t for date $t + 1$ prove correct, then the expectation held for later dates, $t + 2$, $t + 3$, and so on, will not change between dates t and $t + 1$. This last assumption, it will be noted, is essentially the base of Meiselman's model (1962). Work in progress indicates that our weighting structure roughly satisfies consistency requirements. It may also be noted that the explanatory power of the four equations reported above, whether measured by the standard error of the residuals or by R^2, tends to decline as we move to shorter maturities. This finding is not surprising in the light of our model. It is reasonable to suppose, in fact, that expectations about the course of interest rates in the near future should reflect a good deal more information than is provided by the past history of rates appearing in the weighted average. On the other hand, when it comes to the more distant future, the past may still tend to be regarded as providing the most useful guide. Since the influence of nearby expectations dominates the shorter rates and becomes less and less important as we move to longer rates, it is understandable that the weighted average term should prove more useful in explaining the behavior of long-term rates than of short-term ones. Actually, neither R^2 nor the $\bar{S}_e$ is a reliable measure of the extent to which this deterioration occurs because both statistics depend also on the con-

now will be that of testing whether and to what extent the residual error of the above equations can be accounted for by measures of the age composition of the supply of government debt developed above.

The first test, whose outcome is summarized in Table 3, is essentially a replication for each maturity of the last test we reported for the long rate in Table 1. Since each rate should be most affected by the behavior of supply in its own maturity range, we should expect the *spread* between each of our selected maturities and the short rate to be significantly and positively associated with the ratio of the supply in that maturity to the supply in the shortest maturity. The denominator of this ratio, the supply in the shortest maturity, can presumably be best measured by the proportion of short debt I, that is, with three months or less to maturity. For the numerator of the ratio, we choose from among the remaining series that one which most nearly matches the given maturity. In the case of the twelve-year rate, the appropriate series would clearly seem to be the proportion of long-term debt. The result of that test is shown in row (1) of the table. As indicated in the stub on the left, the dependent variable in this row is the spread between the twelve-year and the three-month rate. The entry in the first column is the coefficient of the debt variable—in the present instance, the ratio of the volume of long-term debt to short debt I—when added to equation

tribution of the current short rate, which tends to rise as the maturity shortens. A more useful statistic may be provided by the "net" contribution of the moving average term, as measured by the proportion of variance not explained by the short rate, which is explained by the entire moving average term. This proportion is, respectively, .83 for the twelve-year rate, .75 for the eight-year rate, .48 for the four-year rate, and .22 for the two-year rate.

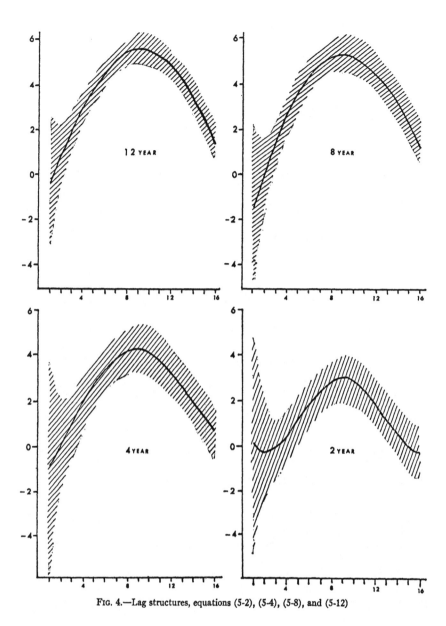

Fig. 4.—Lag structures, equations (5-2), (5-4), (5-8), and (5-12)

(5–12). The entry in the second column is the coefficient of the rate of change of the variable. (As in Table 1, we do not give the remaining coefficients of the equation, since they were in no case significantly affected.) The coefficient of the debt variable has the anticipated positive sign; however, as in the case of the long-term rate, it is far from significant. Similar comments apply to the coefficient of the rate of change reported in the second column of row (1).

able size, and with t-ratios in excess of five; furthermore, in the second column it appears that the rate of change also has a respectable effect in the hypothesized direction.[17]

Because the short-term rate has exhibited in the past a modest seasonal pattern and the same is true of the proportion of short debt I, it is conceivable that the coefficients of Table 3, which are clearly not very reliably estimated as one can infer from the standard errors,

TABLE 3

DEBT EFFECTS FOR SPECIFIC MATURITIES

MATURITY	VARIABLE	COEFFICIENT OF	
		Level	Change
(1) 12 years..........	Ratio of long to short I debt	0.189 (0.162)	0.224 (0.158)
(2) 8 years..........	Ratio of intermediate II to short I debt	−0.234 (0.105)*	0.063 (0.209)
(3) 4 years..........	Ratio of intermediate I to short I debt	0.469 (0.084)*	0.402 (0.174)*
(4) 2 years..........	Ratio of intermediate I to short I debt	5.03 (0.082)*	0.408 (0.175)

* Coefficient is more than twice its standard error.

In row (2) the dependent variable is the spread between the eight-year and the short rate. Accordingly, the numerator of the variable used was chosen to be the proportion of intermediate debt II, which is basically debt in the six-to-ten-year range. Here even the sign is wrong, while for the rate of the change in the second column, the coefficient is totally insignificant. In the next two rows, applying the test to the four- and two-year rates, the numerator of the ratio is the proportion of intermediate debt I— covering basically the maturity range of one to five years. Here for the first time we find statistically significant results in accord with expectations: the coefficients have the predicted sign, are of respect-

could be distorted by these seasonal influences, even though the seasonals are quite mild. Accordingly, the same relations were re-estimated with the addition of seasonal dummies.[18] In no case were the results materially changed, except that for the two- and four-year

[17] The coefficients imply that if in the second quarter of 1965 1 per cent of the debt had been moved from the shortest maturity to maturities in the one-to-five-year range, then the two-year spread would increase nearly ten basis points in the first quarter and then fall back to about 5.5 basis points above its previous level. The four-year spread would settle to about five points above its previous level after an initial increase of nine points.

[18] Because the seasonal pattern in the bill rate has nearly disappeared after 1961, seasonals were separately estimated for the two periods. In every case, however, the mean of the four seasonal constants was restrained to be equal for all years.

yield the estimate of the effect of the rate of change of the debt variable is reduced by some 20 per cent (and the standard error also rises, cutting the *t*-ratio to around 1.5).[19]

A considerable number of further tests have been carried out utilizing the various measures of age structure described above, though none of these other tests is, in our view, as sensitive and reliable as that reported in Table 3. This battery of tests has, on the whole, proved as disappointing and inconclusive as those we have reported above, and we shall not comment on them further. Instead we turn to an over-all evaluation of our results in the next section.

III. EVALUATION OF THE RESULTS AND THEIR IMPLICATIONS

In summary, we feel that the investigation attempted in this paper has provided some quite positive and significant results, some less clear-cut ones, and a few rather negative ones which raise more questions than they settle. Let us briefly review the grounds for these assertions.

At the positive level, the analysis of this paper, when combined with that presented earlier (Modigliani and Sutch, 1966), seems to us to provide impressive empirical evidence for the proposition that the relation between rates for different maturities can be largely accounted for by our Preferred Habitat model or

related variants of the expectations hypothesis. The analysis also provides strong evidence that the prevailing relevant expectations of future rates are, to a surprising extent, shaped in a predictable and stable fashion by the history of interest rates over several past years. The estimated weighting structures indicate that the market tends to expect a short-run continuation of recent trends, together with a longer-run regression toward a long-run "normal" level determined by past experience.

As for risk premiums (or discounts), the habitat model holds that they should reflect the relative strength of the demand and supply for funds in various maturities as controlled by the distribution of preferred habitats of both primary borrowers and primary lenders, by arbitrage operations of intermediaries and by debt management. Accordingly, we have attempted to establish whether variations over time in the spread, not accounted for by our expectation model, were systematically related to the maturity structure of the outstanding supply of the marketable federal debt. It was hoped that this analysis could throw light on the sensitivity of differential premiums to variations in supply and, more specifically, on the effectiveness of debt management as a device for controlling the yield structure, especially the relation between long- and short-term rates. Our findings on this score must be rated as prevailingly negative, though not uniformly so. On the whole, they suggest that the responsiveness of the rate structure to variations in the age composition of the national debt outstanding was at best weak, even in a period in which the national debt was large, both in absolute and relative size.

To some extent this result was foreshadowed by the finding that the be-

---

[19] For the sake of completeness, we note that for the subperiod ending in fourth quarter 1961, the results of these tests did not appear very consistent with those reported above for the entire period. In particular, for the two- and four-year rate, the level of the debt variable had a much smaller and not significant coefficient. However, when the test was carried out with seasonal dummies, the inconsistencies largely disappear; in particular, the coefficients for the two- and four-year rate are again almost identical to those reported. This finding is not entirely surprising since, as noted in n. 18 above, seasonal patterns were distinctly more in evidence up to 1961.

havior of the spread could be accounted for by the expectational part of the hypothesis up to an error which is surprisingly small, particularly for the longer maturities. This suggests that there is relatively little left to be explained by other variables, including debt management.

On the basis of a rather extensive battery of tests based on a variety of measures of age composition, we have been able to uncover persistent and fairly convincing evidence that at least variations in the supply of debt in the intermediate range, especially in the one-to-five-year range, tended to produce moderate variations in the spread for intermediate maturities, that is, maturities in the corresponding age class. On the other hand, we have been unable to uncover solid or even suggestive evidence that the age composition of the supply affects significantly longer rates as measured by the average long-term rate or the twelve-year rate.

It is hard to tell precisely what interpretation should be placed on these negative findings. We are not prepared to take them as conclusive evidence that the long end of the market is insensitive to supply effects. Such a conclusion would be hard to reconcile with the indications of substantial risk differential uncovered by other authors and supported by our own research, and also with the evidence uncovered for the intermediate range, and shorter markets. We are rather inclined to interpret our inability to uncover significant effects as reflecting in good part serious shortcomings of our test procedure, to which reference was made earlier.

The supply effects our model predicts are related to the age distribution of the *total* supply, and the government debt is by no means all or even an overwhelming component of the total. Hence the movements in supply of government debt measured by our variables could very well be swamped by movements in the supply of private, state, local, and foreign securities. Indeed, it is even conceivable that the Treasury in its endeavor to hold down interest costs could have been led to vary the supply of governments in a fashion tending to offset movements in these other components. Unfortunately, this is a shortcoming which cannot be readily remedied with presently available data and might be hard to remedy even if one were prepared to make a large investment in new data collection and estimation.

An admittedly superficial examination of the available information suggests that the shortcomings of our measures may be particularly serious in the case of long-term debt. Our series measuring the proportion of long-term debt exhibits a steady downward drift to the end of 1961 and very little, though prevailingly upward, change since. This movement reflects, in part, variations in the total debt, the denominator of our variable. In terms of actual dollars, the amount of long-term government debt outstanding declined from $31 billion in 1952 to about $19 billion at the end of 1961, and rose back to $23 billion at the end of our period. Indications are that these are not very large figures relative to the total outstanding long-term debt, and that the total outstanding long-term debt may well have *risen* (and appreciably) over the period. Under these conditions, the insignificant effect found for our measure cannot be given much weight. The fact that even the rate of change of our variable comes out with the wrong sign might be more disturbing were it not for the fact that the short-run variations have been really quite modest. One may conjecture that the more significant and well-behaved results obtained with intermediate debt I might reflect the fact that the supply in this maturity segment—ranging from $36 billion at the beginning, down to $17 billion in 1954, up again to $52 billion around 1960, and down to $35 billion at the end—may constitute a more significant and representative component of the total supply and its movement.

Grounds for doubting that supply effects are totally absent are also suggested by specific episodes, such as the experience with pegging of the rate structure during the war and partial pegging in the pre-accord period. Cursory examination of the events of those years suggests that the pegging was feasible, though it necessitated large accommodating changes in the age structure of the publicly held supply. These facts seem inconsistent with the pure expectation hypothesis and are consistent instead with the implications of the habitat (and liquidity preference) model that the yield structure can be modified, within limits, by sufficiently large changes in the composition of supply.

Needless to say, the arguments advanced in the above three paragraphs to "rationalize" some of our more puzzling results are no more than conjectures and not an adequate basis for conclusions. Yet they do provide a basis for an earnest warning against overinterpreting our negative results.

But having sounded such a warning, we must equally warn the reader not to dismiss our results outright as shedding no light at all on the question under investigation. Our results *do* imply that the structure of yields is not very responsive to variations in the age composition of government debt, at least of the order of magnitude experienced in the period studied. Whether this result reflects a large responsiveness of both lenders and borrowers to differentials in expected returns and/or a high degree of substitutability between government and other debt, it suggests that the effectiveness of debt management may be rather limited, much more so than we at least would have suspected when we first embarked on this study.

REFERENCES

Almon, S. "The Distributed Lag between Capital Appropriations and Expenditures," *Econometrica* (January, 1965).

De Leeuw, F. "A Model of Financial Behavior," in J. Duesenberry, G. Fromm, L. Klein, and E. Kuh (eds.). *Brookings Quarterly Econometric Model of the United States Economy.* Chicago: Rand McNally & Co., 1965.

Hicks, J. *Value and Capital.* Oxford: Oxford Univ. Press, 1939.

Luckett, D. "On Maturity Measures of the Debt," *Q.J.E.* (May, 1965).

Malkiel, B. "Expectations, Bond Prices and the Term Structure of Interest Rates," *Q.J.E.* (May, 1962).

———. Discussion of Modigliani and Sutch (1966), *A.E.R.* (May, 1966).

Meiselman, D. *The Term Structure of Interest Rates.* Englewood Cliffs, N.J.: Prentice-Hall, Inc., 1962.

Modigliani, F., and Sutch, R. "Innovations in Interest Rate Policy," *A.E.R.* (May, 1966).

Okun, A. "Monetary Policy, Debt Management and Interest Rates: A Quantitative Appraisal," in Commission on Money and Credit. *Stabilization Policies.* Englewood Cliffs, N.J.: Prentice-Hall, Inc., 1962.

Scott, R. "Liquidity and the Term Structure of Interest Rates," *Q.J.E.* (February, 1965).

Smith, W. Discussion of Modigliani and Sutch (1966), *A.E.R.* (May, 1966).

Wallace, N. "The Term Structure of Interest Rates and the Maturity Composition of the Federal Debt." Unpublished doctoral dissertation, Univ. of Chicago, 1964.

Errata

Page 571, equation (1): "$R(m) - r = $ capital appreciation" should read "$R(m) - r = $ capital depreciation."

Page 574, footnote 6: the first coefficient in the second line of coefficients should be ".044" rather than ".004."

Inflation, Rational Expectations and the Term Structure of Interest Rates

By Franco Modigliani and Robert J. Shiller[1]

In a number of recent papers [11] [12],[2] it has been shown that, for the United States, the behaviour of the term structure of interest rates can be explained remarkably well by combining the "Preferred Habitat" version of the Expectation Theory with a simple and readily tractable model of the formation of expectations, a model in which expected future rates are represented by a linear function of past rates.

The purpose of the present paper is to generalize that approach and to strengthen the evidence supporting it in two major directions.

First, we endeavour to broaden and refine the earlier analysis by making proper allowance for one additional factor, which is entirely consistent with the spirit of the model but was not duly taken into account, namely the effect of expectations of future changes in the price level. Evidence is provided that this additional factor is empirically important and that by allowing for it one can obtain a significant improvement in fit as well as a reduction in the serial correlation of the residual error. Some further improvement can also be achieved by introducing a variable intended to measure the effect of changes in the uncertainty about the future course of interest rates on the risk premium.

Our second goal is to provide independent evidence in support of both the expectation theory and of our model of expectation formation and of the determinants of the risk premium, by exploring the relation between our model and the "rational expectation hypothesis". To this end we first derive expressions for the "optimal" (in the least square sense) linear forecast of all future rates, conditional upon the past history of rates of interest and rates of inflation. We show that the relation between the long rate and the history of short rates and prices which is estimated in the process of fitting our term structure equation is broadly similar to the relation that would hold if, in fact, (1) the long rate were an average of expected future rates—as called for by the expectation hypothesis—and (2) the expected future rates tended to represent optimal forecasts—as called for by the rational expectation hypothesis. These results provide strong evidence in support of both hypotheses, and of our term structure model built on them. Further

---

[1] Part of the results reported in this paper originated in Shiller's doctoral dissertation at the Massachusetts Institute of Technology, which was supported by a Federal Deposit Insurance Corporation Graduate Fellowship.
[2] References in square brackets are listed on pp. 42–3, below.

12

evidence is marshalled by computing at each point of time the average of optimally forecast future rates and showing that the resulting series fits rather closely the behaviour of the long-term rate as computed from the term structure equation, especially once proper allowance is made for factors affecting the risk premium, along the lines hypothesized in our model. This last result also serves to provide independent evidence in support of our modelling of the determinants of the risk premium. Finally, this result, when coupled with the consideration that our term structure equation fits the actual long-term rate quite closely, yields fresh evidence that past interest rates and prices are, in fact, the two major variables on which the United States market bases, directly or indirectly, its forecast of the future course of the short rate.

I. REVIEW OF THE BASIC MODEL AND PAST EMPIRICAL EVIDENCE

1.1 Preferred Habitat Version of the Expectation Theory

As is well established, in a world in which all future rates are known with certainty, with rational behaviour, perfect markets and no transaction costs, the price and yield to maturity of an n-period bond can be expressed as a function of its coupon and of the short-term (one period) rates applying over the n periods till the maturity of the bond. The expectation theory hypothesizes that in a world in which the future short-term rates are not known with certainty, the current yield of an n-period bond can be expressed as the very same function of the short rates currently "*expected*" to rule over the next n periods.

In his well-known contribution Hicks [6] amended this simple model by hypothesizing that the long-term rate would tend to exceed the value implied by the average of expected future rates by a liquidity or risk premium. This premium would arise because when future rates are not known with certainty, the actual short-term yield of long-term securities is uncertain, and, given risk aversion, the holders of long securities will require compensation for bearing the uncertainty. The *habitat model* purports to generalize the Hicksian theory and to combine it with the "market segmentation theory" which, in its extreme form, hypothesizes that the market for bonds of different maturities are isolated from one another, with the rate on each such market determined by the demand and supply for that maturity. It hypothesizes that the actual yield of an n-period security may differ from the value predicted by the simple expectation theory by an n-period "risk premium" which, however, need not be monotonic function of length to maturity and may be positive or negative. This premium arises from a possible imbalance between the volume of funds supplied by lenders and the volume of funds demanded by borrowers whose preferred habitat is in the neighbourhood of n-periods. To bridge the imbalance it is necessary to bring into the n-period market lenders or borrowers with a different preferred habitat. Under the assumption of prevailing risk aversion, this will require offering a premium over and above the expected return from a sequence of one period bonds if the n-period habitat borrowers exceed the lenders, or a discount if n-period lenders exceed the borrowers. The resulting positive or negative premium should, therefore, in general be expected to vary from one maturity to the other, though smoothly because nearby maturities may be expected to be close substitutes for both lenders and borrowers. Furthermore, the premium for a given maturity range might be expected to be relatively stable over the medium term as one would expect the habitat preferences to remain reasonably stable.

1.2 The Model of Expectations

The model of formation of expectations set forth in [11] was derived by focusing attention on the currently expected *change* in the long rate. However, it can be restated readily in terms of expectations of future short-term rates (see Sutch [18]); and this formulation will be adopted here since it is more convenient for our present purposes. We rely on the following basic assumptions.

Assumption 1

The market expectation of next period's short rate is based on an extrapolation of the past history of short-term rates and can be approximated by a linear function of these rates, with coefficients constant in time, or

$$(1.1) \qquad {}_{(t+1)}r_t^e = \sum_{\tau=0}^{\infty} w_\tau^{(1)} r_{t-\tau} + c_1,$$

where ${}_{(t+1)}r_t^e$ is the rate that, at time t, is expected to prevail in the next period, $t+1$. One would expect the sum of the weights in (1.1) to be roughly unity, and the constant term c_1 close to zero, since, if past rates remained constant over a sufficiently long time, the expected future rate should tend to coincide with it. It is quite conceivable, however, that the short-term rate may be expected eventually to regress toward some long-run "normal" level, say r^*, which might be fairly constant in time. In this case, the sum of the weights should be less than one and the constant term positive.

Assumption 2

It follows from Assumption 1 and the further assumption that expectations are "consistent" that the short-term rate expected at time t to hold at any other future date m, i.e., ${}_{t+m}r_t^e$, must be given by Eq. (1.1) after replacing, in the right-hand side, the first $m-1$ short rates, which are unknown at time t, by the expected rates, i.e.

$$(1.2) \qquad {}_{(t+m)}r_t^e = \sum_{\tau=0}^{m-2} w_\tau^{(1)} {}_{(t+m-1-\tau)}r_t^e + \sum_{\tau=m-1}^{\infty} w_\tau^{(1)} r_{t+m-1-\tau},$$

a relation that has been labelled the "chain principle of forecasting" [20]. The expected rates of (1.2) in turn can be expressed in terms of the known current and past rates by recursive application of (1.1) and (1.2). Thus, $_{(t+m)}r_t^e$ can be expressed as a weighted average of only current and past rates, or

$$(1.3) \qquad _{(t+m)}r_t^e = \sum_{\tau=0}^{\infty} w_\tau^{(m)} r_{t-\tau} + c_m.$$

The weights $w_\tau^{(m)}$ are clearly related to the coefficients $w_\tau^{(1)}$ of the basic equation. This relation can, in fact, be expressed by the recursive relation

$$(1.4) \qquad w_\tau^{(m)} = w_{m-1+\tau}^{(1)} + \sum_{j=0}^{m-2} w_j^{(1)} w_\tau^{(m-1-j)}.$$

It has been shown by several authors (cf. Sutch [18], Mincer [10]), that the above model of the formation of expectations encompasses Meiselman's "error learning hypothesis" [9]. According to that hypothesis the market revises its expectation of all future short rates by a constant proportion of the error in the previous period's forecast of the current period short rate, or

$$(1.5) \qquad _{(t+m)}r_t^e - _{(t+m)}r_{t-1}^e = a^{(m)}(r_t - _t r_{t-1}^e).$$

One can readily verify that our model implies (1.5) and that Meiselman's $a^{(m)}$ is simply $w_0^{(m)}$ of Eq. (1.3). It can also be seen from (1.4) that from the vector $w_0^{(m)}$ estimated by Meiselman one can infer the vector $w_\tau^{(1)}$ of the one-period equation, Eq. (1.1).

1.3 Implications of the Model for the Determinants of the Long-Term Bond Rate

In what follows we shall focus on the implication of the above model, with certain modifications to be introduced presently, for the determinant of *the* long-term rate of interest. We shall define this quantity as the yield to maturity (or equivalently, the coupon rate) of an n-period bond selling at par, where n is large—say in the order of 30 years—and the bond is of prime quality so that the yield may be presumed to be reasonably free of any premium for default risk. As is well known, in a world of certainty this long-term rate, $R_t(n)$, can be expressed as a weighted average of the short-term rates from t to maturity, $r_{t+\tau}$, $\tau = 0, 1 \ldots n-1$; more precisely, the long-term compounding factor $[1 + R_t(n)]$ is a weighted average of the short-term compounding factors $(1 + r_{t+\tau})$, each weighted by the product of all compounding factors, from $\tau + 1$ to $n - 1$. In past empirical work it has been generally assumed that this complex weighted average could be approximated by a simple average, or

$$(1.6) \qquad R_t(n) = (1/n) \sum_{\tau=0}^{n-1} r_{t+\tau}.$$

This formulation would seem adequate in the case of pure discount bonds (for it then relies only on the approximation $\log(1+r) \simeq r$, which is certainly satisfactory for realistic values of r), or in the case of relatively short-term bonds. But for a bond of very long maturity, the assumption that it can be treated as a discount bond becomes untenable, since the present value of the principal will contribute but a small fraction to the present value of the bond. It has been shown by Shiller [17] that in the limiting case of perpetuities, and, therefore, also for very large n, a better approximation is to replace the simple average (1.6) by an exponentially weighted average of the form

$$(1.7) \qquad R_t = (1-\gamma) \sum_{\tau=0}^{\infty} \gamma^\tau r_{t+\tau},$$

where R_t stands for "the long rate". The coefficient γ equals $1/(1+r^0)$, and r^0 is a "representative" short-term rate, say the long-run average. This result can be derived by starting from the expression relating the yield to future short-term rates, and expanding it in a Taylor series, to linear terms, around $r_{t+\tau} = r^0$, $\tau = 0, 1, 2, \ldots$

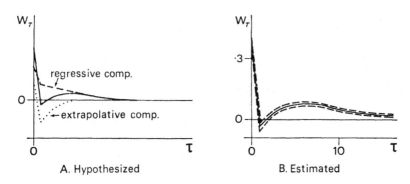

A. Hypothesized   B. Estimated

FIGURE 1   Weighting function in term structure equation for short rate.
A. Hypothesized. B. Estimated distributed lag, Simple M–S equation, E-1, Table 1.

From (1.7) and the expectation hypothesis we now deduce

$$(1.8) \qquad R_t = (1-\gamma) \left[r_t + \sum_{\tau=1}^{\infty} \gamma^\tau {}_{(t+\tau)} r_t^e \right] + K_t',$$

where K_t' is the risk premium hypothesized by the habitat model, which, in principle, could change in time—hence the t subscript. Finally, making use of our model of expectations, and in particular of Eq. (1.3) to substitute for ${}_{(t+\tau)} r_t^e$, we obtain

$$(1.9) \qquad R_t = \sum_{\tau=0}^{\infty} w_\tau r_{t-\tau} + K_t.$$

In this equation the weights w_τ are clearly functions of the coefficients $w_\tau^{(1)}$ of Eq. (1.1) and of γ of (1.7). (For further details on this relation, see Section 4 below.) Finally, K_t depends both on K_t' and on the constant c_1 of equation (1.1).

It has been suggested by de Leeuw [3] and in [11], [12], that the extrapolation of past history on which the market relies in forming its expectation of future rates according to (1.9) may involve both regression towards prevailing past levels, as suggested by Keynes [8], and extrapolation of recent trends, as hypothesized by Duesenberry [5]. If the expectation of future rates reflected primarily regression toward a long-run average of past rates, the weights would tend to look like the dashed line in Figure 1-A. Extrapolative expectations on the other hand imply a pattern of weights of the type shown by the dotted curve, with the first weight positive and the following ones negative, but tending back to zero. When both tendencies are present simultaneously, that is, when the market expects some continuation of recent trends followed by a return towards prevailing past levels, the distributed lag will tend to be of the type shown by the solid curve in the figure, with a sharp initial dip which may even be negative.

1.4 *Review of Empirical Tests of the Original Model*

If, for the moment, we approximate K_t by a constant, (1.9) contains only observable variables; it is in fact, the basic equation derived and tested by Modigliani and Sutch (M–S) in [11]. The results reported there show that when an equation of the form (1.9) is fitted to a variety of data for the United States both in the post-war and the pre-war period, one finds that: (a) the model fits the data very closely; (b) the shape of the weighting function w_τ is indeed of the form shown in Figure 1 with a very sharp dip at the beginning and frequently with negative values of w_1; (c) the value of W is generally quite close to unity, mostly in the immediate neighbourhood of 0·9. As an illustration, we report in row E-1 of Table 1 the results obtained when the M–S equation, originally fitted to data relating to government securities over the decade 1952.1 to 1961.4, is applied instead to corporate securities—the type of securities utilized in the rest of the paper. Accordingly, the dependent variable is Moody's yield on Aaa rated corporate securities rather than the yield of long-term governments, while the short-term rate is measured by the rate on four to six months prime commercial paper rather than by the 3 months treasury bill's rate. Despite these differences in the specific variables used, the two estimated equations are remarkably similar: the distributed lag, reproduced in Figure 1-B (with standard error bands) has pretty much the same shape; the standard error—column 13— is 0·086 (versus 0·093) and the *D.W.* statistic— column 14—is only slightly lower (1·27 versus 1·42).

The favourable experience with the M–S model through the beginning of the '60s has been largely confirmed for the United States by the behaviour of interest rates since the time the paper was published. This conclusion can be supported, for example, by the results obtained when the equation of row E-1 is extrapolated over the next decade. The fit is remarkably close despite the great volatility of interest rates in recent

TABLE 1

ESTIMATED LONG RATE EQUATIONS

						Estimated Coefficients of							
						RCP		p		S			
Eq. No.	Period of fit	Method of Estimation	Lag Length (Qtr.)	Dependent Variable	Const.	Current	Sum Lag Coeff.	Current	Sum Lag Coeff.		R^2	S.E.	D.W.
(1)	(2)	(3)	(4)	(5)	(6)	(7)	(8)	(9)	(10)	(11)	(12)	(13)	(14)
E-1	1952.1–61.4	Almon 4° Const.	17	RS	0·972 0·063	0·396 0·030	0·582 0·036	—	—	—	0·982	0·086	1·28
E-2	1955.3–71.2	Almon 3° Free	18	RS	0·726 0·075	0·265 0·032	0·691 0·046	0·022 0·019	0·137 0·062	0·24 0·12	0·993	0·127	1·01
E-3 (MPS Model)	1954.4–66.4	Almon 3° Const.	19	RS	0·90 0·11	0·211 0·024	0·73 0·05	0·00 0·00	0·07 0·07	0·27 0·072	0·985	0·078	1·20
E-4	1955.3–71.2	Bayesian $K=30$	24	RS	0·706 0·084	0·229 0·029	0·721	0·028 0·022	0·189	0·204 0·126	0·993	0·126	1·00

Definition of Variables

RCP = 4–6 month prime commercial paper rate (per cent. per year).

p = Annual rate of inflation = $400 \times (PCON - PCON_{-1})/PCON_{-1}$. $PCON$ is the price deflator for consumption in the MIT-Penn-SSRC Econometric Model of the United States.

S = 8-quarter moving standard deviation of RCP.

RS = Moody Aaa corporate bond yield average.

years and the fact that they moved far out of the range prevailing in the period of estimation. Though the root mean square error is somewhat higher than in the sample period, it increases only to 0·17 (or 17 basis points); and the increase in the relative error is considerably smaller considering that over the period of extrapolation the long-term rate had an average value some 50 per cent. higher than in the base period. Furthermore, the computed values track quite closely the sharp rise in rates from 1967 to mid '70 (the peak rate of 8·2 per cent in 1970.3 is missed by only 34 basis points) and also catch every significant turning-point in the period.

In the light of these results it is hardly surprising that if one refits the equation for the entire period 1952.1 to 1971.2, one finds that the estimated coefficients are quite close to those of the shorter period, while the standard error improves only negligibly, from 17 basis points to 16.

While this stability of the coefficients is very encouraging and significant, it must be acknowledged that the fit suffers from one serious shortcoming: though the residuals are reasonably small, they exhibit a very pronounced positive serial correlation. This serial correlation was already rather high over the period of fit, as evidenced by the value of the $D.W.$ statistic, of 1·3; but it becomes much more pronounced over the period of extrapolation. This problem is not eliminated even by refitting the equation to the entire period; indeed, the $D.W.$ statistics for the refitted equation is but 0·52. Such a finding suggests that some systematic and presumably highly serially-correlated explanatory variable has been omitted from the list of independent variables. This possibility will be explored in the next section.

II. THE EFFECT OF PRICE EXPECTATIONS ON THE TERM STRUCTURE

2.1 *Generalization of the M–S Model to Allow for Price Expectational Effects*

In the model of expectations set out in Section I, no distinction was made between the expected future level of the money rate and of the "real rate", i.e., the expected money rate less the expected rate of change of prices over the maturity of the instrument. This procedure was justified by the consideration that, regardless of the expected future course of prices, in a well-functioning market with rational participants it remains true that—aside from risk premia—the n-period *money* rate must tend to equal the (weighted) average value of the one-period *money* rate over the same n periods. Hence, to explain the n-period money rate one only needs to have a model of the expected future course of short-term *money* rates. It was hypothesized (at least implicitly) that this future expected course was determined by the past history of the *money* rate alone.

However, in an economy in which prices have been subject to considerable variability, and may, therefore, be expected to continue to change in the future, it may be more reasonable to suppose that, by and large, the future short-term money rate will be expected to reflect the rate of change of prices prevailing then. Denote by $p \equiv \Delta P/P$ the rate of change of prices, and $i_t = r_t - p_t$ the "real" rate. Then the short-term money rate expected at time t to prevail m periods later, $_{(t+m)}r_t^e$, could be thought of as the sum of an expected real rate, and an expected rate of change of prices for that period, or

(2.1) $_{(t+m)}r_t^e = {}_{(t+m)}i_t^e + {}_{(t+m)}p_t^e$ $m = 1, 2 \ldots$

Then, making use of (1.8), the current long-term rate could be expressed as

(2.2) $R_t = (1-\gamma)(i_t + p_t) + (1-\gamma) \sum_{\tau=1}^{\infty} \gamma^\tau {}_{(t+\tau)}i_t^e + (1-\gamma) \sum_{\tau=1}^{\infty} \gamma^\tau \times$
$$_{(t+\tau)}p_t^e + K'$$

Suppose we now make use of the M–S expectation model to account for each of the two summation terms in (2.2). In the spirit of that model each of the terms in the first sum can be approximated by a weighted average of past values of the real rate $i_{t-\tau}$ and, therefore, the weighted sum itself is a weighted average of these past values, or

(2.3a) $(1-\gamma)(i_t + \sum_{\tau=1}^{\infty} \gamma^\tau {}_{(t+\tau)}i_t^e) = \sum_{\tau=0}^{\infty} w_\tau i_{t-\tau} + k_1.$

Applying the same reasoning to the second summation,

(2.3b) $(1-\gamma)[p_t + \sum_{\tau=1}^{\infty} \gamma^\tau {}_{(t+\tau)}p_t^e] = \sum_{\tau=0}^{\infty} v_\tau p_{t-\tau} + k_2.$

Substitution of (2.3) into (2.2) yields

(2.4) $R_t = \sum_{\tau=0}^{\infty} w_\tau i_{t-\tau} + \sum_{\tau=0}^{\infty} v_\tau p_{t-\tau} + K; \quad K = k_1 + k_2 + K'.$

Since the real rate is not directly observable, for purpose of estimation, and also to see the relation to the original M–S model, it is convenient to eliminate i from (2.4) by replacing it with $r - p$. After re-arranging terms, one obtains:

(2.5) $R_t = \sum_{\tau=0}^{\infty} w_\tau r_{t-\tau} + \sum_{\tau=0}^{\infty} v_\tau^* p_{t-\tau} + K$

(2.5a) $v_\tau^* = v_\tau - w_\tau,$ $\tau = 0, 1, 2 \ldots$

It is thus apparent that the M–S original formulation is equivalent to assuming that, at least to a first approximation, $v_\tau = w_\tau$, i.e., that the relation between the expected future course and past history is the *same for the real rate and for the rate of change of prices.*

While there is nothing logically wrong with the above assumption, it is certainly open to question at the empirical level, and, at the very least, deserves explicit testing. Indeed, one would rather be inclined to think that the lesson to be learned from past history in forming expectations about the future would be different for the real rate as contrasted with the rate of change of prices. In particular, for the real rate the extrapolative-regressive mechanism would still appear well suited; on the other hand, one might conjecture that the expectations of the rate of change of prices would tend to be regressive towards a past long-run average, which implies a weighting function of the general form sketched out in Figure 2, panel A1. Note also that the sum of the weights v (the

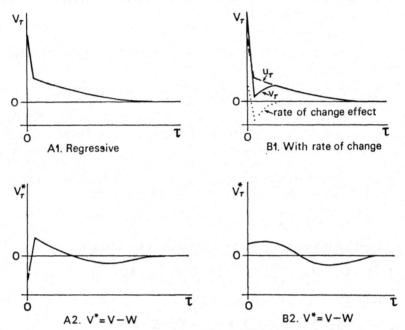

FIGURE 2   Hypothesized weighting structures for the rate of inflation in generalized term structure equation.

area under the curve) should be expected to add up roughly to unity, on the ground that if p had been at some constant level, say p^*, over a sufficiently long time then the expected rate of change should also be p^*. We should then expect the weighting function v^* to have the general shape exhibited in panel A2, obtained by subtracting the solid curve of Figure 1-A from that of Figure 2-A1. The sum of weights $\sum_{\tau=0}^{\infty} v_\tau^* \equiv V^*$ should be close to zero, with the two negative portions offsetting the positive one in the middle.

However, before accepting the hypothesis advanced above about the shape of v_τ, we must pause to consider a possible objection to assumption (2.3a), that the expectation of the real rate is based exclusively on the past history of the observed real rate. If one takes the view, as we do, that, in the short run, the short-term money rate of interest can be manipulated (within very broad limits) by the central bank through its control of the money supply, then it follows that the central banks could force a market level of i quite different from—and, in particular, lower than—the "equilibrium level". "Equilibrium" within this context might be thought of as the level consistent with equilibrium in the commodity markets. One clear evidence of disequilibrium would be provided not by the rate of change of prices—for, in general, equilibrium is consistent with any maintained value of p—but by evidence that the real rate enforced by the money authority was accompanied by acceleration or deceleration in the price level, that is, by a non-zero value of $\dot{p} = dp/dt$. A positive value of $\dot{p}$ would provide indications that the real rate was too low, while a negative value would indicate that it was too high. This suggests, in turn, that (a) the variable whose past history is relevant in forming expectation about the future of i should not be directly the observed i_t but rather some estimate of the "equilibrium" value of i_t; and (b) that this equilibrium value might be inferred by adjusting the observed i_t up or down to the extent that it was accompanied by acceleration or deceleration in p.

We can formalize this hypothesis by replacing in the right-hand side of (2.3a) the observed real rate i_t with the "equilibrium" value, say i_τ^*, and approximating i_τ^* by an expression of the form

$$(2.6) \qquad i_\tau^* = i_t + a \sum_{j=0}^{m} q_j(p_{t-j} - p_{t-j-1}) = (r_t - p_t) + \sum_{\tau=0}^{m} q_j(y_{t-j} - p_{t-j-1}),$$

where the second term is the "acceleration effect" approximated by a distributed lag of observed changes in the rate of change over some immediately preceding interval. One might expect the distributed lag to be short and declining rapidly toward zero. Eq. (2.4) then takes the form

$$(2.7) \qquad R_t = \sum_{\tau=0}^{\infty} w_\tau i_{t-\tau} + \sum_{\tau=0}^{\infty} w_\tau \sum_{j=0}^{m} q_j(p_{t-\tau-j} - p_{t-\tau-j-1}) + \sum_{\tau=0}^{\infty} u_\tau p_{t-\tau} + K.$$

In this expression the last two terms both represent distributed lags on the variable p_t, and since the sum of distributed lags is itself a distributed lag, it is apparent that (2.7) has the same general form as (2.4) and that it can also be expressed in the form (2.5), with (2.5a) still holding. However, the distributed lag v must now be interpreted as representing the sum of the distributed lag u, whose likely shape was shown in Figure 2-A1, and of a second distributed lag embodying the acceleration effect. If the q_j have the general properties suggested above, then the second weighting function should tend to have the broad shape described by the dotted line shown in Figure 2, panel B1; it should start quite positive (with a weight $w_0 q_0$), then become significantly negative, and then tend to remain negative but rising gradually toward zero. In panel B1, we have also reproduced the weighting function of panel A1 shown as a broken curve. The weighting function v should then have the general form shown by the solid curve in panel B1, obtained by summing

The Term Structure of Interest Rates

algebraically the other two weighting functions. It is apparent that the shape of the weighting function v should resemble that of w. This is not surprising since both functions now are the result of extrapolative and regressive elements, even though for very different reasons.

Since w and v might be expected to have similar shapes, it is impossible to draw firm inferences about the behaviour of their difference, v^*. The curve of panel B2 illustrates the outcome under the plausible assumption that the extrapolative component is less pronounced for v than for w—but many other shapes are possible. Unless v and w overlap everywhere, as implicitly assumed by M–S, we should expect at least an alteration of sequences of positive and negative weights on the ground that the sum of the v^* should be zero. Actually even this inference is not firm, since the proposition that v^* should be close to zero holds only if $W = 1$; what we should really expect is $V = 1$, implying $V^* = 1 - W$. If W falls somewhat short of unity, which, as we have pointed out, is fully consistent with the model, then v^* should be positive.

2.2 Empirical Tests of the Generalized Model

Table 1, row E-2 reports the results obtained by fitting Eq. (2.5) to the data described above for the period 1955.3 to 1971.2. The choice of these specific dates is explained below. The distributed lag for both r and p includes 18 quarters. The coefficients of the 17 lagged values are estimated again by Almon's polynomial technique, while the current value of r and p are entered separately, as this appears the most effective way of capturing the shape of the weighting functions sketched out in Figures 1 and 2.

The length of the distributed lag was arrived at as a compromise between the two conflicting requirements. On the one hand, it would seem desirable to let the lag extend a long way in the past. On the other hand, it would seem desirable to avoid using either interest rates or price data before 1951.2, in view of the abnormal circumstances during the war and the immediate post-war period, through the early phase of the Korean War. Lengthening the lag requires either violating this desideratum or shortening the sample period. The specific choice of 17 quarters was based on results of Sutch suggesting that a significantly short lag may be inadequate. This choice also serves to account for the beginning date. The choice of the terminal date, on the other hand, was dictated by the fact that in the third quarter of 1971 price and wage control went into effect, and again one would expect that price expectations could no longer be well accounted for by the past history of p. As we shall presently see this inference receives support for some results reported below.

In addition to adding the distributed lag on p, Equation E-2 introduces other refinements which need to be briefly described.

(a) In [18] Sutch hypothesized that if long-term bonds command a positive premium, as they seem to do, then this premium might be expected to rise if there is greater uncertainty about the future course of interest rates—i.e., greater probability that the actual path might deviate from the expected path, described by the expectation model. He further suggested that a reasonable measure of uncertainty might be provided by the variability of the short-term rate in the immediately preceding period. He accordingly added to the original equation a moving standard deviation of the short rate. He found that this variable had the expected positive sign and contributed moderately to explaining the movements of the long rate (though it did not significantly change the serial correlation of the residuals). Following his lead we have, therefore, added to the explanatory variables an eight-quarters moving standard deviation of the commercial paper rate (RCP), labelled S in Table 1. As can be seen from column (11) of row E-2, this variable comes out with the expected positive coefficient and t-ratio of about two. Furthermore, results obtained by modifications of the basic specifications uniformly confirm the important of this variable and yield rather stable estimates of its coefficient. The Sutch hypothesis and approximation receive, therefore, empirical support, a conclusion that is further confirmed by results to be reported in Section 3.

(b) Sutch has also suggested to us verbally that there is no really sound justification for forcing the right tail of the distribution to zero. This specification is based on the consideration that the weighting function should eventually tend to approach zero, probably asymptotically. But since in empirical work we are generally forced by a variety of "practical" considerations to hold down, somewhat arbitrarily, the number of past quarters included in the distributed lag, it seems preferable to leave the right-hand tail free. One would then expect the right tail to terminate positive, or even with a positive slope, on the ground that when dealing with a relatively sluggish variable, such as interest rates, the most lagged observations may be proxying for the relevant earlier observations, which one could not explicitly introduce. Following his suggestion we have, therefore, left free the right tail of the distribution both for r and for p. At the same time, we have reduced the degree of the polynomial to 3 as this seemed adequate to fit the anticipated shape.

From the summary of the results in row E-2, we can first observe that the addition of the distributed lag on p and the other minor refinements have the effect of reducing the standard error to 12·7 basis points as against 16·9 for the original equation fitted over the same sample period. In addition, the $D.W.$ measure of serial correlation rises from 0·56 to 1·01. Figure 6 (page 40) compares the actual course of the long-term rate, represented by the solid curve, with that computed from our equation E-2, shown as the dotted curve. (The remaining dashed curve can be ignored for the moment.) It is apparent that the fit is extremely close; in the 60 quarters up to the middle of 1970 there are but two quarters in which the error exceeds 20 basis points; the peak rates of over 8 per cent. in the second and third quarters of 1970 are somewhat under-estimated, but only by some 20 basis points, and the subsequent decline and rise are also well caught, as are all major turning-points. We have also extrapolated our equation into the period of price and wage controls, as far as the data permitted, i.e. 1972.1. We should expect these programmes to have produced a significant decline in price expectations relative to past history of p, which our equation cannot account for; hence, the computed values should exceed the actual—and this indeed turns out to be the case. The over-estimate is some 40 basis points in 1971.3, half of which preceded the controls, and rises to 57

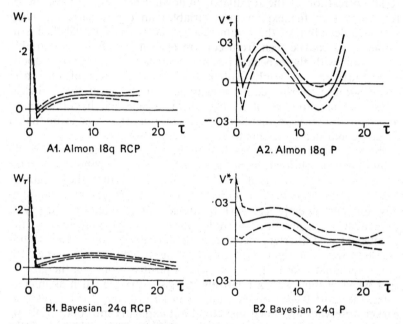

FIGURE 3   Estimated distributed lag coefficient with standard error bands. A1 and A2 from Equation E-2; B1 and B2 from Equation E-4.

points in the following quarter. In 1972.1 it falls back to 35 points which is, in part, to be expected as the anticipated decline in inflation begins to be incorporated in the actual experience; but it might also reflect some loss of confidence in the effectiveness of the programme, though it is yet too early to say.

Turning next to the shape of the distributed lags, the estimates obtained are shown in Figure 3-A1 and A2. In the case of the short rate—panel A1—the form is basically unchanged, except that, as expected, the right tail remains quite positive and tends to rise terminally. The sum of weights W is quite close to one (0·96), and the extrapolative effect is quite marked. As for the weighting function v^*, in panel A2, we first note, by comparing the point estimate with the standard error shown by the band around the central curve, that especially the coefficients of the hump are highly significant, with t-ratios ranging up to 4. Also, we do find the expected alternation of a positive stretch toward the beginning and a negative one toward the end, though the initial dip is somewhat harder to interpret. In any event, it can be verified, by adding up the graph of panel A1 and A2, that the shape of v is pretty much like that shown by the solid curve in Figure 2-B1, except that the curve rises again toward the end, which may be accounted for by truncation. Finally, the sum of the v^* weights is 0·16, which, taking into account that W is 0·96, implies a value of V of 1·1. This exceeds the expected value of 1·0; but the difference is not large, especially considering that the standard error of the sum of the lagged v^* alone is 0·66 (cf. row E-2, column (10)).

On the whole these results seem to provide strong support for our generalized model. One might wonder, however, whether the strong showing of the p component, might not reflect entirely, or largely, the experience of the last three or four years in which prices have been advancing rapidly and attracting great notice. To throw light on this question, we report in row E-3 of the table the results of a replication of E-2 over the shorter time span terminating in 1966.4, before the recent major surge of inflation and presumed novel inflationary psychology. This equation happens to be the one that is used in the present version of the MIT-Penn-Social Science Research Council Econometric Model of the United States.[1] It is apparent that the fit of this equation is even closer, and the $D.W.$ higher which, of course, reflects in part the exclusion of the recent period of extreme fluctuations of rates. What is most relevant for present purposes is that the contribution of the price variable remains substantial, with several coefficients again having t-ratios in the order of 3 to 4. The shape of the weighting function v^* conforms more closely to the graphs of Figure 2-B, and the sum of the weights 0·07, implies that the sum of the v weights—$0·94 + 0·07$—is almost exactly unity. These results, while supporting the previous ones, suggest that the inclusion of the latest years may have tended to exaggerate slightly the contribution of p to the determination of the long rate, and suggest that re-estimation of the equation at a later date, when hopefully inflationary developments will have quietened down and more stable conditions been re-established, might lead to results even closer to those implied by the model.

One more question that deserves some attention concerns the estimated shape of the distributed lags of equation E-2. It is seen from panels A1 and A2 of Figure 3 that both weighting functions terminate with quite high values. Although this feature might be accounted for by the effect of truncation, there is room for concern that it may instead be a spurious result due to the estimating procedure. This is especially true of the distributed lag for p which turns up abruptly at the end. The

[1] This model is a later version of the FRB–MIT–Penn Model, sponsored by the Federal Reserve Board, and developed, in co-operation with the Board staff, under the principal direction of Franco Modigliani and Albert Ando.

third degree polynomial constraint may very well be responsible for this since the polynomial is completely determined by any four points along it; it follows that we could not have the estimated initial hump without the upturn at the end. We have endeavoured to explore this possible problem area by relying on a more suitable procedure, which has recently become available, for estimating the distributed lags.

2.3 *Alternative Estimation of the Distributed Lags by a Bayesian Approach*

The fundamental problem with the Almon estimation procedure is that the polynomial constraint is not an accurate representation of our prior knowledge regarding the lag coefficients. We wish to constrain the coefficients to lie on any "simple" or "smooth" curves, not necessarily a low degree polynomial. Low degree polynomials imply a rather restrictive class of lag shapes. In particular, they preclude an asymptotic behaviour. Yet in many instances, including the one with which we are concerned here, it is precisely this kind of behaviour that one would like to approximate, as one would expect the relevance of past data to vanish asymptotically towards zero. High degree polynomials can approximate as asymptote by, in effect, oscillating around it, but, by the same token, as one readily discovers on trying them, they can approximate many erratic, implausible shapes as well.

We propose, therefore, to rely on an alternative method of estimation which has been developed recently along Bayesian lines [16]. This method does not constrain the lag coefficients to lie on a polynomial of stated degree but imposes instead the condition that the lag curve should be "smooth", by assigning a low prior probability to sudden changes in the slope.[1]

The results obtained by using this alternative procedure were found to be quite close to those reported for Eq. E-2, in every relevant respect, (though in the case of v^* the somewhat puzzling sharp initial dip is appreciably smoothed out). In particular, both distributed lags still turn up at the end and terminate with relatively high values. These results are reassuring as they support the hypothesis that the terminal high values can be attributed to truncation, and that, if the lag were lengthened, the weights would eventually turn down and approach zero. Fortunately, this conjecture can be tested explicitly by relying on the Bayesian estimation, for this method can generate a tail that becomes quite close and eventually coincides with the axis. This also implies that one need not be concerned with the danger of serious distortions in shape, if the chosen lag is unnecessarily long.

In panels B1 and B2 of Figure 3, we show the estimate of the distributed lags obtained when the length of the lag was increased from 18 to

---

[1] This statement holds if one chooses to impose "first order" smoothness. But the same method can be applied to specify nth order smoothness.

24 quarters. The results are seen to support quite well our conjecture. The weights of r decline rapidly after the 18th quarter and by the 24th are quite close to zero, even though no end-point constraints or priors were used which might have forced this. The weights of p, on the other hand, get very close to zero by the 13th quarter, and are practically zero for the last six quarters. In every other respect the results obtained with the longer lag reported in row E-4 are very similar to those reported in row E-2; in particular, W is almost identical, V is only a little larger (by 0·05), and the standard error is but negligibly smaller. There is accordingly no need to modify any of our earlier conclusions.[1]

III. The Term Structure Model and Rational Expectations

3.1 Basic Issues and Method of Attack

In the last section we have shown that our expanded version of the M–S model accounts remarkably well for the behaviour of the United States long rate and that the shape of distributed lags, which are supposed to account for the long-run average of future rates expected by the market, is consistent with a very plausible hypothesis about the forces shaping expectations. However, as was first pointed out in Muth's pioneering contribution [13], to claim that a model is fully consistent with rational behaviour it is not sufficient to show that the process of expectation formation is "plausible"; what should be established is that it is consistent with the hypothesis that the resulting expectations are "rational". Broadly speaking, by this term is meant that the market expectation of any relevant variable must represent the best forecast that could be made of that variable, on the basis of all the information available at the time of the forecast. This consistency was not investigated in the original M–S contributions [11], [12]; Sutch in [18] did recognize the issue, but his attempt at resolving it was not very conclusive. Indeed Nelson, apparently somewhat misinterpreting Sutch's analysis and results, claims that Sutch's evidence establishes that the M–S empirically-estimated distributed lag is *not* consistent with rational expectations, and on this basis, summarily dismisses the M–S model ([14], p. 30).

In this final section we propose to show that the term structure equation we have estimated, and, in particular, the distributed lags, are broadly consistent with the hypothesis that the long-term rate is a weighted average of expected future rates, and that the expectations of future rates are rational.

Our analysis will use a number of propositions concerning rational expectations that have been established by Shiller [17]. We shall

---

[1] It should be noted that while the distributed lags of Figure 3-B were estimated by fitting Eq. (2.5), the statistics reported in row E-4 of the table were obtained by fitting the equation in the form (2.4) which yields directly an estimate of v (used in Figure 5-C, to be discussed presently). However, the results of the two alternative procedures are nearly identical.

paraphrase here somewhat loosely those propositions that bear directly on our immediate problem, referring the reader to [17] for a more rigorous formulation and formal proofs.

Let x be a stochastic process whose history up to t, $x_{t-\tau}$, $\tau = 0, 1 \ldots$ provides information about x_{t+1}. Let

$$_{t+m}\hat{x}_t = \sum_{\tau=0}^{\infty} \beta_{\tau}^{(m)} x_{t-\tau} + \gamma_0^{(m)}$$

denote the best (in the least-squares sense) forecast of x_{t+m} linear in the historical values of x, up to t. In other words, the coefficients β_{τ} and γ_0 are such as to minimize the expectation of $[\epsilon_{\tau}^{(m)}]^2 = [x_{t+m} - {}_{t+m}\hat{x}_t]^2$.

Next, let ${}_{t+m}x_t^e$ denote the (revealed) market expectations or forecast of x_{t+m} made at time t. Suppose one finds the coefficients of the regression:

$$_{t+m}x_t^e = \sum_{\tau=0}^{\infty} b_{\tau}^{(m)} x_{t-\tau} + C_0^{(m)} + \eta_t^{(m)}$$

Shiller's basic proposition then asserts that, if the market expectation ${}_{t+m}x_t^e$ is a rational expectation, in the sense of being the best (in mean square) possible forecast of $x_{t+m}^?$ conditional on all the information available at t, then

(3.1) $\beta_{\tau}^{(m)} = b_{\tau}^{(m)}$ and $\gamma_0^{(m)} = C_0^{(m)}$.

The important point to note is that (3.1) will hold even though there may be other variables, besides x itself, whose past history provides information about x_{t+1}, and these other variables are taken into account in the market forecast—as, indeed they must, if the expectations are rational.

Clearly the proposition will apply as well if ${}_{t+m}x_t^e$ and ${}_{t+m}\hat{x}_t$ are replaced by weighted average, say $\Sigma_j q_{j(t+j)} x_t^e$ and $\Sigma_j q_{j(t+j)} \hat{x}_t$, since the optimal forecast of a weighted average is the weighted average of the optimal forecasts.

The result (3.1) is especially important with regard to the criticism of the model made by Sargent [15]. Sargent estimated relations of the form (1.9) with the addition of a second distributed lag on *future* values of the short rate of interest. The lags appear to be two-sided, although the coefficients of the future values of the short rate beyond the first were generally not significant. Sargent concludes that such results disconfirm the rational expectations hypothesis. He is correct that lags should be one-sided if expectations are based only on a least-square forecasting relation that is linear in the history of short rates alone, (and, of course, if the liquidity premium cannot be explained on the basis of future short rates). But the lags need not be one-sided if the forecasts are based also on other variables besides the short rate. We may therefore interpret his results as lending support to our contention that the history of short rates is not the only basis for forecasts of future short rates. His two-sided distributed lags could arise, for example, if future short rates are related also to past rates of inflation, as we have hypothesized. Yet, it remains true, and this we wish to emphasize, that (3.1) must still hold for distributed lags which are constrained to be one-sided.

3.2 A Test Based on the Basic M–S Equation

The relevance of these propositions to our problem is readily apparent. If the expectation hypothesis holds, then (abstracting for a moment from the risk premium) the long rate RS can be approximated by an average of the current and expected future rates, as shown by the first term of (1.8). Hence, if the expectations are rational, the distributed lag w_τ of the M–S equation should coincide with the distributed lag ω_τ obtained by computing the same average of the optimal linear forecasts conditional on the past short rate. Denote this optimal weighted forecast by RF. Thus,

$$(3.2) \qquad RF_t = (1-\gamma)[r_t + \sum_{m=1}^{\infty} \gamma^m {}_{(t+m)}\hat{r}_t],$$

where

$$(3.3) \qquad {}_{(t+m)}\hat{r}_t = \sum_{\tau=0}^{\infty} \omega_\tau^{(m)} r_{t-\tau} + \Omega^{(m)}$$

is the optimal linear forecast of r_{t+m} at date t.

Substituting (3.3) into (3.2) and re-arranging terms yields

$$(3.4) \qquad RF_t = \sum_{\tau=0}^{\infty} \omega_\tau r_{t-\tau} + \Omega$$

$$\omega_\tau = (1-\gamma) \sum_{j=1}^{\infty} \gamma^j \omega_\tau^{(j)} + g(\tau)$$

$$g(\tau) = 1-\gamma \text{ for } \tau=0; \qquad g(\tau)=0 \text{ otherwise.}$$

To obtain the $\omega_\tau^{(m)}$ of Eq. (3.3) we start by estimating the distributed lag $\omega_\tau^{(1)}$ of the one-period forecasting equation. To this end we regress RCP on lagged values of RCP, relying again on the Bayesian approach to estimate the lag structure. On the basis of the considerations developed in Section 2, we have allowed for a lag of 24 quarters. Also, for reasons touched upon below, the sum of weights was constrained to unity. (The unconstrained estimate yielded a sum of but 1·02, and nearly identical estimates in all other respects.) The results are reported in Table 2, Row F-1, while the distributed lag is reproduced in Figure 4-A.

Several features of the one-period forecasting equation are worth noting. First, the shape of the lag structure shows the same basic features as the solid curve of Figure 1-A, but in even more extreme form, suggesting that the process generating the short-term rate is characterized by the interaction of extrapolative but regressive tendencies. The presence of similar components in the distributed lag of the M–S equation thus appears to have some "rational" basis. On the other hand, the hump in Figure 4-A appears much shallower than that of the M–S lag of Figure 1-B. The peak of the hump is but 0·04 as against 0·08 for 1-B, and, furthermore, no coefficient beyond the 12th has a

TABLE 2

EMPIRICAL FORECASTING RELATIONS

Eq. No. (1)	Period of fit (2)	Method of Estimation (3)	Forecasted Variable (4)	Estimated Coefficients of						R^2 (11)	S.E. (12)	D.W. (13)
				RCP		I		p				
				Current (5)	Sum Lag Coeff. (6)	Current (7)	Sum Lag Coeff. (8)	Current (9)	Sum Lag Coeff. (10)			
F-1	1955.3–71.2	Bayesian $K=45$	One-period RCP	1·095	−0·095					0·93	0·45	1·37
F-2		Computed from F-1 $\gamma=0·99$	Long Run Average RCP	0·430	0·570							
F-3	1955.3–71.2	Bayesian $K=45$	One-Period I			0·597	0·403	0·488	−0·488	0·50	0·794	1·95
F-4	1955.3–71.2	Bayesian $K=45$	One-Period p			0·275	−0·275	0·611	0·389	0·65	0·901	1·96
F-5	—	F-3 + F-4	One-Period RCP			0·872	0·128	1·099	−0·099	0·96	0·378	
F-6	—	From F-3 and F-4 $\gamma=0·99$	Long Run Average RCP			0·262	0·738	0·407	0·593			

Definition of Variables:

RCP = 4–6 month prime commercial paper rate (per cent. per year)

p = Annual rate of inflation = $400 \times (PCON - PCON_{-1})/PCON_{-1}$

See footnotes to Table 1

$I = RCP - p$

t-ratio above 2, while for the M–S equation all 17 coefficients are significant. It is apparently on account of these differences, which had already emerged from the work of Sutch, that Nelson was led to conclude that the M–S distributed lag could not be reconciled with rational expectations.

We have shown, however, that the issue cannot be settled merely from the shape of the distributed lag of the one period equation of Figure 4-A. What we need to compare with Figure 1-B is the graph of the ω_τ, the lag coefficients of long-run average forecast, which are given by Eq. (3.4). These coefficients depend not only on those of the one-period

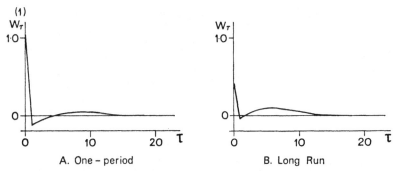

FIGURE 4   Estimated optimal forecasting weights.

equation, but also on those of the optimal forecast equation for *j* periods ahead, $\omega_\tau^{(j)}$, $j = 2, 3 \ldots$ As indicated in Section 1, these can be derived by applying the chain rule, so that Eq. (1.4) holds (replacing everywhere *w* by ω). By applying this equation recursively, one can, in principle, express the vector of coefficients $\omega_\tau^{(j)}$ in terms of the vector of one-period coefficients $\omega_\tau^{(1)}$. Finally, by substitution in (3.4), ω_τ itself can be expressed in terms of the one-period weights $\omega_\tau^{(1)}$. Shiller [17] has shown that this relation can be expressed in the relatively simple form

$$(3.5) \qquad \omega_\tau = A \sum_{j=\tau}^{\infty} \gamma^{(j+1-\tau)} \omega_{(j)}^{(1)} + g(\tau)$$

$$A \equiv (1-\gamma)/(1 - \sum_{j=0}^{\infty} \gamma^{(j+1)} \omega_{(j)}^{(1)}).$$

It should be noted that this simple result depends critically on the approximation (1.7) and the fact that the summation extends to infinity. If, for example, one approximated the long rate by a simple average of future short rates, the relation of ω_τ to $\omega_\tau^{(1)}$ would be a very unwieldy one (see Sutch [18]).

Before applying (3.5) to our data, two observations may prove useful. First, the proportionality factor *A* in (3.5) is very delicate since both the numerator and denominator are close to zero.[1] It was found that with

---

[1] Clearly the denominator must be positive. If this turns out not to be the case for our sample estimates of the $\omega_\tau^{(1)}$, the fault would lie with the approximation (1.7) which is good only in the vicinity of r_0.

minor changes in the sample period or lag length, the $\sum_{\tau=0}^{\infty} \omega_\tau$ (based on the estimated one-period forecasting equations) moved erratically around (falling as low as 0·2, and in some cases, as high as $+\infty$), while the overall shape remained remarkably stable. Clearly, we will not be able to make reliable inferences about the sum of weights from this procedure. Since we should not expect it to be appreciably different from 1·0, in estimating the one-period equation we have, as already noted, imposed the condition $\sum_{\tau=0}^{\infty} \omega_\tau^{(1)} = 1$, which can be shown to imply $\sum \omega_\tau = 1$.[1] Second, since A is not a function of τ, we see from (3.5) that if γ is close to 1 (as it must be for our problem, since $1 - \gamma$ is approximately the interest rate per quarter), ω_τ is approximately proportional to the *sum of the one-period weights starting from τ*. This observation immediately gives us a glimpse of how the shape of ω_τ is related to that of $\sum \omega$ of Figure 4-A. For instance, ω_τ can have a dip at $\tau = 1$, if and only if the extrapolative component of the one-period equation is strong enough to lead to a negative $\omega_1^{(1)}$, as is the case in 4-A; for ω_1 actually to be negative a stronger condition is required, roughly speaking that the leading coefficient $\omega_0^{(1)}$ be larger than one, a condition which again holds in our case.

In the light of these remarks it may not come as a surprise that if one computes the ω_τ explicitly from (3.5) using the values of $\omega_\tau^{(1)}$ underlying Figure 4-A, the results—reported in Figure 4-B and Table 2, row F-2—are strikingly similar to the M–S distributed lag ω_τ of Figure 1-B.[2] Thus, ω_0 is 0·43 as compared with 0·40 for ω_0, and the sum of the remaining weights is 0·57 as compared with 0·58. The peak of the hump in the forecasting relation is at $t-6$, where it attains a value of 0·09; while the peak in the M–S relation is at $t-5$, where it attains a value of 0·08. In the M–S relation the length of the lag, that was decided upon on the basis of the reasonableness of the results, is 16 quarters. In the forecasting relation the curve seems to form an asymptote after 13 quarters.

One point worth noting is that the weighting function ω_τ, just like w_τ, assigns substantial weights to the short rates 4 to 12 quarters back, even though, as noted earlier, in the one-period forecasting equation these weights are small. This result has some bearing on the seemingly paradoxical proposition that to forecast the near future one only needs to look at the recent past, but to forecast far into the future, one should look well into the past. This proposition is seen to be borne out in the case of interest rates: to forecast next quarter's short rate, the only significant information is the rate of the current quarter and, at most, a

---

[1] This condition implies that the stochastic process generating r is non-stationary—but we can see nothing wrong with this assumption.
[2] As shown in Table 2, row F-2, column (3), in computing the ω_τs from (3.5) we have assumed a value of γ of 0·99 (implying a "normal" rate of 4 per cent. per annum). However, the results are not very sensitive to the choice of γ within the relevant range, at least as long as the sum of the coefficients is constrained to unity.

very few quarters back. But for the very long rate, the current rate is far less important while the history of the past few years is also relevant. However, it is also clear from (3.5) that the proposition is not universally valid and depends on the specific form of the one-period relation. One circumstance that will make it valid is when the one-period equation involves a long string of small positive weights extending into the distant past. These small weights will then "pile up" to form a substantive distributed lag for the long-run forecast. This is what we observe in Figure 4-A and B.

In view of the close similarity of the weighting functions w_τ and ω_τ, and in the light of Shiller's proposition, we feel entitled to conclude that the evidence is consistent with the hypothesis that the long rate is an average of expected short rates and that the expectations approximated by the distributed lag of the M–S equation are rational expectations.

The above conclusion rests on a comparison of the M–S weights with those of the optimal forecast of the weighted average future rate derived from the one-period optimal forecast. However, one could also proceed in the opposite direction. The weights w_τ of the M–S equation can be shown to imply a unique vector of weights $w_\tau^{(1)}$ of the one-period expectation equation. If one could derive these weights explicitly, then one could compare them with the weights $\omega^{(1)}$ of the one-period optimal forecasting equation. If expectations are rational the two sets of weights should tend to be equal.

Shiller has shown that, with approximation (1.7), the coefficients $w_\tau^{(1)}$ are related to the w_τ's by the simple formula

$$(3.6) \qquad \omega_\tau^{(1)} = [\omega_\tau - \gamma \omega_{\tau+1} - g(\tau)] / \gamma \omega_0.$$

Since the denominator of (3.6) is not a function of τ, and γ is close to one, the one-period forecasting weights $w_\tau^{(1)}$ are seen to be approximately proportional to the forward first difference of the w_τ. It can be verified readily that if one applies (3.6) to the weights of the M–S equation, one obtains estimates of the one-period weights which are strikingly similar to those reported in Figure 4-A. Thus, the first coefficient is 1·08 versus 1·1; the next $-0·14$ versus $-0·13$; the weights first turn positive with the seventh coefficient and the peak of the hump (0·03 for $w^{(1)}$ versus 0·04 for $\omega^{(1)}$) is reached respectively with the ninth and tenth coefficient.

The approach just described was actually the one followed by Sutch (although, without the simplifications afforded by approximation (1.7) his derivation of the one-period weights was far more laborious), and he also concluded that there was a good deal of similarity between the coefficients $\omega_\tau^{(1)}$ and $w_\tau^{(1)}$. The main drawback of this alternative approach, however, is that it breaks down if expectations depend on more than one variable, as is the case for our generalized term structure equation to which we now turn.

3.3 Tests for the Generalized Term Structure Equation

The task of assessing whether the two estimated lags of the generalized M–S equation are consistent with rational expectations would be relatively simple if we can assume that expectations of future real rates are based only on past real rates and expectations of future prices only on past prices. Then, each distributed lag in the term structure equation could be compared with a long-run forecasting equation derived from a one-period forecasting equation and the chain rule, using expression (3.5). However, as suggested in Section 2, there are reasons for supposing that the expectation of future real rates might depend on p (or more precisely, on its rate of change). This implies a one-period optimal forecasting equation for the real rate of the form

$$(3.7) \qquad _{(t+1)}i_t = \sum_{\tau=0}^{\infty} \mu_{\tau}^{(1)} i_{t-\tau} + \sum_{\tau=0}^{\infty} \mu_{\tau}^{(1)} p_{t-\tau} + c_1.$$

For generality, we may also write the one-period forecasting equation for p as a function of past i's and p's, or

$$(3.8) \qquad _{t+1}p_t = \sum_{\tau=0}^{\infty} \bar{\mu}_{\tau}^{(1)} i_{t-\tau} + \sum_{\tau=0}^{\infty} \bar{\nu}_{\tau}^{(1)} p_{t-\tau} + \bar{C}_1,$$

though there is little *a priori* reason for holding that i should, in fact, have significant informational content in this equation.

The optimal forecasts for i and p for the more distant future $_{t+m}\hat{i}_t$ and $_{t+m}\hat{p}_t$, and hence for $_{t+m}\hat{r}_t = {}_{t+m}\hat{i}_t + {}_{t+m}\hat{p}_t$, can again be derived from the one-period equations and the chain rule. To forecast i two periods in advance, one uses the one-period forecast both of i and p in expression (3.7). Thus, the long-run forecasting equation for either i or p will involve weights that depend on all four distributed lags in (3.7) and (3.8).

Expressions analogous to (3.5) for the long-run forecasting weights in terms of the one-period forecasting weights have been derived (cf. Shiller [17]), although they are substantially more complicated than (3.5). It can be shown that if the sum of lag coefficients are constrained so that: $\Sigma\mu_{\tau}^{(1)} = 1$, $\Sigma\nu_{\tau}^{(1)} = 0$, $\Sigma\bar{\mu}_{\tau}^{(1)} = 0$, $\Sigma\bar{\nu}_{\tau}^{(1)} = 1$, then the sums of each distributed lag in the long-run forecasting equation for r will be one. In the estimation of (3.7) and (3.8), we have imposed this constraint which is analogous to the constraint imposed in testing the original M–S model.[1]

The results of estimating (3.7) and (3.8) are reported in Table 2, row F-3, and F-4, and in Figure 5-A and B. In the forecasting equation for i, the most striking result is the distributed lag for past p, shown in panel A2; its shape provides unequivocal support for the hypothesis, advanced in Section II, that the future course of the real rate is positively associated with the recent acceleration of prices. Indeed, the effect appears quite strong, as the first large positive coefficient is followed by eight negative ones, the first five of which have t-ratios in the order of 3

---

[1] Note that $\Sigma\nu_{\tau}^{(1)} = 0$ is a necessary condition for the real rate to be independent of the *level* of p; similarly $\Sigma\mu_{\tau} = 0$ is a necessary condition for p to be independent of the level of i. They are therefore appropriate specifications to impose if one accepts the dichotomy of monetary and real economics as a good long-run approximation.

and above. The coefficients of lagged i, in panel A1 are, as expected, similar to those of Figure 4-A, except that the right tail remains clearly positive until the very end. In the forecasting equation for p most of the action comes, as expected, from past p, and the shape of the distributed lag for this variable, in panel B2, again supports our hypothesis that

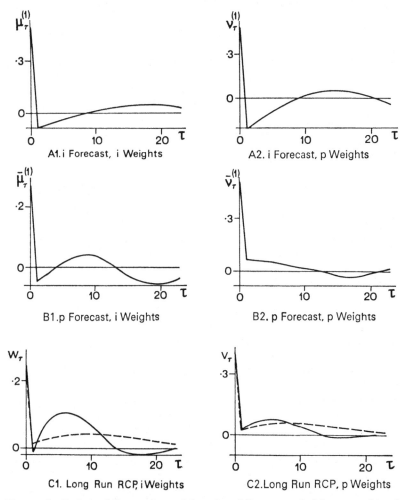

A1. i Forecast, i Weights

A2. i Forecast, p Weights

B1. p Forecast, i Weights

B2. p Forecast, p Weights

C1. Long Run RCP, i Weights

C2. Long Run RCP, p Weights

FIGURE 5   Estimated forecasting weights: A and B—one-period forecast of i and p. C—solid curve: optimal forecast; dashed curve: equation E-4.

the dominant component is regressive. The distributed lag for i in panel B1 has a peculiar shape; the first few coefficients suggest some association between p and the rate of change of i. However, all coefficients, except the first, are small and insignificant (note that the scale for panel B1 is some 50 per cent. larger than for B2).

The Term Structure of Interest Rates   333

Finally, from row F-5 of Table 2 it can be seen that the one-period forecast for *RCP* obtained by summing the forecast for i and p, has a standard error of 0·38 as compared with 0·45 for the forecast based on past r alone, thus confirming that rational expectations of future r should take p into account.

The distributed lag for *RF*, the optimal forecast of the weighted average of future rates, can now be derived by applying Shiller's formulae to the estimated coefficients of (3.7) and (3.8). The results are shown by the solid curves in Figures 5-C1 and C2. For comparison we also report the corresponding distributed lags estimated for our term structure equation, E-4 of Table 1, shown by the dashed curves.

It is apparent that there is again a broad family resemblance in the shape of the dashed and the solid curve: a very high value for the first coefficient, followed by a sharp dip, and then by a hump. However, the shape of the humped portion shows some dissimilarities, distinctly more pronounced than those between Figures 1-B and 4-B of the basic M–S model. It is hard to tell how much significance should be attached to these dissimilarities when one recalls that all estimated coefficients are subject to error. The error is derived from the coefficients of the one-period forecasting equations. Many of these coefficients, we recall, have small t-ratios and, hence, their estimates have a sizeable margin of error. Indeed we have found that variations in the specifications used in estimating the one-period equation, such as length of the lag, constraints on sum of weights, or terminal constraints, while they do not affect the basic shape of the distribution, do have appreciable effects on its detailed features. For instance, the negative tail of the solid curve in Figure C1, which is rather difficult to rationalize, disappears if Eqs. (3.7) and (3.8) are estimated with an eighteen-quarter lag (the specification used in equation E-2) and a terminal zero constraint.

How critical then are the differences observed in Figure 5-C1 and C2? A very natural way of shedding light on this question consists in using the distributed lags estimated for the optimal forecast of the weighted average future rate to compute a time series of the optimal forecasts, RF_t. This series can then be compared with RSC_t, the long-term rate computed from our term structure Eq. E-4. Since by Shiller's proposition the distributed lags should be the same, if the expectations measured by E-4 are rational expectations, it also follows that *RF* should coincide with *RSC*, again abstracting for the moment from risk premia. Of course, since we already know that the distributed lags are not identical, we do not expect that *RF* and *RSC* will be identical. On the other hand, it is well known that the value of a weighted average is not very responsive to moderate perturbations in the weighting structure; or, equivalently, that the very same variable can frequently be approximated nearly as well by a variety of lag structures. In fact, this is a major source of difficulty in obtaining reliable measures of the precise lag structure. What in effect we are proposing is to gauge how "really different" are the weighting structures compared in Figure 5-C by determining how much difference they make in the value of the variable computed from them.

Before we can apply this test we must come to grips with the problem of the risk premium. Under our hypothesis the dependent variable in Eq. E-4 is not merely a weighted average of expected future rates, but rather this quantity plus a risk premium. In our model we have approximated the risk premium by the quantity $C_0 + C_1 S$, where S denotes an eight quarter standard deviation of the short rate. Shiller's proposition therefore implies

(3.9) $RSC = RF + C_0 + C_1 S_1.$

Our test of the rational expectation hypothesis can, therefore, be reformulated as follows: estimate the regression equation

$$RSC - RF = C_0' + C_1' S + u_t.$$

Then (i) C_0' and C_1' should have value close to those obtained for the corresponding coefficient of Eq. E-4 reported in column (6) and (11) respectively of Table 1; (ii) the error term u_t should have a small variance relative to the variance of RSC or, equivalently, the quantity $RF + C_0' + C_1' S$ should explain a large fraction of the variance of RSC.

There remains one purely statistical problem to deal with, having to do with measurement errors in our series for the long rate. There is reason to believe that Moody's Aaa series tends to lag behind the facts, and this hypothesis is supported by a good deal of evidence presented in a forthcoming paper. The main reason seems to be that some of the issues on which it is based are traded infrequently and, hence, the quotations used will tend to reflect past rather than current market values. This suggests that our measured RS may be thought of as an average of the current and the lagged true long rate or $RS = a_1 RS^* + a_2 RS_{-1}^*$, where RS^* is the true long-term rate and $a_1 + a_2 = 1$. Accordingly, (3.9) should be changed to

$$RSC = a_1(RF + C_0 + C_1 S) + a_2(RF_{-1} + C_0 + C_1 S_{-1})$$
$$= a_1 RF + a_2 RF_{-1} + C_0 + C_1 S - C_1 a_2(S - S_{-1}),$$

or, after dropping the last term, as second order of magnitude,

(3.10) $RSC - RF = C_0 - a_2(RF - RF_{-1}) + C_1 S + u.$

Estimates of the parameters of Eq. (3.10) are reported in Table 3, row S-1. The coefficients of both dependent variables have the expected sign and reasonably high t-ratios. In the case of S, the coefficient (0·3) is also reasonably close to that estimated for E-4 (0·2). On the other hand, the estimated value of a_2, the coefficient of ΔRF, implies an improbably long lag in the Aaa series. In addition, the value of $D.W.$ is extremely low. Under these conditions a more reliable estimate of the coefficients can be obtained by using the autoregressive transformation. The results, reported in row S-2 yield a much more plausible estimate of a_2, little change in the coefficient of S (though in the wrong direction) and very high t-ratios for both variables. The standard deviation of the residual error (computed without feeding back the lagged error) shown in the last column is 22 basis points, which is reasonably small considering the large variation of RS and hence RSC in the period. Indeed, the variable RF corrected for risk premium and the lag in RS, relying on the coefficients given in Table 3, row S-2, explain 98 per cent. of the variance of RSC. The association can be seen graphically from Figure 6 by comparing the time series of corrected RF, labelled RSF, shown by the dashed line with that of RSC, shown as the dotted line. The closeness of the fit is especially impressive when it is recalled that RF—by far the major component of RSF—was in no way "fitted" to RSC or to RS, but was instead derived entirely independently from the regression of the short rate on past short rates and prices.

TABLE 3

TESTS OF THE RATIONAL EXPECTATION HYPOTHESIS AND DETERMINANTS OF RISK PREMIUM

Eq. No.	Dep. Variable	Estimated Coefficient of					S.E.	D.W.	S.U.
		Const.	ΔRF	S	RCP	λ			
(1)	(2)	(3)	(4)	(5)	(6)	(7)	(8)	(9)	(10)
S-1	$RSC-RF$	0·55	−0·61	0·30			0·22	0·20	
			0·14	0·10					
S-2	„	0·45	−0·383	0·35		0·95	0·076	1·15	0·22
			0·038	0·08					
S-3	$RS-RF$	0·55	−0·57	+0·30			0·26	0·39	
			0·17	0·11					
S-4	„	0·53	−0·303	+0·30		0·86	0·14	1·63	0·26
			0·074	0·15					
S-5	„	0·43	−0·311	0·27	0·017	0·87	0·14	1·63	
			0·074	0·15	0·037				

From Figure 6 one can surmise that RSF accounts reasonably well also for the actual behaviour of the long rate, RS, shown by the solid line. This, of course, is what one would expect if (i) the expectation hypothesis holds; (ii) market expectations are rational; and, in addition, (iii) the variables used in the "optimal" forecast, RF, namely the short rates and rate of change of prices, are the main variables that can provide information about the future course of interest rates, and hence also the main variables used, directly or indirectly, by the market in forming expectations. The standard deviation of the difference $(RS-RF)$ turns out to be 28 basis points, implying that RF explains over 96 per cent. of the variance of RS.[1] But, once more, this direct comparison is not the

[1] Note that the mean value of $RS-RF$ is not zero but instead a substantial positive number (0·70), as one would expect if RS contains a positive risk premium. In computing the standard deviation (rather than the root mean square difference) to a first approximation, the difference in the mean is accounted for by the risk premium.

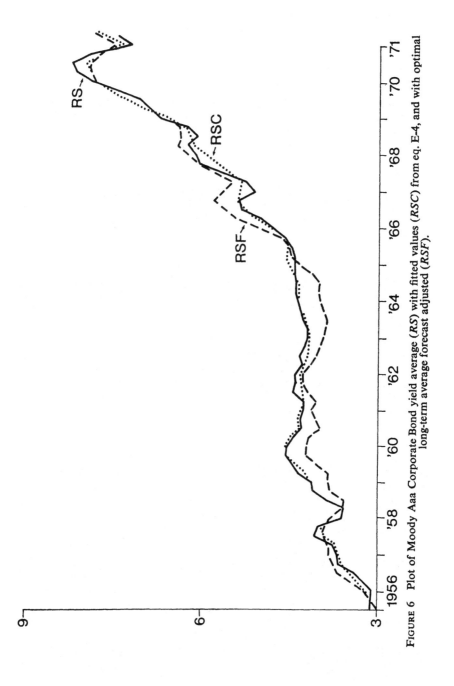

FIGURE 6 Plot of Moody Aaa Corporate Bond yield average (*RS*) with fitted values (*RSC*) from eq. E-4, and with optimal long-term average forecast adjusted (*RSF*).

appropriate one because presumably RS contains a risk premium and also appears to lag appreciably behind the true long rate. The extent to which these two forces account for the spread $RS - RF$, can be tested by regressing the spread on ΔRF and on the moving standard deviation, S, which, according to our model is supposed to account, at least partially, for the variations in risk premium over time. The result, reported in Table 3, row S-3, shows again that both variables have the expected sign and non-negligible t-ratios, but that the coefficient of ΔRF is uncomfortably high, as is the serial correlation of the residuals. The equation has, therefore, been re-estimated with the autoregressive transformation—see row S-4. Both coefficients now appear quite reasonable and, in particular, that of S is roughly consistent with alternative estimates. However, these variables are seen to account only for a modest portion of the spread, as the standard deviation of the residual error, SU, declines only to 26 basis points.

A final test, reported in row S-5, relates to an issue which has been repeatedly debated in the literature, namely whether the risk premium tends to vary with the level of interest rates, and, if so, whether the association should be a positive or a negative one. For instance, Kessel [7] has argued that the association should be positive and provides some evidence for this view, though only with respect to very short-term rates. Cagan [1] also finds some support for this hypothesis. On the other hand, Van Horne [19] and, more recently, Nelson [14] have suggested that the association should be negative and have also provided some evidence, though again, most of the supporting evidence in Nelson's painstaking analysis relates to forward rates from 1 to 9 years, a spread much smaller than that included in our long rate.

These alternative hypotheses clearly could not be tested in the framework of our term structure equation, for, within that structure, it would be impossible to identify whether the coefficients of interest rates, current or lagged, reflected the formation of expectations or instead risk premium effects. A test can be carried out, however, by making use of RF, our "optimal" forecast, which is derived entirely from the one-period equation. Hence, the spread $RS - RF$ should reflect at least, in part, the risk premium—and the significance of our variable S in S-1 to S-4, supports this hypothesis. We can, therefore, test whether the risk premium depends on the level of rates by adding RCP to Eq. S-4. The result, reported in S-5, provides no support for either of the two hypotheses as this variable turns out to be totally insignificant. This test has been repeated by adding RCP to Eq. S-2, since under our hypothesis the spread $RSC - RSF$ should also reflect risk premium. The result is again a totally insignificant value for the coefficient of RCP.[1]

---

[1] This result, in sharp contrast, to those reported by Nelson, presents somewhat of a puzzle since the method used is, at least conceptually, the same. It consists in regressing the spread between a "revealed" expected rate and an optimal forecast of that rate on the short-term rate. There are, of course, considerable differences

CONCLUSION

Summing up, we have developed and tested a model of the determinants of the long-term interest rate based on the hypothesis (i) that this rate is an average of expected future short-term rates, adjusted for risk premium and (ii) that the expectations are primarily shaped by the history of interest rates and rates of inflation over several past years. This model was shown to account remarkably well for the behaviour of the US long-term rate in the post-war period. We have next developed conditions that must be satisfied by the long-term rate equation if the expectations determining the long rate are "rational", and found that these conditions were broadly satisfied. This last result, in combination with the close fit obtained for our equation and for the "optimal linear" forecasting equation support the view that past interest rates and rates of inflation are, in fact, the main variables containing information about the future course of interest rates, and provides a "rational" support for our finding that these same variables very largely shape the expectations of future rates.

Massachusetts Institute of Technology,
University of Minnesota.

REFERENCES

[1] Cagan, P., "A Study of Liquidity Premiums on Federal and Municipal Government Securities", in J. Guttentag and P. Cagan (eds.), *Essays on Interest Rates*, vol. 1, New York, 1969.

[2] Culbertson, J., "The Term Structure of Interest Rates", *Quarterly Journal of Economics*, November 1957.

[3] de Leeuw, F., "A Model of Financial Behavior", in J. Dusenberry *et al.* (eds.), *The Brookings Quarterly Econometric Model of the United States*, Chicago, 1965.

---

in empirical specifications. Thus, our basic one-period forecasting equation is a quarterly, rather than an annual one, and it makes use of a much longer and richer distributed lag than his; furthermore, it also allows for the effect of past rates of inflation. Also, the period of observation is quite different, 1901–58 versus 1955–71—and the years of the great depression can have a pervasive effect on results. Again, his dependent variables are forward rates deduced from a yield curve, data which are known to be quite noisy as compared with our Aaa series. Last, but not least, Nelson's evidence about the inverse relation between risk premium and interest rates is rather impressive for forward rates up to 9 years, but when it comes to the 35 year rate—the only longer rate examined by him—the evidence is mixed, to say the least. This is suggestive, considering that our evidence relates to the average of future rates up to 30 years or so.

Nelson also hypothesized that the risk premium should tend to decline with an improvement in business confidence measured operationally by the reciprocal of the rate of unemployment, and again obtained results strikingly favourable to the hypothesis. We have endeavoured to replicate also this test, by adding the reciprocal of the unemployment rate to each of the Eqs. S-2, S-4 and S-5, even though we do not find Nelson's hypothesis entirely convincing, as when dealing with a measured rate which is supposed to be largely free of default risk. In every instance the coefficient of the variable was negative, as called for by the hypothesis and significant if estimated by ordinary least squares. However, after re-estimation with the autoregressive transformation, the coefficients, though still negative, were in every case less than their standard error, mostly less than half. Thus, our results appear at odds with those of Nelson also with respect to this variable.

[4] Diller, S., "Expectations in the Term Structure of Interest Rates", in J. Mincer (ed.), *Economic Forecasts and Expectations*, New York, 1969.

[5] Duesenberry, J., *Business Cycles and Economic Growth*, New York, 1958.

[6] Hicks, J. R., *Value and Capital*, Oxford, 1939.

[7] Kessel, R., *The Cyclical Behavior of the Term Structure of Interest Rates*, New York, 1965.

[8] Keynes, J. M., *The General Theory of Employment, Interest and Money*, 1936.

[9] Meiselman, D., *The Term Structure of Interest Rates*, Englewood Cliffs, N.J., 1962.

[10] Mincer, J., "Models of Adaptive Forecasting", in J. Mincer (ed.), *Economic Forecasts and Expectations*, New York, 1969.

[11] Modigliani, F. and R. C. Sutch, "Innovations in Interest Rate Policy", *American Economic Review*, vol. 56 (1966), Papers and Proceedings, pp. 178–97.

[12] ——, "Debt Management and the Term Structure of Interest Rates: An Empirical Analysis of Recent Experience", *Journal of Political Economy*, vol. 75 (1967), pp. 569–89.

[13] Muth, J. F., "Rational Expectations and the Theory of Price Movements", *Econometrica*, vol. 29 (1961), pp. 315–35.

[14] Nelson, C., *The Term Structure of Interest Rates*, New York, 1972.

[15] Sargent, T. J., "Rational Expectations and the Term Structure of Interest Rates", *Journal of Money, Credit and Banking*, vol. 4 (1972).

[16] Shiller, R. J., "A Distributed Lag Estimator Derived from Smoothness Priors", *Econometrica*, forthcoming.

[17] ——, "Rational Expectations and the Structure of Interest Rates", Unpublished Ph.D. dissertation, Massachusetts Institute of Technology, 1972.

[18] Sutch, R. C., "Expectations, Risk and the Term Structure of Interest Rates", unpublished Ph.D. dissertation, Massachusetts Institute of Technology, 1968.

[19] Van Horne, J., "Interest-Rate Risk and the Term Structure of Interest Rates", *Journal of Political Economy*, vol. 73 (1965), pp. 344–51.

[20] Wold, H., "Forecasting by the Chain Principle", in Rosenblatt (ed.), *Proceedings of the Symposium on Time Series Analysis, held at Brown University, June 11–14, 1962*, New York, 1963.

Errata

Page 17, paragraph 2, line 9: insert after W, "—the summation of all weights w_τ—."

Page 22, paragraph 2, lines 2 and 3: "i°_τ" should read "i°_t."

Page 22: equation (2.6) should read "$i^\circ_t = i_t + a \sum_{j=0}^{m} q_j(p_{t-j} - p_{t-j-1}) = (r_t - p_t)$

$+ \ a \sum_{j=0}^{m} q_j(p_{t-j} - p_{t-j-1})$."

Page 22, equation (2.7): the second term should read "$\sum_{\tau=0}^{\infty} w_\tau a \sum_{j=0}^{m} q_j(p_{t-\tau-j} - p_{t-\tau-j-1})$."

Page 22, line following equation (2.7): "the last two terms" should read "the last two terms before the constant."

Page 23, 6 lines from the bottom: "support for" should read "support from."

Page 24, line 16: "important of this variable" should read "importance of this variable."

Page 26, line 12: "0.66" should read "0.06."

Page 26, 10 lines from the bottom: "quietened" should read "quieted."

Page 27, paragraph 2, line 11: "as asymptote" should read "an asymptote."

Page 35, equation (3.7): second term on the right-hand side should read "$\sum_{\tau=0}^{\infty} v_\tau^{(1)} p_{t-\tau}.$"

Page 38, 10 lines from the bottom: "both dependent variables" should read "both independent variables."

Page 41, footnote 1, line 1: there should not be a comma after "contrast."

PART IV
The Determinants of Investment

INTERNATIONAL ECONOMIC REVIEW
Vol. 15, No. 2, June, 1974

ON THE ROLE OF EXPECTATIONS OF PRICE AND
TECHNOLOGICAL CHANGE IN AN
INVESTMENT FUNCTION

By Albert K. Ando, Franco Modigliani, Robert Rasche,
and Stephen J. Turnovsky[1]

1. INTRODUCTION

IT IS A SIMPLE TAUTOLOGY that, when prices of inputs and outputs are not expected to remain constant during the planning horizon, real rates of interest and the money rate of interest are not the same. While the investment decision must depend upon a "real" rate of interest, the monetary authority can at best control directly the money rate of interest. Furthermore, the notion of a real rate of interest is itself ambiguous since there are three alternative real rates, namely, in terms of output, of capital goods, and of labor. Therefore, in order to evaluate the effects of monetary policy on investment decisions, it is crucial to specify the way in which the money rate of interest and the expected rate of change of prices both enter the cost of capital which in turn directly influences investment decisions.

To answer this question requires the formulation of an investment function. The purpose of this paper is to investigate this problem, both theoretically and empirically, in the context of the investment function developed by Bischoff [1, 2], which is based on the assumption of a "putty-clay" production function. In this model the equipment in which the investment at any given point of time is embodied is characterized by fixed proportions, and in particular by a fixed output labor ratio, although the proportions embodied in the equipment can be chosen from a set of alternatives describable by an *ex ante* production function allowing for continuous factor substitution. Bischoff has shown that under these conditions the investment function takes the general form

$$(1) \qquad\qquad I_t = \hat{k}_t \Delta X_t^c$$

where I_t and ΔX_t^c denote respectively gross investment and the gross increment to capacity which firms wish to provide for in period t, both for expansion and for replacement, and $\hat{k}_t$ is the optimum (cost minimizing) capital output ratio in the same period t, as determined by the relative prices of relevant inputs prevailing then, and expected to prevail over the relevant future.

In his original contribution Bischoff derived an expression for $\hat{k}_t$ but his analysis was based, in part, implicitly on two rather restrictive, interrelated,

[1] We are grateful to Dale Jorgenson for his comments on an earlier draft of this paper and to Robert Shiller for his comments on the theoretical section and especially for his help in the derivation in Section 2.2. We also wish to thank Al Hoffman for his excellent research assistance. Finally, we owe special thanks to Charles Bischoff on whose work we have drawn freely and whose advice was especially helpful in the final revision of the manuscript.

384

simplifying assumptions. First, he assumed that input prices were expected to remain constant over the life span of the currently acquired equipment. He assumed further that the equipment remained in service until it completely depreciated physically, an assumption which, as we shall see, can be justified if, but only if, the first assumption holds.

Our task is to generalize his analysis by allowing explicitly for the fact that, in general, input (and output) prices will be expected to change over time, both in absolute terms and relative to each other. These expectations will arise in part from prevailing anticipations of *overall inflationary or deflationary trends* and in part from the anticipation of *continued technological progress.*

Thus far, expectational elements have received little attention in either the theory or the empirical estimation of investment functions.[2] One previous attempt to deal with this question is in two papers by Jorgenson and Siebert [13, 14] which are based on the assumption of a putty-putty technology. They show that under this assumption the relevant real rate of interest is the rate measured in terms of capital goods. However, in the putty-putty model even already installed capital is instantaneously malleable and thus factor proportions are free to adjust in response to changes in relative prices as they occur. This implies a myopic investment rule, depending only on the *current* real rate of interest and hence only on the expected rate of change of prices for the current period. Their equations estimated over the period 1949–63 provide some evidence that the incorporation of a measure of the expected rate of change of prices of capital goods leads to some improvement in the quality of the results.

In a putty-clay model, however, since all existing capital is characterized by fixed proportion over its economic life, a myopic rule will, in general, not be optimal. The current choice of technology must depend instead on the current as well as expected future "real" rate of interest and real wage rate, and, therefore, on the expected future course of money wages and prices, as well as on expected technological change over the life of the investment (and even beyond— see below).[3] A somewhat counter-intuitive result of our analysis is that, in the putty-clay model, the relevant rate of interest is the real rate in terms of output rather than of capital goods (or labor).

A further complication arises from the fact that the expected service life can no longer be taken as determined exogenously by technological properties. On

---

[2] For a recent extensive and enlightening review of econometric estimates of investment functions, see Jorgenson [12].

[3] Even in the conventional putty-putty mod the optimalityel of the myopic rule ceases to hold if one assumes the existence of "adjustment costs" so that, for example, the cost of installed capital goods is an increasing function of the rate of investment, as suggested, in particular, by Eisner and Strotz [6], (see also the references cited by Jorgenson [12, (1142)]); this has been shown, for example, by Gould [8]. In our analysis, we have not explicitly introduced adjustment costs related to the rate of investment. Note, however, that our putty-clay model does explicitly allow for the cost of adjusting the existing stock of capital to changes in relative prices—a cost which is, in fact, indefinitely large. Because of this cost, a putty-clay model can readily account for the slow adjustment of the stock of capital to changes in relative prices, suggested by the empirical evidence, without recourse to the somewhat *ad hoc* notion that the cost of capital goods depends on the rate of growth of the stock of capital, gross or net.

the contrary, the expectations of forthcoming technological progress and changes in relative prices may lead to the expectation that it will be advantageous to discard the current equipment before it is physically obsolete. As is well known, this will occur once the marginal cost of producing with the current equipment exceeds the average cost for the latest available vintage. Thus the determination of the "economic service life" of the present investment becomes itself an integral part of the optimization problem which interacts with the choice of the optimum capital-output ratio and thus affects the form of the investment function.

In the light of the above consideration it appears that the derivation of the investment function must be cast in the framework of a "machine replacement problem." That is, given some output X to be produced throughout the indefinite future, and given a (consistent) set of expectations about future prices and technological progress, there is an optimal sequence of machines that minimizes the present value of expected costs. The currently purchased equipment must then be viewed as the first link in this optimal chain.

The rest of this paper is divided into three parts. In 2, we endeavor to establish which are the variables, current and expectational, that determine the optimum capital output ratio $\hat{k}_t$, at any given date, and to derive the parametric form of the function relating $\hat{k}_t$ to these variables. In 3 the results of 2 are utilized to derive an empirically testable investment function, making due allowance for the relevant response lags, and for the nature of the available data. Finally, in 4 we proceed to test the model and estimate its parameters.

The results of our statistical tests are not as clear cut as one might wish, due in part to the well known difficulty of measuring the expectation of the rate of change of prices. However, it is hoped that the theoretical and empirical analysis presented here will provide a useful basis for further research on the difficult problem of explaining the behavior of aggregate investment.

2. THE EFFECT OF EXPECTED TECHNOLOGICAL AND PRICE CHANGES ON THE OPTIMAL CAPITAL OUTPUT RATIO

2.1. *Assumptions.* Since the empirical work in this paper is based on the Cobb-Douglas production function, this shall be assumed throughout.[4] We further assume that Harrod neutral technical progress occurs at the constant rate g, and that firms (correctly) anticipate the indefinite continuation of this progress. Thus at date t the *ex ante* (putty) production function, assumed to be homogeneous of degree one can be denoted by:

$$X_t = AI_t^{1-a}(e^{gt}E_t)^a$$

where,

$X =$ flow of gross output
$I =$ putty content of capital equipment
$E =$ man hours per unit time

[4] The considerations that justify this assumption as a useful approximation in an econometric analysis of investment data are discussed in footnote 29.

g = the rate of "Harrod neutral" (embodied) technical progress[5]
t = the point in time when I is installed.

Since we shall eventually apply our formulation to the explanation of investment in producers' equipment in the economy as a whole, it is more natural to think of I not as one machine but as a collection of machines. We make the following additional assumptions:

(a) A proportion d of all existing equipment becomes physically incapacitated and scrapped per year.

(b) As machines get older, the required labor increases at the rate m per year for surviving machines.

(c) Demand for the output of new machines is exogenously given and firms expect that it will continue indefinitely.

(d) Producers expect that over the "relevant" future, the money wage rate, W, will rise at the constant proportional rate w, the money interest rate, r, will remain constant and the price of capital goods (putty), Q, relative to the price of output, P, will increase at a constant proportional rate q^*. (In the special case of a "one sector" model q^* would of course be zero.)

(e) Finally, as in Bischoff's original formulation, we assume that the output price is set by applying an oligopolistic mark up, M, determined by entry preventing considerations, to the minimum cost achievable, given current and expected technology and factor prices. We further postulate that firms assume that the mark up policy will remain constant over the relevant future. However, in view of the dynamic nature of our analysis the assumed mark-up policy is specified as follows: the price at any date t is such that, given that the same price *policy* will apply at all future dates, the present value of revenue derived from a constant stream of output must be M times the present value of the minimized cost of the same stream of output.

2.2. *Derivation of the optimal capital—output ratio.* As indicated in Section 1, the derivation of the investment function requires determining the current investment I_0 that is optimal for a given output X in the sense that, together with an optimal sequence of later investments, it minimizes the present value (PV) of costs of producing the perpetual stream X. The task of determining the optimal sequence can be accomplished by relying on fairly standard methods; however, since it turns out to be rather lengthy and tedious we shall here merely sketch out the derivation, highlighting those steps which have a bearing on later developments.[6]

In the first place it can be shown that, under our "constant expectations" assumption, the optimal life of each machine in the chain is the same and is independent of the point of time at which the chain starts. The problem can then be conveniently attacked in two stages. We first determine the capital output and labor output ratio that minimize the present value of costs for *given* service

---

[5] The analysis developed in the text assumes that all technological progress is embodied. It can, however, be readily generalized to the case where some constant portion of g is disembodied.

[6] A detailed derivation is available on request from the authors.

life, T. The solution to this suboptimization problem can then be used to express the PV of costs in terms of T and, hence, finally to determine the cost minimizing value of T, which we denote by $\hat{T}$.

When T is given, it follows from assumptions (a), (b) and (d) that the present value of costs of the stream of output resulting from the initial investment can be expressed as

$$(2) \qquad C_0(X, T) = Q_0 I_0 + E_0 W_0 \int_0^T e^{-(r-w+d-m)s} \, ds$$

where X is the initial capacity of the equipment and I_0, E_0, must satisfy the initial production function constraint, $X = A(I_0)^{1-a}(E_0)^a$. The cost in (2) consists of the initial purchase cost of the equipment together with the present value of the payments to labor employed on that machine throughout its life.

Let us define:

$p =$ the proportional rate of change of output price
$R = r - p + d; \ L = m + w - p; \ R^* = r - m - w + d = R - L$
$B(s, T) = \dfrac{1 - e^{-sT}}{s}$ $\qquad$ for all s and T $\quad s > 0, T > 0.$

Note that $r - p$ is the "real" rate of interest in terms of output, R is the "real" rental rate in terms of output, and L is the rate of increase in the real labor cost of operating machines of a given vintage, as those machines grow older.

From the above definition and (2) it follows that the PV of cost *per unit* of initial capacity X, can be written as

$$(3) \qquad \chi_0(T) = \frac{C_0(X, T)}{X} = Q_0 \left(\frac{I_0}{X}\right) + W_0 B(R^*, T)\left(\frac{E_0}{X}\right).$$

Now, let $(\hat{I}_0/X)$ and $(\hat{E}_0/X)$ denote the capital output and the capital labor ratio that minimize $\chi_0(T)$, subject to the production function constraint, and let $\hat{\chi}_0(T)$ denote the minimized value of $\chi_0(T)$, or

$$\hat{\chi}_0(T) = Q_0\left(\frac{\hat{I}_0}{X}\right) + W_0 B(R^*, T)\left(\frac{\hat{E}_0}{X}\right).$$

Relying on standard methods of constrained minimization one finds that

$$(4a) \qquad \left(\frac{\hat{I}_0}{X}\right) = A^{-1}\left[\frac{(1-a)W_0 B(R^*, T)}{aQ_0}\right]^a$$

$$(4b) \qquad \left(\frac{\hat{E}_0}{X}\right) = A^{-1}\left[\frac{(1-a)W_0 B(R^*, T)}{aQ_0}\right]^{a-1}.$$

One can then establish that our assumption about the expected course of W, r, and P/Q and about the constancy of the mark up have the following implications:

i) The minimized PV of costs per unit of capacity expected to result from a machine installed at any later date t, and computed as of that date, must be expected to grow in time at a constant rate, or

(5a)
$$\hat{\lambda}_t(T) = \hat{\lambda}_0(T)e^{pt}$$

where[7]

(6)
$$p = w - g + q^*(1 - a)/a.$$

Similarly, the price set on output must also be expected to rise at the same rate p, or

(5b)
$$P_0(t) = P_0 e^{pt}$$

where $P_0(t)$ is the price which, in period 0, is expected to rule t periods later. (Note that for $q^* = 0$ (6) reduces to the familiar formula, $p = w - g$.)

ii) The minimized PV of cost per unit of producing a constant output X over the infinite horizon starting at time 0, given that service life is T, can be expressed as

$$\hat{c}_0(T) = \frac{\hat{\lambda}_0(T)}{(r - p)B(R, T)} = \frac{1}{(r - p)B(R, T)}$$
$$\times \left[Q_0\left(\frac{I_0}{X}\right) + W_0 B(R^*, T)\left(\frac{\hat{E}_0}{X}\right) \right].$$

Substituting for I_0/X and $\hat{E}_0/X$ from equation (4) we finally obtain

(7)
$$\hat{c}_0(T) = \frac{[(1 - a)B(R^*, T)]^{(a-1)}}{A(r - p)a^a} Q_0^{1-a} W_0$$

which gives the unit cost associated with any service life T, when factor intensities are chosen optimally for that T. The optimal T, $\hat{T}$, is then that value which minimizes the right-hand side of (7); it must satisfy the first order minimum condition[8]

(8)
$$\frac{ae^{-R \cdot T}}{B(R^*, T)} - \frac{e^{-RT}}{B(R, T)} = 0.$$

Hence from equation (4a) we can conclude that the currently optimum capital output ratio, k_0 is given by the right-hand side of that equation with T replaced by $\hat{T}$. That equation, however, expresses k_0 in terms of the ratio of the wage rate to capital good prices, W_0/Q_0 which cannot be taken as an exogenous parameter in our model. Indeed, what our model assumes as exogenously given is

[7] Since by assumption the price of capital goods relative to the price of output is expected to change at the constant rate q^*, it follows that the price of capital goods itself is expected to grow at the constant rate $q = p + q^*$. Note that the conclusion that cost must be expected to rise at a constant rate could be reached without recourse to the assumption of a constant mark up by starting out with the assumption that Q is expected to grow at the constant rate q. With this assumption, cost can readily be shown to grow at the constant rate $(1 - a)q + a(w - g)$. Alternatively, (5) could be established by defining q^* as the growth of Q relative to unit cost. In either case the assumption of a constant mark up would still be needed to establish the constancy of the rate of growth of output price and its equality to the rate of growth of unit cost.

[8] It can be verified that the second order condition, $d^2c_0/dT^2 > 0$, is also satisfied as long as $m + g > 0$ and hence $L > 0$. An approximate explicit solution of (8) for $\hat{T}$ is given in the footnote to Table 2.

the ratio of capital goods to output prices or Q_0/P_0. Hence

$$\frac{Q_0}{W_0} = \left(\frac{Q_0}{P_0}\right)\frac{P_0}{W_0},$$

is determined by P_0/W_0 which, in turn, depends on the mark-up policy. Our mark-up policy assumption (cf. assumption (e)) can now be formally expressed as

(9) PV of Revenue per unit $= M\hat{c}_0(\hat{T})$.

But from equation (5b) it follows that

$$PV \text{ of Revenue per unit} = \int_0^\infty P_0(t)e^{-rt}dt = P_0\int_0^\infty e^{-(r-p)t}dt = \frac{P_0}{r-p}.$$

Substituting this result in the left hand side of (9) and making use of (7) we can therefore write

$$P_0 = \frac{M[(1-a)B(R^*, \hat{T})]^{a-1}}{Aa^a} Q_0^{1-a}W_0^a.$$

Multiplying both sides by $P_0^{(a-1)}$ and solving for P_0, we finally obtain:

(10) $$P_0 = \frac{1}{a}\left(\frac{M}{A}\right)^{1/a}\left[\frac{(1-a)B(R^*, \hat{T})}{q_0}\right]^{(a-1)/a} W_0$$

expressing the price in terms of its "ultimate" determinants: the parameters of the production function, a, A; the factor prices, W_0, R^* and the exogenously given q_0; and the mark-up factor, M.

From (10), we can infer:

$$\frac{Q_0}{W_0} = q_0\frac{P_0}{W_0} = \frac{1}{a}\left(\frac{M}{A}\right)^{1/a}[(1-a)B(R^*, \hat{T})]^{(a-1)/a}q_0^{1/a}$$

and substituting this result for W_0/Q_0 in (4a) yields our final expression for the current optimal capital output ratio:

(11) $$k_0 = \left(\frac{I_0}{X}\right) = \frac{1-a}{Mq_0}B(R^*, \hat{T}) = \frac{1-a}{M}\frac{P_0}{Q_0}\frac{1-e^{-(r-p+d)\hat{T}}}{r-p+d}.$$

This equation is remarkably similar in form to that originally derived by Bischoff. It actually differs from that equation in only two respects, both having to do with the last factor. In the first place, in the denominator Bischoff's money rate r is replaced by the "real rate", $r - p$. We have thus established that, at least under our assumptions, *the real rate of interest relevant to the investment decision is the "own" rate measured in terms of output.*[9] The other difference is

---

[9] It is interesting to observe that this result differs substantively from that obtained for the conventional "putty-putty" model where it turns out that the real rate of interest should be

(Continued on next page)

the term, $e^{-(r-p+d)\hat{T}}$ appearing in the numerator and which brings in the effect of the "economic service life." This term did not appear in Bischoff because, under his simplifying assumptions, $\hat{T}$ could, essentially, be taken as indefinitely large (though, of course, even in his model the capacity of each vintage is dwindling toward zero through the decay factor d). This last term, unfortunately, confronts us with somewhat of a problem. We know that $\hat{T}$ is the solution for T of equation (8) so that to complete our derivation of $\hat{k}_0$ we should, in principle, replace this solution for $\hat{T}$ in the right hand side of (11). The difficulty is that equation (8) does not yield an explicit analytical solution.

One way around this difficulty is to secure some approximation to $\hat{T}$, or possibly to the whole numerator of the last factor, $1 - e^{-R\hat{T}}$. To this end we may note that, given Bischoff's estimate of d as .16, any realistic value of the real rate implies a value of R of no less than .20. Hence, if $\hat{T}$ were to be reasonably large, say somewhere above 10, $e^{-R\hat{T}}$ would be a rather small number compared with unity. But then, especially if $\hat{T}$ turned out to be not very sensitive to variations in $r - p$, the quantity $1 - e^{-R\hat{T}}$ might well be approximated by a constant close to one. These considerations led us to investigate the properties of $\hat{T}$ through the numerical solution of equation (8), for a range of "reasonable" values of the relevant parameters and for a realistic range of values of the real rate $r - p$. Selected results of these calculations are reproduced in Table 1.

Inspection of (8) shows that T is independent of the mark-up factor M, but depends on the coefficient a of the production function and on R and R^*, or equivalently R and L (since $R^* = R - L$). We chose for a a range of .65 to .75, though we regard the neighborhood of the lower bound as somewhat more realistic. It is harder to guess a reasonable range for L, which by definition equals $m + w - p$. However, using (6), this expression can be written more usefully in the alternative form $m + g - ((1 - a)/a)q^*$. For the United States, the rate of technical progress, g, can be estimated at close to 3 percent but we have no direct measure of m. As for the ratio of Q/P, q^*, it has had some tendency to increase at a very modest rate, though this may largely reflect errors of measurement. In the table we present results for a range of L from .03 to .05.

An inspection of the table suggests the following summary conclusions:

i) The only parameter to which $\hat{T}$ is sensitive is L. As might be expected $\hat{T}$ is a decreasing function of L; the faster machines deteriorate (m), and the faster the rate of technological progress (g), the shorter the economic life. In fact, as can be verified by inspection of (8) as L tends to zero (Bischoff's implicit assumption), T approaches infinity (if equipment does not accumulate inferiority with respect to new equipment, it never pays to discard it). It is also apparent from (11) that a larger value of L, (and hence m

(continued)
measured in terms of capital goods. Of course, in the special case $q^* = 0$, and hence $p = q = w - g$ (see (6)), the real rate in terms of output coincides with that in terms of capital goods (putty), and also with the real rate in terms of labor measured in "efficiency" units. Similarly for the general case $q^* \neq 0$, since $p = (1 - a)q + a(w - g)$, we can also say that what matters is the real rate in terms of a "basket," consisting of $(1 - a)$ units of putty and a units of labor in efficiency units.

TABLE 1

VALUE OF $\hat{T}$ AS A FUNCTION OF a, d, L, AND $r - p$

a	d	L	$r - p$	T
.65	.16	.03	.02	20
			.06	19
			.10	18
		.04	.02	16
			.06	15
			.10	14
		.05	.02	13
			.06	13
			.10	12
.75	.16	.03	.02	14
			.06	14
			.10	13
		.04	.02	11
			.06	11
			.10	10
		.05	.02	9
			.06	9
			.10	9
.65	.10	.03	.02	21
			.06	20
			.10	19
		.04	.02	17
			.06	16
			.10	15
		.05	.02	14
			.06	13
			.10	13

and g), by reducing the service life, tends to *decrease* the capital output ratio, as it results in a higher "rental cost."

ii) For the neighborhood of the parameters which we regard as most realistic for the U.S. economy of the postwar period, the value of $\hat{T}$ is in the neighborhood of 15 years ± 2 years, or a little lower if a is closer to .75.

iii) $\hat{T}$ is a *decreasing* function of the real rate $r - p$, but in the relevant range of the parameters, it is clearly very insensitive to variations in this variable.[10]

[10] The finding that $\hat{T}$ tends to fall with R is rather surprising and counter-intuitive. Indeed, the literature on optimal equipment replacement policy suggests that a higher interest rate generally works toward postponing replacement and thus larger $\hat{T}$. Our results come about because as R rises, the optimal labor capital ratio rises, which makes for a decreasing $\hat{T}$. It can be verified that if this ratio were unaffected by R then, in general, $d\hat{T}/dR$ would indeed tend to be positive (although even in this case $d\hat{T}/dR < 0$ is not impossible if the labor capital ratio is large enough and L is large relative to R).

TABLE 2

	(1)	(2)
$r - p$	Elasticity of $\dfrac{1 - e^{-(r-p+d)\hat{T}}}{r - p + d}$ with respect to $(r - p)^1$	Elasticity of $\dfrac{1}{r - p + d}$ with respect to $(r - p)$
.02	−0.103	−0.111
.06	−0.253	−0.273
.10	−0.357	−0.385

[1] In computing this elasticity we relied on the following approximations to T, which is close for $\hat{T}$ sufficiently large:

$$T = \frac{\ln R - \ln R^* - \ln c}{L},$$

where c is a constant. The values of T were obtained from Table 1, under the assumption $L = .04$, $a = .65$, and $d = .16$.

These observations in turn suggest that, in the relevant range of $r - p$, the last factor on the right hand side of (11), $(1 - e^{-RT})/R$ might well be replaced by the very convenient approximation: D/R, D a constant. As a further check on this approximation, we provide in Table 2 a comparison between the elasticity with respect to $r - p$ of $(1 - e^{-RT})/R$ and of the proposed approximation, D/R.[11] These elasticities are seen to be quite close, though that of the approximation is, of course, systematically slightly higher. This suggests that a better approximation might be $D/(R + c)$ where c is some small positive constant. This is the approximation we have actually employed, with c estimated from the data.

2.3. *Allowing for the effect of taxes.* Before we can utilize (11), or its approximation, for empirical tests we must make proper allowance for the effect of major tax provisions: the corporate income tax, depreciation provisions and investment tax credit. In this respect our treatment is analogous to that of previous authors (see e.g., Bischoff [2], Hall and Jorgenson [10], Jorgenson [11]), so that again we need only summarize the results.

Taking tax considerations into account, the present value (at time zero) of the "tax adjusted" cost per unit of initial capacity, resulting from the investment I_0—i.e., the right hand side of (3)—must be modified to:

$$(1 - u)\, \frac{E_0}{X}\, W_0 B(R^*, T) + Q_0\, \frac{I_0}{X}\, (1 - k - uz')$$

where

u = rate of direct taxation of business income

$z = \displaystyle\int_0^J e^{-rs} D(s)\, ds$

J = lifetime of the machine for tax purposes

$D(s)$ = proportion of the original cost of an asset of age s that can be deducted from taxable income

k = rate of tax credit on investment

$z' = (1 - k')z$, k' = rate of tax credit that can be deducted from original cost to obtain the depreciation base.

Also, in order to make proper allowances for taxes, our mark-up rule is modified to:

PV of tax adjusted revenue per unit $\equiv \dfrac{(1 - u)P_0}{r - p} = M \cdot PV$ of minimized

tax adjusted cost per unit.

Then a step-by-step repetition of the derivation in 2.2 leads to the following generalization of (11)

$$k_0 \equiv \left(\frac{l_0}{X}\right) = \frac{(1 - a)(1 - u)P_0}{MQ_0(1 - k - uz')} \cdot \frac{1 - e^{-(r-p+d)\hat{T}}}{r - p + d}.$$

This equation is again similar to (3.6) of Bischoff [1, (73)] from which it differs again only in the last factor. It can also be readily verified that the optimal economic life is totally unaffected by the kind of taxes we have allowed for and hence $\hat{T}$ is again given by the solution of equation (8). It follows that our arguments supporting the approximation of the last factor by $D/(R + c)$ remain valid. We thus conclude that the optimal capital-output ratio implied by our model can be approximated by

$$(12) \qquad \hat{k}_t = \frac{(1 - a)}{M}\left(\frac{(1 - u)}{1 - k - uz'}\right)\left(\frac{P}{Q}\right)\left(\frac{D}{r - p + d + c}\right).$$

This result, it should be acknowledged, depends on a number of rather stringent assumptions. However, some of these assumptions can be considerably relaxed. In particular, it should be apparent from our derivation that, given the constancy of g and q^*, our results remain valid even if r and w are expected to change, as long as $r - w$ (the real rate in terms of labor) is expected to remain constant. Finally, while we have developed the theory for the Cobb-Douglas production function, the crucial proposition in our derivation, namely that prices and unit costs both rise at the same constant rate p, generalizes for any production function homogeneous of degree 1, provided $p = q$, i.e., in essence, for a single sector model.

3. DERIVATION OF THE INVESTMENT FUNCTION

3.1. *Short-run adjustments.* Equation (1), with $\hat{k}_t$ defined by (12), gives the static equilibrium relationship among I, ΔX^c, P/Q, and $r - p$. Since actual data are generated by the economy in which these variables are continuously changing, we must modify (12) in order to accommodate adjustment processes. This is one of the problems thoroughly discussed by Bischoff. In this paper, we will simply list the more important considerations which led Bischoff to his formulation of the dynamic adjustment.

(a) In our theoretical discussion we did not distinguish among decisions to add to capacity, placement of orders for, and shipment of equipment, and actual additions to capacity. In actual practice, these are clearly distinct actions which take place sequentially. After the need for addition to capacity is recognized, specifications for the equipment required for this addition to capacity corresponding to anticipated relative prices are drawn up. The order containing these specifications is then placed, and the equipment is finally produced, shipped and installed. We have no information on the timing of decisions to add to capacity, but we feel that the timing relationship between the decision to add to capacity and orders for equipment is much less variable over business cycles than that between orders and shipments. We therefore take orders for equipment as the dependent variable for our investment equation. The relationship between orders and the national income definition of expenditures on producers durable equipment will be discussed in Section 3.4.

(b) Orders reflect recent past decisions, and decisions are based on the anticipated need for additions to capacity and anticipated relative prices. Like Bischoff, we assume that anticipated relative prices are functions of past relative prices, and that anticipated need for capacity is proportional to anticipated output which is, in turn, a function of past outputs.

These considerations, together with a variety of statistical reasoning, led Bischoff to the following specifications:

$$(13) \qquad OPD_t = \sum_{i=0}^{n} \alpha_i VPD_{t-i-1} XB_{t-i} + \sum_{i=1}^{n+1} \beta_i VPD_{t-i} XB_{t-i}$$

where n is the length of the orders lag, OPD denotes orders for producers durable equipment, XB is gross domestic business product (our approximation to X), and

$$(13') \qquad VPD \equiv A' \frac{1-u}{1-k-uz'} \frac{PXB}{PPD} \frac{1}{d+\rho^*+c}$$

is our operational empirical approximation to $\hat{k}$ of equation (12).[11,12] The

[11] It should be readily apparent that this formulation of the investment function is broadly consistent with the findings about the determinants of replacement expenditure reported by Feldstein and Foot [7]. Our dependent variable is (order for) *gross* investment, and we make nowhere use of the assumption that replacement expenditure is proportional to the stock of capital. Furthermore, our distributed lags of past sales can, at least in principle, account for the variables that are found to affect replacement expenditure, except for "available funds" whose role in *total* expenditure, however, cannot be inferred from the equation for replacement alone.

[12] As has been pointed out by Gould [9], the use of actual output XB as the independent variable in (13) is not altogether satisfactory. It would be clearly preferable to use a variable like orders booked, since, strictly speaking, actual output must be regarded as an endogenous, "optimizing" response of the firm to orders received. Unfortunately, there seems to be at present no feasible alternative to XB at the level of aggregation with which we deal in the present paper. Indeed, there exists no comprehensive series of aggregate orders corresponding to XB, and even the partial series available cannot be readily utilized because they involve a great deal of duplication. In any event, while the (attenuation) bias resulting from the use of actual output could be serious in dealing with individual firms, or even very disaggregated industry totals, it is unlikely to be very significant at the very aggregate level of our analysis, especially since the output variable that finally determines orders is an average of some twelve terms.

constant A' stands for the factor $(1 - a)D/M$, PXB is the deflator for XB, (our approximation to p) and PPD is the NIA price index for producers durable goods (our approximation to Q). Finally, ρ^* denotes a measure of the required real rate of return, or cost of capital, which we have denoted by $r - p$ in Section 2. It is only with respect to the measurement of this variable that our procedure differs significantly from Bischoff's.[13]

3.2. *The measurement of the cost of capital.* Following Modigliani-Miller [15 and 16], Bischoff proposed to measure ρ^* as

$$\rho^* = \rho(1 - ul)$$

where ρ is the market capitalization rate of an unlevered stream, and l is the target leverage or ratio of debt to debt-plus-equity. Note that since he did not explicitly face the problem of price expectations he did not need to specify whether this measure was an approximation to r or to $r - p$.

According to Modigliani-Miller $(M - M)\rho$ itself can be inferred from market data as

$$\rho = \frac{\hat{Z}(1 - u)}{S + D - uD} G$$

where D is the (market) value of firms' debt, S the market value of equity, Z the expected stream of before tax returns from current assets and G an adjustment factor for special growth opportunities incorporated in the market valuation of equity, S. Denoting by i the average rate of interest on outstanding debt and by $\Pi = (1 - u)[Z - (iD)]$ net of tax profits, we can rewrite $\hat{Z}(1 - u)$ as $\hat{\Pi} + (1 - u)(iD)$. Expected net profits $\hat{\Pi}$ is unobservable, but Bischoff suggested approximating it from dividends (Div) by relying on the hypothesis that dividend payments are proportional to expected profits, or $\Pi = Div/\delta$ where δ is the "target" payout ratio. We can then approximate ρ by

(14)
$$\rho \simeq b_1 i + b_2 \frac{Div}{S}$$

(14')
$$b_1 \equiv \frac{G(1 - u)D}{S + (1 - u)D}, \quad b_2 \equiv \frac{G}{\delta} \frac{S}{S + (1 - u)D}.$$

Bischoff next assumed that G, δ and S/D are reasonably stable over time, justifying treating b_1 and b_2 as constants. He further approximated Div/S and i respectively by a linear function of an index of dividend yields, RDP, and of corporate bond yields, RCB. He was thus led to measure ρ, by a linear function of RCB and RDP, say

(15)
$$\rho' = c_0 + c_1 RCB + c_2 RDP.$$

Accordingly, in (13'), he used the approximation

[13] Eisner and Nadiri have raised certain objections against the specification (13), (see [4, footnote 30]). These objections are discussed in footnote 17.

(16) $d + \rho^* = d + (c_0 + c_1 RCB + c_2 RDP)(1 - ul)$

(the constant c_0 does not appear in Bischoff since it is related to our approximation to e^{-RT}). He further assumed l to be constant (0.2) and estimated the coefficients c_0, c_1, c_2, simultaneously with the coefficients α_i and β_i of (13) by the method of maximum likelihood.

One striking feature of Bischoff's results is that his estimate of c_1 was consistently quite large relative to c_2, typically about one and a half times as large. Taken at face value, these estimates would seem to be inconsistent with (14), since, as is apparent from (14'), the ratio c_1/c_2 should be of the order of $b_1/b_2 = (1 - u)\delta D/S$. With the corporate tax rate u around .5, the dividend pay out ratio δ also in the order of .5 and since D/S is certainly less than one, c_1/c_2 should be less than 1/4, instead of over 1.5. His results, however, might be accounted for by the consideration that ρ' of equation (15) is a measure of ρ subject to errors on at least two counts: i) because dividends are an imperfect measure of expected profits $\hat{\Pi}$ and ii) because the growth component G may be subject to variations in time. At the same time, the long rate RCB also contains important information about ρ. Indeed the required return on equity capital, ρ, should differ from the long rate only by a "risk premium." If this premium were constant—or more generally a linear function of the long rate—then the long rate would be a perfect proxy for ρ. Thus, one might think of RCB as an alternative measure of ρ subject to error, this time error resulting from variation in time in the risk premium. Under these conditions the weights c_1 and c_2 may be expected to reflect in part the relative informational content of the two variables ρ' and RCB with respect to the non-directly observable variable ρ.[14]

However, our analysis of Section 2 shows that the appropriate measure of the required rate of return ρ^* is not the money rate of return r, but rather the real rate $(r - p)$. Now, as is well known, the capitalization rate of profits, $\hat{\Pi}/S$ is a real rate, and hence RDP itself can be regarded as a measure of the real rate up to proportionality factor.[15] However, RCB is a money rate. These considera-

[14] A possible additional explanation for the large relative weight of RCB is that the MM measure may be directly relevant for firms having reasonable access to the equity markets, while for other investors the required rate might be some linear function of the long rate. The cost of capital would then be an average of the MM measure and the long rate.

[15] This statement is only approximately valid. While it is correct to say that ρ, the capitalization rate for an *unlevered* stream, is a real rate, in the sense that it should be unaffected by the rate of inflation p, this is not strictly valid in the case of the capitalization rate for a levered stream, $\hat{\Pi}/S$. It was shown in [16, (equation (12c))], that $\hat{\Pi}/S = \rho + (1 - u)D/S(\rho - i)$. This equation can be shown to remain valid also in the presence of inflation, if D is expected to remain constant, while if one assumes, more reasonably, that the target leverage *ratio* remains constant in the face of inflation, then the right side should contain an additional term $-u(Dp/Si)\rho$, where i is the "real" rate of interest. Thus, in principle, $\hat{\Pi}/S$ is a (decreasing) function of the expected rate of inflation, p, because the last term contains p explicitly, and because, even in the absence of this term, it depends on the money rate which, in turn, will tend to increase with p. However, since D/S is quite small (around .2, as already noted) and u is roughly .5, the effect of p on $\hat{\Pi}/S$ should be quite small as long as p remains moderate. Some numerical calculations based on NIA and Flow of Funds data, fully confirmed this conjecture and lead to the conclusion that this effect could be safely disregarded, for the period of observation, and for foreseeable rates of inflation.

tions lead us to approximate $d + \rho^* + c$ by

(17) $d + \rho^* + c = d + [c_0 + c_1(RCB - p) + c_2RDP](1 - ul) + c$.

p measures the expected rate of change of prices, as in Section 2.[16,17]

3.3. *The measurement of the expected rate of inflation.* Unfortunately, the estimation of p in equation (17) poses a very difficult problem because what is needed is a subjective, anticipated rate of change of prices for which there are no direct data. One possibility, which has been used extensively in earlier work, is to rely on a weighted average of the past actual rate of change of prices as a proxy. However, it did not seem feasible to estimate the weights as a part of the estimation of the investment equation due to the severe non-linearity of the equation. We were thus led to attempt to approximate the expected rate of change by the following weighted average of past cited price changes:

(18) $$p_s = 400 \frac{1}{\sum\limits_{j=0}^{11} (.87)^j} \sum\limits_{j=0}^{11} (.87)^j \frac{PXB_{t-j} - PXB_{t-j-1}}{PXB_{t-j-1}}.$$

The weights are taken from a paper by Modigliani and Shiller [17], in which they have estimated a set of weights similar to the one in the above equation

---

[16] In the actual estimation of (13) the last constant c was dropped. This is because l is assumed constant and u has had no significant changes in the period of estimation. Under these conditions it would be impossible to secure reliable separate estimates of the constants c_0 and c. The estimated value of the constant c_0 reported in Table 3A below must thus be regarded as standing for $c_0 + c/(1 - ul)$, and since the first term should be close to zero, we should expect this estimated value to be positive, or at least non-negative.

[17] This measure of the cost of capital should be immune to the criticism levied by Eisner and Nadiri [4, (373-74)], against a somewhat related measure used in some of Jorgenson's work in computing the rental price of capital (c_1), namely the earning price ratio. This ratio, they argue, is "an implicit measure of expected future profits," rather than the desired measure of the ratio of *expected* earnings to market value. They further suggest that the latter ratio should tend to be more or less proportional to the interest rate. Accordingly the influence of the cost of capital on investment could be more reliably estimated by using the interest rate rather than the earning price ratio. Indeed the association of the latter variable with investment might reflect the role of expectations rather than the true effect of the cost of capital.

In our measure of the cost of capital we have replaced earnings with dividends which we regard as a better measure of expected future profit. At the same time, we acknowledge that even the dividend price ratio will not provide a perfect measure of the ratio of expected profit to price. On the other hand, as indicated in the text, the (real) interest rate will also not provide a perfect indicator—except if the risk premium is constant. There is no justification for such an assumption on a priori ground or in the light of the post-war experience. This period was characterized by a *declining* trend in the earning and dividend ratio, at least until the early 60's and a *rising* trend in interest rates, strongly suggesting a declining trend in the risk premium. (These opposite trends, incidentally readily explain the negative correlation between Jorgenson's c_1 and c_2 measures which so puzzled Eisner and Nadiri in [5, (220, Footnote 17)]. Since both the (real) interest rate and the dividend price ratio contain some, but only some, information about the true cost of capital, the measure we have used is a weighted average of these two. Finally, since the estimated weight of the interest rate turns out to be twice as large as that of the dividend-price ratio, there seems very little danger of significant upward bias in our estimate of the effect of the cost of capital, of the type suggested by Eisner and Nadiri for Jorgenson's c_1.

as a by-product of their study of the term structure of interest rates. We are not on very firm ground in transplanting the weights obtained in the estimation of a term structure equation to the investment equation, but we could not come up with a better alternative to it. Under the circumstances, we have tried to locate some information, however indirect, on the accuracy of this approximation.

The only continuous time series covering the period of 1950–1969 related to the price expectations of business decision makers that we have been able to locate is a semi-annual survey of so-called business economists conducted by Mr. J. A. Livingston of the *Philadelphia Bulletin.* In his survey, Mr. Livingston asks his respondents to state what they think the level of Consumer Price Index (CPI) and Wholesale Price Index (WPI) will be six months and twelve months after the date of the survey. Since the questionnaire used in the survey provides the latest figures on these indices, we can interpret the responses to these questions as giving the respondents' idea of the expected rate of change of these indices.

There are several serious difficulties in using these time series of expectations generated by Mr. Livingston's surveys. First, they are on the WPI and CPI, while what we need for our purposes is the expectation of the rate of change of *PXB*, domestic private business output in the national income accounts. Second, Livingston's data are expectations for the period of one year or less from the time when the survey is conducted, while what we need are much longer run expectations; short run expectations of prices may be influenced much more by very recent special circumstances than the longer period expectations would be.

To get around the first of these two difficulties, we have calculated the weighted average of the past actual rate of change of CPI in the same way as in equation (18) above, and compared the resulting series with the Livingston data on expectations of the rate of change of the CPI for a period of a year from the time when the survey is given.[18] This comparison is shown in Figure 1.

All we can say about Figure 1 is that the Livingston expectations and our proxy move in broadly similar patterns, though the levels are different, after 1962 or so, while the two series have totally different patterns before 1960. Perhaps all we can conclude from this comparison is that, for the period since 1965, any series based on the past rate of change of prices catches the broad pattern of the movements of the price expectations, while it does not provide much reliable information about price expectations before 1960.

Under the circumstances, we conclude that we have to be very cautious in using equation (18) as the mechanism generating price expectations, and that we should not be surprised if it served as a very rough approximation since 1965 but did not work at all before.

We would like to make a final comment on the measurement of *p.* It is quite possible that some of the decision makers do not pay much attention to the expected rate of change of prices unless their recent experience indicates that it

---

[18] Since the Livingston data are only six-monthly, we have interpolated them to give quarterly predictions.

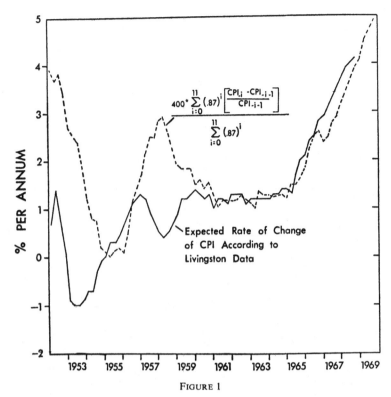

$$400^* \frac{\sum_{i=0}^{11} (.87)^i \left[\frac{CPL_i - CPL_{-i-1}}{CPL_{-i-1}} \right]}{\sum_{i=0}^{11} (.87)^i}$$

Expected Rate of Change
of CPI According to
Livingston Data

% PER ANNUM

FIGURE 1

COMPARISON OF EXPECTED RATE OF CHANGE OF CPI ACCORDING TO THE
LIVINGSTON SURVEY AND A WEIGHTED AVERAGE OF PAST VALUES OF CPI

is quite important to do so. If the actual rate of change of prices has been very small in the recent past, those decision makers who did not correct for the rate of change of prices in their calculation of cost of capital find that, *ex post*, they have not been seriously wrong, and they may then continue to ignore the rate of change of price in their calculation of the cost of capital in their current decisions. If a substantial proportion of the decision makers behaved this way, then at any point of time, some proportion would take account of the expected rate of change of prices while the remainder would assume that it is either zero or a small constant, the proportionality depending on the recent actual rate of change of prices.

To take this kind of consideration explicitly into account would be an impossible task since the estimation of our investment function already involves fairly complex non-linearities. We shall attempt to account for this possibility by supposing that if some fraction of the decision makers adjust the money interest rate for the rate of change of prices and the rest do not, then this is similar, in effect, to a situation in which all decision makers adjust only partially.

Thus we hypothesize that the rate of interest that enters the cost of capital in our investment equation is a weighted average of the form:

$$w_1 RCB + w_2(RCB - p) = RCB - w_2 P$$

$$w_1 + w_2 = 1.0$$

where w_2 depends on the recent past actual rate of change of prices. We have experimented with the following approximations for w_2:

$$w_2 = \frac{1}{12} \sum_{i=0}^{11} D_i$$

(19)

$$D_i = \begin{cases} 0 & \\ 1 & \text{otherwise} \end{cases} \quad \text{if} \quad \frac{PXB_{t-i} - PXB_{t-i-1}}{PXB_{t-i-1}} \leq C.$$

We shall refer to w_2 as defined above as "threshold weights."

3.4. *New orders and their relation to expenditure on producer durables.* We have noted that OPD, the dependent variable in equation (13), represents (net) orders for producers' durable goods. Unfortunately, data for this variable do not exist at present. We have, therefore, constructed a time series for this variable based on current and later expenditure on producers' durables (EPD) as given in the national income accounts, orders for machinery and equipments, and shipments of machinery and equipments.[19] This constructed series is used as the dependent variable in (13).

The variable OPD plays an important direct role in the FMP model, particularly in the inventory equation and in the price equation. However, for our present purpose interest centers on actual expenditure, EPD. We hypothesize that EPD can be accounted for by a distributed lag of current and past values of OPD, with the weights reflecting the prevailing time required for execution of different types of orders. We also allow for the possibility of a variable lag because the time required to process an order might tend to change over the business cycle, depending on the volume of orders outstanding, relative to existing capacity. Lacking an explicit measure of capacity of the equipment industry we have approximated the last mentioned effect by the ratio of unfilled orders ($OUPD$) to deliveries, or EPD.

Thus our investment expenditure equation takes the form:

(20a)
$$EPD = \sum_{i=0}^{5} \left[a_i + b_i \left(\frac{OUPD}{EPD} \right)_{-(1+i)} \right] OPD_{-i}.$$

The coefficients of this equation have been estimated subject to the constraint that

$$\sum_{i=0}^{5} a_i = 1, \qquad \sum_{i=0}^{5} b_i = 0$$

[19] A detailed description of the procedure used for generating the OPD data and a discussion of the reliability of the data so generated is available from the authors.

to insure that, given time enough, deliveries must match orders. The estimated value of coefficients and other characteristics of this equation are:

$$
\begin{aligned}
a_0 &= .4357 & b_0 &= -.5378 \\
a_1 &= .3378 & b_1 &= -.1752 \\
a_2 &= .2102 & b_2 &= -.0768 \\
a_3 &= .0290 & b_3 &= .2181 \\
a_4 &= -.0145 & b_4 &= .2489 \\
a_5 &= -.0521 & b_5 &= .1691 \\
R^2 &= .9261 & \text{Sample period: 54.3--66.4} \\
\sigma_\epsilon &= .8462 \\
D.W. &= 1.14
\end{aligned}
$$

Unfilled orders, $OUPD$, are in turn given by the perpetual inventory formulation

$$(20\,\mathrm{b}) \qquad OUPD = .25(OPD - EPD) + OUPD_{-1}.$$

In interpreting the coefficients of equation (20), it is helpful to note that the average value of the ratio $OUPD/EPD$ over the sample period is roughly .37.[20] Thus, the pattern of the b_i coefficients of equation (20) implies that, as $OUPD/EPD$ rises, the weight of the most recent orders declines, while the weight of orders placed further back correspondingly rises, lengthening the average delivery period.

It is apparent from the content of this section that there are two ways in which one can judge the performance of our model. One method consists in comparing the actual values of OPD with the values generated by (13). This test, however, is of limited value in that the series for OPD is our own construction, and, furthermore, because of the method used to construct it, the current and very recent values of this series are subject to large revisions. A more telling test is how well (13) together with (20) can account for actual expenditure, EPD. In this test, the results of which are reported below, EPD is always computed from (20), using the values of OPD, current and lagged, generated by (13).

4. ESTIMATION AND TESTS

Table 3 reports the results of our estimation of equation (13), with the cost of capital given by (17), for alternative periods of estimation and alternative specifications of the crucial variable p.[21] Part A provides summary measures of

[20] It should be remembered that EPD is measured at an annual rate, while $OUPD$, being a stock concept, is not affected by the length of period. This accounts for the coefficient .25 in (20b).

[21] The estimates were carried out before the revision of the National Income data in summer '71, '72 and '73. Since the period of estimation extends at most through 1968, and the revision did not affect the pre-1967 data, and affected 1968 to a relatively minor extent, we can safely conclude that revised data would not perceptibly affect the estimates reported in Table 3. The data used in the extrapolation tests of Table 4 are also unrevised, and here the effect of the revisions is considerably more serious, as the revisions for more recent years are non-negligible and affect not only EPD and OPD, but also the independent variables used in the extrapolation of (13). Some comments on the implications of the revised data are provided in footnotes 27 and 28.

TABLE 3

PART A

SUMMARY CHARACTERISTICS OF ALTERNATIVE SPECIFICATION

	Sample Period: 1953 : 1—1965 : 4			Sample Period: 1953 : 1—1968 : 4		
	(1)[6]	(2)[7]	(3)[8]	(4)[9]	(5)[10]	(6)[11]
R^2[1]	.979	.968 (.974)	.974 (.977)	.984 (.987)	.987 (.990)	.910 (.982)
Se[2,4]	1.095	1.370 (1.238)	1.227 (1.169)	1.397 (1.273)	1.253 (1.143)	3.234 (1.517)
DW[3,4]	1.71	1.29 (1.75)	1.27 (2.07)	1.25 (1.77)	1.232 (1.915)	0.32 (2.00)
λ[4]	0	.35	.35	.45	.40	.96
c_0[5]	0	.37494	.30465	0	0	—
c_1[5]	3.64316	3.49123	6.83889	2.35035	2.08971	—
c_2[5]	2.28964	5.81559	−.66020	1.82362	1.38398	—

1. The ratio of explained variance to total variance adjusted for the degrees of freedom.
2. Standard error of estimate, adjusted for degrees of freedom.
3. Durbin-Watson Statistic of the residual.
4. λ represents the first order serial correlation of residuals. The estimation program does not minimize the residual sum of squares with respect to λ. We have, therefore, followed the procedure in which we first estimate parameters assuming λ to be zero, and calculate the serial correlation of residual, and then re-estimate the equation assuming the true serial correlation to be equal to the one so calculated. The second round estimates almost always gave residuals whose serial correlation was very close to zero. Whenever λ is other than zero, for R^2, Se, and DW, we report, *without* parenthesis, their values calculated with $\lambda = 0$, which are, for present purpose, the relevant statistics to judge goodness of fit. For the sake of completeness we also show in parenthesis the values obtained allowing for the estimated value of λ as reported in the table.
5. c_0, c_1, and c_2 are, respectively, the constant and the coefficients of $RCB\text{-}p$ and RDP in the cost of capital terms. See equation (17) in the text.
6. Estimated under the assumption that p is constant.
7. p is assumed to be given by (21a).
8. p is assumed to be given by (21c).
9. p is assumed to be zero for the period 1954–64, and given by (21a) for the period 1965–68. Because of the way the depreciation rate, d, and c_0 enter the cost of capital, this could be reinterpreted to mean that p is a constant $\bar{p}$, for 1953–64, and it is $p_s − 1.2 + \bar{p}$ for 1965–1968.
10. p is assumed to be zero for the period 1953–1964, and given by (21b) for 1965–68. The same comment as in footnote 13 applies to this case.
11. VPD is assumed constant throughout the straight acceleration model.

PART B

ESTIMATED STEADY STATE ELASTICITIES OF OPD WITH RESPECT TO $RCB\text{-}p$ AND RDP

	(1)		(2)		(3)		(4)		(5)	
	$RCB\text{-}p$	RDP	$RCB\text{-}p$	RDP	$RCB\text{-}p$	RDP	$RCB\text{-}p$	RDP	$RCB\text{-}p$	RDP
1953, 1st quarter	−.34	−.38	−.05	−.37	−.42	.05	−.28	−.38	−.29	−.34
1958, 1st quarter	−.41	−.32	−.08	−.32	−.36	.05	−.35	−.33	−.35	−.29
1963, 1st quarter	−.50	−.25	−.19	−.23	−.35	.04	−.42	−.25	−.41	−.22
1965, 1st quarter	−.53	−.22	−.20	−.20	−.33	.04	−.44	−.22	−.42	−.20

TABLE 3

PART C

PERCENT APPROACH TO EQUILIBRIUM

Changes in XB	(1)	(2)	(3)	(4)	(5)
1	310	138	270	284	230
2	262	160	280	275	235
3	230	169	273	263	234
4	209	168	252	247	227
5	195	161	224	229	215
6	185	150	192	209	199
7	175	137	161	188	179
8	164	126	133	167	187
9	150	116	112	146	136
10	135	108	98	127	117
11	118	103	94	112	104
12	100	100	100	100	100

Changes in V

	(1)	(2)	(3)	(4)	(5)
1	0	0	0	0	0
2	18	87	49	20	28
3	38	143	80	38	54
4	59	173	98	54	75
5	78	183	107	67	91
6	92	181	109	78	103
7	103	170	108	86	110
8	108	153	106	92	112
9	110	135	103	96	111
10	107	119	101	99	107
11	103	107	100	100	103
12	100	100	100	100	100

fit as well as the estimated value of the three coefficients c_0, c_1, and c_2 of (17). When, as in column (1), the value of c_0 is given as zero, the estimation was carried out constraining this coefficient to be zero. This was done because the unconstrained estimation tended to yield a large negative value of c_0 which cannot be readily reconciled with *a priori* specifications.[22] It also implied an implausibly high value of the elasticity of the capital output ratio, and hence of investment, with respect to the long-run cost of capital. In every instance imposing this constraint increased but slightly the sum of squared residuals while yielding much more plausible estimates of the elasticities. The long-run elasticities implied by the estimates are shown in Part B of the table for each component

[22] Cf. footnote 16.

of the cost of capital, namely *RDP* and the "real" interest rate, *RCB-p*. Since these elasticities are not constant under our specifications, we report the values computed for four representative periods; we recall here that, over the period of observation, *RDP* has tended on the whole to decline, especially till the mid 60's, while *RCB* has tended to rise steadily. It should also be observed that in the steady state, *RDP* can be expected to change roughly in proportion to the real rate of interest; hence, the overall longest-run effect of a change in the real interest rate, both directly and indirectly through *RDP*, is roughly equal to the sum of the elasticities for each component.

The coefficients α_i and β_i of the distributed lag of equation (13) were estimated, as in Bischoff [1] by Almon's method using third degree polynomials. We do not report the values of the individual coefficients α_i, β_i, because they are not easy to interpret economically. Instead we report in Part C, the essential economic implication of the estimated pattern. Specifically we show in the upper part of the table the time path of response to a step change in output, *XB*, as a percentage of the steady state response; this steady state response is simply the rate of investment which is needed to *maintain* the additional capacity, installed in response to the change in *XB*. The initial response on the other hand shows the path of investment through which the *additional* capacity, needed to produce the incremental output is provided for; in other words, it shows the time path of the "accelerator." As did Bischoff, we assume that the process of providing the additional capacity is completed within three years. Our model, like most others, implies that the entries in the upper half should rise to a peak (which could occur in the very first quarter) and then decline monotonically toward the steady state value, which is normalized to be 100.

The lower part of Table 3C gives the path of response of orders to a step change in the optimal capital output ratio, *VPD* (the counterpart of $\hat{k}$ of Section 2), whatever the source of change in *VPD*, (cost of capital, *P/Q*, or tax provisions). The entries show the implicit response in quarter *j* after the step change, as a percentage of the long-run response. (In the long run, we recall, investment is unit elastic with respect to *VPD*). As shown by Bischoff, it is an essential implication of the putty-clay model that this response should rise monotonically from zero to 100. By contrast the putty-putty hypothesis implies an "accelerator type" path, greatly overshooting the steady state response and reflecting investment expenditure for the purpose of modifying the capital intensity of the stock of capital *already in place*.

In columns (1) to (3) of Table 3A the parameters were estimated over the sample period 1953 through 1965. 1953 was chosen as the beginning of the sample period so as to avoid the severe disturbances due to the Korean war, and we terminated the sample period at 1965 so as to exclude the period of increasingly inflationary expectations that began in 1966. The last three equations based on the period 1953–1968, incorporate the more recent inflationary episode.

In column (1) we have assumed *p* to be zero; the resulting equation is thus a replication of Bischoff's original equation, except for the effect of revisions in the data. This equation is seen to perform quite well in terms of R^2 and DW, though the implied elasticity of investment with respect to RDP and RCB given in Part B are rather higher than the *a priori* values computed in Table 2. The pattern of dynamic response in Part C also conforms reasonably well with *a priori* specification. To be sure, there is a slight overshooting in the response to a change in VPD, but it is small enough to be consistent with an "almost" putty-clay hypothesis.[23]

In columns (2) and (3) we have tested two alternative specifications of p. Our intention was to test three possible specifications, to wit:

(21a) $$p = p_s - 1.2$$

(21b) $$p = w_2 p_s$$

(21c) $$p = p_L - 1.2$$

where p_s is defined by equation (18), w_2 is defined by equation (19), and p_L is the one year expected rate of change of the CPI taken from the Livingston survey data. The reason for subtracting 1.2 will be discussed a little later. Unfortunately, we were unable to obtain estimates using specification (21b), as the non-linear estimation program ran into a singular matrix in the process of minimization, presumably reflecting multicollinearity of the variables. Estimates using the definitions (21a) and (21c) are reported in columns (2) and (3) respectively.

It is readily apparent that explicit introduction of p, in either specification, worsens the result in every aspect. In columns (2) and (3) the standard errors of residuals are 35% and 20% larger than that in column (1). Furthermore, the Durbin-Watson statistic has deteriorated sufficiently that we felt it necessary

---

[23] In [4, (footnote 30)], Eisner, commenting on a similar result reported by Bischoff in a paper presented at the 1966 San Francisco meetings of the Econometric Society, has hypothesized that he "obtained his results in support of the putty-clay role of relative prices from the particular constraints introduced into the Almon lag estimator." Although the nature of these biassing constraints is not specified in [4], Bischoff has kindly informed us that Eisner objected to the fact that in the distributed lag there was no term in current VPD, a specification which is also retained in our equation (13). Eisner conjectured that a very different pattern of coefficients would be obtained if one added, to the second summation, the term $VPD_t XB_t$.

This objection has already been largely invalidated by the results reported by Bischoff in [2, (362, Section III)]. He showed that using the very same method of estimation employed by Eisner and Nadiri in [4], even though this method is not entirely appropriate under a putty-clay hypothesis, one obtains a set of estimated coefficients for VPD and for XB which "are in accord with the suggestion of the "putty-clay" hypothesis", (p. 365) that the change "in relative prices operates more slowly than..... ....changes in output", (p. 366, cf. also Table 5, columns (4) and (5)). Bischoff has also kindly made available to us the results of a recent test in which he relied on the specification (13) used also in his original contribution [1] but, following Eisner's suggestion, he added the term $\beta_0 VPD_t XB_t$. For the purpose of this test he used the specification of VPD underlying column (5) which is our preferred specification (see below) and a period of observation only slightly different from that used in column (5), 1954.1 to 1968.1V. Since our putty-clay hypothesis implies that the coefficient β_0 should be close to zero, it could not be expected to lie on the 3rd degree polynomial on which the weights β_i, $i = 1$ to 11 were required to lie. Accordingly, this coefficient was estimated freely. The point estimate of β_0 is negative but numerically small (less than 10% of the steady state response), and statistically insignificant (t ratio of 0.7), and, contrary to Eisner's conjecture, the remaining coefficients, and hence the approach to equilibrium, are essentially unchanged.

TABLE 4

DYNAMIC SIMULATION ERRORS OF SELECTED EQUATIONS[1]

PART A *OPD*

	OPD ACTUAL ($, bill.)[2] (0)	Simulation Error					
		(1)	(1a)[3]	(1b)[4]	(2)	(4)	(5)
1965 I	44.2	0	0	0	0	−.9	.1
II	45.3	.1	0	−.2	−2.5	−1.0	−.3
III	46.6	−.6	−.9	−1.5	−4.5	−2.0	−1.3
IV	49.9	.7	.2	−.8	−3.2	−.8	−.3
1966 I	52.8	2.3	1.7	.2	−1.5	.5	.9
II	54.1	4.3	3.4	1.7	0	1.9	2.1
III	54.4	3.7	2.2	.4	−.9	.6	.6
IV	51.8	3.7	1.4	−.5	−.7	−1.0	−.8
1967 I	48.4	3.0	−.2	−2.1	−1.3	−2.1	−2.2
II	49.9	5.2	1.1	−1.3	.3	−.4	−1.1
III	51.5	7.2	2.2	−.8	1.5	1.1	−.3
IV	51.5	7.9	2.1	−1.5	.5	1.1	−.8
1968 I	51.3	7.2	.6	−3.8	−.8	−.2	−2.4
II	51.7	7.9	.5	−4.3	2.2	−.3	−2.4
III	54.1	10.9	3.0	−2.1	5.1	1.7	−.5
IV	57.3	14.8	6.3	.8	7.6	4.4	1.6
1969 I	58.3	16.4	7.1	.6	7.3	4.9	.8
II	59.5	18.3	8.3	1.2	8.7	6.2	1.4
III	58.0	17.7	7.1	−.5	9.3	5.1	.4
IV	58.0	19.6	8.8	1.0	11.7	7.0	2.3
1970 I	56.0	19.8	9.2	1.6	12.1	7.5	3.1

1. Dynamic Simulation of equations (13), (20a) and (20b) together starting in the first quarter of 1958.
2. The actual and computed figures reported in part A and B of this table are based on the data available at the time the estimation was carried out, basically those reported in the July 1970 issue of the Survey of Current Business. Since then the data have been repeatedly and substantially revised. The effect of these revisions is taken up in footnote 28.
3. The difference between actual *OPD* (*EPD*) and its simulated value, using the estimate given in column (1), Table 3, and assuming that p is zero for 1953–64 and given by (21a) thereafter.
4. The difference between actual *OPD* (*EPD*) and its simulated value, using the estimate given in column (1), Table 3, and assuming that p is zero for 1953–64 and given by (21b) thereafter.
5. Actual values of *EPD* (same as "Investment in Producers' Durable Equipment; Billions of 1958 dollars" as reported in Table 1.2, National Income Accounts). The effect of the recent revision of the *EPD* figures for the comparisons made in the table is briefly touched upon in footnote 28.

TABLE 4

DYNAMIC SIMULATION ERRORS OF SELECTED EQUATIONS[1]

PART B *EPD*

	Actual Value ($, bill.)[5] (0)	Simulation Error					
		(1)	(1a)[3]	(1b)[4]	(2)	(4)	(5)
1965 I	42.1	.3	.3	.3	−.4	−.4	.3
II	42.7	−.2	−.2	−.3	−1.4	−1.1	−.4
III	45.0	.7	.6	.4	1.1	−.3	.4
IV	46.4	.6	.4	0	−1.9	−.6	.1
1966 I	48.1	.7	.4	−.3	−2.2	−.6	0
II	49.4	.9	.5	−.5	−2.5	−.7	−.2
III	50.9	1.4	.7	−.6	−2.4	−.6	−.2
IV	52.0	2.5	1.3	−.2	−1.7	−.3	0
1967 I	49.8	1.0	−.8	−2.5	−3.4	−2.5	−2.4
II	51.1	3.3	.8	−1.2	−1.3	−1.0	−1.0
III	50.6	3.8	.5	−1.8	−1.1	−1.1	−1.5
IV	50.8	5.1	1.0	−1.8	−.5	−.5	−1.4
1968 I	52.7	7.7	2.7	−.5	1.3	1.4	.1
II	51.5	7.0	1.2	−2.6	.6	0	−1.6
III	52.6	8.6	2.0	−2.2	2.2	.9	−1.0
IV	54.3	10.9	3.6	−1.1	4.2	2.3	.1
1969 I	55.4	12.5	4.5	−.7	5.3	3.0	.3
II	57.0	14.7	6.0	.2	6.8	4.3	1.0
III	57.3	15.8	6.3	−.1	7.4	4.5	.7
IV	57.8	17.4	7.4	.4	8.8	5.5	1.3
1970 I	56.5	17.7	7.2	−.1	8.9	5.4	.9

3, 4. See bottom of Part A.

to reestimate these equations allowing for first order serial correlation of residuals. In column (3), c_2 has the "wrong" sign, so that the elasticity of *OPD* with respect to *RDP* is positive (though it also is negligibly small). In column (2), the elasticities are not altogether unreasonable, but the dynamic reaction pattern shown in Part C of the table does not seem to be sensible. The acceleration seems to be unusually weak, and the overshooting of the reaction to changes in *VPD* is very large.[24]

However, if we extrapolate these equations into the period of rapidly rising prices and uncommonly high interest rates beginning with 1966, the results turn out to be quite different from those obtained over the period of fit, and are altogether rather disquieting. This can be verified from Table 4. In Part A of

[24] If the true nature of the production function is putty-putty, the over-shooting in the response to changes in *XB* and *VPD*, should roughly be the same, and this possibility cannot be ruled out completely. However, our experiences in the past suggest that strong overshooting in response to changes in *VPD* leads to an unrealistic degree of instability of the full model.

this table, column (0) gives the actual value of *OPD*, from 1965 through the first quarter of 1970. The remaining columns—except for (1a) and (1b) to be discussed presently—show the difference between this value and the value computed from the corresponding estimated equation. Similarly, in Part B column (0) gives the actual value of *EPD* while the remaining columns show the difference between this value and that computed from (13) and (20).[25]

It is seen that equation (1) begins to underestimate *OPD* seriously immediately following the sample period; and this underestimate, in turn, generates a similar error in *EPD* beginning a few quarters later. By 1970 the underestimate for both equations approach the 20 billion level!

We do not present results of extrapolating equation (3) based on the Livingston measure of *p*, both because this equation is inconsistent with our model and because, in any event, this series is supposed to measure short-run expectations of the cost of living rather than long-run expectations of output prices. However, the extrapolation of equation (2), shown in the corresponding column of Table 4 is rather instructive. Despite its inferior performance through 1965, this equation manages to go through the middle of 1968 with errors which are not significantly different from those of the sample period. It is only in the third quarter of 1968 that it begins to significantly underestimate both *OPD* and *EPD*. But, once it begins, it becomes rapidly worse, reaching $12 billion for *OPD* and $9 billion for *EPD* by the first quarter of 1970.

A possible clue to this rather puzzling set of results might be found in the Livingston survey data. As we argued in our earlier discussion of these data, they suggest that there was a break in the formation of expectations in the mid 1960's. Indeed, an earlier study (Turnovsky [18]) concluded that before 1965, expectations could be regarded as rather constant, averaging about 1.2% per annum, and it was only after the early 1960's that they were found to be closely related to actual price changes.

To pursue this clue that a radical change in the prevailing mechanism of formation of price expectation on the part of firms might have occurred around 1965–1966, we began by carrying out the following experiment. We took equation (1) which, it will be recalled, is estimated through 1965 assuming that *p* was zero, and we extrapolated it from 1966 on by replacing *RCB* by *RCB-p* with *p* defined by equation (21a). Because there is a long lag in the reaction of *OPD* to *VPD*, we have replaced *RCB* by *RCB-p* in the first quarter of 1965 so that by the first quarter of 1966 some of the effect of this replacement will be felt. The resulting predictions of *OPD* and *EPD* are given in columns (1a) of Table 4. This result is very similar to that given in column (2), though generally somewhat superior. To the extent that the dynamic reaction pattern of (1.a) is more plausible than that of (2), this result provides some support for the hypothesis that one should explicitly allow for a break in the mechanism of price expectation formation around the mid-sixties, instead of assuming that the same mechanism was operating through the whole period, as specified in equation (2).

[25] These so-called "extrapolations" reported in Table 4B are dynamic simulations of equations (13), (20a), and (20b) starting from the first quarter of 1958.

The experiment was also repeated using the alternative specification of p given by (21b) and the results, reported in column (1b) are striking. The fit remains remarkably good down to the very end of the period.

Encouraged by these results we have reestimated two versions of equation (13) incorporating in it formally the hypothesis of a break in expectations by specifying that p is a constant through 1964 and is given by either (21a),—equation 4 or by (21b)—equation (5). The period of estimation in both cases is 1953 to the end of 1968. Turning first to Table 3, we find that the fit of both equations is rather good, especially that of (5). It is, in fact, comparable to that of equation (1), when we allow for the generally higher level of *OPD* in the more recent period. The estimated elasticities in Part B of Table 3 are generally somewhat lower, which is in the right direction, though even the elasticities of (5), which are the lowest, remain above the *a-priori* values of Table 2. The dynamic response characteristics in Part C are again broadly consistent with the putty-clay formulation, though (5) implies a slight overshooting. But, in terms of extrapolation for the five quarters following the period of fit (5) performs distinctly better. Indeed this equation performs roughly as well in the post 1966 period as in earlier periods. To illustrate, the ratio of the root mean square error to the mean value of *OPD* is 2.8% for the period 1966-69, as compared with 3.1% for the entire period '58-'69. In the case of *EPD* the relative errors are 2% and 2.1% respectively[26]

On the whole then equation (5) appears to be the most satisfactory in that it is consistent with the *a-priori* specifications of the model and is also capable of accounting for the behavior of *EPD* throughout the postwar period. It should be added that since the completion of the calculation given in Table 4, the National Income Account estimates of *EPD*, and of other series relevant to the estimation of our series of *OPD*, have been significantly revised. On the whole, these revisions have tended to make the errors of extrapolation for *EPD* appreciably smaller than those reported in Table 4B.[27] Equation (5) (together with (20)) also appears to account rather well for the behavior of *EPD* since 1969, down to the very present (1973.I), though this conclusion must be regarded as somewhat tentative because the National Income Account estimates of *EPD* are subject to surprisingly large revisions, at least up to three years back. For the years 1969-70, which are by now unlikely to undergo significant revisions, the computed series tracks remarkably well the actual series, including its flat peak in the second half of 1969, and its subsequent rapid decline: indeed the RMS is only about 1 billion or less than 2%. For the most recent nine quarters the RMS is substantially higher, around 2.6 billion or over 4%. Most of this error can be traced to substantial underestimates in 1971 and the first quarter of 1972,

[26] It will also be noted that (5) implies a more plausible initial response of investment to changes in output. Even in the case of (5) this response may appear suspiciously large in the first few quarters, suggesting the possibility of some simultaneous equation bias. While this possibly cannot be excluded, it is most unlikely to be serious because as dependent variable we use not investment but new orders, which have a relatively small feedback on current sales.

[27] The errors implied by the latest revision of the data (July 1973) are reported in the table in footnote 28.

averaging over three billion, whereas for the latest four quarters the error again averages below one billion (see footnote 28). Even the relatively large under-estimates for 1971, cannot, in our view, be reliably assessed at this time, and for two reasons. In the first place, this period was affected by a series of ab-normal circumstances which our model is not designed to handle, including, in the first half of the year, the aftermath of the automobile strike at the end of 1970, and, in the second half, the uncertainty over the reinstatement of invest-ment credit and its "buy American" clause, and the introduction of wage and price controls. In the second place, as already noted, the data for *EPD* are still subject to substantial revisions as far back as 1971, and past experience indicates that such revisions (as well as the usually smaller revisions of the independent variables used in the *OPD-EPD* equations), typically reduce the error, sometimes rather dramatically.[28]

[28] This conclusion is supported by the following table which reports the error of *EPD*, from 1969 to date, as calculated from the data provided in successive July issues of the Survey of Current Business, following the July 1970 issue underlying the estimation through 1968, and the extrapolation through 1970.I, reported in Table 4B:

Error of *EPD* calculated from the data in *SCB* of:

YEAR and Quarter	July 1971 (1)	July 1972 (2)	July 1973 (3)
69.I	−.6	.6	.7
II	−.4	−.5	−.4
III	−.5	−.5	−.3
IV	.3	−.2	.1
70.I	−.9	−.8	−.9
II	.5	.5	.2
III	3.2	2.7	2.5
IV	1.6	−.1	−.1
71.I	4.7	2.5	2.6
II	6.8	4.1	3.8
III		3.7	3.0
IV		4.8	4.0
72.I		4.5	3.4
II		2.9	.9
III			−1.2
IV			−.8
73.I			−.7

It is readily apparent that the errors based on the latest revision, in column (3), for the five quarters 1969.I to 1970.I, are generally smaller than those reported in column (5) of Table 4B, and substantially so in three of the five quarters. For the remaining quarters the latest error is also uniformly smaller than that implied by the first available estimates, with reductions rang-ing up to 3 billion. It is also generally smaller than that implied by the first revision of the data.

Before concluding brief mention should be made of one more test, the outcome of which is reported in column (6) of Table 3. The major effect of switching the specifications of p from a constant up to 1965 to (21b) beginning in 1965 is that of offsetting, to some extent, the unprecedented rise in the corporate bond rate RCB which has occurred in the post 1965 period. Under these conditions one could suspect that our procedure has primarily the effect of preventing the occurrence of large changes in the cost of capital term and, hence, in VPD. If so, might we not obtain at least as good a fit by taking VPD as a constant, i.e., with the straight accelerator model? We have carried out this test and, as can be seen from column (6) the answer is rather unequivocally negative. The root means square error of (6) for the entire period 1953–68 is nearly three times as large as that of specification (5), and the errors exhibit very high serial correlation, as evidenced by the value of DW and by the estimate of the autoregression coefficient of .96. Clearly, allowing for variations in the optimal capital output ratio makes a very substantial contribution to the explanation of EPD.[29]

This completes the survey of the empirical results that we have been able to obtain so far on the ability of our investment function to explain the behavior of aggregate data under several alternative assumptions concerning the behavior of the cruical, but unobserved variable, the expected rate of change of prices.

---

[29] This test compares only two very specific alternatives; a zero elasticity of capital with respect to relative prices (E_p) versus a unit steady state elasticity, implicit in our maintained hypothesis of a Cobb Douglas. The empirical validity of the latter specification has been questioned in a well known contribution of Eisner and Nadiri [4]. From an extensive analysis of the data used by Jorgenson, they have concluded that "Results contradict Jorgenson's assumption of a Cobb-Douglas production function" though "they are generally consistent with the implications of a CES production function with elasticities of substitution nearer zero than unity" (p. 381). This serious indictment of the Cobb Douglas has been challenged by Bischoff [2] who has shown that "with an improved stochastic specification the result does not contradict the Cobb-Douglas assumption" although the point estimate of the elasticity E_p of capital with respect to relative prices (our VPD) is typically well below unity. He has also shown, however, that a similar analysis of data for producers durable equipment—the data used in our analysis—yields point estimates of both E_p and E_q (the elasticity with respect to output), numerically close to, and not significantly different from, unity—(cf. Section 3 and Tables 3, 4). Besides this test, both Bischoff and ourselves have, in the past, worked with the variant of (13) implied by a CES production function, and endeavored to estimate the elasticity of substitution without prior constraint. We have consistently found that the estimated E_p was close to unity and that the difference from unity was not very robust. More recently, Bischoff has carried out one further test relying on the specification of VPD used in our preferred variant, that underlying column (5) of Table 3—but replacing specification (13) with a specification analogous to that employed by Eisner and Nadiri in [4] namely

$$\log OPD_t = \sum_{i=0}^{7} w_i \log VPD_{t-i} + \sum_{i=0}^{7} v_i \log XB_{t-i} + \sum_{i=1}^{2} q_i \log OPD_{t-i} + u_t .$$

E_p is then given by $\quad \sum_{i=0}^{7} w_i / \left(1 - \sum_{i=1}^{2} q_i\right) \quad$ and $\quad E_q = \sum_{i=0}^{7} v_i / \left(1 - \sum_{i=1}^{2} q_i\right) .$

The resulting estimates are found to be $E_p = 1.17$, $E_q = .92$, quite representative of similar results obtained in earlier tests. Also the fit is somewhat poorer than that of (5) as the standard error is 3.7%. On the whole we suggest that imposing the assumption of a Cobb-Douglas and constant returns to scale, $E_p = E_q = 1$, involves at most a modest specification bias, and is preferable to trying to estimate E_p and E_q from the data, along with the other parameters.

The conclusion of our survey is fairly clear: the hypothesis that is capable of accounting for the behavior of the aggregate data within the overall framework of our investment function is that the expected rate of change of prices was roughly constant and close to zero until about 1964, and thereafter is given by equation (21b). Within our theoretical framework, we have not been able to find any other formulation that can account for the behavior of *EPD* and *OPD* for the period 1953–69 as a whole.

Our evidence, of course, is far short of establishing that the estimate given under column (5) in Table 3, is the best specification and estimate of the investment equation for the next several years. For one thing, the threshold weights are a bit too arbitrary to accept blithely without much more careful tests against alternative weighting structures. Such tests cannot be readily performed in the context of our investment function because the estimation of this function, even without a complex lag structure in the price expectations, is a difficult enough non linear estimation problem. Furthermore, some plausible alternative explanation of the investment behavior in 1966–69 could be found. One such alternative hypothesis, which does not require serious changes in our theoretical construct, would say that *p* is constant before 1964, given by (21a) thereafter, and in addition, there was an unusually high level of investment in public utilities beginning around 1968–69. In order to test an alternative such as this, however, we need detailed data on investment by industries. Very recent data on *EPD* are subject to substantial revision, and as *EPD* is revised, *OPD* will change further back as we have indicated earlier. The more detailed the data are, the more subject to revision they tend to be. Thus, we do not feel that the time is ripe, in terms of data availability, to undertake a detailed study of investment behavior during the post 1968 period, and unfortunately, the choice between columns (4) and (5) must be largely based on their performance in this later period.

We, therefore, conclude our discussion at this time by accepting specification (5) as the best working hypothesis available within our framework for the explanation of investment behavior, and hope to be able to reach a more definitive judgment in the coming years, as more and sounder data on investment become available for the more recent period and especially if we also manage, in the near future, to bring the rate of inflation back to levels prevailing before 1966.

University of Pennsylvania, U.S.A.,
Massachusetts Institute of Technology, U.S.A.,
Michigan State University, U.S.A., and
The Australian National University

REFERENCES

[1] BISCHOFF, C. W., "A Study of Distributed Lags and Business Fixed Investment," unpublished Ph.D. dissertation, Massachusetts Institute of Technology, (1968).

[2] ———, "Hypothesis Testing and the Demand for Capital Goods," *The Review of Economics and Statistics*, LI (August, 1969), 354–68.

[3] _____, "The Effects of Alternative Lag Distribution," in G. Fromm, ed., *Tax Incentives and Capital Spending* (Washington, D. C.: The Brookings Institution, 1971).

[4] EISNER, E. AND M. I. NADIRI, "Investment Behavior and Neoclassical Theory," *Review of Economics and Statistics*, L (August, 1968), 369-82.

[5] _____ AND _____, "Neoclassical Theory of Investment Behavior: A Comment," *Review of Economics and Statistics*, LII (May, 1970), 216-22.

[6] _____ AND R. STROTZ, "Determinants of Business Investment," in *Impacts of Monetary Policy*, Research Study Two, prepared for the Commission on Money and Credit (Englewood Cliffs, N. J.: Prentice-Hall, Inc., 1963).

[7] FELDSTEIN, M. S. AND D. K. FOOT, "The Other Half of Gross Investment: Replacement and Modernization Expenditure," *Review of Economics and Statistics*, LIII (February, 1971), 49-58.

[8] GOULD, J. P., "Adjustment Costs in the Theory of Investment of the Firm," *Review of Economic Studies*, XXXV (January, 1968), 47-55.

[9] _____, The Use of Endogenous Variables in Dynamic Models of Investment," *Quarterly Journal of Economics*, LXXXIII (November, 1969), 580-99.

]10] HALL, R. E. AND D. W. JORGENSON, "Tax Policy and Investment Behavior," *American Economic Review*, LVII (June, 1967), 391-414.

[11] JORGENSON, D. W., "Capital Theory and Investment Behavior," *American Economic Review*, LIII (May, 1963), 247-59.

[12] _____, "Econometric Studies of Investment Behavior: A Survey," *Journal of Economic Literature*, IX (December, 1971), 1111-47.

[13] _____ AND C. D. SIEBERT, "A Comparison of Alternative Theories of Corporate Investment Behavior, *American Economic Review*, LVIII (September, 1968), 681-712.

[14] _____ AND _____, "Optimal Capital Accumulation and Corporate Investment Behavior," *Journal of Political Economy*, LXXVI (November-December, 1968), 1123-51.

[15] MODIGLIANI, F. AND M. H. MILLER, "The Cost of Capital, Corporation Finance and the Theory of Investment," *American Economic Review*, XLVIII (June, 1958), 261-97.

[16] _____ AND _____, "Corporate Income Taxes and the Cost of Capital: A Correction," *American Economic Review*, LIII (June, 1963), 433-42.

[17] _____ AND R. SHILLER, "Price Expectations and the Term Structure of Interest Rates," *Economica*, new series, XL (February, 1973), 12-43.

[18] TURNOVSKY, S. J., "Some Empirical Evidence on the Formation of Price Expectations," *Journal of the American Statistical Association*, LXV (December, 1970), 1441-54.

Errata

Page 385, footnote 3, line 1: "putty-putty mod the optimalityel" should read "putty-putty model the optimality."

Page 388, equation (4a): disregard the marks that appear in the denominator.

Page 389: equation 7 should read "$\hat{c}_0(T) = \dfrac{[W_o B(R^*, T)]^r Q_0^{1-a}}{Aa^a(1-a)^{1-a}(r-p)B(R,T)}$."

Page 390: unnumbered equation above (10) should read

$$\text{``}P_0 = \frac{M[W_o B(R^*, \hat{T})]^r Q^{1-a}}{Aa^a(1-a)^{1-a}B(R,\hat{T})} \text{.''}$$

Page 390: equation 10 should read

$$\text{``}P_0 = \left[\frac{M}{AB(R, \hat{T})}\right]^{1/a} \left[\frac{q_0}{1-a}\right]^{(1-a)/a} \frac{W_0 B(R^*, \hat{T})}{a} \text{.''}$$

Page 390: unnumbered equation following (10) should read

$$\text{.}\frac{Q_0}{W_0} = \left[\frac{Mq_0}{AB(R, \hat{T})}\right]^{1/a} \frac{(1-a)^{(a-1)/a}}{a} B(R^*, \hat{T}). \text{''}$$

Page 412, last line: "of the cruical" should read "of the crucial."

PART V
The Determinants of Wages and Prices

Reprinted from THE REVIEW OF ECONOMIC STUDIES, Vol. XL (2), April, 1973, FRANCO MODIGLIANI and EZIO TARANTELLI, pp. 203-223.

A Generalization of the Phillips Curve for a Developing Country [1,2]

FRANCO MODIGLIANI

MIT

and

EZIO TARANTELLI

University of Rome

INTRODUCTION AND SUMMARY

The aim of the present study is to propose and test a generalization of the Phillips curve for a developing country which starts out with a substantial volume of structural unemployment and gradually works it down in the development process. The central conclusion of the paper is that, while an expansion of effective demand and employment beyond the previous crest gives rise in the short run to inflationary pressures on the labour market, it also induces an on-the-job training effect for the labour force previously excluded from the productive process. The resulting permanent improvement in the skill and competitiveness of the labour force thereafter reduces the inflationary pressure associated with any given level of employment. Accordingly, in a developing country, the Phillips curve can be pictured as a frontier which in the process of development tends to the left and downwards. This inference will be shown to be supported by empirical data drawn from the experience of the Italian post-war period. In this analysis we focus on the industrial sector on the ground that in a developing country the latter tends to set the pace for the entire wage structure.

The pioneering studies of Stigler [14] and [15], Alchian [1], Holt and David [4], and Phelps [11] have recently laid the foundations for a new micro-economic theory of employment and inflation and stimulated a growing literature on the theoretical basis of the Phillips curve.[3] These studies, however, have the common characteristic of dealing with a labour market close to full employment. Thus, like the previous work on the Phillips curve, they are directly relevant only to already developed countries. We propose to show, however, that the new approach and, in particular, the formulation of C. C. Holt can be readily generalized to analyze the labour market of a developing economy.

Part I briefly reviews Holt's analysis. Part II extends its implications to a developing system. In Part III, the central hypothesis of the paper is tested. Some implications are then examined in Part IV.

[1] *First version received November* 1970; *final version received March* 1972 (*Eds.*).

[2] The equations proposed here are part of the Econometric Model of the Bank of Italy, which fully sponsored and financed the present work, and whose aid we gratefully acknowledge. We wish to express our thanks to G. M. Rey who contributed to the development of the ideas set out in this paper and to F. Caffè, C. C. Holt, R. Schiller and T. Ter Minassian for their criticism of an earlier draft of the paper and for their valuable suggestions.

[3] This literature includes the studies of G. C. Archibald, A. Hynes, R. E. Lucas, D. T. Mortensen and L. A. Rapping, all of which can be found in Phelps [11].

I. A SUMMARY OF THE THEORY RELEVANT TO THE PRESENT ANALYSIS

Let $\dot{w} = d \log W/dt \cong \Delta W/W$ represent the rate of change of the average wage rate, W; T_u, the average duration of unemployment, and T_v, the average length of time required to fill a vacancy. Then, from his analysis of the search process and the level of wage aspiration mechanism Holt is lead to the conclusion that $\dot{w}$ should be an increasing function of $1/T_u$[1] and of T_v[2]; thus

$$\dot{w} = \Phi\left(T_v, \frac{1}{T_u}\right), \quad \Phi_1, \Phi_2 > 0, \qquad \ldots(1)$$

where Φ_1 and Φ_2 represent the partial derivatives of Φ with respect to the first and second arguments respectively.

In turn, T_u and T_v are related to the stock of unemployment, U, and of vacanices, V, through the flow, F, of separations per unit of time. Indeed, when U and V are stationary so that F also equals the flow of accessions, we have

$$T_u = \frac{U}{F}; \quad T_v = \frac{V}{F}.$$

If we further call LF the labour force, $u = U/LF$ and $v = V/LF$, the " rate " of unemployment and vacancies, respectively, the above two equations can be conveniently restated as

$$u = T_u f, \qquad \ldots(2)$$

$$v = T_v f, \qquad \ldots(3)$$

where $f = F/LF$ can be considered approximately constant for a system hovering close to full employment.[3]

Next, Holt shows that v must itself be related to u by a functional relation of the form

$$uv = kf, \qquad \ldots(4)$$

where k is some constant.[4]

To derive equation (4), we may first note that the flow of new hires per unit of time, say H, can be expressed as

$$H = VP_v, \qquad \ldots(4')$$

where P_v is the probability per unit of time of filling an existing vacancy. Now, Holt argues, P_v may be expected to grow in proportion to the rate of unemployment, or

$$P_v = \frac{u}{k}. \qquad \ldots(5)$$

---

[1] See especially Holt [6], pp. 63-66.
[2] See e.g. Holt [5], p. 138, and Holt [7], p. 98.
[3] The flow F of accessions and separations can be best thought of as proportionate to the stock of employment, E, say

$$F = f^*E$$

where f^* is constant. But

$$E = LF(1-u)$$

and hence

$$f = \frac{F}{LF} = f^*(1-u)$$

can be also taken as roughly constant as long as u varies within modest limits.
[4] See Holt [6], p. 70.

Substituting into (4′) and equating H with F one obtains (4).[1]   From (4) and (3) (or directly from the consideration that $T_v = 1/P_v$) we can, in turn, infer

$$T_v = \frac{v}{f} = \frac{k}{u} = \frac{1}{P_v}. \qquad \qquad ...(5')$$

We may also note for later reference that from (5′) together with (2) and (3) we can deduce

$$T_u = \frac{u}{v} T_v = \frac{u}{v}\frac{k}{u} = \frac{k}{v}. \qquad \qquad ...(5'')$$

If we now substitute into the right-hand side of (1) for T_v from (5′) and for T_u from (2), we obtain

$$\dot{w} = \Phi\left(\frac{k}{u}, \frac{f}{u}\right) = \Psi(u; f). \qquad \qquad ...(6)$$

The specific form of Ψ depends on the form of Φ, though, in view of the properties of (1) we can unequivocally infer that $\partial\Psi/\partial u < 0$.   In particular, if we assume that Φ can be approximated by a linear function of its arguments,

$$\Phi\left(T_v, \frac{1}{T_u}\right) = A + BT_v + C\frac{1}{T_u},$$

then Ψ reduces to the well-known non-linear hypothesis discussed by Lipsey [8].   Indeed, substituting for T_v and T_u we find

$$\dot{w} = A + B\frac{k}{u} + C\frac{f}{u} \equiv A + b\frac{1}{u}, \qquad \qquad ...(7)$$

where $b = Bk + Cf$.

II. EXTENSION OF THE THEORY TO A DEVELOPING COUNTRY

The fundamental feature of the labour market in a developing country is the strong heterogeneity of the available labour force.   For the following analysis, it will be useful to separate the labour market into three micromarkets.   The first relates to the " employed ", the fraction of the labour force currently absorbed in the productive process.   The second includes the " trained unemployed " who constitute the fraction of the labour force already integrated

---

[1] Holt actually derives the equivalent of (4) in " Improving the Labor Market . . ." [5], pp. 137-8, starting from

(i) $H = UP_u$, (ii) $P_u = \frac{V}{K}$,

where P_u is the probability per unit of time of an unemployed worker finding a job.   But since $UP_u = VP_v$, (ii) implies

(iii) $P_v = \frac{U}{V}P_u = \frac{U}{K}$.

This equation differs from our (5) in that it makes P_v proportional to the *number* of unemployed rather than to u, the number of unemployed relative to the labour force.

The choice between (iii) and (5) depends on the role of economies of scale.   In later works, Holt has suggested that to allow for such scale effects (as well as cyclical variations in F) (4) should be stated in the more general form

(iv) $u^\alpha v^\beta LF^\gamma = kf$.

(Cf. " The Unemployment Inflation Dilemma . . ." [7], pp. 95-9).   Equation (5) would then take the form

(v) $T_v = \frac{v}{f} = \frac{k'LF^{-\gamma/\beta}}{u^{\alpha/\beta}}$, $k' = k^{\frac{1}{\beta}}f^{\frac{1-\beta}{\beta}}$.

Since we have no reason to suppose that α/β is appreciably different from unity, equation (5′) should provide a good approximation to (v), at least as long as LF can be taken as roughly constant.   Accordingly, in what follows we shall rely on (5′) which greatly simplifies the development of the argument.   It will be apparent that our major conclusions would not be seriously affected if we used (v) in place of (5′), except possibly if α/β were in fact quite different from unity.

in the productive process but presently looking for a job. The third, finally, includes the " untrained unemployed ", i.e. the fraction of the labour force which lacks previous experience in the industrial sector, and which we denote by Un.

The presence of an army of untrained unemployed workers creates further elements of selection in the hiring criteria adopted by firms, due to elements such as the higher cost of training an untrained worker, his lower productivity in the initial period of work, the degree to which he can be absorbed into an industrial type of work, his age, etc. Accordingly, the probability of filling a vacancy will increase with the size of the pool of *trained* unemployed, but will respond much less to the availability of untrained labour, both because it is untrained and because it is new to the industrial environment and often less available in the developing regions.[1] This consideration suggests that for a country in process of development, in equations (5) and (5'), the conventional measure of unemployment, $u = U/LF$, should be replaced by the following alternative measure of labour availability

$$u' = \frac{U - \beta' Un}{LF - \beta' Un}, \qquad \qquad ...(8)$$

where Un denotes the number of the untrained unemployed and β' should be greater than zero—since the untrained unemployed are less readily employable than the trained ones— but less than unity—which would imply that they are altogether unemployable.

In order to test any hypothesis involving u', we need, of course, a suitable operational measure of the size of the untrained labour force, Un. Conceptually, Un represents the difference between the total and the trained labour force. While we have no direct measure of the trained labour force, we suggest that for a developing system, a reasonable proxy at any date t may be provided by the maximum level of employment reached by the system in any year preceding t, say $E_M(t)$ or

$$Un(t) = LF(t) - E_M(t).$$

One possible improvement is to recognize that unemployment may be expected to have a positive lower bound which may be taken as roughly proportional to employment and labelled minimum frictional unemployment (cf. III.3 below). Accordingly, we can write

$$Un(t) = LF(t) - (1 + \gamma) E_M(t),$$

where $\gamma E_M(t)$ represents the frictional unemployment accompanying $E_M(t)$. If we further assume that the labour force changes slowly as compared with the growth of employment, we can conveniently use the approximation

$$E_M = LF - U_m,$$

where U_m denotes the minimum level of unemployment previously reached by the system. With this approximation, we obtain

$$Un = LF - (1 + \gamma)(LF - U_m) = (1 + \gamma)U_m - \gamma LF. \qquad ...(9)$$

Substituting (9) into (8) yields

$$u' = \frac{U - \beta'((1 + \gamma)U_m - \gamma LF)}{LF - \beta'((1 + \gamma)U_m - \gamma LF)} = \frac{u - \beta'((1 + \gamma)u_m - \gamma)}{1 - \beta'((1 + \gamma)u_m - \gamma)}$$

$$= \frac{u - b'(u_m - \gamma')}{1 - b'(u_m - \gamma')}, \qquad \qquad ...(10)$$

where $b' = \beta'(1 + \gamma)$ and $\gamma' = \gamma/(1 + \gamma)$.

---

[1] It may be argued that there is an appropriate wage differential at which untrained workers would be a perfect substitute for trained workers. We suggest, however, that as a rule and on the average, a host of institutional factors, both on the demand and supply side, will prevent the emergence of a differential large enough to eliminate the incentive for firms to discriminate against untrained labour.

We thus hypothesize that for a developing country, equation (5′) should take the form

$$T_v = \frac{k}{u'} = k\frac{1-b'(u_m-\gamma')}{u-b'(u_m-\gamma')}. \qquad \qquad ...(11)$$

Similarly, in equation (7), k/u should be replaced by k/u', with u' defined by (8). It is seen that the essence of generalization (11) is that T_v depends not only on u as in (5′) but also on u_m. This relation is shown in Figure 1 for two different values of the minimum rate of unemployment previously reached, u_{m_1} and u_{m_2}, with $u_{m_1}>u_{m_2}$.

As the system develops and E_M grows towards full employment, u_m declines, the asymptote of the function shifts to the left and the curve relating T_v and u recedes downwards and to the left, that is, towards the origin.

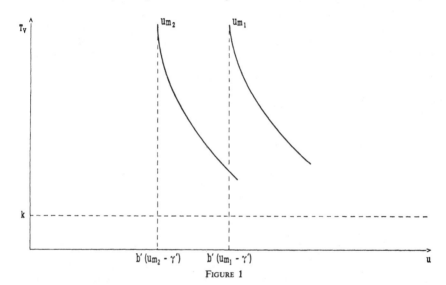

FIGURE 1

Consider now the last term of (7), f/u, which is essentially meant to reflect the downward pressure exercised on the wage rate by the level of unemployment. Here again, we suggest that the untrained portion of the labour force will not be exerting as much downward pressure on wages as the trained counterpart. This is so for a number of reasons. In a segmented labour market like the one previously described, the untrained worker is not effectively integrated into the competitive market economy and often not even present in the developing regions. Further, he knows from long experience that his chance of finding a job depends more on a brisk demand for labour than on any effort to underbid going wages when demand is slack. Further, underbidding requires information on bids of potential rivals and, as first suggested by Stigler [15], the less-trained portion of the labour force has in general a lower degree of information on the present level of demand and on changes in market conditions than the more specialized workers. In other words, any given level of unemployment will tend to produce a smaller downward pressure on wages, the larger the portion of U that is accounted for by Un. This suggests that in f/u the variable u might again be replaced by some alternative measure of the form

$$u'' = \frac{U-\beta''Un}{LF-\beta''Un}, \qquad \qquad ...(12)$$

where β'' should again lie between zero and unity. Substituting for Un from equation (9), and rearranging terms, we can again express u'' in terms of u and u_m, thus

$$u'' = \frac{u - b''(u_m - \gamma')}{1 - b''(u_m - \gamma')} \qquad \qquad ...(13)$$

with $b'' = \beta''(1+\gamma)$.

Finally, making use of (10) and (13), the wage equation (7) can now be reduced to the following expression that represents our proposed generalization of the standard Phillips curve

$$\dot{w} = A + B' \frac{1 - b'(u_m - \gamma')}{u - b'(u_m - \gamma')} + C' \frac{1 - b''(u_m - \gamma')}{u - b''(u_m - \gamma')}, \qquad ...(14)$$

where $B' = Bk$ and $C' = Cf$. It can be readily verified that for an already " developed " country, (14) reduces precisely to the standard Lipsey equation (7). Indeed, for such an economy, U_m—the lower bound of recorded unemployment—must tend to coincide with the minimum frictional unemployment, say, FR_m, i.e. $U_m \simeq FR_m$. But, in turn, frictional unemployment can be expressed as $\gamma \hat{E}_M$, where $\hat{E}_M$ is the maximum *feasible* volume of employment. Thus

$$FR_m = \gamma \hat{E}_M = \gamma(LF - FR_m),$$

implying

$$FR_m = \frac{\gamma}{1+\gamma} LF = \gamma' LF$$

and

$$u_m = \frac{U_m}{LF} = \frac{FR_m}{LF} = \gamma'.$$

But when $u_m = \gamma'$, (14) is seen to reduce to

$$\dot{w} = A + b \frac{1}{u},$$

where

$$b = B' + C'.$$

So far we have been focusing on the way in which the rate of change of wages is affected by unemployment (and its composition) both directly and through its relation to the average length of vacancies, T_v. In recent work on the Phillips curve, it has become customary to include as an additional variable some measure of the rate of change of prices current and/or lagged. Whether such a variable really belongs and how large its coefficient should be is a controversial issue intimately related to whether one is primarily concerned with the long or with the short run. For our present purpose, which is that of testing the mechanisms outlined in the previous section by relying on data generated by the Italian experience, we do not have to face squarely that thorny issue. First, in our test, we shall be concerned primarily with the short run Phillips curve; second in the Italian economy, the institutional and legal practice is to tie wages explicitly to prices through escalator clauses. It seems, therefore, reasonable to add the rate of change of consumer prices, denoted by $\dot{p}_c$ to our equation (14)—though, strictly speaking, one can argue that even the existence of explicit escalator clauses does not necessarily imply that $\dot{p}_c$ must appear as argument in the wage equation. On *a priori* grounds, one should expect the coefficient of this variable in a short-run wage equation to be non-negative. At the same time, we should expect it to be less than unity since, among other reasons, escalator clauses apply directly only to minimum wage rates as established in collective bargaining agreements (*salari contrattuali*) which represent but some sixty to seventy per cent of actual wage rates (*salari di fatto*).[1]

We finally note that in equations (7) or (14), the constant term will reflect essentially the response of the wage rate at high levels of unemployment. Thus in a competitive

[1] See Sylos Labini [16].

market subject to a high degree of information, we would expect the constant term to be low and possibly negative, implying a falling wage level at sufficiently high rates of unemployment. But this inference does not necessarily apply in a prevailingly unionized market, and/or in a market characterized by substantial segmentation between the trained and untrained labour force unable to compete very effectively with the trained pool. All of the above qualifications apply very clearly to the Italian industrial labour market, where unions are strong and also very much aware of the rapid growth of productivity which has averaged around 6 per cent in the relevant period. Under these conditions, even when unemployment is relatively high, unions may be expected to hold out for a minimum rate of increase of wages commensurate to productivity gains in an endeavour to ensure that labour shares in these gains. Accordingly, in the case of Italy we should expect a positive and rather high constant term.

Clearly, the above analysis could be further refined to allow for the introduction of a variable reflecting the change in trade union power in the period under consideration. Unfortunately, this approach would hardly seem relevant for the purposes of an empirical test, since suitable data are not available at present.

III. EMPIRICAL TESTS

1. The basic data for our proposed test

For an empirical test of our model, we rely on data generated by the Italian experience in the post-war period. Italy seems well suited for this purpose, since between the end of the Second World War and the present, the Italian economy has been characterized by a sustained process of development which has gradually transformed the country from a minor industrial power with a large fraction of the labour force unemployed, underemployed and engaged in non-industrial activities to one of the leading industrial countries. The share of national income accounted for by the industrial sector grew from some 33 per cent in 1951 to 45 per cent in 1968. Industrial employment grew from 20 per cent to 32 per cent of the labour force and, at the same time, the total measured unemployment shrunk gradually—from some 9 per cent of the labour force in 1951 to 2·5 per cent in 1963—though, following the recession of 1964, it has tended to increase again somewhat and, recently, has been averaging around 3·5 per cent.

Enough statistical information is available to enable us to estimate reasonable approximations to the variables called for by our model, though, unfortunately, adequate information covering the entire period 1951 to date is, at present, only available on an annual basis.

The money wage per worker in industry was measured by the ratio of total earnings of employees (*lavoro dipendente*) to an estimate of the number of equivalent full time employees.[1] For the cost of living, we used the implicit deflator for private domestic consumption, p_c.[2] There are two available measures of the unemployment rate. The conventional one

$$u = \frac{\text{total labour force} - \text{total employment}}{\text{total labour force}}\ [3]$$

[1] The number of equivalent full-time employees is estimated by adding to the number of full-time employees one-third of so-called " marginal employees ", essentially defined as those with less than 32 hours worked per week (even though they would be willing to work longer). It could be argued that the inclusion in the money wage per worker index of one-third of marginal employees, who account for 2 to 3 per cent of total full-time employees in the period under examination, could bias upwards the estimated coefficient of our " modified " unemployment rate (see equation (16) below), if there is a negative correlation between the unemployment rate and the number of hours worked per marginal employee. Unfortunately, the data are not adequate enough to test for this hypothesis. But it should be noticed that, first, if a bias exists, it is likely to be very slight given the small proportion of total employment accounted for by this group; second, the tendency of marginal employees to diminish in periods of high employment and to increase in depression should further reduce the empirical relevance of the bias. The data were drawn from " Quadri della contabilità nazionale italiana ", Istituto Nazionale per lo Studio della Congiuntura and " Annali di statistica ", Istituto Centrale di Statistica.

[2] Data from " Quadri della contabilità nazionale . . .", *op. cit.*

[3] Data from SVIMEZ, "L'aumento dell'occupazione in Italia dal 1950 al 1957", 1959, and ISTAT, "Annuario di statistiche del lavoro".

and a non-agricultural unemployment rate estimated by Sylos Labini [16].

$$\frac{\text{non-agricultural labour force} - \text{non-agricultural employment}}{\text{non-agricultural labour force}}$$

denoted hereafter by *Dis*. We have tested both concepts since it is not entirely clear which comes closer to the concept called for by our model.[1] In any event, the two alternative measures are highly correlated.

Even though all the data are to be taken with the usual qualifications, they have already been extensively and satisfactorily used in several econometric studies of the Italian economy [16], [17].[2]

2. *A test of the standard version of the Phillips curve*

Before proceeding to a test of equation (14), it is useful to exhibit the results obtained by relying on the standard Phillips-Lipsey version for an already developed system, represented by equation (7) with the addition of the variable $\dot{p}_c$. The equation was estimated for the period 1952-68 by ordinary least squares. The estimated equations are given in Table I, for both measures of the unemployment rate. All variables, including u, are measured as percentages. The figures in parenthesis under the coefficients are t-ratios.

TABLE I*

(a) $\quad \dot{w} = 0.59 + 17.4u^{-1} + 1.11\dot{p}_c$
$\qquad\quad (0.4) \quad (2.6) \qquad (3.5)$

$\qquad R^2 = 0.71 \quad \text{S.E.} = 2.24 \quad \text{D.W.} = 1.75$

(b) $\quad \dot{w} = 1.07 + 19.1\,Dis^{-1} + 1.13\dot{p}_c$
$\qquad\quad (0.7) \quad (2.5) \qquad\quad (3.5)$

$\qquad R^2 = 0.69 \quad \text{S.E.} = 2.28 \quad \text{D.W.} = 1.72$

* The data on which these and the following estimated equations are based are available on request.

In both forms of the equation, the coefficients of both variables are fairly significant, and the overall fit, as measured by R^2 is reasonably good, though the standard error of the regression, denoted by S.E., some 2·2 per cent, is still fairly high even when compared with the average rate of change of wages which amounted to some 8 per cent over the period of observation. The point estimate of the coefficient of u inverse is of the same order of magnitude as has been reported in empirical studies for advanced countries; it implies, e.g. that a reduction of u from 8 to 2 per cent would cause the annual rate of change of wages to increase by seven percentage points. On the other hand, the coefficient of the rate of change of prices is clearly much larger than expected; indeed, it is larger than unity, which is inconsistent with a stable long-run Phillips curve.[3]

[1] One would conjecture that by and large the unemployed of the agricultural sector should be regarded as part of "untrained unemployment" both from the point of view of the industrial employability and from the point of view of the pressure they might exercise on industrial wages. Indeed, a case could be made for defining our measure of u' (and u'') as

$$u' = \frac{U - b_1' Unn - b_2' Ua}{LF - b_1' Unn - b_2' Ua},$$

where Ua denotes agricultural unemployment and Unn, the non-agricultural untrained unemployed; we should expect $0 < b_1' < b_2' < 1$. We have not pursued this course because the final wage equation would contain far too many parameters to estimate in relation to available observations. If one supposes $b_2' \simeq b_1'$, we are led back essentially to equation (8) and the appropriate measure of u and u_m is the conventional one. If, on the other hand, one supposes $b_2' \simeq 1$, then it would be appropriate to redefine u as non-agricultural unemployment, so that *Dis* would be the more appropriate measure (except that the denominator of *Dis* excludes not only Ua but the entire agricultural labour force).

[2] Tarantelli [17] also tested the hypothesis analyzed here in its linear form, obtaining results consistent with those reported below. (Cf. also for further references.)

[3] A similar result has been reported by Sylos Labini (see the Italian version of [16] in Moneta e Credito, September 1967). His estimated coefficient for $\dot{p}$ is about the same as ours (1·15) or even larger (1·30) in an equation in which u entered linearly. He also finds that "interpretation is not easy" for this result, though he tries to rationalize it by the supposition that trade union pressure might increase with the cost of living, because of expectations of further increases.

We may also note that the coefficient of autocorrelation of the errors, D.W., indicates some positive serial correlation though not very pronounced. In fact, an examination of the residuals reveals that the equations do tend to underestimate the actual change of wages in the early years and to overestimate it in the most recent period. This is what our model would lead us to expect since in the early years when much of the unemployment was untrained, the measured rate of unemployment should tend to overstate the downward pressure on wages (cf. Section IV.3 below). Finally, both equations substantially underestimate the unusually high rate of change of wages in 1963 (amounting to about 20 per cent).[1] This extreme observation has posed problems for analysts of the Italian economy and has sometimes been attributed to political factors accompanying the shift in the government coalition from centre right to centre left. In fact, the addition to the equations of a dummy variable for that year improves the fit considerably, lowering the standard error from 2·2 to about 1·6 (it also yields a much more reasonable estimate for the coefficient of $\dot{p}_c$).[2]

3. *A test of the proposed generalization*

Taking into account the price variable, the equation suggested by our model becomes

$$\dot{w} = A + B'\,\frac{1 - b'(u_m - \gamma')}{u - b'(u_m - \gamma')} + C'\,\frac{1 - b''(u_m - \gamma')}{u - b''(u_m - \gamma')} + D\dot{p}_c. \qquad \text{...(15)}$$

Unfortunately, there are statistical problems in trying to estimate the parameters of (15) as it stands. That equation contains seven parameters (A, B', b', γ', C', b'', D) and is non-linear in three of them (b', b'', γ'), and we have but 17 observations at our disposal. One possible approach to make the problem more manageable would be to fix the value of at least some parameters from prior information. The approach seems feasible only with respect to the parameter γ' which essentially measures the minimum feasible frictional unemployment rate. We know that this coefficient must be positive and presumably somewhat smaller than the historically observed minimum rate of unemployment. Since this minimum was 2·5 per cent for the u measure and 3 per cent for the Dis measure, we cannot be seriously off by assuming a value somewhat lower than these minima; we have accordingly assumed for γ', a value of 1·5 per cent when using the u measure and 2·0 per cent for the Dis series.

In order to reduce still further the number of parameters to be estimated from the data, we feel that a good case can be made for merging the second and third term into a single term, say:

$$B^*\,\frac{1 - b(u_m - \gamma')}{u - b(u_m - \gamma')}.$$

Clearly, if b' and b'' were equal or very close, this procedure would be strictly valid and B^* would be simply $B' + C'$. But the approximation should remain a satisfactory one as long as b' and b'' are not very different and we have no reason to suppose that they should

---

[1] The underestimate is 6·7 per cent in equation (*a*), and 4·8 per cent in equation (*b*).

[2] Denoting the dummy by d, the estimated equations are:

(*a*) $\dot{w} = 2\cdot8 + 11\cdot6u^{-1} + 0\cdot68\dot{p}_c + 7\cdot9d$
$\quad\quad\;\; (2\cdot3)\;\;(2\cdot3)\quad\;\;(2\cdot7)\quad\;(3\cdot8)$
$\quad\quad\; R^2 = 0\cdot86 \quad \text{S.E.} = 1\cdot60 \quad \text{D.W.} = 2\cdot03$

(*b*) $\dot{w} = 3\cdot1 + 12\cdot7Dis^{-1} + 0\cdot69\dot{p}_c + 8\cdot1d.$
$\quad\quad\;\; (2\cdot7)\;\;(2\cdot2)\quad\quad\;(2\cdot6)\quad\;(3\cdot8)$
$\quad\quad\; R^2 = 0\cdot86 \quad \text{S.E.} = 1\cdot63 \quad \text{D.W.} = 2\cdot01$

These results would imply that in 1963 the rate of increase of wages was some 8 per cent larger than could be accounted for by the standard Phillips-Lipsey hypothesis.

be. Furthermore, under these conditions the quantities $(1 - b'(u_m - \gamma'))/(u - b'(u_m - \gamma'))$ and $(1 - b''(u_m - \gamma'))/(u - b''(u_m - \gamma'))$ would be expected to be highly collinear so that one could not hope to secure reliable estimates of the individual coefficients B' and C'.

For the purpose of estimation and testing, we therefore propose to simplify (15) to

$$\dot{w} = a + B^* \frac{1 - b(u_m - \gamma')}{u - b(u_m - \gamma')} + D\dot{p}_c. \qquad \qquad ...(16)$$

The equations actually estimated and reported in Table II differ slightly from (16) by the introduction of one further conceptual refinement. First note that (16), just like our original, (14) has the property that for a developed country operating in the neighbourhood of full employment, so that $u_m = \gamma'$, it reduces to the standard Phillips-Lipsey version. However, in our view, this version suffers from one shortcoming: it implies that u has a lower bound of zero and, hence, could be smaller than minimum frictional unemployment, which is an obvious contradiction. We would suggest instead that, while the average duration of unemployment, T_u, will tend to decline as the vacancy rate rises (cf. equation (5″)) it may be expected to have a lower bound, say, $\hat{T}_u$; but this, in turn, implies that, given the

TABLE II*

(a) $\quad \dot{w} = 3 \cdot 7 + 1 \cdot 58 \dfrac{1 - 0 \cdot 54 \left(\frac{u_m - 1 \cdot 5}{100} \right)}{u - 1 \cdot 5 - 0 \cdot 54(u_m - 1 \cdot 5)} + 0 \cdot 72 \dot{p}_c$
$\qquad \qquad (6 \cdot 2) \ (6 \cdot 8) \qquad \qquad \qquad \qquad (3 \cdot 5)$
$\qquad R^2 = 0 \cdot 90 \quad$ S.E. $= 1 \cdot 33 \quad$ D.W. $= 2 \cdot 01$

(b) $\quad \dot{w} = 3 \cdot 4 + 2 \cdot 38 \dfrac{1 - 0 \cdot 56 \left(\frac{Dis_m - 2 \cdot 0}{100} \right)}{Dis - 2 \cdot 0 - 0 \cdot 56(Dis_m - 2 \cdot 0)} + 0 \cdot 80 \dot{p}_c$
$\qquad \qquad (5 \cdot 2) \ (6 \cdot 4) \qquad \qquad \qquad \qquad \qquad (3 \cdot 8)$
$\qquad R^2 = 0 \cdot 89 \quad$ S.E. $= 1 \cdot 39 \quad$ D.W. $= 1 \cdot 86$

* The unemployment variable differs from formula (16′) because there u and u_m are defined as ratios, whereas in Tables I and II they are measured as percentages.

flow, f, u will also have a lower bound $\hat{u} = \hat{T}_u f$, where $\hat{u}$ is our minimum frictional unemployment and for a developed country coincides with γ'. Hence, we suggest that the standard Phillips equation for a developed country should be written as

$$\dot{w} = a + b \frac{1}{u - \gamma'}; \quad u > \gamma'.^{[1]} \qquad \qquad ...(17)$$

In order to ensure that (16) will reduce to (17) when $u_m \to \gamma'$, we rewrite the second term of (16) as

$$B^* \frac{1 - b(u_m - \gamma')}{u - \gamma' - b(u_m - \gamma')}. \qquad \qquad ...(16')$$

[1] Note that (17) ceases to hold once u reaches γ': for then $\dot{w}$ no longer bears a one to one correspondence to u and is instead determined by the rate of vacancies. In other words, the mechanism described in equations (2), (3) and (4), implies that there is a well-defined relation between u and v, say

$$u = g(v); \quad g' < 0. \qquad \qquad ...(18)$$

As long as (18) holds, $\dot{w}$ could be expressed indifferently as a function of u, as we have chosen to do, or, just as well, as a function of v. What we are suggesting, however, is that (18) actually can hold only for $v < \hat{v}$, where $\hat{v}$ is defined by $\hat{u} = g(v)$. Once v has reached the neighbourhood of $\hat{v}$, or exceeds $\hat{v}$, u will no longer respond to variations in v, and (18) should be replaced by $u \simeq \hat{u}$; $\dot{w}$ can then no longer be expressed as a well-behaved function of u, but only as a function of v.

With this final modification and γ' fixed *a priori*, (16) is still non-linear in the parameter b. A maximum likelihood estimate of this parameter was estimated by scanning over the *a priori* admissible range, $0 < b < 1$, and selecting that value which minimizes the standard error.[1]

The results of our test are reported in Table II. It is seen that with the first measure of unemployment, the best fitting value of the parameter b turns out to be 0·54 and with the second of 0·56. These coefficients, which may be thought of as weighted averages of b' and b'', imply that with respect to the effect on wage behaviour an "untrained unemployed" person counts, as it were, half as much as a trained one. It is also seen by comparison with Table I that our hypothesis produces a very substantial improvement in overall fit as the standard error declines by almost 40 per cent.[2] Furthermore, our modified unemployment measure is by far the most significant variable in the equation. The plot of actual and fitted values for equation (a) of Table II is given on p. 214 (similar results hold for equation (b)).

Of particular interest is the estimated coefficient of the cost of living which is now substantially below unity, and is in line, in both equations, with *a priori* expectations. Finally, it is rather significant that either of the equations in Table II accounts quite well for the exceptionally large increases in 1963 without any need to appeal to extra-economic factors. Indeed, if a dummy for 1963 is added, its coefficient in (a) is only 2·9 and its t-ratio barely 1·2, while in (b) the coefficient is actually negative but totally insignificant (t-ratio of 0·2).

It is also worth noting that the constant term, which had a value between 0·5 and 1·0 per cent in the standard Phillips-Lipsey equations (a) and (b) in Table I increases in the estimate of the " modified " Phillips-Lipsey equation (17) reported in Table III below[3] and increases still further in our generalized equations of Table II. The constant term in the latter equations, amounting to some 50-60 per cent of the long-run industrial productivity trend, reflects more accurately in our view the strong trade union power and the labour market segmentation that, as noted earlier, characterizes the Italian economy. Thus, our equations indicate that even in the early stages of development, the trade union awareness of the long-run rate of increase of productivity tends to set a lower limit to the rate of increase of wages. More generally, as is clearly brought out by Figure 2 below, our parameter estimates imply that wages are very responsive to unemployment for values of u close to or smaller than u_m, but not for larger values of u.[4] This has the credible interpretation that when effective demand pressure is high, wages rise rapidly in response to competitive forces (one manifestation of which is the so called wage-drift—the increase of actual relative to contractual wages). On the other hand, even when unemployment is high, trade union power succeeds in forcing increases in wages commensurate to the productivity trend.

Table II also suggests that there is no appreciable difference in results as between the two alternative measures of unemployment. The first measure, including the agricultural sector used in (a), has a slight edge in terms of standard error, a lower coefficient for $\dot{p}_c$ and a better fit to 1963, but the difference is very marginal. On the other hand, the constant term and the estimate of B^* seem somewhat more plausible in equation (b). It is possible that more refined approximations for the measurement of the trained and untrained unemployment allowing for compositional effects within each aggregate might improve the explanation further. However, such refinements are hardly worth trying unless one has a larger sample, possibly by relying on quarterly data, which we hope will soon be available.

[1] By scanning at intervals of 0·1 we found that the minimum was between 0·4 and 0·6. Within this interval we proceeded to scan with an interval of 0·01 to obtain the results presented in Table II.
[2] The standard errors reported in Table II have been adjusted for the additional degree of freedom lost in scanning for the optimum value of b.
[3] Cf. Section IV.
[4] It is also to be noted that the parametric family of curves obtained from our generalized equations should be interpreted, for any practical purposes, in some interval close to the value of u_m for which each curve is drawn, since it is obviously in that interval that the observations from which they are derived apply.

E—40/2

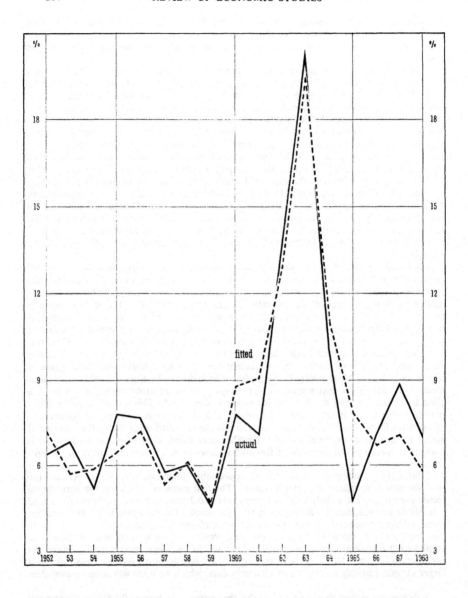

But even at this stage, it would appear that the evidence strongly supports our generalization of the Phillips curve for a developing country.[1]

In the next section we examine some implications of this generalization relying explicitly on equations of type (a) using u_m, though very similar conclusions would hold with the alternative measure of the unemployment rate.

IV. SOME IMPLICATIONS

The main implication of our analysis and empirical results boils down to the fact that while a country is in the process of development with the trained labour force gradually growing relative to the total labour force, there is no unique relation between the rate of growth of wages and the level of unemployment as postulated in the standard Phillips curve applicable to developed countries. This is because the pressure exercised on wages by a given level of unemployment depends on the composition of that unemployment as between the trained and untrained labour force which itself shifts in the process of development. Thus, instead of a single " Phillips curve ", we get a whole " parametric " family of curves. The relevant parameter is the composition of unemployment which we approximate through the variable u_m, the lowest previous level of unemployment. Figure 2 illustrates this point by showing a sample of such curves drawn for selected values of u_m by relying on the parameter estimates of Table II, equation (a) (and assuming $\dot{p}_c = 0$).

Each such curve must be looked upon as a short-run curve for two reasons; because it only holds for the stated value of u_m and because it takes $\dot{p}_c$ as exogenously given, which is not a valid assumption in that, at least in the longer run, $\dot{p}_c$ itself will depend on $\dot{w}$. It is convenient, initially, to disregard this interdependence. But even with $\dot{p}_c$ taken as exogenous, say at zero, as in the graph, any given short-run curve represents an only partially reversible curve. Specifically, the curve corresponding say, to $u_m = u'_m$ is reversible for values of $u > u'_m$. But once u reaches a value smaller than u'_m, say, u''_m, then the original curve continues to hold only for the " year " in which the crossing first occurred; but thereafter, it is replaced by a new short-run curve to the left of the original one with $u_m = u''_m$,

[1] One problem with the method of estimation used in Tables I and II is the possibility of simultaneous equation bias resulting from the fact that there is a second relation between wages and prices reflecting the dependence of prices on unit costs of which wages are a major component. This bias would most likely result in an overstatement of the coefficient of $\dot{p}_e$ in equations (a) and (b). With quarterly data, this bias could be at least reduced by using the lagged value of $\dot{p}_c$ (or some average of lagged values); but this approach is not feasible for annual data since the lag of $\dot{p}_c$ is presumably much shorter than one year. In order to get some idea of the magnitude of this bias in our annual equations, the two equations have been re-estimated by a two-stage procedure. To this end we relied on the following price equation suggested and successfully tested for the Italian industrial sector by E. Tarantelli [17]

$$\log p = a_0 + a_1 \log w - a_2 \log \Pi + a_3 \log K^{occ} + a_4 RM + a_5 p_{-1},$$

where Π is (long run) labour productivity, K^{occ} denotes the rate of capacity utilization as estimated by G. M. Rey [13] and the variable RM is an index of international prices of raw materials relevant to the Italian market (derived from data obtained from Confindustria-ISCO). By taking the first difference and recalling that the first difference of the logarithm is approximately equal to the percentage change, we derive

$$\dot{p} = a_1 \dot{w} + a_3 \dot{K}^{occ} + a_4 \dot{R}M + a_5 \dot{p}_{-1},$$

where the rate of change of productivity is approximately constant. Substituting for $\dot{w}$ from (16) and solving for $\dot{p}$, one obtains

$$\dot{p} = a'_3 \dot{K}^{occ} + a'_4 \dot{R}M + a'_5 \dot{p}_{-1} + a_6 u^*,$$

where u^* denotes our modified measure of unemployment defined in equation (16) and used in Table II. The above equation was used to obtain a first-stage estimate of $\dot{p}$, say $\dot{p}^c$, which was then used to replace the actual $\dot{p}_c$ in equation (a). This procedure yields an estimate of the coefficient of the unemployment variable rather similar to that reported in equation (a) $-2 \cdot 27$ instead of $1 \cdot 58$—but the estimated coefficient of $\dot{p}_c$ is reduced substantially from $0 \cdot 72$ to $0 \cdot 41$. This rough test confirms that the coefficients of equations (a) and (b) may be somewhat biased. But the bias does not appear large enough to seriously affect conclusions based on those equations, though the long-run Phillips curve may well be less steep than might be inferred from those equations. (Cf. Section IV below.)

and in principle, the $u_m = u'_m$ curve never becomes relevant again. Furthermore, since the new curve is lower than the previous one in the Phillips plane, the value of $\dot{w}$ corresponding to any u will be smaller than that implied by the $u_m = u'_m$ curve. The economic interpretation of the above phenomenon is straightforward. To any given u_m corresponds a given pool of " trained " labour. As long as u fluctuates in a range larger or equal to u_m, the trained labour force tends to remain unchanged as vacancies tend to be filled from the

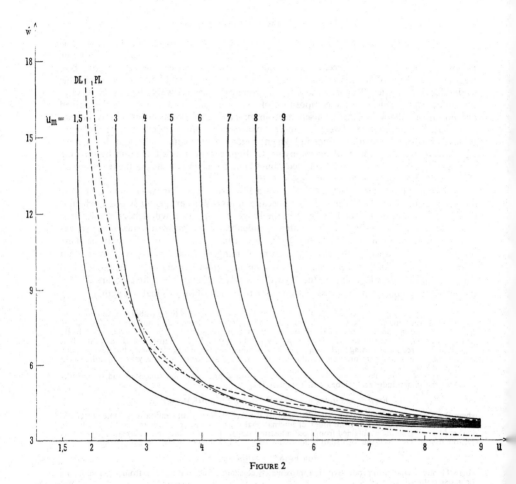

FIGURE 2

trained pool. As the pressure of demand rises and u approaches u_m, the pool of trained unemployed gradually shrinks towards the minimum frictional level u_m, as the average duration of unemployment of trained workers shortens, and, correspondingly, the average length of vacancies increases. This puts growing upward pressure on the wage rate, as employers bid for the dwindling stock of trained labour; but at the same time, the rising cost of securing and holding labour and the growing difficulties and time required to fill vacancies induce firms to lower their standard requirements for hiring. Thus, previously untrained unemployed get trained on the job by firms and pass into the ranks of the trained labour force.[1]

Since the larger and more established firms typically provide more attractive employment opportunities, they are likely to secure the lion's share of the initially trained pool, and the absorption of untrained labour may tend to be carried out by the smaller firms, though this need not be universally true. In any event, the larger the pressure of demand, the smaller will u become relative to u_m, and, hence, the larger the increment in trained labour, which is essentially $u_m - u$; though also, $\dot{w}$ will be larger as we move up the short-run curve past u_m. At the same time, training permanently upgrades the labour force by increasing the trained pool, and thus, in the future, any given level of employment, up to the newly reached value of E_M, and corresponding u_m, is permanently accompanied by a lower pressure on wages. This outcome is described by the shift to a new short-run curve with a lower u_m equal to the newly reached u, and, thus, lying everywhere below the previous curve.

Thus, in the process of development, the relevant short-run curve gradually shifts " permanently " to the left until u_m reaches its lowest possible value, which we have denoted by γ' and which in Figure 2 has the value 1·5. Once this value has been reached, the corresponding " short-run " curve is no longer subject to either rightward or leftward shifts and, hence, it becomes also a " long-run " curve. It is, in fact, precisely the " modified " Phillips-Lipsey curve of equation (17).

For any given u_m curve, the value of $\dot{w}$ at the point where u crosses u_m can be inferred from equation (a), Table II, by setting $u = u_m$. This yields,

$$\dot{w} = 3\cdot7 + 3\cdot4 \ \frac{1 - 0\cdot54\left(\dfrac{u - 1\cdot5}{100}\right)}{u - 1\cdot5} \qquad \qquad ...(19)$$

which is essentially the " envelope " of the family of short-run curves. It represents the relation between the rate of change of wages and u *if* that level of u, once reached, were indefinitely maintained (and $\dot{p}_c$ remained equal to zero). The locus of equation (19) is shown by the dashed curve in Figure 2. Any given u_m curve is reversible until it crosses this curve from below, once it crosses it, it loses its relevance.

We propose to label equation (19) and its graph in Figure 2, the " Development Locus ", DL, on the ground that it may be expected to represent roughly the relation between the rate of unemployment at any date t, $u(t)$, and the corresponding $\dot{w}(t)$ which one might expect to observe for a country undergoing a reasonably steady and orderly development process. Indeed, for such a country $u(t)$ may be expected to be highly correlated with $u_m(t)$. For, once a given value u_m has been reached, u itself is unlikely to rise again very much above u_m. At the same time, $u(t)$ is unlikely to ever fall significantly below $u_m(t)$ because the training can only occur at a relatively modest pace. (In other words, $E(t)$ is unlikely to ever significantly exceed $E_M(t)$.)

The above considerations suggest that, if one were to fit the standard Phillips-Lipsey hypothesis (7) (or the modified version (17)) to data pertaining to a steadily developing country, the estimated parameters should tend to be reasonably close to those of the " development curve ". This expectation is fairly well borne out in the case of Italy as can be seen by comparing (19) with the results obtained by fitting (17) (with the addition of the variable

---

[1] Additional strong evidence on this hypothesis is shown in the work of Tarantelli [17] which essentially uses a vintage model to show that short-run man-hour productivity movements in the Italian industrial sector are counter cyclical. Thus, " Okun's Law " does not seem to hold for a system in the process of development characterized by strong heterogeneity of the stock of available capital, since, when demand expands, vintages of human and physical capital progressively less efficient are absorbed in the productive process. Consistently with the results of the present paper, it is found that at any given point of time productivity is an increasing function of u/u_m. Accordingly, productivity is *lowered* by a *lower* level of unemployment, given u_m, but is *raised* by a *lower* level of u_m, given u, because a lower u_m implies a larger pool of trained personnel and a consequent overall upgrading of the stock of human capital.

$\dot{p}_c$) to the Italian data, reported in Table III.   The estimated coefficient of the unemployment variable is reasonably close to that of (19)—though somewhat larger, a fact which can readily be accounted for.[1]   The graph of (a) of Table III is shown in Figure 2 by the dot-dashed line *PL* (for Phillips-Lipsey) and its similarity with the *DL* curve—the graph of (19)—is readily apparent.

It may be noted in passing that our modified version (17) of the Phillips-Lipsey curve tested in Table III fits the data somewhat better than the conventional version (7) of Table I and yields more sensible estimates of the cost of living effect.   However, a comparison with II confirms that even (17) is distinctly inferior to our generalized hypothesis.   Indeed, if that hypothesis is valid the fitted equations of Table III just like the Development Locus basically describe the broad historical covariation of $\dot{w}$ and u in the development process but will yield biased estimates of short-run, cyclical developments.[2]

TABLE III

(a) $\dot{w} = \underset{(2\cdot1)}{2\cdot1} + \underset{(3\cdot3)}{7\cdot8} \dfrac{1}{u - 1\cdot5} + \underset{(2\cdot8)}{0\cdot88}\dot{p}_c$

$R^2 = 0\cdot75$ S.E. $= 2\cdot05$ D.W. $= 1\cdot72$

(b) $\dot{w} = \underset{(2\cdot6)}{2\cdot6} + \underset{(3\cdot3)}{8\cdot0} \dfrac{1}{Dis - 2\cdot0} + \underset{(2\cdot7)}{0\cdot87}\dot{p}_c$

$R^2 = 0\cdot75$ S.E. $= 2\cdot07$ D.W. $= 1\cdot65$

So far, we have proceeded as though the value of $\dot{p}_c$ was exogenously given.   But this procedure is hardly justified when examining the long-run implications of our generalized Phillips curve, for $\dot{p}_c$ itself is significantly affected by $\dot{w}$—though possibly with some lags—and hence again by u.   Indeed, in the case of the standard Phillips-Lipsey curve, if the equation contains a term in $\dot{p}_c$, that equation must be looked on as a " short-run " curve, i.e., one providing information only on the short-run trade-off between $\dot{w}$ and u.   To estimate the long-run trade-off between $\dot{w}$ and any permanently maintained level of u, one must express $\dot{p}_c$ itself in terms of u—or, what comes to the same thing, the wage equation and the " price " equation must be solved simultaneously to express both $\dot{w}$ and $\dot{p}_c$ in terms of final determinants, notably u.

For present purposes, we shall assume that in the *long-run* prices are determined by a constant mark-up on unit labour costs—a hypothesis which seems to fit well data for both the United States and Italy.[3]   This hypothesis can be expressed as

$$\log p = m + \log w - \log \Pi \qquad \qquad \dots(20)$$

where m is the logarithm of the mark-up assumed roughly constant in the relevant run. From (20), in turn, we derive

$$\dot{p} \simeq \dot{w} - \dot{\Pi} \qquad \qquad \dots(20')$$

and $\dot{\Pi}$, the rate of growth of productivity, can also be taken as roughly given and constant for present purposes.   Let the Phillips curve be written quite generally as

$$\dot{w} = \phi(u) + d\dot{p}. \qquad \qquad \dots(21)$$

[1] The scatter diagram of the point $(\dot{w}(t), u(t))$ may be expected to be somewhat steeper than implied by the " development curve " because it reflects in part the short-run curves for fixed u_m, which are steeper than the development curve.

[2] In particular, the equations of Table III, just like the *DL* curve should tend to overestimate $\dot{w}$ for levels of unemployment higher than the latest u_m and to underestimate it if and when u first rises significantly above the latest u_m.   This expectation is borne out reasonably well for equation (a) in Table III.   In the years following 1963, when u fluctuated above the value of $2\cdot5$ reached in 1963, that equation appreciably overestimates $\dot{w}$ in three years and never underestimates it significantly.   The average overestimate in the equation is $1\cdot7$ per cent whereas for our equation (a), Table II, the average error is close to zero.   Similar results hold for equation (b).

[3] For Italy, see [16] and [17]; for the United States, the price equation presently embedded in the FRB-MIT-PENN econometric model is of this general form.   For a description and empirical estimation, see deMenil and Enzler [2].

Solving (20′) and (21) simultaneously yields

$$\dot{p} = \frac{\phi(u) - \dot{\Pi}}{1 - d}; \qquad \qquad ...(22a)$$

$$\dot{w} = \dot{p} + \dot{\Pi} = \frac{\phi(u) - d\dot{\Pi}}{1 - d}. \qquad \qquad ...(22b)$$

Equation (22a) can then be interpreted as the long-run price-Phillips curve and (22b) as the corresponding wage-Phillips curve. It is seen that this long-run curve is essentially a " stretching " of the short-run curve (21), whose slope with respect to u is everywhere higher by the factor $1/(1-d) > 1$, for $0 < d < 1$. Furthermore, the short and long-run curve intersect for that value of u, say $\hat{u}$, for which $\phi(\hat{u}) = \dot{\Pi}$, for at this value of u, $\dot{p} = 0$, and both the short-run and the long-run wage equations yield the same value of $\dot{w}$, namely $\dot{\Pi}$.

Our own analysis, however, leads to the conclusion that for a developing country in equation (21) $\phi(u)$ must be replaced by $\phi(u^*)$ and $\phi(u^*)$ can be approximated by

$$\phi(u^*) = a + B^*(1 - b(u_m - \gamma'))/(u - \gamma' - b(u_m - \gamma')),$$

i.e. a family of curves each defined by the parameter u_m. It would, then, appear from (22b) that the " long-run wage-Phillips curve " corresponding to any given u_m would be given by

$$\dot{w} = \frac{\phi(u^*) - d\dot{\Pi}}{1 - d} = \left\{ a + B^* \frac{1 - b(u_m - \gamma')}{u - \gamma' - b(u_m - \gamma')} - d\dot{\Pi} \right\} \bigg/ (1 - d).$$

Using the empirical estimates of Table II which underlie Figure 2,

$$\dot{w} = \left\{ 3 \cdot 7 + 1 \cdot 58 \frac{1 - 0 \cdot 54 \left(\dfrac{u_m - 1 \cdot 5}{100} \right)}{u - 1 \cdot 5 - 0 \cdot 54(u_m - 1 \cdot 5)} - 0 \cdot 72\dot{\Pi} \right\} \bigg/ 0 \cdot 28.$$

Again, each long-run curve intersects the corresponding short-run curve for $\dot{w} = \dot{\Pi}$. Since for Italy the value of $\dot{\Pi}$ can be estimated at around 5 per cent per year, the relation $\dot{w} = \dot{\Pi}$ can be represented in Figure 3 by the dashed horizontal line drawn to intersect the ordinate at 5 per cent.[1]

Thus, in Figure 3, the long-run curves for any given u_m can be generated by stretching the corresponding short-run curve around its point of intersection with the horizontal line, until its slope is roughly three times as large as that of the short-run curve.

This relation between the short- and the long-run wage-Phillips curve is illustrated in Figure 3 for two particular values of u_m. The two curves on the left are the short- and long-run curves for $u_m = 1 \cdot 5$ which, as it will be recalled, is the lowest member of the family and corresponds to the conventional " developed country " curve. The relation between these two curves can be interpreted as follows. Suppose that initially u was indefinitely maintained at 3·0 per cent (after having once reached the value of 1·5 per cent); then $\dot{w}$ would remain indefinitely at 5 per cent and $\dot{p}$ at zero. If new demand pressure were to cause u to fall to say 2·5 per cent, then initially, we would be moving along the short-run curve, which is drawn for $\dot{p} = 0$, and $\dot{w}$ would grow to 6 per cent. However, sooner or later this would cause $\dot{p}$ to move toward 1 per cent which, in turn, would cause a further rise

---

[1] This figure represents the average rate of growth of productivity for the system as a whole which seems more relevant than industrial productivity in relating the rate of change of the cost of living to that of wages It is also assumed that industrial wages set the pace for all wages. This assumption—which implies a constant wage structure—and that of a constant mark-up, allows us to simplify the analysis by treating $\dot{p}$ as though it were $\dot{p}_c$, for our illustrative purposes of the long-run Phillips curve; though none of our basic conclusions would be affected by its absence, as also supported by the results of the Econometric Model of the Bank of Italy. In the latter, a wage model similar to that proposed here was also successfully tested for the services sector in which, even more than for the industrial sector, the concept of " trained " should not only be rigidly interpreted as referring to skill differences, as our formal analysis could at times suggest, but also to the other characteristics, noted in Section II above, which distinguish one group from the other.

in $\dot{w}$, and so on; thus, with u fixed at 2·5, $\dot{w}$ would gradually rise until it would reach the value of $\dot{w}$ given by the steeper long-run curve, namely 8 per cent; and $\dot{p}$ would similarly reach 3 per cent. At this point a new steady state has been reached, $\dot{w}$ and $\dot{p}$ rising indefinitely at 8 per cent and 3 per cent respectively.

However, the conclusion that for every value of u_m there exists a long-run wage-Phillips curve derivable by stretching the corresponding short-run curve around its point

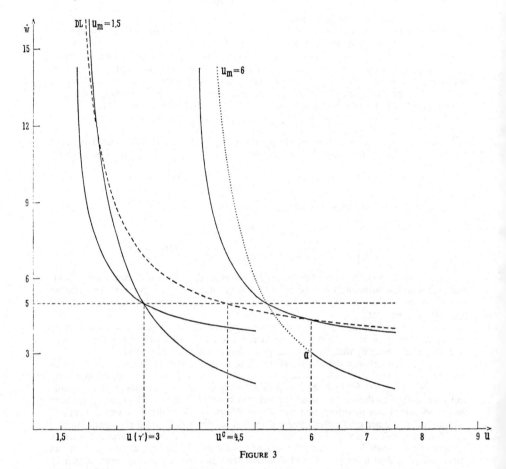

FIGURE 3

of intersection with the line $\dot{w}. = 5$ per cent is subject to one important qualification. The long-run curve gives the behaviour of wages for an indefinitely maintained level of u. But, we have seen that the short-run curve corresponding to some $u_m = u'_m$ ceases to hold once u falls below u'_m. Hence, the long-run curve corresponding to u'_m is well defined only for $u > u'_m$. This point is again illustrated in Figure 3, which shows the short-run curve for $u_m = 6$ per cent and the corresponding long-run curve; only the solid portion of this curve, but not the remaining dotted portion, is a valid long-run curve. Note that, in the region of validity, $\dot{w}$ is less than 5 per cent and hence $\dot{p}$ must be negative. This conclusion can readily be seen to hold for any curve whose u_m is higher than the critical value u^c at which our so-called development curve crosses the horizontal line $\dot{w} = 5$ per cent.

One peculiar implication of the above is that for u higher than u^c, there exists no value of u which, if indefinitely maintained, would lead to a stable price level. To illustrate in terms of Figure 3, suppose we started out with $u_m = 6$ per cent and u also indefinitely maintained at 6 per cent. Then, as we see from Figure 3, we would be in a steady state equilibrium at point " a " with $\dot{w}$ constant at 3 per cent and $\dot{p}$ at -2 per cent. There will be some value of u say u'' for which $\dot{w}$ will initially rise to 5 per cent but it will be smaller than 6 per cent. If u were to be maintained at u'', the relevant short-run curve would shift down and, hence, $\dot{w}$ could not stay at 5 per cent; on the contrary for $\dot{w}$ to remain at 5 per cent, u would have to continuously decrease until it would eventually reach 4·5 per cent. Once this level had been reached, by maintaining u permanently at 4·5, there would be a steady state $\dot{w} = 5$ per cent and $\dot{p} = 0$ (i.e. a constant price level). The same conclusion holds if we start from any other position with u_m higher than 4·5 per cent.

On the other hand, for values of u_m less than the critical u^c, and down to the lowest feasible bound γ'—or 1·5 per cent in our case—there is a whole range of values of u which, if indefinitely maintained, would be consistent with stable prices; indeed, there is one such u for each u_m in the range (1·5 $\leqq u_m \leqq$ 4·5) and that value of u is given by the intersection of the short-run (or the long-run) curve corresponding to u_m and the line $\dot{w} = 5$.

A useful alternative way of bringing out the implications of our generalized Phillips curve is as follows. If we start out from any u_m above the " *critical value* " u^c, where the development curve intersects the line $\dot{w} = \dot{\Pi}$, there will exist some appropriate path of aggregate demand so that the price level could be maintained constant while u steadily decreases and (asymptotically) approaches u^c.[1] To the left of u^c, on the other hand, every value of u (down to a lowest bound determined by the intersection of the developed country curve and $\dot{w} = \dot{\Pi}$) is consistent with the maintenance of price stability. But, in order to move from a given value of u_m to a lower one the system must be at least transiently exposed to enough demand pressure to produce a lower value of u, and concomitant expansion of the trained pool, and this must be accompanied by at least a transient burst of rising prices. We see once more that, even when prices are treated as endogenous, a burst of demand pressure sufficient to lower u below the previous u_m, though it will initially generate strong inflationary pressures, also lays the groundwork for a permanent, more favourable trade-off between $\dot{w}$ and u.[2] A further interesting implication of the above analysis is that, contrary to conclusions of Friedman *et al.*, [3], [6], [10], [11], for a developing country, a permanent reduction of u below some initial natural rate (achieved after an an even larger temporary drop) does not generate an increasingly rapid inflation but, on the contrary, is consistent with any stable value of $\dot{p}$ and $\dot{w}$, including $\dot{p} = 0$.[3]

In conclusion, we should like to call attention to one feature of our analysis which might well find application in other problems. The essential mechanism which accounts for most of the implications examined in this section is that, for a developing country, as demand expands significantly above previous peaks, pressures are generated which result

---

[1] In particular, it is our own intention to show in a forthcoming article that on the basis of the above analysis: (i) there is an appropriate path to full employment in a developing country for every given permissible rate of increase of prices; (ii) the path essentially exhibits an asymptotic approach to full employment so that the sharpest cuts in the unemployment rate can be achieved only at the beginnings of the development process; (iii) in a world of uncertainty and imperfect information, the stochastic nature of the unemployment rate will make the target of approaching lower levels more risky (and thus less desirable for a risk-averse policy-maker) at later stages of development, when the flatter and flatter possible path asymptotically approaches frictional unemployment values. (Cf. F. Modigliani and E. Tarantelli [9]).

[2] In principle, the trained pool could be increased without relying on demand pressure and on the job training by appropriate man-power training programmes. In a country like Italy, where an important portion of industrial activity is carried out through enterprises directly and indirectly controlled by the public sector, a promising alternative might be for such firms to endeavour to partly fill their incremental requirements by hiring and training the " untrained " labour pool (including non primary groups of the labour force) rather than competing for the " trained " pool.

[3] For a discussion of this point see Modigliani and Tarantelli [9].

in some inflation but which, at the same time, help to break the barrier set by the previous high mark. Once this barrier has been pushed further, the inflationary pressure accompanying a given level of demand should tend to abate. Thus, the inflationary bursts are akin to growth pains which the economy must undergo as the price of reaching maturity. In our own model, the barrier is represented by the pool of trained labour. However, the principle should be generalizable and applicable to other factors of production and to productive organizations.[1] These considerations reinforce our conclusions that the inflationary pressures generated by an expansion of employment beyond accustomed levels should be largest in the beginning but should then tend to *abate*. This is, of course, diametrically opposite to the conclusion of Friedman *et al.*, that the expansion of demand and employment would tend to be accompanied by *growing* inflation.

To be sure, our conclusions are strictly applicable in the process of development and not to a fully developed system. But then the notion of " fully developed " is a convenient abstraction and many so-called developed countries may possess some untapped margin. In this connection, we should also acknowledge that our formal analysis is probably too rigid,[2] in its assumption that the process of development is a one-way, irreversible street: once some additional labour has been trained, it stays trained forever. In reality, of course, given enough slack and enough time, the trained portion may decrease again, especially when account is taken of births, deaths, and retirements. Thus even for a developing country, the short-run frontier may under appropriate circumstances tend to retrace to the right its leftward movement—though this is likely to take substantial time. Similarly, for a so-called " developed " country, if unemployment rises substantially and for long periods of time above previous minima, phenomena akin to those proposed and tested here for a developing country may become significant. In particular, a rapid reflation of demand may generate inflationary pressures which decrease rather than increase in time.

REFERENCES

[1] Alchian, A. A. " Information Costs, Pricing and Resource Unemployment ", in E. S. Phelps *et al.*, *Microeconomic Foundations of Employment and Inflation Theory* (W. W. Norton & Co., 1970).

[2] deMenil, George and Enzler, J. J. " Wages and Prices in the FRB-MIT-Penn Econometric Model ", presented at the Conference on the Econometrics of Price Determination, Washington, D.C. (October 1970).

[3] Friedman, M. " The Role of Monetary Policy ", in *American Economic Review* (March 1968).

[4] Holt, C. C. and David, M. H. " The Concept of Vacancies in a Dynamic Theory of the Labor Market ", *Measurement and Interpretation of Job Vacancies* (National Bureau of Economic Research, New York, 1966).

[5] Holt, C.C. " Improving the Labor Market Trade-off between Inflation and Unemployment ", in *American Economic Review*, Papers and Proceedings (May 1969).

[6] Holt, C. C. " Job Search, Phillips Wage Relation, and Union Influence: Theory and Evidence ", in E. S. Phelps *et al.*, *Microeconomic Foundations of Employment and Inflation Theory* (W. W. Norton & Co., 1970).

[1] One such application is reported in footnote 1, page 217.
[2] It is also oversimplified in that at the last stages of development, parameters other than u_m are likely to become the most relevant, such as the composition of physical and human capital for different groups of the labour force and, particularly in a unionized market, the degree of awareness and acceptance of the mark-up adopted by firms and, in general, of the distribution of income.

[7] Holt, C. C., MacRae, C. D., Schweitzer, S. O. and Smith, R. E. " The Unemploy-
     ment-Inflation Dilemma: a Manpower Solution " (The Urban Institute, Washington,
     D.C., 1971).

[8] Lipsey, R. G. " The Relation between Unemployment and the Rate of Change of
     Money Wage Rates in the United Kingdom, 1862-1957; a Further Analysis ", in
     Economica (February 1960).

[9] Modigliani, F. and Tarantelli, E. " Curva di Phillips, sottosviluppo e disoccupazione
     strutturale ", *Quaderni di Ricerche dell'Ente per gli Studi Monetari, Bancari e Finan-
     ziari* L. Einaudi (Rome 1971).

[10] Mortensen, Dale T. " A Theory of Wage and Employment Dynamics ", in Phelps,
     Microeconomic Foundations of Employment and Inflation Theory (W. W. Norton &
     Co., 1970).

[11] Phelps, E. S. (editor). *Microeconomic Foundations of Employment and Inflation
     Theory* (W. W. Norton & Co., New York, 1970).

[12] Rees, A. " The Phillips Curve as a Menu for Policy Choice ", in *Economica* (August
     1970).

[13] Rey, G. M. " Una misura della capacità produttiva utilizzata nel settore industriale ",
     in *L'Industria* (July-September 1965).

[14] Stigler, G. J. " The Economics of Information ", in *Journal of Political Economy*
     (June 1961).

[15] Stigler, G. J. " Information in the Labor Market ", in *Journal of Political Economy*,
     Vol. LXX (Supplement October 1962).

[16] Sylos Labini, P. " Prices, Distribution and Investment in Italy, 1951-66: an
     Interpretation ", in *Banca Nazionale del Lavoro, Quarterly Review* (December 1967).

[17] Tarantelli, E. " Produttività del Lavoro, Salari e Inflazione ", *Quaderni di Ricerche
     dell'Ente per gli Studi Monetari, Bancari e Finanziari* L. Einaudi (Rome, 1970).

Errata

Page 212, line 8: the comma that appears after "original" should appear after "(14)."

Page 212, footnote 1, 3 lines from the bottom: "$\hat{u} = g(v)$" should read "$\hat{u} = g(\hat{v})$."

Page 215, footnote 1, line 10: in the equation, the variables "RM" and "p_{-1}" should read "$\log RM$"
and "$\log p_1$," respectively.

Reprinted for private circulation from
THE JOURNAL OF POLITICAL ECONOMY
Vol. LXVI, No. 3, June 1958
PRINTED IN U.S.A.

NEW DEVELOPMENTS ON THE OLIGOPOLY FRONT[1]

FRANCO MODIGLIANI

Carnegie Institute of Technology

I

IN MY opinion the two books reviewed in this article represent a welcome major breakthrough on the oligopoly front. These two contributions, which appeared almost simultaneously, though clearly quite independently, have much in common in their basic models and method of approach to the problem. But, fortunately, they do not significantly repeat each other; for, having started from the same point of departure, the authors have followed divergent paths, exploring different implications of the same basic model.

Sylos deals almost exclusively with *homogeneous* oligopoly defined as a situation in which all producers, actual and potential, are able to supply the identical commodity (more generally, commodities that are perfect substitutes for each other) and have access to the very same long-run cost function. He thus focuses on barriers to entry resulting from economies of scale. Bain, on the other hand, also analyzes the effect of competitors being altogether unable to produce perfect substitutes—that is, product-differentiation barriers—or being able to do so only at higher costs—absolute cost-advantage barriers. Furthermore, Bain's book is greatly enriched by fascinating empirical data, painstakingly collected

through a variety of means, and by a courageous attempt at an empirical verification of the implications of his model. However, Bain is concerned primarily with the analysis of long-run market equilibrium, while Sylos devotes more than half of his book to examining the implications of his model for many other issues, such as (1) the effect of short-run or cyclical variations in demand and costs, (2) the validity of the so-called full-cost pricing model, (3) the effect of technological progress, and (4) the impact of oligopolistic structures on the formation and reabsorption of unemployment. His analysis is primarily theoretical and does not purport to provide new empirical evidence, with one rather significant exception. In an appendix to the introductory chapter Sylos presents indexes of concentration for various sectors of the American economy, based on the Gini coefficient.[2] Sylos finds that, according to this measure, concentration has tended to increase appreciably over the period considered—generally from the first decade of the century to the end of the 1940's—for all but one of the distributions analyzed. These include the distribution of plants by value added and by value of sales for manufacturing as a whole and by size of labor force for all manufacturing and for selected industries[3] and the distribution of cor-

[1] A review article of Paolo Sylos Labini, *Oligopolio e progresso tecnico* ("Oligopoly and Technical Progress"). Milan: Giuffrè, 1957. Pp. 207. L. 1,000. Joe S. Bain, *Barriers to New Competition*. Cambridge, Mass.: Harvard University Press, 1956. Pp. xi+329. $5.50. A preliminary edition of Sylos' book was published in 1956 for limited circulation. References in this article are to the final edition.

[2] The Gini coefficient is a measure of the area lying between the actual Lorenz curve and the equi-distribution Lorenz curve.

[3] The individual industries, chosen on the ground that their definition has remained reasonably stable over time, are: (1) steel works and rolling mills;

porations by size of assets. These findings are rather striking, since they run counter to widely accepted views based on well-known studies of the share of the market of the four or eight largest firms. They will undoubtedly deserve close scrutiny by the experts on the subject.

It would be impossible within the scope of a review article to summarize adequately the content of both books and take a good look at the promising new horizons they open. Under these conditions it appears wise to devote primary attention to Sylos' work. The reader can do full justice to Bain's contribution by reading the original, while in the case of Sylos this possibility is open only to the "happy few." With respect to Bain's book, therefore, my only goal will be to whet the reader's appetite.

II

Until quite recently little systematic attention has been paid in the analysis of monopoly and oligopoly to the role of entry, that is, to the behavior of potential competitors. This neglect is justified for monopoly, which is generally defined as the case of a single actual as well as potential producer whose demand curve is not significantly influenced, either in the short or in the long run, by his price policy. Oligopoly could also be defined to exclude entry, fewness being then the result of the impossibility, for firms not now in the group, of producing the commodity—whether for physical or legal reasons. And, undoubtedly, the impossibility of entry is frequently

at least implicitly assumed in the analysis of oligopoly, following the venerable example of Cournot, with his owners of mineral wells. But such a narrow definition leaves out the far more interesting case where fewness is the result of purely economic forces, entry being prevented by—and within the limits of—certain price-output policies of existing producers. This is precisely the essence of homogeneous oligopoly analyzed by both Sylos and Bain.

One might suppose that, as long as potential entrants have access to a long-run cost function identical in all respects to that of existing firms, entry must tend to occur whenever the market price is higher than the minimum long-run average cost. (Cost is used hereafter in the sense of opportunity cost, including therefore an appropriate allowance for "normal" profits.) But then long-run market equilibrium would have to involve a price equal to minimum average cost and a corresponding output[4] and would be undistinguishable from perfectly competitive equilibrium. This supposition is, however, invalid whenever the output of an optimum size firm represents a "non-insignificant" fraction of pre-entry output. The price that is relevant to the potential entrant is the price *after* entry. Even if the pre-entry price is above the lowest achievable cost, the additional output he proposes to sell may drive the price below cost, making the entry unprofitable.

Unfortunately for the theorist, the exact anticipated effect of the entry on

[4] This is, in fact, the conclusion reached by H. R. Edwards, "Price Formation in Manufacturing Industry and Excess Capacity," *Oxford Economic Papers*, VII, No. 1 (February, 1955), 194–218, sec. 4.2, which is, in turn, an elaboration of the model developed by P. W. S. Andrews in *Manufacturing Business* (London: Macmillan & Co., 1949). In other respects Edwards' stimulating analysis anticipates many of the conclusions of Sylos and Bain.

(2) electrical machinery; (3) petroleum refining; (4) lumber and timber products; and (5) shipbuilding and iron and steel. For these industries indexes are given for 1914 and 1947. The distribution for lumber is the single instance in which concentration has decreased.

price is not independent of the (anticipated) reaction of existing producers. The more they are willing to contract their output in response to the entry, the smaller will be the fall in price; in the limiting case the price may even be completely unaffected. Both authors have wisely refused to be stopped by this difficulty. They have instead proceeded to explore systematically the implications of the following well-defined assumption: that potential entrants behave as though they expected existing firms to adopt the policy most unfavorable to them, namely, the policy of maintaining output while reducing the price (or accepting reductions) to the extent required to enforce such an output policy. I shall refer to this assumption as "Sylos' postulate" because it underlies, more or less explicitly, most of his analysis, whereas Bain has also paid some attention to the possibility of potential entrants, assuming a less belligerent behavior on the part of existing firms.

The significance of Sylos' postulate lies in the fact that it enables us to find a definite solution to the problem of long-run equilibrium price and output under homogeneous oligopoly, or at least a definite upper limit to the price, to be denoted by P_0 and a corresponding lower limit to aggregate output, say, X_0. Both authors have essentially reached this conclusion, though through somewhat different routes.

I shall not attempt to reproduce faithfully their respective arguments, but shall instead concentrate on developing the logical essence of their approach. To this end, let $X = D(P)$ denote the market demand curve for the product and let P' denote the pre-entry price, $X' = D(P')$ being then the corresponding aggregate output. Under Sylos' postulate the prospective entrant is confronted not by an infinitely elastic demand at the price P' but by a sloping demand curve which is simply *the segment of the demand curve to the right of* P'. I shall refer to this segment as the marginal demand curve. Note that it is uniquely determined by the original demand curve and the pre-entry price P'. Suppose P' to be such that the corresponding marginal demand curve is *everywhere* below *the* long-run average cost function. Clearly, under these conditions, entry will not be profitable; that is, such a P' is an *entry-preventing price*. The critical price P_0 is then simply the *highest* entry-preventing price, and the critical output X_0 is the corresponding aggregate demand, $D(P_0)$. Under perfect competition, where the output of an optimum size firm is negligible relative to market demand, the marginal demand curve is itself infinitely elastic *in the relevant range;* hence the familiar conclusion that the long-run equilibrium price cannot exceed minimum average cost. But, where the output of an optimum plant is not negligible, P_0 will exceed minimum cost to an extent which depends on the nature of the demand and the long-run cost function.

In order to explore the factors controlling P_0, let us denote by $\bar{x}$ the optimum scale of output, that is, the scale corresponding to the lowest point of the long-run average cost curve. (If this scale is not unique, $\bar{x}$ will mean the smallest scale consistent with minimum cost.) If k denotes the corresponding minimum average cost, then the perfectly competitive equilibrium price is $P_c = k$, and the corresponding equilibrium output is $X_c = D(P_c) = D(k)$. Finally, let us define the size of the market, S, as the ratio of the competitive output to the optimum scale; $S = X_c/\bar{x}$. (This definition is not the same as that of either

Sylos or Bain; it appears, however, to be the most convenient for theoretical purposes, even though it may have drawbacks for empirical investigations.)

Now, following Bain, consider first the simplest case in which the technology of the industry is such that, at a scale less than $\bar{x}$, costs are prohibitively high, so that an entrant can come in only at a scale $\bar{x}$ or larger. In this case the entry-preventing output X_0 is readily found to be

$$X_0 = X_c - \bar{x} = X_c\left(1 - \frac{\bar{x}}{X_c}\right)$$
$$= X_c\left(1 - \frac{1}{S}\right), \tag{1}$$

or $(100/S)$ per cent below the competitive output. Suppose in fact that aggregate output were smaller; it would then be profitable for a firm of scale $\bar{x}$ to enter. Indeed, the post-entry output would then still be smaller than X_c, and hence the post-entry price would be larger than P_c, which is in turn equal to the entrant's average cost. By the same reasoning an output X_0 (or larger) would make entry unattractive. The critical price P_0 corresponding to X_0 can be read from the demand curve or found by solving for P the equation $X_0 = D(P)$. The relation between P_0 and the competitive equilibrium price P_c can be stated (approximately) in terms of the elasticity of demand in the neighborhood of P_c; if we denote this elasticity by η, we have

$$P_0 \simeq P_c\left(1 + \frac{1}{\eta S}\right),$$

or $100/\eta S$ per cent above P_c.[5]

We can now replace the very special

[5] This approximation will not be very satisfactory for small values of S. In particular, if the demand curve has constant elasticity, then, for small values of S, the extent of price rise will be significantly underestimated.

cost function assumed so far with the more conventional one, falling, more or less gradually, at least up to $\bar{x}$. In this general case the critical output may be somewhat larger, and the critical price may be lower, than indicated in the previous paragraph. Indeed, while at the output X_0 given by (1) it is not profitable to enter at the scale $\bar{x}$, it *may* still be profitable to come in at a *smaller* scale.

This possibility and its implications can be conveniently analyzed by means of the graphical apparatus presented in Figure 1. (This graphical device is not to be found in either of the books under review, but I believe that it is quite helpful in bringing out the essence of the authors' arguments.)[6] In panels IA and IIA, the light lines falling from left to right are the (relevant portions of the) market demand curve. For the sake of generality it is convenient to take $\bar{x}$ (the optimum scale) as the unit of measurement for output X and to take k (the corresponding minimum cost) as the unit of measurement for price, P. It follows that the competitive equilibrium price is, by definition, unity, while the corresponding output is precisely the size of the market S. Thus panel IA of Figure 1 relates to an industry of size 2 and panel IIA to an industry of size 10. The two demand curves have constant unit elasticity in the range shown, but, as will become apparent, the effect of different assumptions about the elasticity of demand can readily be handled.

The two heavy lines in each of the two panels represent alternative cost curves, graphed on the same scale as the demand curve, for outputs up to $\bar{x}$ (that is, for values of X up to 1). Because of the choice of units, each curve shows the

[6] In the case of Sylos, I am less sure of my ground, since his argument rests almost entirely on a detailed analysis of two numerical examples.

behavior of costs, in percentage of minimum cost, as a function of plant scale, expressed in percentage of optimum scale. The steeper of the two curves is the kind of traditional, well-behaved cost function that underlies Bain's analysis and involves marked economies of scale. It is, in fact, based on the information reported by him for the cement industry, which appears to have more marked economies of scale than any other of the twenty industries analyzed in his book. It is obtained by joining with a smooth curve the data provided there for discrete scale sizes. The other cost curve, involving less pronounced economies of scale, depicts the kind of cost

function that underlies Sylos' numerical examples. Sylos explicitly assumes, on grounds of presumed realism, the existence of very pronounced discontinuities in the available technologies. Plants can thus have only sizes that are very specific and far apart—only three sizes in his examples and in my graph. The rounded

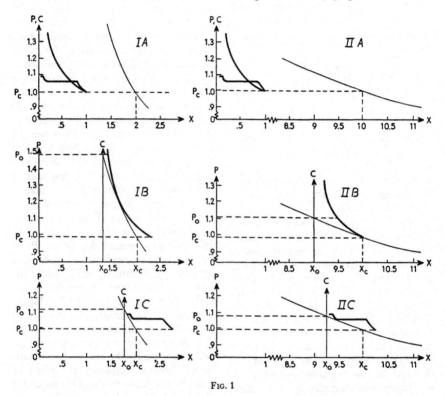

Fig. 1

portions of the curve result from the fact that, beyond certain critical outputs, it pays to shift to a plant of a larger size, even though such a plant could not be utilized to capacity.[7]

[7] If Sylos' assumption is taken literally, the portions of the curves shown as straight lines parallel to the X-axis should really have a scalloped shape. This refinement can, however, be ignored, since it does not affect the results.

The critical price and output, P_0 and X_0, for a given cost curve can now be readily located by means of the following simple device. Slide the cost curve to the right parallel to itself, together with its co-ordinate axis, until no point of this curve lies inside the demand curve. This step is illustrated in panels IB and IIB for the steeper cost curve and in panels IC and IIC for the flatter one. The point at which the Y-axis so displaced cuts the demand curve represents P_0; the point at which it cuts the X-axis is X_0. For, clearly, the portion of the demand curve to the right of the displaced axis is precisely the marginal demand curve when the aggregate output of the existing firms is X_0. If the cost curve is nowhere below this marginal demand curve, there is no possibility of profits for a new entrant.

As can be seen from Figure 1, the cost curve in its terminal position may be either tangent to the demand curve, as in IB, or may touch it at a "corner," as in IC and IIC, or, finally, may touch it at its lower extreme, as in IIB.[8] The X co-ordinate of the point where the two curves touch, referred to the axis of the cost curve, indicates the size of firm which represents the most immediate threat of entry. Where this immediate threat comes from an optimum size plant, as in IIB, X_0 is precisely that given by formula (1) above; it is now seen that this possibility represents a limiting case—and that, in general, the formula provides only a lower bound to X_0.

With the help of Figure 1 we can also establish several interesting propositions in comparative statics. First, by comparing panel IB with IC and IIB

with IIC, we see that, for given market size, P_0 will tend to be higher the steeper the cost curve, that is, the greater the economies of scale. The common sense of this result is apparent: when economies of scale are important, the effective threat will tend to come from large-scale plants, which must widen the gap between X_0 and X_c. Similarly, by comparing IB with IIB and IC with IIC, it appears that, for a given cost curve and elasticity of demand, P_0 will tend to fall with the size of the market; it will, in fact, approach unity (the competitive price) as the size of the market approaches infinity. Furthermore, since, for given size S, a higher elasticity of demand implies a rotation of the cost curve in a counterclockwise direction around the competitive point, it is apparent that a higher elasticity will act in the same direction as a larger size with given elasticity; that is, it will tend to lower P_0.

In summary, under Sylos' postulate there is a well-defined, maximum premium that the oligopolists can command over the competitive price, and this premium tends to increase with the importance of economies of scale and to decrease with the size of market and the elasticity of demand.[9]

III

I have now laid down the basic long-run equilibrium model common to both Bain and Sylos. Hereafter, their roads part, and I shall first follow Sylos in his explorations of some of the fascinating implications of the model.

The first of these implications refers to the size distribution of firms (or, more

[8] It may, of course, also have several discrete points of contact with the demand curve or overlap a portion of it.

[9] As Bain points out, it is conceivable, though not likely, that P_0 will be higher than the price that "maximizes the profit" of the existing firms, in which case it will have no bearing on long-run equilibrium. See below, Sec. VIII.

precisely, of plants) within the group—its *internal structure*, as I shall call it. If we look, for example, at panel *IC*, we see that the price P_0 is considerably above the average cost of the medium-size firms and even slightly above that of the smallest. If then any such firm *happened* to be a member of the group—Sylos here, in good Walrasian tradition, speaks of the initial structure as "criée par hasard"—it could survive and even prosper.

But would it not be profitable for the larger firms to expand, eliminating the smaller ones and securing for themselves the small firms' share of the market? In Sylos' model this possibility can be largely dismissed, thanks to his assumption of sharp technological discontinuities. Suppose, for instance, that there are only two possible scales: (*a*) large plants, producing 10,000 units, and (*b*) small plants, producing 500 units. Suppose further that X_0 is 15,000 and that this output is initially produced by one large firm and ten small ones. There is, then, no real incentive for the large firm to drive the small ones out of the market, for, in order to produce the extra 5,000 units, it would, in fact, have to operate ten small plants (at least as long as the average cost of a small plant is less than the average incremental cost of producing an extra 5,000 units by operating two large plants at 75 per cent of capacity). But the cost of a small firm must be such as to yield very little, if any, abnormal profit at the price P_0. In fact, this price must be such as not to give an inducement to enter the market with a small plant. Hence there will generally be no incentive for the large firm to undertake the price war necessary to eliminate the smaller firms.

If there existed a technology of inter-mediate size, say, size 5,000, the situation might look somewhat different, since at price P_0 such a plant would make some profits. However, even in this case the elimination of small firms would involve a costly price war. The price would have to be kept below prime cost of the small firms for a time long enough to induce them to fold up or below their average cost until their fixed plant wears out. Sylos suggests that usually the war will not be worth the prize and that it will be preferable for the larger firms not to disturb the delicate balance that always prevails in a homogeneous oligopoly structure.

Are we then to conclude that any structure, "criée par hasard," will tend to perpetuate itself as long as it is consistent with a price not higher than P_0? Sylos does not investigate this issue systematically, confining himself to illustrating various possibilities on the basis of his specific numerical examples. I suggest, however, that with the help of Sylos' model it is possible to throw some interesting light on this question. To this end I shall first introduce a definition. Consider any two structures A and B consistent with no inducement to entry: let us say that A is more rational than B if the total profits accruing to the members of the group are larger under structure A than under B.[10] It follows from this definition and our previous analysis that there exists a *most rational* structure, namely, that structure (not necessarily unique) which produces at the smallest total cost the output X_0 that can be sold at price P_0.[11] This

[10] It is apparent that this notion bears a close affinity to that of *dominance* in the theory of games.

[11] This statement is valid only to a first approximation. It is possible that the output X_0 cannot be produced with an integral number of plants of various sizes working at capacity, in which case profit maximization may involve an output somewhat

most rational structure has two features worth mentioning. (1) From a welfare point of view, it has certain optimal properties in that X_0 is being produced at the smallest (social) cost; but it still involves a departure from the usual conditions of Pareto optimality in that the output X_0 is, generally, too small and P_0 too high. (2) From a technological point of view, it has the property that the total capacity of the plants of a given size must necessarily be no larger than the capacity of one plant of the next larger size.

It seems reasonable to suppose that, if a structure B is less rational than a structure A, it will be less likely to be observed. For there is some incentive to a shift from B to A, since such a shift is accompanied by a net gain; that is, losses, if any, are more than compensated by gains. But there will be no corresponding incentive to move back from A to B. It does not follow, however, that structures other than the most rational have no chance at all of ever existing or surviving. As Sylos rightly points out, moving from one structure to another generally involves costs—at best, the cost of reaching an agreement; at worst, that of war—and the potential gain may not be worth the cost, especially when the gain, and even more the cost, may be problematic and uncertain.

The conclusions to which we are led are therefore, as it were, of a probabilistic nature. Less rational structures are less likely to be observed than more rational ones, and very irrational structures are unlikely to maintain themselves for any length of time. But certainly structures

other than the most rational can exist and survive, especially in a world that is moving and in which the most rational structure is itself continuously changing. Similar considerations apply to the price; while we should not expect prices higher that P_0 to be long maintainable, lower prices may have a certain degree of permanence. But, again, a gap between P and P_0 will provide a stimulus to reorganization of the structure, and this stimulus will be more powerful, and hence more likely to produce a response, the greater the gap.

By drawing together the analysis of market equilibrium and that of internal structure, we may venture some tentative conclusions about the factors which, according to Sylos' model, tend to control the degree of scatter in the size distributions of firms. We already know that only those sizes can survive whose average cost is no larger than P_0. From an analysis of the figure it can therefore be inferred that the possible range of the scatter of sizes will tend to be greater the smaller (a) the economies of scale, (b) the size of the markets, and (c) the elasticity of demand.

These implications, as well as those relating to P_0, are in principle testable. Indeed, it is to both Bain's and Sylos' credit that, by moving us away from conjectural variations and similar subjective notions and focusing instead on objective market and technological data, they have provided us with theories rich in empirical content and capable of being disproved by the evidence. To be sure, such tests may not be easy to carry out, especially with the information presently available, as is amply attested by Bain's gallant efforts in this direction. But, with a clear theoretical framework available as a guide in the collection of data, one may hope that more reliable

---

above X_0. However, the departure from X_0 will tend to be negligible, at least as long as the output of the smallest size consistent with P_0 represents a minor fraction of X_0.

and abundant evidence will sooner or later accumulate.

Even at this stage, ingenuity can do much to remedy inadequacies of the data. For instance, in order to compute the actual value of P for a given industry, one would need to know not only the market price but also the minimum average cost of an optimal plant. Bain ingeniously suggests that, even in the absence of precise information on this point, some notion of the relative height of P for various industries may be gotten by ranking them in terms of the rate of profits of the largest firms in each industry, since the average cost of such firms will presumably tend to be reasonably close to the minimum.[12] It should be noted, however, that, contrary to what Bain seems to imply in some of his empirical tests, there is no reason to expect any simple association between P_0 (or its proxy, the rate of profit) and the degree of scatter in plant sizes, at least within Sylos' model. While it is true that a large scatter is not to be

expected when P_0 is very close to unity— for then only firms of near-optimum size can survive—it does not follow that there is a positive association between P_0 and scatter. The only safe statement we can make is that, for given P_0, the scatter should tend to be smaller the steeper the cost curve and that, for given cost curve, the association between P_0 and scatter should be positive, both variables tending to decline as the size of the market and the elasticity of demand increase. A cursory examination of Bain's data for those industries in which product-differentiation and absolute-cost advantages are not supposed to be dominant does not seem to contradict this inference conspicuously. Unfortunately, the data in question provide no information on the elasticity of demand and, what is more serious, leave too much room for personal judgment in ranking industries in terms of any variable.

IV

It is tempting to explore the extent to which the implications we have derived from Sylos' model would be affected if we relaxed some of his very rigid assumptions. This question is especially pressing with respect to his assumption of technological discontinuities. Indeed, Bain has emerged from his empirical investigation with a strong conviction that, although there exists a fairly definite scale $\bar{x}$ at which average cost reaches its minimum, costs do not generally tend to rise for scales larger than $\bar{x}$. This possibility in no way affects our analysis of long-run equilibrium price and output but has considerable bearing on the conclusions concerning the size structure. Clearly, under a Bain-type cost function, the "most rational structure" must be such that all the output X_0 is produced by plants of size $\bar{x}$ or

---

[12] In his book and in earlier contributions Bain measures the rate of profit as the rate of return, net of taxes, on the book value of equity. It would seem preferable to use the rate of return before taxes and interest on the book value of assets, since such a measure is not affected by financial structure. Perhaps a still more relevant measure, for the purpose of testing the model, could be derived from the rate of profit on sales. In fact, letting p denote the market price, we have

$$P = \frac{p}{k} = \frac{px}{kx} = \frac{\text{Sales}}{\text{Sales} - \text{Profit}} = \frac{1}{1 - \dfrac{\text{Profit}}{\text{Sales}}}.$$

By profit I mean here earnings over and above a "normal" rate of return on the book value of assets, which may not be easy to estimate in practice. One may also have some reservations about the assumption that minimum long-run average cost can be approximated from the actual average cost of the dominant firms in the industry. Franklyn Fisher has suggested that a better approximation may be obtained by utilizing, at least as supplementary evidence, the rate of profit on sales of the most profitable firms.

larger. It would follow that structures involving smaller plant sizes would tend to be unstable, especially where the cost function is steep in the range of (relative) costs from 1 to P_0.

The reader can decide for himself just how serious this conclusion is for Sylos' construction.[13] I shall limit myself to suggesting that Sylos' case may be considerably strengthened when we recognize the existence of product differentiation of a type not altogether inconsistent with the notion of homogeneous oligopoly, such as spatial differentiation or modifications in product design to meet customers' specifications. Under these conditions the area of the market supplied by smaller firms may be such that the dominant firms would have little to gain by capturing it, either because they have no cost advantage or because this would require an unprofitable price policy on other lines of product.

Consider, for example, the case of spatial differentiation. Suppose the large firm has a cost of 10 and the cost of transportation to a given distant market is 1. Suppose further that the highest f.o.b. price preventing entry that the large firm can charge is 12. The delivered price in the given market is then 13, and it may well be that, at this price, the market can be profitably supplied by a small local firm at, say, a cost of 12.5. In order to capture that relatively small market, the large firm would have to keep the price well below 11.5 for some considerable length of time and then keep it no higher than 11.5 in-

definitely—a policy which may well be unprofitable.[14] There is thus room for smaller firms in the industry, but this room is generated by market "exploitation" on the part of the large firm, and all customers are paying a higher price (by 2 per unit) than under competitive equilibrium.

Consider next the case of product modifications. It may well be that a class of customers is willing to pay an extra premium of 1 for a specific variation of the standard product. If the large firm charges 12 for the standard line, even though it has a cost of 10, these customers are therefore willing to pay 13. Now, suppose that, given the size of the market for the specialty, the average cost of the product is again, say, 12.5, whether it is produced by the larger firm or by a smaller one specializing in that line. If such a smaller firm exists, it is not worthwhile for the large firm to try to capture the market. But note once more that the existence of the smaller firm is made possible by the larger firm's oligopoly power. Under competitive conditions the small firm could not exist, since, if customers could get the standard product for 10, they would not be willing to pay enough for the specialty to cover its production cost of 12.5.

In short, in many situations the presence of a variety of sizes may be rendered reasonably stable by the fact that the larger firms find it advantageous to skim the fattest segment of the market, leav-

[13] Rosenstein-Rodan has pointed out to me that Bain's long-run cost function may not be too relevant where plant is very long lived. For, even though it may be possible to design a plant having cost k at sizes larger than $\bar{x}$, nonetheless an existing firm wishing to undertake a moderate expansion may have to utilize a smaller-scale technique with higher costs.

[14] It is assumed that the alternative, and more profitable, course of quoting a delivered price of 12.5 is not available. It is interesting to note in this connection that the prohibition of freight absorption as an antitrust measure will have a desirable effect if it induces the producer to choose a lower price in order not to lose distant markets to smaller local firms but that it will have an undesirable outcome if the producer finds it more advantageous to abandon those markets, in which case the demand will be supplied at a higher social cost.

ing it for smaller firms to supply less profitable pockets. Nor should one forget altogether, even within the realm of pure theory, the public relations advantages that tend to accrue to the large firms from the coexistence of smaller and weaker partners. The argument that prices cannot be lowered without playing havoc with large numbers of honest and industrious small enterprises is always one of great public appeal. And, where antitrust laws are a potential threat, the advantages of having smaller competitors is even more evident.[15]

V

Before closing the subject of longrun static analysis, I must report one more observation on which Sylos lays a great deal of stress and which has to do with the effects of technological progress. While improvements in technology that are applicable to all scales must necessarily tend to depress price and expand output, he argues that improvements applicable only at, or near, the largest scale will not affect the critical price and hence will tend to result in higher profits for the larger firms. Furthermore, Sylos seems to feel that technological changes are very commonly of

this type, and he is inclined to account in this fashion for a presumed tendency of the profit margin of large firms to grow over time. Here, however, I cannot avoid feeling that Sylos is going too far. For, in the first place, even a change that affects only the largest scale may well lower P_0 when the immediate threat is, in fact, from firms of size $\bar{x}$; and, in the second place, any innovation that affects only plants of suboptimal size (and such innovations are by no means inconceivable) will also result in a fall in the critical price and thus will reduce the profit of the largest firms whose costs have remained unchanged. There is therefore serious doubt whether Sylos' argument can account for a long-run relative rise in large firms' profits, not to mention the equally serious doubt whether such a relative rise has in fact occurred. The model does suggest, however, that changes in technology may cause radical changes in the most rational structure and thus eventually may lead to pervasive changes in the actual structure, including the possible elimination of whole layers of small-scale plants.

VI

I now proceed to consider with Sylos some implications of the model for the effect of short-run changes in demand and cost conditions. Note, first, that in the analysis of market equilibrium I have made no mention of the standard categories of monopolistic competition theories, namely, marginal cost and marginal revenue. To be sure, with sufficient ingenuity, the analysis could be forced into that cast,[16] but such an undertaking would be merely an exercise in semantics

[15] The considerations of this section clearly point to the importance of factors other than those discussed in Sec. III above in controlling the scatter of the size distribution of firms and plants. In particular, under a Bain-type cost function, the model has nothing to say about the size distribution of firms above the optimum size $\bar{x}$. Here one may have to fall back on stochastic models of the type advanced, for example, by H. Simon in *Models of Man* (New York: John Wiley & Sons, 1957), chap. ix. In any event the analysis presented casts most serious doubts on the argument advanced by some authors and well exemplified by the following quotation: "Actually, we find that in most industries firms of very different sizes survive, and we may infer that commonly there is no large advantage or disadvantage to size over a very considerable range of outputs" (George Stigler, *The Theory of Price* [New York: Macmillan Co., 1952], p. 144).

[16] For such an attempt see, for example, J. R. Hicks, "The Process of Imperfect Competition," *Oxford Economic Papers*, VI (February, 1954), 41–54.

and formal logic and would in no way increase our understanding of what is involved. On the other hand, our result can readily be recast in the framework of the so-called full-cost pricing principle. According to this principle, prices are determined by adding to prime cost a markup to cover overhead per unit and by adding further an "appropriate" profit margin. So far, however, it has never been convincingly explained just at what level of output the overhead charge is computed or what determines the "appropriate" profit margin. Sylos' and Bain's models do provide answers to both questions. The large firms, which typically set the pace in the market, must base their price on long-run average cost (so that the overhead must normally be computed at capacity operation, with due allowance for normal seasonal and cyclical variations in the rate of utilization) and apply to this cost the largest profit markup that "the traffic will bear," namely, the markup P_0—for P_0, it will be recalled, is precisely the ratio of the highest possible price to average cost.

The usefulness of translating the result of the static analysis into the language of full-cost pricing becomes fully apparent when we proceed to examine the effects of a variation, say, an increase, in some element of prime cost. Such a change will generally affect all firms and hence will raise the long-run cost curve more or less uniformly. This development in turn will raise the level of the critical price and make it profitable to raise the actual price to this new level. Now it can be verified that, at least for moderate variations in costs and well-behaved demand functions, a good approximation of the new critical price can be obtained precisely by adding to the new average cost the very same profit margin that prevailed before the change; and nearly as good an approximation can be obtained by applying to the new prime cost the original total percentage markup. Thus full-cost pricing may well represent a very useful rule of thumb in reacting to cost changes affecting the entire industry, at least as long as such changes are not too drastic.

Now that we have a solid rationale for the full-cost principle, we need not have qualms about acknowledging two other sets of factors that tend to give it further sanction. (1) In an oligopolistic situation, with its precarious internal equilibrium, there is much to be gained from simple and widely understood rules of thumb, which minimize the danger of behavior intended to be peaceful and co-operative being misunderstood as predatory or retaliatory.[17] (2) The experience of those who, like myself, have conducted extensive personal interviews with executives suggests that these respondents have a strong propensity to explain their behavior in terms of simple mechanical principles, especially when they feel that these principles are blessed by general respectability.

So much about the effect of variations in costs. Let us now turn to the effect of cyclical variations in demand. For the sake of concreteness, let us start out from the prosperity phase, in which plants are being operated at, or near, capacity rates. If the demand curve now shifts to the left as a result of a fall in aggregate income, our model suggests that the optimum markup may have a slight tendency to increase. There are two main reasons for this contention:

[17] See, for example, A. Henderson, "The Theory of Duopoly," *Quarterly Journal of Economics*, LXVIII (November, 1954), 576–79, Sec. VII, and T. C. Schelling "Bargaining, Communication, and Limited War," *Conflict Resolution*, I (March, 1957), 19–36.

(1) the critical price P_0 tends to rise when the size of the market falls and (2), with substantial idle capacity and sharply reduced profits, or even losses, prevailing in the industry, even a price somewhat higher than P_0 is not likely to encourage entry, especially where the effective threat is from plants large enough to require a substantial investment. This tendency for the critical markup to rise may partly be offset or even more than offset if, as the demand shifts, its elasticity increases; it will be reinforced if the elasticity falls—a case which Sylos regards as more typical, though, in our view, not very convincingly.

On the whole, then, the critical price P_0 may have some mild tendency to rise; but this does not mean that the actual markup will necessarily rise, for, with much idle capacity, the temptation for individual members of the oligopolistic group to secure a larger share of the shrunken business is very strong. Thus the self-discipline of the group may well tend to break down, with a resultant fall in the effective price if not in the officially quoted one.

In the course of the recovery the markup will of course tend to retrace the path followed in the contraction. But here some new interesting possibilities arise which Sylos himself has not considered. In an expanding economy the recovery will tend to push demand to levels higher than previous peaks. As a result of a rise in demand that is rapid and larger than expected, or as a result of circumstances beyond its control, such as war, the industry may be caught with capacity inadequate to satisfy the demand at the critical price P_0. In terms of traditional patterns of thinking, one would expect firms in the industry to be eager to exploit the situation by charging higher prices. But such

a price policy may not be so appealing to the larger firms whose long-run interest is to secure for themselves as much as possible of the additional demand at the profitable price P_0. A higher price may tend to encourage entry, which would not only reduce their share but possibly also threaten the maintenance of self-discipline in periods of depressed demand. Thus the dominant firms may have an incentive to "hold the price line" by such devices as lengthening delivery schedules and informal rationing (even at the risk of gray markets), while at the same time expanding capacity—but only to an extent that seems warranted by the anticipated long-run demand at the price P_0. These considerations may help to explain the otherwise rather puzzling behavior of certain important sectors of the economy in the early postwar period.[18]

On the whole it would appear that no very definite general conclusion can be reached about the cyclical behavior of the markup, although the model may have a good deal to say for well-defined classes of situations. One might, however, go along with Sylos on the following two tentative generalizations: (1) on the average, the markup is not likely to change much in the course of the cycle, but one should expect some scatter around this central tendency, and (2)

[18] A similar explanation is advanced in Edwards, *op. cit.*, and in Kuh and Meyer, *The Investment Decision* (Cambridge, Mass.: Harvard University Press, 1957), esp. chap. xii. It has also been suggested that the price policies in question may be explained by the concern that higher prices and consequent higher profits would have led to irresistible pressure for wage concessions, difficult to reverse. By contrast, the abnormally high profits of dealers or gray-market operators could be counted on to disappear automatically as the supply gradually caught up with demand. I am indebted to Albert G. Hart and Richard Cyert for stimulating discussions on the relevance of Sylos' model to the explanation of the postwar experience.

prices should tend on the average to fluctuate more in relation to prime cost where there is more chance for the discipline of the group to break down, and this chance presumably should tend to increase with the size of the group and decrease with degree of concentration (in Sylos' sense). These generalizations appear to be consistent with the evidence assembled by Stigler in his well-known criticism of the kinky demand curve,[19] though they may be less easy to reconcile with certain empirical studies of price flexibility.[20]

Sylos attempts to dispose of the latter evidence by an ingenious argument which is not entirely convincing in this context but which is of interest on its own merit. Specifically, he suggests that, where the full-cost principle is widely adhered to, it may be in the interest of the larger firms to sustain the prices of factors entering into prime cost; in fact, provided that the shifted demand curve has a sufficiently low elasticity, such a policy will increase the over-all profit of the industry. Where the large firms are themselves important producers of some critical raw materials, they may best achieve this purpose by sustaining these particular prices; where this is not possible, they may acquiesce to an increase in real wages.[21] However, the advantage of an increase in prime costs is realized only where full-cost pricing is adhered to in spite of widespread excess capacity. Hence this policy can be sensible only where discipline is maintained, which, as suggested earlier, may be related to small number and heavy concentration. Sylos suggests that these considerations may help to explain certain empirical results indicating a positive association between cyclical wage rigidity and degree of concentration.[22]

VII

The last two parts of Sylos' book expound the thesis that monopolistic and oligopolistic market structures are an important factor contributing to the development of unemployment, especially technological unemployment. In spite of the importance of the subject, this part will be reviewed in very sketchy form, both for lack of space and because Sylos' argument is not so convincing as his partial equilibrium analysis.

The main thread of his argument in Part II seems to run as follows. Starting from a stationary situation with full employment, a labor-saving innovation initially displaces labor. The reabsorption of this unemployment requires some net saving to be invested in the equipment necessary to outfit the displaced workers. (The alternative possibility of a fall in real wages leading to an appropriate change in capital coefficients is excluded by assumption.) Under perfectly competitive market structures, the fall in cost would lead to higher real income for all those who have not lost their

[19] George Stigler, "The Kinky Oligopoly Demand Curve and Rigid Prices," *Journal of Political Economy*, LV (October, 1947), 432–49.

[20] Richard Ruggles, "The Nature of Price Flexibility and Determinants of Relative Price Changes in the Economy," in *Business Concentration and Price Policy* (A Conference of the Universities–National Bureau Committee for Economic Research [Princeton, N.J.: Princeton University Press, 1955]), pp. 441–505.

[21] Note that this argument is applicable even to long-run equilibrium analysis. That is, when the market demand is sufficiently inelastic, an increase in wage rates may increase the total excess of receipts over (opportunity) costs accruing to the group. It may then be profitable for existing firms to tolerate high wages, as long as these are enforced by a trade union strong enough to impose the same wage scale on any potential entrant.

[22] The major piece of evidence quoted in this connection is J. W. Garbarino, "A Theory of Interindustry Wage Structure Variation," *Quarterly Journal of Economics*, LXIV (May, 1950), 282–305.

The Determinants of Wages and Prices

employment, and this rise in real income, especially profits, supposedly produces the saving and investment necessary for the reabsorption. On the other hand, under oligopolistic structures, the fall in cost will frequently not be accompanied by a proportionate fall in prices and will thus result in an increase in the value added of the sector where costs have fallen. (I have already expressed some doubt about the validity of this conclusion in Sec. V above.) To the extent that the increase in value added is absorbed by higher wages, the necessary saving will not be forthcoming, since, by an assumption which is particularly unpalatable to me, workers have a marginal propensity to consume equal to 1. To the extent that the increase in value added results in higher profits—and even if these profits give rise to savings—there may still be difficulties. Sylos suggests in fact that the entrepreneurs to whom the profits accrue will be disinclined to invest outside their own industry, whereas the investment required should be spread throughout the economy.

The conclusion Sylos draws is that, with widespread oligopolistic market structures, the forces making for reabsorption, though not entirely absent, will be lagging and weak. In a world of continous technological change this weakness is sufficient, in his view, to account for a substantial permanent pool of unemployment, whose continuing existence is therefore an essentially dynamic phenomenon. He further argues that the kind of innovations the larger firms in the oligopolistic group will be inclined to adopt are likely to aggravate the technological displacement of labor. He maintains in fact that, though these firms will tend to be quite progressive in searching for, and adopting, innovations that cut

costs at current level of output, they will nonetheless shun improvements that would cut costs only at a large scale of operation. But this argument is not quite consistent with his own model, since the new, larger-scale, and cheaper technique may itself become the immediate threat to entry. Nor is it clearly relevant—for it does not per se establish a bias in favor of labor-saving innovations.

Part III purports to explore the implications of the previous analysis for the standard Keynesian theory of effective demand. This part again contains many interesting observations but also has its shortcomings. In particular, the author does not seem to be sufficiently aware that the implications of the analysis of Part III are profoundly different for an economy poor in capital and savings like the Italian economy and for one in which the main threat to unemployment springs from a lack of effective demand. In the former case, labor-saving innovations may indeed tend to aggravate the problem of unemployment, especially when coupled with powerful unions and downward wage rigidity. But, in the latter case, such innovations are, as it were, a blessing, since they increase the required stock of capital and thus make possible the absorption of full-employment saving.

This sketch of Parts III and IV may well fail to do justice to Sylos' argument. But such a failure would serve to confirm the earlier statement that these final chapters do not quite match the high level of performance that characterizes the rest of this remarkable book.

VIII

Let us now look briefly at that part of Bain's analysis that does not overlap Sylos'.

Still with respect to barriers from economies of scale, Bain makes a halfhearted attempt to explore the consequences of dropping Sylos' postulate (see Sec. II). Unfortunately, as long as we are dealing with homogeneous oligopoly, it is hard to find a well-defined sensible alternative. Certainly, the diametrically opposite assumption that existing firms will adopt a policy of maintaining price, by contracting their output, would generally be a rather foolish one for the entrant to make. It implies that established firms will graciously allow the entrant to carve out for himself whatever slice of the market he pleases, while suffering losses on two accounts: (1) by losing sales and (2) by incurring a higher average cost, at least in the short run and possibly even in the long run, if their original plant was of no more than optimal size. Furthermore, such a policy, if consistently followed, would unavoidably result in the original members' being gradually squeezed out of the market.

The only alternative systematically explored by Bain is for the entrant to assume that price will be maintained but only provided he is contented with a share of the market no larger than that of the existing firms—which are conveniently assumed, for this purpose, to be all of equal size. There is, then, in general, a well-defined critical price (and corresponding output) such that entry is unprofitable even if a prospective entrant proceeds on the stated "optimistic" assumption.[23]

As Bain is well aware, this alternative assumption is but one of a large class of assumptions that could be constructed and explored. But he has wisely refrained from following this line, which is rather unpromising at this stage. For the moment, at least, we must be satisfied with the conclusion that there exists a well-

defined upper limit to the price that can be maintained under oligopoly in the long run, and this upper limit is P_0, obtained under Sylos' postulate. It is the upper limit because, at a price higher than this, entry will be profitable even if the existing firms are bent on doing the entrant as much damage as they possibly can.[24] But a price lower than P_0 cannot be excluded a priori, even in the long run, especially where P_0 would cover the cost at a scale of output which represents a small fraction of X_0 and where a plant of such scale would require a relatively small investment. But, broadly speaking, these are precisely the conditions under which P_0 is close to 1, and the classical competitive model may provide a reasonable approximation. Conversely, Sylos' postulate may well provide a reasonable approximation precisely where it makes a real difference —where it implies a value of P_0 appreciably above unity.

Dropping the assumption that all producers, actual and potential, have access

[23] It is easy to verify that the stated critical price, say, p_0, and corresponding output are given by the simultaneous solution of the following two equations:

$$X = D(p) \qquad (1)$$

$$p = c\,\frac{X}{(n+1)}, \qquad (2)$$

where $c(q)$ denotes the minimum long-run average cost of producing the quantity q, and n is the number of plants. In general, p_0 is an increasing function of n and is larger than the competitive price, at least as long as n is larger than S. Furthermore, for sufficiently large n, each firm is of less than optimal size, and the equilibrium bears a close resemblance to that described by Chamberlin in *Monopolistic Competition*, chap. v, sec. 5.

[24] A somewhat higher price could conceivably be maintained if the industry produced an output smaller than X_0, but had enough capacity to produce X_0 or more and a record of readiness to exploit the extra capacity to *expand* output in the face of entry. Such behavior would presumably require more or less open collusion, of a nature likely only with a very small and well-disciplined group.

The Determinants of Wages and Prices   415 to identical cost functions enables us to analyze another set of forces which can account for a long-run excess of price over cost, and which Bain labels "absolute cost advantages." Such differential costs, arising from factors like control of scarce resources, patents and trade secrets, and generally superior technical and managerial know-how, have already been extensively analyzed and understood in the received body of theory. They underlie the traditional theory of monopoly, oligopoly without entry, and rents. Of course, with cost differential in the picture, there is no longer a specific entry-forestalling price, even under Sylos' postulate. Rather the critical price depends on the cost of the most efficient potential entrant and, hence, on just which firms are already in the group. It may then not be in the interest of existing firms to try to prevent the entry of very efficient producers, since this might require an unprofitably low price. When the price-output policy of existing firms is not intended to discourage potential entrants, Bain speaks of "ineffectively impeded" entry, in contrast to "effectively impeded" entry, in which price and output policy is designed to make entry unprofitable, and to "blockaded entry," in which the price and output policy that is most advantageous to the group, without regard to entry, happens to make entry unattractive.

But Bain's most significant finding about absolute cost barriers is probably at the empirical level. He finds in fact that, at least for his sample of twenty industries, such barriers are generally not important. Natural scarcity appears to be a significant factor in at most two industries—copper and possibly steel. In only three other cases do patents and/or technical know-how possibly play some role and apparently not a major one.

Bain also provides a valuable tabulation of available information on the size of the investment required by a new entrant (with an optimum scale plant). These capital requirements represent a somewhat special type of barrier to entry whose possible significance has been repeatedly mentioned earlier.

The remaining barrier to entry—resulting from the inability of potential competitors to produce a commodity that is a perfect substitute for the product of existing firms—is again one that has received considerable attention in the past. Bain's new contribution in this area consists of a penetrating empirical investigation of the specific barriers that impede the production of perfect or near-perfect substitutes for each industry and their consequences. The main factors may be classified roughly as follows: (1) Allegiance to brands, supported by large advertising outlays, and possibly also, by a long record of reliability; this factor is found to provide the main barrier, and a significant one, almost only in the case of inexpensive durable or non-durable consumers' goods such as cigarettes, liquor, and soap. (2) Control by the manufacturer of an extensive and exclusive dealers' organization attending to the sale and the servicing of the product; as one might expect, this phenomenon is of major importance for expensive durable goods, such as automobiles, typewriters, and tractors and other farm machinery, but it is apparently also of some significance for other commodities, such as petroleum and rubber tires. (3) Patents protecting some feature of the product or related auxiliary services. (4) Special services provided to customers. These last two factors are rarely mentioned and generally do not seem to offer very effective protection.

It is worth noting that factors (2) and (3), and in part also factor (1), could be largely treated as economies of scale in marketing. Both Bain and Sylos are aware of this possibility; in fact, the latter—though he pays only passing attention to product differentiation fostered by advertising—hints that the effect of this type of barrier could be analyzed along lines similar to those utilized in the homogeneous oligopoly model. That is, a new entrant could hope to match the profit performance of the successful large firms only by securing a market of the same absolute size. But, given the over-all size of the market, even if the entrant succeeded in capturing a share comparable to that of existing firms, each member would be left with too small a market, so that the final result of the entry would be to make the business unattractive for all.

After evaluating for his twenty industries the over-all barriers to entry resulting from the joint effect of economies of scale, absolute cost advantages, and product differentiation and after summarizing the effects that these over-all barriers should have on various aspects of market performance on the basis of his theoretical analysis, Bain proceeds to check his deductions against available evidence on actual performance. To be sure, the present evidence on barriers to entry as well as on market performance is frequently far from adequate, and one may have reservations about the details of some of the test procedures. Nonetheless, Bain's courageous attempt at systematic testing and his candid admission of occasional failures of his predictions is a highly welcome novelty and one whose importance can hardly be overestimated.

Finally, the implications of the analysis for public policy designed to foster workable competition are set forth in a very cautious and restrained spirit in the concluding chapter viii. On the whole, the outlook for effective public policy is not too optimistic, although it is by no means as gloomy as that of Sylos. But, then, Sylos' gloom is understandable. His inspiration comes from the Italian economy, where markets are naturally small and are made still smaller by tariffs and other artificial restrictions. According to his own model, the tendency to oligopolistic structures, and their power of market exploitation, will tend to be greater the smaller the size of the market.

I hope I have succeeded in justifying the glowing statement with which this review begins and in showing how well the two books complement each other. To be sure, much work still remains to be done in the area of oligopolistic market structures. In particular, the analysis of both authors is still largely limited to a static framework, and there is reason to believe that certain aspects of oligopolistic behavior can be adequately accounted for only by explicitly introducing dynamic elements into the analysis.[25] In my view, the real significance of Bain's and Sylos' contributions lies not merely in the results that they have already reached but at least as much in their having provided us with a framework capable of promising further developments and leading to operationally testable propositions. In addition, Bain deserves high credit for having led the way on the path of empirical testing.

[25] Some promising beginnings in this direction are already to be found in Sylos and, even more, in Bain. The latter's notion of ineffectively impeded entry, for example, is an essentially dynamic one. Similarly, Sylos hints that, where demand is growing, existing firms, to discourage entry, may have to keep their capacity somewhat larger than X_0 and their markup somewhat below P_0. Needless to say, the mere emphasis on the problem of entry is, per se, a significant movement in the direction of a dynamic analysis.

Errata

Page 222, column 2, line 7: "that P_0" should read "than P_0."

Page 230, footnote 23: equation (2) should read "$p = c\left(\dfrac{X}{n+1}\right)$." Five lines from bottom of footnote, after "larger than S," insert "This conclusion is valid provided that the equilibrium with n firms is stable in the sense that an increase in output would not reduce costs more than price, which is analogous to the Marshallian stability condition."

FRANCO MODIGLIANI
Massachusetts Institute of Technology

and

LUCAS PAPADEMOS
Massachusetts Institute of Technology

Targets
for Monetary Policy
in the Coming Year

MOST OBSERVERS would agree that the present state of the economy can be traced largely to the monetary policy pursued during the last few quarters, in particular the severe monetary squeeze of mid-1974. We see this policy as resulting from the pursuit of inappropriate targets framed in terms of monetary aggregates and "orderly markets"—since we disbelieve that policymakers intended to achieve 9 percent unemployment, so far off any target announced by the administration or sanctioned, even indirectly, by Congress. In order to avoid similar episodes in the coming difficult quarters, monetary policy should be aimed at explicitly stated targets for real output and employment, and at consistent targets for money income. The purpose of this paper is to propose appropriate real targets for the next two years and to examine their implications for monetary policy.

In the light of the high unemployment of mid-1975, and of the importance of an orderly reduction of the current high rate of inflation, the aim proposed is to bring down the rate of unemployment over the next two years to

Note: We wish to express our appreciation to Arlie Sterling for helping us with the computations.

141

a level that we label the noninflationary rate of unemployment (NIRU). It is defined as a rate such that, as long as unemployment is above it, inflation can be expected to decline—except perhaps from an initially low rate. The existence of NIRU is implied by both the "vertical" and the "nonvertical" schools of the Phillips curve. Postwar data (for the years 1953–71) are consistent with the hypothesis of a well-defined NIRU, stable over time, provided that the measure of unemployment is adjusted for changes in the composition of the labor force. Because the present labor force is heavily weighted with groups exhibiting high relative unemployment rates, NIRU as measured by the official unemployment rate is currently estimated at somewhat over 5½ percent. Some evidence suggests, however, that over the last two decades NIRU was held down by a favorable trend in the terms of trade between the private nonfarm sectors on the one hand and imported goods and farm products on the other. A termination or reversal of this trend would tend to raise NIRU, at least temporarily.

On the basis of these and other considerations, we conclude that a conservative interim unemployment target for mid-1977 is 6 percent. Achieving this target will require a growth of output of at least 17 percent over the next two years. Of this total, more than half should be achieved in the first year, to allow the growth rate to abate as the ultimate target is approached. Taking into account the price implications of this growth path, we conclude that in the first year money income should grow at an annual rate above 15 percent. From this it is argued that even if the primary stimulus to recovery comes from fiscal policy, as seems necessary to ensure an early and vigorous revival, the money supply will have to increase for a while at a rate well above 10 percent. There is wide concern that such a sharp acceleration in the money supply would have an unfavorable effect on the rate of inflation. But we allay this concern by showing that the evidence is clearly inconsistent with *any* influence of money on inflation outside of its indirect effect through its contribution to the determination of aggregate demand and employment.

We conclude that the monetary authority should be prepared to accommodate the temporary rapid rate of growth of the money supply required for the strong recovery we advocate, which we believe is consistent with a gradual abatement of inflation. By contrast, holding to monetary growth targets of the 1974 magnitude would very likely make for a sluggish recovery with rising unemployment, and might even produce a new downturn.

The Lessons of 1974

Monetary policy in 1974 represented an unfortunate blend of two targets: (1) an endeavor to keep the growth of monetary aggregates within rigid bounds, and in particular to bring the growth of M_1 roughly within the 6 percent target foreshadowed in the 1974 report of the Council of Economic Advisers; and (2) an endeavor to prevent interest rates from falling too rapidly.

The first target was operative through July. Unfortunately, that 6 percent money growth rate was far too small to satisfy the increasing transactions requirements implied by the administration's targets for the economy for 1974: a modest growth of real income of 1 percent, an increase in unemployment between the end of 1973 and the end of 1974 from 4.9 percent to around 5¾ percent, and a concomitant price increase estimated somewhat optimistically at 7 percent. Taken together, the price and output projections implied a growth of money income of about 8 percent. Warnings about the inadequacy of the 6 percent limit and the dangers of concentrating on the growth of monetary aggregates had been sounded since early in the year by many analysts, including one of the authors.[1]

The inconsistency became dramatically apparent as the monetary squeeze of the second quarter drove the federal funds rate from below 9 percent in early March to 13.5 percent in early July. The Federal Reserve's tolerance of such a drastic rise in short-term market rates must have reflected its aversion to significant deviations of the growth of monetary aggregates from its initial targets. The violence of the squeeze may be attributed partly also to the unreliability of the monetary statistics on which the decisions were based. Later revisions of these statistics have in fact reduced the estimated annual rate of growth of M_1 in the critical four-month span from February to May from 9.7 to 7.6 percent.[2]

The resulting conditions in the credit market are generally assigned the major responsibility for the decline in real gross national product in the

1. Franco Modigliani, "The 1974 Report of the President's Council of Economic Advisers: A Critique of Past and Prospective Economic Policies," *American Economic Review*, vol. 64 (September 1974), pp. 544–57. Although this paper was published in September, it was written in March–April, well before the squeeze.
2. We are indebted to Benjamin Friedman for bringing these figures to our attention.

third and, especially, the fourth quarter. The *Economic Report of the President, February 1975*, for example, attributes to this squeeze the aborting of the mild recovery in housing in the spring and the subsequent collapse, and points out that "housing accounted for fully half of the decline in real output from 1973 to 1974...." (p. 41.) The credit squeeze also reduced investment, had disastrous repercussions on the stock market and hence on consumption, and directly and indirectly contributed to the desire to liquidate inventories.

After the economy began to sag, the demand for money eased and interest rates began to drop, though the decline was initially cushioned by a very slow growth of the money supply that may well have reflected the Board's desire to make up for what it perceived as the excessive growth of the first half of the year.[3] In the latter part of the year, the second target—achieving a gradual fall in interest rates—became operative. To force the money supply to grow at 6 percent or thereabouts would have led to a precipitous decline in short rates, which the Board presumably regarded as undesirable. Given the sharp decline in the demand for money—due in part to falling business activity, but in part to still unsettled causes—the endeavor to bring about an "orderly" decline of interest rates meant that the money supply increased little, and even declined in early 1975, according to the data now available.

The most important lesson of this experience is that monetary policy should not be directed to the achievement of purely monetary targets, such as rigid growth rates of monetary aggregates, or to the preservation of so-called "orderly" markets. The monetarists may be right that, given enough time and enough pain, and perhaps enough ups and downs, the economy may adjust to a M_1 growth of 4 percent—provided that fiscal policy and the

---

3. If this interpretation has merit, the Board's actions even in July and possibly August resulted again from the unreliability of the monetary statistics; the text interpretation is suggested also by the "Record of Policy Actions of the Federal Open Market Committee" of July 16, in *Federal Reserve Bulletin*, vol. 60 (October 1974), especially pp. 716–17, and of August 20, ibid. (November 1974), especially pp. 766–67. The data now available indicate, in fact, that M_1 remained consistently below a 6 percent trend beginning in December 1973, except for June 1974, when it was negligibly above that trend. But in terms of the data published in the *Federal Reserve Bulletin* of July and August 1974, the cumulated growth of M_1 was above 6 percent from March to July. A revision of these estimates apparently became available shortly before the August FOMC meeting.

rest of the world are kind enough not to make new waves! But 1974 shows that this is not a satisfactory way to manage an economy. Instead, monetary targets should be set, and adjusted, in the light of explicitly stated goals for real output and employment and money-income targets consistent with them. Only explicit targets will make it possible to monitor the success of policymakers. In this way, too, inconsistency among the targets becomes apparent; for example, if the desired unemployment path goes along with more inflation than had been expected, a new set of targets and their policy implications should be worked out.

Real Targets for the Next Two Years

Clearly, two major problems demand urgent solution today: unemployment and inflation. Unemployment must be reduced with deliberate speed, but at the same time its planned path should lead to a steady decline in the rate of inflation. With these considerations in mind, unemployment should be gradually reduced over the next two years to an "interim" target level defined above as the noninflationary rate of unemployment, or NIRU.

The past performance of the economy permits us to identify NIRU, within bounds, and we can do so without confronting the conceptual question of the shape of the Phillips curve at extreme values. Rather, we address the more relevant question of what unemployment path is consistent with slowing inflation. For this purpose, all major views about the relation between inflation and unemployment imply the existence of a NIRU. The two extreme views carry this implication—the first that even in the long run, the Phillips curve has a negative slope throughout the entire range of unemployment; and the second that in the long run it can have no negative slope and must be vertical at some natural unemployment rate. The existence of a NIRU is also implied by intermediate positions such as our own, that the Phillips curve is relatively flat for high unemployment rates but approaches verticality (or may even be slightly backward sloping!) for sufficiently low rates of unemployment. The diagram below illustrates how the concept of a NIRU fits into these different views. The rate of inflation is measured along the vertical axis, and the rate of unemployment along the horizontal. The line F—F' is a vertical Phillips curve, à la Friedman. In this case, the NIRU is the value of U at which F—F' cuts the horizontal axis, because a value of

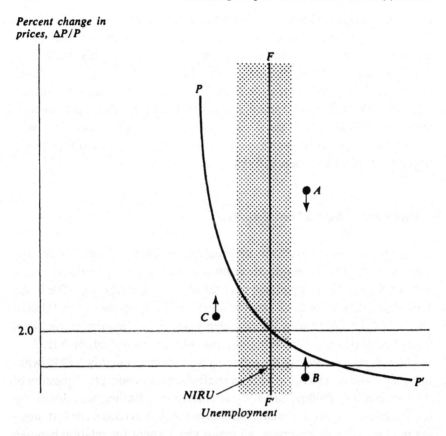

*Percent change in
prices,* ΔP/P

2.0

NIRU

Unemployment

U larger than NIRU must be accompanied by declining inflation, as indicated by the direction of the arrow from point A. Curve P—P′ is a conventional Phillips curve; it may become vertical for sufficiently low unemployment and horizontal for sufficiently high unemployment, but over some middle range it has a negative slope. Here NIRU can be found by first establishing a "negligible" rate of inflation; in the diagram this rate is illustrated by 2.0 percent. The point at which the 2.0 percent inflation line intersects the P—P′ curve is the NIRU corresponding to the nonvertical Phillips curve (drawn here to intersect the F—F′ line so that NIRU is the same whatever the view of the inflation tradeoff). Again, whenever U exceeds NIRU, but with an initial inflation rate above the negligible level, inflation must decline, as shown again by point A. For our purposes, the only difference between the vertical and nonvertical schools is that, for the former, the rate of change of prices must necessarily decline for U above NIRU even if it was zero or negative to begin with, whereas for the latter it may increase if inflation was initially below the Phillips curve, at a point such as B.

The shading of an area on either side of NIRU indicates both uncertainty about the exact location of NIRU and the implausibility that any single unemployment rate separates accelerating and slowing inflation. Unemployment rates left of the shaded area imply a high probability that inflation will accelerate. So long as this process involves unacceptable rates of inflation, it matters little whether inflation would accelerate indefinitely (as F—F' would predict) or would approach a limit (as P—P' would predict). And as an empirical matter, unemployment rates have not been low long enough to test whether P—P' or F—F' is the better description of the trade-off. The expectation is for accelerating inflation whenever the initial condition is little or no inflation and unemployment is to the left of the shaded area, as illustrated by point C.

The practical problem is determining the value of NIRU and establishing its stability over time. As to stability, the Phillips curve is known to shift with the composition of the labor force. For any given demand pressure (as measured, for example, by vacancies), various segments of the labor force tend to differ in rates of unemployment. Because significant changes in the composition of the labor force in recent years have tended to shift the trade-off to the right and thus to increase NIRU, the stability of NIRU must be judged in light of a measure of unemployment adjusted for this composition. What follows, therefore, uses an adjusted unemployment rate, UA, provided by the Council of Economic Advisers, which is based on the composition of the labor force in 1956. The analysis seeks to identify a NIRUA corresponding with this employment concept.

The evidence presented in figure 1 strongly suggests that for the postwar period there exists a stable NIRUA that can be located within fairly narrow bounds. The horizontal axis measures UA, the adjusted unemployment rate; the vertical axis measures whether inflation went up or down in a given year, and by how much. For purposes of this figure and the subsequent regression analysis, we measure inflation by the rate of change of the consumer price index excluding food ($p\dot{c}x$). This price index is used because year-to-year changes in food prices reflect, to a considerable extent, circumstances specific to agriculture, such as weather, rather than demand pressures. The points plotted in the figure show how UA and the change in the

Figure 1. Relation between the Unemployment Rate[a] and the Change in Inflation, 1953–74

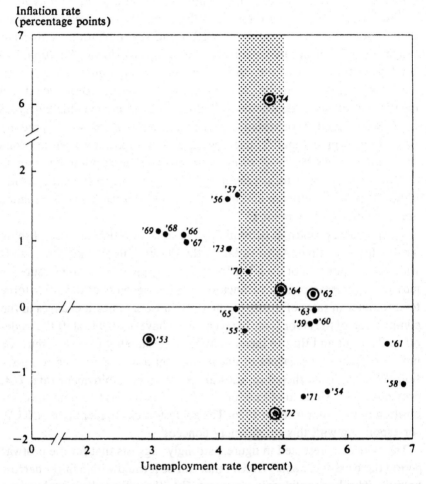

Sources: The data for the adjusted unemployment rate were provided by the Council of Economic Advisers; the change in the inflation rate is measured by the rate of change of the consumer price index excluding food, from the National Bureau of Economic Research Data Bank.

a. Adjusted, using 1956 composition of the labor force, to compensate for the changing composition of the labor force over time.

inflation rate were related each year from 1953 to 1974. Points above the solid horizontal line are years in which inflation increased and points below it are years in which inflation decreased.

The points that are circled in the figure require special comment. First, 1962 and 1964 each followed years in which inflation was at a very low rate;

they correspond roughly to points like *B* in the diagram, where inflation may speed up merely to reach a low rate of inflation predicted by current unemployment. The speedup in each of these years was less than 0.2 percentage point. Second, price and wage controls marked 1972. Third, unusual movements of raw materials prices and, in the immediately preceding years, of food prices, characterized 1953 and 1974: in 1953, these prices fell; in 1974, they rose. As the model developed below and the accompanying regression analysis will show, these price movements help account for the outlying behavior of *pcx* in these two years.

In eight of the years plotted in figure 1, *UA* exceeds the vertical line drawn at 5 percent. In all but 1962 (circled), inflation decreased. The inference is that NIRUA is at most 5 percent. It could be somewhat lower, but the figure is ambiguous on the issue, because the next three lower observations, lying between 4.8 percent and 5.0 percent, are subject to the special factors just discussed. In nine years, *UA* equals or falls short of the vertical line drawn at 4.3 percent. In all but two of these years, the rate of inflation increased noticeably. The exceptions are the circled year 1953, and 1965, a year again somewhat special because of the elimination or reduction of excise taxes at midyear. This evidence strongly suggests that a *UA* of 4 percent or thereabouts represents what could be labeled the inflationary rate of unemployment, which policymakers should vigorously avoid because it leads to increasing inflation. In this region, the Phillips curve appears to be quite steep, if not vertical. On the other hand, for the two remaining years in which *UA* fell between 4.3 percent and 4.8 percent—1955 and 1970—the response of inflation is not so consistent. The area between 4.3 and 5.0 percent *UA* is shaded in the figure and represents the region of uncertainty about inflationary behavior.

An Alternative Approach to the Estimation of NIRU

The conclusion suggested by figure 1 can be made more precise by regression analysis. In equation (1) of table 1, estimates from a reduced-form equation are presented relating the rate of inflation in a given year to the rate of unemployment and the rate of productivity change in the same year, and to the rate of inflation in the previous year. All the variables have very significant coefficients of a priori reasonable value and the fit is fairly close, as indicated by the standard error and the $\bar{R}^2$. The equation was estimated

Table 1. Determinants of the Rate of Inflation as Measured by the Consumer Price Index Excluding Food[a]

Equation	Constant	$1/UA$	$\dot{p}(-1)$	$\dot{\pi}$	Determinants[b] $p\dot{m}x$	$\dot{bf}(-1)$	$\dot{M}$	$\dot{M}(-1)$	Standard error	Durbin-Watson statistic	R^2
(1)	−0.67 (0.84)	8.2 (2.9)	0.80 (0.11)	−0.25 (0.12)	...	...	...	...	0.69	1.32	0.83
(2)	−0.42 (0.73)	8.2 (2.4)	0.68 (0.10)	−0.24 (0.10)	0.081 (0.044)	0.059 (0.033)	...	...	0.58	1.80	0.88
(3)	−0.78 (0.88)	12.2 (4.1)	0.77 (0.14)	−0.29 (0.14)	0.110 (0.054)	0.055 (0.033)	−0.004 (0.124)	−0.21 (0.15)	0.58	1.84	0.88
(4)	−0.77 (0.73)	12.1 (3.5)	0.77 (0.11)	−0.29 (0.10)	0.109 (0.046)	0.055 (0.032)	...	−0.21 (0.14)	0.55	1.85	0.89

Sources: Adjusted unemployment rate—Council of Economic Advisers; price index of imports—U.S. Department of Commerce, *Indexes of U.S. Exports and Imports by Economic Class: 1919 to 1971* (1972), and Department of Commerce, *Overseas Business Reports*, various issues; consumer price index excluding food and M_1—NBER Data Bank; productivity and price index of farm products—SMP Data Bank.

a. The equations are estimated from annual data for 1953–71. The numbers in parentheses are standard errors.

b. UA = unemployment rate, standardized for composition of the labor force

$\dot{p}$ = rate of inflation measured by the rate of change of the consumer price index excluding food

$\dot{\pi}$ = rate of change of productivity in the private nonfarm business sector

$p\dot{m}x$ = rate of change of price index of imports excluding crude and manufactured foods, constructed from the index of crude materials, semimanufactures, and finished manufactures, published by the U.S. Department of Commerce (see sources above). It is a Paasche index calculated by dividing the sum of the three components by the sum of their quantity indexes weighted by the values of the base year (1967).

$\dot{bf}(-1)$ = rate of change of price index of farm products, lagged

$\dot{M}$ = rate of change in M_1 (currency plus demand deposits).

for the period 1953–71 to minimize distortions from price controls and, more recently, from increases in oil prices. The form of the equations is derived from an underlying model, presented in an appendix available from the authors on request.

Briefly, the model has three main characteristics: (1) a wage equation that accounts for the percentage change in wages in terms of the unemployment rate and expectations on the rate of change of prices; (2) a price equation that determines the long-run or target price level as a markup on unit labor cost; and (3) an allowance for the gradual adjustment of prices to their target levels and for the effect of deviations of actual productivity from its trend.

In equation (1), the dependent variable is the rate of inflation, p, but this equation can be readily transformed into one accounting for the acceleration of inflation—the variable used in figure 1—by simply subtracting $p(-1)$ from both sides. If the coefficient of $p(-1)$ were one, the acceleration would turn out to be independent of $p(-1)$, which is the essential feature of the vertical Phillips curve. In equation (1), the estimated coefficient of $p(-1)$ falls short of unity, though not by very much (roughly by 0.2 with a standard error of 0.1). Accordingly, estimating NIRUA requires specification of a "negligible" rate of inflation: we use 2 percent. Solving equation (1) for the unemployment rate consistent with this inflation rate yields 4.88, reported in the first row of column (8) of table 2, which shows in the first five columns the data from table 1 for equations (1) and (2), and provides additional estimates in the other columns. This rate agrees closely with the value suggested by figure 1. To translate NIRUA into an official unemployment rate, NIRU, 0.8 percentage point must be added to allow for the current composition of the labor force. Thus, the NIRU implied by equation (1) is around 5.7 percent (table 2, column 10).[4]

This estimate is rather high compared with traditional targets for unemployment, although it is not inconsistent with recent results of others.[5] It might result from using UA as a measure of unemployment, which is only one of many ways to account for the effect of changes in the composition of the labor force. Table 2 summarizes a number of tests designed to assess the

---

4. Allowing for the error term, when unemployment equals NIRU, inflation may temporarily rise or fall, even if it was initially in the neighborhood of 2 percent, but not systematically.

5. See, for example, Robert E. Hall, "The Process of Inflation in the Labor Market," *BPEA* (2:1974), pp. 343–93.

Table 2. Estimates of the Noninflationary Rate of Unemployment for Alternative Specifications, and Assumptions about Terms of Trade

						Noninflationary unemployment rate			
	Specifications and measures of fit					Using unemployment index in column (1), by growth trend in terms of trade		Using official unemployment index, by growth trend in terms of trade	
		Exogenous prices[b]							
Index of unemployment used in equation[a]	$\hat{p}mx$	$\hat{p}f(-1)$	Standard error	Durbin-Watson statistic	Prediction error for 1974[c]	Zero	Historical	Zero	Historical
(1)	(2)	(3)	(4)	(5)	(6)	(7)	(8)	(9)	(10)
Equation									
(1) UA	...	...	0.69	1.3	5.2	...	4.88	...	5.7
(2) UA	0.081 (0.044)	0.059 (0.033)	0.58	1.8	−1.0	5.8	4.8	6.6	5.6
(5) UMM	...	...	0.66	1.6	5.2	...	3.01	...	5.8
(6) UMM	0.077 (0.045)	0.051 (0.033)	0.58	2.0	−0.6	3.9	2.9	6.7	5.7
(7) U	...	...	0.73	1.3	5.3	...	5.1	...	5.1

Sources: Same as table 1. The equations are estimated from annual data for 1953–71. The numbers in parentheses are standard errors.

a. UA = unemployment index adjusted to the 1956 composition of the labor force
UMM = unemployment index for married men
U = official unemployment index.

b. $\hat{p}mx$ = rate of change of price index of imports; $\hat{p}f(-1)$ = rate of change of price index of farm products, lagged.

c. Actual minus predicted.

sensitivity of the estimate of NIRU to alternative specifications of the estimating equation.

Equation (5) of table 2 shows estimates obtained when UA is replaced by another frequently used measure, the rate of unemployment for married men, UMM. Without reproducing the regression equation, which is quite similar to (1), we report in columns (4) and (5) some measures of fit; in column (8), the noninflationary rate of unemployment using the index of unemployment of married men; and in column (10) the estimate of NIRU implied by this value and the relation between UMM and U in the early seventies. Comparison with the statistics for equation (1) reported in table 2 shows similar fits and implied estimates of NIRU. Finally, equation (7) shows the effect of measuring labor market tightness by the official unemployment rate, U, itself, making no allowance for compositional effects. Here the estimate of NIRU is reduced somewhat, to 5.1. However, it is most unlikely that NIRU has remained stable over the last two decades, and the somewhat poorer fit of the equation supports this view. Hence, this estimate is not a reliable guide to the current value of NIRU.

The specification underlying equation (1) suffers from allowing only for the effect of changes in unit labor costs. The rate of change of a price index like pcx, the consumer price index excluding food, should depend also on the current rate of change of imported inputs, the other major component of costs (that to some extent enters into pcx directly). In addition, even though pcx excludes food, insofar as wage changes respond to the actual and expected behavior of prices of the basket of goods bought rather than produced by workers,[6] the rate of change of pcx $(p\dot{c}x)$ should also depend, with some lag, on the rate of change of food prices. These effects might not be important for most of the period 1953–71, when the movement of these prices was relatively moderate (which may explain the reasonably good fit of equation 1), but they may be critical for years of extreme fluctuations, like 1973 and 1974 (and, incidentally, 1953). In this light, it is not surprising

6. This is not a universally acceptable hypothesis. Robert J. Gordon has emphasized the influences on wages of prices in the product markets. In his various contributions to *Brookings Papers*, he has stressed that prices of products produced by labor and prices of products consumed by it have independent effects on wages. Hall, in "Process of Inflation," ignores the effect of price expectations in the wage equation and questions the theoretical rationale for such a feedback (except that it may reflect the excess demand for labor). In his model, which he built around the distinction between the scale wage and the marginal effective wage, expectations on the rate of change of wages play the role of price expectations as determinants of the wage rate.

that extrapolation of equation (1) somewhat overestimates the price change in 1972, a year of price controls, underestimates moderately in 1973, and underpredicts conspicuously the 10 percent rise of 1974. For that year the error is over 5 percent (see table 2, column 6).

Equation (2) in table 1 reports the results of adding to the specification of (1) the current rate of change of a price index of imports excluding food, $p\dot{m}x$, and the lagged rate of change of an index of farm prices, $\dot{p}f(-1)$. Both variables display fairly significant coefficients and the standard error is reduced appreciably, while the serial correlation of the errors as measured by the Durbin-Watson statistic also falls substantially. The point estimates of the coefficients are not unreasonable, though they appear somewhat high. This is especially true in the case of imports, whose coefficient is larger than the share of nonfood imports in nonfood consumption or private nonfarm GNP. This result suggests that import prices affect domestic ones not only directly through their weight as inputs but also indirectly by influencing the domestic markup on labor costs (especially in the case of raw materials). In addition, the estimate of the $p\dot{m}x$ coefficient may be biased upward since, in view of U.S. dominance in world trade over the period covered, the behavior of import prices may themselves be influenced by U.S. domestic prices. Equation (6) of table 2 shows that very similar results are obtained when these additional price terms are added to the equation in which UMM is used as the measure of unemployment.

The coefficient estimates are rather sensitive to the sample period and especially to the exclusion of 1953; in one sense this is understandable because 1953 was the only year up to 1971 in which these indexes behaved much differently from domestic prices. Nonetheless, this sensitivity implies that these coefficient estimates are subject to a fair margin of error. It is encouraging, however, that the equation tracks experience of recent years well. After overestimating both 1972 and 1973 somewhat, equation (2) accounts quite closely for the 10 percent rise of 1974. It does so by explicitly recognizing the importance of food prices and import prices, including those of oil, in the nation's recent experience. In 1974, it attributes some 3 percentage points of the inflation in the CPI less food to import prices and somewhat over 2 percentage points to the sharp rise of food prices in 1973. The equation actually overestimates 1974 by 1 percent (table 2, column 6), which again suggests some upward bias in the coefficient, since some underestimation might have been expected in that year.

Our main interest here is in the estimate of NIRU implied by equations

(2) and (6), which now depends on the relation between the exogenous prices and $p\dot{c}x$. Using the historical relations inferred from the mean values of these prices over the period of fit, one obtains the estimates of NIRUA and NIRU reported in columns (8) and (10) of table 2, which agree closely with those derived earlier.

Two further, interrelated, objections to the specification of equation (2) require attention: (1) especially when dealing with annual data, one should not expect the rate of inflation to respond to unemployment without at least some lag;[7] (2) our specification omits the rate of change of unemployment despite some evidence that this variable tends to have a negative effect on the rate of inflation. While each objection is valid in itself, they apparently cancel out in the annual model in which the expected lag structure interacts with the rate-of-change effect.[8]

A simple model, in which the effect of unemployment on price change is approximately linear, demonstrates how this can happen. The combined effect of current and lagged U and of ΔU can be expressed as

$$\dot{p} = aU + bU(-1) + c\Delta U = (a + b)U + (c - b)[U - U(-1)],$$

in which the constants a, b, and c are all negative. If b approximately equals c, neither the variable $U(-1)$ nor the variable ΔU will add significantly to the explanation of $\dot{p}$, given U. The reason is that for *given* U, a higher value of $U(-1)$ has two offsetting effects on $\dot{p}$: it tends to raise $\dot{p}$ through the rate-of-change effect, but it also tends to lower it through the lagged level effect. In our case, these two effects seem roughly to offset each other.[9]

Although the estimates of NIRU summarized in column (10) of table 2

7. Starting from a quarterly model of the form outlined earlier, one can deduce an annual model by first deriving a four-quarter change equation through recursive substitution of the lagged dependent variable, and then aggregating the four-quarter equations into an annual one. Under reasonable assumptions about the speed of adjustments, the current annual rate of change of prices in a given year depends on a distributed lag of unemployment, including the four quarters of that year and at least the six previous ones, with weights heavily concentrated in the previous year and most of the remaining weight in the current year.

8. When equation (2) is reestimated, replacing UA with $UA(-1)$, the fit deteriorates somewhat. Similarly, if one adds $UA(-1)$ to UA, the new variable is barely significant (*t*-ratio of 1.2). Alternatively, the fit is also somewhat worsened by using unemployment lagged two (or three) quarters—in a given year using the average unemployment rate for the four quarters ending with the second quarter of that year.

9. This explanation receives some support from a test in which ΔUA is added to the specification of equation (2); that variable is found to have the expected negative sign, but a very small coefficient (-0.13) which is entirely insignificant (*t*-ratio of 0.5).

are consistent with one another and with the implications of figure 1,[10] they are based, explicitly or implicitly, on the relation between the index *pcx* and the exogenous prices prevailing, on the average, over the period 1952–71. Now, in this period farm and import prices tended to increase at appreciably lower rates than the prices of the basket of goods produced off the farm, as measured by the CPI excluding food; in other words, the terms of trade moved in favor of the nonfarm population. The average rate of improvement was in fact rather substantial: 2.9 percentage points per year in terms of food and 1.7 percentage points in terms of imported nonfood commodities. If one assumes less favorable behavior of the terms of trade in the future, then any of our equations allowing for the effect of exogenous prices will imply a shift to the right in the locus of the long-run tradeoff between inflation and unemployment, and in particular a higher NIRU than in the period 1953–71. This conclusion is illustrated by columns (7) and (9) of

10. This conclusion is supported by a number of additional tests, one of which consisted in replacing *pcx* with the private nonfarm business deflator. For this index the specification of equation (1) yields results quite similar to those of table 1, but the implied NIRU is somewhat larger—6 percent. In specifying an equation corresponding to (2), the deflator does not *directly* include the price of exogenous inputs—farm products and imports—but at most a markup on these costs (which are but a small portion of total cost). It will, however, be affected *indirectly* to the extent that the rate of change of wages depends on the basket of goods bought; thus, in the equation below we include the change in a lagged index of farm and import prices (which were combined by simple averaging to reduce multicollinearity). In addition, we include the current rate of change of nonfood import prices on the ground, discussed in the text, that the behavior of these prices may affect the size of the domestic markup on labor costs. A test of this specification yields the following estimates (obtained using the autoregressive transformation because of a rather high negative serial correlation of the residuals):

$$\dot{p} = 0.005 + 6.9(1/UA) + 0.598\dot{p}(-1) - 0.24\dot{\pi}$$
$$\quad (0.52) \quad (1.5) \qquad (0.080) \qquad (0.09)$$

$$+ 0.086pmx + 0.043[\dot{p}f(-1) + pmx(-1)]/2,$$
$$\quad (0.03) \qquad (0.03)$$

with standard error = 0.49 (adjusted to include the lagged residual) and autocorrelation equal to −0.54.

These results are open to some question. The coefficient of current nonfood imports seems high, perhaps because of the upward bias mentioned earlier. The coefficient of lagged farm and import prices seems low and is subject to a large standard error. Nonetheless, the equation accounts surprisingly well for the 11 percent inflation rate for the deflator in 1974, underestimating it by 1 percent.

What is important for our purpose is that the NIRU implied by this equation, using historical values for the terms of trade, turns out to be 5.7, in close agreement with the estimates reported in table 2.

table 2, which also serve to provide a notion of the sensitivity of NIRU to the terms of trade; they give the estimate of NIRU implied by each equation on the assumption of a zero growth trend in terms of trade. The effect is an increase in the estimated NIRU by about 1 percentage point.

Taken at face value, this result is rather disturbing, considering that the continuation of the favorable trend in the terms of trade after 1971 is very much in question. It is, however, subject to a number of important qualifications. First, the estimated response of NIRU to the terms of trade depends sensitively on the value of the coefficients of the exogenous prices; for reasons stated earlier, these estimates are not very reliable and are probably biased upward. Second, while, in the short run, unfavorable developments in the terms of trade seem very likely to bring higher inflation for a given unemployment rate, as our equations imply, the long-run effects are much more doubtful. A change in the trend of the terms of trade is entirely analogous in its effects to a change in the trend of productivity. In the long run, the wage Phillips curve should shift to accommodate such changes, producing a similar accommodating shift in the price Phillips curve and hence leaving NIRU roughly unchanged.

To summarize, analysis of the postwar experience points to a NIRU of just over 5 ½ percent, an estimate robust with respect to alternative specifications. In the years to come, this value will be affected by the composition of the labor force and, to some extent, by developments in the terms of trade. Considering that neither of these factors is expected to shift significantly in the near future, we propose an official rate of unemployment of around 6 percent as a reasonable, if conservative, operational target for the end of the second year following the beginning of recovery.

If, over the next two years, unemployment approaches this target from above, the rate of inflation will almost certainly decline steadily. In fact, the proposed interim target may well be too conservative; but given the present national concern with inflation, erring on that side may, in the end, provide greater assurance that a program of orderly reduction of unemployment will be adhered to.

We look forward to a significantly lower target for later years. This development might be made possible by greater sensitivity of wages to the aggregate demand for labor. But even without that, a lower unemployment target, within the nonvertical range of the Phillips curve suggested by our analysis, may be socially desirable, as James Tobin has long maintained, even though it implies a somewhat higher rate of inflation.

Implications of the Real Target for Monetary Policy

The next question is, how much must real GNP grow over the next two years if the nation is to meet the 6 percent unemployment target? By the time income begins to recover around mid-1975, unemployment will have passed 9 percent, thus exceeding the target by 3 percentage points. Given Okun's law and the expectation of recapturing some of the recent extraordinary loss of productivity once output turns around, the recovery should start with output around 10 percent below the rate consistent with the interim unemployment target. In addition, over the two years of the plan, potential GNP should rise about another 7 percent. Thus, to meet our target, real GNP should grow by somewhat over 17 percent from the second quarter of 1975 to the second quarter of 1977, or at an average annual rate of 8 percent. However, the optimal path of recovery to the 6 percent target presumably should not be pursued at a uniform pace; rather, the rate of growth should be faster in the first year, when there is plenty of slack, and less rapid as the target is approached. Indeed, in the final quarter, the growth rate should not be much above the long-run figure of 3 ½ to 4 percent. Hence, for the first year, the real GNP growth target should be about 9 to 10 percent. While such growth is rapid by postwar standards, it is not excessive in light of the unusual slack in the economy. This conclusion is consistent with the modest effect of the change in the adjusted unemployment rate on inflation reported earlier. Furthermore, the recovery from the Great Depression was often marked by growth rates of at least that size; and they occurred even in the emergence from the 1958 contraction, without significant inflationary pressures.

Judging the implications of this real growth rate for the growth of money income calls for a realistic expectation for inflation in 1975. The administration's official target was 11 percent, but that included the effect of the oil taxes, estimated to account for 2 percentage points. The 9 percent forecast excluding the energy taxes is roughly consistent with equation (2) or the corresponding equations relying on *UMM*. If average unemployment in the first year is set at somewhat over 8 percent, if productivity growth returns to its trend value, and if import prices rise 15 percent,[11] these equations would predict a decline in inflation of around a modest 1.5 percent.

---

11. Based on a forecast for the import deflator from Wharton Econometric Forecasting Associates, which, however, includes food prices.

However, with an improvement of productivity growth to, say, 5 percent—
which is not implausible in the initial phase of output recovery—the decline
in inflation could exceed 2 percent, reducing the year-to-year rate of change
of prices below 8 percent. Variations in the rate of unemployment, on the
other hand, would have minor effects; a change of 1 percentage point
around a level of 8 would affect the rate of inflation by only around 0.15
point. Because of the very rapid growth of prices in 1974, however, a year-
to-year growth of 8 to 8 ½ percent implies a growth of only 6 to 6 ½ percent
within the year itself. Given the target real growth of 9 to 10 percent and the
implied rate of price increase estimated above, the target annual rate of
growth for money income over the coming year should be in the neighborhood of 16 percent.

Achieving a rate of growth of income of this magnitude obviously will require a large expansion of the money supply, though the precise figure
would depend on the concomitant fiscal policy. A recovery as rapid and
vigorous as that advocated would have to rely initially on massive fiscal
stimuli. Monetary policy alone would not be adequate because of long lags
and possible effects on the international value of the dollar that could aggravate inflation.

But even if the increase in income is achieved initially through fiscal
measures, monetary policy must accommodate the increase without letting
interest rates rise above current levels, at least for the first few quarters of
the recovery, in particular to ensure a strong recovery of housing. Now, if
income is to grow at a 16 percent rate with short-term interest rates stable,
the money supply will have to rise at a rate not much lower than that. Simulations of the SMP model, as well as of some others, suggest that the
achievement of this rate would require fiscal stimulants considerably
stronger than those enacted so far. In their absence, the recovery would
have to rely more heavily on expansionary monetary policy, and in this
case, the required growth of the money supply would have to be even larger,
so as to reduce interest rates below current levels.

The Impact of Monetary Growth on Inflation

At this point the analysis confronts a widely held concern, encouraged by
at least some monetarists, that such a rapid rate of growth and sudden acceleration of the money supply, implying a two- to three-fold increase over

recent rates, would unfavorably influence prices and inevitably set off a new round of inflation. Our analysis indicates that such concerns are unfounded; it implies that inflation systematically accelerates only when unemployment falls below NIRU, and the M_1 growth that we expect will be needed as a component of a policy package aimed at approaching NIRU from above over the next two years.

Conceivably, one might still oppose the large growth of M_1, even in the months immediately ahead, out of fear of its causing unemployment to fall below NIRU *after the first two years*—that is, beyond mid-1977—and in a fashion that no action after mid-1976 could correct. Even with all due allowance for long lags, such an objection can hardly be taken seriously.

Another concern of the monetarists is that an increase in the money supply somehow has a direct effect on inflation, whatever the slack in the economy. This view is hard to credit, unless one presumes that manufacturers and merchants all over the country avidly follow the monetary statistics from the St. Louis Federal Reserve Bank and immediately raise their prices whenever the annual rate of money growth exceeds 4 percent for a month (or week). No doubt, a few people in the financial markets pore over those statistics, but mostly because they hope to infer something about the forthcoming behavior of the Federal Reserve. It is hard to believe that anybody else—except economists like us—wastes his time in this way.

But such a priori reasoning does not settle the issue; for what is incredible to us is apparently self-evident to others. The remedy is empirical evidence. On this point, the analysis already presented cannot reject the hypothesis of a direct impact of monetary growth on inflation because this possibility was not even entertained. Tests are needed to deal squarely with this issue.

In an exploration for direct correlations between money growth and inflation, the simplest relations fail. Year by year, the acceleration (or deceleration) of inflation and the acceleration (or deceleration) of money growth show no positive relation. In the post-Korean period these two variables moved more often in opposite directions than together, and the correlation between them for the 1953–71 period is about zero. Allowing for a one-year lag of prices behind money scarcely changes this result, with the correlation still only 0.08 and observations for nine out of twenty-one years going in the "wrong" direction.

Allowing for long distributed lags from money to prices sharply improves the fit of regression equations between the two. Among several tried with annual data for the 1953–71 period, the best was

(8) $$\dot{p} = -0.09 + 0.27\dot{M}(-1) + 0.71\dot{p}(-1),$$
$$(0.12) \qquad (0.15)$$

Standard error = 0.83; $\bar{R}^2 = 0.75$.

where $\dot{p}$ is defined as in table 1 and $\dot{M}$ is the growth rate of the money supply; the numbers in parentheses are standard errors.

Such an equation is consistent with many views of the inflation process. It implies the monetarist position that, in the long run, the rate of inflation tends to equal the rate of growth of money, up to a constant reflecting the growth trend of income and possibly of velocity (although the lag in adjustment implied by equation 8 is very long indeed). The equation is even more consistent with the view widely held by nonmonetarists that the money supply is only one of the determinants of aggregate demand, and hence of the rate of unemployment, and that monetary policy works with long lags. For instance, the SMP model, which is nonmonetarist and embodies a Phillips curve relation to explain inflation, implies a long-run relation between money and prices consistent with (8).[12] However, nonmonetarists would also expect that, since in the short run $\dot{M}$ is but one of the many forces controlling aggregate demand and unemployment, the explanatory power of this variable in an equation like (8) would be rather low—which it is.[13] The standard error is rather high in (8) compared with those of the equations without money in tables 1 and 2; also, $\dot{M}(-1)$ has a relatively low *t*-ratio, and in fact accounts for only about one-quarter of the variance of $\dot{p}$ that is not accounted for by $\dot{p}(-1)$. Equation (8) also fails completely to account for the high inflation of 1974, predicting a rate of only 4.7 percent.

The critical issue, then, is not whether in the long run money affects prices, but whether this effect results from the contribution of M to the determination of unemployment or derives, at least in part, through some independent channel. This question can be readily answered by adding $\dot{M}$ to

12. Franco Modigliani, "Monetary Policy and Consumption: Linkages via Interest Rate and Wealth Effects in the FMP Model," in *Consumer Spending and Monetary Policy: The Linkages*, Proceedings of a Monetary Conference (Federal Reserve Bank of Boston, 1971).

13. When $\dot{M}$ replaces $\dot{M}(-1)$ in (8) yielding a somewhat different distributed lag pattern, $\dot{M}$ has a smaller and insignificant coefficient; $\bar{R}^2$ drops to 0.69 for the equation and lagged inflation does most of the explaining.

equation (2) of table 1: if money has an independent effect on inflation, then the coefficient of $\dot{M}$ should remain positive and significant.

The result of this test, shown as equations (3) and (4) in table 1, is striking and unequivocal: when $\dot{M}$ or $\dot{M}(-1)$ is added to (2), singly or in combination, the estimated coefficients turn out to be actually negative, although not very significant. The safe conclusion is that absolutely no evidence supports any systematic effect of the rate of growth of the money supply on inflation except insofar as it helps determine aggregate demand in relation to the available labor force (and possibly in relation to other determinants of productive capacity). Put somewhat differently, the evidence supports the view that the rate of inflation depends on aggregate demand through its impact on unemployment, but does not depend on the mix of fiscal policy and growth of monetary aggregates that determines the aggregate demand for labor. It follows that, in assessing the impact of monetary policy on inflation, only its influence on aggregate real demand and employment is of concern, after due consideration of concomitant fiscal actions.

For the present purpose, the essential implication of this latest test is that a rate of growth of money well above 10 percent for the next few quarters is perfectly consistent with decreasing inflation, unless one is prepared to maintain that such growth would cause unemployment to dip significantly below 6 percent within the first two years. Again, the experience of the Great Depression supports this conclusion: from 1934 to 1936, the money supply grew 37 percent with no effect on prices.[14]

Needless to say, a two-digit rate of growth of M_1 will not be appropriate forever, or indeed for very long. By 1976, the required growth will undoubtedly be appreciably lower. In particular, if a 9 to 10 percent growth rate is achieved beginning in mid-1975, then by mid-1976 the target growth rate of real income might be down to 7 percent, and the rate of inflation for the next year should also be down by 2 to 3 percent. Hence, the required growth in M_1 might well be below 10 percent. And later on, the required rate should decline appreciably to let interest rates begin to move up appropriately. Indeed, by the time the economy nears our interim target of 6 percent unemployment, it should no longer be growing very fast, lest policy fall once again into the error, made both in 1965–66 and in 1972–73, of

14. The fact that prices did not actually fall is consistent with our analysis, given a very flat Phillips curve in the high unemployment range, and considering that, contrary to the case of 1975, there was no inherited high inflation at the beginning of the period.

accelerating the growth of demand just as the critical noninflationary rate of unemployment is about to be reached.

The conclusion about the high rate of growth of money that is likely to be needed to achieve the proposed targets should not be interpreted as a recommendation that the Federal Reserve adopt a rigid target of 10 or 12 percent or any other specific size. We expect the recovery to be brought about primarily by fiscal stimuli—some already in place and some yet to be enacted—and by the now somewhat easier conditions in the credit markets and their attendant interest rates. Once the recovery gets going, rapid growth of the money supply will be necessary for maintaining current market interest rates for a while, which is appropriate to sustain the recovery. Especially in light of the puzzling behavior of money demand in recent quarters, it would not be surprising if the appropriate growth rate in some future quarters were appreciably smaller or larger than the average estimate. The important point is to avoid the wild gyrations in interest rates of the last year by focusing on interest rate targets. In the initial phase of the recovery, the target should be the maintenance of current rates; after the recovery is well established, a rise in rates may become appropriate.

If the Federal Reserve should fail to accommodate the recovery in money income and insist on containing the growth of monetary aggregates within some historical average range, as in 1974, one can confidently predict that short-term market interest rates will again escalate into the two-digit range, taking the wind out of the sail of recovery and possibly causing a new recession, much as in 1974. This time, however, the episode would start from an unemployment rate of 8 percent or more, and the consequences would be far more tragic.

Errata

Page 148: the vertical axis which is labeled "Inflation rate" should be labeled "Change in inflation rate."

NOTE: The acronym "SMP model" that appears on pages 159 and 161 refers to the MIT-University of Pennsylvania-Social Science Research Council Econometric Model of the United States, more commonly known as the MPS model (previously known as the FMP model).

CONTENTS

Volume 2   The Life Cycle Hypothesis of Saving

Part IV. Policy Applications

Contents of Volumes 1 and 3

Acknowledgments

Name Index

CONTENTS

Volume 3   The Theory of Finance and Other Essays

ACKNOWLEDGMENTS

The author, editor, and The MIT Press wish to thank the publishers of the following essays for permission to reprint them here. The selections are arranged chronologically, with chapter numbers in brackets.

"Liquidity Preference and the Theory of Interest and Money," *Econometrica* 12 (January 1944): 45–88. Copyright 1944 by The Econometric Society. Plus "Postscript" of the paper in *The Critics of Keynesian Economics,* edited by Henry Hazlitt, pp. 183–184. Copyright 1960 by D. Van Nostrand Company, Inc. [2]

"New Developments on the Oligopoly Front," *Journal of Political Economy* 66 (June 1958): 215–232. Copyright 1958 by The University of Chicago Press. [14]

"The Monetary Mechanism and Its Interaction with Real Phenomena," *Review of Economics and Statistics* 45 (February 1963): 79–107. Copyright 1963 by North-Holland Publishing Company. [3]

"Innovations in Interest Rate Policy," (with Richard Sutch), *American Economic Review* 56 (May 1966): 178–197. Paper presented at the seventy-eighth annual meeting of the American Economic Association, Dec. 28–30, 1965. Copyright 1965 by The American Economic Association. [9]

"Debt Management and the Term Structure of Interest Rates: An Empirical Analysis," (with Richard Sutch), *Journal of Political Economy* 75, part 2 (August 1967): 569–589. Paper presented at the Conference of University Professors, The American Bankers Assoc., Sept. 19, 1966. Copyright 1967 by The University of Chicago Press. [10]

"Liquidity Preference," *International Encyclopedia of the Social Sciences,* edited by David L. Sills, vol. 9, pp. 394–409. Copyright © 1968 by Cromwell, Collier and McMillan, Inc. [4]

"Central Bank Policy, the Money Supply, and the Short-Term Rate of Interest," by Franco Modigliani, Robert Rasche, and J. Philip Cooper, is reprinted by permission from the *Journal of Money, Credit, and Banking,* Volume 2, Number 2 (May 1970), 166–218. Copyright © 1970 by the Ohio State University Press. [7]

"The Dynamics of Portfolio Adjustment and the Flow of Savings Through Financial Intermediaries." Reprinted by permission of the publisher, from *Savings Deposits, Mortgages, and Housing: Studies for the FMP Econometric Model* edited by Edward M. Gramlich and Dwight M. Jaffee (Lexington Mass.: Lexington Books, D. C. Heath and Company. Copyright 1972, D. C. Heath and Company). Pp. 63–102. [8]

"Inflation, Rational Expectations and the Term Structure of Interest Rates," (with Robert J. Shiller), *Economica,* February 1973, pp. 12–43. Copyright 1973 by Economica Publishing Office at the London School of Economics. [11]

"A Generalization of the Phillips Curve for a Developing Country," (with Ezio Tarantelli), *Review of Economic Studies* 40 (April 1973): 203–223. Copyright 1973 by University of Essex. [13]

"On the Role of Expectations of Price and Technological Change in an Investment Function," (with Albert K. Ando, Robert Rasche, and Stephen J. Turnovsky), *International Economic Review* 15 (June 1974): 384–414. Copyright 1974 by University of Pennsylvania. [12]

"The Channels of Monetary Policy in the Federal Reserve-MIT-University of Pennsylvania Econometric Model of the United States," *Modelling the Economy,* based on papers presented at the Social Science Research Council's Conference on Economic Modelling, July 1972, edited by G. A. Renton, pp. 240–267. Copyright 1975 by Heinemann Educational Books. [5]

"Targets for Monetary Policy in the Coming Year," (with Lucas Papademos), *Brookings Papers on Economic Activity* 1 (1975): 141–163. Copyright 1975 by The Brookings Institution. [15]

"Impacts of Fiscal Actions on Aggregate Income and the Monetarist Controversy: Theory and Evidence," (with Albert Ando, and with the assistance of J. Giangrande), *Monetarism,* edited by Jerome L. Stein, pp. 17–42. Studies in Monetary Economy, vol. 1. Copyright 1976 by North-Holland Publishing Company. [6]

"The Monetarist Controversy or, Should We Forsake Stabilization Policies?" *American Economic Review* 67 (March 1977): 1–19. Copyright 1977 by The American Economic Association. [1]

Name Index

Printed in the United States
by Baker & Taylor Publisher Services